1,000,000 Books
are available to read at

Forgotten Books

www.ForgottenBooks.com

Read online
Download PDF
Purchase in print

ISBN 978-0-282-24090-5
PIBN 10845230

This book is a reproduction of an important historical work. Forgotten Books uses state-of-the-art technology to digitally reconstruct the work, preserving the original format whilst repairing imperfections present in the aged copy. In rare cases, an imperfection in the original, such as a blemish or missing page, may be replicated in our edition. We do, however, repair the vast majority of imperfections successfully; any imperfections that remain are intentionally left to preserve the state of such historical works.

Forgotten Books is a registered trademark of FB &c Ltd.
Copyright © 2018 FB &c Ltd.
FB &c Ltd, Dalton House, 60 Windsor Avenue, London, SW19 2RR.
Company number 08720141. Registered in England and Wales.

For support please visit www.forgottenbooks.com

1 MONTH OF FREE READING

at
www.ForgottenBooks.com

By purchasing this book you are eligible for one month membership to ForgottenBooks.com, giving you unlimited access to our entire collection of over 1,000,000 titles via our web site and mobile apps.

To claim your free month visit:
www.forgottenbooks.com/free845230

* Offer is valid for 45 days from date of purchase. Terms and conditions apply.

English
Français
Deutsche
Italiano
Español
Português

www.forgottenbooks.com

Mythology Photography **Fiction**
Fishing Christianity **Art** Cooking
Essays **Buddhism** Freemasonry
Medicine **Biology** Music **Ancient Egypt** Evolution Carpentry Physics
Dance Geology **Mathematics** Fitness
Shakespeare **Folklore** Yoga Marketing
Confidence Immortality Biographies
Poetry **Psychology** Witchcraft
Electronics Chemistry History **Law**
Accounting **Philosophy** Anthropology
Alchemy Drama Quantum Mechanics
Atheism Sexual Health **Ancient History**
Entrepreneurship Languages Sport
Paleontology Needlework Islam
Metaphysics Investment Archaeology
Parenting Statistics Criminology
Motivational

THE SHILLUK PEOPLE
THEIR LANGUAGE AND FOLKLORE

BY DIEDRICH WESTERMANN

WITH EIGHT PLATES
AND A SKETCH MAP

PHILADELPHIA, PA.
THE BOARD OF FOREIGN MISSIONS OF
THE UNITED PRESBYTERIAN CHURCH OF N. A.

DIETRICH REIMER (ERNST VOHSEN) BERLIN

COPYRIGHT, 1912, BY
THE BOARD OF FOREIGN MISSIONS OF THE
UNITED PRESBYTERIAN CHURCH OF N. A.
PRINTED BY J. J. AUGUSTIN, GLÜCKSTADT.

NOTE OF APPRECIATION.

The Board of Foreign Missions of the United Presbyterian Church of N. A. desires to express to the Trustees of the Arthington Fund its profound appreciation for financial help which made it possible to carry on linguistic investigations in Southern Sudan and then to give publicity to their findings by the publication of this book.

PREFACE.

In the summer of 1910 the Prussian Board of Education provided me with the means to undertake a journey to the Northern Sudan. My object was to make linguistic studies. During my stay in the Sudan the material for this work was collected. My studies in the Shilluk language and people are due to a request made to me by the Reverend C. R. Watson D. D., of Philadelphia Pa., Corresponding Secretary of the Mission of the United Presbyterian Church of North America. Mr. Watson, having heard of my intended journey to Egypt and the Sudan, asked me to visit the United Presbyterian Church's Mission on the Sobat, and to study the language of that district which lies within the sphere of their activity. By supplying the necessary funds for this part of the journey and for my stay in the Sudan, I was enabled to carry out this proposition, which was at the same time of importance for my linguistic studies.

I left for the Sudan at the beginning of August 1910, where I staid in Khartum and on the Sobat till the middle of November.

The results of my work obtained during this comparatively short time would not have been possible had it not been for the extremely active and kind support rendered me everywhere in the Sudan by the American missionaries. Not only was I able to profit by their kind hospitality, but they also most generously placed at my disposal their extensive knowledge of the country, people and language. I owe my practical introduction to the language to Dr. Thomas A. Lambie, medical missionary at Khartum, in whose house I was privileged to stay for over a month. In addition to the contributions signed by him he also supplied me with several native texts from his collection which will be found incorporated in this book.

The missionaries on Doleib Hill, Mr. C. B. Guthrie and the Reverend D. S. Oyler also helped me on all possible occasions; above all they introduced me to the Shilluks and put me into touch with those natives who were necessary and useful to me in my researches. Both these gentlemen and the Reverend E. McCreery and Mr. R. W. Tidrick have supplied me with very valuable information in answer to questions addressed to them since my return to Germany, some of which appears as signed contributions. Part of it has been included in the introduction. During the winter of 1911 I had the pleasure of receiving the Reverend McCreery while he was in Berlin, and thus had an opportunity of discussing grammatical questions with him.

I must express my sincere thanks to all those who have assisted me in their cooperation and by placing the necessary funds at my disposal, which enabled me to complete this work.

I am indebted to the Arthington Trustees, who by their financial support made the printing of this book possible.

My gratitude is also due to Mr. L. Hamilton of the Oriental College, Berlin, who has read and corrected the English text.

The Reverend C. R. Watson was kind enough to read and correct that part of the work which relates to Folklore.

Berlin, August 1912.   DIEDRICH WESTERMANN.

CONTENTS.

NOTE OF APPRECIATION V
PREFACE VII
ABBREVIATIONS XVI
AUTHORS QUOTED XVII
INTRODUCTION .... XIX—LXIV

FIRST PART. GRAMMAR.

FIRST SECTION. THE SOUNDS.

The Vowels. 1—8 .... 1—4
The Consonants. 9—11 .... 4—6
Change of Vowels. 12—27 .... 7—12
Change of Semivowels. 28—36 .... 13—14
Change of Consonants. 37—46 .... 14—18
Intonation. 47—60 .... 18—22

SECOND SECTION. FORMATION OF WORDS.

Form of the Stem. 61—76 .... 23—27
Composition of Words. 77—85 .... 27—29

THIRD SECTION.
GENEALOGICAL RELATIONS OF THE SHILLUK LANGUAGE.

The Dialects or Divisions. 86—89 .... 30—32
The Position of Shilluk among other African Languages. 90—101 .... 33—45
Comparative Lists of Words. 98—101 .... 36—44
Appendix: Names of Languages .... 44—45

FOURTH SECTION.
THE PARTS OF SPEECH.

THE NOUN. Singular and Plural. 102—124 ... 46—55
Examples showing plural-formation. 113—124 .. 49—55
Gender. 125—126a .... 56—57
Case. 127—129 .... 57—59

THE PRONOUN. The Personal Pronoun. 130
— 137 .... 59—64
Demonstrative Pronouns. 138—141 .... 64—66
Interrogative Pronouns. 142—144 .... 66—67
Relative Pronouns. 145 67
The Reflexive Pronoun. 146 .... 67—68
The Reciprocal Pronoun. 147 68
THE ADJECTIVE. 148—151 .... 68—71
Comparison. 151 .... 70—71
THE NUMERALS. 152—154 .... 71—72
THE VERB. Conjugation of the Verb. 156—196 72—90
Examples of Conjugation. 157—178 .... 73—79
Present. 157—158 .... 73—74
Perfect. 159—161 .... 74—75
Future. 162 75
Habitual. 163 75
Imperative. 164 76
The Verb with a Noun as Object. 165—169 76
Verbal Noun. 170 .... 76—77
Noun Agent. 171 77
The Passive Voice. 172—177 a. .... 77—79
Doubling of a Verb. 178 79
Change of Sounds in Verbs. 179—193 .... 79—89
Changes in the second consonant. 179—185 .... 79—84
A List of Verbs in their different forms. 181 .... 80—81
Changes in the stem-vowel. 186—188 .... 84—86
Changes in the semivowel. 189—193 .... 86—89
Auxiliary Verbs. 194—195 .... 89—90
Negation of the Verb. 196 .... 90—91
ADVERBS. 197—203 .... 91—93
PREPOSITIONS. 204 .... 93—94
SALUTATIONS. 205 94

SECOND PART. FOLKLORE.
I. OCCUPATIONS.
1. Housebuilding .... 96—98
2. Soil................................. 98
3. Field-produce........................ 98

| Contents | XI |

4. Kinds of duras .... 98—99
   Agriculture .... 99—102
5. Foods .... 102—103
6. Seasons 103
7. Months 103
8. Day-times 103
9. Stars 104
10. Household-things 104
11. Handicrafts .... 105—106
12. Tools 106
13. Clothings and ornaments .... 106—107
14. Names for cows .... 107—108

II. SOCIAL INSTITUTIONS AND SCENES FROM DAILY LIFE.

15. Marriage 109
16. Burial 111
17. Inheritance 113
18. Murder 114
19. Blood Revenge 115
20. Quarrel between Husband and Wife .. 116
21. The Husband who wanted to cook ... 117

III. SICKNESS.

22. Treatment of Sick People 119
23. Another Report on Sickness 119
24. Sicknesses 120

IV. POLITICAL INSTITUTIONS.

25. Election of a King 122
26. Another report on Election 123
27. Clothes for the Royal Court 125
28. Boats for the King 126
29. Provinces of the Shilluk country .. 127
    The Clans or Divisions of the Shilluk People ... 127
30. The Shilluk Kings 135
31. Burial of a King 135
32. The Man who took the Law into his own Hand . 136
33. A killed Crocodile is the Property of the Magistrate 137

34. How Fashoda became the Royal Residence 138
35. A Law-suit about Dowry 139

V. HISTORICAL TRADITIONS.
36. Nyadwai......................... 141
37. Golit............................. 141
38. Nyimo 142
39. Nyadoke.......................... 142
40. King Dokot....................... 143
41. Nyakwach........................ 144
42. The False Prophets 146
43. The Prince who refused to be King 147
44. The Cowardly King 148
45. Queen Abudok 149

VI. WAR STORIES.
46. War............................... 151
47. Tribal War....................... 153
48. The War of Nyeker 153
49. The War of Deng 153

VII. TRADITIONS ON NYIKANG.
50. Nyikang's Parents 155
    The Origin of the Shullas 157
51. Early Wanderings of Nyikang............ 158
52. Different Doings and Adventures of Nyikang ... 161
53. The Man who sacrificed himself 165
54. Nyikang and the River-people............ 165
55. The Lost Low 165
56. The Liar......................... 166
57. Nyikang's Quarrel with Duwat 166
58. The Fish Ocholo 167
59. Nyikang and the Sorcerers 168
60. A War against Turtles 169
61. Praising Nyikang.................. 170

VIII. PRAYERS AND RELIGIOUS CEREMONIES.
62. A Prayer to God 171
63. A Prayer for Rain 171

64. A Religious Ceremony 172
65. How Cattle is brought across the River 172
66. Preparation for War 173

IX. STORIES ABOUT SORCERERS.
67. The Cruel King 175
68. King Nyadwai trying the Sorcerers 175
69. The Vision of the Sorcerer 176
70. Agok 177

X. CREATION.
71. The Creation of Man 178
71 a. On Totemism 178

XI. ANIMAL STORIES.
72. Hare and Hyena 180
73. Monkey and Lion 184
74. Dog and Fox 185
75. Hare and Hyena 185
76. Lion and Fox 186
77. Starling and Centipede 188
78. Hare and Tapero 189
79. Who is King 190
80. The Hare 193
81. Camel and Donkey 196

XII. ADVENTURES BETWEEN MEN AND ANIMALS.
82. The Country of the Dogs 201
83. Akwoch 202
84. Girl and Dog 205
85. Anyimo and the Lion.. 208
86. An Adventure in the Forest 210
87. Boy and Hyena 211
88. Nyajak 213
89. Ajang 217
90. The Snake 219
91. The Crocodile Hunter 221

XIII. ANECDOTES.
92. The Travellers 224

93. A Goat-story 225
94. The Glutton 225
95. Bachet 226
96. The Country where Death is not 228
97. The King and the People 230
98. Wealth cannot be imitated 231
99. Increase of Cattle 232
100. The Haughty Prince 232
101. The Hyena with the Bell 233

XIV. A HUNTING MATCH, AND A JOURNEY.

102. Elephant Hunting 234
103. A Journey 235

XV. SONGS.

104. War Songs 237
105. Mourning Songs, and others 239

XVI. RIDDLES.

106. Riddles 241

THIRD PART. DICTIONARY.

Shilluk—English 244
English—Shilluk 290

REGISTER 307

PLATES.

1: The Goldencrested Crane. Young Warriors with Clubs and Spears. Shilluk Dug-out. Typical Shilluk pose. The Marabou-stork XXIV
2: A Typical Shilluk XXXII
3: Boys and Maidens Dancing. View of Sobat River XXXVI
4: Shilluk war dance XXXVI
5: Village scene. "House of Nyikang". A Shilluk giant. Group of Shilluks XL

6: Shilluk Girls showing the way they wear the skin dress. Lotus flower XLVIII
7: Group of Native Huts. Group of Boys. Girls Sewing School XLVIII
8: Shilluk Women in arms. Two men in arms. A Shilluk Warrior LVI

MAP.

Sketch map of Tribes of the Shilluk Cluster indicating their principal migrations as shown by traditions and language, compiled and drawn by Bernhard Struck LXIII

ABBREVIATIONS.

a. = adjective
adv. = adverb
A. E. S. = The Anglo-Egyptian Sudan; vide "Authors Quoted"
interr. = interrogative
n. = noun, also verbal noun
prep. = preposition
rel. = relative
v. = verb
v. a. = verb active
v. n. = verb neuter
verb. n. = verbal noun

ff. = and the following
* before a word means that the word or form is not really existing, but hypothetical
- standing between two nouns designates the first of the two as a singular, the second as a plural, e. g. $àd\underline{e}rò$-$àd\underline{e}r$ means: $àd\underline{e}rò$ is the singular, $àd\underline{e}r$ the plural
⟨ means: is derived from
⟩ means: changes into.

The verb in the present tense has generally low tone on both syllables, therefore the tones are not designated in this case.

Names of Languages and Dialects abbreviated.

Al. = Aluru
Any. = Anywak
Ba. = Bari
Bo. = Bongo
Di. = Dinka
E. = Ewe
Ef. = Efik
G. = Gã
Ga. = Gang

Ju. = Jur
La. = Lango
Nu. = Nuba
Nr. = Nuer
N. = Nupe
Shi. = Shilluk
T. = *Twi*
Y. = Yoruba
V. = Vai

Ja. = Ja-Luo (Nyifwa).

AUTHORS QUOTED.

Anthropos 1910. (Hofmeyer.)
O. Baumann, Durch Massailand zur Nilquelle. Berlin 1894.
J. Bruce, Reise nach Abyssinien (Translated from the English). From: Sammlung merkwürdiger Reisen in das Innere von Afrika. Leipzig 1791.
F. Cailliaud, Voyage à Méroé. Paris 1826.
S. Crowther, Vocabulary of the Yoruba Language. London 1843.
K. Giffen, The Egyptian Sudan. Second Edition. Newyork 1911.
Count Gleichen, The Anglo-Egyptian Sudan. London 1905. Quoted: A. E. S.
C. R. Hall, English-Teso Vocabulary.
R. Hartmann, Die Nigritier. Berlin 1876.
— —, Die Nilländer. Leipzig 1883.
A. C. Hollis, The Masai. Oxford 1905.
Sir H. Johnston, The Uganda Protectorate. London 1904.
A. L. Kitching, An Outline Grammar of the Gang Language. London 1907.
R. Lepsius, Nubische Grammatik. Berlin 1880.
E. Marno, Reisen im Gebiet des Weißen und Blauen Nil. Wien 1874.
J. C. Mitterrutzner, Die Dinka-Sprache. Brixen 1866.
L. Reinisch, Die Nuba-Sprache. Wien 1879.
E. Rüppell, Reise in Abessinien, Frankfurt (Main) 1838—40.
J. v. Russegger, Reisen in Europa, Asien und Afrika. Stuttgart 1841—50.
G. Schweinfurth, Im Herzen von Afrika. Leipzig 1878.
Schweitzer, Emin Pascha. 1897.
B. Struck, An Unlocated Tribe on the White Nile, Journal of the African Society. London 1908.
— —, Über die Sprachen der Tatoga und Irakuleute. Mitteilungen aus den Deutschen Schutzgebieten, Ergänzungsheft 4, 1910.
H. L. Tangye, In the Torrid Sudan. London 1910.
F. Werne, Reise durch Sennaar. Berlin 1852.
D. Westermann, Die Sudansprachen. Hamburg 1911.
— —, The Nuer Language. Mitteilungen des Seminars für Orientalische Sprachen. Berlin 1912.

INTRODUCTION

I. DESCRIPTION OF THE COUNTRY AND ITS PEOPLE.

NAME

The inhabitants are called: *óchŏlọ,* "a Shilluk", plural *wạte chŏl,* "children of Shilluk", "Shilluks"; the country is called *fọ̀ẹ̀ chọ̣l* "country of the Shilluks." The word *chŏl* perhaps means "black", vide below. A second name of the people is *okāṅọ,* "descendants of *kāṅọ,*" this name is connected with Nyikang, the national hero of the Shilluks. The name "Shilluk" (singular Shilkawi) is given to them by the Arabs, and has now become their common designation; it is of course derived from *ochŏlọ.* Other appellations, which are in use among the neighbours of the Shilluks, vide page 44.

EXTENSION OF THE COUNTRY

The Shilluk country is situated on the western banks of the White Nile, from Kaka to Lake No, that is from about 10°5′ to 9°5′ northern latitude, a length of nearly 350 km, and a width of 5 to 6 hours. Near the mouth of the Sobat (Bahr El Asraf, "Yellow River") a number of Shilluks live on the eastern shore of the White Nile, on both sides of the lower Sobat, chiefly on its northern bank. They extend about 35 miles up the Sobat, the last Shilluk village up river being Nagdyeb. There is also a group of Shilluk settlements at Shakwa El Shilkawi (= Shilluk), near Bahr El Zeraf, on the right bank of the Nile, and on Khor Atar, south of Tonga *(Tūṅọ).* North of Kaka the first Shilluk settlements are found on Aba Island, on the north- and south-end of which there is a small Shilluk village each. Near Masran Island there is also a Shilluk village on the right bank of the Nile. Again single settlements are met with on Masran Island, Wad Dakona Island, and on the north-end of the Gezira Wad Beiker.

The Shilluks themselves designate the extension of their country by naming the most northern and the most southern village and district of their Kingdom, viz. Mwomo and Tonga *(Mwọmọ, Tūṅọ),* which term corresponds exactly to the expression of the ancient Hebrews: from Dan unto Bersheba.

In former times the country of the Shilluks seems to have been larger than it is now. According to older reports it not only extended farther northwards, whence they were driven back by Arab tribes, but they are also said to have, in the 17th century, inhabited both sides of the White Nile south of Kawa; Kawa is situated a little south of El Dueim; so, provided this report is right, they owned at that time a trait of territory nearly three times as great as that they inhabit to-day.

CLIMATE

From January to April the climate of the country is dry and warm. April is the hottest month of the year. June to September constitutes the rainy season, and from October to December the larger part of the country is flooded with water, but the marshes and smaller Khors [1] all dry up by April. From November to April the climate is not unhealthy for Europeans. During the wet season mosquitoes are numerous. Malaria and black water fever are the diseases most dangerous to white people.

The country is a plain with only inconsiderable elevations, on which the villages of the natives are built. The soil is black and fertile near the river and the khors, back from the water courses it is in most places poorer, sometimes sandy. SOIL

The chief vegetation is high grass, interspersed with shrubs. A light forest of acacia trees is found mainly along the Nile. The acacia is the chief representative of the tree-flora: heglig (Balanites aegyptiaca), sont-acacia (Acacia arabica), Talh (Acacia Seyal), different kinds of gum-acacias, etc. A characteristic feature of the landscape are groups of deleib- and dom-palms (Borassus flabellifer and Hyphaena Thebaica); a beautiful tree is the mahogany tree (Khaya senegalensis); it is most useful as timber, but seems to be rather rare in the Shilluk country; other notable trees are: different kinds of Ficus (Sycomore fig), the ardeib tree (Tamarindus indicus), nabag (a fruit tree) etc. The vegetation on the river is most luxuriant. Though this is not the region of the sudd, yet the river is at most times largely covered with single plants and swimming islands, formed of papyrus, ambach (Herminiera Elaphroxylon), several kinds of reeds, lotus, Umm Suf (Vossia procera), Potamogeton, Ottelia, and many others. The floating vegetation often serves birds for a fishing place. Trees are much hampered in their growth by the fires which the natives light while the grass is dry; the reason for burning the grass is to hunt up game, and to get the ground cleared for cultivation. VEGETATION

The country being thickly populated, game is not very numerous. But at some distance from the settlements large animals are still frequent, chiefly near the river towards Lake No; the neighbourhood of Kaka and north of it are also rich in game. Elephants, giraffes, buffaloes are met with, though not very frequently; antelopes and gazelles abound: bushbuck (Tragelaphus scriptus), reedbuck (Cervicapra bohor), white-eared cob (Cobus leucotis), ariel (Gazella soemmeringi), dorcas (G. dorcas), isabelline gazelle (G. isabella), oryx, waterbuck (Cobus defassa), Mrs. Gray's waterbuck (Cobus maria), gazella rubifrons, roan antelope (Hippotragus equinus bakeri), hartebeest (Bubalis jacksoni), tiang or Bastard Hartebeest (Damaliscus tiang), Oribi antelope (Ourebia) etc. Of the carnivorous family the most notable are: lion, leopard, jackal, hyena, fox, Zorilla (a little black-and-white animal resembling the American skunk), ANIMALS

---

[1] Khor (Arab) = water course drying up in the rainless season.

XXII   *Introduction*

ichneumon (mangouste). The natives also hunt the hare, porcupine, ground-squirrel, rat, and hedgehog. The rivers and khors, and chiefly their sidearms, are populated by crocodiles, hippos, and numerous fish, some of which weigh up to lbs. 200. The birds are mainly riverain: cranes, storks, herons, egrets, fish-eagles, marabous, pelicans, ibises, ducks, geese; the guinea-fowl is very common; numberless swarms of dura-birds (Pyromelana franciscana) are a great nuisance to the farmer; besides them quails, pigeons, turtle-doves, hawks, crows, swallows, owls, and starlings are frequent. Of snakes the largest ist python; of poisonous species the puff-adder and some others occur; harmless snakes are numerous.

PULATION The population amounts to about 60000 souls,[1] who live in a little more than 1200 villages, and 10000 "domiciles", each of which consists of three to five huts. Accordingly the average number of people living in a village is 50, and one domicile is inhabited by about six persons. The largest village is Atwadoi in a district of the same name north of Kodok; it consists (1903) of 120 domiciles. The villages generally lie in the belt between the swamp of the Nile-bank and the forest. There are, however, eight groups of villages 12—22 miles inland, away from the river. The country is, for its size, and considering the fact that only in the higher parts settlements are possible, thickly populated. "Right away from Kaka to Lake No is a continous string of villages lying about a mile from the river. There are only two points in the whole of this distance, at which the interval between villages exceeds two miles, and these are the points where grazing is bad, between Akurwar and Nun, and between Nielwag and Nyagwado." A. E. S., p. 193.

According to Schweinfurth, the population was much larger formerly. In 1871, when the Egyptians had conquered the country, a census was taken; the villages on the left bank of the Nile were almost exactly 3000. The inhabitants of this part numbered one million, each village consisting of 45—200 huts, a hut comprising four persons. No part of Africa, not even of the world, is so densely populated. "The whole western Nile bank, as far as the boundaries of the country reach, is like one single village, whose parts are separated by a distance of only 500 to 1000 steps. The hut-clusters are built in an astonishing regularity, and are so crowded together that from a distance they look like a cluster of mushrooms."

The statement of a population of more than one million is probably too high; the Shilluks have doubtlessly suffered cruelly from wars and raids, but in spite of this a decrease from one million to 60000 within a time of forty years is hardly thinkable.

Since the time the people live under the peace of Anglo-Egyptian rule, they

---

[1] This is the number of the White Nile and Sobat Shilluks only; if all the Shilluk speaking people are included, the population will amount to several hundreds of thousands.

are increasing in numbers. The average number of children reared in one family may be from three to four. The number of children born by one woman is not low; women with ten children are no exception. But as a rule no more than three or four children grow up to maturity in one family, the rest dying from want of reasonable nursing. If in course of time the natives are taught to take better care of their children, the population will no doubt strongly increase. A cause of the low birth rate in many families is the fact that a man is not supposed to have intercourse with his wife while a baby is nursing, that is, till the baby is from two to two and a half years old. They consider it a great shame for a woman to become pregnant before this time has elapsed. If such a case happens, they generally will say that the woman has committed adultery.

The Shilluks are tall in figure, the average height of the men being nearly 1.80 m.¹ They are generally lean, rather narrow in the shoulders, and have but thin calves; their arms and legs are long, especially the legs below the knees and the forearms; hands and feet are small. A characteristic posture of the Shilluk man is to stand on one leg, and bending the other, press the sole of his foot against the inner surface of the knee, while one hand holds a spear stuck into the ground; he will stand thus for hours, looking admiringly at his cattle. They are very clever in running and jumping, and are capable of sustaining considerable fatigue. [OUTWARD APPEARANCE OF THE PEO...]

Their skin is dark, almost black; albinoes seem to be rare. The physical appearance of the Shilluks is not that of pure negroes, they might rather be called negroids, in spite of their dark colour. Most of them have a fierce, sometimes a proud, haughty look. The cheek-bones and lips are protruding, but not excessively; the nose is flat, but high noses are not infrequent. Young people of both sexes are finely built, while in old age they generally become very thin and bony. Their gait is erect and elastic.

What makes the Shilluks look most ugly and almost frightful in the eyes of a newcomer, is their habit of smearing the whole body. While the lower part is covered with ashes, the breast and head are painted with red earth or with chalk, or, if they can afford it, with oil or butter. Sometimes the whole body is painted white or red, and lines or figures are drawn across the face. [PAINTING THE BODY]

Like most Nilotic negroes the Shilluk remove the lower incisors; this is done in early childhood; its omission would, in the belief of the natives, cause sickness; for instance, a case occurred where the teeth were taken out to cure sore eyes; a woman who had just had them removed from her child, said that unless they were taken out, her child would undoubtedly be deformed in some way, when it grew to maturity. Another explanation for extracting the teeth [EXTRACTION OF INCISORS]

---

¹ five feet ten inches.

is, that this will keep them from using abusive language. — Some natives say, members of the royal family do not remove the incisors; but of this I am not sure.

TRIBAL MARKS The tribal marks of the Shilluks, women as well as men, are from three to five rows of dots across the forehead. The regular instrument for tattoeing these dots into the skin is a crude iron similar in shape to our scalpel. But not infrequently individuals are met with who have not these marks. Sometimes women have from one to three rows of small scars across their foreheads. These are in most or all cases simply caused by wearing bands of buttons drawn tightly across the forehead. Tattoeings on other parts of the body are seldom.

SHAVING The women wear either no or only short hair on the head; they shave their heads with a razor consisting of a straight piece of thin iron, whose edge is sharpened, or with a short piece of iron with one side beaten out to a thin edge. But lacking a razor they use almost any metal instrument they can get hold of for this purpose. Both sexes scrupulously remove any hair on the body by pulling it out with a kind of pincers; the men even pull out their beard and eyelashes. — They do not circumcise.

HAIR-DRESSINGS The men, chiefly youths, indulge in elaborate hair-dresses of varied forms. Such hair-dressing takes several hours to arrange, and has to last for weeks, the natural occassion for renewing it being a village-dance, where everyone wants to appear at his best; in dressing it, the hair is first loosened with a stick, which serves at the same time for scratching the head. Then it is twisted and brought into the right form by means of a mixture of gum, mud, and sometimes cow-dung; from time to time oil or butter is poured on it. In order not to spoil the hair-dressings while sleeping, the neck is supported by neck-supports. Sometimes the hair is bleached either yellowish-red or grey. Bleached hair is generally not twisted or dressed, but is left standing out in all directions "like the feathers of a fighting cock." Bleaching is done by smearing a thick plaster of ashes, chalk and cow-dung on the hair and leaving it there for about two or three weeks. Another mode of bleaching is to rub the plaster well into the hair, then gathering it up from the back, and bringing it forward, forming it into the shape of a horn. While in this state, they must be very careful not to break it, lest the hair is broken off. The same result is obtained by washing the hair continually with cow-urine. These processes take the kink as well as the colour out of the hair. This bleached bristle-like hair together with their tall, thin body covered with ashes or brick-dust, and the want of eyelashes sometimes gives the people, in the eyes of one who has never seen them before, a rather frightful appearance. Boys wear their hair in little knobs, formed with red earth and fat. Cowrie-shells, in strings or single, are often twisted into the hair, and

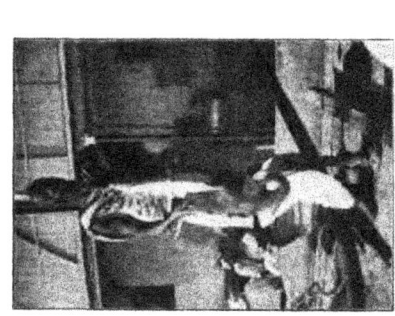

1. The Goldencrested Crane, the most beautiful Bird in the Sudan
2. Shilluk Dug-out
3. Typical Shilluk pose. In the background a killed crocodile
4. Young Warriors with Clubs and Spears
5. The Marabou-stork

youg men are very fond of adorning their hair with ostrich or other fine feathers.

The men and generally also unmarried girls go naked. In recent times many men wear a cotton cloth, which is knotted on the left shoulder, and slung round the right hip; chiefly people living near the mission have partly adopted this clothing; the desire to possess such a cotton-cloth is a stimulus for many a Shilluk to work for a few days or weeks in the mission-compound; the number of those who do so is apparently increasing. Animal-skins are generally not worn by men as an every-day dress. Women, and sometimes girls are dressed in cow, calf, or antelope skins, which are either wrapped round the body, or hung over the shoulder. CLOTHING AND ORNAMENTS

[The full dress of a woman is described by Mrs. Giffen in "The Egyptian Sudan" as follows: First of all there is a small apron. This is a piece of coarse cloth — originally white — about two feet long and eighteen inches wide. It is made of two thicknesses, and it is tied by strings fastened to two corners around the waist, but just below the abdomen, and falls down to the knees.

Then there are two skins, of sheep, goat, calf, gazelle or whatever it may be, tanned with the hair on, and worn with the hair side out. One of these is tied around the waist, using one foreleg and one hindleg of the skin for strings to tie with. The tail and the other two legs — or the skin of them — dangle and flap around the legs as ornaments. Indeed these are sometimes ornamented with beads, brass or iron rings. This skin is tied in front so as to show the white apron underneath.

The other skin is worn on the upper part of the body. The fore and hind legs on one side are fastened together at their very tips; this is then slipped over the head, the legs of the skin thus tied together resting on the right shoulder, and the other side passing under the left arm. This is the full dress of a woman. Of course in addition to this they may wear as many beads and other ornaments as they can afford; strings of beads around the waist, neck, and arms, and armlets, of brass; sometimes as many as ten or twelve brass or iron rings, weighing several pounds, and extending from the hand half way to the elbow. These are not loose, but drawn tight to the flesh, and each made fast by the blacksmith. Similar rings of iron are often worn by the elder women on the ankle. These are very heavy and produce great knots in the flesh.

The little girls wear the apron only, and when a little older, put on the shoulder skin, and when full grown wear the skin about the waist.]

When meeting for a dance both sexes are richly dressed. While present at a great dance. I have noted the ornaments and clothings worn by the young men and girls on the occasion. They are a) for the men: above the ankles a strip of sheep or goat skin with the hair on it outside; the same just below the knee; above it are the knee-bells, a number of metal bells each consisting in a hollow, oblong piece of iron, in which a small iron ball moves, thus producing a rattling noise; about the loins there is a skin of leopard, gepard, wild cat, or jackal, suspended on a eight to twelve-fold girdle of ostrich egg shells; the girdle may also consist of European beads; on the wrist a bracelet of brass or iron, above the elbow an ivory ring, above it a six- to eight-fold ring of ambach; about the neck they wear one or more necklaces of beads; on the head ornaments of horse-tail or other long hair, and ostrich feathers; round the forehead strips of red or white bristles are fastened; each man holds two lances, two clubs, one club-shield, the lances generally being adorned with ostrich-plumes; sometimes the skin-cloth round the waist is adorned with bells or iron chains. Face, arms, and the upper part of the body are smeared with red earth, over wich melted butter is poured and stripes of ashes are drawn. Several, if not all, of the dancers carry a dancing-stick, a long stick, bent at its upper end like the handle of a walking stick, and covered with brass or some other metal. b) The girls present the following appearance: above the ankles a bundle of heavy iron rings, on the loins a large antelope- or more frequently calf-skin suspended by a bundle of ostrich egg shell chains; round the neck and hanging down on the breasts a large bundle of blue or green beads; on the wrists bracelets of beads; round the forehead a string of beads; the hair is sometimes dressed on the occasion; in the hair an ostrich or some other good feather is stuck, in one or two cases I saw even flowers instead of a feather; the girls are not painted, only anointed with oil.

The most characteristic adornments of the men are thick, heavy bracelets and armlets of iron, brass, ivory, twisted ambach, tree-bark, and cowrie shells. A wreath consisting of a strip of skin with the hair on the outside is laid round the head. Rings of metal, ambach, cowrie or bark are worn above the ankle. Women and girls also wear armlets, but not ivory ones. The legs below the knee are loaded with heavy metal rings. Men as well as women, but chiefly the latter, pierce their ears at the top, and wear rings of brass or iron in them; sometimes merely a piece of metal or a stick is fastened in them. Both sexes wear strings of ostrich egg shells about the loins; besides these chains of cowries, of river shells, of leather, and of varied beads are frequent. Many grown-up men and youths wear a necklace of a peculiar kind of small, well-shaped, and marble-like stones, which have about the size of a pigeon-egg; they are very much valued, and the natives always ask an ox in exchange for them. These stones are collected by the Arabs of Kordofan about the numerous mountains there. The amount of labour required to work them into the proper shape accounts for their high value, as well as their scarcity among the Shilluks.

A Shilluk man hardly leaves his home without carrying a spear or two, and ARMS a club. They have two kinds of spears, one whose blade has the form of a laurel-leaf, another with a cylindric blade, ending in a sharp point, the surface being either smooth or barbed. The shafts are of common wood without any ornaments. The spears often have a tuft of short ostrich feathers or of wool, near the butt. The cylindrical (round) spears are used not only as arms, but also in fishing. Besides the spears, they have two species of clubs, at least one of which a man always carries with him. One is simply a thick stick about one meter long, and heavy at one end. The other is about two feet and a half long, made in one solid piece of hard, heavy wood, with a big round knob at one end.

The Shilluks are a haughty, proud people. They are much inclined to consider CHARACTER themselves and everything belonging to them as superior to the strangers, including the white men. "The things of the Shilluks are good, and the things of the strangers are bad", is a common saying among them. They do not in any way want the foreigners and their mode of life. This strong disinclination is not only due to their innate character, but also to the evil experiences they have had with Arabs, Turks, Abyssinians, the Dervishes etc.

The well-founded feeling of suspicion and even of contempt for white people will grow less intensive or may disappear altogether in consequence of the peaceful intercourse they now have with the representatives of the white race. In conversing with a white man they at the best treat him as their equal, but hardly ever as their superior. It requires therefore considerable tact to deal with them. Once having gained confidence they are frank, open-minded, and always ready for a joke, but they are also quickly offended.

As warriors the Shilluks are brave; they make excellent soldiers in colonial troops, and are renowned as the best soldiers in the Sudan; generally they become really attached to their leaders, whether white or black.

Working for the white man is done only in times of dearth, when no food is obtainable in other ways. But in spite of this difficulty the mission has, during the last few years, had remarkable results in educating the natives to regular voluntary work. — If one sees a Shilluk standig for an hour or longer almost without ever moving, except now and then scratching his head or chewing his tooth-stick, or if one meets them lying in the ashes of the village place for hours together, one might believe them to be an extremely lazy people. But this would be only partly right. Indeed during the dry season they have not much work

XXVIII   *Introduction*

to do except hunting, fishing, building or repairing the houses, or practising some craft: their chief occupation in this time is idling about, seeing friends, dancing, etc. But in the rainy season all people, including women and children, are engaged in farm-work; during these months they are really hard-working.

To give an opinion on the mental abilities of the natives would require a long and intimate acquaintance with them. From my personal experiences I can only say that I feel an admiration for the few men who have been working with me during my studies. They were never tired in giving explanations, in procuring folklore and helping me to acquire a thorough knowledge of the language. Whenever their store of tales was exhausted, they used to go to their families in the evening to get new informations; historical reports being provided by old men, chiefly from those belonging to the royal family, while for stories, riddles, etc. women were the best source. Though we were at work day after day, which meant for them a considerable and quite unaccustomed mental exertion, they never showed any unwillingness, but were really interested in the work. I consider them an intelligent, quick-witted people. This is confirmed by their folklore. They have a decided sense and predilection for historical traditions, being the only black people of the Eastern Sudan who are able to trace back their own history for centuries. The fact that they have had, up to the European occupation of the country, a kingdom with a well-ordered provincial government, shows no doubt certain political capabilities.

II. OCCUPATIONS.

HOUSEBUILDING Vide page 96 and 97.

The homestead is surrounded by a fence of dura-stalks. The villages are built in a circle, the open space in the centre containing sometimes a meeting-house for the men, and a small, narrow hut which is dedicated to Nyikang or some other ancient king.

AGRICULTURE Vide page 99.

CATTLE-BREEDING The favourite occupation of the Shilluks is cattle-breeding; cattle mean wealth and a social position, while the cultivation of the ground is merely the means of procuring daily food. Besides cattle goats and sheep are kept. The number of cattle has in earlier times undoubtedly been much larger than it is to-day, the desire of robbing cattle being one of the chief reasons for the raids of Arabs, Turks, and other enemies. The cattle census of 1903 showed 12 173 head of cattle and 63 473 sheep and goats, which is very little compared with that of the Dinkas. But the number of cattle is increasing now.

The cattle are of the zebu race, with a hump behind the neck; they are tall,

Occupations

with rather long legs, a slender body, and large horns. The horns, while young, are dressed into most manifold strange forms, this being the business of a particular craftsman, the "dresser of horns". Sometimes in a large herd one sees hardly any cattle with the horns in their natural shape. An illustration of how cattle are cherished and almost regarded as personal beings is the fact that they have about 40 different names for cattle, according to their colour, the configuration or size of the horns, etc. Vide page 107. — Domestic animals are not butchered, except when sick or exceedingly old. Oxen and goats are killed on festal occasions, such as funeral or marriage meals, or as sacrifices to Nyikang and Jwok. Neither do they sell cattle; for a stranger it is practically impossible to purchase a cow or an ox. The price of a cow is about £ 5; an ox is half the value of a cow which has calved; a young heifer has double the value of a cow. — Slaying a cow is done by stabbing it with a spear in the nape, so that the aorta is pierced. The blood is collected and cooked as food.

. The cows are milked morning and evening, usually by boys, sometimes also by old men, but not by women, the latter having nothing to do with cattle. The quantity of milk obtained is but poor. A gourd is the usual milk vessel. These are washed with cow-urine, which gives the milk an unpleasant flavour. They also wash their hands in cow-urine; but they do not mix the milk with it, as is the custom with Dinkas and Nuers.

Each village possesses a common cow-shed, but into it the herd is put at night during the rainy season only, when the mosquitoes are very bad. The rest of the year they are kraaled in the open yard, where they are tied with ropes to short pegs driven into the ground. This cattle-court is a semi-circular enclosure; at the entrance to it there is a small circular place built of corn stalks and covered with ashes, in which the young men who watch the herd sleep. A fire of dried cow dung is kept smouldering all night in this place. Sick cattle are nursed in the cow-shed during the daytime, to keep them out of the sun and away from food, but not in the night, unless it is the season when all the cattle are housed. Many cattle die every year, from intestinal worms and other diseases. A considerable number of cows are barren.

The cattle are herded by young men and boys. As soon as the dew has dried off the grass, the herd is driven into the pasture. During the dry season, when grass is getting rare, the herds migrate into the lower and swampy parts of the country, where the grass is still flourishing; the Shilluks along the White Nile cross over to the east bank; likewise the cattle of the Sobat Shilluks descend to the lagoons south of the Sobat. So in both cases they have to cross the rivers, which is, on account of the many crocodiles living in them, not undangerous, and is therefore done with much care and accompanied by weighty ceremonies, in order to keep the crocodiles away; this forms an important part of the duties of the witch-doctor; vide page 172. All the youths and boys over ten years accompany the herds, leaving their homes for several weeks or even months, and enjoying the free life in temporary huts. When after the first rains the new grass springs up, they return home. The struggle for the best pasture grounds very often becomes the cause of bitter quarrels, and has in the past not unfrequently led to tribal wars.

GOATS
SHEEP
FOWLS
DOGS

The Shilluk goats have rather high legs, they almost unvariably look thin and not well fed; their colour is mostly grey, but black ones too are not unfrequent. The sheep have no wool, but hair. They have a kind of mane on shoulder, neck and breast, the rest of the body being covered with short hair. Most sheep are white, brown-white, or black-white. — A race of small fowls is kept, but the natives do not make much of them; many chickens are stolen by snakes and other small animals. — Dogs are very numerous, they are a kind of greyhound, of red or yellow colour, and have a black, long snout. They are exceedingly quick in running and most clever in jumping. They overtake gazelles with easiness, and are much used in hunting.

HUNTING

Hunting is practised by all men occasionally, but is, as a rule, not very successful. They use spears, clubs, and traps in killing or catching animals. Sometimes, chiefly in procuring animals whose skins form part of the revenue of the king, all the people of a village assemble for a hunting match, vide page 125; a large circle is formed, and the animals inside it, when wishing to escape, are killed. When an animal is wounded, but runs away, they will persecute it for days, till it breaks down. The skin of a killed leopard belongs to the king, and could, at least formerly, be worn by privates only by special permission of the king. A lion's skin is considered as evil, and is not worn.

Hippopotamus hunting is done by combined parties in canoes, harpooning the animal and dispatching him with spears, when he comes to the surface to breathe.

FISHING

Their way of fishing is that with the round barbed spear, and with traps, which are made of corn stalks and reed. Fish-spearing is done in muddy water, where they cannot see anything below the surface, and therefore cannot aim. But nevertheless by this rude mode they sometimes have good results, the fish in the White Nile and Sobat being numerous and large. Sometimes they carry on fishing during the night time by holding burning grass-torches over the water, and thus enticing the fish, which are then speared. In recent time nets and fishhooks are bought from the white people, and are employed in fishing.

HANDICRAFTS

The Shilluks practise a great number of crafts, which are carried on in families for generations, the father and mother imparting their skill to their children.

A list of craftsmen and their trade vide page 105. A few words may be added here
on some particular crafts. They have skilful blacksmiths; these make spears, BLACKSMITH
hoes, axes, harpoons, picks, arm-rings of brass and of iron, bells, chains. Their
handicraft, which is carried on chiefly during the dry season, is a travelling
one; they take their tools and go about from one place to another. While
among the Dinkas the blacksmiths are considered a low, despised class of
people, who live separate from the villages in the bush, with the Shilluks they
are respected persons, and accordingly their pay is good. The employer has
to support the blacksmith working for him, and pays him a sheep beside. Iron
is not found in the Shilluk country. Previous to the opening up of the country to
the traders the iron secured by the Shilluks came from the Dinkas and Nuers,
who seemed to buy it from the natives of the Upper Nile regions (Jurs, Bongos),
where iron is smelted; some may also have come from Darfur through Kordofan. In recent years, however, nearly all of it is procured from the north, and
is of European origin. A remarkable proof of the growing willingness on the
side of the natives to work for wages is the fact that during the last two years the
American missionaries have introduced and sold to the natives some thirteen
tons of raw iron, together with a great number of good iron tools, as axes, etc.
Not only the raw material, but even the finished articles of native manufacture
are gradually being replaced by European imports. Their good spears are still
made by their own blacksmiths, but many cheap spears are bought from the
traders; so are their crude axes, mattocks and hoes. Iron bracelets and other
ornaments are made by their blacksmiths from iron rods. If the rod is too
large, it is heated and beaten out. Whatever the Shilluk blacksmith makes, is
superior to the imported article that he gets from the Arab or Greek trader.
It may be mentioned that the word bọ̈do, which means originally and properly
"blacksmith", has also the wider sense of "craftsman", and has become a
designation for all other crafts they practise.

An important craft is that of the thatch-maker. The roofs of the Shilluk OTHER CRA
houses are of a peculiarly neat description. While the Dinkas generally leave
the roof with the appearance of being unfinished, the grass not being smoothed
down and cut at the ends, the Shilluk thatcher makes his thatch with a
neatness which really excites admiration. The framework of the roof is always
made on the ground and placed on the circular wall like a great conical cap.

Plaiting is pratised by both sexes. Men make the large, coarse mats for
enclosing yards, and also the large grain baskets. Women plait small fancy
mats for covering food, and also very nice small coloured baskets, sieves, etc.

Most of the men make their own ostrich shell girdles. The shells are first
broken into irregular pieces, which are pierced in the center with an awl-

shaped iron instrument. The hole is made by holding the sharpened point of the iron on the piece of shell and rapidly revolving it between the palms of the hand. The pierced pieces are then rounded by crushing the edges against a stone with a cow's hoof.

Skins for wearing apparel, such as the hides of calves, goats, gazelles and other small animals are usually prepared by drying them first and dressing, then curing in ashes. After this they are stretched tight on poles stuck in the ground, and grease or oil is rubbed on them; then they are rubbed and worked for several hours, till they are soft, and the oil well worked into them. The hair is left on; a skin with a large amount of the hair gone would be considered very poor. The skin is worn with the hair on the outside.

Ropes are made from plant fibres, grass, and the leaves of the dom palm.

BOATS Canoes are hollowed out of trees; this is, considering the poor tools they have, a very tiresome work, but the boats they make are fairly well; they are propelled by means of long sticks. A peculiar kind of boat or raft is made of the ambach tree; it is composed of a thick bundle of that pith-like, light cane tied together, turned up at the bows, and propelled by a paddle. These boats are so light that they are easily carried by one man.

MUSICAL RUMENTS Their musical instruments are small and large drums, a stringed instrument called *tom* and a wind instrument consisting in a cow's or antelope's horn; this is used in wars and in war-dances. The drums are logs of wood hollowed out and braced with skin; they are beaten either with the flat hand or with a stick. The *tom* is made by splitting in the middle a small section of a log and hollowing out the flat side a little. A piece of raw cow hide is stretched wet over this, and the flat side becomes the face of the instrument. A round stick some 18 inches long is fastened at each end. The ends of these two upright pieces pass through a cross-stick, which is large enough in diameter to allow them to pass this and still be quite strong. The holes are made in it by burning. The strings are made of tendons of animals or of the root bark of a certain plant. These are attached to the head, drawn across the face over a small wooden bridge, and wound about the cross-stick. They are then tightened, and the instrument is tuned by wettening these strings and tightening or loosening them about the crosspiece. They are tied to this stick, and by winding over themselves, keep from slipping.

POTTERY Pottery is the handicraft of women. They make pots of different kind and size, for carrying water, cooking, brewing beer; they also make pitchers, cups for drinking beer, heads for smoking pipes, etc. Gourds and calabashes are also much used household tools. The pipe-heads are made of clay; they are large and rather clumsy, and are generally ornamented with some simple designs,

A Typical Shilluk, showing head dress

mostly consisting of ring-shaped lines with dots in them. The pipe-stem is a long, thick, hollow reed of about 1½—2 cm in diameter. The juncture between the stick and the head is tightly closed with a leather cover. On the upper end of the stick a small, oblong gourd with a pointed head is fastened; here again the juncture is made tight by a leather cover wrapped about it. Along the stick four or five strings are fastened, by which the pipe is carried; a long, pointed stick for cleaning the pipe is tied to the stem with a string. They are exceedingly fond of smoking, both men and women. The smoking materials is a little tobacco and much charcoal. The pipe being rather heavy, they usually sit down, bowing their head deep over the pipe while smoking. When sitting in a circle they take only one or two draughts, and after that hand the pipe over to their neighbour. — Tobacco is not only smoked, but also chewed passionately; this habit is more common among women and girls than among men. *[SMOKING AN CHEWING OF TOBACCO]*

In cases of sickness the doctor is called. His chief means of curing consists in charms, but they also know some reasonable medicines, among which cutting stands in the first place; but although they inflict much pain, they often heal a sickness. — Sick people are nursed by their relatives with care; temporary residences are fixed for them by screening off a place in the yard.

Building houses, making fences, dressing skins, working neck supports, carving and polishing clubs and spear sticks, making ambach boats and other common work is understood by every Shilluk. The neck supports are "invented by Nyikang." They are carved of wood, and are made to resemble the forms of animals, viz. of hippopotamus, giraffe, tiang, camel, ostrich and another bird, which seems to be an ibis. The Shilluks have no chairs or stools; old men sometimes sit on a piece of ambach wood, young people squat or lie on the ground. *[NECK SUPPO]*

The craftsmen do not practise their trade with the exclusion of all other kind of work; each one of them cultivates his farm and tends his cattle, and only during the time there is no farm-work, he works at his craft.

There are villages which are renowned in practising certain crafts; some in fishing or hunting, some in cattle-breeding or cultivating dura, some in making pots or baskets, etc. As these goods are exchanged between the villages, a little trade is going on; but in this trade among the natives no money is used, and it is practised only occasionally; they have no markets. The very little development of trade is illustrated by the expression used for it: *ṅgawọ*, which means "to sell" as well as "to buy"; all trade being done by barter, selling and buying are identical actions; the native cannot "buy" anything without at the same time "selling" another thing; be exchanges one thing for another. In trading with the Arab or Greek merchant they have, however, learnt the use of money;

here articles of purchase and sale are calculated in silver currency.

The daily work of the women is cooking, carrying water, cleaning the house and yard, etc. During the time of farmwork they help the men in cultivating the fields.

FOOD

The staple food is dura. It is cooked, baked into a bread *(kwen)*, roasted, brewed and, when green, eaten raw. For different kinds of food vide page 102. Their diet is rather monotonous, dura being its constant chief component. The dura is pounded and ground. The mortar is either a log of wood hollowed out, or a flat excavation in the ground, limed out with clay. The mill-stones — a large and a small one, with the latter the grinding is done — are secured from districts west of the Shilluk country. — Fire is made by twirling a hard stick on a soft piece of wood.

Besides dura they eat sesame, duchn, maize, beans, some onions, various grass seeds, the seeds of the lotus plant and of some kinds of nymphaeae. The fruit of several trees, as deleib, nabag, etc. also serve as food; they even rob ant hills to procure the winter store of hoarded seeds. White ants, when in the winged state, are a delicacy to them. — Milk is used in the household in many ways: it is drunk fresh, sour, or boiled, or dura meals are prepared with it. They also make butter, by shaking or rolling the milk in a gourd. — As domestic animals are almost never slain, meat forms no part of the daily food, but is rather an exceptional delicacy, which is, however, sought for with eagerness; of game they hardly leave any piece uneaten, skin and bowels not excepted; they do not even despise dead animals. The blood of killed animals is kept and cooked, but they do not tap the blood from living cattle, as is the custom with the Bari and Masai. — Generally they prefer the meat of castrated animals.

Two chief meals are taken daily; one from nine to ten in the morning, and the second at sunset.

BREWING OF BEER

A large quantity of the dura the people reap is used in cooking merisa or beer. The grain is put into jars and water poured on it. Thus it is left till the grain begins to sprout. Then it is spread in the sun to dry, and then pounded or ground; this wet meal is mixed with flour from the fresh grain and put a second time into jars which are filled with water. After stirring and mixing well, a little dry meal is sprinkled on it; the jars are covered with small mats and allowed to remain a day or two, until it begins to ferment, when a little more water and meal are added. When the whole mass is well fermented it is filtered through a grass funnel, and the following day is ready for use. It will keep about a week. Though this drink is slightly intoxicating, it does not seem to do great harm; it is very nourishing, and the natives regard it rather as a food than a beverage.

III. FAMILY LIFE.

When a young man wants to marry, he himself asks the girl he has selected; MARRIAGE if she assents, she directs her lover to her parents and the old people of the village; if these also do not object, they ask him to bring the dowry, which consists of cattle. From four to six head of oxen and one milch cow is the ordinary price for a woman, besides a number of sheep and goats. But the whole of this dowry is in most cases not paid to the father-in-law at once, before the marriage takes place. One ox is paid to the elders of the village when they arrange the marriage business, one or more at the celebration of the marriage, another when the first child is born. The ox which is slaughtered at the marriage festival is driven to the village of the bride by all the young men of the bridegroom's village. They decorate this ox by tying tassels of cows' tails on the top of the horns. In case the horns have not a good shape for tying these tassels, they are pierced and the tassels are fastened in the holes. A young man in buying an ox is always particular about the shape of the horns for this reason. On the marriage festival vide page 109. — A man cannot reach a social position without being married, and he cannot get a wife without cattle; so every young Shilluk's highest ambition consists in procuring cattle in order to buy a wife. But, as already mentioned, they usually marry before the full dowry is paid, and in such a case the debts of the young husband may become the source of quarrels between husband and wife, and still more between husband and father-in-law. As long as the price is not paid, the father has a legal right to take his daughter back from her husband; but this, though often threatened, is seldom done. Those who have sufficient means will as a rule not be satisfied with one wife, but marry a second and a third; only a very few exceed this number.

A young man may not marry a girl from his own division or clan, (vide page 127 ff.) but from any other division; the girl may live in the same village or in any other village, but they prefer to marry in a distant village. These marriage laws are a well established tribal custom, and people fear to break them, lest death follow marriage.

The position of the woman is no doubt a higher one than with most Moham- POSITION O medan peoples of the Sudan. She is generally well treated and is shown remark- WOMEN able respect. The women sometimes take part in public assemblies with the men, discuss the affairs that interest them and partake in dances and religious ceremonies. Even in their war-dances the women play an active *rôle*, vide page XXXIX. — If refractory or lazy, the man may give his wife a thrasing with a rope.

XXXVI	*Introduction*

REARING AND EDUCATION OF CHILDREN

On the average number of children in a family vide page XXIII. The birth of twins is regarded as the greatest of good fortune.

Affection of parents for their children is not wanting. The mother often places the infant in a long basket or bed made of grass; this she carries on her head or covers with a mat in some secure place, while the child sleeps. Education is limited to teaching the children the work and skill which the parents command.

The naming of the children is done by some member of the family, in most cases by the parents or grandparents. The name generally has some connection with circumstances attending the birth. The name *Atou* ("she died") is often given when the birth occurs in close proximity to a death in the family. *Ñawailo* is a very common name; it indicates that the mother of the child has prayed for a child by sweeping a sacred house (a temple of Nyikang or of some other ancient king) with a bunch of straw. Men often acquire a second name when grown up; this one is in most cases called after the name of a cow or an ox.

When the boys are from thirteen to fifteen years old, they start the cultivation of a small field of their own, for the result of which they try to acquire cattle. — The boys and young men of a village born in the same year form a companionship, all member of such a "class" having a common name. The young men of a village do not sleep in their parents' houses, but their common sleeping place is in the cow-shed of the village. The act of sleeping in the barn is called "sleeping in the ashes" from the fact that they during this time sleep in the ashes of the fire kept smouldering in the barn.

SLAVES The Shilluks have some slaves secured before the present régime. Some of these are Shilluks, others are from the Kordofan and also from farther up the Nile. They were secured in war or purchased from the Arabs. In single cases Shilluk parents sold their children for food in time of famine, or gave them away to chiefs.

BURIAL When a grown-up man dies, he is buried in or just before his hut. An ox is killed as a funeral feast, and its horns are planted on the grave so that they are visible from without. Women and children are buried in the bush. — For a description of a burial vide pages 111 and 135.

Some time after the death of a man a funeral ceremony is held; it takes place when the property of the deceased is divided among his heirs; this may be from about one month to one year after the person has died. The warriors of the neighbouring villages are invited. An ox is killed on the occasion. The ceremony consists in dancing, making displays of arms, feasting on the meat of the slain ox, and drinking merissa. The women also partake in it. Whether any religious actions are connected with it, I do not know.

1. 2. Boys and Maidens Dancing; the Maidens in cow skins
3. View of Sobat River with Doleib Hill in the distance

Shilluk war dance at Doleib Hill

Family Life XXXVII

The sons inherit the property of their father. The wives of the deceased INHERITANC[E] father are divided among the children, who may, and in most cases do, marry them, except their own mother. It is said that sometimes, when a husband is very old and infirm, his wives put him to death, in order to get a younger companion. On inheritance vide page 113.

Their chief amusement is dancing. The houses of a village are built in a DANCING AN[D] circle, leaving an open place in their midst. Here the inhabitants assemble in WAR-PLAYS the evening, stretching themselves in the warm ashes or on a skin, or squatting on a piece of ambach; several small fires of cow dung are burning and spread a smoke of strong smell, which is the best protection from mosquito-stings. The events of the day are discussed here, the tobacco pipe and merisa pot going from hand to hand. In the middle of this open place the trunk of a large tree is erected, in which the drums are suspended. With them signals are given in times of danger, but more frequently they are used to accompany the dances of the young people. These public dances are among the greatest events in the lives of the young Shilluks; even old men and women, though not taking an active part, are highly interested in them; sitting before the huts in front of the dancers they constitute a chorus, who accompanies the transactions of the younger generation with loud acclamations or blamings. The dances generally take place during the dry season; they begin at about four o'clock in the afternoon, or, in case there is moonshine, later in the evening, and last from three to five hours or longer. As a rule one village invites its neighbours by a drum signal given in the early morning of the day fixed for a dance. On hearing this signal the young people show a great zeal in preparing their body, hairdress and the ornaments worn on the occasion. They go to the village in groups or single, men and girls separately. Usually the youths perform some war-dance in full arms at first, in which the girls do not partake; they form a large circle in four or two rows, and while the drum is being beaten, begin dancing and singing war songs. The dance consists in jumping on the toe and at the same time moving slowly forward. These rhythmical movements are from time to time interrupted by a group of dancers violently rushing out of the circle, howling and shouting aloud, brandishing their spears with fierce looks, and performing mock fights or playing pantomimes, in which they exhibit very remarkable ability. Scenes from the hunting, pastoral and agricultural life are represented with such a dramatic vivacity that they richly deserve the applause they earn.

On a given signal, spears, clubs and shields are laid aside and put together in one place, and now the second part, in which the girls partake, begins. The latter have till then been waiting in a separate place, where the female lookers-on are gathered. Each girl selects her own dancer. First the men form again a

circle. Then the girls rush into this ring, each looking out for the man she
intends to favour. She draws up in front of him, so that they look each other
in the face; again two or four rows are formed, and the same dance begins
anew, accompanied by drumming and singing.

The dances are in many cases repeated on four successive afternoons or
nights; on the fourth day they frequently end in quarrels or real fights. The
cause of this is the young men of one village casting their eyes on the girls of
another village, and thus arousing jealousy. In such fights clubs are used, in
exceptional cases also spears.

[Of a great war-play which was performed in honour of the missionaries,
Dr. Giffen in "The Egyptian Sudan" gives the following description:
"The first intimation we had of their coming, or rather of their presence,
was a whoop and the sound of a horn that sent a chill, and kept it shooting up and down the spinal column. We rushed out on the veranda, and
saw at the foot of our hill, and only a few rods away, that the clans had
assembled. There were about one hundred men and boys with their
spears and war clubs, their bodies shining with oil, and their spears shining
from vigorous rubbing, while their faces were hideous with white and
red paint of brick-dust and ashes. They kept leaping in the air, yelling
and blowing that soul-sickening horn. Little by little they came toward
us, stooping low, hiding behind trees, gliding back and forth until they
were in front of the house. Then I stepped out and smiled at them, while
suddenly with a yell that was not earthly, they sprang in the air, the
first line made as if throwing the spear, and suddenly dropped down
for the following ranks. Again they all sprang up into the air, yelling,
dancing, singing, and brandishing spears, then circled around the house
and attacked from another quarter.

These manoeuvers were kept up for some time, and they grew more
excited and more wild all the while. Then, at a command from their chief,
they ceased and began to dance. Dancing with the Shulla (Shilluk) means
jumping up and down in the same spot, accompanied with a sort of
chanting sing-song, throwing the arms over their heads and flourishing
spears and clubs.

Again they formed in line of battle, five ranks deep, with a front of
twenty, each man with spear and shield. The horn sounded the advance,
and away they charged to the Doctor's house. They seemed to get the
very spirit of murder in their faces. They charged in good order; the
front rank, striking at an imaginary foe, dropped to their knees to allow
the other ranks to strike over their heads, and then the horn sounded the

retreat. Around our house they went in a regular stampede, and forming in a line again in front of the house for another charge.

This they repeated a number of times. Then a crowd of women, who had followed their husbands and sweethearts to battle, acted the part of foe, only to be overcome by the brave warriors and driven back. This part was very amusing. One old body with great bravery marched out and charged, using her pipe as her weapon. The men were a bit rough in driving her back, and she was evidently afraid her dear pipe would come to grief, so she took it inside our house and when next we saw her she was in the thick of a fray with a long weed as her weapon of offence and defence".]

The dry season is also the time for travelling. Relatives pay mutual visits, and marriageable young men go to the Nuers and Dinkas with spears, wire, stuffs, and dura, which they exchange for sheep and calves.

IV. RELIGION.

In the religion of the Shilluks three components ary clearly distinguishable: 1. Jwok (*jwǫk*) or God; 2. Nyikang (*Ńikäṅǫ*), the progenitor and national hero of the Shilluks; 3. ajwogo (*ȧjwǫ̊gǫ́*), the witch doctor or sorcerer. These three do not exist separate from each other, but have many relations amongst one another. There are still other forms of religious service, but they are not so prominent as the three mentioned.

"Jwok (*jwǫk*) is a supreme being, residing above". Whether he is regarded JWOK as creator is not sure. According to the sayings of some natives he surely is, but it seems probable that this belief, if there is such a one, is young, and must be traced back to Mohammedan or Christian influences. — On certain occasions an ox is killed as a sacrifice to Jwok, though this is done more frequently to Nyikang; prayers are also offered to Jwok, but according to my information, they have only one prayer to Jwok (for which vide page 171), while to Nyikang there are many. "Praying" to Jwok is expressed by a different word from that which serves for designating a prayer to Nyikang; the first is *lāmǫ* "to pray"; its original meaning is probably: to conjure. In praying to Nyikang *kwachǫ* "to ask for, to beg" is used. While the prayers to Nyikang are sung, and accompanied by dances, that one to Jwok is only spoken, not sung, and not accompanied by dancing. Jwok has no visible symbols or temples, nor are the prayers to him offered by a priest or sorcerer, but by the chief or village-elder.

In the heart and mind of the Shilluk Jwok does not possess a deep-rooted rank. In some way they do attribute good and evil to him, and chiefly the latter; when a person is ill, they may say: *erɛ jwọk* "Why, Jwok?" The sudden and violent death of a man is regarded as being caused by Jwok. But I do not think there is any ethical motive in our sense underlying this belief; Jwok has simply killed the man for having offended him, probably without knowing it. The name of Jwok is used in a favourable sense in the following phrases of salutation: when a person arrives, he is saluted: *yi kạl jwọk* "you have brought Jwok"; to one starting on a journey they say: *yi mīṭe jwọk*" you may hold fast Jwok". — Jwok has also the meaning of "sickness"; the reason for this is the conviction that Jwok is the causer of sickness; "he is sick", they express by "he has Jwok", "Jwok is upon him".

Although the Shilluk does certainly not connect with the word Jwok the same notion as we do with "God", Jwok is doubtless the only word fit for being used in the Christian sense. It is true the word occurs in stories in rather a disrespectful sense, any being with more than natural powers being called a Jwok; but this is so in analogous cases with many African peoples, and will almost always be so in heathen languages; it can therefore not form a real obstacle for using the word in Christian preaching and literature.

[In older literature the name Kelge appears as that of the "creator of the Shilluks." I have never heard this name].

NYIKANG, AND THE ORIGION OF THE SHILLUKS

The tradition on the origin of man or rather of the Shilluks leads to the second and most important part of the religious practice of the people, viz. the worship of Nyikang. This tradition runs thus: A white or rather greyish cow, *ḍeaṅ aduk*, came out of the river; she brought forth a gourd; when this gourd split, a man and animals came forth out of it (vide page 178). The name of this man was *Kọlọ*; *Kọlọ* begat *Omarọ*, who begat *Wat Mọ̄l* ("son of *Mọ̄l*"); *Wat Mọ̄l* begat Okwa. Okwa used to go to the riverside; here he met repeatedly two maidens who had come from out the water, they were very beautiful and had long hair, but the lower part of their bodies was like the form of a crocodile. One day Okwa seized the girls and carried them away. Their screams brought out their father, who till then had not been seen by Okwa. His face and the left side of his body were like human, but his right side was green of colour and had the form of a crocodile. When asked he declared his name to be Odiljil, he protested against his daughters being taken away by force, but afterwards consented. Okwa married the girls. The names of the two maidens were Nyakayo and Ongwat (*Ńakāyọ* and *Oṅwāt*). One of Nyakayo's sons was Nyikang; according to some this was the eldest child, while others say he was the youngest. Nyakayo had more children beside Nyikang; of one son the name is known, he was *Omọi*; the names of her daughters are (according to A. E. S.) Ad Dui, Ari Umker, and Bunyung. Okwa's second wife Ongwat gave birth to one son, Ju or *Bworọ*. Okwa married

1. Village scene   2. "House of Nyikang"   3. A Shilluk giant
4. Typical group of Shilluks; bodies covered with ashes; at the left a Shilluk dog

Religion

a third wife, whose eldest child, a son, was called Duwat *(Duwạt)*. The name *Dimǫ* also occurs as that of a son of Okwa, but I could not make out who his mother was. Nyikang was in form partly a man, and partly a crocodile.

[The exact pronunciation of Nyikang is *Ńĭkȧnǫ̀*, but the final *ǫ* is often omitted: *Ńĭkȧn*; the form *Ńȧkȧn* also occurs; in older literature the name is written Nyakam, Nyekom. *Ńĭkȧnǫ̀* is a composition from *ńi*, *ńa* "son" and *Kāńǫ*, which is probably a proper name; thus *Ńĭkȧnǫ* means: "son of *Kāńǫ*." The name *Kāńǫ* occurs also in *Okāńǫ*, which is composed from *O* and *Kāńǫ* and means "descendant of *Kāńǫ*; *Okāńǫ* is another name designating the Shilluk people. But about *Kāńǫ* the traditions, as far as they are kown, say nothing. — Frequently Nyikang is simply called *riṭ* "king".]

Nyakayo (*Ńakāyǫ*), the mother of Nyikang, exists up to the present time. NYAKAO, THE MOTHER OF NYIKANG Her residing place is about the junction of the Sobat and the White Nile. This is remarkable, as according to the tradition she did not emigrate with her son Nyikang, and yet does not now live in her original place, but in the Shilluk country. She sometimes appears from out the river, generally in the form of a crocodile, but at times in other forms. No worship or sacrifices are offered to her, but when a man or animal is taken by a crocodile, this is attributed to *Ńakāyǫ*. When she does this, the people must not complain; it is rather an honour, when she takes her sacrifice from a village.

In dubious judicial cases Nyakayo is resorted to as judge. The accused one is tied in a river, and a goat is bound and laid on the river-bank near by. This latter is done to allure a crocodile. If the accused one is taken by the crocodile (i. e. by Nyakayo), he was guilty. But not infrequently the delinquent, from fear of being lacerated by the crocodile, confesses his crime.

Between Nyikang and one of his brothers, probably Duwat, there arose a NYIKANG'S EMIGRATION quarrel after their father's death; according to some, about who should follow the father in the chieftainship, others say it was a quarrel about cattle. As they did not come to an agreement, Nyikang together with *Omǫi*, his brother, and his half-brother Ju (and his three sisters), left the country,[1] seeking for a new abode; when he started, *Duwạt* threw a digging stick after him, wherewith to dig the ground (or to bury the dead). Several tribes whom he met on his way, joined him, thus increasing the band of his followers. Nyikang settled about the mouth of the Sobat, and here founded the kingdom of the Shilluks. To increase the population of his new foundation, he changed animals and fabulous beings whom he found in the place, into men, built villages for them, and made them his subjects.

While residing in the Shilluk country, Nyikang fought many wars, among NYIKANG'S

---

[1] "acquiring wings and flying away to the mouth of the Sobat", A. E. S.

others one against the sun and his son; vide page 159.

When he felt his end approaching, he assembled all the chiefs of his kingdom for a splendid festival. While all were merry, suddenly a great wind arose, and scattered all those present. In this moment Nyikang took a cloth, wound it tightly round his neck, and thus choked himself.[1]

But many Shilluks firmly believe that Nyikang is still alive. The Rev. Oyler writes to me: "When I asked how Nyikang died, they were filled with amazement at my ignorance and stoutly maintained that he never died. If he dies, all the Shilluks will die. Hǫ, *Dāk*, and five other kings ascended to heaven, where Nyikang prays for the Shilluks (!). They say that he disappeared as the wind".

NYIKANG ADORED- Nyikang is the ancestor of the Shilluk nation and the founder of the Shilluk dynasty. He is worshipped, sacrifices and prayers are offered to him; he may be said to be lifted to the rank of a demi-god, though they never forget that he has been a real man. He is expressly designated as "little" in comparison with God.

In almost every village there is a little hut dedicated to Nyikang, or to some other ancient king. In form it is like the common houses, but much smaller and more slender. On its walls sometimes rough drawings in white, red, and black colour are seen, consisting simply in line-ornaments or representing animals. These drawings are made by women, with white, red and black earth, and are renewed every year before the chief prayers are offered. These huts are commonly called *kęn rit* "place of the king" i. e. of Nyikang. Besides these small huts they have a number of greater temples, which are in form like the Shilluk-hut, but of much larger size. They are found in most of the villages devoted to Nyikang. These "sacred villages" are, Akuruwar, Wau,[2] Fenyikang, Nyibodo (*Ńibǭdǫ*), *Otǫnǫ*, Nyelwal, *Oshārǫ, Otigǫ, Dīdīgǫ*. These houses, the small as well as the larger, are the places where Nyikang is worshipped. In them, at least in some, a number of reliques are preserved, which are considered holy and are held in great veneration. Among these are a statue of Nyikang made of ambach-wood; the holy spear, drum, and shield of Nyikang, a digging stick, ancient metal ornaments and clothes, etc. Spoils from wars are also dedicated to Nyikang, and are preserved in the temples.

In times of need, when sickness or war are threatening, but above all when rain does not come in due time, the people assemble round the house of Nyikang and pray to him. This is done by dancing and at the same time singing prayers. At the beginning of the rainy season, when they are about to plant dura, the regular chief prayers take place; on this occasion an animal is slain as a sacrifice to Nyikang. Before the transaction of any serious business the elders of the village assemble around the temple of Nyikang, to ask for his counsel.

---

[1] Till the subjection of the Shilluks by the British all succeeding Shilluk kings have finished their lives by the same form of death.

[2] This Wau is not the place in the Bahr Ghazal Province, but is situated on the left bank of the White Nile between Taufikia and Kodok.

Religion

SWEARING OATHS BY NYIKANG

By Nyikang also oaths are sworn. The expressions mostly used in swearing an oath are: *Ńikań shęt!* i. e.: "Nyikang indeed", "by Nyikang!" *Ńikań anan!* i. e. "Nyikang here!" or: "Nyikang now!" Another form is to couple his name with any of the sacred villages, as *Ńikań a Wau!* i. e. "by Nyikang of Wau!" Likewise *Ńikań a Ńelwal*, etc. In their conversations they are constantly using these oaths; they often make promises under oath, which they, however, readily break without any fear of penalty. They swear also by Dak, or any other of the ancient kings.

Another mode of swearing, which is used in judicial cases only, is to swear by the holy spear (of Nyikang): the *ajwōgǫ* who keeps the spear, sacrifices a sheep and puts the blood upon the accused and the accuser, and offers a prayer that justice may follow. Now the accuser or the accused or both swear by the holy spear. If a person perjures himself, death is sure to follow as penalty.

HOW NYIKANG APPEARS

Nyikang at times appears in the forms of certain animals, as ichneumons, rats, snakes, lizards, or in birds. The tree on which such a bird alights, is considered holy, and is henceforth dedicated to Nyikang; beads and pieces of cloth are suspended on its branches, sacrifices and prayers are offered below it. When once the Turks felled such a tree without knowing its destination, terror fell on the by-standing Shilluks; they walked in procession round the tree, filled the air with lamentations, and killed an ox to propitiate their ancestor.

NYIKANG AN*D* THE "PROPHETS"

Though Nyikang is considered inferior to Jwok, sometimes the names of both are called simultaneously in the same prayer. In some prayers the name of Dak, a son of Nyikang, is also invoked beside that of Nyikang; but this is not frequent. It seems, however, that in some measure the nearest descendants of Nyikang, or rather the ancient kings of the Shilluks, enjoy some kind of veneration, though perhaps this may not be called religious. They sometimes talk about the *rōr*, which is the plural of *rįt* king, and has in this connection the meaning of "Prophets", or one analogous to that of the "Judges" of the ancient Hebrews. In several villages there are huts, like those of Nyikang, dedicated to one of these ancient kings or "*rōr*".

JWOK AND NYIKANG

In the political, religious and personal life Nyikang takes a far more important place than Jwok. Nyikang is the national hero, on whom each Shilluk feels proud, who is praised in innumerable popular songs and sayings; he is not only a superior being, but also a man. He is the sublime model for every true Shilluk; everything they value most in their national and private life, has its origin in him: their kingdom and their fighting as well as cattle-breeding and farming. While Nyikang is their good father, who only does them good, Jwok is the great, uncontrollable power, which is to be propitiated, in order to avoid his inflictions of evil.

THE COWS OF NYIKANG

The natives frequently speak of the "cows of Nyikang". This expression is used in two different meanings, one mythological and one real.

Once Nyikang caught a cow in the river in a fish-net. It had no ears or horns. This cow was the beginning of a sacred herd; if anyone touched them who was not of their attendants, he died. They live in the river and come out to feed at night. This herd was carried away; some say the Dervishes took them, while others affirm that it was the Turks. From the dung of this herd the "ashes of denying" were gained. The ashes were made by burning the dung of the sacred cattle. They are preserved at Wau and other villages dedicated to Nyikang, and are applied in ordeals, when cases of adultery are to be tried. When the woman has confessed, but the man denies, they take recourse to the "ashes of denying". An old chief, taking a spear in his hand, stands erect and offers the following prayer: "You Nyikang, the ashes are yours! If this man has not had intercourse with this woman, may he escape! But if he has had intercourse with the woman, may he die! If this woman accuses falsely, may she escape!" After this the chief takes some of the ashes on his hand and strikes the man with it. Then the one who has sworn falsely, will die.

The other application of the term is to cows devoted to Nyikang by the king. Each year the king gives a steer and a cow to the villages in which the cows of Nyikang are kept. The male is killed and used for food. If any person not belonging to the attending herdsmen, eats of the meat of these animals, he becomes a servant of Nyikang, and must take up his residence in that village. The female is kept for breeding purposes. The *Kwa Obọ̄gọ* (vide page 130) herd these cattle. The chief of these villages of Nyikang seems to be Wau. If an outsider tried to milk one of these cows, he would die.

SORCERY

The third factor in the religion of the Shilluks is the *ájwȯgọ́*, and what is connected with him; *ájwȯgọ́* is the witch doctor or sorcerer; the word is probably derived from *jwọk* "God", and would then mean: "one who is dependent on God", or "who has to do with God". As his most prominent business is to procure rain, Europeans generally call him rain-maker. He is the mediator between the people and Nyikang; he leads the dances and prayers to Nyikang, and presides at the sacrificial ceremonies. He heals also sicknesses by administering charms. Sick people apply to him with the present of a sheep or goat, or even an ox; the animal is killed, and the contents of its stomach are laid on the sick person's body; or the skin of the animal is cut into strips and these are fastened below the knee of the patient. This is also applied as a protection against dangers on a journey. When in the dry season the cattle are brought across the river, the sorcerer has to prepare charms to protect them from being seized by crocodiles. Besides this he is able to perform miracles, to kill a man by witchcraft, to prevent rain, and to cause the cattle to be barren. — There exist two kinds of sorcerers, the one whose functions are just mentioned, who plays an important and mostly beneficient *rôle* in public life and the official religion of the community, and another one whose doings are secret and who works for mischief. If this latter is convicted of his evil doings, he may be severely fined, or even sentenced to death. — Besides these the word *jal yaṭ* "man of medicine" is sometimes used; whether this is a synonym to *ajwōgọ*, or whether it designates still a third class of "witch"-, or ordinary "doctor", I do not know.

When possessed by a spirit (or by Jwok?) the sorcerers become ecstatic; ECSTASY the same seems to be the case with a newly elected king; here it seems to be the spirit of Nyikang, which falls on his follower, vide page 149.

The texts contain many mythological tales and allusions, which may in former MYTHOLOGY times have formed part of the strictly religious belief of the people, but exist now merely as historical traditions, without having any active meaning to the present generation; this domain of their mental life is, however, not sufficiently known as yet to allow a decisive judgment. A reminiscence of sun-service is evident from 55, page 166. The Nile and Sobat are populated by water-people, who in figure are partly like men, partly like crocodiles or fish. They had, in the past, many intercourses with men. — According to some older writers the spirits of the Nile are worshipped. They have their own cattle-herds, which live with them in and on the banks of the Nile. They often dive up from the water, chiefly in misty weather. When a cow is fished out of the river, it is placed under the protection of the Nile-spirits and the sun-god ¹.

The Shilluks have two expressions which may be translated by "soul" or SOUL, SPIRIT "spirit" of a living person: *wei* and *tipọ*; *wei* means "breath", and is the life-giving factor in man; the meaning of *tipọ* is "shadow" of a man, or "image", as seen when looking into clear, still water. — The spirit of a dead person is called *anękọ*; the word is derived from *nạgọ* to kill; *anękọ* probably means "one who kills", or "who is killed". The *anękọ* is feared.

On the abode of deceased persons the Shilluks have but vague ideas; in one ABODE OF of the texts the dead are called "the people of the village of God", *jē pā jwọk*. THE DECEAS Whether they have a general belief in a life after death, is not known.

Islam does up to now not find much sympathy with the Shilluks. They ISLAM prefer their own religion to that of foreigners. Only a few people who have for a longer time lived in close touch with Mohammedans, chiefly those who have served as soldiers, adopt the religion of Mohammed, or at least wear Mohammedan amulets beside their own charms. It is admirable that these people, Shilluks, Dinkas Anywaks, and Nuers, though having lived for centuries side

---

¹ This doubtlessly relates to the cows of Nyikang, vide the preceding.

by side with Arabs and other Mohammedan people, should have preserved their own heathen form of worship, and should, with a few exceptions, look down rather with contempt on the religion of the foreigners. Partly this is explained by their conservativeness and self-confidence, and partly by the fact that their intercourse with Mohammedans was almost exclusively hostile. Whether now that the Pax Britannica makes slave-dealing and raiding impossible and new ideas slowly penetrate the country, Islam will make greater progress, the future will show. A gradual peaceful conquest of the country by Islam is not improbable, because civilisation, as it comes to these people, wears an outspoken islamic stamp.

On Christian Mission work among the Shilluks vide the end of Introduction.

V. POLITICAL INSTITUTIONS.

RESIDENCE OF THE KING — The Shilluks are the only people of the Sudan who have a Kingdom [1]. The king resides at Fashoda. His residence consists in a large number of huts for himself, his numerous wives and other members of his family and for guests. He possesses large herds of cattle, goats and sheep. When a person of some respect pays him a visit, the king presents him with an ox. — The royal robe consists in a leopard skin. They have also a coronation robe of leopard skin and ostrich feathers, which has been handed down from many generations. The present king has a gorgeous red robe presented by the governor, which he wears on occasions when he meets the higher English officials.

ELECTION — The kingdom of the Shilluks is hereditary in so far as the king must always be a member of the royal family, that is, of the descendants of Nyikang, and only a person whose father has been a king, may be elected. There are three houses of the royal family, and the king is elected from each of these royal branches in turn. If there are several brothers in the branch whose turn it is to have the kingship, upon the death of the king one of these brothers will be elected. But in case there is no vacancy during the life of these three brothers, then the sons of the eldest will be in line for the throne.

Fadyet is the present king. He is of the house of Kwat Ker. When he dies, the kingship will pass to the house of $Y\bar{\varrho}$; at the death of the king from the house of $Y\bar{\varrho}$ it will be the turn of the house of *Ñeḍok*. Thence it will return to the house of Kwat Ker, but not to a son of *Fadyet*, but to one of the king's brothers. When it has gone around the circle again, it will be the turn of a son of *Fadyet*. There seem to be two branches of each house, so that when a king dies, it will be the turn of his eldest son to become king, after five kings have reigned and died. There have been other royal houses, but they have lost their

---

[1] "king" is in Shilluk *riț* or *reț*; in older literature the word "bondu" is given as the Shilluk name for king. By Europeans the king is commonly called mek, which is a contraction of the Arab malik.

right to the throne. If all the sons of a king die, before it is the turn of one of them to become king, that family loses its royal prerogatives. A left-handed or otherwise deformed man cannot be crowned. When from such or a similar reason the son of a king fails to be crowned, his posterity loses the right to the throne.

As a rule only a man can be king; though once a queen reigned, she apparently did not command a great authority, vide page 149; and it is characteristic that in the lists given by Banholzer and Dr. Giffen her name is not mentioned.

The way in which the king is elected, vide page 122 ff. Of course frequently party intrigues are at work on these occasions, and it may have been not quite an uncommon occurrence that there were several candidates for the throne, supported by different factions; sometimes there were even two kings, residing in different places of the country.

The power of the king was, previous to the British occupation, absolute; he disposed on life and death of his subjects. The subjects had to pay heavy taxes in cattle, dura, boats, skins for clothes, and under certain circumstances, in persons also. **POWER OF THE KING**

All judicial cases may be brought before the king, with whom lies the final decision. They have an unwritten code of law, providing fixed penalties and fines. Cattle thieves were formerly killed on the spot by the owner of the stolen property. If the thief escaped, but was located with the stolen thing, the owner demanded it. In case the thief refused to give it up and the owner was unable to get it by force, he then reported to his chief, and if he failed there, the matter went to the king, who punished the man perhaps by taking his property and some girls from his village for himself. **JURISDICTION**

In the case of certain infractions of the law the convict became the slave of the king, and could no more return to his home. These slaves are known as *tygi orǫk* ("men of crime") or *adẹ̄rǫ*. The king gives to such a man a wife. Their children are slaves at the royal court and are called *adẹ̄rǫ*. To the male descendants of such the king gives wives, and the females are taken to be given to male members of the *adẹ̄rǫ* class as wives. If the king does not have enough girls in the *adẹ̄rǫ* class to supply all the young men with wives, he buys free girls for the purpose, their descendants become also slaves.

In some cases the criminal becomes the slave of a chief; these are also called *adẹ̄rǫ*.

Murder cases were tried by a court of chiefs and the king. If the man was condemned, he was disgraced in many ways before the people. Sometimes he was led about the village with a cow-rope around his neck, and then executed by hanging. If a man was executed on account of a crime, his whole family

XLVIII　　　　　　　　　　　　　　　　　*Introduction*

and everything he possessed became the property of the king.

DIVISION OF COUNTRY
The country is divided into 63 districts (vide page 127), every one of which is presided by a district chief; each village again has its own chief. The district and village chiefs are appointed and may be deposed by the king. Quarrels and law-suits may be judged by the local or district chief, but an appeal to the king is always possible. Common affairs of a village and minor judicial cases are judged by the local chief together with the old men of the village. They sit on such occasions in a circle in the village yard, in the shade of a tree, if there is one. If the meeting is secret, or if the weather is bad, they assemble in the cow-house.

VI. ETHNICAL COMPONENTS OF THE SHILLUK PEOPLE.

EARLY INHABITANTS OF THE COUNTRY
When Nyikang arrived in what is now the Shilluk country, the latter was inhabited by other tribes, who probably were partly of dark, and partly of fair colour. These inhabitants were either expelled or subdued and then incorporated into the Shilluk nation. This process is clearly reflected in the traditions. Among others Nyikang found the "red strangers" in the country, which he either defeated and made them tributary, or drove out of their residences (vide page 163 ff). These "red strangers" seem to be Arabs. But apart from them the traditions speak of fabulous beings who were partly man and partly animal; Nyikang fought with them, and when defeated, transformed them into real men and settled them in villages. They are probably the original negro inhabitants of the present Shilluk country, who up to this day form the essential part of the Shilluk people, a discrimination being made between them and the "people of Nyikang."

SOCIAL ORGANISATION
The latter form, so to say, a nobility. The first in rank is the royal family and all members of it, that is all persons who can claim descendency from Nyikang. The male members of the royal family bear the title *Kwa riṭ* "descendant of the king", and are shown special deference. In several of the historical traditions the king or the royal family expressly distinguish themselves from the common Shilluks; in these connections the name "Shilluk" is even used in an abusive way: "merely a Shilluk", vide page 233. Probably the name of the Shilluks *chŏlǫ* means "black"; in some nearly related languages the word has this meaning. This makes it probable that Nyikang and his people, or, the members of the royal family, were originally of lighter colour, as only this would give them a reason for calling the population they found inhabiting the country, "blacks".

1. Shilluk Girls showing the way they wear the skin dress
2. Lotus flower along the Sobat River

1. Group of Native Huts
2. Group of Boys
3. Girls Sewing School at Doleib Hill

So the coming of Nyikang into the Shilluk country would in fact mean an immigration of light-coloured people into a region already inhabited by black tribes. — Probably the word *Okāṇọ*, which, as is shown on page XLI, is connected with *Nĭkàṅọ*, and means a descendant of *Kāṅọ*, also designates only or mainly members of the royal family, and not the common Shilluks; on the Sobat the word is rarely used; but it is well known at Fashoda, the seat of the royal court.

There live among the Shilluks a number of "Nubians", called by them *Dọṅ*; the word is derived from Dongola, and designates the Nubians (and perhaps other tribes) living west of the White Nile. These Nubians came into the country as captives, during wars, others came as fugitives. They are exceptionally numerous in Faina, a sub-district of Nyagir; they are known here as good cultivators of dura. Originally these were driven into this district by the Khalifa's people, and inhabit five villages, consisting of 104 domiciles; they are subject to the Shilluk chief of the district. — The Nubians play a certain rôle in the election of the king, vide page 122 ff. They bear the title *Ńadwai*. RELATIONS WITH THE NUBIANS

The Shilluks do not, as a rule, agree well with the Dinkas, their northern and eastern neighbours. The Dinka possesses more cattle than the Shilluk, and therefore looks down on the latter rather contemptuously. The Dinkas are said to have formerly lived on the right bank of the lower Sobat, but were driven inland by the Shilluks. Incited by Arabs, the Shilluks in former times frequently raided the Dinkas and carried away their women and cattle. They however live peaceably now, thanks to the fear they have of the new Government. The two tribes now and then pay mutual visits and also intermarry occasionally; a certain amount of trade is carried on between them. RELATIONS WITH THE DINKAS

There are a few Selim Baggara in the neighbourhood of Kaka, but these people appear to visit the district only after the harvest to purchase dura from the Shilluks, which they are too indolent to cultivate themselves. The Kenana Arabs occupy the wells at Atara. They are disliked by the Shilluks on account of their dirty habits. Another branch of the Kenana Arabs inhabit a village close to Fadiang (*Fa ḍeaṅ* "village of cattle"). RELATIONS WITH THE ARABS

VII. MIGRATIONS AND HISTORY.

South of the Shilluk country there live, under different names, a number of tribes who likewise speak the Shilluk language (vide page 30 ff.), and who, in their physique, show strong resemblances to, and in some cases identity with, the Shilluks of the White Nile. It must be supposed that originally all these tribes lived in one place. Some of them still have traditions pointing to a common ORIGINAL SEATS OF T SHILLUKS, WANDERIN origin and a common home. The southern mass of the Shilluk speaking people, the Gang, pretend to have come from north (vide Schweitzer, Emin Pascha; Berlin 1898, page 155), and, as will be seen below, the White Nile Shilluks have migrated into their present seats from south; so the original habitat of the whole people will have been in the country situated about the middle of their present seats, that is, along the shores of Bahr el Jebel. Here one division of the Shilluks, the Beri (*Bęri*, also written Beir), are still living. The rest of the Shilluks were forced to emigration probably by the arrival of more powerful and warlike tribes coming from east, viz. the Bari and Latuka, who up to the present time inhabit this country. The Shilluks, being thus expelled from their seats, emigrated in three directions: south, north-east, and north-west. The division wandering southwards are now known as Gang or Acholi, Shuli (on the identity of the names Acholi, Shuli, and *Chōlǫ* vide page 31); the north-eastern branch are the Anywaks (Anuaks). These two branches, viz. the Gang and the Anywak, have practically almost no differences in their dialect; they may be said to speak the same dialect, which differs from the rest of Shilluk dialects by the relative primitiveness of its sounds; to give one example, they have generally preserved *ch* and *p*, where other dialects have adopted the younger corresponding sounds *sh* and *f*. So these two may be regarded as direct branches of the original stock, who both must have branched off about the same time. That Gang and Anywak have been separated from the north-western section at an earlier period than that in which the latter was again divided into different sub-groups (vide below), is evident from the fact that all these north-western sub-groups still know of their common origin, whereas I have never met with a tradition pointing to relationship with the Anywaks and Gang.

The Anywaks have again been divided into three sections, whose residences vide page 30. From the Gang a number of smaller divisions have branched off into south-west, south and south-east: the Lur, (Aluru), Jafalu *(Jafaluǫ, Japaluǫ)*, Lango, Ja-Luǫ (Nyifwa Kavirondo), Wagaya.

The third division first wandered north-westward, crossing the Bahr el Jebel, and subsequently probably resided in a place situated about the 10° eastern long. and 7° northern lat. That they have settled and lived in this region for a considerable time, is practically proved by the fact that on older maps a number of villages are situated here whose names begin in *Pa, Fa*; e. g. Fatil in the Dinka district *Rǫl*; Fayot, Fawer, Fayak, in the Dinka district Kich, and Fagak, in the Dinka district Twi (Twich). *Pa, Fa* is a word of the Shilluk language meaning village, home (Many villages in the Shilluk country have this same prefix *pa, fa,* vide 80; it is also freqent in the Jur country: Famir, Fabuchak,

Fashien, and in the Acholi country: Fanyikuara, Fandikir, Faggeir, Fadjulli, Fadibek (from Schweitzer, Emin Pascha). This district is now inhabited by Dinkas, and their occupation of the country no doubt forced the Shilluks to emigrate once more. From here they went in north-eastern direction and thus came into their present seats on the White Nile and Sobat. *These last wanderings were carried on under the leadership of Nyikang;* they form the object of the traditions on pages 158 ff. Another part of this north-western section went westwards and formed the Ber (= Beri, vide 87) and Belanda or rather *Bǫr*, vide page 44. The third part of this branch are the Jurs and the Dembos. Jur is a nickname given to the people by the Dinkas, it means "uncivilised tribe", "bushman". They call themselves *Luǫ,* a name which occurs again among several southern Shilluk tribes, vide 89; by the Bongos they are called Ber (vide above), thus showing in their very names the near relationship they have with other Shilluk divisions. — The Jurs have no cattle, they are renowned as iron smelters.

According to Schweinfurth (page 63) the Jurs themselves say that they are a part of the Shilluk people who (on account of over-population) emigrated from north (i. e. The White Nile region) into their present habitat, and that they call the name of their ancestor Oshuola = *Ochōlǫ*. But on the other hand, Hofmeyer states that the White Nile Shilluks call the Jurs *Odimǫ,* that is descendants of *Dimǫ*. Now *Dimǫ* is a brother of Nyikang, whom the latter left. All the Shilluk traditions are unique in the assertion that Nyikang did *not* go northwards together with Dimo. So this would mean that the Jurs never wandered into the White Nile country, but went their way directly westward into their present seats.

[The suggestion on the migration of the north-western section, viz. that of the White Nile Shilluks, Jurs, Dembos, Belandas and Bers, as it has been outlined above, is in a remarkable way supported by traditions of the White Nile Shilluks, which Hofmeyer gives; according to these the origin of the nation was in the far east (i. e. east of the Bahr el Jebel). Nyikang led his people *from the east towards north-west.* After a long march *they crossed the Nile* (i. e. the Bahr el Jebel) and came into that region which is now called Bahr el Ghazal. From here the Belanda went westwards, the rest, after some time, travelling farther northwards.]

While nothing is known concerning the *time* of the earlier Shilluk migrations, we are able to fix the approximate date of the wanderings which resulted in the final settlement of the "Proper Shilluks" on the White Nile and Sobat. Mr. B. Struck, by taking into consideration all the available (written or unwritten) chronicles of African dynasties, has made a calculation on the average duration

THE RULING ELEMENT AMONG THE SHILLUKS

of the reign of an African ruler. The number of years thus reached at is between 13 and 14 for each king. Now from the reign of Nyikang, who was the first Shilluk king, till to-day the Shilluks have had 28 to 30 kings; 29 multiplied with 13 1/2 leads back to the first quarter of the sixteenth century. About this time, then, the Shilluk kingdom was founded, or, in other words, during this period a probably fair-skinned tribe or clan became in some manner united with the Shilluks, and made itself the ruling factor among the latter. The first of these leaders and rulers was Nyikang, or possibly Nyikang is only a personification — the heros eponymos — of the foreign element in the Shilluk population. From those early days up to the present never a "Shilluk", i. e. a member of the original population, has been king, solely the "descendants of Nyikang" forming the royal family, from which the king is elected. Even to-day the descendants of Nyikang do not intermarry with the "Shilluks", they live in districts and villages of their own and enjoy certain privileges, thus forming the aristocracy of the nation. Second in rank are those Shilluks which migrated into the country together with Nyikang as his "followers" or "servants." They also possess several social privileges and state functions. The lowest class of Shilluks are the natives found in the country, when Nyikang and his adherents arrived. They may be designated as the "common people", the "subjects" in the state community. The second and third categories, and also the first, have no doubt been mixed by intermarriage. From the earlier centuries of the Shilluk dynasty but scanty historical data are known. The only reports we have are the list of kings (vide page 135), and a considerable store of traditions, dealing with prominent acts of single kings and important events which occurred during their reign. Some of these native records are printed on pages 141 ff.

RELATIONS WITH THE FUNJ The first time the Shilluks enter history is about the beginning of the sixteenth century, that is at the same time when they took possession of their present seats. Beginning at this period they have, during almost two centuries, played an essential part in the history of the *Funj* people. The question of the origin of the Funj is as yet unsettled. In order to introduce the reader into the problem, I shall give a short survey of this remarkable people and their history.

The most common form of the name is Funj or Fonj, and Fung. Funj is in phonetic writing probably *Foñ*, ending in a palatal n, and Fung = *Fuṅ*, ending in a velar n. Of these two forms I suppose Fonj = *Foñ* to be the older one. Foreigners who are not used to a palatal n standing at the end of a word, find its pronunciation difficult, and frequently substitute ṅ for ñ, a mispronunciation which I myself have often heard in the Sudan. This Funj, Fonj is probably identical with the Shilluk word *bwoñ* "stranger"; in Shilluk as well as in Nubian b and f are interchanged; in Nuer the word for "stranger" sounds *foñ*, and in the Funj language the word "bunj" means "Arab", i. e. stranger; the identity of this bunj with Shilluk bonj, Nuer fonj and the name Funj can hardly be doubted. Now Bruce gives the singular of the name by "fungo", and the plural "fungi". *This is a pure Shilluk form;* ọ being in Shilluk the ending of the noun in singular, and i that of the plural. The meaning of the word "fungo" Bruce renders by "free citizen". (R. Hartmann [Die Nigritier] identifies the word Funj with the Ptoemphanae of the ancients, and morever compares it with a great number of African names of similar sounding; but his deductions have not convinced me.)

The present Funj are a negro people living in Sennar. Their colour is dark, but somewhat lighter than that of the Shilluks; they are of a strong, tall figure, with thin legs. Both sexes wear most artful hair dresses. They have leather shields in form almost like those of the Shilluks; their fighting arms are swords and missiles. The huts of the Funj consist in round walls with conical roofs. Their chief occupation is agriculture, but they have also some cattle. They are clever in smelting and working iron and other metals.

Their religion is Islam, but the older records are unique in stating that at the end of the 15th century they were heathens, and even when Bruce was in the country, many pagan practices had survived; it almost seems that at that time the people still were in their hearts rather pagans than true followers of Islam, though the latter had long before become the official religion.

The Funj country, Dar Fung, stretches on both sides of the Blue Nile. Its present boundaries are: on the north, Jebels Gereiwa and Rera; on the east, Jebel Agadi and the Fazogli district. Southwards, it extends to the Abyssinian frontier, and including the district of Keili and the northern Burun country, extends westwards towards the Dinkas of the White Nile. In the days when the Fung were a great power of the Sudan, their country included parts of Abyssinia, and large districts west of the White Nile.

About the beginning of the 16th century the Funj appear in history. At this time they founded the kingdom of Sennar, which, from then till about the end of the 18th century, was governed by a Funj dynasty.

Since the early days of their history the Funj must have lived in some connection with the Shilluks. This fact is stated by all travellers and explorers who have been in the country and have written on the subject. Sir James Bruce, a distinguished English traveller and writer, who visited Sennar in 1770, asserts *the identity of the Shilluks and Funj.* In his Travels into Abyssinia he says that in 1504 a hitherto unknown negro nation, which had till then inhabited the western shores of the Bahr el Abiad about the 13° northern lat., landed in canoes in the Arab provinces of the Gezira; they defeated Wed Ageeb, the king of Sennar, and forced a treaty upon him by which the kingdom of Sennar became subject to the Funj, who subsequently took possession of the whole Gezira. *"This negro nation is in their own country called Shillook".* [1] In 1504 Amru, the son of Adelan, who was the first of their regents, founded his monarchy on the eastern shores of the Blue Nile, and built Sennar, which ever since has been the capital. "From this period until the time of my sojourn (1770) 266 years had passed, during which twenty kings had reigned [2]. When the monarchy was founded, *the king and the whole nation of the Shillook were pagans.* Soon after they accepted Mohammedanism, and took the name Fungi, which they sometimes translate by "lord" or "victor", and sometimes by "free citizen" .... but this term should be applied to those born east of the Bahr el Abiad only".

So the essence of James' report is this: The Funj are a portion of the Shilluk people, which, in the beginning of the 16th century, crossed the White Nile, conquered Sennar, founded a kingdom there, and henceforth were called and called themselves Funj. The source from which Bruce got this information, was the executioner of the royal court, whose chief office it was to put the king to death, as soon as in the opinion of the state ministers he was, from old age or on account of his misdoings, no more apt to govern the country. This same practice has been in use with the Shilluks up to the nearest past, with the sole difference that the Shilluk kings were strangled by their chief wife, not by an official. Bruce, having cured the executioner from a severe disease, gained the full confidence of this important person, who no doubt was well acquainted with the history of his people. Bruce also mentions the presence of Nubian (heathen) priests at the court of Sennar, who were, according to the executioner's statement, "great conjurers and sorcerers". From these Nubians Bruce heard of the "large mountains Tegla and Dyre" (= Jebel Tagale and Jebel Eliri in south-eastern Kordofan), from which their, the Nubians', forefathers had come into this country a long time ago, after they had been escaped there from a great flood.

According to the report given in The A. E. S. the rise of the kingdom of Sennar began in 1493. In that year Amara Dunkas (= Amru of Bruce?), the Sheikh of a sub-section of the Fung, either through the fortune of war or his superior capacity, succeeded in getting himself declared king of all the Fung tribes. These districts were inhabited by negroes belonging to the Nuba tribes, some of whom after the conquest remained in the country, while others emigrated into the mountains of Fazogli and Kordofan. Those who remained, embraced Islamism, intermarried with their conquerors, and, losing their language and nationality, were soon lost in the tribes known collectively under the name

---

[1] Bruce has never been in the Shilluk country, and had probably never before heard the name "Shilluk", he can only have learned it in Sennar from the natives.
[2] Thus the average reign of each king was a little more than thirteen years! vide above.

Migrations and History

of Fung. King Baadi Abu Dign, who reigned from 1635—1671, *attacked the Shilluk negroes and took a large number of slaves*. The Shilluks at that time inhabited the country on both sides of the White Nile south of Kawa. Thence he invaded the mountains of Tagale and destroyed Kordofan, where he again took a large number of slaves. On his return to Sennar he built a number of villages in that district for his prisoners. The prisoners named these villages after those they had left, hence the number of villages now near Sennar with names similar tho those in Jebel Nuba, Tagale, and other districts about Kordofan. In time these slaves supplied the kings of Fung with recruits for their armies. — In 1719 a king whose name was *Gaadi Abu Shilluk* ascended the throne.

In the first half of the 18th century the Fungs drove the Darfurians back, which had at that time dominion over the country east of the White Nile as far as the Atbara; the Fungs then again established their own authority on the banks of the White Nile. In 1770 they even wrested the province of Kordofan from the Darfur kings, but it was retaken by the latter five years later. This was about the time when the Dinkas emigrated from the Bahr el Ghazal and took possession of the right bank of the White Nile, under their great chief Akwai Chakab; by them the Fungs were expelled from the eastern shores of the White Nile into the Blue Nile region.

According to Cailliaud, a French writer, who was in Sennar about 1820, the "Foungi" came from the Sudan, crossed the White Nile and arrived at "Arbaguy" (= Herbagi of Bruce); here a great battle was delivered, in which the Funj were victorious, so that they became lords of the country; "they gave their name to a part of the Sennar kingdom in the Bouroum (= Burun) country, called also Jebel Fungi, *where the soldiers of the mek live*".

R. Hartmann, who visited the country in 1859/60, is of the opinion that the original home of the Funj is in Sennar. "They recruited their (black) soldiers from their military colonies, which were situated at the foot of the Sennar hills, and from Kordofan Nubas." "Between 1499 and 1530 the christian state of Aloa (Alwa) succumbed under the invasion of the Funj, who broke forth from the south of Sennar, and *whose military force consisted partly of Shilluks*". "*The Shilluks are relatives of the Funj*, whose intimate allies they were during the conquest of Sennar in the 16th century."

Cailliaud and the A. E. S. as well as Bruce give a list of the Funj kings, which, though differing in severel items, is on the whole consistent. Bruce fixes the beginning of the dynasty in the year 1504, Cailliaud in 1484, and A. E. S. in 1493.

Leaving the question of the provenience of the Funj alone, the following can be regarded as sure: 1. The kingdom of Funj was founded in the beginning of the 16th, or at the end of the 15th century. 2. the political influence of the Funj extended at times westward beyond the White Nile, as far as Darfur and Kordofan; consequently the Shilluks must also have been under the dominion of the Funj, as their country is situated on the way to Kordofan. 3. All writers confirm that the Funj have repeatedly transplanted great numbers of Shilluk and Kordofan prisoners into the Funj country, where they were settled, formed large colonies of their own, and finally submerged in the "Funj" nation. It was these large numbers of new settlers who formed the bulk of the Funj armies and enabled them to carry on their great conquests. 4. But it is not at all unprobable that portions of the Shilluk people should have emigrated into Sennar of their own will; the coincidence of the arrival of the Shilluks in the White Nile region and the foundation of the Funj kingdom is remarkable; both events took place about the beginning of the 16th century; at that time the Shilluks inhabited *both* shores of the White Nile as far north as Kawa; consequently they lived in close contact with the people of Sennar, and it seems not unlikely that parts of them should have pushed forward into Sennar, the more so as they had only just arrived in the country and were not yet finally settled; such an emigration would also explain their now being limited to a relatively small district compared with the former much larger size of the Shilluk country. 5. The Shilluks themselves tell in their traditions of repeated and severe fights against the people of Sennar; they call the place where these wars were fought, Chai, and say it is close to Roseires on the Blue Nile, that is *east* of Jebel Gule, where the old capital of the Funj was situated. 6. Cailliaud in his book "Voyage à Méroé, names 50 villages beginning in *Fa*, in the Bertat and Fazoql country on both sides of the Blue Nile; as shown above, *Fa* is the characteristic prefix of Shilluk villages, being an abbreviation of *fa, pa* "village". It seems evident that these villages are originally settlements of the Shilluks who emigrated into these regions. 7. The Shilluks living in Sennar called the aboriginal inhabitants *"bwoń* or *fwoń"* (= Fonj, Funj) that is "strangers", just as to-day they call every one who is not a Shilluk: *bwoń* (= *bwonj*), and finally this became the name of the "Funj nation". 8. It is possible that this Shilluk population in Sennar came to political influence and took part in the government of the state. This becomes even highly probable by a very curious remark of Bruce; where he translates the name Fungi by "free citizen" he continues: "Methinks they should not boast of the title "free citizen", because the first name of nobility in this country is that of 'slave', indeed they have no other title except this. If a man in Sennar feels himself not sufficiently respected, he will ask at once: 'Do you not know who I am? Do you not know I am a

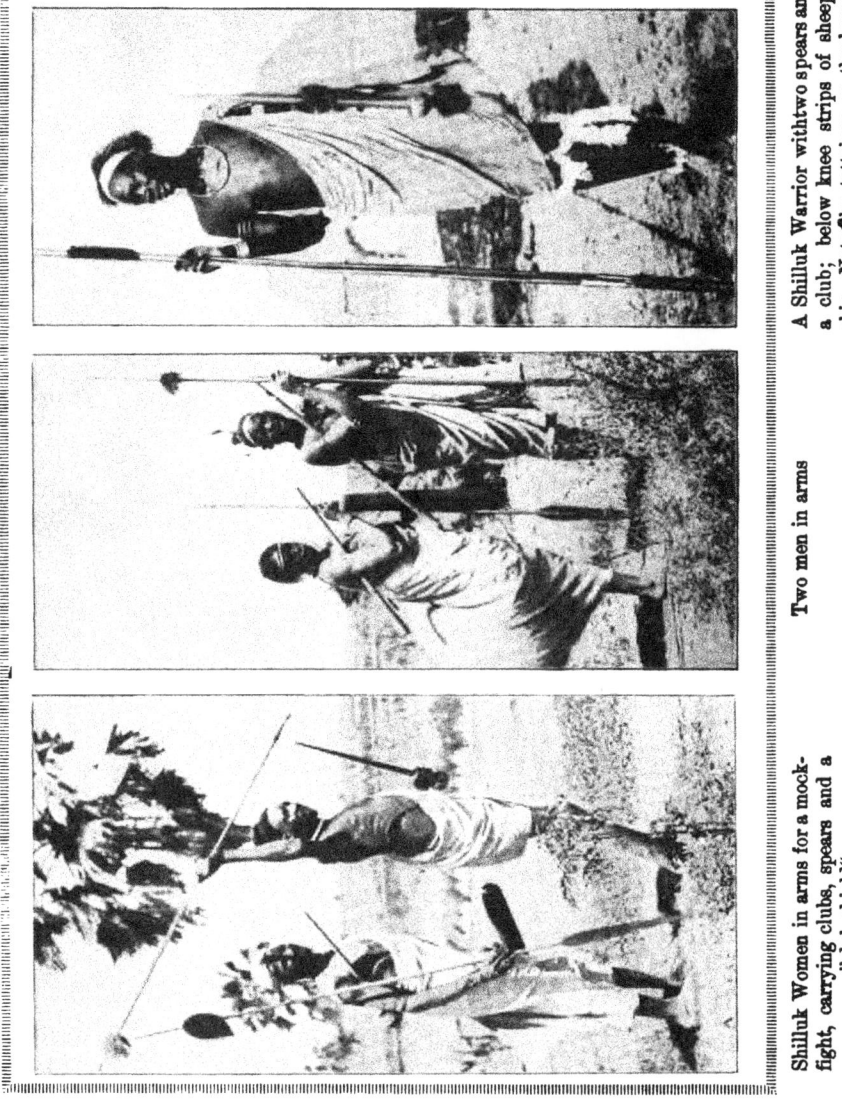

Shilluk Women in arms for a mock-fight, carrying clubs, spears and a "club-shield"

Two men in arms

A Shilluk Warrior with two spears and a club; below knee strips of sheep-skin. Note the tattooings on the breast

Migrations and History

slave?" Connecting with this word the same notion of pride, as one in England would say: 'Do you not know I am a peer of the kingdom?" All titles and offices are not respected, if they are not in the hands of a man who is a slave. Slavery is in Sennar the only true nobility". This subversion of social ranks becomes intelligible, if we assume a state of facts as suggested above, viz. that the Shilluks, and perhaps also, in a limited number, the Nubians, who lived in the country as a kind of military caste and still were designated as slaves, had in fact become the ruling race. They may even at times have possessed the throne, as the name of one of the Funj kings indicates: Gaadi Abu Shilluk. — Thus we understand also the report of the executioner from whom Bruce got his information: he was a descendant of the Shilluk immigrants, and considering the position the latter held at that time, he was not wrong in saying the Funj were originally Shilluks. The same is to be said of the Nubian priests, who claimed for their home the region of the Eliri mountains. 9. The present language of the Funj, of which Marno gives some 150 words, is not identical with the Shilluk language, but it shows unmistakable signs of a connection with the latter, a number of words being common to both, notably

Funj.		Shilluk.	
bunj	Arab	*bwoṅ*	stranger, Arab
ibibia	ant	*bĭ*	white ant
kamas	to eat	*chāmọ*	to eat
ṅaṅ	hippo	*ṅaṅ*	crocodile
lei	giraffe	*lại*	game
jok	God	*juọk*	God
kạlu	star	*kyẹlọ*	star
mine	dumb	*miṅ*	dumb
kaj an	to-day	*kach an*	this time
ko-song	spear	*toṅ*	spear
luss	stick	*loṭ, loṣ*	stick, club

Thus out of a number of about 150 Funj words given by Marno 11 are Shilluk words; and, what is remarkable, these eleven words the Funj has *not* in common with its neighbouring languages Tabi and Bertat, they can therefore not be borrowed from these languages.

In 1786 the kingdom of the Funj totally disappeared. King Adlan was deposed by the Hameg (Hamej), a tribe living south of Roseires. Anarchy prevailed throughout the country, and the kings succeeded each other in such rapid succession that in the year 1788 four kings successively reigned. During the succeeding 33 years of anarchy the Hameg continued supreme, and under Sheikh Nasser they devastated the northern and eastern part of the Sudan with fire and sword.

In 1820 the Turkish-Egyptian troops under Ismail Pasha occupied the country and defeated the Funj in the battle of Abu Shoka.

Apart from these expansions towards the Blue Nile the Shilluks of the White Nile have frequently waged wars against the Dinkas and Nuers, of which their traditions tell. More severely they suffered from never-ending raids by Arabs and Turks, undertaken for the purpose of stealing cattle and slaves.

CONQUEST OF THE SHILLUK COUNTRY

a) By the Turks. As early as 1820—1830 the Sudan was conquered by the Turko-Egyptian government, and was considered as part of the Turkish empire; but this hardly affected the political situation of the Shilluk kingdom, the Turkish rule not being strong enough to make its influence felt, except in levying at intervals heavy taxes in cattle and corn, and in making slave raids.

b) By the Baggara Selim. In 1861 the Baggara Selim under Faki Mohammed Kher invaded the Shilluk country and plundered it thoroughly. Mohammed Kher married the daughter of the Shilluk king and practically made himself the ruler of the country. —[1] In the same year Sir Samuel Baker started for his expedition into the Sudan. His description of the Sudan at this period gives a melancholy picture of the results of Egyptian rule. He describes the provinces as utterly ruined and only governed by military force, the revenue unequal to the expenditure, and the country paralysed by excessive taxation; the existing conditions rendered these countries so worthless to the State that their annexation could only be accounted for by the fruits of the slave trade. — On this expedition Baker founded the military post of Taufikia on the right bank of the White Nile, near the mouth of the Sobat; this place has since then consistently been continued as a station for troops.

SIR SAMUEL BAKER'S EXPEDITION

On Ismail Pasha coming to the throne in 1863 orders for the suppression of the slave trade were issued and on Baker's return journey in 1865, he found an Egyptian camp of 1000 men established at Kodok in the Shilluk country for the purpose. — Khartum was at that time the headquarters of the slave traders, who carried out their traffic under the cloak of legitimate commerce. The traders organised armies of brigands, and formed chains of stations, of about 300 men each, throughout their districts, which they had leased from Government. Raids were made on native tribes, who were obliged to submit, fly the country, or ally themselves to the slave hunters, to be used against other tribes.

CONQUEST BY THE EGYPTIANS 1871

In 1871 the Shilluk country was finally conquered by the Egyptians and became a province of the Turkish empire.

In 1874 Charles Gordon was appointed Governor of the Equatorial Provinces, and at the close of the same year he could report to the Egyptian Government that the slave trade on the White Nile had received a deadly blow.

---

[1] The following data have with few exceptions been taken from The A. E. S.

During Gordon's absence in 1875, the Shilluk tribes in the neighbourhood of Kodok rose in rebellion against the oppression of the Government, and, had it not been for the presence of Gessi, an Italian adventurer who had joined Gordon's staff, Kodok would probably have been lost. *REBELLION OF THE SHILLUKS 1875*

A great cause of disturbance in the Sudan was the appearance of the Mahdi Mohammed Ahmed, a native of Dongola; he began his career in 1881. The Shilluks and their country were in many ways affected by these troubles; not only did they with their own troops fight against the Mahdi, but their young men also formed a considerable and valuable part of the Anglo-Egyptian army. *DISTURBANCE OF THE MAHDI BEGINNING IN 1881*

The Mahdists extended their invasions far into the Sudan and took possession also of the Shilluk country. But in 1890 the Shilluks rebelled against their oppressors: an Emir of the Mahdi Zeki, Tumal, was sent thither to quell the rebellion, with a force chiefly consisting of the Gallabat men who had fought bravely against the Abyssinians in 1889. During the whole of 1891 the war against the Shilluks continued, the Mahdists ("Dervishes") on more than one occasion being heavily defeated, and the communications between Omdurman, the residence of the Khalifa, and Bahr el Jebel being completely interrupted. Two steamers had stuck in the sudd in the winter of 1888, and had been taken by the Shilluks; desperate efforts were now made by the Dervishes to effect their recapture. In August, 1891, the Nuers were used as allies by the Dervishes, and succeeded in killing the king of the Shilluks. Soon afterwards, however, the Nuers turned against their allies and expelled them from the country south of Kodok, whilst the Shilluks inflicted a severe defeat on their enemy near Kodok, in December, 1891, and again in January, 1893. The war was waged with indecisive results till 1894, when the Dervishes finally crushed the Shilluks and murdered their king's wife. After that the Dervishes merely kept a small tax-collecting outpost at Kodok.

On the 10th September, 1898, Kitchener left Omdurman for the south with five gunboats and troops, and having destroyed a Dervish force of 700 at Renk, arrived at Kodok on the 19th, where he found the French expedition under Marchand. He left a garrison at Fort Sobat. This place has been relinquished since as a military post.

On 19th January, 1899, an agreement was signed between Great Britain and Egypt, defining the status of the Sudan, and laying down broad principles for its government.

In the same year, on the 24th November, the power of the Khalifa Abdallah, who was the successor of Mohammed Ahmed, was utterly defeated by the Anglo-Egyptian army at Um Dubreika; the Khalifa himself was killed. This victory finally stamped out the Dervish dominion in the Sudan. *FINAL DEFEAT OF KHALIFA 1899*

?EDITION OF THE SSINIANS 1898	In summer 1898 an Abyssinian force came down the Sobat. It arrived at Sobat mouth at the end of June, but, owing to the death of the leader, the expedition returned almost immediately, without having a hostile encounter with the Shilluks.
LATEST EVENTS	In April, 1903, the Shilluk king Kur Wat Nyedok (*Ńeḓǫk*) was deposed for malpractices; his successor, Fadyet Wat Kwat Ker (*Kĕr*), is now limited in power, and is subservient in most things to the Governor of the Upper Nile Province, a Britisch officer resident in the town of Kodok (Fashoda). Gradually the whole Shilluk population was now brought under the more direct control of the Anglo Egyptian Government. The election of their king is now subject to the approval of the Governor General.

CHRISTIAN MISSIONS IN THE EGYPTIAN SUDAN.
BY CHARLES R. WATSON, PHILADELPHIA.

The "American Mission" of the United Presbyterian Church of North America and the Church Missionary Society of Great Britain are the two missionary agencies representing Protestant Christendom in the Egyptian Sudan. Both Missions began their work after the opening up of the Sudan through Kitchener's victory over the Mahdi forces at Omdurman: the Church Missionary Society in 1899 and the American Mission in 1900. In Northern Sudan they labor alongside of each other in a spirit of comity and cooperation, each developing such missionary work as the other may not have taken up at each station occupied by both societies.

The stations occupied by the American Mission in Northern Sudan and the forces and work maintained at these stations in 1911 were as follows:

Khartum: An ordained American missionary; a native ordained native pastor; an organized native congregation with 142 members; a boys' school with an enrolment of 210; regular congregational services; a clinic; a boys' orphanage or home.

Khartum North: Two unmarried American women missionaries and an American doctor; a girls' boarding school with an enrolment of 133 in both day and boarding departments; a boys' day school with an enrolment of 143; a clinic; regular preaching services.

Omdurman: An ordained American missionary; a boys' school with an enrolment of 80; regular preaching services.

Wad Medani: A colporteur evangelist with regular preaching services; a mixed school with an enrolment of 8 boys and 12 girls.

Christian Missions LXI

Atbara: A boys' school with an enrolment of 87; also informal services.

Wadi Halfa: A girls' school just opened, and informal services.

Port Sudan, Merowe, Suakin and Dueim: There are native Evangelical Church members at these centers, and informal services are held at the first three places.

The stations occupied by the Church Missionary Society in Northen Sudan and the forces and work maintained at these stations in 1911 were as follows:

Khartum: One unmarried English missionary; four native Christian women workers; a girls' school with an enrolment of 68.

Omdurman: A medical English missionary; two unmarried English women missionaries; three native Christian women workers; a girls' school with an enrolment of 51; a hospital and a clinic.

Atbara: An unmarried English woman missionary; two native Christian women workers; a girls' school with an enrolment of 38.

In Southern Sudan, among the pagan tribes, each Mission labors in a distinct territory. The American Missions's sphere of work and influence lies along the Sobat River; that of the Church Missionary Society lies along the upper reaches of the White Nile.

The American Mission opened work at Doleib Hill, in 1902 on the Sobat River just six miles from where this river empties into the White Nile. The American force here consists of two industrial missionaries, an ordained missionary and a doctor. A regular Sabbath morning service is held, and those engaged in industrial work, ranging in number from ten to two hundred, attend daily morning service. Evangelistic itinerating is done in adjoining villages. A boys' school has been maintained but with some irregularity. Some 3600 clinic patients have been treated. Agricultural and industrial training forms the chief feature of the Mission's work. The population of this region is from the Shilluk tribe, but Dinka and Nuers are also reached. The Mission is about to open another station farther up the Sobat River in the vicinity of Nasser, and a doctor and an evangelistic missionary have been appointed to this task.

The Church Missionary Society began its work at Malek, on the White Nile, about 1000 miles south of Khartum, in 1908. The Britisch missionary force consists of two ordained men, a lay worker, and a doctor. The work is chiefly among the Thain, Bor and inland Dinkas.

The following sketch of the early missionary efforts of the American Mission will be of interest. In 1899, the Rev. Andrew Watson, D. D., and the Rev. J. K. Giffen, D. D., were commissioned to visit the Egyptian Sudan and investigate the possibilities for missionary work. This missionary reconnaissance resulted in a recommendation that the American Mission, whose work in Egypt extended from Alexandria to Assuan and whose Evangelical Church members and adherents were going into the Sudan in considerable numbers as Government employes, should extend its work to the Sudan. Accordingly, the Rev. J. H. Giffen, D. D., and Dr. H. T. McLaughlin were commissioned as the first missionaries of the proposed Mission. They reached Omdurman in December, 1900. For some time, a rigorous prohibition of the Government forbade all missionary work among the Moslems of Northern Sudan. The work was therefore limited to the Evangelical and other Christian communities. In March, 1902, work was begun at Doleib Hill, among the black tribes of Southern Sudan. In establishing this mission station practically everything remained to be done. Houses needed to be provided; at first of mud, later of burnt brick, and later still of concrete. Provisions needed to be secured and gardening became a necessity, for no vegetables or fruit were to be had unless grown by the missionaries themselves. Problems of health became acute, as life and work were thus undertaken in a region and a climate where hitherto no white community had established itself. To these difficulties were added those of safety from wild animals, and especially innumerable snakes which infested the place until the land was somewhat cleared by agriculture. There were also the problems of establishing just and sympathetic relations with the people of the neighborhood. The early attitude of suspicion which prevailed is well illustrated by the following incident narrated by the Rev. Dr. Giffen in his interesting book "The Egyptian Sudan."

"We had been there for some months, and thought we had gained much confidence from the people. We had a friend visiting us and this chief, Ariu, had called in honor of our guest. After some conversation, our friend said to Ariu: 'Now you have a good and righteous Government; it will protect you, and will help you; it will fight your battles if need be. And these missionaries will teach your children, will help you to cultivate your lands, will find a market for your grain, and they have The Book and will teach you of God; you ought now to be quiet and peaceable. Till your lands and care for your herds.'

"After a good deal of deliberation and smoking, Ariu laid his pipe aside and replied: 'Master, you speak well. We had here the Turks (the old Egyptian Government) and they said, "Be submissive to us; we will protect you, we will fight your battles four you, we will teach you of God." But they took our cattle, they destroyed our villages, and carried our women and children into slavery, and they are gone. Then came the Ansar (the Mahdists) and they said: "Come with us, we have a great army; we will care for you and protect you; we will give you plenty to eat, and a good place to live; we have The Book and we will teach you of God". But they slew our men, and right here where these missionaries built their houses many of our men fell fighting for their women and children. They took away our cattle, destroyed our villages, carried off our women and children, and they too have gone. Now you come and say: "We will care for you; we will protect you; we will fight for you; we have *The Book;* we will teach you." Master, you speak well; but we will see.'

"This brief, pathetic story, a review of their whole history, reveals everything."

The supreme problem in the new work was, however, the language, for the Shilluk language had never been reduced to writing, neither was any grammar of the language in existence. The missionaries sent to the Southern Sudan mission field labored successively to reduce the language to writing and to work out its grammar and vocabulary, but they were greatly hampered both by the burden of other work and by an entire lack of acquaintance with cognate African languages. However, the Rev. Ralph Carson and the Rev. Elbert McCreery especially were able to bring together considerable material bearing upon the structure and vocabulary of the Shilluk language, but it remained for the efforts with which this book is connected to set forth with adequate definiteness the grammatical structure of the language. These efforts became possible through a generous grant made by the Trustees of the Arthington Fund, to the Board of Foreign Missions of the United Presbyterian Church of North America under whose care the American Mission in the Sudan is operated.

Among the successes of missionary work during the brief period of about a decade which has elapsed since this work was begun, may be enumerated the following important achievements: the ministry to the religious life of many Christians, Egyptians, Levantines and Europeans who entered the Sudan in Government service; the establishment of preaching centers and of both educational and medical missionary institutions whose Christian influence is steady and far-reaching; the solution of problems of health, of residence and of agricultural possibilities; the solid foundations laid for the mastery of the language; the winning of the sympathy of the people; and, finally, a hopeful beginning in the winning of some to Christianity and in the awakening of a spirit of inquiry in a much larger circle.

The most serious problem is the rapid advance of Islam into pagan territory through the aggressive efforts of Moslem traders and the pervasive influence of military posts at which are stationed Moslem troops.

SKETCH MAP
TO ILLUSTRATE "WESTERMANN, THE SHILLUK PEOPLE, THEIR LANGUAGE AND FOLKLORE".

FIRST PART
GRAMMAR

FIRST SECTION: THE SOUNDS.

THE VOWELS.

Enumeration of the Vowels and their Pronunciation.

1. The *quality* of vowels is marked by signs *below* the letters, the *quantity* is marked by signs *above* the letters. *Long* vowels are marked by a line, thus: ā = long a. All vowels which have no mark above, are *short*.

2. *a* is the pure short "Italian" a, the same sound as in English father, only *short*, while a in father is long. The short pure a does not exist in English, but in French, as ami, and in German hatte. Ex.: *kal* fence, *mak* catch!

   ạ is a little narrower than *a*, but wider than *ę*. The Shilluk *a* sometimes, especially when pronounced rapidly, has a tendency to turn into *ạ*, for instance *ńa* "child", and *má* "which", when standing in compound words, are generally spoken *ńạ, ńę* or even *ńe; mạ, mę*.

   ę (Bell ae low-front), as in English fat, man, perhaps a little more tending towards e, as in English let, well. Ex.: *kęt* go! *bęt* fish-spear.

   e (Bell e mid-front) as in French *été*. This sound is not frequent. Ex.: *atet* ichneumon.

   ẹ (Bell eh mid-mixed), a very short, and almost voiceless sound, like e in below, fishes, or like a in idea. It is the so-called 'helping vowel'. The short *e* does not occur at the end of a word, whereas *ẹ* very often finishes a word. In all these cases *e* is written instead of *ẹ*. Thus *e* at the end of a word is always to be read *ẹ*. Only where *ẹ* stands in the middle of a word, it is marked *ẹ*; ex.: *nẹk* killed.

   i (Bell i high-front) like *i* in bit, pity; ex.: *wiṭi* arrived, *kinau* thus.

   i as in beer, keen, he, but *shorter*; ex.: *abikyel* six.

   ạ (Bell a mid-back), a sound between *a* and *ǫ*, like u in but; ex.: *gạt* river.

   ǫ (Bell ɔ low-back), as in not, folly; ex.: *gǫ* him, *gǫl* court, *ńǫl* cut. If *ǫ* stands at the end of polysyllabic words, it is pronounced very faintly, so that often merely an *ẹ* is heard. But on close attention one will in most cases hear the *ǫ*. In analogy with *ẹ*, this *ǫ* ought to be written *ǫ*, but as it occurs at the end of words with more than one syllable only (and *ǫ* never occurs here), I always write *ǫ* instead of *ǫ*.

   o like o in note, mote, but shorter and narrower, and without the final sounding of u, which the English o in note has. In French seau, German so, ital. dolore. Ex.: *loṭ* club.

ṳ (Bell *u* high-back), as in English full, put, ex.: *bṳ* to have not.
u like Engl. fool, mood, but *shorter*. French sou. Ex.: *kudǫ* to be silent.

System of the Vowels.

Long Vowels.

All vowels, including *ẹ*, may be long.
ā (Bell a mid-back) engl. father, ital. padre, German Vater.
ą̄ between *ā* and *ǭ*, almost as u in further; ex.: *fąd̦ǫ* to fall.
ē̦ almost as a in careful, ai in laird, ei in heir; ex.: *tē̦rǫ* people, *ṅē̦ṅǫ* much.
ē as *a* in save, bale; ex.: *yējǫ* to sweep.
ē̤: *yē̤t* roads.
ī̤: *chī̤n* bowels.
ī (Bell i high-front) as in meal, bear; ex.: *rīṅǫ* to run.
ō (Bell o mid-back), as o in mole, note, but narrower, and without the final sound of u, which is peculiar to this English o; ex.: *chōți* it is finished.
ǭ: *nǭți* not yet.
ū as oo in fool, cool; ex.: *rūmǫ* to think.

Remarks.

1. The vowels are pronounced with a soft aspiration (the so-called gradual glottid).
2. *i* and *u*, when standing in a closed syllable, that is a syllable ending in a consonant, generally are pronounced almost *i̦* and *u̦*.
3. In forming *ṳ* and *i̦* the mouth is wider opened than in the formation of *u* and *i*; *ṳ* and *i̦* may therefore be called wide vowels, while *u* and *i* are narrow. (In forming *u* the hind-part of the tongue is raised, in forming *ṳ* it is lowered; likewise in the formation of *i* the forepart of the tongue is raised, and in forming *i̦* it is lowered.
4. According to their place of formation in the mouth *u*, *ṳ* and *o* are back (or velar) vowels, *i*, *i̦* *e*, *ẹ* are front (palatal) vowels.
5. The language has no nasal vowels.
6. *o* and *ǫ*, *e* and *ẹ* are not so strictly distinguished as is done in some other languages.

Diphthongs.

6. *ai* as y in spy.   *au* as ow in fowl.   *ǫi* as oi in oil.
ou as o in note, but the *u* sound is more distinct than in the English o.
ei almost as ei in eight, but the *i* is heard more distinctly than in English; *ei* and *ou* are almost two-syllabic.

7. The sounds *ch, j, sh* and *ń*, when following a vowel, generally have a slight *i* sound before them, which combines with the preceding vowel to a diphthong. This *i* sound is, however, not expressed in writing, because 1. it occurs regularly before the said consonants, and 2. some individuals pronounce it so slightly, that in some cases one may doubt, whether it really exists. Thus *pach* "home" is to be pronounced *paich*; *gǫch* "beaten": *gǫich*; *bańǫ* "to refuse": *baińǫ*.

This *i* sound is best heard in those cases, where the preceding vowel is *a*, *ǫ* or *ę*.

If, however, a vowel follows the above mentioned consonants, so that the word does not end in a consonant, but becomes two-syllabic, the *i* sound sometimes disappears altogether. The reason for this is, the connection between the first vowel and the second consonant not being so narrow here as is the case in a monosyllabic word. Thus "*gǫch*" is pronounced "*gǫich*", but *gǭjǫ* hardly has any *i* sound. Likewise "*lach*" = "*laich*", but *lājǫ* = *lā-jǫ* without an *i* sound.

Semivowels.

8. *y* as y in yes; it has never the vocalic value as in the English spy.
w as w in well; *w* is sometimes pronounced with almost unrounded lips.
y and *w* are unsyllabic *i* and *u*.

When following a vowel, also when beginning a word, *y* and *w* have a slight *i* and *u* sound before them; thus *yḕyǫ* to believe almost sounds *iyḕyǫ*, *wąr* night and *awa* yesterday almost sound *uwąr*, *auwa*. These *i* and *u* sounds are not expressed in writing.

Combinations of consonant and semivowel are very frequent.

THE CONSONANTS.

Enumeration of the Consonants and their Pronunciation.

9. *b* as in English; Ex.: *bańǫ* to refuse.
ch is a palatal *t*; in phonetic writing *t'*; it is therefore not quite the same sound as in church, child. The sound is articulated *further back in the mouth,* and therefore is *thinner*. Ex.: *chǫl* Shilluk. See also *j* and *sh*.

The Consonants

d as in English; Ex.: *dęmǫ* to fall; when standing between two vowels, it is hardly distinguishable from *r*.

ḍ is an interdental *d*; put the tongue between the teeth-rows, so that it is visible from without between the teeth, then press it lightly against the upper teeth, and pronounce a *d*. Ex.: *ḍǫk* mouth.

f as in English; sometimes *f̜*, that is, an *f* pronounced with both lips (while *f* is formed by pressing the lower lip against the upper teeth, in forming *f̜* both lips are pressed together) is used instead of *f*. Ex.: *fańǫ* to divide.

g always hard, as in garden, gold, never as in George. Ex.: *gǫn* him.

h occurs only in some exclamations; it is sounded a little stronger than the English *h* in he; e. g. *búh* exclamation of surprise (*u* followed by a strong aspiration).

ɣ might be called a fricative *g*; it is in the same relation to *g*, as v is to b. It might be compared with the Arabic Ghain, but is much softer, and its place of articulation does *not lie so far back in the throat* as that of Ghain. Ex.: *ɣęn* him, *ɣɑ̄m* thigh. In forming *ɣ* the *back* part of the tongue has nearly the same position as in the pronunciation of *u*, but the lips are of course not rounded.

j is a palatal *d*; in phonetic writing *d'*; it is therefore not quite the same sound as the English *j* in jest, just. It is articulated a little *further back* in *the mouth*, and therefore sounds thinner. Ex.: *jāgǫ* chief. — *ch* and *j* have the same place of articulation; the middle of the tongue's back is pressed against the hindpart of the hard palatum.

k l m n are as in English. But *l*, when standing at the end of a word, is rolled, almost as the English pronounce the *ll* in well.

ń is a palatal *n*; it is pronounced like ñ in cañon, or like Italian and French gn in signore, seigneur. Its pronunciation is somewhat difficult, if it stands at the end of a word; here sometimes foreigners pronounce *ṅ* instead of *ń*. This can easily be avoided by adding the so-called 'helping vowel' to *ń*; instead of saying *leń* war, say *leńe*. Compare also such French words as Compiègne, Champagne, where also *ń* ends a word. Ex.: *ńa* child.

ṇ is an interdental *ṇ*, pronounced by putting the tongue between the teeth, as in *ḍ*. Ex.: *yaṇ ęni* this tree.

ṅ is a velar *n*; it is pronounced like ng in singer, or like n in Con-go. Its pronunciation is only difficult at the beginning of a word. Divide: si-nger, and pronounce "nger" only; this ng is exactly the sound of *ṅ*. Ex.: *faṅǫ* to divide, *ṅālǫ* to cut.

p as in English.

r is formed with the tongue's end. It is not rolled (trilled), but pronounced very slightly, so that often between two vowels, *r* and *d* are hardly distinguishable.

sh is formed farther back in the mouth than the English sh. *It is nearly the same sound as the German ch in "ich, dich"*; in phonetic writing *ʃ*. When *ch*, *sh* and *j* stand before the vowels *a ǫ o ụ u*, they are accompanied by a hissing sound, so that they tend somewhat more to the English ch, sh and j, but they are never identical with them.

ṣ is an interdental *s*, it is pronounced as the sharp th in thing.

t as in English.

ṭ is the interdental *t*; it is formed just in the same way as *ḍ*, only the tongue is pressed more tightly between the teeth, and thus a t is produced.

ẓ is an interdental *z*, like th in these.

10. System of the Consonants.

	Mutes		Fricatives		Liquids	Nasals	Semi-vowels
	Voiceless	Voiced	Voiceless	Voiced			
Velars	k	g	—	r	—	ṅ	—
Palatals	ch	j	sh	—	—	ñ	y
Alveolars	t	d	—	—	r l	n	—
Interdentals	ṭ	ḍ	ṣ	ẓ	—	ṇ	—
Labials	p	b	f, ḟ	—	—	m	w

Remarks.

11.   1. The consonants *m*, *n*, *l* and *r* may form a syllable, thus having the quality and function of a vowel; in these cases they are designated thus: *ṃ, ṇ, ṛ, ḷ*; they may then also have their own tones.

2. The consonants *g, k* may have a twofold pronunciation. When standing before a velar vowel they are articulated further back in the mouth than before a palatal vowel; the *g* in *gu* and *k* in *ku* lie farther back than the *g* in *gin*, and *k* in *kịnau*; but this difference in pronunciation is not marked by different signs.

3. Double consonants are rare, but are sometimes pronounced, for instance the *l* in *Chǫlǫ* "Shilluk" is frequently pronounced distinctly long: *Chǫllǫ*; I also heard *pǫnnǫ lūm* to weed grass, besides *pǫnǫ*; *kọṭ é mmọ̀kọ* it is raining.

CHANGE OF SOUNDS.

12. The change of sounds takes a large and important part in the *grammar* of the Shilluk language.

In order to show the changes which certain sounds have undergone, it is in some cases necessary to take the neighbouring related languages into consideration; they in many instances help to clear up transformations of sounds and to demonstrate older forms of sounds which from the Shilluk alone cannot be seen.

Change of Vowels.

Quantity.

13. Long and short vowels are in Shi. not always so strictly distinguished as is done in other Sudan languages. There is, in certain cases, some liberty in using a long or a short vowel; but in other cases again the lengthening or shortening of a vowel means different grammatical functions. The most important of the changes will be given here.

Frequently a vowel is long when standing in an open syllable, that is, a syllable ending in a vowel, but it becomes short, when standing in a closed syllable (a syllable ending in a consonant) *of the same word:* yán I, but yá I; yín you, but yí you; ńal boy, ńāra my boy; jal man, jālǫ man; fá not, fát not.

The demonstrative n (see 138) causes the preceding vowel to become long. The reason for this may be that n was originally an independent word (én), with a vowel of its own, the quantity of this vowel being added to the vowel preceding n: ńate man, ńān this man.

A vowel may be lengthened at will, in order to intensify the meaning of a word, e. g.: é kùdǫ he was silent; é kùdǭ he was silent for a long time, he remained in a deep, musing silence; é tígǫ he is strong, e ńùdǫ he is (something) in a high degree; é tígǭ yi rājǫ, or: é ńùdǭ yi rājǫ he is very, very strong in badness, he surpasses everything in badness, is exceedingly bad. Chiefly some adjectives may lengthen their vowel exceedingly, so that instead of one line above the vowel, two or three ought properly to be written: kệch strong kệch very strong, ràch bad, ràch or ràch, very bad; often when such an adjective is said twice (see 151), the second time the vowel is lengthened: kệch kệch, ràch ràch.

Interjections also may have short, long or very long vowel according to the degree of excitement which is to be expressed.

In fluent speech frequently a vowel is shortened, which is pronounced long, if the word is spoken alone.

In the vocative case the (last) vowel becomes long: *nàtè* man, *nàté* o man! (see also 129).

14. Regular changes of vowel-quantity take place in forming singular and plural of nouns, and in forming the tenses of the verb. Of these only a few examples are given here, for more see 123, 156 ss.

Singular short vowel
òkǫ̀k-òkǫ̀k egret;

Plural long vowel
òrǫ̀k-òrǫ̀k astuteness.

Singular long vowel
óbậgǫ̀-óbǫ̀k albino;

Plural short vowel
gǒjì-góchì sword.

In Verbs:
yậ gệjǫ I am beating   *yậ gộch* I was beaten   *yậ nậgǫ* I kill
yậ nęka dận I killed a man.

Frequently a change of quantity coincides with a change of quality; see below.

Quality.

15. Here again the changes in the formation of singular and plural and in the tenses and modes of the verb are of prominent importance; a few examples will suffice here; for more see 124.

It is particularly to be observed in the following examples that, as mentioned above, frequently change of quality and of quantity coincide, and that in some cases a change of tone is added to these two. No doubt these changes have influenced each other, one causing, or cooperating in causing, the other.

16. A most prominent change is that of a long or short *a* or *ậ*, and in some cases *ę*, being reduced to *ę*:

a 〉 *ę*: *agàk-agę́kì* crow   *ógwàl-ógwę́kì* frog   *óywàk-óywę́kì* crane
ólák-ólę́kì a fish.

ā 〉 *ę*: *ólàm-ólę́mì* sycamore   *fâl-fę̂t* spoon   *kwàrǫ̀-kwǫ̂rì* pole.

ạ 〉 *ę*: *rạt* king (older form), *rit* (properly *ręt*)¹ king (present form); *rạt* is still used in a composition: *rạt lạbǫ* king of the people, and when possessive pronouns are added: *rạda* my king.
wạtǫ and *węṭǫ* to arrive; *wạt* heads, *węṭę ńu* heads of lions; *dạk* third, *adęk* three. Here always *a* represents the older, *ę* the younger form.

ậ 〉 *ę*:
bậgǫ to boil	past *bę̂k*	*fậdǫ* to be tired	past *fę̂t*
fậnǫ to hide	past *fę́nì*	*kậdǫ* to bring	past *kę̂l*
kậgǫ to ache	past *kę̂k*	*kậdǫ* to twist	past *kę̂l*
nậgǫ to kill	past *nę̂k*	*kậbǫ* to take	n. *kę̀pǫ̀*
pậnǫ to fill	and *pękǫ* to fill	*kậdǫ* to bring	and *kęlǫ* to bring
fậdǫ to be tired	and *fędǫ* to be tired		
kậdǫ to twist	and *kędǫ* to twist.		

---

¹ In some words my materials give *i*, where *ę* was to be expected; this is doubtless misheard. For "king" *rit* being introduced already, I keep this orthography instead of writing *ręt*, which would be more correct.

ẹ, ē ⟩ ẹ: ódẹ̀k-údẹ́kì a mat   ótẹ̀t-ótị́tị̀ a pot   ótwẹ̀l-ótwẹ́lị̀ a fish
aḷ̀bó-aḷ́pì a bird   ólẹ̀t-ólẹ́tị̀ hawk.

In all these cases except a few, the vowel ẹ has high or high-low tone. Even in the verbs with double forms, e. g. fạdọ and fẹdọ to be tired, the second form originates from a form with high tone, see 188. It is therefore hardly to be doubted that *the high tone is the cause of the vowel being reduced to* ẹ.

ọ ⟩ ọ ⟩ ẹ. The singular of the noun, and the present tense of the verb end in ọ, which was no doubt originally ọ. This ọ is very often pronounced ẹ. The reason for this is that the emphasis (stress-tone) always lies on the stem-syllable, consequently the pronunciation of ọ (ọ) is neglected and is reduced to ẹ.

In the first instances it is the high tone, in the last the absence of a stress, which causes the reduction of a full vowel to ẹ.

A short, pure *a*, when lengthened, often becomes *ạ*; there is a general tendency in the language to pronounce a long *a* as *ạ̄*, so that it is sometimes difficult to decide, whether one ought to write *ā* or *ạ̄*; often there are no doubt individual differences.   17.

àchwát̟-àchwọ̀t̟ guinea-fowl kàl-kạ̀lị̀ fence   dák-dạ̀k pot
chạbọ to mix   past *chapa*   lạgọ to inherit   past *laka*.
But mark the opposite: ńwālọ to touch   past *ńwat̟ị*   ńārọ to gnarl   past *ńat̟ì*.

Long or short *a* or *ạ* ⟩ short *ẹ*. Here the coincidence of change of quantity with change of quality is the rule: *a long ā or ạ̄ becomes a short ẹ*. The shortening of the vowel is probably the prius; its consequence was *a* and *ạ* becoming *ẹ*.   18.

má and mẹ́ which   ńa and ńẹ child
kepā and kepẹ because   jāgọ and jẹkọ to rule
kādọ and kẹdọ to go   kwālọ and kwẹtọ to steal
lwāń and lwẹń poor, worthless   gwāńọ to err, past *gwẹń*
gwārọ to snatch, past *gwẹr*   mā-mẹk aunt
yat̟-yẹń tree   ya and yẹńa (from *yańa*) to be
lạgọ and lẹkọ to dream   yạ̄bọ and yẹbọ to open
pạ̄ńọ and pẹkọ to fill   lạbọ and lẹpọ mud.
But mark: *rach* bad rẹ̄ńọ to become bad; atẹ̀ń-atàń hat; yɛi-yat̟ boat.

In the double forms of verbs the form with *ā* is the primitive, from which that with *ẹ* is derived; see 188.

a and *ē* change in: ńājọ and ńējọ to know.   19.
e and *ẹ* change in: átẹ̀t-átẹ̀t mangouste   ańẹ̀nọ-ańẹ̀n red ant   ówẹ̀t-ówẹ̀t a mat.
i and *e* change in: wīdọ to exchange   past *wēla*
                         lībọ to come stealthily past *lēpa*.
vice versa: yèt̟-ytt̟ scorpion,   yèt̟-ytt̟ a well.

i and *ę* change in: *rŭnǫ* to run; past *a reńi*.
ǫ and *y̨*, *u* change in: *gǫrǫ* and *gyrǫ* to tattoo, *rọ̈mǫ* and *rūmǫ* to meet
ǫ̀kǫ̀dǫ̀-ǫ̀kùtì hedgehog *mǫgǫ-myki* beer *kǫch-kuchi* axe.
vice versa: *kudǫ* to pull out,   past *kǫla*,   *fudǫ* ⎱ to pull
ṅudǫ to cut,   past *ṅǫla*   *fǫnǫ* ⎰ out
lūgǫ to turn   past *lǫgi*;   *rum-orǫm* nose.
o and *ǫ* change in: *áṅǫ́ṅ-aṅǫ̀ṅì* a knife   *chōr-chǫ̀r* vulture
bǫ̀r-bǫ̀r boil; and: *toch-toach* gun; this last example suggests
that *o* was changed into *ǫ* by an inserted *a*.
o and *u* change in: *kōdǫ* to fasten n. *kûdǫ̀*; *chudǫ* and *chōlǫ* to avenge,
kuno and *kōdǫ* to blow up.

20.   The vowels *ę* and *ǫ* can in many cases be shown to be not primitive.
ę 〈 *a*.

lęk tooth	Any. *lak*			*węlǫ* to travel	Ba. *wala*	
kęnǫ gourd	Ju. *kano*			*kęch* ⎱ bitter,	Nu. ⎱ *kagal*	
ṅwęch smell	Any. *ṅwai*			⎰ sharp	⎰ sharp	
nęnǫ to sleep	Nu. *nalu*			*nę̄no* to see	Nu. *nale*	
kwęn bread	Ju. *kwǫn*	Nr. *kwǫn*, Bo. *kōa*		*ṅę̄nǫ* much	Nr. *ṅwan*	
kyęṅ horse	Ju. *akaja*	Ga. *kaṅa*;		(*chwe* fat	Nr. *chwat*)	
aṅwęn four	Nr. *ṅwān*			*nyęṅ* metal	Ju. *gaṅa*.	

In these words the form with *a* is doubtless the older one; in Shi. *a* has, from reasons not known, changed into *ę* (or *e*).

21.   *ę* 〈 *ia*.
pęk to be heavy   Any. *pyak*
tęk to be hard   Di. *tyek* (*tyęk?*)   Bo. *tigo*
pę̄chǫ, pyę̄chǫ to ask   Ba. *pija*
rę̄mǫ blood, Ba. *rima*,   Bo. *trama*,   Nr. *ryęm*.

These words have originally the vowels *ia*, of which *i* probably is the oldest; see Bo. *tigo* and Ba. *pija*, *rima*, here the second vowel, *a*, is not yet added. When *a* was suffixed, the first vowel, *i*, became unsyllabic, that is, it turned into *y*; this form is preserved in *pyak*; *a* was then assimilated to *i* (*y*) and thus turned into *ę*: *tyęk*, *pyę̄chǫ*, *ryęm*; finally in Shi. the *y* was absorbed wholly by *ę*, and *ē* remained; but, as the examples show, in many words both forms, *ē* and *yę*, are still existing.

22.   *ǫ* 〈 *wa* or *ua*.
w or *u* preceding an *a* has often assimilated the *a*, so it became *ǫ*; in certain cases the *u* or *w* has then been wholly absorbed by *ǫ*, so that *ua*, *wa* 〉 *wǫ* 〉 *ǫ*.
Compare the following examples:
wá and *wǫ́* we; *wá* is the primitive, *wǫ* the influenced form; likewise: *gwāṅǫ*

and *gwǭnǫ* to scratch, *ñudǫ* to cut, *ñālǫ* to butcher, *ṅǫtǫ* to cut.

tǭ to die	Ba. *tuan*	*rǭnǫ* to dive	Di. *rwan*
ywǭnǫ to cry	Ga. *ywak*	*lwǭkǫ* to wash	Nr. *lah* Ba. *lalaju*
bǭrǫ afternoon	Ga. *abwar*	*rǭdǫ* thirst	Ga. *orwar* Ju. *ryau*
abwǫk maize	Any. *abach*	*ñwǭlǫ* to bear,	Ga. *ñwala*
kwǭrǫ cotton	Ga. *waro*	beget	
gǭjǫ to beat	Any. *gwai* Bo. *gba*	*ānǫ* what	Nr. *ñu*, Di. *eña*
chwǫu man	Ga. *chwa* Nr. *chau*	*yǫ* road *yu toch* narrow road	
chwǫtǫ to call	Nr. *chal*	*ogwǭk* fox	Nr. *gwak*.

In these words *ǫ* is evidently an original *a*; in Shi. the *a* has in all cases been assimilated by the preceding *u* or *w*, while in other languages the primitive *a* is preserved. In Shi. *ñudǫ* "to cut", the vowel, *a*, is not yet added; in *ñālǫ* "to butcher", the suffixed *a* has dropped the *u*; here is no assimilation, but simply the elision of *u*; whereas in *ṅǫtǫ* both vowels are contracted to one; an analogous case is *ānǫ* what; the primitive vowel is *u*: Nr. *ñu* what; later an *a* was added; before this *a* the primitive vowel *u* dropped in Di.: *eña* what; in Shi. both vowels were first assimilated and then contracted: *nǫ* (the beginning *ā* does not belong to the stem, see 124) what. Note also *yǫ* road, but *yu toch* narrow road, and *yu Fakǫi* the way to F., from original *yu*; this older form is preserved in connections of the word with a determinative; later an *a* was added, which united with *u* to *ǫ*.

Compare also the following words:

23.

omǫrǫ roan antelope	Ju. *omar*
yǭmǫ wind	Ga. *yamo*
okǫk blossom	Di. *gak*.

These either have the same origin as the examples given above, the *w*, *u* having been dropped in both respective languages, or the original vowel is simply *a*, which, for reasons unknown, has become *ǫ* in Shi.

It is of course probable that, in analogy with the development shown above, many, if not all, words with *wǫ*, *yǫ*, and perhaps also those with *ǫ*, *ę* had the original vowel *a*, or *ua*, *ia*, though this *a* may no more be visible now in any of the related languages.

Some of these words show that the first of the two vowels (*ia*, *ua*) was *i*, *u*, and that the *a* was added later; compare *ñudǫ*, *ñālǫ*, *ṅǫtǫ*; and *atudǫ* goose, Di. *twol* (*twǫl?*), Nr. *twǫr*; *ñudǫ* and *atudǫ* are the eldest forms; then *a* was suffixed, see above; in Nr. *twǫr*, *ua* became *uǫ* > *wǫ*, whereas in Shi. *atudǫ* was preserved, no second vowel being added here.

24.

If *a* is a secondary vowel, it must of course have been added for a certain purpose, by adding it the meaning of the word must undergo a change; this is the case in ñudǫ to cut and ñālǫ to butcher. For more examples of the addition of a second vowel see 70.

A good example for w being dropped altogether in Shi. is this: māgǫ to catch, Ga. mako, Ba. mok, Di. mwǫk ⟨ *mua or *mwa.

25. A different evolution have

twǫn male, Di. wton; chǭnǫ to heap up, assemble, Di. wchan. Here again the primitive vowel is a, as is evident from wchan; now an u — in Di. preserved as w — was prefixed to the stem, and in Shi. was received into the stem, so wchan ⟩ chwǫn, wton ⟩ twǫn. See also the formation of the passive 173 ss.

So we have two forms of adding a second vowel to the stem:
a) consonant + vowel + vowel: $t + u + a$ ⟩ twa, twǫ, tǫ;
b) vowel + consonant + vowel: $u + t + a$ ⟩ wta, twa, twǫ, tǫ.

Assimilation of Vowels.

26. Some assimilations are treated above: ia ⟩ ię, yę; ua ⟩ uǫ, wǫ. Others are: wich head and wuch; witǫ to arrive, and wutǫ: i has been assimilated by the preceding w and thus become u;
ya ú "I shall" is often pronounced yo u̯, ya u̯;
bugin "there is not", and bigin;
bu "not to be", and bogǫn "there is not" ⟨ bu + gǫn;
yigǫ to become, and yǫgǫ;
tyęl foot, tyāla my foot;
bànęn it is, and bę̀nęn;
kį rę "with its body" becomes kę rę;
yí rè why you, but ę́ rę̀, why he;
kį́ "and", but: wú kú bǭdǫ you and the smith: i is assimilated to the preceding u. àn this, ę́ní that; an i has been affixed to an, and has turned the a to ę. (Note the change of tone in this last example: the low tone designates the nearer, the high tone the farther distance).

27. ### Contraction and Elision of Vowels.

Some have been shown above: ia ⟩ ya, yę ⟩ ę; ua ⟩ wa, wǫ ⟩ ǫ. Others are:
yí ú "you will" ⟩ yú.   mi ęn his mother ⟩ męn.   wi ęn his father ⟩ węn.

Where two vowels of different words meet together, generally one is dropped:
kwārǫ a my grandfather ⟩ kwāra.
kwārǫ i thy grandfather ⟩ kwāri, and likewise all these connections.
afoachi ak these rabbits ⟩ afoach ak.
yi gwǭk āṅǫ what are you doing ⟩ yi gwǭ ṅǫ?
yi kǭbǫ adi what do you say ⟩ yi kǭb adi, or: yi kō di?

In the nasalization of final consonants a final vowel is dropped: jāgǫ chief ⟩ jāṅ; see 127.

Change of Semivowels.

28. In forming the singular and plural of nouns and the tenses of verbs, frequent changes of semivowels are to be observed. As is said above, the semivowels *within* a word are probably original vowels, w ⟨ u, y ⟨ i. In many of those cases where the *u* or *i* had a *high tone*, it has not become a semivowel, but has retained its original form. If the *u*, *i* with a high tone did become a semivowel, its tone was transferred to the following vowel; it is sometimes difficult to decide whether one ought to write úǫ̀ or wǫ́.

29. A few examples of the changes may be given here; for more see 124 [14] [15].
ǫ and wǫ: gō̩gǫ to work passive gwǫ̣k   kǭbǫ to speak passive kwǫ́p
ógwǫ̣k-ógǫ̣kì jackal   ó̩twǫ̀n-ó̩tǫ̀n cock
kǭtǫ and kwǫtǫ to drive   okwǫr-ókǫ̀rì serval.
vice versa: mǫ̀k-mwǫ̀k dog-head fish.
o and wo: kōṅǫ and kwōṅǫ to help   ṅotǫ and ṅwotǫ to spit.
vice versa: kwōt-kōt shield.
wǫ, wo and uǫ, uo: ṅwotǫ, ṅuotǫ and ṅutǫ to show.

30. The vowel *u* has been preserved in:
kúǫ̀nǫ̀ to taste, past a kwǫṅa; kwōjǫ to sew, n. kúòjǫ̀.
ṅwǫbǫ to knead, n. ṅùòbǫ̀;
gwòk-gúòk dog; kwòm-kúòmì chair; tōjǫ and túòjǫ̀ to tie.

31. Changes between ę and yę:
gę̄dǫ and gyę̄dǫ to build; kę̣dǫ and kyę̣dǫ to dig
fyę̀r-fę̀rì back-bone; ṅę̣rǫ to let the milk down, ṅyę̣dǫ to milk.
The vowel *i* has been preserved in:
gę̄tǫ to sacrifice, and gíę̣tǫ̀; òbę̀ch-óbíéch reed
lyech-líèch elephant; kyę̣dǫ to refuse, n. kíèdǫ̀.

32. y ⟨ w: yei soul   Di. wei   gwę̄lǫ and gyę̄lǫ ring
gyę̄nǫ fowl   Any. gwę̣nǫ   kyę̣dǫ to refuse Ga. kwero
lyę̄lǫ to save   Nr. lwę̣l   fyou heart   Di. pwou
kyęṅ horse   Any. okwęṅ.

In most of these words the cause of *w* being transformed into *y* may be the following vowel ę, e, which, being palatal, assimilates *w* into the palatal *y*.

33. Elision of an original *w*:
wōrǫ and ōrǫ to send, ǫ́rù relative by marriage Ga. wor.
leṅ war   Ga. lweṅ Ju. lwiṅ   jē people   Ba. gwea
dę̣l skin   Ga. odwel   tǫṅ egg.   Nr. twǫṅi
ṅę̣ṅǫ much   Nr. ṅwan   māgǫ to catch   Di. mwǫk
ṅę̣ṅǫ is probably ⟨ *ṅyęṅ ⟨ *ṅwęṅ ⟨ *ṅwaṅ.

34. In many of these examples it is to be noted that often a vowel preceded by a semivowel is short, but when the same word appears without a semivowel, the vowel is long: the quantity of the semivowel is added to that of the vowel.

Elision of ɣ: ɣén and én he.

Change between w, ɣ and r. — Though r is not a semivowel, it is to be treated here.

In a considerable number of words these three sounds may be interchanged at will. Compare what is said of the nature of ɣ in 9. ɣ and w are closely related (they are interchanged in just the same way in Ewe); now the friction which is produced in forming ɣ is, by some individuals, transferred from the back-mouth to the point of the tongue, the velar friction becoming a lingual one, that is, instead of ɣ an r is pronounced.

wǫt, ɣǫt, rwǫt house	wūmǫ, ɣūmǫ and rūmǫ to finish
wūmǫ, ɣūmǫ and rūmǫ to cover	wǭmǫ, ɣǭmǫ and rǭmǫ to carry water
ɣēȷǫ and rēȷǫ fish	wōr and rōr kings
wa, wǫ we, Di. ɣǫk	ɣǭnǫ and rǭnǫ to elect.

ɣ does not stand before i, o, and seldom before u; here w takes its place: ńaɣǫlǫ-ńawuli axe; ɣéṙ and wóṙ a season, ɣǭdǫ and wīdǫ to pound.

In ɣéṙ-wóṙ the change from ɣ to w has caused a change from e to o.

35. Change between y and ɣ:

yé and ɣén he;   yá I   Di. ɣa.

y sometimes corresponds to j in Nr. and Any.:

yan I	Nr. jan	yaṭ tree	Nr. jaṭ
yín you	Nr. jin	yiep tail	Nr. jip
yǫ road	Any. jǫ	yǭmǫ wind	Any. jamǫ
ywǭńo to cry	Any. jwǫkǫ and juńǫ.		

Here probably j is the older sound; compare the analogous case, where in Shi. a j turns into y: 46.

36. When a noun ending in u receives a vowel-suffix, a w is inserted between both; ńu lion ńuwi lions; or, if u is part of a diphthong, it becomes w: fyóu heart, fyówá my heart; see 135.

Change of Consonants.

Interchange.

37. Some consonants may be interchanged at will, one individual preferring the one, another the other consonant; often the same individual in the same words now uses the one, a little while later the other consonant. The younger generation of the people, and chiefly all strangers speaking the language, prefer the fricative sounds.

These consonants are:
ch and sh   ḑ and ʓ   ʈ and ʓ   p and f or f.

According to the general laws of evolution in African languages, ch ʈ ḑ p are to be regarded as the older, sh ʓ ʓ and f f as the younger sounds. — t never changes with its corresponding sound, which would be s; the natives are not able, unless expressly taught, to pronounce an s.

Assimilation.

38. The consonants k ch t ʈ p, *when standing at the end of a word*, can be pronounced in two ways. They are voiceless, that is a real k ch t ʈ p is to be pronounced, if 1. the word stands alone or at the end of a sentence; 2. if it is followed by a voiceless consonant. They are voiced, that is, they are to be pronounced g j d ḑ b 1. if they are followed by a voiced consonant, 2. if they are followed by a vowel (an exception to this rule see 139 and 143). *But these consonants are always written voiceless.* This rule is suggested merely by practical regards: it would, for instance in school-practice, be troublesome, to write the same word with different sounds.

Real pronunciation	Usual writing	
ḑog jal	ḑok jal	the cattle of the man
ḑok tęrǫ	ḑok tęrǫ	the cattle of the people
riḑ labǫ	riʈ labǫ	the king of the people
riʈ ʈọ	riʈ ʈọ	the king died
kwǫb obwoń	kwǫp obwoń	the talk of the stranger
kwǫp tęrǫ	kwǫp tęrǫ	the talk of the people.

39. If one consonant of a word is interdental, the rest of the consonants in the same word, if t, d or n, become in most cases likewise interdental:

ḑaṇ man, ḑiḑǫ to make straight, ḑǫḑin hot season, ḑǫḑǫ to suck, ḑuoḑǫ to rise, ʈaʈęḑi a pole for pulling boats; in some connections even the consonant of another word may become interdental: yaʈ tree, duǫń large, yaṇ ḑuǫń a large tree; between ṇ and ḑ the tongue does not change its position. But observe: ʈa tyęlǫ heel, literally "base of the foot", here each of the two words is still felt as independent, therefore no assimilation takes place.

40. Assimilation is also to be observed in the *law of nasalization:*

$$k + n > ń \qquad ch + n > ń$$
$$t + n > n \qquad ʈ + n > ṇ$$
$$p + n > m \qquad gǫ + n > ń$$
$$jǫ + n > ń \qquad dǫ + n > n$$
$$ḑǫ + n > ṇ \qquad bǫ + n > m$$

Examples see 140.

Consonants influenced by vowels.

41. a) A mute voiceless consonant standing between vowels generally shows a tendency of becoming voiced. Thus nearly in all verbs in the present tense the second consonant is voiced: *kụdọ, gēdọ, gōgọ, kọ̄bọ* etc.; and in those which have preserved a voiceless consonant, often, when the word is spoken rapidly, the consonant is pronounced almost voiced, or at least not as *k t* etc., but as a somewhat hard *g, d,* etc. (what in German phonology is called "voiceless lenis").
b) See 38.

42. Change between voiced and voiceless consonants.
1. See 26, Assimilation.
2. See 41, Consonants influenced by vowels.
3. Sometimes the consonant beginning a word shows a change between voicedness and voicelessness:
Bachōdọ and *Pachōdọ,* Fashoda   *dạkạ̣gi* and *tạkạgi* dura-stick
bà and *pà,* or *fà* not   *dọk* mouth Any. *tọk; dāk* pot Nr. *tạk*
    gệ they, probably reduced from *kwẹ;* see 131.
4. In the formation of plural a voiced consonant often turns voiceless: *afudọ* pl. *afuti;* see 107.

43. Combination of Consonants.

The Shi. does not combine two or more consonants in a word without an intervening vowel. A consonant may be combined only with one or more vowels or with a semivowel, never with a second consonant.

44. If in the connection of noun and possessive pronoun or in the formation of plural two consonants meet together, one is always dropped:
ńal boy *ńal ra* my boy ⟩ *ńara*   *yinọ* fisherman plural *yiṭ* ⟨ **yinṭ*
    ńal ri thy boy ⟩ *ńari*   *yech* belly plural *yẹṭ* ⟨ **yechṭ*
pach village *pach rẹ* his village ⟩ *pārẹ*   *dyẹl* goat plural *dyẹk* ⟨ **dyẹlk*
wich head plural *waṭ* ⟨ **wachṭ*   *lwọl* gourd plural *lọ̄t* ⟨ **lwọlt.*

An *n* has been dropped in certain cases of genetive-formation, *dọk n tẹ̄rọ* becoming *dọk tẹ̄rọ;* see 127.

45. If two consonants of two different words meet together,
a) both consonants may be preserved; this is generally the case, when the first of the two consonants is a liquid or a nasal one; *jal mẹ̄kọ* some man; *Gol bańọ* a proper-name, *Agun jwọk* a proper-name; but *ágòn gẹ́n* "where are they" becomes *ágò gẹ́n;* and *kal wun* your fence ⟩ *kal ūn.*
b) the 'helping vowel' is inserted: *lẹch* tooth, *lẹche lyech* the tooth of the elephant; see 127.

c) a mute consonant is sometimes dropped:
ḍǫk cattle, dǫ riṯ cattle of the king
pach village pā riṯ village of the king
bat arm ba jal arm of the man.
d) ch turns into y, that is, an unsyllabic i:
wich head wiy pa̰m head of the table
yech middle yey nam middle of the river.

Changes of single consonants.

k. An original k is dropped in:
wa, wǫ we   Nr. kǫn ⟨ *kwǫn   warǫ shoe   Nu. kwari
wiṅǫ bird   Ba. kwen   orāp spider   Nu. korābe
um nose   Ju. kum   wūmǫ to cover   and kūmǫ ⟨ *kwumǫ.
The opposite state is in:
kwǭrǫ cotton   Ga. waro   kōṅǫ to pour out   Ga. oṅo ⟨ *kwoṅǫ.
Perhaps the primitive state in all these words is a beginning kw.
An original k has turned into ch in
cha̰tǫ to walk   Di. kat, kawt   kech bitter   Nu. kagal, stem *kak
kwach leopard   Bo. kǫgo, Ba. koka.
An original k has turned into t in alilit bat, Di. alich, Ga. olik; here k ⟩ ch
⟩ t, k being the oldest, t the youngest form.

g. A primitive g has turned into j:
jĕ people, Ba. gwea tribe.
ch. ch has become y in connections described in 127.
j. j has become y in wājǫ aunt, and wāi (wāy).
t d, and ṭ ḍ.
   1. At the beginning of a word; t ⟩ r.
     rēmǫ blood Bo. trama   rōmǫ and tōmǫ to fetch water, Ga. twomo.
     ṭ ⟩ r: ṭumǫ and rumǫ to finish.
   2. Within or at the end of a word.
t ⟩ r: dwatǫ and dwerǫ to wish, tyetǫ and tērǫ to carry; gǫr and gǫt corner.
t, d ⟩ l: kētǫ and kēlǫ to throw   kwātǫ and kwālǫ to steal
   kwǫtǫ to drive   past kwǫla   lēdǫ to shave   and lyēlǫ
   ṅotǫ to spit   past ṅol   yādǫ to curse   and yālǫ
   gōdo to scratch   past gōl   gwidǫ to wink with the lips, gwēlǫ to wink.
ṭ ḍ ⟩ r: nẹ̄tǫ to laugh, n. nyẹ̄rò   yiedǫ to cut, past a yier
riṯ king pl. rōr,   obeṯ and byerǫ womb
rōḍǫ thirst Ga. orwor
waṯ steer, but wạre gǫt, and wạr nam tai a certain kind of steer.

WESTERMANN, The Shilluk People.

Concerning $t > r$ (and $\underset{.}{t} > r$?) it may be remarked that in Nr. a final t is followed by a strong hissing sound, which sometimes turns into a rolled r, and thus makes the t disappear altogether. In the same way t may have become r in Shi., the tr in Bo. meaning an intermediate stage between t and r. $t\ \underset{.}{d} > l$: $t\bar{a}\underset{.}{d}\underset{.}{o}$ to cook, past $t\underset{.}{\bar{a}l}$ $w\widetilde{i}\underset{.}{d}\underset{.}{o}$ to change, past $w\bar{e}la$.

More examples for these changes are to be seen in 182; there also the functions of some of the changes are described. The changes of consonants into the corresponding nasal sounds are treated in 140.

The changes of $t\ d$, $\underset{.}{t}\ \underset{.}{d}$ to 1. r, 2. l, and 3. n are doubtless to be traced back to different causes. — Observe also that $t\ \underset{.}{t}$ at the beginning of a word change into r only, in the middle or end of a word they may change to r or to l.

INTONATION.

47. As in other Sudan languages, the intonation is an important and essential part in Shilluk grammar. Without paying close attention to it, it is not possible to master the language. Intonation is not to be confounded with *accentuation*, which means the stress laid on a particular syllable or word. Intonation means exclusively the highness or lowness of a syllable compared with other syllables. Each syllable has its own tone, which cannot, as is the case in European languages, be changed at will, but is altered only under certain conditions.

The tone can lie on vowels, and on consonants which have the function of vowels: $\underset{.}{n}\ m\ \underset{.}{l}\ r$. If in diphthongs only the first vowel has a tone-mark, it is understood that the second vowel has the same tone.

48. The Shi. has three original tones: a high tone, marked thus: $\acute{a}$, a low tone: $\grave{a}$, and a middle tone: $\bar{a}$. Two tones, and in some cases even three, may combine on one syllable. Generally it is the high and the low tone, which unite on one syllable; so we have the combinations low-high $\check{a}$ (rising tone) and high-low $\hat{a}$ (falling tone). In the first case the vowel begins with a low tone and then rises; in $\hat{a}$ it is the reverse: at first a high tone, which is lowered at the close of the sound. According to my observation in both cases the high tone is of longer duration than the low, and it seems to me that a particular stress lies on it (see below).

There are also combinations of the high and middle tone $\acute{a}$, these are fairly frequent, while I have not met with a middle and high tone. One example of three tones on one syllable is given below.

49. The rising and the falling tone generally occur on syllables with a long vowel, but they are also met with on short vowels, just the falling tone often does so.

Intonation

In this case the high tone is clearly prevalent, only just before the sound is stopped, the tone is lowered.

50. It is difficult to describe the tones or to give analogies for their pronunciation from European languages. In this particular case it is still less advisable, as the author of this book does not write in his own language, and does not feel sufficiently acquainted with English to give examples from it for illustrating the pronunciation of the tones.

[The English as well as other European languages does have different tones, one syllable or word being pronounced higher than others. The difference between European and Sudan languages is, that in the first the observation of the tone is not indispensable in speaking, the meaning of a word is not altered, whether it be pronounced with a high or a low tone; but in Sudan languages the tone is just as essential and integral as are vowels and consonants. Two words with the same sounds, but different tones, are quite different words, which in their etymology and meaning have nothing to do with each other, the conformity in the sounds is in this case to be considered as mere accidental. — On the other hand in European languages the *stress* or *strength* laid on a word is essential, it distinguishes the syllable or word which conveys the chief thought from those which are less important.]

Only some examples of each tone and combination of tones are given here; their pronunciation must be acquired by hearing them from the natives. The student should let a native pronounce these and other examples repeatedly, so long till he is not only able to hear the differences, but to imitate them to the satisfaction of the native. (To do that, one must really try to wholly quit the European mode of pronouncing a word; to give one example: When we pronounce a single word, or, the last word of a sentence, we generally lower the tone of the sound; the Shi. cannot do so, unless the word has a low tone; if it has a high tone, he will pronounce it high, whether it stands at the end of a sentence or not; just mark the first examples which follow here.)

51. Examples.

High tone: lén war, fén ground, yán I, gén they, dyél goat, óbói foam.

Low tone: t̀rò people, ànàn now; d̀eàn cattle, pì water. The high and low tone are easily distinguished, when both meet together: ákyèl one, ádèk three, tyèlò foot, pl. tyél; ká è kò and he said; ják àk these chiefs.

Middle tone: is not so easily distinguished, and may be confounded with the high tone. Examples: ótwǫ̀n cock; the second tone is a little lower than the first, yet it is distinctly not low; gát pl. gát riverbank; kífá in order that.

Rising tone: gę̌ bę̌n all of them, ótwǒn hyena; (these examples are easy, because a high tone precedes the rising one, the tones are like this: ~; mark the difference between "cock" and "hyena"!); fák a water-pot, yŏ road, Dák a proper-name.

Falling tone: ę̂ tǫ̂k he is absent, tę̂k is hard. When a high tone is followed by a low tone in the following syllable, the high tone itself sometimes is lowered at its end, so that instead of *ábà, sometimes *ábà is heard.

High and middle tone: dwęn when? wú kí męn you and who? ê yes.

High-low-high tone: dǔt dowry.

In the texts and dictionary the high-middle tone is generally rendered by high-low tone.

52. Examples of words which have the same sounds but different tones:

ótwǫ́ṅ cock	ótwǫ̀ṅ hyena	lę́u hot season	lę̀u a small lizard
làṅǫ́ nebbak-tree	làṅǫ̀ to spend the night	má which	má aunt
		màr green	már because
láu skin	làù spittle	ókǫ́k a fish	òkǫ̀k egret
lę́lǫ́ flint-stone	lę̀lǫ̀ to be smooth	wáṅ year	wáṅ eye.

53. But such words are not nearly so frequent here as they are in western Sudan languages; this is so chiefly from three causes:

1. the words consisting of only one consonant and one vowel, which prevail in the western Sudan, are not numerous in the eastern languages, these last having augmented the primitive stem by prefixes and chiefly by suffixes; see 63. These additions were in most cases a sufficient means for distinguishing the stems from each other, thus the distinction by tone became in many words superfluous, and consequently disappeared, or was mechanized.

54. 2. In the eastern languages, at least in some of them, the tone developed into quite a different function, which the western Sudan languages do not have. Here the tone is exclusively *etymological*, that is two or more words which have the same sounds but are of quite different etymology, are distinguished from each other by different tones. In the eastern languages this function is also preserved, but it is almost being suppressed by the *grammatical* function of the tone, that is, *grammatical categories are expressed by difference of tone*. Copious examples for this rule, which is a characteristic feature of the Shi., are given in 122 ss.

55. A few illustrations will suffice here:

a) singular and plural by different tones:

kyę̀ṅ pl. kyę́ṅ horse	dàk pl. dą̂k pot
byę̀lǫ̀ pl. byę́l dura	jàch pl. jách shoulder
bǫ́i pl. bǫ̀i net	ótǫ́r pl. ótǫ̀r ford
dǫ́k pl. dǫ̀k mouth	alǔṅ pl. alùṅ somersault.

Intonation

b) the vocative always receives high tone on the last syllable:
   bǫ̀dǫ̀ smith, but in addressing: *bǫ̀dǫ́!* o smith!
   màyò mother, but in addressing: *màyó!* o mother!
   ṅàtè man, but in addressing: *ṅàté!* o man!
   Dăk a proper-name, but in addressing: *Dăgí!* o Dăk!
c) The personal pronouns have high tone; see 130. Note also the mechanized tone in the possessive pronouns and the numerals, 134, 152.
d) the tenses and modes of the verb are distinguished by tone:
   to eat: present active *chàmò*, passive *chăm*, verbal noun: *chăm*
   to work: present active *gògò*, passive *gwǫ̆k*, verbal noun: *gwǫ̆k*
3. Into the Shi. the accentuation or stress (the dynamic tone) has, probably by hamitic influence, been introduced, and it is often difficult to distinguish intonation from accentuation. This is not so much the case in single words, but in groups of words, in which stress is laid on a particular word; generally this is a word with high tone, so that high tone and stress unite on the same word or syllable; and on the other hand, a stress falling on a low tone, raises the tone of the syllable.

Change of Tones.

The intonation is in Shi. not of that regularity which is found in the western Sudan languages. Though most changes obey fixed laws, yet many seem rather arbitrary, and I have sometimes met with the baffling fact that a word or a connection of words were, at different times, pronounced with different tones. Generally a word, when pronounced single, has its fixed tone, but in connection with other words the intonation changes very strongly, adapting itself to or contrasting with, its neighborhood (*rhythmical* tone).

Most of the changes may be classified under two headings, viz. assimilations and dissimilations.

Assimilation of Tones.

yít pl. *yìt* ear; but *yìté kyeṅ* ears of the horse
òkǫ̀k pl. *òkǫ̀k* flower, but *òkǫ̀kí yat* blossoms of the tree
àt̪ǎp pl. *àt̪ǎp* bag; but *àt̪ǎpé ṅàtè* the bags of the man.

In all these words the plural has low tone; but in connecting the words with a genetive, a high-toned *é* is added; the high tone of this *e* causes the preceding syllable to become also high.
gúòk dogs *á* my, *gúòká* my dogs; this is analogous to the preceding examples.
kà "and", *é* "he", *kò* "said" but connected: *kà è kò*.
yă I *gògò* work, *yă gògò* I am working; the low tone of *gògò* causes the *ă* of

56.

57.

58.

yá to add a low tone to its high tone; this low tone on á is, however, pronounced but very faintly, sometimes only á is heard.

Dissimilation of Tones.

59. gìn thing àn this, but gín àn this thing, gík àk these things.
ǹàǹ crocodile àn this, but ńàń àn this crocodile.

Here the reason of the low-toned noun becoming high-toned is the stress which is laid on the noun.

Many references to intonation will be found in the following paragraphs, they are treated there together with the grammatical functions they exercise.

Accentuation.

60. In words with more than one syllable the accent (or stress) lies on the stem-syllable. When a syllable with low tone has the accent, this low tone frequently becomes high.

SECOND SECTION:
FORMATION OF WORDS.

61. The stems of the Shilluk-words are monosyllabic. A word may consist in
1. **a vowel.**

62. *á* sign of the past, *í* it is, *â* which, *ú* forming the future; and the personal pronouns when suffixed: *a, i, e̩*; but these last, being unseparably connected with another word, are not independent words; and the rest are likewise mere particles; no noun or verb in Shi. consists in a vowel only.

2. **a consonant and a vowel.**

63. This is the oldest form of the word in the Sudan-languages (comp. Die Sudansprachen, page 14), but is not very frequent in Shi. now. Examples: *bá, fá* not, *be̩* in order to, *bú* to have not, *cha* time, *cha* to be going to, *chi* wife, *che̩* to begin, *chū* bones, *dà* to have, *dè* sign of perfect, *dè̩* but, *ga* piece, copy, *gé* they, *go̩* him, *gū* a big fish, *jé* people, *kā* to go, *ká* place, *kí* with, *ko* to say, *kū* thief, *má* aunt, *ma* because, *mi* mother, *ná* as, *né* as, *ní* to use, *ńa* child, *ńu* lion, *pi* water, *rè* why, *wá* we, *wú* you pl., *yá* I, *yí* you, *yo̩* road.

64. Not in all these words the primitive form, consonant + vowel, is original, some are apparently shortened from longer forms, but in others it is not clear, whether the short forms are mutilated from longer ones, or whether the words consisting in more than one consonant and one vowel have evolved from the corresponding primitive forms. Compare these examples:

bá, fá not, *fáṭ* it is not
    be̩ in order to, probably from *bia* to come
    bi to come — *bia* to come
    bú to have not — *buṇo̩* to have not
    cha time — from *chaṅ* "day, sun"
    cha to be going to — *chamo̩* to be going to

    chi wife — *chyek* wife
    che̩ to begin — *chāgo̩* to begin
    chū bones, sing. *chōgo̩*
    gi thing — *gin* thing
    kā place — *kāch* place
    kā to go — *kādo̩* to go
    ko to say — *kōbo̩* to say
    ma because — *mar* because.

3. **a consonant and a diphthong.**

65. *bai* buttermilk, *be̩i* mosquito, *bói* net, *lai* game, *láu* cloth, *lḍu* far, *lau* spittle, *nau* thus, *ńau* cat, *ye̩i* boat, *ye̩i* hair.

4. **a consonant and two vowels.**

66. *bia* to come; this is probably derived from *bi* to come.

5. **a consonant, vowel, and consonant.** This is by far the most fre-

67.

quent form; it may be called the characteristic form of the word in Shi., about 90 % of all *stems* of the language having this form.
bàt arm, *bák* fence, *báṅ* a cow, *báṅ* behind, *bar* long, *bech* bundle, *bet* spear, *bol* a mat, *gol* fence, *kal* fence, *kot* rain, etc.

68. In my comparative study "Die Sudansprachen", I have shown the original word in Sudan to consist in one consonant and one vowel, all other elements in a word being later additions. As is seen under 2., this original form is not frequent in Shi., the standard form being here consonant + vowel + consonant. Accordingly these words ought to be demonstrated as having evolved from words with one consonant and one vowel only; the second consonant should be traced as a later element. That is, however, until now possible only in a small minority of cases. This may be explained from the fact that the eastern Sudan languages have, for a comparatively long time, had their own development, separate from that of the western languages, and under the influence of languages of different character.

I have found, however, a number of words which, being identical in their first consonant and vowel, and differing only in the second consonant, have the same or a similar meaning, which makes it probable that they are of one origin, and consisted originally in one consonant and one vowel, but differentiated their meaning by adding a second consonant. In some of the examples there is a semivowel between the first consonant and the vowel, which, according to 21, 22, has arisen from a vowel, so that here two vowels are to be supposed.

69. Examples.

bāgo to make a fence ⎫
bājo to tie together ⎬ < *bā*

bāno, ⎫
baṅo, ⎬ to make a mistake ⎫
bājo to err ⎭ < *bā*

chōk it is finished ⎫
chōṭi it is finished ⎬ < *chō*

chwōbo to pierce ⎫
chwayo to pierce ⎬ < *chua*

gōdo to scratch, dig ⎫
gōṅo, ⎬ to scratch ⎫
gwaṅo ⎭ < *gua*
gōbo to scratch ⎭

fago to be sharp ⎫
fālo knife ⎬ < *fā*

fecho, ⎫
fyecho ⎬ to ask ⎫ < *fe, *fia, with
femo to gainsay ⎬ the supposed
fedo to lie ⎭ meaning of "to say"

fōgo to be bruised ⎫
fōjo to rub, brush ⎬ < *fo, fua

gōdo to loosen ⎫
gōṅo to loosen ⎬ < *go, gua

kāgo, ⎫
kago ⎬ to ache, pain ⎫
kājo to bite, ache, pain ⎭ < *kā

kēto to throw ⎫
kēto to dash, shatter, split ⎬ < *kē

kā to go ⎫
kādo, kedo to go ⎬ < *kā

Formation of Words 25

kōd̲o̲ to blow	} < *kō	ṅō̲g̲o̲ to vomit	} < *ṅua	
kōṅo̲ to blow		ṅoto̲, ṅwoto̲ to spit		
kwōd̲o̲	} pole < *kua	kāgo̲, kẹ̄to̲ split < *kā		
kwāro̲		fwō̲jo̲	} to thank < *pua	
kū thief	} < *ku, kua	pāko̲		
kwālo̲ to steal		ro̲bo̲ to string beads	} < *ro̲	
kwāṅo̲ to take	} < *kua	ro̲to̲ to sew		
kwōgo̲ to take		tẹ̄no̲ to pour out drop by drop	} < *tẹ	
kwayo̲ to herd	} < *kua	tẹ̄no̲ to strain beer		
kwodo̲ to drive, herd		tō̲no̲ to pick	} < *tua	
muo̲no̲ to plaster	} < *mu, mua	twāro̲ to pick, gather, clean		
mūlo̲ to plaster				
má because	} < *ma	wōd̲o̲ to pull out	} < *wo, wua.	
már because		wo̲ro̲ to pull out		
awa yesterday	} < awa			
awar-awa the day before yesterday				

6. Consonant, semivowel, and vowel, which may again be followed by another augment.

These forms are also very frequent.

70. *kwā* grandfather, *kwi* some, *kwot* shield, *gwo̲k* work, *kwó̲p* talk, *lwak* cow-house, *lwo̲l* gourd, *kwach* leopard, *kwālo̲* to steal, *kwako̲* to embrace, *kwāṅo̲* to swim; *fye̲cho̲* to ask, *kye̲d̲o̲* to refuse, *gyẹ̄no̲* fowl, *tyẹ̄lo̲* foot, etc.

In 21, 22 I have, with the help of related languages, tried to show that in many, if not in all, cases the semivowel is to be traced to an original vowel, so that here also the primitive stem would be one consonant and one vowel. Compare:

ṅudo̲ to cut	} < *ṅu + a	kū thief	} < *ku + a
ṅālo̲ to butcher		kwālo̲ to steal	
ṅo̲lo̲ to cut		kwāṅo̲ to swim	} < *ku + a.
		Nu. kuje to swim	

For more examples see 69.

71. 7. The forms 5 and 6 may have a vocalic suffix, which consists a) in the vowel o̲; it is added to the verb in the present tense, and to the singular of many substantives.

gō̲go̲ to work, *kād̲o̲* to go; *jâgò̲* chief, *jālo̲* man, *obwo̲ṅo̲* white man, *aṅṅò̲* an ant, *àchwât̲ò̲* loin-cloth, etc.

In certain words this o̲ may be pronounced or dropped at will: *obwo̲ṅo̲* or *obwo̲ṅ*, *jālo̲* or *jal*; moreover it is sounded so slightly, that one very often overhears it. — In the Nuer language ǫ is a suffixed demonstrative pronoun; it may originally have had the same meaning in Shi.

In the following cases a verb is formed from a noun by adding ǫ: *wich* head, *wijǫ* to make a roof ("a head") *lach* urine, *lājǫ* to piss.

b) in the vowel *i*: stem *rūm* to cover, *rūmi* a cover; stem *chām* to eat, *chāmichami* a bait; stem *gǫj* to strike *gǒjì-gòchìs* word.

c) the plural-suffixes see.

72. 8. Words with prefixes.

The Shi. has two vocalic prefixes, *a* and *o*. In most cases these prefixes have a distinct function: *by prefixing a or o to a verb, the verb becomes a noun.* This is a law prevailing in very many Sudan languages, eastern as well as western.

73. Examples.

bù to have not — *àbù* poor
chāgǫ to compose a song — *achak* poet
chęmǫ to make straight, to aim — *àchę́m* straight
gē̤tǫ to bless — *àgę̄tǫ́* blessed
gwēnǫ to pick up — *àgwę́n* a bastard child (a child "picked up")
kārǫ to branch off — *akar* branch
kwǫrǫ to winnow, *àkwǫ́r* husk
lūnǫ to be turned upside down — *alún* somersault
mạ̈t (to be) slow — *àmạ́t* a stork
nạ̈gǫ to kill — *ànę́kǫ̀* spirit of a deceased person

bugǫ to press the bellows — *òbừk* bellows
chōdǫ to break off — *óchǒdǫ̀* a cow whose horns are broken, a hornless cow
dįkǫ to darken (said of the sun) — *odįng* cloud-shadow
rō̤gǫ to hollow — *órę̄gǫ́* hollow
tįnǫ to raise, lift up — *ótįnò* stones raised up, dam
tǭrǫ to make a ford — *ótǫ́r* ford
dǭlǫ to swing — *òdǭlǫ̀* swinging
kā̤gǫ to blossom — *òkǭk* flower
kǫnǫ to stimulate — *òkǭn* stimulating
rǭnǫ to be astute — *òrǫ̀k* astuteness
tgwǫ to wag — *òtè̤u* wagging.

The prefix *o* often designates persons as descendants of other persons, as members of a tribe or nation:

wājǫ sister *owājǫ* the child of the sister
nāyǫ the mother's brother, *onāyǫ* the mother's brother's child
chōl Shilluk *óchǒlǫ̀* a Shilluk man
jāṅǫ Dinka *ojāṅǫ* a Dinka man

māyǫ the mother's sister *omāyǫ* the mother's sister's child
Dăk name of a king *Ódăk* the son of *Dăk*.
bwoń foreign *obwǫnǫ* a stranger, foreigner.

In some cases *a* or *o* are prefixed to a *noun*, thus giving it a peculiar sense:

lwẹ̄dọ finger — alwẹ̄dọ a dura which has four ears, like the four (long) fingers of the hand

mal front — àmál*ọ̀* the first
tuṅ horn — atuṅakyel "unicorn" : rhinoceros.

Not all words with a prefix can be derived from words without a prefix, for example:

àbàch a certain cow, ábàṅ hammer, ábich five, àbúr*ọ̀* bushbuck, and many others.

In some words the prefix may be omitted at will:

atẹ̄gọ and tẹ̄gọ bead   oyino and yino fisherman.

74. There are some other words beginning with a vowel, but here apparently the vowel is not a prefix:

àk these, àn this, àchà these, áfà in order that, *ę̀n* he, him, ōrọ to send, *ọ́rọ̀* relative by marriage, àn*ọ̀* what?

In some of these a beginning consonant can be shown to have been dropped: *ę̀n* ‹ *ŕ̥ęn*, ōrọ to send ‹ wōrọ; *ọ́rọ̀* relative by marriage is in Ga. wor; in àn*ọ̀* "what" *à* is evidently the deictic particle: "it is".

9. **Reduplication** is very rare. I have only met with one single example: 75. yiyi to be possessed by a spirit.

The Shilluks like to *repeat* a word or grammatical form which is to be emphasized: *é kẹdọ, kẹdọ, kẹdọ* he was going, going, going: was going on for a long while; *gẹ bẹ̀n*ọ̀ *bẹ̀nè bẹ̀nè* they came all, all, all: all of them came; *láu láu láu* very far away; *é chák*í *chák*í he approached slowly, stealthily; *yá nẹ̀n, yá nẹ̀n* I looked closely.

Recapitulation.

76. The word in Shi. may have the following forms:
1. a, 2. ba, 3. bau, 4. bia, 5. bat, 6. bwa, bwat, 7. batọ, bwatọ, 8. obat, obatọ, obwatọ; 9. baba.

COMPOSITION OF WORDS.

77. Nearly all compound words in Shi. consist in two or more nouns, which stand to each other in genetive relation; they are, properly speaking, no compound words, but two distinct, independent nouns; compare:

waṅ àgàk	"eye of the crow"	a kind of red dura
waṅ Ńíkàṅ	"eye of Nyikang"	east
waṅ ṅu	"eye of lion"	a kind of red dura
wiy ṅu	"head of lion"	story, tale
wiy kyạ̀ṅ	"head of horse"	riddle

28   *Formation of Words*

    wan̄ wot̯ "eye of house" window
    t̯a tyėl̯o̭ "basis of foot" heel.

78. Sometimes the single part of combinations cannot be identified:
wá jàl n̄é n̄árò a kind of red dura *t̯at̯ėd̯i* a pole for pulling boats
wan̄ wure lwal south *t̯ákugi* a little axe (these last three
t̯àyè dè gāk a cow, black with white are compounds with *t̯a* "ba-
  throat sis").

  Proper-names are often compounds: *Kwat̯ Ke̯r, Koyikwo̯n, A̯t̯wo̭d̯wo̭i, Akùrù-wâr, Awarejwo̯k, Óbàyàbwíjȧp,* etc.

  Many of these combinations are no doubt whole sentences, which have been united into one word.

79. Some nouns, being frequently combined with other words, help to form certain grammatical categories:

  n̄a, in compositions often *n̄e* "child, young one" forms deminutives, it frequently also designates nouns with a certain quality, similar to the Arab *abu* "father":

n̄a yat̯ a small, young tree *n̄a rō̯jo̯* a young heifer, a calf
n̄a rit̯ son of a king, prince *n̄a kō̯ro̯* cotton seed
n̄a go̯l "child of the enclosure": wife
n̄a bán̄ "child behind": slave, servant, liege-man
n̄a kwâch, n̄a let̯, n̄a félwot̯ names for cows;
Ń̄elwâk, Ń̄en̄árò̯, Ń̄ejwàd̯o̭, Ń̄egèr, Nelye̯ch, proper names of persons and places.

80. *pà* ⟨ from *pàch* "village, settlement, home" is frequently used in forming names of places:

  Páchȯd̯o̭, Fámat̯, Fádèt, Fát̯áù, Fábùr, Fàd̯eàn̄,[1] *Fan̄ikan̄* (also *Fen̄ikan̄*), *Fákán̄,* etc.

81. *jal*, pl. *jo̯k* "man" may designate the acting person or a possessor, it can be combined with a verbal noun or an original noun:

    jale lwo̯k "man of washing" washerman
    jal n̄al "man of butchering" butcher
    jal lén̄ "man of war" warrior
    jal yat̯ "man of tree" medecine man, doctor
    jal ke̯r "man of richness" rich person.

82. *n̄ate*, pl. *tye̯n̄* man, person, is used in the same way as *jal*:

    n̄ate ne̯k "man of killing" murderer
    n̄ate kwȧyo̭ "man of herding" herdsman
    n̄ate n̄al "man of butchering" butcher
    n̄ate ke̯r "man of richness" rich man
    n̄ate jwo̯k "man of sickness" sick person.

---

[1] Note the assimilation of tone!

Composition of Words

83. A peculiar kind of compound nouns is formed by ñān, the nasalized form of ñate "man, person"; ñān is properly "*the* man", "this man", see 138. It may be combined with a noun, or, what is more frequent, with a verb in the present tense, and with a verb in the passive:

ñān e ḍachǫ, ñān a ḍachǫ	"the person is a woman"	the woman
ñān lōjǫ	"the man (is) black"	a black man
ñān chwǫr, ñān e chwǫr	"the man is blind"	a blind person
ñān e lẹdǫ, ñān lẹdǫ	"the man (he) is shaving"	one who is shaving
ñan e kók	"the man (he) is hired"	a hired person.

84. In the following compound nouns the first part of the composition is known, but no more existing independently in the language.

tedigǫ a red-brown cow, teduk a grey cow, tẹtań a black cow, from *te cow; compare Nu. ti cow, Ba. ki-teń cow. Compare also: ḍeań cow < *ḍe yań, Nr. yań; ḍǫk < *ḍe rǫk cows, Nr. rǫk. In both cases the word in Shilluk has two components: *ḍe and yań, rǫk.

85. The last consonant of the ruling noun undergoes a change in these words:

wǫrnamtai a certain cow ⎫
wǫregòt a certain cow ⎬ from waṭ "steer".
wâtyḷbyêk a certain cow ⎭

THIRD SECTION:
GENEALOGICAL RELATIONS OF THE SHILLUK LANGUAGE.

THE DIALECTS OR DIVISIONS.

86. The Shilluk language is not confined to one single territory, but is spoken in different parts of the White Nile region, some of which are situated at considerable distance from one another. The largest section of Shilluk-speaking people live in what is generally called the Shilluk country, and only this part is known under the name of Shilluk people. The rest of the tribes speaking the same language have each their own name, both for people and language, but their languages are essentially one in structure and vocabulary with the Shilluk proper. There are, of course, dialectical differences, which are the natural consequences of the language being separated into locally different branches, so that each branch had its own way of development, and was in some measure influenced by its respective neighbour; but the following examples will make it evident that they are to be regarded as dialects of one language. It is to be noted that not only the selection of words given below are identical, but, as far as I have been able to judge, about 90 % of all words in these dialects are uniform, and so is the grammatical structure; the only remarkable deviation is that Gang (Acholi) has a noun-forming prefix *la*-, pl. *lu*-, which is Hamitic and corresponds to the Masai "article" *ol* pl. *il*.

87. The dialects or divisions of the Shilluk language are:
1. *Shilluk* proper.
2. *Anywak (Añwak, also Anuak);* it is spoken a) on both sides of the Sobat between the Dinka Tribe Gnok *(Ŋǫk)* and the Nuers, south-east of Abwong; b) in Abyssinia on both sides of the river Baro; c) in Abyssinia between the rivers Gelo and Akobo.

The Anywak has been somewhat influenced by its neighbour, the Nuer; some grammatical formations coincide with those of Nuer. But during my stay in the Shilluk country I have convinced myself that it is possible without considerable difficulty to converse with an Anywak man in Shilluk. The Abyssinians call the Anywaks Jambo.

3. *Jur;* is spoken between the 7th and 8th degree of n. lat. and about the 28th and 29th degree of eastern longitude.

The Dialects or Divisions. 31

4. *Dembo;* is spoken to the north-west of Jur, on both sides of the Bahr Dembo.
5. *Belanda;* is spoken south to south-west of the Jur, the habitat of both being separated by the Bongo or Dōr.
6. *Ber (Bẹ̄r);* is spoken south of the Bongo country and east of the Belanda, on the right bank of the Suē river.
7. *Beri (Bẹ̄ri)* is spoken in the province of Mongalla, on the right bank of the Nile, north-east of Lado.

On the map of A. E. S. the Beri ("Berri") are also called Beir; from this it is probable, that Beri and Ber are identical, Beri being the plural form of Ber. Again according to Schweinfurth[1] the Bongo designate the Jur by the name of "Behr", and on the map of A. E. S. in the habitat of the Ber the name "Jur" is put in; this seems to show the very near relationship of Jur, Ber and Beri; and as Belanda lies close to Ber, these two can also be nearly or totally identical.[2]

8. *Gang (Gaṅ)* or Acholi; is spoken in the country situated east, north-east and north of the Nile between Lake Victoria and Lake Albert. — The name Acholi, also Shuli, is evidently identical with the name of the Shilluk: *Chōlọ,* the *i* in Acholi, Shuli denoting the plural.
9. *Nyifwa (Ñifwa)* or Ja Luo, also called Kavirondo; is spoken in part of the Kavirondo-country, in the north-east coastlands of Lake Albert, round the Kavirondo-bay.
10. *Lango* (Kitching: Umiru); is spoken in the Bukedi district, north and north-east of Lake Kioga. Kitching in his Grammar of the Gang Language page VII says: "The northern Bakedi or Lango seem to be distinct from the Umiru, and their dialect is unintelligible to the Acholi." But the words which Johnston gives under "Lango", are clearly a dialect of Acholi and Shilluk proper.
11. *Aluru* (Kitching: Alur); is spoken in the country north and north-west of Lake Albert and west of the Nile.
12. *Chopi;* is, according to Kitching, spoken between Bunyoro and the Victoria Nile. Sir Harry Johnston does not mention this name in "The Uganda Protectorate", but he says that the name *Luọ,* which is given to several Shilluk dialects, also occurs in the north of Unyoro.
13. South of Nyifwa, on the eastern shore of Lake Victoria, lives a small tribe called *Gaya;* they seem also to speak a dialect of Shilluk; but it is not sure.
14. The same is to be said of the *Jafalu,* who live to the north-east of Lake Albert.

These are the dialects or divisions of the Shilluk which are known to-day. It is, however, to be observed that the word "dialect" is not employed here quite in its usual meaning, as of some "dialects", chiefly Ber, Beri, Belanda,

---

[1] Linguistische Ergebnisse einer Reise nach Central-Afrika (Berlin 1873) p. 61.
[2] Compare also B. Struck "An Unlocated Tribe on the White Nile", in Journal of the African Society 1908 page 75—78.

Dembo, it is not known whether they do at all differ from each other, or whether they are rather divisions of one identical dialect. The distinctions which do exist between some of the divisions will best be seen from the examples following in the list below. In this list most of the dialects or divisions are illustrated:

Anywak from my own unpublished materials;
Jur in Schweinfurth, Linguistische Ergebnisse;
Ber is represented by a few words[1] in Petherick, Egypt, the Sudan and Central Africa, p. 481:

forehead	*wiy*	Shilluk *wich*	
eye	*wang*	Shilluk *wan̄*	
nose	*koum*	Shilluk *wum*	The orthography of the original has been retained.
lip	*dack*	Shilluk *ḍǫk*	
tooth	*lack*	Shilluk *lęk*	
tongue	*laeb*	Shilluk *lęp*	

Gang in Kitching: An Outline Grammar of the Gang Language, London 1908.
Nyifwa in O. Baumann, Von Masailand zur Nilquelle, also in Sir H. Johnston, The Uganda Protectorate.
Lango and *Aluru* in Johnston, The Uganda Protectorate.

Of *Dembo, Belanda, Beri* and *Chopi* I have not found any materials. *Dembo* and *Belanda* I include amongst the Shilluk dialects on the strength of Schweinfurth's statement ("Im Herzen von Afrika" page 63): north of the Jurs the more numerous Dembo and some smaller tribes of the same origin have their residence; and the Belanda live 80 (German) miles south of the Jur; they, in spite of the great differences in their habits, which have evidently been influenced by the Bongo, still have preserved the Shilluk language in a more or less pure form." The native traditions also designate the Belanda as belonging to the Shilluks.

Of *Beri* Emin Pasha says that they speak the same language as the Shilluks.

Chopi is mentioned by Kitching as belonging to the Shilluk group.

It is remarkable that many dialects bear the same name. As stated above, Acholi, also called Shuli, is doubtless identical with *Chōlǫ*, the name of the Shilluk proper. Likewise the name Luǫ occurs repeatedly: the Jurs call themselves Luǫ; the Aluru of Albert Lake, according to Johnston, more often pronounce their name Aluǫ, and this form appears again in the north of Unyoro and among the Ja-Luǫ (Nyifwa). Note also the names *Bẹ̄r, Bẹ̄ri, Bạr*, (this last name is given to the Shilluk proper by the Dinkas), and *Bǫr*, which is the proper name of the Belanda.

---
[1] These words are also given by Struck, An Unlocated Tribe.

THE POSITION OF SHILLUK AMONG OTHER AFRICAN LANGUAGES.

The Shilluk belongs to a clearly circumscribed group of African Languages, which is usually styled "Nilotic Languages". It is difficult to give the characteristic marks of the languages belonging to this group, as sufficient materials of all of them are not available. Some chief points are: 90.

1. Mute and fricative sounds are in some cases interchangeable, chiefly p and f are often so.
2. Many, if not all, of the languages have interdental sounds ($t\ d\ n$). I have found them in Shilluk, Anywak, Nuer and Dinka, and according to some German authors Masai and Ndorobo also have them.[1]
3. The stem in most cases consists in a consonant, vowel, and consonant, generally ending in a consonant.
4. Stems with a semivowel between the first consonant and the vowel are frequent. The stem-vowel is often a diphthong.
5. Probably in most of them intonation plays an important rôle.

The Nilotic languages consist of two sub-divisions: 91.
        a) The Niloto-Sudanic group.
        b) The Niloto-Hamitic group.

It is probable that the Nilotic languages originally belong to the family of the Sudan-languages (vide below 95). The phonology, the form of the word and some grammatical peculiarities in all Nilotic languages point to this common origin. The vocabularies of all of them have certain sudanic elements. But at a certain former period all these languages have more or less strongly been influenced by languages of a different character, which are generally called Hamitic languages. They differ from the Sudanic languages chiefly in the grammatical gender, in the prevalence of accentuation instead of intonation, and in their more extensive possibilities of expressing formative elements. Rudiments of the grammatical gender are found in Shilluk also, see 126; likewise accentuation exists in Shilluk, but the means of forming words are scanty. On the other hand numerous Shilluk-words, which most probably are Sudanic, are found in languages generally counted as Hamitic.

So the line between Niloto-Sudanic and Niloto-Hamitic languages is not easy to define; they all have components of Sudanic and of Hamitic origin, only that in some cases the first is prevalent, in others the latter. But nevertheless the groups may be distinguished; the languages belonging to the Niloto-Sudanic group having a large number of words common to all of them, and

---

[1] See for instance Meinhof on Ndorobo in Mitteilungen des Seminars für Orientalische Sprachen, Band X, 111; and Struck in „Die geographischen Namen im Gebiet der ostafrikanischen Bruchstufe". Reprinted from „Mitteilungen aus den deutschen Schutzgebieten", Nr. 2, 1911.

many of which are clearly genealogically connected with the Western Sudan languages. In the formation of words and in the structure of their grammar they are essentially uniform; they have not the grammatical gender or only faint traces of it. On the other hand the Niloto-Hamitic group has not nearly so many words in common with the Sudanic group, as the idioms of the Sudanic group have with each other; in formation of words and in the wealth of formative elements they considerably deviate from the Sudanic group; and they have the grammatical gender. Whether accentuation is more, and intonation less prevalent in them than in the Sudanic group, is as yet unknown, but it is probable.

92. To the Niloto-Sudanic group belong:
   a) Shilluk with its divisions or dialects.
   b) Dinka and Nuer.
   c) Mittu, Madi, Madi-Kaya (Abo-Kaya), Abaka, Luba, Wira, Lendu, Moru.

Dinka is spoken a) in the northern part of the Bahr Ghazal province, b) on both sides of the White Nile between the 6th and 7$^{th\,0}$ n. l. (Bor), c) on both sides of the lower Sobat, d) on the right bank of the White Nile from near the mouth of the Sobat to Jebelein. Bahr Ghazal and Bor are probably the eldest seats of the Dinkas, from here they emigrated northwards. The dialect of Bor *(Bǫr)* seems to differ considerably from the dialects of the north. Dinka has in its vocabulary remarkable similarity with Bari; in accordance with this the Dinkas seem in their bodily appearance and their culture to be more strongly influenced by Hamitic tribes than the Shilluks are.

The *Nuers* live a) on the White Nile north of Bor, b) south of Tonga and of the lower Sobat, c) on both sides of the Sobat near Nasser.

Dinka and Nuer differ in their phonology and structure but slightly from the Shilluk dialects; they have, in common with Acholi and Anywak, the particles *chi* and *bi* for expressing past and future; these particles are not found in Shilluk proper. A great, probably the greater part of the words of both languages are essentially the same as in Shilluk, but to a considerable extent the vocabularies differ, so that both are to be considered as separate languages. They are nearer related to each other than to Shilluk.

c) Some tribes lying between the upper course of the rivers Rohl and Suē speak languages which seem to be in some broader way connected with the Niloto-Sudanic group, so that they are perhaps to be regarded as a sub-group of these. To this sub-group belong: Mittu, Madi, Madi-Kaya (Abo-Kaya), Abaka, Luba, Wira, Lendu, Moru. According to Schweinfurth and A. E. S. the six first-named of these tribes have really one language, which differs only dialectically, so that individuals of the different tribes understand each other.

The Position of Shilluk

In their vocabularies these languages considerably distinguish themselves from the Shilluk dialects as well as from Dinka and Nuer.

According to their topographical situation the three groups of Niloto-Sudanic languages may be designated thus:
a) The High Nilotic Group, comprising Mittu, Madi, Madi-Kaya, Abo-Kaya, Abaka, Luba, Wira, Lendu, Moru.
b) The Middle Nilotic Group, comprising the Shilluk cluster.
c) The Low Nilotic Group, comprising Dinka and Nuer.

93. The *Niloto-Hamitic group* may, according to B. Struck,[1] be divided into the sub-groups of Bari-Masai and Nandi-Tatoga. To the first belong: Masai, Ngishu, Elgumi, Teso, Suk, Karamojo, Turkana, and Bari; to the latter: Tatoga, Ndorobo, Nandi, Kamasia, and Burkeneji. All these languages are situated in British- and German East-Africa.

94. The *Niloto-Sudanic languages* are a sub-group of the *Eastern Sudan Languages*, to which belong Nuba in the north, Kunama in the north-east, most languages of the southern Gesira (between White and Blue Nile), and others.

95. The Eastern together with the Central and Western Sudan-languages form the family of the *Sudan Languages*, which extend from near the Red Sea and Abyssinia through the whole continent to the Atlantic Ocean from the northern Cameroons to Senegambia.

96. In order to demonstrate the genealogical connection between Shilluk, the Niloto-Sudanic group and the Eastern Sudan languages on one side and the Western Sudan languages on the other side, the chief characteristics of the Sudan languages, as shown in my "Sudansprachen" may be given here:
1. they are monosyllabic, each word consisting in one syllable;
2. each syllable or word consists in one consonant and one vowel;
3. they are isolating, that is they have no inflection, and only few formative elements; the "class-prefixes" of the Bantu-languages and of some Hamitic languages are absent;
4. they have no grammatical gender;
5. intonation is prevailing in a higher degree than it is in Bantu- and Hamitic languages.

These characteristics are not preserved in their pure form in all Sudan languages, almost all of them showing some marks of development from the primitive stage to a more developed state, chiefly by adding augments to the original stem; this is still more the case, where a language has been strongly influenced by an idiom belonging to a different family. But in each Sudan language it will, to a certain extent, be possible to trace the later additions to a stem as such, that is to show that these words were originally simple stems

---

[1] B. Struck, Über die Sprachen der Tatoga und Irakuleute. Reprinted from the "Mitteilungen aus den Deutschen Schutzgebieten", Ergänzungsheft 4, 1910.

consisting in one consonant and one vowel, to which, certain elements were added at a later time.

97. In Shilluk the characteristics mentioned above can easily be traced:
1. the stems are monosyllabic; see 61;
2. though the majority of the words do not consist in one consonant and one vowel, it is shown in 68 that a number of stems can be traced to the original primitive form;
3. the language has no inflection; the vowel-changes occurring in the verb and noun, which come near to what might be called inflection, are most probably of Hamitic origin. The nouns have no class-prefixes;
4. grammatical gender is absent; the rudiments of it which do exist, are of Hamitic origin;
5. Intonation dominates in the language.

Comparative Lists of Words.

98. Their object is to show in a number of words:
a) the identity of Shilluk proper and its dialects or divisions.
b) the genealogical relation between Shilluk and other Niloto-Sudanic languages, viz. Dinka and Nuer.
c) the genealogical relation between Shilluk and other Eastern Sudan languages. Of these Nuba is treated in the list; it has a good number of words in common with Shilluk; in other Eastern Sudanic languages such common words are rarer.
d) the genealogical relation between Shilluk and Bongo; this language, though having its habitat amidst the Shilluk languages, shows remarkable connections with Central Sudanic languages, particularly with Bagirmi. Some of the Bongo-words which it has in common with Shilluk, may of course be loan-words.
e) the genealogical relation between Shilluk and a Niloto-Hamitic language, viz. Bari.
f) the genealogical relation of Shilluk and some other Eastern Sudan languages to the Western Sudan-languages.

a)—e) are comprised in one group; f) forms a group for itself. Both groups might without difficulty have been multiplied, but the examples given will suffice.

[In order to show more fully the affinities in vocabulary between the Niloto-Sudanic and the Niloto-Hamitic group, a number of words common to languages of both groups are given in their Hamitic form in the *Dictionary*. It will be seen that the conformities with Shilluk are more nume-

The Position of Shilluk   37

rous in the Bari-Masai than in the Nandi-Tatoga group. The Dictionary contains also some hints regarding the very few words which are identical in Shilluk and in the High Niloto-Sudanic group.]

In the comparative lists some letters are used, which do not occur in Shilluk, and need therefore an explanation.   99.

ǫ is the German ö in nötig "necessary"; it is pronounced in rounding the lips as if pronouncing an o and then saying an e. — Mitterrutzner's *å* I render by ǫ. ˜ is the mark for nasalization: *ã* is nasalized *a* as in French an "year". ģ is a palatal g, it sounds almost like j. In Nuer and Anywak the pronunciation of final mute consonants and even of y is in certain cases followed by a pressing of the larynx, so that the consonant sounds very abrupt, and is sometimes hardly audible. These sounds are rendered by ': *k*, *y*', etc. (Some divisions of Shilluk as well as Masai and Nandi have the same sounds; see Johnston page 888.) — Kitching frequently writes "or" at the end of a word, where other languages have ǫ; I suppose that here "or" simply expresses ǫ, "or" being frequently used by English speaking authors for ǫ.

Most of the authors quoted do not distinguish o and ǫ, e and ę, some not even long and short vowels; none has marked interdental sounds; thus the differences between Shilluk and the other languages look greater than they really are, the difference being only one of orthography.

The following remarks belong to the second group only.

ų, į are narrow vowels; u, i are wide vowels.

ḍ and ḷ are cerebral sounds; they are formed a little further back in the mouth than where the usual d and l are articulated.

ḳ is a transformed *k*; the changes which it undergoes in certain languages are different from those of the usual *k*.

χ is the German ch in "ach".

v is the English v.

ü is an i with rounded lips, as in German "übt".

ẃ is ü with a following short y.

First Group.   100.

Shi. *bąr* long	Any. *bat* arm	Ju. *bęt* sharp, pointed
Ga. *bor* long	Ju. *bat* arm	Any. *będi* sharp, pointed
Ju. *bār* long	Ja. *bāt* arm	Di. *bit* fish-spear
Di. *bar* long	La. *bāt* arm	Nr. *biţ* fish-spear
Nr. *bąr* long	Shi. *bęţ* fish-spear	Shi. *dbich* five
Shi. *bàt* arm	Ga. *bit* sharp	Ga. *abich* five
Ga. *bat* arm	Ju. *będi* fish-spear	Ju. *abich* five

Any. *abíyù* five
Ja. *abīch* five
Al. *abi* five
Ba. *bu* five

Shi. *bǭdǫ* artist, smith
Ju. *bōdo* artist, smith
Bo. *bǫro* artist, smith
Ba. *bōdo* artist, smith

Shi. *būl* drum
Ga. *bul* drum
Ju. *būl* drum
Any. *būl* drum
Nr. *būl* drum
Ja. *būl* drum
La. *būl* drum
Al. *vūl* drum

Shi. *bur* ashes
Ga. *buru* ashes
Ju. *bur* ashes
Nu. *oburti* ashes
Bo. *buruku* ashes

Shi. *butǫ* to lie down
Ga. *buto* to lie down
Ju. *budo* to lie down
Any. *butǫ* to lie down
Di. *but* to waylay

Shi. *byḗl* dura
Ga. *bel* corn
Ju. *bęl* dura
Any. *byḗl* dura
Nr. *bḕl* dura
Di. *bel* dura

Shi. *chāk* milk
Ga. *chak* milk
Ju. *chak* milk
Any. *chāk* milk
Nr. *chăk* milk
Di. *cha* milk
Nu. *ichi* milk

Shi. *chāmǫ* to eat
Ga. *chamo* to eat
Ju. *shame* to eat
Any. *chama* to eat
Nr. *cham* to eat
Ja. *chamo, chyęmǫ* to eat
La. *samǫ* to eat
Di. *cham* to eat

Shi. *chul* penis
Ju. *shul* penis
Any. *chul* penis
Nr. *chul* penis
La. *sūl* penis
Al. *chūl* penis
Ba. *toluto* testicles
Nu. *sorot* penis
Di. *chul* penis

Shi. *chuń, chwiń* liver
Ga. *chwiń* liver
Ju. *shwiń* liver
Nr. *chwoń* liver
Di. *chweń* liver

Shi. *chūnǫ* to stop
Ga. *chuño* to stop
Ju. *chuń* to stop
Any. *chūnǫ* to stop
Nr. *chuń* to stop

Shi. *chwǫr* vulture
Ga. *ochur* vulture
achut vulture
Ju. *achut* vulture
Nr. *chwǫ́r* vulture
Di. *chwor* vulture

Shi. *ddęk* three
Ga. *adek* three
Ju. *adak* three
Any. *àdágò* three
Ba. *bu-dǫk* eight, that is: five and three
Ja. *adek* three
La. *adek* three
Al. *adek* three

Shi. *ḍāk* pot
Ga. *dak* pot
Ju. *dak* pot
Any. *dak* pot
Nr. *ṭak* pot
Ba. *ḍāk* pot

Shi. *ḍāṇ* man
Ga. *dano* man
Jur. *dano* man
Any. *ḍāṇ* man
Ja. *dānǫ* man
La. *danǫ* man
Al. *danǫ* man
Di. *ran* man
Nr. *rān* man

Shi. *dǫ̀k* mouth
Ga. *dok* mouth
Ju. *tio* mouth
Any. *dǫ̀k* mouth
Ja. *dōk* mouth
La. *dǫk* mouth
Al. *dǫk* mouth
Di. *wtoch* mouth
Nr. *ṭǫk* mouth
Nu. *ak* mouth
Bo. *ndu* language
Ba. *ka-tok* mouth

Shi. *gǭjǫ* to beat
Ju. *goi* to beat
Any. *gwai* to beat

Ja. gōjǫ to shoot
Bo. gba to beat
Ba. gwai to beat

Shi. ogwal frog
Ga. ogwal frog
Ju. ogwal frog
Any. ogwal frog
Nu. guglati frog

Shi. gwok dog
Ga. gwok dog
Ju. guok dog
Any. gwok dog
Ja. gwok dog
La. guōk dog
Al. guōk dog
Di. jo dog
Nr. jǫk dog
Ba. dyoṅ dog

Shi. gyēnō hen
Ga. gweno hen
Ju. gyeno hen
Any. gwęnǫ hen
Ja. gweno hen
La. gwēno hen
Al. gwēno hen
Bo. ṅgono hen

Shi. jĕ people
Ga. ji̇̄ people
Any. jō people
Bo. ji̇̄, ǵi̇̄ people
Ba. gwea tribe

Shi. jwǫk God
Ga. jok demon
Any. jwǫk God
Ju. jwok fortune
Ja. juogi ghost
La. ęǫk God

Al. jǫk God
Di. ajyek, ajǫk demon
Ba. ajwok, jwek demon

Shi. kąbǫ to take away
Ga. kabo to bring
Ju. kābi to bring
Di. kap to bring, take
Nr. kạ̈p to take

Shi. kādǫ salt¹
Ga. kado salt
Ju. kada salt
Any. kadǫ salt
Nr. kădĕ salt

Shi kāgǫ to split
Ga. kak to split
Nu. kage to split
Ba. kagu to split

Shi. kęch bitter
Ga. kech bitter
Ju. kęch bitter
Any. kęch bitter
Nu. kag-al sharp
Di. kech bitter
Bo. ke bile

Shi. kich bee
Ga. kich bee
Ju. kich bee
Any. kich bee
Ja. kĭch' bee
La. kits bee
Al. kĭch bee
Di. kyech bee
Nu. kit, kuti bee
Ba. chi, chiwo bee

Shi. kǫt rain
Ga. kot rain
Ju. kǫt rain

Any. kǫt rain
Ja. kōt rain
La. kǫt rain
Al. kǫt rain
Nr. kǫt rain, God
Ba. kudu rain

Shi. akur pigeon
Ga. akuri pigeon
Di. kure pigeon
Nr. kŭr pigeon
Nu. kuru pigeon
Ba. gure pigeon

Shi. kwālǫ } to steal
 kwętǫ
Ga. kwalo to steal
Any. kwętǫ to steal
Ja. kwalǫ to steal
La. kwalo to steal
Di. kwal to steal
Nr. kwal to steal
Ba. kola-nit theft

Shi. kwęnǫ to count
Ga. kwano to count
Ju. kwēno to count
Nr. kwǫn to count
Di. kwen to count
Ba. ken to count

Shi. kwāṅǫ to swim
Ga. kwaṅo to swim
Ju. kwaṅ to swim
Any. kwal to swim
Nu. kuǵe to swim

Shi. kwōrǫ cotton
Ga. waro cotton
Ju. wara cotton
Ba. waro cotton

---

¹ salt made of grass-ashes.

Shi. *kwā́rọ* grandfather
Ga. *kwaro* grandfather
Ju. *kwā* grandfather
Di. *kọkwar* grandfather
Nr. *kwāro* chief
Ba. *ńa-kwari* grandchild

Shi. *kwā́rọ* red
Ga. *kwar* red
Ju. *kwar* red
Nr. *kwâr* red
Nu. *kor-gos* yellow

Shi. *kwach* leopard
Ga. *kwach* leopard
Ju. *kwach* leopard
Any. *kwach* leopard
Ja. *kwach* leopard
La. *kwach* leopard
Al. *kwach* leopard
Di. *kwach* leopard
Nr. *kway'* leopard
Bo. *kọgo* leopard
Ba. *koka* ⎱ leopard
    kwaru ⎰

Shi. *kwẹn* bread
Ga. *kwon* bread
Ju. *kwen* bread
    kwọn bread
Any. *kwon* bread
Nr. *kwạn* bread
Bo. *koā* bread

Shi. *ákyẹ̀l* one
Ga. *achel* one
Ju. *akyẹlo* one
Any. *àchyẹ́lọ̀* one
Ja. *achyel* one
Al. *achyel* one
Bo. *kotu* one
Ba. *bu-ker* six = five + 1

Shi. *kyén* horse
Ga. *kana* horse
Ju. *akaja* donkey
Any. *okwẹń* horse
Ja. *kańima* horse
Bo. *akasa* horse
Nu. *kach* horse, donkey
Ba. *kaine* horse

Shi. *lachọ* to piss
Ga. *layo* to piss
Ju. *alach* urine
Any. *la* to piss
Ja. *lāch'* urine
La. *lās* urine
Al. *lāch* urine
Di. *lach* to piss
Ba. *lode* urine

Shi. *lại* game
Ga. *le* game
Ju. *lai* game
Any. *lại* game
Nr. *lẹi* game
Ba. *lai* game

Shi. *lāmọ* to pray
Ga. *lamo* to sacrifice
Di. *lam* to pray
Nr. *lam* to pray
Bo. *loma* God
Ba. *lọm* to insult

Shi. *léń* war
Ga. *lwen* war
Ju. *lwiń* war
Ja. *lueń* war
Any. *leń* war
Bo. *lań* gun

Shi. *alilit* bat
Ga. *olik* bat

Any. *aligá* bat
Di. *alich* bat
Ba. *lukululi* bat

Shi. *lwọ̄kọ* to wash
Ga. *lwoko* to wash
Ju. *lwok* to wash
Any. *lwọk* to wash
Di. *lọk* to wash
Nr. *lah* to wash
Bo. *dogu* to wash
Ba. *lalaju* to wash

Shi. *māch* fire
Ga. *mach* fire
Ju. *mach* fire
Any. *māyọ* fire
Ja. *mach'* fire
La. *māch* fire
Al. *māch* fire
Di. *mai* fire
Nr. *māch* fire

Shi. *mạ̄dọ* to drink
Ga. *mato* to drink
Ju. *māde* to drink
Any. *mādọ* to drink
Ja. *madọ* to drink
La. *matọ* to drink
Di. *mat* to drink
Nr. *mạt* to drink

Shi. *māgọ* to catch
Ga. *mako* to catch
Ju. *mau* to catch
Any. *mak* to catch
Di. *mwọk* to catch
Nu. *māge* to catch, steal
Ba. *mok* to catch

Shi. *mạnọ* to hate
Ga. *mon* to hate

Di. *man* to hate
Nu. *mōne* to hate
Ba. *man* to hate

Shi. *mạt* slow
Ga. *mot* slow
Ju. *māde* slow
Di. *māt* slow
Nr. *mạt* slow
Bo. *mēt* slow
Ba. *madaṅ* slow

Shi. *nẹnọ* to sleep
Ga. *nino* to sleep
Ju. *nen*, *nendo* } to sleep
Di. *nin* to sleep
Nr. *nyẹn* to sleep
Nu. *nalū*, *nēre* } to sleep

Shi. *nẹnọ* to see
Ga. *neno* to see
Any. *nẹna* to see
Ja. *neno* to see
Nr. *nẹn* to see
Nu. *nale* to see

Shi. *ṅaṅ* crocodile
Ga. *ṅaṅ* crocodile
Ju. *ṅaṅ* crocodile
Any. *ṅaṅ* crocodile
Ja. *ṅaṅ* crocodile
La. *aki-ṅaṅ* crocodile
Al. *ṅaṅ* crocodile
Di. *ṅaṅ* crocodile
Nr. *ṅaṅ* crocodile
Bo. *ṅaṅa* crocodile
Ba. *ki-ṅoṅ* crocodile

Shi. *ṅājọ* to know
Ga. *ṅeyo* to know

Ju. *ṅo*, *ṅaya* } to know
Ja. *ṅeyo* to know
Any. *ṅạ* to know
Nr. *ṅẹch* to know

Shi. *ạṅọ̀* what?
Ga. *aṅor* what?
Any. *ạṅọ̀* what?
Di. *ṅo, ṅu* what?
Nr. *ṅu* what?
Ba. *iṅo* what?

Shi. *peṅ, feṅ* earth
Ga. *piṅ* earth
Ju. *piṅ* earth
Any. *feṅ* earth
Ja. *piṅ* earth
La. *piṅe* earth
Di. *piṅ* earth
Nr. *peṅ* earth

Shi. *pi* water
Ga. *pi* water
Ju. *pfi, fi* water
Any. *pi* water
Ja. *pi* water
La. *pi* water
Al. *pi* water
Di. *pi* water
Nr. *pi* water
Ba. *piom* water

Shi. *faṅọ* to divide
Ga. *poko* to divide
Ju. *paṅ* to divide
Nu. *fage* to divide
Bo. *eke-bake* to divide

Shi. *rējọ* fish
Ga. *rech* fish
Ju. *rēyo* fish

Any. *reo* fish
Ja. *rech'* fish
La. *rech* fish
Al. *rech* fish
Di. *rēch* fish
Nr. *rech* fish
Nu. *ka-rē* fish

Shi. *rẹmọ* blood
Ga. *remo* blood
Ju. *remo* blood
Any. *rẹmọ* blood
Ja. *remọ* blood
La. *remu* blood
Al. *remo* blood
Di. *ryam* blood
Nr. *ryẹm* blood
Bo. *trama* blood
Ba. *rima* blood

Shi. *rīṅọ* meat
Ga. *riṅo* meat
Ju. *riṅo* meat
Any. *rīṅọ* meat
Ja. *riṅo* meat
La. *riṅo* meat
Al. *riṅo* meat
Di. *riṅ* meat
Nr. *rīṅ* meat
Nu. *arich, arji* meat

Shi. *rọ̄dọ* thirst
Ga. *orwor* thirst
Ju. *ryau* thirst
Any. *ryo* thirst
Di. *rou* thirst
Ba. *rọdu* to wither

Shi. *rọmọ* sheep
Ga. *romo* sheep
Ju. *rōmo* sheep

Any. rǫmǫ sheep
Nr. rŏm sheep
Bo. rǫmbō sheep

Shi. rǭmǫ to meet
Ga. romo to meet
Ju. romo to meet
Di. rom to meet
Nr. rōm to meet
Ba. rum to meet

Shi. rugǫ to dress
Ga. riko to dress
Di. ruk to dress
Ba. ruk to dress

Shi. wūm nose
Ga. um nose
Ju. hum nose
Ja. um nose
La. um nose
Al. um nose
Any. óm nose
    wum nose
Di. um nose
Nr. rum nose
Bo. hǫmo nose
Ba. kume nose

Shi. dryàu two
Ga. aryor two
Ju. aryau two
Any. àrèau two
Ja. areio two
La. ariŏ two
Al. ariŏ two
Di. rou two

Nu. ora, ore twenty
Ba. ǫri two
    bu-ryǫ seven = five + two

Shi. tęk (to be) hard
Ga. tek hard
Ju. tęk hard
Any. tęk hard
Di. tyek hard
Bo. tigo hard

Shi. tęn, pl. tǫnǫ small
Ga. tidi small
Any. tēn small
Ja. tēn small
Nu. tin, tüń small
    tod small

Shi. tǫwǫ to die
Ga. tor to die
Any. tǫu to die
Ja. tǫ to die
La. tŏ to die
Di. tou to die
Ba. tuan to die

Shi. wārǫ shoe
Ga. war shoe
Any. war shoe
Di. war shoe
Nr. wăr shoe
Nu. kwari shoe

Shi. wǫr night
Ju. war night
Any. warǫ night
Ja. wǫr night

Nr. wăr night
Nu. awar night

Shi. wēkǫ to give
Ga. weko to give away
Di. yek to give
Ba. yek to give

Shi. wēlǫ to travel
Ga. wel to travel
Ba. wala to travel

Shi. wińǫ bird
Ga. wińo bird
Ju. wińo bird
Any. węyǫ bird
Ja. weńǫ bird
La. wēn bird
Al. wińō bird
Ba. kwen bird

Shi. wōrǫ to sing
Ju. wǫr song
Ga. wer song
Ja. wir song
La. wer song
Al. wer song
Nu. owe to sing
Ba. yoyu, yolo to sing

Shi. yęi boat
Ga. yeya boat
Ju. yei boat
Any. yai boat
Ja. ńjie boat
La. yede boat
Al. yei boat
Bo. yēi boat.

101. Second Group.
The words in the first line designate the "original Sudanic form", which has been gained by comparing the sounds of a word in the different languages, and thus finding out those sounds which may be considered as the most primi-

tive. This "original Sudanic form" is of course merely hypothetical. For more on this see my "Sudansprachen", from which the greater part of these words are taken.

S. *bi̯a to come*
E. *vá* to come
  bá to come
T. *ba* to come
  ǫbra coming into the world
G. *ba* to come
  bla coming into the world
Y. *ba* shall, should
Ibo *bia* to come
Isoama *bia* to come
Eafeng *ba* to come
Abouré *va* to come
Alaguiang *va* to come
Avikam *ba, iba* to come
Mékyibo *ba* to come
Di. *abi* prefix of future
Nu. *bi* prefix of future
Shi. *bi, bia* to come
Any. *bi* prefix of future
Nr. *bi* prefix of future
Ga. *bino* to come

S. *buagi to fear*
E. *vǭ* to fear
Ef. *bak* to fear
Shi. *bōkǫ* to fear
  bwǫkǫ to frighten
Any. *bwǫk* to fear

S. *bu̯a open place*
E. *ablǫ* open place
F. *abǫ-nteṅ* } main street,
  abrǫ-ntseṅ } open place
G. *blǫ* street

V. *bar* large, open place
Nu. *bud* place before the house
Di. *bur, abora* market place
Shi. *byra* open place

S. *ga place*
E. *gà* place
T. *ɛha* this place
N. *ga* this, that
Nu. *aga, agar* place
Shi. *ga* this
  agak these

S. *gaga cowrie*
E. *àgàgà* cowrie
Di. *gak* cowrie
Shi. *gāgǫ* cowrie
Ga. *gage* cowrie
Nr. *gak* cowrie
Bo. *gaki* cowrie

S. *guaṅi antelope*
E. *gbàgbà* antelope, "unicorn"
G. *ṅman*
  ṅma   } antelope, "unicorn"
  ṅmaṅma
Y. *agbaṅ-rere* "unicorn"
Shi. *aṅwak* waterbuck

S. *kuagi, kuali to embrace*
E. *kplà* to embrace
T. *kwaṅ* to wind around
G. *kplā* round about
Ef. *ukwaṅ* winding
  kpaṅ to fold (hands)

Y. *kpǭ* to carry on the back
Nu. *kat* to envelop
Di. *kwak* to embrace
Shi. *kwakǫ* to embrace
Ga. *kwaka* to embrace

S. *kuagi, ku̯iagi leopard*
E. *kpǭ* leopard
T. *etvói* leopard
Ef. *ekpe* leopard
V. *kori* leopard
N. *ɛkū* leopard
Ku. *uṅka* leopard
Di. *kwach* leopard
Shi. *kwach* leopard
Ga. *kwach* leopard
Ju. *kwach* leopard
Any. *kwach* leopard
Ja. *kwach* leopard
La. *kwach* leopard
Al. *kwach* leopard
Di. *kwach* leopard
Nr. *kway'* leopard
Bo. *kǫgo* leopard
Ba. *koka* leopard
  kwaru leopard

S. *kuani bread, pudding*
E. *akplḙ* pudding of maize
Shi. *kwḙn* bread
Ga. *kwon* bread
Ju. *kwǫn* } bread
  kwǫn
Any. *kwon* bread
Nr. *kwǫn* bread
Bo. *koā* bread

S. kuani to count, read
E. χlẹ́ to count, read
T. kan
kane } to count, read
G. kane to count, read
Y. ka to count
V. kara, karañ to learn
Di. kwen to count
Shi. kwẹ́nọ to count
Ga. kwano to count
Ju. kwēno to count
Nr. kwen to count
Ba. ken to count

S. nḷụ́, nḷua to lick, suck
E. dọ́ to lick, suck
dụ́dọ́ to lick
Y. adun
adọn } taste
Nu. dugs
dach } to lick
Shi. ḏọ̄dọ to suck, lick

Shi. ḏwọ̄dọ to suckle
Ga. doto to suck
Ju. dot to suck
S. pagi to divide
E. afā part, half
T. pae to split
G. afā half
Y. apa part
Ku. fak to split, divide
Nu. fage to divide
Shi. pạ̄nọ to divide
S. puy to beat
E. fo to beat
T. po to beat
Ef. foi to beat
Plaoui po to beat
Téoui po to beat
Shi. pwōdọ to beat
Di. pwot to beat
S. tiagi to be hard
E. sẹ̄ to be hard, strong

Di. chẹk to be hard
Shi. tẹ̄k to be hard, strong
Ga. tek to be hard
Ju. tẹk to be hard
Any. tẹ̄k to be hard
Bo. tigo to be hard

S. tịị hand
E. ashí hand
Ku. shi-ma hand
Di. chin, chyen hand
Shi. chyẹ̄nọ hand
Ju. shyeno hand
Any. shyẹnọ hand

S. tịị to bear a child; wife
E. ashi wife
Ku. shi to beget, bear
shā begetting
Nu. ash, ashi daughter
Di. tik wife
Shi. chi wife.

Appendix.

Some Names of Languages, Peoples, and Rivers, as they are in use among the natives.

The *Shilluks* call themselves: *Óchȯ́lọ̀* a Shilluk man, pl. *Chọ́l*, or *wate Chọ́l* "children of *Chọl*"; their country: *fọ̀tẹ̀ chọ́l*; their language: *dọ̀ chọ́l*. The Shilluks are called by the Arabs: Shilluk, by the Dinkas: *Bạr*, by the Nuers: *Tẹ̀t*.

The *Anywaks* call themselves: *Añwak*, they are called by the Nuers: *Bálạ̀k*, by the Dinkas: *Pálạ̀k*, by the Abyssinians: Jambo.

The *Dinkas* call themselves: *Jäñe*; they are called by the Shilluks: *ójáñọ̀* pl. *jáni̯*; by the Arabs: Dinka, or Denka.

The *Nuers* call themselves: *Gánạ̀t* a Nuer man, pl. *Kẹ́gánạ̀t*; their language: *tọk Nạ́t*; they are called by the Shilluks: *Nuẹ́r*, by the Dinkas: *Núạ̀r*; by the Arabs: *Nuẹ̀r* or *Nawár*.

The Jurs call themselves De-Luọ or Luọ, by the Shilluks they are called Odimọ, "descendants of Dimọ", by the Bongo: *Bẹ̄r*. The Belanda call them-

The Position of Shilluk

selves *Bǫr*. Belanda is a Bongo word, *landa* = stone, hill; so Belanda is probably "hill-country".

The Nubians are in all three languages called: *Dǫñ*, from "Dongola". According to Schweinfurth in Golo the Nubians are called Turuku, in Jur Oturu, in Bongo Turu; these names are doubtlessly derived from "Turk".

The Bahr Zeraf is called in Shilluk: *Oñęl*, in Nuer: *Fạu*, in Dinka: *Piau* The Bahr Jebel is called in Shilluk: *Kēr*; in Dinka: *Kēr*, in Nuer: *Konam*; the Khor Filus is called in Shilluk: *Olūt*, in Dinka: *Pelūt*, in Nuer: *Pulūt*.

FOURTH SECTION:
THE PARTS OF SPEECH.

THE NOUN.
Singular and Plural.

102. Singular. Many nouns have in the singular the suffix $ǫ$; in some nouns it may be dropped at will; on this and on the original meaning of $ǫ$ see 71.

Some nouns denoting a plurality, are in their form singular, and are treated as such; e. g.: *lǫbǫ, tẹdǫ* people.

102a. Plural. The Shilluk is remarkable for its manifold means of forming the plural of nouns. These means may be divided into three principles; they are: plural-formation

a) by affixes,
b) by change of tone,
c) by change of vowel.

Generally in forming the plural of a noun, not only one of these means is employed, but several.

103. a) Plural-formation by affixes. In most Sudan languages the plural of nouns is formed by affixing to the singular a particle, which in most cases originally is a noun or a pronoun: "people, they". In Shi. this formation is represented by several vocalic and consonant affixes.

1. The most frequent plural-affix is the suffix i. Although by no means all nouns have this suffix in the plural, yet it is a question of feeling with the natives that they prefer it; if a foreign word is introduced into the language, it receives i in the plural; and on the other hand there are numerous genuine Shilluk words which sometimes are used with i, and sometimes without it in the plural. This leads to the supposition that possibly the ending i was formerly more employed than it is now, and that it may be the oldest and originally only ending for the plural. — The plural-suffix i occurs also in **Masai** and in Nuba and Kunama; in Kunama i is the personal pronoun of the third person plural: "they". It may be that the suffix i is of common origin in all these four languages.

Besides the vowel-suffix, there are several consonants which serve in forming the plural:

104. 2. *k*; *gin* thing pl. *gik*; *k* may be shortened from the demonstrative pronoun *ak* "these"; in Di. the plural is formed in the same way, viz. by adding the

The Noun 47

demonstrative pronoun *ke* "these".

105. 3. *ṭ; t* is possibly identical with the Anywak word *ṭoṭ* "many"; so that originally the word was common to both languages, but in Shi. it was exclusively retained for forming the plural, a different word being employed for "many". In Anywak the plural is frequently formed by simply adding "*ṭoṭ*". In some cases the plural is formed by adding *t* instead of *ṭ*; whether this is misheard by me, or whether there is really a class with *t* in plural, I do not know. — Di. also has the plural in *t (ṭ?): puou-puot* heart.

106. 4. A nasal consonant; some nouns form their plural in changing their last consonant into the corresponding nasal one, according to the rule given in 40; here doubtlessly a nasal consonant has been suffixed, which may be shortened from the demonstrative pronoun *an* "this, these".

While *i* is used very much, and may, in a certain measure, be employed at will, *k, ṭ* and the nasal consonant are restricted to a small number of nouns.

107. 5. Words whose second consonant is a voiced mute followed by a vowel, change this consonant into the corresponding voiceless one in the plural: *áfùdǫ* pl. *áfútị*. In connection with this it is to be remarked that in those nouns which in their plural end in a mute consonant, *this consonant is always voiceless*, even when a vowel follows: *lęk* teeth, *lęka* my teeth, *lęk ak* these teeth; this is contrary to the rule in 38; perhaps this voicelessness is the rest of a voiceless consonant which was suffixed for forming the plural, but assimilated itself in all cases with the preceding consonant.

108. 6. Many nouns form their plural by dropping the singular-suffix *ǫ*: *gyēnǫ* hen pl. *gyęn*.

109. 7. A few nouns with the prefix *o* drop this prefix in plural; such are names of persons as belonging to a nation (patronymica): a Dinka man, a Shilluk man; here the plural-form may be the first, noting the nation as a collective mass, from this the singular was derived by prefixing *o*, which probably means: "he" or "one": "he a Shilluk". The opposite formation see in *rúm* pl. *órǫm* nose.

8. A peculiar kind of plural-formation in nouns designating relatives is that of prefixing *né* in the plural; *nà* (also *nè*) means "child"; it is low toned, but when expressing the plural, its tone rises. Examples:
ákḁyǫ-nékḁi nephew; or: *nàkḁi-nékḁi* nephew.

[The partial conformity of the plural-affixes in Shilluk and Masai is remarkable. Just as in Shilluk one of the most frequent plural suffixes is *i*, so it is also in Masai. Likewise *k, t* and a nasal suffix (*n*) are found in both languages. The plural-formation by dropping the final vowel *ǫ* of the singular (see 108) has also its analogy in Masai, where a final *a* or *o* (*ǫ?*)

is dropped: *ol abura* plural *il abur* "froth"; *ol kurto* pl. *i kurt* "caterpillar". Hollis is probably right in supposing that in these words the plural is the original form, from which the singular was formed by adding ǫ or *a*.
— According to Hollis, Masai has no plural-distinction by tone. See Hollis page 18 ss.]

10. b) Plural-formation by change of tone. As stated above, the predomination of intonation is a characteristic of Sudan languages; but in none of these the change of tone is known to be a means of distinguishing singular and plural. In the western languages, of whom a greater number is thoroughly known, this function of the tone is sure not to exist; but it may be expected that on close investigation it will be found in other eastern Sudan languages.

By the change of tone the nouns are grouped into classes, a certain tone or group of tones in the singular always corresponding to a certain tone or group of tones in the plural. There do not seem to be very many nouns without the distinction of tone in singular and plural.[1]

This distinction is probably younger than the plural-formation by affixes. Though the intonation is no doubt genuine Sudanic, this particular employment of it, viz. the distinction of number, may be of foreign origin, a foreign element getting into the population and using the tone in quite a new way, which, until then, was not known to the primitive inhabitants. This is the more probable, as the change of tone is a process analogous to that of the change of vowel, which will be shown below. It might be supposed that both are of the same foreign origin, i. e. Hamitic. The older plural-formation by affixes seems gradually to be suppressed by the modern means, viz. change of tone and of vowel.

It is to be remarked that, as a whole, in plural the low tone is more frequent than in the singular, the low tone, together with the long vowel (see the following) conveying the notion of greatness or plurality.

c) Plural formation by change of vowel.[2] A plural-formation likewise unknown in western Sudan languages is that by changing the quantity or quality of the stem-vowel. This vowel-change is common in Semitic and Hamitic languages, and is in Shilluk probably to be traced to Hamitic influence. How far it is spread in the eastern Sudan group, cannot be stated now, but the Di. also has it. Quite of Hamitic character is the interchange of certain vowels in this way: the vowel-changes in one group are contrary to those in another group; the first group has long vowel in singular and short in plural; a second group short vowel in singular and long in plural; likewise the quality changes: one group has ǫ in sing., *u* in pl.; a second group *u* in in sing., ǫ in pl.; this peculiarity was first shown by Meinhof as existing in

---

[1] According to Kitching in Gang most nouns have the same form for singular and plural; is it not possible that a distinction is made by tone, which has not been noted?

[2] Plural-formation by change of vowel-quantity and quality is also largely used in Dinka; see Mitterrutzner page 15.

The Noun 49

the Hamitic languages, and has been called by him "polarity".

The same tendency of interchange is to be seen in other formations, see for instance 119: singular prefix *o*, plural no prefix, and 119: singular no prefix, plural prefix *o*.

111.

Though this formation be probably foreign and relatively young, it may contain some primitive principle of language building: It is worth noting that the large majority of nouns have short vowel in the singular and a long one in the plural; this may lead to the supposition (which is supported by results of studies in other African languages. In Ewe for instance adjectives with long vowel and low tone designate large things or beings, the same adjectives with short vowel and high tone express small things or beings.) that in an early stage of language the long vowel is expressive of the idea of "much, big, great".

112.

Examples illustrating the different ways of forming the plural.

a) Plural-formation by Affixes.

113.

1. Suffix *i*. *akǫ̌l-akǫ́lị̌* drum-stick   *ámáṭ-ámáṭị̌* a stork
   dṅǫ̌n-dṅǫ̀nị a knife   *dywóm-dywòmị* monkey
   áchùṅǫ̀-áchúnị an ant   *pǎm-pǎmị* board
   γěrɔ̀-γěrị a bead   *kàl-kǎlị* fence
   ṅù-ṅuwị lion   *lęu-lęwị* lizard.

For more examples see below.

The ending *i* has in most cases low tone; where the tone is middle, the stem-vowel too has middle tone, that is, the tone of the suffix is assimilated to that of the stem.

2. suffix *k*. *pi-pik* water *gin-gik* thing *dyęl-dyęk* goat *jal-jǫk* man
   lǎjǫ-lęk tooth *mā-męk* aunt *męn-mǫk* this one.

114.

3. suffix *ṭ*. *ṭdu-ṭǎṭ* buttocks *wich-wǫ́ṭ* head *yęi-yąṭ* boat
   yiṅǫ-yỉṭ fisherman *yech-yęṭ* belly *kęu-kōṭ* breast
   (*lwǫl-lǭṭ*) a gourd (*yǫ-yẹ̆ṭ*) road.

115.

When in a noun with a consonant plural-ending the stem also ends in a consonant, the final consonant of the stem is dropped, the consonantal suffix taking its place; see 44.

4. nasal consonant as suffix.

116.

ṭǎgɔ̀-ṭǎnị dura-basket *kwàch-kwànị* leopard *àṅàdǫ̀-àṅànị* breast-bone
yàṭ-yęṇ tree *àtǎbǫ̀-àtǎm* tobacco *ṭabǫ-ṭami* dish.

Vice versa: *waṅǫ-wǫch* paper.

WESTERMANN, The Shilluk People.

117. 5. voiced mute consonant becomes voiceless.
áfúdọ-áfútị a fish   *átúdọ-átútị* a wild goose   *bọ̣dọ-bọ̣tị* blacksmith
gójị-góchị sword   *búdọ-bútị* a melon   *dạkạ̀gị-dạkạ́kị* dura-stick
òkọ̀dọ-òkọ̀tị basket.

Vice versa: *fúk-fúgị* tortoise   *órọk-órọgị* bell   *lwóp-lwóbị* company.

118. 6. dropping the singular-suffix *ọ*.
fạlọ-fāl knife   *gyẹ̀nọ-gyẹ̀n* hen   *byẹlọ-byẹl* dura
wínọ̀-wín bird   *tọ̀nọ-tọ̀n* egg   *gwẹlọ-gwẹl* ring.

119. 7. dropping the prefix *o*.
obwong-bwon white man   *óchọ̀lọ-chọ̀l* Shilluk-man   *ójǎnọ-jǎn* Dinka-man.[1]
Vice versa: *rúm-órọ̀m* nose.

120.   b) **Plural-formation by Change of Tone.**
For completeness' sake the nouns which do *not* change their tone in plural, are also enumerated here. — Nouns with prefixes and those without them are separated, as they show differences of tone.

In some cases nouns with a slight deviation of tone have been grouped under the same heading; this has been done, because the differences do not seem to be essential and perhaps have been misheard. On the difference between ′ and ⌃ see 51.

Some nouns have two plural-forms.

Nouns with prefixes.

121. 1. *àchwàtọ̀-àchwàtị* loin-cloth   *àmàlọ-àmàlị* camel
     òkọ̀k-òkọ̀k egret   *òkọ̀k-òkọ̀k* flower
     òkwọ̀k-òkwọ̀k a goose   *òmẹ̀dọ-òmẹ̀t* fire-fly
     òrọ̀k-òrọ̀k craft.

  2. *àdẹ̀rọ-àdẹ̀r* arm-ring   *òchọ̀yọ̀-òchọ̀yị* melon
     òpárọ̀ a gourd   *òṭwól* blue
     àlútọ̀-àlútị fist   *àwâk-àwâk* a bird.

  3. *òbáu-òbáwị* lungs   *ògwẹ̀rọ̀-ògwẹ̀rị* } blue heron.
     òbẹ̀r-òbẹ̀rị feather   *ògwẹ̀rị*

  4. *àkùr-àkùrị* pigeon   *àṭẹ̀rọ-àṭẹ̀rị, àṭẹ̀r* a spear
     àwóch-àwóch a shell   *òlóó-òlòó* duck
     ògwól-ògwọ̀l a bird.

  5. *àchúṭ-àchúṭ* arm-ring   *àgwẹ́n-àgwẹ́n* bastard child.

  6. *àkyẹ́n-àkyẹ̀n* gun-cock   *òbírọ-òbìr* a pot
     àbúrọ-àbùr bush-buck   *àchwáṭ-àchwàṭ* guinea-fowl
     àdẹ̀rọ-àdẹ̀r donkey   *àṭẹ̀p-àṭẹ̀p* bag.

---

[1] In one example the plural is formed by suffixing *r*: *ríṭ-rōr* king.

The Noun

7. òkọ̀dọ̀-òkúti̩ hedgehog òlẹ̩lọ̩-òlẹ̩li̩ club
   òṅwáṅọ̀ an ant   òṅwẹ̀rọ̀ whip   òtọ̩lọ̩ a white dura.

8. ówáṅọ̀-ówáṅi̩ heron   ókwáṅọ̀-ókwáṅi̩ broom
   ótyẹ̀ṅọ̀-ótyẹ̀ṅ a fish   ótâgọ̀-ótâṅi̩ a fish
   ówájọ̀-ńéwájọ̀ cousin   órộk-órộk small bell
   óyi̩ṅọ̀ crocodile-hunter.

9. áchán-áchán a fish   áchwi̩k-áchwi̩k anus
   ákwán-ákwán ear-lap   álún-álún somersault
   ámá̩t-ámá̩ti̩ a stork   áṅón-áṅọ̀ni̩ a knife
   átĕ̆t-át̩ẹt mangouste   áywóm-áywòmi̩ monkey
   órá̩t-órá̩t a snake ómí brother ómẹ̆ṅ his brother
   ólwĕ-ólwè marabout   ófwộṅ-òfwún loaf
   ógik-ógi̩k buffalo   ókộk-ókọ̀k a fish
   ókwól-ókwòli̩ gourd   ókyệl-ókyẹ̀li̩ an ant
   óṅyẹ́ṅ-óṅyẹ́ṅi̩ a snake   ópâp-ópàp hip-bone
   ótwóṅ-ótwòṅi̩ hyena   ótwọ̀ṅ-ótọ̩ṅ cock.

10. ábáṅ-ábáṅ hammer   ákộl-ákọ́li̩ drum-stick
    ókwọ̀r-ókộri̩ serval   ólák-ólẹ́ki̩ a fish
    ótwẹ̩l-ótwẹ̩li̩ a fish   ólám-ólẹ́mi̩ sycomore
    òlẹ̩t-ólẹ́ti̩ hawk   óti̩ẹ̀t-óti̩ẹ̀ti̩ a pot.

11. ágàk-ágẹ́ki̩ crow   álẹ̀ṅ-álẹ̀ṅi̩ a fish
    áchùṅọ̀-áchúni̩ an ant   ádàlọ̀-ádàli̩ a gourd
    ádọ̀lọ̀-ádọ́l a fish   áfúdọ̀-áfúti̩ a fish
    ódẹ̀k-údi̩ki̩ a mat   ógọ̀ṅọ̀-ógọ̀ṅi̩ bracelet
    ógwál-ógwẹ́li̩ frog   óywàk-óywẹ́ki̩ a crane.

12. átùdọ̀-átùti̩ wild goose   áyọ̀mọ̀-áyọ̀m tin
    áfẹ̀dọ̀-áfẹ̀t skunk   ágẹ̀rọ̀-ágẹ̀r a hair dress
    ágọ̀rọ̀-ágọ̀r neck-bone   áṅẹ́ṅọ̀-áṅẹ́ṅ a red ant
    átwâk-átwâk a bird   áyl̩ẹr-áyl̩ẹri̩ quail
    ódẹ̀rọ̀-ódẹ̀r kiddle   ógwộk-ógộki̩ jackal
    ómẹ̆rọ̀ red dura   ómộdọ̀ a cow
    óṅọ̀gọ̀ a cow   órâp-óràp spider
    ótộr-ótọ̀r a ford   ówáù-ówáu ibis
    ówêt-ówẹ̀t a mat   órộch-óròch ram
    óṅwộk-óṅwộk male goat   ómọ̀rọ̀-ómọ̀r roan antelope
    ómáyọ̀-ómái cousin   óbọ̀gọ̀-óbọ̀k albino
    óbwòyọ̀-óbwòi̩ a shrub   ódệlọ̀-ódẹ̀l a cow

	ódằbò-ódằp blanket	ógâl-ógàl mule
	ógàlọ̀-ógàlị̈ mule	ónằyọ̀-óndi cousin.
13.	ókọ̀dọ̀-ókọ̀tị́ basket	órọ́k-órọ̀gị́ bell.
14.	óchyẹ̀nọ̀-óchyẹ̀n loin-cloth.	
15.	ógwé-ógwê bow.	
16.	dlẹ̀bọ́-dlípì a bird	ónẹ̀lọ́ red earth.
17.	ddị́nọ̀-àdị̈n a fish	àtẹ́n-àtàn hat
	ókwọ́n-òkọ̀n feather	ókwọ̀k-òkwọ̀k goose
	ókọ̀k-òkọ̀k egret.	
18.	dchyẹ̀nọ-àchyẹ̀n an ant	áywàk-áywàk crest
	òrọ̀-òr ant-hill	órọ̀-òr relations by marriage.

Perhaps in these last two examples ō and ǫ are not prefixes, but vowels of the stem, the first consonant (perhaps w) having been dropped; see 33.

19.	ókọ́t-òkọ̀t bell	
20.	àkọ̀n-àkọ̀nì gazelle	ànàdọ̀-ànằní breast-bone
	(àtằbó-àtằm tobacco).	
21.	àjwọ̀gọ́-àjwọ̀k sorcerer.	
22.	òtyêm-ótyẹ̀m dragon-fly.	
23.	òlẹ̀t-ólétì hawk	òbẹ̀ch-óbíẹ́ch reed.

122. *Nouns without prefixes.*

1.	bọ̀lọ̀-bọ̀l face	bọ̀nọ̀-bọ̀nì lizard
	bọ̀t-bọ̀tị̈ bachelor	bwọ̀nọ̀-bwọ̀nì a fish
	byẹ̀rọ̀-byẹ̀r root	chòr-chọ̀r vulture
	chùt-chùt tooth-brush	chwài-chwàyì broth
	chwọ̀k-chwọ̀k ambassador	chwàrọ̀-chwàr bug
	dàtọ̀-dàt hoof	dẹ̀n-dẹ̀nì jaw-bone
	fàlọ̀-fàl knife	gàt-gàt river-side
	gìn-gìk thing	gòk-gòk ring
	gwẹ̀lọ̀-gwẹ̀l ring	gyèk-gyèk water-buck
	kwòm-kòm back	kyẹ̀t-kyẹ̀t a fish.
2.	gẹ̀lọ̀-gẹ̀lị̈ slope	gằgọ̀-gằk cowry
	bûdọ̀-bût a shell	búdọ̀-bútị̈ melon
	chằmị̀-chằmị̀ bait	dằkằgì-dằkằkì dura-stick
	dọ̀rọ̀-dọ̀rì axe	fàl-fẹ̀t spoon

The Noun

	fóḍọ̀-fọ̀ṭ	country	fọ̱lọ̀-fọ̱l	cloud
	jágọ̀-ják	chief	kwéṭ-kwéṭ	dung-hill.
3.	gọ̱lọ̀-gọ̱l	bight	γèrọ̀-γèrì	a bead
	kàl-kḁlḭ	fence	kèdọ̀-kèṭ	a fish
	kwàch-kwáṅì	leopard	pàm-pàmḭ	board
	fuḍọ̀-fúṭ	lame person.		
4.	chògọ̀-chòk	a fish	fúk-fùgḭ	tortoise
	fyèr-fèrḭ	back-bone	gàṅọ̀-gàṅ	button
	jòp-jòpḭ	buffalo	kàṅ-kàṅḭ	trumpet
	kàwọ̀-kàwḭ	beam	kàt-klṭḭ	rock
	kù-kùwḭ	thief.		
	fùk-fùkḭ	pot	gúṭ-gúṭḭ	hammer.
5.	byèlọ̀-byèl	dura	byèrọ̀-byèr	belly
	pàr-pérì	hippo	kyèṅ-kyéṅ	horse
	(dèl-dèl	skin).		
6.	bọ́i-bọ̀i	net	bọ́r-bọ̀r	boil
	chùrọ̀-chùr	a fish	dọ́k-dọ̀k	mouth
	gòjì-gòchì	sword	gúlọ̀-gùl	cannon
	gùt-gùt	navel	òrọ̀-òr	relations by marriage
	kwânọ̀-kwànì	solo-singer	kọ́ch-kùchì	axe
	kwọ́ṅ-kwọ̀ṅ	report	kyèlọ̀-kyèl	star.
7.	gyèlọ̀-gyèl	ring	bák-bák	fence
	bàṅọ̀-bàṅ	locust	bọ̀ḍọ̀-bọ̀ṭḭ	blacksmith
	chùl-chúl	penis	ḍàṅ-ḍáṅḭ	dancing-stick.
8.	bànọ̀-bànì	meat on the skin	bàt-bàt	arm
	chùgọ̀-chúk	charcoal	dàk-dàk	pot
	fyèn-fyénì	skin	gwòk-gúòk	dog
	gyènọ̀-gyéṅ	hen	jàch-jàch	shoulder
	kènọ̀-kènì	gourd	kwàrọ̀-kwérì	pole
	kwòt-kòt	shield	kwòm-kùòmì	board.
9.	kwọ̀ṭọ́-kwọ́ṭ	farting	fàrọ́-fárì	mat.

c) **Plural-formation by vowel-change.**
Change of the quantity of the stem-vowel.

1. Singular short vowel, plural long vowel.

òkọ̀k-òkọ̱k	igret	òkọ̀k-òkọ̱k	flower
òrọ̀k-òrọ̱k	craft	àwàk-àwâk	a bird

123.

The Parts of Speech

òrǫ̆k-òrǫ̱k	a small bell	chŭt-chŭt	tooth-brush
găt-gàt	river-side	chwǫ̆k-chwǫ̱k	ambassador
òkwǫ̆k-òkwǫ̱k	a goose	ògwǫ́l-ògwǫ̱l	a bird
àchŭt-àchŭt	arm-ring	àgwĕn-agwĕ̱n	bastard
àchwăt-àchwa̱t	guinea-fowl	ótwǫ̆n-ótǫ̱n	cock
átwâk-átwàk	a bird	òrâp-òràp	spider
ówĕ̂t-ówĕ̱t	a mat	ótwǫ̂k-ótwǫ̱k	male goat
ógâl-ógàl	mule	dtĕ́n-àtǎn	hat
òkwǒn-òkwǫ̱n	feather	òkǫ́t-òkǫ̱t	bell
dàtǫ̆-dàt	hoof	kàl-kǎl̥	fence
fyĕr-fĕri̱	back-bone	bǎk-bǎ̱k	fence
dak-dǎ̱k	pipe.		

In the first eight examples the short and long vowel are the only distinction between singular and plural.

2. Singular long vowel, plural short vowel.

chămi̱-chămi̱	bait	ògwǒrǫ̀-ògwǫ̱ri	blue heron
òlăm-ólĕmi̱	sycomore	òlĕt-ólĕ̱ti̱	hawk
óbǫ̂gǫ̀-óbǫ̱k	albino	óchyĕnǫ̀-óchyĕ̱n	loin-cloth
àjwǒgǫ́-àjwǫ̱k	wizard	òlĕt-ólĕ̱ti̱	hawk
chòr-chǫ̱r	vulture	byĕ̂lǫ̀-byĕ̱l	dura
pàr-pĕ̱ri̱	hippo	bŏr-bǫ̱r	boil
gòji̱-góchi̱	sword	kyĕ̂lǫ̀-kyĕ̱l	star
gyĕ̀nǫ̀-gyĕ̱n	hen	kwàrǫ̀-kwĕ̱ri̱	pole.

Only in the first word the plural is distinguished from the singular by the short vowel only.

[24.] *Change of the Quality of the Stem-vowel.*

1. The stem-vowel of the singular turns *ę* in plural.

àgàk-àgĕ́ki̱	crow	pàr-pĕ́ri̱	hippo
ógwàl-ógwĕ́li̱	frog	ódǎk-ǔdǐki̱	a mat
óywàk-óywĕ́ki̱	crane	ótwǒl-ótwĕ́li̱	a fish
ólăk-ólĕ́ki̱	a fish	ótĕt-ótĭ́ti̱	a pot
òlăm-ólĕ́mi̱	sycomore	àlĕ̀bǫ́-àlĭ́pi̱	a bird
fâl-fĕ̱t	spoon	òlĕt-ólĕ́ti̱	hawk
kwàrǫ̀-kwĕ́ri̱	pole	ògwǒrǫ̀-ógwĕ́ri̱	blue heron.

In some words the vowel in plural is not *ę*, but *e* or *i*; as these are closely related to each other, and perhaps *e*, *i* are misheard for *ę*, I have classed them together.

In all these nouns the stem-vowel has high tone in plural; probably the

The Noun 55

high tone and the reduction of the vowel to *ę* are in some causal connection; vide 16.

2. The stem-vowel of the singular — mostly *a* — turns *ą* in plural.
    àchwáṭ-àchwą̄ṭ guinea-fowl   *kàl-kął́į* fence
    bàk-bą̄k fence   *dàk-dą̄k* pot, pipe
    òkwòk-òkwą̄k a goose   *òkwêk-òkwą̄k* a goose.

Here the short vowel of the singular becomes long in plural; the lengthening of the vowel may be the reason of its turning into *ą*; see 17.

3. singular *a* pl. *ę*.   *mā-męk* aunt   *yaṭ-yęṇ* tree.
4. singular *ę* pl. *a*.   *átęn̄-átàn̄* hat   (*yęi-yąi* boat).
5. singular *a*, pl. *o*. *raṭ* (*riṭ*, see 16) *-rōr* king.
6. sing. *ę* pl. *e*.   *gyèṭ-gyèt* waterbuck.
7. sing. *e* pl. *ę*.   *átęt-dįęt* mangouste   *ánénọ̀-ánèṇ̄* red ant
                òwêt-òwęt a mat   *yech-yęi* belly.
8. sing. *e*, pl. *i*.   *yèṭ-yìṭ* a well   *yèṭ-yìṭ* scorpion.
9. sing. *i* pl. *ą*.   *wich-wąi* head.
10. (sing. *a*, *ę* *ē*) pl. *ǫ*.   *jal-jǫk* man   *mēkǫ-mōko* some
                ṭēn-tǫṇǫ small   *ánò-ǫ̀nò* what
                męn-mǫk these.

The plural-vowel *ǫ* is remarkable, as it does not correspond to a certain vowel in singular, but is a class of its own; it not only forms the plural of nouns, but also of pronouns and adjectives. Note also *ā́nǫ-ǭnǫ*; *ā* is the deictic pronoun "it is"; but here it is treated like a radical vowel and thus changed in plural.

11. sing. *ǫ*, pl. *u*, *ų*.   *ńaṛǫlǫ-ńawulį* an axe   *kǫ́ch-kùchį̀* an axe
                òkǫ̀dǫ̀-òkùṭį̀ hedgehog   *mǫgǫ-mųki* beer.
12. sing. *u* pl. *ǫ*.   *rúm-ṭrǫ̀m* nose.
13. sing. *o* pl. *ǫ*.   *ánón̄-ánǫ̀nį̄* a knife   *bór-bǫ̀r* boil
                toch-toach gun; see 22   *chór-chǫ̀r* vulture.
14. sing. *ǫ* pl. *wǫ*.   *mǫ̀k-mwōk* dog-head fish.
15. sing. *wǫ*, *wo* pl. *ǫ*, *o*, *u*.   *óṭwǫ̀ṇ-óṭǫ̀n* cock   *ókwǫ̀r-ókįrì* serval
                ógwǫ̀k-ógǫ̀kì jackal   *ókwǫ̀n-ókįn* feather
                lwǫl-lòṭ a gourd   *ṭwol-ṭōlį* snake
                kwòm-kòm back   *kwòt-kòt* shield
                ófwǫ̀n-ófùn loaf.
16. sing. *wo* pl. *uo*.   *gwòk-gùòk* dog   *kwòm-kùòmį̀* board.
17. sing. *yę* pl. *ę*.   *fyèr-fèrì* backbone.
18. sing. *yę* *ę*, *i* pl. *ię*.   *lyęch-lįęch* elephant   *yęṭ-yìęṭ* neck
                òbich-òbìęch reed.

Gender.

125. Gender is expressed in the noun only, not in pronouns. The natural gender may be marked in two ways:
a) by different words.

  chwogu man   *ḍächọ* woman   *waṯ* bull   *ḍeaṅ* cow
  óṅwọ̈k male sheep or goat   *dyệl* female goat.

b) by adding *óṯwọ̈n* for the male, *màṯ* for the female gender.

  ṅù óṯwọ̈n male lion   *ṅù màṯ* or *màṯ ṅù* female lion
  ộṇí ṅù male lions   *màṯí ṅù* female lions
  kyệṅ óṯwọ̈n or *kyệṅ à ṯwọ̈n* male horse   *kyệṅ a màṯ* or *màṯ kyệṅ* female horse
     kyệṅ à ṯộṇ male horses   *kyệṅ à màṯ* female horses
  ṯwọ̈n ómọ́rọ̀ male roan antelope, pl. *ṯộṇ ómọ́rọ̀*
  màṯ ómọ́rọ̀ female roan antelope, pl. *màṯ ómọ́rọ̀*.

126. *In one single word, however, the Shilluk expresses the gender by phonetic means:*   *ṅa* child   *ṅal* boy   *ṅan* girl.

Here evidently *l* and *n* are added to the word *ṅa* in order to mark its gender, *l* for the male, *n* for the female gender.

[That this case is not merely accidental, will be clear from the fact that by the same means gender is expressed in the Bari language; here it is not the nouns, but demonstrative pronouns which receive the affixes *l* and *n*:

   lo this m.   *lu* that m.
   na this f.   *nu* that f.
  pl. *chi-lo* these m.   *chi-lu* those m.
   chi-ne these f.   *chi-nu* those f.
   lu-yu that one yonder m.   *chi-lu-yu* those yonder m.
   nu-yu that one yonder f.   *chi-nu-yu* those yonder f.
   li-o my m.   *il-ot* your m.
   ni-o my f.   *in-ot* your f.

In the noun, feminine is distinguished from masculine by the suffix *et*. The same distinction by the same means has Masai.

The distinction of a grammatical gender is surely not Sudanic, it is not known in other Sudan languages; so we have doubtlessly Hamitic influence here. The Shilluks must have been in contact with (a Hamitic) people who expressed in their language the grammatical gender by *l* and *n*, but this contact was not long or strong enough, to make the distinction of gender a living factor in the language; so only a faint trace of it was left. There is one more *Sudan language*, which has a similar distinction: the Songhai (on both banks of the middle Niger). This language has, in

The Noun

the same way as Bari and Masai, a kind of article, *di* for living beings, *ni* for inanimate things. I believe that *di* is identical with *li*, *l* and *d* often changing in African languages; vide the examples in the comparative Lists of Words in Third Section. If this is right, the Songhai (in which, though, this distinction will not be original, but borrowed from some Hamitic language) represents an elder stage in the development of grammatical gender: living ⟩ masculine, inanimate ⟩ feminine or neuter (which may originally be the same, as with primitive men woman is rather a thirg, a merchandise, than a person).]

A second way of distinguishing gender by phonetic means is represented in the following word: 126 a.

ógwḙl an ox with the horns turned toward the eyes
ágwḙlò a cow with the horns turned toward the eyes.

Case.

Genetive.
The ruling noun is a singular.

1. The genetive follows the noun determined by it. The noun ends in a consonant; in these cases the two nouns unite without any connecting element or phonetic changes: 127.

wọt house;	wọt jằgò house of the chief
lot club;	lot obwoń club of the stranger
àṭp bag;	àṭp jal ẹni bag of this man
okọk blossom;	okọk yaṇ ẹni blossom of this tree
yit ear;	yit kyèń ear of the horse.

There are, however, a few exceptions, chiefly if the final consonant is *k* or *ch*, and the next word begins with a consonant;
a) sometimes the "helping vowel" is inserted:

kidọ colour;	kite lōjọ black colour
ńẹdọ rib;	ńẹte jal rib of man
lẹch tooth;	lẹche lyẹch tooth of the elephant
mọgọ beer;	mọke fōte wọn beer of our country
bōdọ artist.	bōte tọń one who makes spears.

These are treated like nouns in the plural.
b) *ch* and *k* may be dropped:

pāch village;	pā rit village of the king
kẹch, kạch hunger;	ka jal ẹni the hunger of this man
dọk cattle;	dọ rit the cattle of the king.

c) *ch* softens into *y*:
    mach fire;   *may kwǭrǫ* "fire of cotton"; see 45.
    One word changes its vowel before a genetive:
    yǫ way;   *yu Fakǫi* the way to F.;
likewise when an adjective follows: *yu toch* a narrow way; see 22.

2. Nouns which have the final vowel *ǫ*, and whose second consonant is a voiced — in some cases also a voiceless — mute (*gǫ, jǫ, dǫ, ḍǫ, bǫ*), drop, when followed by a genetive, the *ǫ*, and turn the consonant into the corresponding nasal one: *gǫ* ⟩ *ṅ, jǫ* ⟩ *ṅ, dǫ* ⟩ *n, ḍǫ* ⟩ *ṇ, bǫ* ⟩ *m*; see 40.

    jāgǫ chief;   *jāṅ fōṭe wǫn* the chief of our country
    afoajǫ rabbit;   *afoaṅ ṅal ṭēṇ* the rabbit of the child
    tẹdǫ people;   *tẹn fān ǥni* the people of this village
    ómǫ̣ḍǫ̣ a cow;   *ómǫ̣ṇ riṭ* the cow of the king
    tạbǫ plate;   *tạm ṅan* the plate of the girl
    mutǫ neck;   *mune ḍeaṅ* the neck of the cow.

This nasalization is caused by a nasal consonant, *n*, which is no doubt identical with the demonstrative *n* (vide 138), and has originally the meaning "that": *jāgǫ n pāch* "the chief, (namely) that of the village". There are some examples which show the *n* in existence at the present time: *lāu* cloth, *lān ḍāchǫ* the cloth of the woman; here *n* is preserved, the *u* having dropped before it; *riṭ* king, an older form *rāṭ*, see 16; *rāṇ lạbǫ* the king of the people; here the *n* is preserved, though the word ends in a consonant; this is generally not the case; it is evident that after a vowel the *n* is easily preserved, *jāgǫ n pāch* offers no difficulty. in pronouncing, but in words ending in a consonant the *n* was liable to disappear, the more so, as the consonant was voiceless, and *n* is voiced; thus *ḍǫk n tẹdǫ* ⟩ *ḍǫk tẹdǫ*, but *jāgǫ n tẹdǫ* ⟩ *jāṅ tẹdǫ*. This *n* has high tone.

[This *n*, originally probably always a demonstrative pronoun and serving to express the genetive relation, exists in a great number of central and eastern Sudan languages. In Di. it effects the same changes as in Shilluk, besides it is found in Nuba, Logonē, Mandara, Tedā, and also in Haussa and Ful.]

The ruling noun is a plural.

If the ruling noun is a plural, the *n* does not appear, but when the noun ends in a consonant, the 'helping vowel' is suffixed to it. When the plural ends in *i*, this *i* is generally preserved. A change of tone is to be noted here: while the plural-forming *i* (see 103) and the helping vowel have low tone in those cases where no genetive follows, they receive high tone when standing before a following genetive. *This high tone most probably indicates the lost genetive-forming* n, the sound n itself having disappeared, but its tone (see 127) was perserved. — Examples:

pāch village,	pl. *myɛr;*	*myɛré rit* villages of the king
wọt house,	pl. *wọ̀ti;*	*wọ̀tí rit* houses of the king
yit ear,	pl. *yit;*	*yité kyɛ̀n* ears of the horse
mọgọ beer,	pl. *myki;*	*mykí fōte wọn* beers of our country
okọk blossom,	pl. *òkọ̀k;*	*òkọ̀kí yat* the blossoms of the tree
atɛ̂p bag,	pl. *àtɛp;*	*àtɛpé ńate wɛ̄lọ* the bags of the traveller
kɛch hunger,	pl. *kańí;*	*kańí fōte wọn* the famines of our country
jàgò chief,	pl. *jàk;*	*jāké fōte wọn* the chiefs of our country.

In my materials I find one exception to this rule: *gwòk-gúòk* dog; *gúòkè jal ɛni* the dogs of this man; but this may be a misunderstanding.

The Objective Case.   128.

The direct object or accusative follows the verb: *á chām byɛ́l* he ate dura. Sometimes the particle *kí* "with" is added: *á chām kí byɛ́l* he ate (with) dura.

But when *kà* "and" begins a sentence, the object always precedes the verb: *kà byɛl chām* and dura ate (he).

What in European languages is an indirect or dative object, the Shilluk transforms into a direct object, and what we would call the direct object, is in this case always introduced by *kí*; instead of saying: "he gave money to the child", they say: "he presented the child with money": *a wēki ńal ki ńyen*.

But in very many, probably in most cases the direct and indirect object are not expressed at all, the passive voice being used instead, "I saw him" is expressed by "he was seen by me"; "he gave the child milk" by "the child was given milk by him". — On the passive voice see 173.

The Vocative Case   129.

is formed by lengthening the (last) vowel, by raising the tone, and sometimes by adding *i* "you": *ńàtè* man, *ńàtéi* o man! *Dàk* a proper name, *Dàgí* o Dak!

THE PRONOUN.

The Personal Pronoun.

Connected Form, standing before the verb.
This form is generally used as the subject of verbs.   130.

| yá I | yí thou | yɛ́, ɛ́ (ò) he |
| wá, wọ́ we | wú you | gɛ́ they. |

The forms are often pronounced with a short vowel. *yɛ́* and *ɛ́* (sometimes *é*), likewise *wá* and *wọ́*, are used promiscuously, but *ɛ́*, apparently the younger form, is employed more frequently than yέ; ὸ is seldom used; in the 3rd person gὸ also occurs, but it is very rare as a subject. Note that ὸ and gὸ have a low tone, but all other personal pronouns have a high tone.

I. [It is at least remarkable that in two West African Sudan languages the personal pronouns of the 3rd pers. sing. are the same as in Shilluk: Ewe é and wò, Twi e and o (In Ewe even the tones are equal to those in Shi.); Ewe makes some distinction in the use of é and wò, while in Shi. they seem to be employed at will. Gang too has e and o, apparently without making any distinction between the two.

On the *form of the pronoun* note the following remarks:
The corresponding forms for the singular and the plural seem to have originally the same vowels, only yí and wú being different. But besides yí, yú also occurs, and in Nuer the possessive pron. of the 2nd pers. sing. is du (d is prefixed), so it seems probable that the original vowel was u, which was assimilated by the palatal semivowel y and thus became i. This palatalization must, however, have taken place at an early period, as neighbouring languages — with the exception just stated — have i and yi for the 2nd pers. sing. So we get as primitive vowels of the personal pronoun: á, ú, έ, which were differentiated into singular and plural by certain prefixes.

a) Singular.
In all three persons the pronoun begins with y, but the 3rd person has a third form, which is not mentioned above: γέn (n marks the absolute form, see 132, so the form is properly γέ); γέ I regard as the older form of yέ (on the change between y and γ see 35); in Dinka and Nuer the pronoun of the first person is γa, which is likewise the older form for Shilluk ya; from this it is probable that the 2nd person also originally began with γ, though, as far as I can see, it is nowhere retained. Thus we get these (hypothetical) primitive forms: γa, γu, γέ; a, u, ε designating the persons, and γ the singular.

b) Plural.
In plural all persons begin with w except gέ. What is the origin of this g? In Nuer the 1st pers. is kό, the third kέn and kyέn, in Dinka ke (probably kέ); kό is evidently contracted from kwa, see 22; analogous to this kyέ may be derived from kwέ (kwέ > kyε see 32), and the 2nd person, wú, would be originally kwu, but, as in the singular, here the hypothetical form seems nowhere preserved. So the primitive forms of the plural would be: kwa, kwu, kwέ; a, u, ε again designating the persons and kw the plural. (As for the prefixing of k note that in Dinka the personal

pronouns in the absolute form suffix a *k!*). — The evolution of *gẹ* in Shi. would then be thus: *kwẹ* 〉 *kyẹ* 〉 *kẹ* 〉 *gẹ*. While in the first and second person the *k* before *w* was dropped (see 46), in the 3rd pers. *kẹ* turned into *gẹ*. The changing of a voiceless into a voiced consonant is not so uncommon in the Eastern Sudan languages, see 42; here the process was facilitated by *gẹ* being a much used word, whose pronunciation may easily be slighted. — Hence perhaps *gọ̀* "he" may also be explained. It may be formed from the primitive pronoun *ò* "he", by prefixing to it, in analogy with *gẹ́*, a *g*, and to make the analogy perfect, the vowel *ò* was also pronounced wide, that is *ọ̀*, in accordance with the *ẹ* in *gẹ́*. This is, indeed, a mere hypothesis, but it is supported by the fact that *gọ̀* and *ò* both have low tone, while all other personal pronouns have high tone.]

Absolute Form. 132.

yán I, me	*yín* thou, thee	*ẹ́n, ɣẹ́n* he, him	*gọ̀* he, him
wán, wọ́n we, us	*wún* you	*gẹ́n* they, them	

These differ from the connected form only by a suffixed *n*; *ẹ́n* and *ɣẹ́n* are used promiscuously; *gọ̀n* occurs frequently as objective, but seldom as subjective pronoun. The suffixed *n* may be identical with the deictic *n* mentioned in 127 et passim; so that *yán* really means: "it is I".

These absolute or separable pronouns do not stand immediately before a verb, they are used when the person is to be emphasized. They are employed as subjective and objective alike. When they emphasize the subject, the connected form of the pronoun has to follow them: *yán yạ chǎm* (it was) I (that) ate.

The absolute pronouns may again be emphasized by adding *á*: *yáná*, *yíná*, *ẹ́ná*. This has the meaning of "it is", and is often used in addresses: *ẹ́ná Páchòdọ̀* that is Fashoda; *yíná jwọ̀k* "thou art God" "o God".

If a personal pronoun in the singular is connected with another pronoun or noun, the plural form is always used instead of the singular: *wọ́ ki yin* I and you; *wú ki mẹ́n* you (sing.) with whom?

Objective Form. 133.
It is suffixed to the verb. Example: stem *chwọl* to call.

Common form.		With more emphasis.	
á chwọ̀lá	he called me	*á chwọ̀lá yán* or *yáná*	
á chwọ̀lí	he called thee	*á chwọ̀lá yín* or *yíná*	
á chwọ̀lẹ̣	he called him	*á chwọ̀lá ẹ́n* or *ẹ́ná*	
á chwọ̀lẹ̣ wọ́n	he called us	*á chwọ̀lá wọ́n* or *wọ́ná*	
á chwọ̀lẹ̣ wún	he called you	*á chwọ̀lá wún* or *wúná*	
á chwọ̀lẹ̣ gẹ́n	he called them	*á chwọ̀lá gẹ́n* or *gẹ́ná*	

The first *á* is the sign of the past; in the second form the final *a* of the verb marks the verb as being followed by an object.

Note the change of the tone in the objective form. *The objective form has low tone, whereas the subjective form has high tone.*[1]

134.   Possessive Form.[2]

This form is also always suffixed. Example *wǫt* house pl. *wǫtí*.

wǫ́dá my house	*wǫ́dí* thy house	*wǫ́dę̂* his house
wǫ̂t wǫ́n our house	*wǫ̂t wún* your house	*wǫ̂t gę́n* their house
wǫ́tá my houses	*wǫ́tí* thy houses	*wǫ́tę̂* his houses
wǫ́tí wǫ́n our houses	*wǫ́tí wún* your houses	*wǫ́tí gę́n* their houses.
	gwǫk pl. *gúǫk* dog.	
gwǫ́gá my dog	*gwǫ́gí* thy dog	*gwǫ́gę̂* his dog
gwǫ̂k wǫ́n our dog	*gwǫ̂k wún* your dog	*gwǫ̂k gę́n* their dog
gúǫ́ká my dogs	*gúǫ́kí* thy dogs	*gúǫ́kę̂* his dogs
gúǫ́ké wǫ́n our dogs	*gúǫ́ki wún* your dogs	*gúǫ́ké gę́n* their dogs.

If the final consonant of the noun is a liquid or nasal, the *w* in *wǫn* and *wun* is often ommitted: *kal ūn* your fence; *tyęn un* your people.

If both the possessor and the thing possessed are a singular, the possessive pronoun has a middle tone, if either of them or both are a plural, the poss. pr. has a high tone.

135. In the connection of noun and pronoun the rule given in 40 is to be observed, as these examples show:

jâgǫ̀ chief,   *jánâ* my chief   *afoajǫ* rabbit,   *afoaná* my rabbit

but in pl.: *jâk* chiefs,   *jáká* my chiefs   *afoachi* rabbits,   *afoachá* my rabbits.

If the final vowel of the noun is *u*, it turns into *w*; if *u* is the sole stem-vowel, a *w* is inserted: *fyóu* heart, *fyówá* my heart; *nù* lion, *nuwa* my lion.

In some few cases the possessive pronoun is prefixed by *r: ra* my, *ri* thy etc. Before this *r* the final consonant of the noun drops:

ńal boy   *ńára* my boy   *pach* village   *pára* my village, etc.

This *r* is a shortened form of *ré* "body, self."

136. As the intonation shows certain irregularities in the connection of nouns with possessive pronouns, some more examples may be given.

ówę̂ę̂ mat	pl. *ówę̂ę̂;*	*ówę̂dá* my mat;	*ówę̂tá* my mats
yį̂ę̂ ear	pl. *yį̂ę̂;*	*yídá* my ear;	*yįtá* my ears
kǫ̂ę̂ rain	pl. *kǫnį́;*	*kǫda* my raining;	*kǫ́ńá* my rainings
lyęch elephant	pl. *lięch;*	*lyę́já* my eleph.;	*lèchá* my elephants
ałę̂p bag	pl. *ałę̂p;*	*ałę̂bá* my bag;	*ałę́pá* my bags
kwǫm chair	pl. *kuǫ́mį;*	*kwǫmá* my chair;	*kúǫ́má* my chairs
rę̄jǫ fish	pl. *réch;*	*rę́ná* my fish;	*réchá* my fishes

---

[1] In Ewe *e*, the pronoun of the 3rd pers. sing. has high tone, when subjective, but low tone, when objective; the same is the case in Yoruba: *ó* he, *ò* him; see Crowther page (4) and (8).

[2] The suffixed subjective form see 160.

The Pronoun 63

yɛt neck	pl. yiɛt;	yɛ̤dá my neck;	yɛ̤tɛ́ wɔ́n our necks
kwāch leopard	pl. kwāni;	kwdjá my leopard;	kwdná my leopards
ṅù lion	pl. ṅuwi;	ṅúwá my lion;	ṅúwá my lions
rɛ̤t king	pl. rór;	ra̤dá my king;	rŏrá my kings
ɔkɔ̤k blossom	pl. ɔkɔ̤k;	ɔkɔ̤gá my flower;	ɔkɔ̤ká my flowers.

In all personal pronouns the singular is not unfrequently used instead of the plural of the corresponding person.

Sometimes the possessive pronoun of *the 3rd person sing.* is employed instead of the first plural, chiefly in names of relatives: *wāṅɛ* "his" *and* "our" grandmother.

The possessive pronoun can also be affixed to an adjective: *wú bì bɛ̤nú* (instead *bɛn wu*) have all of you come?

Some much used nouns have shortened forms, when they are connected with possessive pronouns:

wich father		má mother	
wíyá my father		máyá my mother	
wóu thy father		máyi thy mother	
wɛ́n his father		mɛ́n his mother	
wɛ̤ our father		máy wɔ́n our mother	
wiy wun your father		máy wún (māyu) your mother	
wiy gɛ́n their father		máy gɛ́n their mother	
dɛ̀àṅ cow		mi mother	
dɛ̀á my cow		mia my mother	
dɛ̆ (dɛ̀i) thy cow		miu thy mother	
dɛ̤ his cow		mɛ́n his mother	
ómɨ brother		ṅámí sister	
ómiá my brother		ṅámiá my sister	
ómiòu thy brother		ṅámióu thy sister	
ómɛ́n his brother		ṅámɛ́n his sister	
ómɨ̤ our brother		ṅami yi wɔ́n sister	
ómi wu your brother		ṅami yi wún sister	
ómí gɛ́n their brother		ṅami yi gɛ́n sister.	

The *ɛn* in *wɛn, om-ɛn* etc. is the absolute pronun *ɛn* he.

re body, self	
rea myself	re yi wɔn ourselves
rei thyself	re yi wun yourselves
rɛ himself	re yi gɛn themselves.

In names of relatives the possessive pronoun of the 2nd person sing. (and plural) is generally *u, wu:*

kwāyu your grandfather   māyu your mother   mīu your mother.

137. The Possessive Pronoun as a Substantive.

It is formed by the help of *mé* pl. *mǫk* or *gìn* pl. *gìk*; *gin* is "thing", *me* probably has a similar meaning.

Singular of the thing possessed:

méá mine	*méí* thine	*mǫ́* his
méi (me yi) wǫ́n ours	*méi wún* yours	*méi gę́n* theirs
gìná mine	*gìní* thine	*gìnǫ́* his
gìnè wǫ́n ours	*gìnè wún* yours	*gìnè gę́n* theirs.

Plural of the thing possessed:

mǫ́ká[1] mine   *mǫ́ wǫ́n* ours   *gìké wǫ́n* ours   *gìká* mine.

Demonstrative Pronouns.

138. In connecting nouns in the singular with demonstrative pronouns, the rule described in 40 obtains, with the one difference however, that here not only the nouns ending in a vowel change their last (mute) consonant, but also the nouns whose final sound is a mute consonant; accordingly the rule given in 40 is to be enlarged thus: final *gǫ* and *k* ⟩ *ṅ*, *jǫ* and *ch* ⟩ *ṅ*, *dǫ* and *t* ⟩ *n*, *ḍǫ* and *ṭ* ⟩ *ṇ*, *bǫ* and *p* ⟩ *m*.

These consonant changes, without any further addition, represent the simplest form of the demonstrative pronoun. The changes are no doubt caused by suffixing an *n*, which possesses a demonstrative power. It is employed in nouns ending in a mute consonant or in *gǫ, jǫ, dǫ, ḍǫ, bǫ* only, at least I have not heard it used in others (as for instance in *jal* "man", which would become **jaln* or rather *jan*, see 44).

The meaning of this primitive form is *a reference to a person or object just mentioned or just spoken of*. It has somewhat the character of the definite article in English (as in such a sentence: we saw a man walking in the bush; *the man* called to us).

gwok dog,	*gwoṅ* the (identical) dog, the dog just spoken of
jāgǫ chief,	*jāṅ* the chief just mentioned
māch fire,	*māṅ* the fire just mentioned, this fire
lẹjǫ tooth,	*lẹṅ* the tooth just spoken of, this tooth
wǫt house,	*wǫn* the house just spoken of, this house
yigp tail,	*yigm* the tail just spoken of, this tail, etc.

tyęṅ fōṇ the people of this country, from *fōṭe*
tyęṅ wǫn the people of this house, from *wǫt*

---

[1] *mǫ́gá* also is heard.

The Pronoun

yēi gwoṅ the hair of this dog, from gwok
yiţe yaṇ the leaves of this tree, from yaţ
    kū place,   kūṅ this place, here
    ḍukį to-morrow, ḍuṅ this to-morrow, the next day.

139. Besides these the Shi. has several demonstrative pronouns denoting different distances between the speaker and the person or object spoken of.

Singular: ȧn this, ẹní that, ȧchȧ that over there.

Plural: ȧk, ȧn, ȧgȧk these, ẹní those, ȧchȧ those over there. ȧn and ẹní are probably of the same origin; i was suffixed to an; a has become ẹ by assimilation to i; see 26.[1] Note the difference of tone, the low tone designating the object near by, the high tone that one in some distance.

To mark a great distance, they use chínẹ́; this is pronounced with an exceedingly high tone, and the last vowel may be lengthened at will, according to the greatness of the distance.

Be it noted that according to 138 the changes of the final consonants take place only in singular, never in plural; in the plural the final mute consonants are always to be pronounced voiceless, that is as a real k, ch, t, ţ p.

140. Some examples of nouns connected with demonstrative pronouns (The intonation-marks in my materials are incomplete here).

jȧgọ̀ chief;		jȧṅ ȧn this chief,	
jȧṅ ẹní that chief,		jȧk chiefs;	
jȧk ȧk these chiefs,		jȧk ẹní those chiefs,	
jȧṅ ȧchȧ the chief over there		jȧk ȧchȧ the chiefs over there	
ȧjwọ̄gọ́ sorcerer;		ajwoṇ an this sorcerer	
djwọk pl.;		djwọk ȧk pl.	
chwak voice;		chwȧṅ ȧn; pl. chwak; chwak ȧk	
kwach leopard;		kwȧṅ ȧn; pl. kwȧñį; kwȧṅ ȧk	
afoajọ hare;		ȧfóȧṅ ȧn; pl. afoachį; ȧfóȧch ȧk	
riţ king;		rḭṇ ȧn; pl. ror; ror ȧk	
kọţ rain;		kọṇ ȧn; pl. kọṇ ȧk	
yiţ ear;		yíṇ ȧn; pl. yiţ; yiţ ȧk	
ȧţẹp bag;		ȧţệm ȧn; pl. ȧţẹp; ȧţẹp ȧk	
ḍukį to-morrow,		ḍuṅe chínệ the day after to-morrow	
ówẹt a mat;		ówẹṇ ȧn, ówẹṇ ẹní pl. ówẹt; ówẹt ẹní, ówẹt ȧchȧ	
tẹ̇dọ̀ people;		tẹ̇n ȧn.	

The last example, though virtually a plural, is treated as a singular.

Nouns ending in other consonants or in vowels, have no changes:

rör kings;	rör ȧk these kings	gin thing;	gin ȧn this thing
léṅ war;	léṅ ȧn this war	pi water;	pi ȧn this water.

---

[1] It is, however, difficult to distinguish the beginning vowels in ȧn and ẹní; ȧn sometimes sounds ẹn or even ẹm, and ẹní is sometimes heard as ȧní.

WESTERMANN, The Shilluk People.

141. The demonstrative pronoun standing for a noun.
mɛ́n àn this one   mók àk these ones.

Interrogative Pronouns.

142. They imply the same consonant-changes as the demonstratives Pronouns.
ànǫ̀ what, which? pl. ǫ̀nǫ̀; on this plural see 124.
à which?
àmɛ́n (also ámɛ́n) who?   pl. àmók (ámók).

Examples: Singular.
ogwǫk jackal;   á ogwǫ̀n ànǫ̀ which jackal is it?
lyɛch elephant;   á lyɛn ànǫ̀ which elephant is it?
wǫt house;   á wǫn ànǫ̀ which house is it?
yat tree;   á yan ànǫ̀ which tree is it?
rit king;   á ran ànǫ̀ which king is it?
atɛ̄p bag;   á atɛm ànǫ̀ which bag is it?
gin thing;   á gin ànǫ̀ which thing is it, what is it?

Plural.

143. In the plural the final mute consonants are always to be pronounced voiceless, that is as a real k, ch, t, ṭ, p; see 139.
wǫti houses;   á wǫt ǫ̀nǫ̀ which houses are they?
rōr kings;   á rōr ǫ̀nǫ̀ which kings are they?
yɛn trees;   á yɛn ǫ̀nǫ̀ which trees are they?
ógǫ̀ki jackals;   á ogǫk ǫ̀nǫ̀ which jackals are they?
atɛ̄p bags;   á atɛ̄p ǫ̀nǫ̀ which bags are they?
lyɛ̂ch elephants;   á lyɛ̂ch ǫ̀nǫ̀ which elephants are they?
gik things;   á gik ǫ̀nǫ̀ which things are they?
àmɛ́n á bì who has come?
àmók á bì who have come?
jal amɛ́n which man?
jǫk amók which men?

144. amɛ́n á á wòri yín? who (is it that) sent you?
wá rɛ̄ni mɛ́nâ whom shall we elect?   [this?
wǫn an á wǫt mɛ̂n this house is house whose? whose house is
wǫt ak á wǫti mǫk whose houses are these?
wǫn â which house?   ran â which king?
ogwǫn â which fox?   ógǫ̀ki â which foxes?

mɛ́n (amɛ́n) and probably also â are no original interrogative pronouns, but are demonstratives; see mɛ́n in this sense 141; â is probably the deictic element

The Pronoun

"it is", see 196; buth both are in the same time employed as interrogative, and *mɛ̣n* even as a relative, see 145; originally it was: "this man!" and then, just as in English: "this man?" likewise: "it is a tree!" and: "it is a tree?" Here not even the position of the words is changed, but only their *tone; just so in Shilluk;* only the changing of tone goes the opposite way, the interrogative tone being low; see 206.

Relative Pronouns.

a) What we express by a relative sentence, the Shilluk generally says in a simple sentence. Instead of saying: "the man who came yesterday, was my father" they say: "the man came yesterday, he was my father"; (compare the English "the man I saw" instead of "the man whom I saw").

    jal á bì áwà the man came yesterday, or: the man who came yesterday; *á* is not a relative pronoun, but a particle denoting the past tense;

    wot a gɛ̣rɛ̀ wón the house (which) was built by us;

    ḍean á nɛ̣kɛ̀ yi tɛ̣dọ the cow (which) was killed by the people.

b) In a similar sense *mɛ̣n* is employed; *mɛ̣n* is "this, this one", see 141, but it serves also in expressing relative sentences:

    yá fà dwátá mɛ̣n é lòjò, yá dwátá mɛ̣n à tàr literally: "I do not want this one, it is black, I want this one, it is white" that is: "I do not want the one which is black, I want the one which is white".

    mɛ̣n may also be employed in a local sense: *e muḍọ pi, mɛ̣n àn lūm bogọn* he drank water in a place, where there was no grass.

c) A real relative pronoun seems to be *má* who, which:

    jal má bi the man who came   *kɛ̣n má bɛ̣n* the time which comes.

But this has rather the meaning of a participle: the coming time, the man having come. It is frequently used in connection with adjectives, see 149.

The Reflexive Pronoun.

It is formed with the help of *rɛ́* pl. *rei* "body".

    rɛ́á my body, that is: myself
    rɛ́i thy body, that is: thyself
    rɛ́ his body, that is: himself
    rɛ́i wón our body, that is: ourselves
    rɛ́i wún your body, that is: yourselves
    rɛ́i gɛ̣n their body, that is: themselves
    á nɛ̣ka rɛ́ he killed himself

gé nẹka reị gẹ́n they killed themselves.
They say also:
    a nẹka chwakẹ he killed his throat: himself.
"I myself" is expressed in a similar way:
    á gwọ́kè yá kị́ réá "it was done, I with my body": I myself did it;
    á gwọ́kè yí kị́ réí "it was done, you with your body": you yourself did it;
    á gwọ́kè ẹ́ kẹ́rẹ́ he himself did it
á gwọ́kè wọ́ kị́ reị wọ́n we ourselves did it
á gwọ́kè wú kị́ reị wún you yourselves did it
á gwọ́kè gẹ́ kị́ reị gẹ́n they themselves did it
or with kẹ̄te "alone":
    á gwọ́kè yá kẹ̣́tá I did it myself
    á gwọ́kè yí kẹ̣́tí you did it yourself
    á gwọ́kè ẹ́ kẹ̣́tẹ́ he did it himself
á gwọ́kè wọ́ kẹ̣́tè wọ́n we did it ourselves
á gwọ́kè wú kẹ̣́tè wún you did it yourselves
á gwọ́kè gẹ́ kẹ̣́tè gẹ́n they did it themselves.
This has also the meaning: I did it alone.
And: yá kị́ chwáká I with my throat: I myself; yi kị chwaki etc.

The Reciprocal Pronoun.

147.
    wọ́ fōta reị wọ́n we beat each other
    gẹ́ fōta reị gẹ́n they beat each other.

THE ADJECTIVE.

148. Most adjectives do not distinguish between singular and plural, there are, however, a few which have different forms for both, and, what is very remarkable, the plural always has the ending ọ, which, in the noun, is the specific ending of the *singular*.

    dúọ́n pl.   dọ̣̄nọ̀ big, great   tẹ̀n pl.   tọ̀nọ̀ small, little
    chyẹk pl.   chyẹ̣̄kọ̀ short   bar pl. bárọ̀, bẹ̀rọ̀ long
    ràch pl.   rẹ̣chọ̀ bad.

Note that all the plural-forms have low tone, and some, whose vowel in singular is short, have a long vowel, see 110.

Many adjectives have two forms, one denoting the gradual entering of a state, the growing into a state, and the second denoting the accomplished state.

The Adjective 69

dọ̀nọ̀ becoming big, growing up;   dúọ́n big, great, grown up
rẽ̀nọ̀ acting badly, growing bad;   ràch bad
lạ̀ṇọ̀ becoming hot, feeling hot;   lẹ̀t hot.

When adjectives are connected with nouns, the final consonant of the noun undergoes the changes described in 138.

In this connection, however, the adjective may be prefixed by the relative pronoun *má* (often *mę́*) "which", in this case no changes take place; but it is to be noted that *before má the final consonant of the noun is*, contrary to the rule in 107, *to be pronounced voiced*, whereas in all other connections the voice-less consonant is the characteristic of the plural. This deviation from the common rule is analogous to the fact stated above, that the plural form of the adjective has the ending of the singular of nouns. In order to set forth the difference between the form without *má* and that with *má*, in the following examples the voiced final consonant is written voiced (contrary to the rule 38).

149.

Note: *má* (*mę́*) has always distinctly high tone. The adjectives with *má* are in their meaning more emphatic than those without *má*: *duọn* large, *maduọn* very large, large indeed.

wọt house pl. wọti.	wọn dúọ́n big house	pl. wọ̀ti dọ̀nọ̀
	wọd máduọ́n big house	pl. wọd mádọ̀nọ̀
yat tree pl. yẹn.	yan tẹ̀n small tree	pl. yẹ́n tụ̀nọ̀
	yad mátẹ̀n small tree	pl. yẹ́n mátụ̀nọ̀
rít king pl. rȯr.	rụn dọ̀ch good king	pl. rȯr dọ̀ch [mádọ̀ch
	rid mádọ̀ch good king	pl. rȯr mádọ̀ch, or
atệp bag pl. atệp.	àtệm làch broad bag	pl. àtệp làchọ̀
	atệb málàch broad bag	pl. atệb málàchọ̀
ọkọk flower pl. ọ̀kọ̀k.	ọkọn kwàrọ̀ red flower	pl. ọkọ̀kí kwàrọ̀
	ọ̀kọ̀g mákwàrọ̀ red flower	pl. ọ̀kọ̀g mákwàrọ̀
lyẹch elephant pl. llèch	lyẹ́n lòjọ̀ black elephant	pl. liechí lōjọ
	lyẹj málòjọ̀ black elephant	pl. liej málòjọ̀
gwȯk dog pl. gúȯk.	gwȯn tàr white dog	pl. guoki tàr
	gwȯg mátàr white dog	pl. guȯg mátàr
mọgọ beer pl. mọki, mụki.	mọ̀n mẹt sweet beer	pl. mọkí mẹt
	mọg mámẹt sweet beer	pl. mọki mámẹt
yít leaf pl. yít	yin bẹl bitter leaf	pl. yiti bẹl
	yid mábẹl bitter leaf	pl. yite mábẹl

rêjǫ fish pl. rech, rechi	reṅ chyẹk short fish	pl. réchi̧ chygkǫ
	rej máchyẹk short fish	pl. rej machyękǫ
yęt neck pl. yiẹt.	yęṅ bar long neck	pl. yiẹte barǫ (bęrǫ)
	yęḍ mábâr long neck	pl. yiẹḍ mábậrụ̀
lȩ̣jụ̀ tooth pl. lẹk.	lẹṅ tar white tooth	pl. lẹki tar
	lẹj mátâr white tooth	pl. lẹg mátâr
yŏ road pl. yȩ̣t.	yū toch narrow road	pl. yẹte toch
	yǫ matoch narrow road	pl. yẹḍ matoch.

150. All the connections without *má* may have two meanings, viz. 1ˢᵗ attributive, as they are rendered above: *a big house*, etc.; 2ⁿᵈ *predicative, the house is big* etc., that is, the adjectives have the quality of verbs, and are treated as such, they may be conjugated like any verb; but the adjectives with *má* are only used in an attributive sense.

Comparison.

151. The means of comparing an object with another are rather scanty, the people not feeling the need of comparison as we do. They simply say: this thing is big, and that one is not big, or: is a little big.

a) The most common way of expressing a higher degree of quality or quantity is to lengthen the vowel, and at the same time to raise the tone.

But generally this is only possible in words which have the high or middle tone, not with the low-toned ones; with these the low tone is so essentially connected that a high tone would be incompatible with them. Examples of adjectives whose tone may be raised, are: *di̧ch* good, *gír* many, *ṭȩ̣n* small, *tóch* narrow.

b) Words with low tone may be intensified in their meaning by still lowering their tone, as for instance *ràch* bad, *dǫ̀nǫ̀* big, *ṅènǫ̀* much, many.

Other means for expressing a higher degree of an adjective are:

c) lengthening of a vowel only: *mẹ̀dǫ̀* sweet, *mẹ̄dǫ̀* very sweet; *ṅēnǫ* many (the first vowel to be lengthened).

d) repetition of the adjective: *ràch* bad, *ràch ràch* very bad. In these repetitions generally the vowel in the second word is long.

e) the word is repeated and the second gets the prefix *ma*: *di̧ch mádi̧ch* "good which is (really) good": very good, exceedingly good.

f) "*rach*" is very much used in this sense; e. g. *ràch kí̧ di̧ch* "bad with goodness" that is: exceedingly good; *rach kí̧ lạu* "bad with being far": very, very far.

g) by adding *wǫk* "outside": *ṭěṇ wǫk* "small outside", that is "small beyond anything", very, very small.

h) *chàr, chàrǫ̀* "very" may be added.

i) by *fōdǫ* "to surpass"; this form together with those under k expresses a real comparison: *yḗ dà dǫk máfôṭ d̥ǫ̀k pyàrǫ̀* "he has cows surpassing cows ten": he has more than ten cows; *jè á ṭou̯, gě jódǫ́ jè ddḛk* "people died, they surpassed people three": more than three people died.

k) *rǖnḗ á màl, rǖná yà chán* "his years are above, my years are behind": he is older than I;
yá mǫ̀lá běṇ ḗ tok "I was first coming he was absent": I came earlier than he;
ba duǫ̀ṅ nḗ yán (he is) not (so) old as I.

THE NUMERALS.

Cardinal Numbers.

152.

ákyěl 1	*áryàu̯* 2	*áděk* 3	*ánwěn* 4
dbích 5	*dbíkyěl* 6	*dbíryàu̯* 7	*dbíděk* 8
dbínwěn 9	*pyàrǫ̀* 10	*pyàrǫ̀ wíy ákyěl* 11	
pyàrǫ̀ wíy áryàu̯ 12		*pyàrǫ̀ wíy áděk* 13	
pyàrǫ̀ wíy ánwěn 14		*pyàrǫ̀ wíy dbích* 15	
pyàrǫ̀ wíy dbíkyěl 16		*pyàrǫ̀ wíy dbíryàu̯* 17	
pyàrǫ̀ wíy dbíděk 18		*pyàrǫ̀ wíy dbínwěn* 19	
pyàr áryàu̯ 20		*pyàr áryàu̯ wíy kḭ ákyěl* 21	
pyàr áryàu̯ wíy kḭ áryàu̯ 22		*pyār áděk* 30	
pyār ánwěn 40		*pyār dbích* 50	
pyār dbíkyěl 60		*pyār dbíryàu̯* 70	
pyār dbídêk 80		*pyār dbínwěn* 90	
pyàr pyàr 100		*pyàr pyàr wíy kḭ ákyěl* 101.	

Only the numerals from one to five and ten are primitive, all the rest are compositions. The beginning *á* in the names for one to five is secondary, and is probably identical with *á* "it is"; the ordinal numbers do not have it. Mark the mechanical intonation in the numbers from one to four. *pyàrǫ̀* pl. *pyàr* is a substantive; *dbíkyěl* is of course 5 + 1; *pyārǫ wiy akyěl* means "ten, on its head one" i. e. ten, added to it one; this is still more evident in the following forms, which are also used: *pyàrǫ̀ wíjě dà ákyěl* "ten, its head has one", or: *pyàrǫ̀ wíy kḭ ákyěl* "ten, (its) head with one".

153.

The numeral follows the noun: *woṭ dryạu* two houses; often *ga* "copy" is inserted between both: *chǎn gá pyārọ* ten days.

Ordinal Numbers.

54. They are rarely used. In forming them the prefix *á* is dropped and the simple stem is used, with the exception of "the first", которая is formed from *mal* "above".

  ámáḷọ the first   *ryạu* the second   *dọk, dẹk* the third
  ṅwẹn the fourth   *bích* the fifth   *pyārọ* the tenth.

THE VERB.

55. The *stem of the verb* is uniform. It always consists in a consonant, a vowel, and a consonant, or a consonant, a semivowel, a vowel, and a consonant. But the sounds of the stem may undergo certain changes, on which see 187.

Conjugation of the Verb.

56. The verb has two principal modes or tenses:

1. The Present Tense. This denotes an action as going on, as being done just now, as one not yet finished. This action may be going on in the present as well as in the past or future; the emphasis does *not* lie *on the time*, but on the fact that the action is *not finished*, but is being done, it "has not become", but "is becoming".

 Generally the Present in Shilluk corresponds to the English Present, but it may also describe the Past or the Future: "I am going", "I was going", "I shall be going".

2. The Perfect denotes the action as complete, it describes that which "has become", a state, an accomplished fact. While the Present means: "he is going" the Perfect is: "he is gone", "he is away".

[These same two tenses with exactly the same meanings are found in the Semitic languages, they are there called Imperfect and Perfect. I have retained the name "Present" because it is introduced already, and a new term might lead to confusion. In these two forms there is another conformity between Shilluk and Semitic languages: in Hebrew the verb in the Imperfect (= Shilluk Present) is always preceded by the subject, in the Perfect the subjective pronoun follows the verb; in Shilluk the verb

The Verb 73

in the Present (= Hebrew Imperfect) is preceded by the subject, in the Perfect the subjective pronoun or noun may precede *or follow* the verb. In Nama (Hottentott) and Fulfulde, two Hamitic languages, the subject may also precede *or* follow the verb.]

Besides these two the verb has the following modes:
3. The Future;
4. The Habitual; it denotes action which is done repeatedly, usually, habitually, either in the Present or in the Past.
5. The Imperative.
6. The Verbal Noun; is a real noun, corresponding to the English "going", "eating".
7. The Noun Agent; denotes the doer of the action expressed in the verb. There are two forms, one for expressing an occasional, and the other the habitual doer.
8. The Passive Voice.

Examples showing the conjugation of the verb. 157.
The Verb without an Object.
Stem: *cham* to eat.
Present.

yà chàmọ̀ I am eating	*yí chàmọ̀* you (s.) are eating
è (yé) chàmọ̀ he is eating	*wú chàmọ̀* we are eating
wú chàmọ̀ you are eating	*gé chàmọ̀* they are eating

The verb in the present always ends in *ọ*; this *ọ* is sounded very faintly, see 2.

Nearly all verbs have in the present exactly the same form: the first vowel is long, and both syllables have a low tone. There are only a few exceptions to this rule, viz.

a) the first vowel may be short; in this case the vowel is often high: *kẹ́dọ̀* to go; but at the same time: *kàdọ̀* to go; *ryèrọ̀* to come forth.

b) the first vowel, being long, may have the falling tone; in connection with it the second vowel has sometimes middle, but generally low, tone: *gwânọ̀* to dig, *gôtọ̀* to be vexed. As this is the form and intonation of the infinitive (see 170) these "present forms" may properly be infinitives, these having taken the place of the low-toned present tense.

In most cases the second consonant, if mute, is voiced.

A second form of the present tense is formed by putting *dè* between the subject and the verb:

yà dè chàmọ̀ I am (or was) engaged in eating, I have been eating.

158.

Perfect.

yá chàm I ate	yá kệ̀t I went
yí chàm you ate	yí kệ̀t you went
á chàm he ate	á kệ̀t he went
wá, wú, gé chàm we, you, they ate	wá, wú gé kệ̀t we, you, they went
yá ǹèti I laughed	wá ǹèti we laughed
yí ǹèti you laughed	wú ǹèti you laughed
á ǹèti he laughed	gé ǹèti they laughed.

159.
Characteristics of the Perfect are:

1. the vowel á; appears in the 3rd p. sing. only; the personal pronoun is then dropped.
2. the final vowel ǫ is dropped.
3. With a few exceptions the second (mute) consonant, which in most cases is voiced in the Present, becomes voiceless.
4. The Perfect ends either in the second consonant, or the vowel i is added to the stem.
5. As a rule the tone of the stem-vowel is low; the vowel has, however, not unfrequently a high or falling tone.
6. On vowel- and consonant-changes in the Perfect vide below 182, 187.
7. While in the Present the subject, whether noun or pronoun, always precedes the verb, in the Perfect the subjective noun or pronoun may follow the verb, and very often does so. In this case the tone on both syllables, that is on verb and noun, is high, in the singular; where the suffixed pronoun is a single vowel, the final vowel of the verb, if there is one, is dropped; in the plural a final vowel of the verb is preserved; if the verb ends in a mute consonant, and has no final vowel, the "helping vowel" is sometimes inserted; the same is the case when the subject is a noun beginning in a mute consonant.

This form retains a, the sign of the Imperfect, through all persons, *but its tone is low* (contrast-tone, see 59). — The second consonant, if mute, becomes voiced again, except where the helping vowel is inserted.

à rẹ̀ná I ran	à rẹ̀ní you ran
à rẹ̀ṅé he ran	à rẹ̀ṅ wá we ran
à rẹ̀ṅ wú you ran	à rẹ̀ṅ gé they ran
à nạ̀gá I killed	à kẹ̀dá I went
à chwọ́lí you called	à gwẹ̀dé he wrote.

If the subject is a noun, sometimes the helping vowel is added to the verb, and sometimes not:

à kẹ́t obwoṅ the stranger went;	à kẹ́t óțwǒṅ the hyena went;
à gǫ́ché rịt the king struck;	à bẹ̀n ṅal the boy came

The Verb

but: *ńal e bẹ̄nǫ* the boy is coming   *obwoń e kẹdǫ* the stranger is going.
   Sometimes the subjective noun is placed at the head, the corresponding subjective pronoun following the verb:
   ḍāṇ kẹṅ à tǫ́wẹ́ a man, when he dies: when a man dies.
8. Verbs who have instead of the second consonant a semivowel.
   a) *y*. No *i* is added in the Perfect. The *y* unites with the preceding vowel to a diphthong: *toyǫ* to pierce, perfect *toi*.
   b) *w*. Here likewise generally no *i* is added: *tǫwǫ* to die, perfect *tǫ̀u* (also *tò*). *ṅgawǫ* to trade, perfect *ṅgau*, seldom *ṅgawi*.

160.   Sometimes the subjective pronoun is employed twice, before and behind the verb; for the last not the suffixed, but the emphatic or the subjective form are used; note the changes of the tone!

yí rè gwàl yìn why [re] are you (so) thin?	*ḗ rè gwàl ḕn* why is he (so) thin?
gḗ rè gwàl gḕn why are they (so) thin?	*wú rè gwàl ùn* why are you (pl.) (so) thin?
ḗ rè kẹ́ḍḗ why did he go?	*yí rè kẹ́ṭ* or: *kẹ́ḍí* why did you go?
wá bẹ̀n wà we came	*wú rè kẹ́ḍùn* why did you go?
gḗ kẹ́ḍ gḗ kẹṅ where did they go?	*gḗ bẹ̀n gḕn* they came
	wú kẹ́ḍ wú kẹṅ where did you go?

161.   If *kà* "and" introduces a sentence, the subject, if a pronoun, always follows the verb, and the object always precedes the verb.

   kà kyèṅ gǫ̀já and I struck the horse   *kà kyèṅ gǫ̀jí* and you struck the horse.

Future.

162.   The characteristic of the Future is the particle *ú*,[1] which is placed before the verb. In most cases the present form of the verb is used, but not unfrequently that of the Perfect as well, but in this last case with a slight changing of tone: if the tone is low in the Perfect, it becomes middle in the Future.

yá ú chàmǫ̀ I shall eat	*wá ú chàmǫ̀* we shall eat
yí ú, or *yú chàmǫ̀* you will eat	*wú chàmǫ̀* you will eat
ú chàmǫ̀ he will eat	*gḗ ú chàmǫ̀* they will eat
yá ú ṅẹ̀ṭì I shall laugh	*wá ú kẹ́ṭ* we shall go.

   As the Present, so too the Future has a second form, with *dè* placed between pronoun and verb: *yá ú dè chàmǫ̀* I shall eat. There may be (or at least may have been) a difference of meaning between the two forms, but I have found none.

Habitual.

163.   The *Habitual* is formed by putting the auxiliary verb *ńí* "to use to" between subject and the Present form of the verb.

---

[1] In Masai the Future is formed by suffixing *u*. Hollis page 59.

yá ní chàmọ̀ I use or used to eat gé ní kệdọ̀ they use or used to
é ní gwệdọ̀ he uses or used to write. go

Imperative.

164.
chàm eat! kệt, kẹ́dí go! bi kẹ́dọ̀ come, (let us) go!
pl. chàmùn eat!¹ pl. kẹ́dùn go! chàm wá let us eat!
kệt wá, kẹ́dè wọ̀n let us go! chùní be quiet! pl. chùnún be quiet.

In the singular *i*, the suffix of the 2ᵈ p., may be added or not.

165. The Verb with a Noun as Object.

Present.

The second vowel receives a middle tone.
yá chàmọ̀ byẹ́l I am (or was) eating dura.
yá kẹ́dọ̀ gat I am (or was) going to the river-bank.

Perfect.

166. If the Perfect ends in *i*, this *i* is retained, if it ends in a consonant, an *a*, in some cases *i* is added. I am not quite clear as to the tones; "a" always seems to have a low tone, "i" has sometimes a middle, sometimes also a low tone.

yá chàmà byẹ́l I ate dura yá ßnì kwọf I heard a talk
yá kệtà pach I went home yá màtì (mádi) pi I drank water.

Future.

167. The final vowel has a middle tone.
yá ú chàmọ̀ byẹ́l I shall eat dura yá ú kệtì pach I shall go home.

Habitual.

168. Follows the rules of the Present.

Imperative.

169. In the 2ⁿᵈ p. sing. almost always *i* is added; the 2ⁿᵈ p. pl. has *u* suffixed instead of *un*.

chàm byẹ́l } eat dura! pl. chàmu byẹ́l eat dura!
chàmí byẹ́l
chàm wá byẹ́l let us eat dura! nẹk wá ńarọ̄jọ let us kill a calf!
kẹde wá pach let us go home! māḍe wá pi let us drink water!

Verbal Noun (Infinitive).

170. The Verbal Noun occurs in two chief forms:
a) without the final vowel; the stem-vowel has a middle tone;
b) with the final vowel ọ; the stem-vowel has a falling, and the final vowel a low tone.

Deviations from this rule do occur, but are not frequent. Sometimes a semivowel occurs. Examples:

yá gùgọ̀ I am working n. gwọk working

---

¹ This **un** is of course the personal pronoun of the second person plural.

The Verb

yá gwĕdọ̀	I am writing	n.	gwḗt writing
yá chwọ̀tọ̀	I am calling	n.	chwọ́t calling
yá nágọ̀	I am killing	n.	nḛ́k killing
yá rûmọ̀	I am thinking	n.	rûmọ̀ thinking
yá tábọ̀	I am cheating	n.	tâbọ̀ cheating
yá mắdọ̀	I am drinking	n.	mât drinking.

In adding a genetive, or an adjective pronoun to the verbal noun, the changes described in 138 occur: *gwọ̀n ȧn* this working.

Noun Agent.

171. The language distinguishes two kinds of noun agent, one for the person who does something just now or occasionally, the other denoting the habitual doer of the action.

The first is formed by a connection of words which is really a sentence: *ñān e gō̄gọ* "this man is working" (see 83), *ñate* + the demonstrative *n* is connected *with the present tense of the verb*; this means "one who is working just now". In the second form *ñate* without a pronoun is combined *with the verbal noun*: *ñate gwọk* "a man of working", a man whose habit or calling it is to work, a workman.

ñān e mắdọ a man drinking just now
ñate mât one who drinks habitually, a drinker.

The Passive Voice.

172. The Shilluk forms a Passive Voice, whose chief characteristic is the high-low (the falling), and in some cases the high tone. It consists merely in the stem, no final vowel being added. The stem-vowel is a little shorter than in the Present and Perfect, it may be described as half-long, but is marked as short in this book. In some cases a semivowel is inserted between the first consonant and the vowel.

173. Probably the Passive Voice was originally an intransitive form of the verb, *denoting a state*: from *gō̄gọ* to work, *gwọk* "worked", *á gwộk* "it is worked"; *chảmọ̀* to eat, *châm* "eaten"; *byęl á châm* the dura is eaten, properly "is an eaten one"; *fòdọ̀* to beat, *fwót* "beaten", "a beaten one"; so we can hardly speak of passive tenses, it is rather a mood, an accomplished condition or situation. But nevertheless the form clearly conveys the meaning of a real Passive, which is best shown by the fact that the doer of the action is added to the verb, so its grammatical construction corresponds exactly to that of the Passive in European languages; sometimes, though not frequently, even a Future of the Passive is formed by prefixing *ú*.

174. The doer of the action may be expressed by a noun, or by a pronoun.
a) by a noun.

Here always *yì* "by" is added:
byḗl a châm yì jál ḗní the dura was eaten by this man
ńal á fwôt yì jâgọ̀ the boy was beaten by the chief.
The original meaning of *yì* "by" is not known; perhaps it is some deictic pronoun "it is": "he was beaten it is the chief" (who did it); it can be identical with *yì* "towards".

[75. b) by an absolute pronoun.
The 'helping vowel' is added to the verb. In this case the stem-vowel has a high tone, the 'helping vowel' being low. Perhaps the 'helping vowel' here is the shortened *yì*.
á châmè yán it was eaten by me *á châmè yín* it was eaten by you
á châmè gḗn it was eaten by them.
Sometimes *yì* is also used here: *á châm yì ḗn* it was eaten by him.

[76. c) by the suffixed pronoun.
Here a very peculiar distinction between singular and plural is made: for both numbers the pronouns of the singular are used, but if the doers are a plurality of persons, the last consonant of the verb becomes voiceless; this is of course only possible in verbs ending in a mute consonant; in the rest no distinction is made; but if a distinction seems necessary here, the plural of the pronoun may be employed.
á gwộgà it was worked by me, *á gwộkà* it was worked by us
á kwộbà it was spoken by me, *á kwộpà* it was spoken by us
á mâḍà it was drunk by me, *á mâṭà* it was drunk by us
á gwêdì it was written by you sing., *á gwêtì* it was written by you, pl.
á lédè it was seen by him, *á létè* it was seen by them.
[The verbs following in their intonation the rule demonstrated here, are in the majority; but besides them some examples have been written down by me which deviate in their tones:
á chwộlà he was called by me, *á lwộgà* it was washed by me,
á nḍdá it was cut by me, *á lìná* it was heard by me,
á nágá it was killed by me.
But these are possibly misunderstandings.]

[77. Most foreigners have considerable difficulties in distinguishing the active voice from the passive, the difference between both lying in most cases solely in the intonation. Misunderstandings are easily possible, where the imperfect (active) has a high tone, as *yótọ̀* to find. — The natives generally prefer to speak in the passive voice; therefore the foreigner can best avoid misunderstandings by using the passive voice as much as possible and by supposing that what a native tells him, to be passive, and not active.

The Verb

The chief characteristics of the passive have been given above; the following examples may serve to illustrate the difference in sounds and intonation between active and passive: **177a**

    yá gɔ̀chà jal an I beat this man
    yá góch yì jal an I was beaten by this man
    yá gɔ̀chà yín I beat you
    yá góchè yín I was beaten by you
    yá chàmà ṅàtè I cheated somebody
    yá chăm yì ṅàtè I was cheated by somebody
    á chàmà yán he cheated me
    á chámè yán he was cheated by me
    yá chàmì ɛ́n I cheated him
yá chámè ɛ́n or *yì ɛ́n* I was cheated by him
    á chwɔ̀là ṅal he called the child
    á chwól yì ṅal he was called by the child.

Doubling of a Verb.

In order to intensify the meaning of a verb, it can be doubled; examples for this have been given in 75; a particular kind of doubling a verb is this: the verb is pronounced twice, the first being high toned on its first syllable, the second being low toned on both syllables: **178.**

    yá chámɔ̀ chàmɔ̀ I shall surely eat;
    yí nágà nàgɔ̀ I shall surely kill you;
    yí chámè chàmɔ̀ you will by all means be eaten.

Different tones has: *á dòyì dóyɔ́* it increased gradually, by and by. Mark the long vowel in the second verb.

Change of Sounds in Verbs.

Many verbs undergo certain changes of sounds in their conjugation, these have not been treated in the preceding pages. **179.**

The changes may be classified thus:
    a) changes in the second consonant.
    b) changes in the stem-vowel.
    c) changes in the semivowel preceding the stem-vowel.

a) Changes in the second consonant.

The second consonant, if mute, may change in the perfect, passive and verbal noun. Not all mute consonants change, and in some the form with a changed consonant is employed besides the unchanged form, both having exactly the same meaning. There is no rule to show when the second consonant does change, and when not. **180.**

181.

A List of Verbs in their different Forms.

English	Present	Perfect	Future	Passive	Imperative	Verbal Noun	Noun Agent
beat tell lies	e fĕdè	fĕt, fyĕt	ú fĕdè	—	yi ky fĕt	fyĕt, fyen an	nān e fĕdè nate fyet
hoe, till hoe the field	yá fŏdè ė fŏdè kyet	yá fŏt ė fŏtà k.	ú fŏdè ú fŏtà k. ú fŏdè k.	fwŏt	fŏt, fŏdèn fŏt k.	fŭddè fŭon k.	nān e fŭŏt
build build a house	fŭrè fŭrè fwodè	fŭr fŭrà f.	ú fŭrè ú fŭrè f.	fŭr	fŭr, furun fŭr f.	fŭr	nān e fŭrø nate fŭr
write write a book	gĕrè gĕrè vøt	gĕr gĕra vøt	ú gĕrè ú gĕrè vøt	gĕr, gyĕr gĕr vøt	ger, gerun	gyer, gyer an	nān e gĕrè nate gyer
work	gwĕdè gwĕdè waŋø	gwĕt gwĕdà w.	ú gwĕdè ú gwĕdè w.	gwĕt	gwøt, gwĕdèn gwĕdi v. gwĕdu v.	gwøt gwĕdé v.	nān e gwĕdè nate gwøt
go	gĕgè	gĕk	ú gĕgè	gwŏk	gŏk, gwŏk gŏgun	gwŏk gwŏŋi àn	nān e gĕgè nate gwŏk
speak speak a word	kĕdè kĕdmè kwŏp	kĕt, kĕt kŏp kømà k.	ú kĕt ú kĕdè ú kømø k.	—	kĕt, kĕdèn kŏp, kŏbàn	kĕdè, keŋ àn kwŏp, kwŏm àn	nān e kĕdè nate kĕdè nate kwŏp
hear hear a talk	lĭnè lĭnè kwŏf	lĭn lĭnà k. lĭni k.	ú lĭnè ú lĭnè k.	lĭn lĭni k.	lĭn, lĭnùn	lĭnè	nān e lĭne nate lĭni
see see a bird	lĭt̀, lĭdè lĭt̀ vùnø	lĭt, lĭt̀ lĕdà v.	ú lĭt ú lĭt̀ v.	lĕt	lĕt, lĕtun leti v. letu v.	lĭt̀, lĕn àn	nān e lĭt̀ nate lĭt̀
wash wash a cloth	tøgè tøgè lau	tøgi luokì lau	ú tøgè ú tøgè l.	lwŏk	lwŏk tøgùn lwŏk l.	lwøk lwøŋi an	nān e tøge nate lwøk
drink drink water	mødè mødè pi	mǿt mødì pi mødà pi	ú mødè ú mødè pi	mǿt (not mǿt!)	mǿt, mødùn mødi pi mødu pi	mǿt	nān e mødè nate mǿt
give give money	tŏk, mŭjø tŏk nyet	tŏk tŏkà n. tŏk n.	ú tŏk ú mŭjø ú mŭjø n.	tŏk, mŭch	mŭch, tŏk, muy n., køt n.: køtu n.	tŏk, mŭjø mŭn àn	nān e mŭjø nate mŭch

The Verb

Continued.

English	Present	Perfect	Future	Passive	Imperative	Verbal Noun	Noun Agent
kill, kill a sheep	nẹgọ̀, nẹgọ̀ dyẹ̀l	nẹ̀kị̀, nẹ̀kị̀ d., nẹ̀kị d.	ú nẹ̀kị̀, ú nẹ̀kị̀ d.	nẹ̀k	nẹ̀k, nạ̈gụ̈n, nẹ̀k d. nạ̈gụ d	nẹ̀k, nẹ̈n ạ̈n	nān e nẹ̀ gẹ̀, nate nẹ̀k
sleep	nẹ̈nọ̀	nẹ̈n	ú nẹ̣ni	—	nẹ̣ni, nẹ̈nụn	nẹ̈nọ̀	nān nẹ̈n
laugh	nị̈tẹ̀	nị̈tị̀	ú nị̈tị̀	—	nị̈tị́, nị̈tạ̈n	nị̈tẹ̀, nyẹ̀tọ̀ nyẹ̀r ạ̈n	nān a nị̈tị̀
hew	niudẹ̀ riudẹ̀ yat	niut niudi y. riọta y.	ú niudị̀ ú niudẹ̀ y.	nọ̀t, nịọ̀l	niudi, riudụn rioti y. rioṭu y.	nọ̀t rion an	nān e riudọ̀ nate rị̀ọt
eat, eat dura	chạ̀mọ̀ chạ̀mẹ̀ byẹ̀l	chạ̀m chạ̀mi b. chạ̀mụ̀ b.	ú chạ̀mọ̀ ú chạ̀mẹ̀ b.	chạ̄me	chạ̀m chạ̀mun chạ̀mi b. chạ̄mu b.	chạ̀m	nān a chạ̀mẹ̀ nate chạ̀m
call, call a child	chuọ̀tẹ̀ chuọ̀tẹ̀ ń.	chuọ̀ṭị̀ chuọ̀tị̀ ń. chuọ̀ḷà ń.	ú chuōḷị̀ ń.	chwōl	chuọ̀tị̀ chuọ̀tun	chuọ̀t	nān e chuọ̀ḷẹ̀ nate chuọ̀t
run	rt̀nị̀ọ̀	rẹ̀n	ú rẹ̀nị̀	—	rẹ̣nị̀, rẹ̣nạ̈n	rẹ̣nọ̀	nān a rẹ̣nị̀
buy	nẹ̀awọ̀	nị̀ạ̀u	ú nẹ̀awọ̀	nị̀ạ̀u	nẹ̀au nẹ̀awun	nị̀ạ̀u	nān e nị̀ạ̀u
bring, carry, bring a tree	tẹ̀dẹ̀ tẹ̀dẹ̀ yat	tẹt tẹra y.	ú tẹ̀dẹ̀ ú tẹ̀dẹ̀ y.	tẹ̀r, tyẹ̀r	takị, tẹ̀r, tẹ̣rụ	tẹ̀r	nān e tẹ̀dẹ̀ nate tẹ̀r
play	tugẹ̀	tak	ú tak	—	takị	tugọ̀, tụ̈n ạ̈n	nān e tak
search, search a cow	yabọ̀, yabẹ̀ dẹari	yap yafa d.	ú yabọ̀ ú yabẹ̀ d.	yaf	yaf, yạ̈bạ̈n yaf d.	yabọ̀, yạ̈m ạ̈n	nān e yabọ̀
sweep, sweep a house	yẹ̀jị̀ yẹ̀jọ̀ vọt	yẹ̀ch yẹ̀chạ̀ vọt	ú yẹ̀jị̀ ú yẹ̀jị̀ vọt	yẹ̀ch	yẹ̀ch, yẹ̀jụn yẹy vọt	yẹ̀ch, yẹ̀t ạ̈n	nān e yẹ̀jị̀ nate yẹ̀ch
find, find a thing	yọ̀tị̀, yit̀ẹ̀ yọ̀tà gin	yị̀tị̀ (g.) yọ̀tà g.	ú yọ̀tọ̀ (g.) ú yị̀tị̀ (g.)	yọ̀t, yuọ̀t		yōdẹ̀ yọ̈n ạ̈n	nān e yẹ̀jị̀ nate yẹ̀ch nān e yitẹ̀

Present		Imperfect	Passive	Verbal Noun
t, d > l				
baṭǫ	to throw	á bala gin	bâl	
budǫ	to roast	á but, or á bul	bûl	
chudǫ	to compensate	á chût, á chôl		chŏlǫ̀
chwǫtǫ	to call	á chwǫta,[1] á chwǫla	chwǫ́l	
dǭdǫ	to brew	á dwǫla	dwǫ́l	dwǫ́l
gǭdǫ	to scratch	á gǭla	gól	gǫ́l
kạdǫ	to bring	á kạdi	kệl	
kudǫ	to pull out	á kǫla	kǫ́l	kǫ́l
kwātǫ	to steal	kwati, kwāla	kwâl	
kwǫtǫ	to drive	kwǫti, kwǫla	kǫ́l	kǫ́l
lẹdǫ	to shave		lyêl	
ṅwatǫ	to touch	ṅwati	ṅwâl	ṅwạ̀tǫ̀
ṅādǫ	to cut	ṅàt	ṅâl	
ṅǭdǫ	to cut	ṅǫ̀t, ṅǫ̀l	ṅǫ́l	
wōdǫ	to pound	wólà	wól	wól
yiẹdǫ	to save		yiệl	
t, d > r				
tyɛtǫ	to carry	tyɛti, tɛ̄ra	têr	
t, d > n				
yɛtǫ	to curse	yɛni		yɛ̀n
ṭ ḍ > l				
ṭādǫ	to cook	ṭāla	ṭâl	
widǫ	to change	wēla	wêl	wil
ṭ ḍ > r				
ṅẹ̄tǫ	to laugh	ṅɛ̀ti		ṅyɛ̀rǫ̀
yiẹdǫ	to cut	yiɛti, yiɛra	ylɛ̂t ylêr	
ṭ ḍ > ṇ				
ṅwǫdǫ	to be weak	ṅwǫ̀ṇ		
b > m				
l̤ibǫ	to be cold	l̤imi		l̤ibǫ̀
kǭbǫ	to speak	kǫ̀mà kwǫ́p	kwǫ́p	kwǫ́p

182. In these words the forms with a mute consonant are doubtlessly primitive; from them the present tense was formed by suffixing *ǫ*, so the primitive mute consonant is preserved here in the present; in a later period the mutes were, by different influences, transformed; the primary cause of their transformation was perhaps their position at the end of a word. See note in 46 concerning *t ṭ > r*.

In frequent cases, however, the consonant was also changed in the present tense; but in these cases the unchanged form of the present also exists beside the changed one; thus many verbs have two present (and perfect) tenses.

---

[1] In the forms ending in *a* a noun as object is to follow.

The Verb

different in their form, but uniform in their meaning; sometimes not only the second consonants, but also the vowels of two forms differ, the vowel of the changed form always being identical with that form of the primitive verb which has the changed consonant, so that one can say: *from the changed form of the primitive verb a new verb has been formed;* an example will illustrate what is meant: Present *chwǫtǫ* to call, past *chwǫ̀t, chwǭtị,* or *chwǫ̀l,* passive *chwǫ́l;* now from the form *chwǫl* the present of a new verb is formed: *chwǭlǫ* to call, past *chwǫ̀l,* passive *chwǫ́l.*

183. Double forms in which the second verb is derived from a tense or mood of the first:

{ *chudǫ* to compensate	perf. *chût* and *chól*	n. *chól*
{ *chōlǫ* to compensate	perf. *chól*	n. *chôlǫ̀*
{ *dōdǫ* to brew	perf. *dwǫla*	pe. *dwǫ́l* n. *dwǫ́l*
{ *dwǫlǫ* to brew	perf. *dwǫla*	pe. *dwǫ́l*
{ *gę̄rǫ* to build	perf. *gɛra*	pe. *gyêr*
{ *gyę̄rǫ* to build	perf. *gyɛra*	pe. *gyêr*
{ *kạdǫ* to bring	perf. *kạdị, kạl*	pe. *kɛl*
{ *kạlǫ* to bring	perf. *kạl*	
{ *kudǫ* to pull out	perf. *kǫla*	pe. *kǫ́l* n. *kǫ́l*
{ *kǭlǫ* to pull out	perf. *kǫla*	
{ *kwātǫ* to steal	perf. *kwati, kwāla*	pe. *kwál*
{ *kwālǫ* to steal	perf. *kwāla*	
{ *lędǫ* to shave		pe. *lyêl*
{ *lyęlǫ* to shave		
{ *ṅwątǫ* to touch	perf. *ṅwątị*	pe. *ṅwál*
{ *ṅwālǫ* to touch	perf. *ṅwāla*	
{ *ṅādǫ* to butcher	perf. *ṅàt*	pe. *ṅàt, ṅál*
{ *ṅālǫ* to butcher	perf. *ṅàl*	
{ *wōdǫ* to pound	perf. *wǒlà*	pe. *wól*
{ *wōlǫ* to pound	perf. *wǒlà.*	

184. Some verbs have double forms in which the derivation of the second verb from a tense or mode of the first is not visible, both verbs retaining their second consonant unchanged through all tenses and modes. The meanings of the two verbs are in most cases identical, but in some there is a difference.

    dęgǫ and *dạṅǫ* to move into
    lugǫ and *lūṅǫ* to turn
  dwatǫ and *dwɛrǫ* to search, want, wish
        gwidǫ lɛp to "wink" with the lips, and *gwę̄lǫ* to wink
    fudǫ and *fuṅǫ* to pull out

>   kō̰dǫ and kuṇǫ to blow up a fire
>   fō̰dǫ to pass and fōṇǫ to pass
>   ṅyẹ̰dǫ to milk and ṅẹ̄rǫ to let the milk down.

[85.] Those verbs which are virtually adjectives (see 150), have some peculiarities. Example: ràch "(to be) bad"; this form corresponds in its sounds and its meaning to the Perfect of the common verbs: it ends in a mute consonant, and it designates a state, not an action; this form as such does not change the final consonant; a regular present may be formed from it (though not from all verbs of this kind): rājǫ "to become bad, act badly"; but besides this regular form of the present it has a second, in which the second consonant turns into the corresponding nasal one: rẹ̄ṅǫ "to become bad, act badly".

>   nǫk little   nōṅǫ to become little or few
>   tẹ̰k hard   tẹ̄gǫ and tẹ̄ṅǫ to become hard, feel hard
>   dǭch good   dō̰jǫ and dō̰ṅǫ to become good, act well
>   kẹ̰ch strong   kẹ̄ṅǫ to become or be strong
>   ràch bad   rājǫ and rẹ̄ṅǫ to become or be bad, act badly.

In one case, however, such a word has the nasal consonant in the adjective (perfect) form already:

>   duǫṅ big   dō̰ṅǫ to become big, grow up; here a form with a mute consonant does not exist.

b) Changes in the Stem-vowel.

[86.] Here the very same process as in the change of consonants is to be observed. Present $a > e$ in perf. and passive.

>   ka̰dǫ to bring   pe. kẹ̰l
>   ba̰gǫ to boil   pe. bẹ̰k
>   fa̰dǫ to be tired   pe. fẹ̰t
>   fa̰nǫ to ride   perf. a fa̰ni and a fẹ̰ni
>   ka̰bǫ to take by force   n. kẹ̰pǫ
>   ka̰dǫ to twist   perf. kẹ̰t, kẹ̰l
>   ka̰gǫ to ache   n. kẹ̰k
>   ka̰gǫ to plant   perf. kẹ̰k
>   na̰gǫ to kill   perf. nẹ̰k
>   bājǫ and ba̰jǫ to tie   pe. bẹ̰ch and bẹ̰ch
>   dẹ̄ṅǫ and da̰gǫ to scatter perf. dẹṅ.

Present $a > a$ in imp. and passive.

>   cha̰bǫ to mix   perf. chapa   pe. châp and chảp
>   fa̰gǫ to be sharp   perf. fâk
>   ka̰bǫ to take by force perf. kapa   pe. kâp   n. kẹ̰pả

	lạgọ to inherit	perf. *laka*	pe. *lák*	n. *lák.*
Present *a* ⟩ *ę* in perf. and passive.				
	bājọ to tie	perf. *bęcha*	pe. *bęch*	
	gwāṅọ to tie	perf. *gwęṅ*		
	gwārọ to snatch			n. *gwarọ*
Present *i* ⟩ *e*:				and *gwęrọ*
	wiḍọ to change	perf. *wēla.*		
Changes between *ọ, o* and *u.*				
	tugọ to crush			n. *tọ̑k*
	lūgọ to turn	perf. *lọgi*		n. *lọ̑k*
	kudọ to pull out	perf. *kọla*	pe. *kọ́l*	n. *kọ́l*
	nōṅọ to become little,	*nọk* little		
	kŏdọ̀ to fasten			n. *kŭdọ̀*
	chudọ to compensate	perf. *chól.*		

187. Double forms with different vowels; the second verb is derived from a tense or mood of the first:

	chudọ to compensate	perf. *chól*		
	chōlọ to compensate	perf. *chól*		
	fādọ to be tired	perf. *fęt*		
	fędọ and *fidọ* to be tired	perf. *fęt*		
	fēdọ to raise			n. *fidọ̀*
	fidọ to raise			
	kābọ to take by force			n. *kępọ̀*
	kępọ to take by force			
	kādọ to twist	perf. *kęt*		
	kędọ to twist			
	kāgọ to plant		pe. *kęk*	
	kęgọ to plant			
	kudọ to pull out	perf. *kọla*	pe. *kọ́l*	
	kọ̄lọ to pull out.			

188. Double forms in which the derivation of the second verb from a tense or mode of the first is not visible, both verbs retaining their vowel unchanged through all tenses and modes. The meaning of the two verbs is in most cases identical, but in some there is a difference:

dāgọ and *dēgọ* to move into   *dwoṅọ, dwęṅọ* and *dwuṅọ* } to evaporate
dwatọ and *dwotọ* to want, wish
gọrọ and *gurọ* to tattoo   *gwaṅọ* and *gwoṅọ* to scratch
kādọ and *kędọ* to go   *mōtọ* and *mitọ* to hold fast
ṅājọ and *ṅējọ* to know, recognise *ṅādọ* to butcher, *ṅudọ* to cut

pano and peko to fill   kwālǫ and kwgtǫ to steal.

c) Changes in the Semivowel.[1]

189. The Semivowels *w* or *y* are inserted in the stem in order to form certain tenses or modes of the verb.

dǭdǫ to brew beer	perf. dwǫla	pe. dwǫ́l	n. dwǫ́l
fōjǫ to make butter		pe. fwóch	
gāgǫ to work		pe. gwôk	
gǭṅǫ to scratch	perf. gwǫ́ṅa		n. gwǫ́ṅǫ̀
kǭgǫ to stick		pe. kwôk	
kǭtǫ to drive	perf. kwǫti, kwǫla	pe. kôl, kwôl	
kǭbǫ to speak		pe. kwǫ́p	n. kwǫ̀p
lǭdǫ to wade	perf. lwǫ́t	pe. lwǫ́t	
lǭgǫ to wash [forth	perf. lǫgi, lwǫka	pe. lwǫ́k	
ṅǫ̀dǫ̀ to bear, bring	perf. ṅòt, ṅwǫ́l	pe. ṅwǫ́l	n. ṅwǫ̀dǫ̀
ṅǭmǫ to marry	perf. ṅǭmi	pe. ṅwǫ́m	
ṅotǫ to spit	perf. ṅwoti		
rǭmǫ to fetch water	perf. rwǫma	pe. rwǫ́m	n. rwǫ́m
tōdǫ to tell lies	perf. twota	pe. twót	n. twót
yǭbǫ to bewitch	perf. ywǫba	pe. ywǫ̀p	
bǭkǫ to fear,	bwǭkǫ to make one fear, to frighten		
dǫ̀dǫ̀ to suck,	dwǫ́dǫ̀ to suckle a child		
dǭgǫ to go back	dwǭgǫ to come back		
fęchǫ to ask	perf. fęcha	pe. fyêch	
fędǫ to lie	perf. fęt	pe. fyệt	n. fyệt
fęmǫ to gainsay			n. fyệm
gḗrǫ to build	perf. gḗra	pe. gyệr	
gḗtǫ to sacrifice	perf. gyęta	pe. giệt	
kḗrǫ to dig out		pe. kyệr	
lędǫ to shave	perf. lęl	pe. lyệl	
męnǫ to twist	perf. myęn	pe. myện	
ṅḗtǫ to laugh [guest	perf. ṅḗti		n. ṅyệrǫ̀
rejǫ to receive a	perf. recha	pe. ryệch	
tḗnǫ to strain beer	perf. tyęṅa	pe. tyệṅ	n. tyệṅ
tędǫ to bewitch	perf. tyệt		n. tyệt
ṅḗrǫ to milk	ṅyḗdǫ to let the milk down.		

190. In these examples the infixed semivowel has a function analogous to that of the changing of the second consonant and of the vowel: it is a means of forming tenses and modes of the verb; in most cases the passive, and in some also the imperfect and infinitive differ from the present by the infixed semi-

---

[1] Only the semivowels standing between the first consonant and the stem-vowel are meant here, not those beginning a word.

The Verb

vowel. In a few examples — *bu̱ō̱ko̱, dwō̱do̱, dwō̱go̱, ṅyē̱do̱,* — a *causative* form (or a form of similar meaning) is formed from the common form by infixing a semivowel.

Double forms, the one with a semivowel, the other without it; the one verb is derived from a tense or mood of the other:

191.

{ dō̱do̱ to brew beer	perf. *dwo̱la*	pe. *dwo̱l*	n. *dwo̱l*
{ dwō̱lo̱ to brew beer	perf. *dwo̱la*		
{ jō̱jo̱ to make butter		pe. *fwôch*	
{ fwō̱jo̱ to make butter		pe. *fwôch*	
{ gō̱ṅo̱ to scratch	perf. *gwō̱ṅa*		n. *gwô̱ṅo̱*
{ gwō̱ṅo̱ to scratch			
{ kō̱ṅo̱ to help	perf. *kwō̱ṅa*		
{ kwō̱ṅo̱ to help			
{ kō̱to̱ to drive	perf. *kwo̱ti̱, kwo̱la*		
{ kwō̱to̱ to drive			
{ lō̱do̱ to wade	perf. *lwo̱t*	pe. *lwo̱t*	n. *lwo̱to̱*
{ lwo̱to̱ to wade			
lō̱go̱ to wash	perf. *lwo̱ka*	pe. *lwo̱k*	
lwō̱go̱ to wash	perf. *lwo̱ka*		
{ ṅō̱do̱ to bear, bring forth	perf. *ṅo̱t, ṅwo̱l*	pe. *ṅwo̱l*	n. *ṅwo̱do̱*
{ ṅwō̱lo̱ to bear, bring forth	perf. *ṅwo̱l*		
{ ṅō̱mo̱ to marry	perf. *ṅō̱mi̱*	pe. *ṅwô̱m*	
{ ṅwō̱mo̱ to marry	perf. *ṅwō̱mi̱*	pe. *ṅwô̱m*	
⸺{ ṅo̱to̱ to spit	perf. *ṅo̱ta, ṅwo̱ta*	pe. *ṅôl*	
{ ṅwo̱to̱ to spit	perf. *ṅwo̱ta*	pe. *ṅôl*	
{ yō̱bo̱ to bewitch	perf. *ywo̱ba*	pe. *ywô̱p*	
{ ywo̱bo̱ to bewitch	perf. *ywo̱ba*	pe. *ywô̱p*	
{ fē̱cho̱ to ask	perf. *fe̱cha*	pe. *fyêch*	
{ fye̱cho̱ to ask	perf. *fye̱cha*	pe. *fyêch*	
{ fe̱do̱ to lie	perf. *fêt, fyêt*		n. *fye̱t*
{ fyē̱do̱ to lie	perf. *fyêt*		n. *fye̱t*
{ gē̱to̱ to sacrifice	perf. *gye̱ta*		n. *gíê̱t*
{ gie̱do̱ to sacrifice			
{ kē̱ro̱ to dig out		pe. *kyêr*	
{ kyē̱ro̱ to dig out	perf. *kye̱ra*	pe. *kyêr*	n. *kye̱ro̱*
mē̱no̱ to twist	perf. *mye̱n*	pe. *myê̱n*	
myē̱no̱ to twist			
{ re̱jo̱ to receive a guest	perf. *re̱cha*	pe. *ryêch*	
{ rye̱jo̱ to receive a guest	perf. *rye̱cha*		

{ fẹ̄dọ to bewitch   perf. tyêt̟   pe. tyệt̟
{ tyẹ̄dọ to bewitch

192. Double forms in which the derivation of the second verb from a tense or mode of the first is not visible, both verbs retaining their vowel or semivowel unchanged through all tenses or modes. The meanings of the two verbs are identical:

 bọ̄dọ and bwọ̄dọ to cast iron
 kọ̄dọ and kwọ̄dọ to blow up fire
 fẹ̄jọ and fyẹjọ to pull.

193. The function of the inserted semivowels *w* and *y* are evident from the preceding examples: they serve in forming certain tenses or modes of the verb, and from these modes and tenses new verbs are formed, just as in the changing of the last consonant.

In by far the most cases the infixed *w* (which must originally have been *u*, see 22) forms the Passive and the Perfect of the Verb.

[It is remarkable that in Hamitic languages *u* or *o* have the same function:

 Haussa: *fashe* to break   *fasu* broken
            būde to open   *būdu* open
            buga to beat   *bugu* beaten
 Ful Fulde: *omo nana* he hears   *omo nanọ* he is heard
            omo wara he kills   *omo warọ* he is killed.

In both these languages the forms in *u*, *ọ* correspond to the Shilluk Passive as well as to the Perfect, as they express an accomplished state, as opposed to action.]

It is evident that this last process was chiefly liable to lead to many confusions in the use of *w* and *y* (*and the same holds good for the changing of the second consonant*); once the second verbs, derived from the imperfect or passive of the first verb, came into use, it was scarcely avoidable that the semivowel should not enter the present or any other tense of the first verb, where it did not belong; and again it was easily liable to be dropped where it ought to stand, viz. in a form of the second verb; this was the more possible, as in almost all cases the meanings of the two verbs are absolutely identical. And indeed the natives often do confuse the two verbs, using the one for the other, when asked for the different forms of a verb.

How the semivowel was infixed into the verb, is not clear (but see 25); as they do not always have the same function, the way on which they got into the word may also have been different.

Now it is remarkable, that in all cases, where the *passive or past are formed by infixing w or y* (active present *kọ̄bọ* passive *kwọ́p*, active present *fẹ̄chọ* passive *fyĕch*),[1] *w* occurs exclusively before *ǫ*, and *y* exclusively before *ę*, so that we have only these combinations: *wǫ* and *yę*. The combinations *wa, wę, we, wi, ya, ye* with preceding consonant[2] do also occur frequently, but never in the said function, viz. where the Passive or Perfect are formed from the Present by infixing a *w* or *y*. This leads to the conclusion that there are two different groups of semivowels which have entered the stem, probably at different periods and for different purposes. The second group has in by far the most cases retained the original vowel before *w* and *y*. But the *first group* has in *all cases the same vowel*: *ǫ* after *w* and *ę* after *y*; this can in my opinion be explained only by assimilation; it is not at all probable that here the original vowels were solely *ǫ* and *ę*, and that always before *ǫ* a *w* was infixed and before *ę* a *y*. I suppose that here originally only *one* semivowel was infixed, viz. *w*, and this *w* partly assimilated the following vowel to itself and partly itself was assimilated to the vowel, in this way: *wa* ⟩ *wǫ, wǫ* ⟩ *wǫ, wo* ⟩ *wǫ; wę* ⟩ *yę, we* ⟩ *yę*. If verbs with the stem-vowel *i* or *u* infixed a *w* in order to form the passive or perfect, this *w* must have been assimilated to the following vowel *i* and *u*, so that *wi* ⟩ *yi* ⟩ *i*, and *wu* ⟩ *u*.

Auxiliary Verbs.

da "to have".

ę dà ṅyęṅ he has money; *yá dà jwǫk* I have sickness: I am sick.

"To be".

"To be" is rendered by different words, but in most cases it is not to be translated at all; all adjectives are treated as verbs, and therefore are not connected with "is": "you are great" is rendered *yi dugṅ*. If the predicate is a noun, and the subject is a pronoun, generally the subject is put before the pronoun without a copula: *yá rit* I am king; *yánd rit* I am king; or the demonstrative *á* is employed: *ęn á rit* he is king.

But frequently the particle *bá (fá)* or its emphatic form *bánę, bánęn* is placed between subject and the predicative noun:

ya ba rit I am king; *jal ęni ba rit* this man is king; *fanę rit* (this one) he is king.

I suppose *bá* does not originally mean "to be", but is the negative particle "not", and the sentences in which it is employed, are properly questions: Am I not king? Is this man not king? The negro generally likes to express an assertion by a negative question.

If the predicate is an adverb, *yá, yęṅà* ("to be") or *bēdǫ* ("to stay, remain") are used; *ę ya kęṅ* where is he? *gę yęṅa mal* they are above; *yá bēdǫ wǫt* I am, stay, in the house. Sometimes *bēdǫ* is also employed, when the predicate is a noun.

194.

195.

---
[1] This group is called 'first group' in the following.
[2] This group is called 'second group' in the following.

kámá and chámá "to be going to, to wish, want"; they are used only in the past form.

e kama (also kǫmǫ) bḛnǫ̀ he is going to come, he says he will come, wants to come.

e chama fạdǫ he is near falling, going to fall; chama is often shortened into cha.

In a similar sense dwata "to wish" is often employed.

"Can"

may be expressed by yēyǫ: ya ba yēi bḛn I can (could) not come; but its negation is generally expressed by bu kḛn "there is not a place" (an opportunity): bu kḛn à bḛnd "there was no place for me to come": I could not come.

96. The Negation of the Verb.

1. bạ, fạ not;
2. nụtí not yet, not; hardly a distinction is made between the two; both of them negate the indicative of the verb; a fa kḙṭ, a nụti kḙṭ he did not go.
3. fáṭ, fáṭe negates a single word: faṭe yan not I; faṭe riṭ it is not the king; but it may also negate the verb "to be": faṭe yan riṭ I am not the king; faṭe ki wǫṭ he is not in the house; fa jal maduǫ̇n he is a great man; faṭ ki jal maduǫ̇n he is not a great man.
4. bu, buṇǫ, to have not, to be not;
5. bógǫ̀n, bógìn there is not; ṅygn bógǫ̀n kḭ yà "money is not with me": I have no money; yá bú ṅygn I have no money.
6. ṭǫ̀k to be absent; ńal ṭǫ̀k the boy is not here.
7. kú is prohibitive: kú kḙṭ, yí kú kḙṭ do not go! kú wḕr, also: yi ku wḕr do not be angry! The personal pronoun may also be suffixed: ku kwǫti do not steal! Plural: wú kú kḙṭ do not go! You must not go! kú bì he shall not come.

Sometimes kú is employed where we do not see a prohibition: wá kú kḙṭ shall we not go? But also: wá fa kḙṭ? ńan kú ṅwǫ́l kḭ tǫ́n gyḛnù, nạ̀gà nạ̀gù the man who does not lay a hen-egg, I shall surely kill.

ADVERBS.

97. Most adverbs are originally nouns or verbs.

Adverbs of Place.

The adverbs which are mostly employed are kḙn and kūn; both are nouns and mean "place". Their primitive forms are kḙch, kach and kū, both have affixed a demonstrative n, kḙch + n 〉 kḙn, kū + n 〉 kūn according to 40. They may as adverbs have different meanings: 1. of place: this place, that is: here; 2. then interrogative: where? On the different tones of these two meanings

Adverbs

see 205 aa. "Where is he" is in Shi. literally: "is he here?" *kẹń* does not really mean "where", but simply "this place".

Bi kẹń come here.
kẹti wọk ki kẹń go out from here.
kā "place": there.
ẹ bẹ̄da kā he is there;
a lẹ̄ṭe yán kā he was seen by me there.
mal "heaven", "the upper place", serves for "above, ahead":
a rẹña mal he ran upward, upstairs, ahead.
kundọ (from *kū* place) direction: there.
chuñi kundọ stop there.
chām left hand, *kẹch* right hand, *ánàn* here, *chín̄ẹ* there, yonder, *chán* behind, *lọñ* this side.

Adverbs of Time.

198. Here again *kẹń* "this place" takes the first place, the notion of "time" having its origin in "place"; *kẹń a bi* when he came; *kān* "this time" from *kāke* time: while: *chuñi kan chām wa* stay while we eat; *tịn* soon, at once; *ánàn, ánàn ánàn* presently, at once, this very moment; *chọn* formerly; *de chañ tịn* to-day; *dụki* to morrow; *awa* yesterday; *awar awa* the day before yesterday; *ki chañ* daily; *ki de chañ* at daytime; *ki war* at night.

Kẹń á bi when did he come? *ẹn awẹ̄n á ñwọ́lè yin* when were you born? *wọ́ nẹ̄nà yọ́ yẹti chañ adẹk, ká è bẹ̄n* we were on the road reached three days, then he came: when we had been on the way three days, he came; *ka duóki wọn, chuñẹ a yiga mámẹ̄t* when we told him that, he became glad; *ká lẹ̄t́ẹ́ wọn, ka é ñẹ̀t́ọ̀* when he saw us, he laughed; *ka liñ wa mẹn an, ka chuñe wọn yiga mámẹ̄t* when we heard that, we became glad.

Adverbs of Manner.

199. *ne, neya* thus; *kíndù* just so; *ádi* how? *tyau* also; *chẹt* just, very, surely; *shārẹ* very; *kẹ̄tè, dkyẹl* alone. Much used is the adverb *kine* thus: it always introduces the direct speech; it does not only follow the verbs which express speaking, but frequently also those expressing "to mean, think, wish, ask":

rịt e ko kine, kẹt the king said thus: go!
e fẹchọ kine, ágọ̀n ẹn he asked: where is he?
duoki kine, e bẹ̄nọ tell him, he may come!
e dwata kine, wu kẹdọ wu ki ẹn he wants to go with you
ya dwata kine, wọ chām byẹ́l I wish that we may eat dura.

Frequently an English adverb is in Shilluk rendered by a verb, e. g.:
jwān kẹdọ hurry going, that is: go quickly;
a rūmị chámè yá it is finished was eaten by me: I have already eaten;

kęt, kān a ngti bęno kǫt go, while rain has not yet come: before it rains;
wa kędǫ chāki pach we went approached the village: we came near the village.

Adverbs of Cause and Causal Sentences.

200.   *Bu kęń a bęná yiká dě réd jwǫk* I could not come, *because* I was sick; *bu kęń didá, yika búńí wáńǫ yá* I cannot learn, because I have no book; *ya bugin māga rējǫ, yika búńí abdt kì yá* I cannot catch fish, because I have no hook; *tyęń Nwār chúńé gęn rājǫ kí wǫn, ki yika kǫla dǒ gęn* the Nuer-people hate us, because we (I) have taken away their cattle; *byęl wǫn rechǫ, ki yika bụni kǫt ki rei gęn* our dura is bad, because it did not rain on it; *ba yel gwǫk tin, máré* (or *mdé*) *dà jwǫk* he cannot work to-day, because he is sick; *ba kwópè ręn, mdé bǫkǫ* he does not say it, because he is afraid; *yá bụ dǫró, bęnęn á ddlé yán yi gwǫk* I have no adze, therefore it is impossible for me to work; *tyęlá lęt, bęnęn à bà kędá* my foot was sore, therefore I did not go.

Sometimes a causal relation is expressed without a causal particle: *yá fá chigi chātǫ kęté, yá fędǫ̀* I shall walk no more, for I am tired; *wa kęti wǫt, fen a yígà mōdǫ* we went home, because it grew dark.

Conditional Sentences.

201.   *Kęn chwǫlę yin, yi ku kęt* if he calls you, do not go; *kęń yik ya u lēti kí ńu, ú ńękè yán* if I see a lion, I shall kill him; *ú yǫ́k yú bí, yú u tǫ̀tá ńyęń* if you come, I shall give you money; *u yik yí fá gùgǫ̀ yi ú fwóté yán* if you do not work, I shall beat you; *ká yik u fyęchè wǫn, wǫ́ kwǫ́ńè ęn* if we ask him, he will help us.

The Condition in the unreal case is expressed by *ré: ká lǫgǫ́ ę yá mánút, wǫ́ ré kwǫ́ńè ęn* if he *were* here, he *would* help us; *ká lǫgí yá dà gìn chám, yí ré tǫ̀tá* if I had food, I should give you; *ka lǫgǫ fen dé yá mádǫ̌ch, wǫ́ ré dè bęnǫ̀* if the weather had been fine, we should have come.

Intentional Sentences.

202.   *Yá kęti wǫk bę yáf kí dǫga* I went into the bush, in order to search my cattle; *wǫ kǫlǫ dǫ̀ wǫ́n gę mūjè wǫ́n bwǫ́ń, kífá kine wǫ́ tǫ̀tí byęl* we gave our cattle to the strangers, in order to get dura; *jwáńí ręnǫ, kípá yí kú chwǫ́ń* run quickly, lest you be late!

Interrogative Sentences.

203.   In a question the position of words is the same as in an assertion. To designate a sentence as a question, either interrogative adverbs are employed, or a change of tone takes place. Those cases are difficult particularly, in which an adverb may have a positive meaning as well as an interrogative one, for instance *kęń* "place" may mean "here", and "where". Here the distinction can be made by the tone only.

Prepositions 93

The most important rule is this: if the last syllable of a sentence has a high or middle tone, a low tone is added to it; this low tone expresses the question:

ḗ kwàlà byḗl he stole dura	ḗ kwàlà byêl did he steal dura?
ḗ lḗṭà kwà he saw my grandfather	ḗ lḗṭà kwâ did he see my grandfather?
gḗ lḗṭà rìṭ they saw the king	gḗ lḗṭà rîṭ did they see the king?

But frequently the question is expressed in quite a different way, by laying a high tone, and a strong stress on the word which is questioned; this is particularly the case with *kẹ́ń*:

ḗ yẹ́ń kẹ́ń where is he?	ḗ yà kẹ̀ń he is here
gḗ yẹ́ń kẹ́ń where are they	gḗ yà kẹ̀ń they are here
rìṭ yẹ́ń kẹ́ń where is the king?	rìṭ yà kẹ̀ń the king is here
á bi àwà he came yesterday	á bi àwà did he come yesterday? (the first *a* in *awa* has a very strong emphasis)
jal an ye da ṅyẹ́ń this man has money	
jal an ye da ṅyẹ́ń has this man money? (The ḗ in *ṅyẹ́ń* with very strong emphasis).	

If the sentence contains an interrogative adverb, the tone does generally not change:

yḕ dà ḍọ̀k ádì how many cows has he?
ḗ gwộ ṅọ̀ what does he do?
a fyêch kí yi ẹ́ń, kine: àgọ̀n ẹ́ń mụ̀dì he asked him: where is your friend?
á wọt mên whose house is it?
kipaṅọ à bọ̀kí why are you afraid?
ápaṅọ a kẹṭ why did he go?

In questions introduced by "shall", the subjective pronoun is suffixed and the low interrogative tone is added to the high tone of the pronoun: *kḗḍâ* shall I go? *gwḗḍḕ* shall he write?

PREPOSITIONS.

They are likewise originally nouns and verbs. 204.
Nouns:
wich head: on, upon, for, instead of:
wiy wọt on the house, wiy yaṭ on the tree, wiy rìṭ instead of the king.
bāṅ back: behind, after, besides: bāṅa after me, bāṅ wọt behind the house;
bāṅẹ besides him; kwọm back: on, upon: kwọm aḍẹ̄rọ on a donkey.
bọ̄l and ṅim face, front: in front of, before, at the head of: bọ̄l nam in front of the river; ṅim tḗrọ before the people, at the head of the people.
kẹ̀lé middle: in the midst of, amidst, among: kẹ̀lé jè amidst the people.

ńāch back: behind: ńāch jal ẹni behind this man;
būtọ side: beside: būte wọt beside the house;
yech belly: in: yẹy pi in water;
dyẹr, often shortened into di, middle: amidst, in, di nam in the water.
ṭa the base, the lower part: under, below: ṭa yaṭ under the tree.

Verbs:
wiṭọ to reach: wiṭe awa a ba bi reaching yesterday he did not come: until y...
giṭọ to reach: giṭọ ḍuki till to-morrow.

Particles which cannot traced back to nouns or verbs:
kí may have very different meanings; its original meaning is: with; ki mẹn with whom; ki tọń with a spear;
yi towards, by: a nẹk yi jal an he was killed by this man; kẹṭi yi jal duọń go to the master; yi is connected with personal pronouns as follows: ya to me, yi to you, yẹ to him, yi wọn, yi wun, yi gẹn.

Salutations.

205. Some of the most used forms of salutations are given here. A. is the villager, B. the stranger.

Instead of our knocking the door, the Shilluks, before entering a courtyard, say: yá nẹ́n I am waiting (may I come in?) A. answers: bi come! If the salutation is going on in the open place of the village, as is usual, this phrase is not said.
A. yí bi you have come?
B. yá bì I have come, or: yá nút.
A. yí kál jwọk you have brought God.
B. yí míṭi jwọk you have held fast God.
A. yí nin did you sleep (well)?
B. yá nin I slept (well).
A. yí kwai (meaning not known).
B. á, yá bì.
A. woṭọnọ nút are the little ones well (existing)?
B. Nút they are well.
A. tyẹń gól án your women (are well)?
B. Nút they are well.
A. Tẹ̄lọ bẹ̄di yau? Are the people well?
B. Nut they are. — These enquiries after the well-being of the people in the house can be extended at will, to grandparents, grandchildren, cousins etc. On leaving:
B. says: yá kẹdọ fach I am going home.
A. kẹ́t go! or: kạli jwọk go with God!

SECOND PART
FOLKLORE

1. OCCUPATIONS.

1. Housebuilding.

Tyęle wǫt kyêr, ka tęk (têk), ka lųbǫ kųl, ka lęṅ tyęl, ka mǫgǫ kǫ́ṅ tyęl wǫt, ka chwâch, maka tyęl aṅwęn, ka ḍǫgę dôl, ka gêr. Ka maka chán díbíkyęl, ka wiję lę́ù, ka kwêr dwai, ka gę ráù, ka gę męch féṅ, ká tęgùtì ṅǫ́t, ka dôl kót, ka tyęlę kyêr, ka tyęl têk, ka tęgutí kwôṅ, ká wǫ̀t mâk, ká dôl kítì. Ka dyęṅ kęt, ka tát, ka tęgutí wórò wǫ̀k. Ka wǫt tíṅ, ká lępù gúlà chấp, ka kíti, ka shę̀nę̀ twóch, ká tát, ká lům ṅâr, ká bǫ̀ḍò dwai, ka yęta mal, ka tǫ̀l mắgę́, ka lum kítì, ka e wijǫ. Ka waṅ kājǫ e dǫ̀ṅù, ka e kūnǫ kị kwêr, męn nųk waṅ kājǫ, ka waṅ kājǫ nęk, ká dyęl wékè bǫ̀ḍǫ. Ka wiy wǫt twâk, ka chęne wǫt ṅǫ́l, ka tádḍǫt (tẹde wǫt) tyéṅ, ka wǫt tǫ́r, ka mwǫ́ṅ, ka tịgǫ gwǫ́k, ka kal tát, ka jē dę́ká yeję. Ka gyēnǫ kųl, ka gū̀ch féṅ, ka jē dę́na yey wǫt.

The foundation trenches of the house are dug out, and are smoothed off. Mud is brought, and thrown into the foundation trenches; and beer is poured into the foundation trenches. Now the walls are built; after four days the door-opening is made round; then they build again, and when five days have passed, they begin to make the roof. Poles are brought, they are burnt (to make them hard), and then cut, so that they are of equal length. Roof-sticks are cut, and they are tied up in a circle, and a circular ditch (corresponding to the poles tied together) is dug, and the ends of the roof-sticks are put into it, and buried. Now the roof is constructed; grass is twisted into a rope, with which the poles are tied together. When this is done, the roof-sticks are taken away, and the roof is lifted upon the wall. The junction between the wall and the thatch-poles inserted into it is made tight with mud, the lower roof-ends are tied to the wall, and are tied together. Then grass is cut, and the craftsman[1] is sent for; he climbs on the roof, takes a rope, and binds the grass on the poles. Thus he makes the roof, till only the point of the roof is left. The proprietor of the house now brings a hoe, which is for the making of the roof-point. (When he has given it to the craftsman), the roof-point is made. Then a sheep is given to the craftsman. The surface of the roof is beaten smooth, the dripping-eaves are cut even, a door is made, the floor of the house is filled up with mud, and is made hard and even. A door is worked, the fence is constructed, and then the people move into the new house. A fowl is brought, and left on the ground (as a sacrifice), and the people move into it.

---
[1] thatch-maker.

A Second Report on Housebuilding.
By R. W. Tidrick, of Doleib Hill.

Housebuilding among the Shullas[1] is a trade which comparatively few men learn, whether it is because apprentices are discouraged from learning it, or whether they do not want to learn, or cannot learn the trade well, I do not know. A well constructed tukl is neat and of really fine appearance. Dwelling houses are usually of the same size, conical in shape, walls of mud, sometimes reinforced with poles or corn stalks. The roofs are thatched with two kinds of grass. Family class prescribes which kind may be used in thatching the house.

Every adult member of the family as a rule has a part in construction. The women cut and carry in the grass and corn stalks and bring the water for mixing the mud for the walls. The men bring in the poles for the roof, make the rope, mix and carry the mud and do the real building of the house.

The material is usually collected for some time beforehand. Grass is cut and cocked, poles are brought from the timber and by wetting and heating are brought into the proper shape for rafters. Large circular bands for bracing the rafters and tying the thatch and grass to are made of withs of long coarse grass wrapped closely with rope. The rope for their use and for tying the grass down is made from a tall grass that has a long sheath. The grass is cut and brought in, and these sheaths are stripped off and after being soaked in water are bruised with clubs until the fiber comes apart easily. It is then dampened and twisted into rope. The rope maker sits on the ground holding the rope between his toes, and forms the rope by constantly adding new fiber and rolling the rope between the palms of his hands. It is made two-ply about one fourth of an inch thick.

The mud is prepared by mixing manure, ashes or fine broken dry grass with sandy earth. The mixing is done with the feet. The first step in construction is naturally the foundation. This is made by digging a shallow circular trench where the wall is to stand. The men carry the mixed mud in their hands, which must be quite stiff, and drop it in the trench. The builder forms it into the desired shape with his hands. A layer about six inches deep is put on at a time. But two or three layers a day are added. A little above the foundation an elliptical band of grass about three feet in depth is put in place to form the door. As the wall is built up the mud is built against this, which retains its form leaving the door the desired shape. Later the grass is removed. Toward the top the wall is flanged out like the mouth of a bell to receive the roof. Few houses have windows; when windows are made, they are scarcely six inches in diameter. In forming the roof the first step is the same as for the wall: a shallow circular trench is dug with the same circumference as the inner

---

[1] i. e. Shilluks.

WESTERMANN, The Shilluk People.

circumference of the finished wall. About two feet inside the trench are set forked stakes about two feet high and four feet apart. The rafter poles are now placed with heavy end in trench and resting in the forks of these poles, their tops are brought together and securely tied. The heavy grass bands are now fastened both above and under the poles at regular distances from bottom to top of roof. Corn stalks or cane are woven in between the bands and poles thickly. The roof now has its final conical shape. The roof is ready to be raised and is picked up and placed evenly upon the wall. A layer of mud is then put over the lower end of the rafter poles, to keep it firmly in place. The first work in thatching is to put on what the Shullas call the apron of the house. A short layer of grass is put around the top of the wall and tied securely to the thatching. The thatcher then starts his course straight up the roof and works around the house, finishing the entire length of the roof as he goes around. The grass is tossed up to him in small bundles, which he places in position several at a time and removes the bands and ties then down tightly. With a paddle-shaped stick he evens up the ends of the grass, so that when the roof is finished nothing but the but ends of the grass are exposed, and these lie as evenly as though they had been laid separately by hand. At the top the grass is brought together like a spire and wrapped with rope and rope bands. The grass lies on the roof from six inches to a foot thick, and if kept free from white ants, will last for five or six years.

2. Different kinds of Soil.

Dọ̀dọ̀	black, rich earth	áṅáṅ	brownish earth as found on river-banks, used for making pots
kwójọ̀	sandy ground		
óṅèló	red earth as found on river-banks, used for making pots		
		àněkó	red sand
		àyéch	sand, dust.

3. Field-produce.

byél	dura	ókwọ̌l	an eatable gourd
ńmọ̀	sesame	kḛnọ	a gourd for calabashes, not eatable
ṅọ̀rọ̀	bean		
kwọ̀rọ̀	cotton	òshọ́yó	melon
búdọ̀	a small, sweet gourd, is eaten.	ọ̀tábọ	tobacco
		abwok	maize.

4. Different kinds of duras.

The common name: byél. The common name for white dura: dgọ́nọ̀.

Kinds of white dura.

d̥ọl is very long in ripening.　　　àbwòk maize.
mèr has a longer ear than d̥ọl.　　ràwọ̀ Duchn (panic grass).
àlwẹ̆d̥ọ̆ "finger", has four ears, which stand upright like the fingers of the hand.
lẹ̀k-dẹ́n, shálọ̀, àd̥ùròk, ofyẹ̀t lyẹch ("kills the elephant"), otọlọ, álál, olách-mách, ńémẹ̆k, awẹ̀t, chẹ̀ṭáńá, ákách, ólwĕ.
The stalks of many of the white duras are sucked like sugar cane.

Kinds of red dura.

The common name for red dura is: lwàli.

óṭòrò, wájàl-fá-d̥ímọ̀, wájàl-fá-ńéńárọ̀, òd̥ọ̀ǹ ("the Nubian"?), ṭad̥ẹ̆i-fèńi-dwai, ńákiṇọ̀, óṭól, aṭábọ̀, ńwẹ̀ch, ńàfẹ́gyẹ̀nọ̀, àkwọ́l, bwòńọ̀ ("of the white man"), ókwọ̆ńfi, óm̥ẹ̀rọ̀, wáńù ("lion's eye") wáńágàk ("crow's eye") wòráu, ńàchọ́lọ̀, ńàyọ́mà-bwòk, àwài, ńàfẹ́lwọ̀t, yìgbrọ̀mọ ("sheep-tail"), yìẹpkygá ("horse-tail"), ńáyọ, àdúké.

Agriculture Among The Shullas.[1]
By R. W. Tidrick, of Doleib Hill.

The Shullas have hardly begun their agricultural life. Scarcely one half century ago they were purely a pastoral people. Only within the last decades has his lordship, the Shulla man, begun to assume the burden of providing for his family. In those earlier days the task of tilling the small patch of ground planted annually in dura fell to the woman. Her hoe was made from the shoulder blade of a giraffe or buffalo, or sometimes from the shin or rib bones of these animals.

Boys tended the large herds and flocks, young warriors danced, went on the chase and raid. The old men idled their time away in the village.

But they say the cattle plagues became more prevalent. The Turk and Arab came and took away not only slaves, but cattle, and so necessity forced the Shulla to a larger tillage of the ground.

The change came naturally first in the northern end of their territory, where they came earliest in contact with the murderers and plunderers from down the Nile.

One man when questioned as to the food of the people in his boyhood days said: "We used to eat grass like cattle". There was as much truth as sarcasm in this statement. For even yet when the crop fails, the Shulla women gather grass seed from the swamps and plains. They rob the ants of their winter's provision of seeds. A little sugar is obtained by bruising and boiling a certain reed, which grows in the swamp.

---

[1] i. e. Shilluks.

The Shulla has not yet learned to grow a very large variety of plants. His one main crop is dura, the kaffir corn of America.

All planting except tobacco, which is planted in small plots on the river bank during the dry season and watered by sprinkling the ground from a water jar, is done in the beginning of the rainy season.

A small amount of Indian corn is grown, most of which is eaten when in hard roasting ear. With the dura they plant a few beans, pumpkins, squashes, sesame and occasionally peanuts. No fruits of any kind are grown, and as there are no wild fruits worthy the name, the Shulla has never known fruit until he has recently seen it in our garden or at the government stations.

The Shulla plants his dura in the same field year after year, until his crop fails once or twice. Then he hunts for a piece of high dry ground, preferably in the timber, for his early dura, and a low plain growing a certain rank wild grass for his late variety. He clears off the timber and digs up the grass for his new field which he tills, till another failure comes; if by that time his former field is growing of grass, he will return to its tillage.

His methods of farming are extremely crude, but in some respects accomplish good results. He has neither plough nor spade and never uses the mattock except to dig up the grass and bushes from new ground.

He prepares his ground by raking up the old stalks into piles with a deleib palm limb and burning them.

As soon as the rainy season opens and sufficient rain has fallen to soften the ground, he puts his seed to soak over night, so it will sprout the quicker, and thus more likely escape being eaten by white ants. With a long slender pole which has one end shaped like the bowl of a spoon, he opens up the ground, and drops in the seeds. As he steps forward to make another hole, he presses down the earth over the seed with his foot. The hills are made promiscuously, but are usually some eighteen inches apart in all directions. He plants a large number of seeds in a hill, and later thins out and transplants where hills are missing.

Often he has to replant, for there are many enemies of the sprouting grain. Some years pests of rats devour it, even after it is several inches high. The golden-crested crane also pulls up much of the grain as it comes through the ground. And as before mentioned the white ant destroys the grain in the ground unless it sprouts quickly. But under normal conditions the grain comes up very soon after planting. And the warm rains and tropical sun cause the crop to shoot up like Johnnie's bean pole. Weeds come on quickly too, and so the Shulla begins hoeing his fields at once. It is the only real cultivation he does. His hoe is either a thin circular or rectangular piece of iron with a short wooden handle. The hoer sits on the ground or squats on one knee or both, as he chooses, and catching the grass with one hand cuts it off just under the surface with the hoe. Shaking the dirt from the roots of the weeds he throws them into piles, leaving the ground clean and smooth. It is a good surface cultivation, suitable for this soil and climate, and when the season is favorable, the yield for the amount of ground tilled is very good.

The Indian corn grown by the Shullas is a small early variety, which is in roasting ear a fortnight before the early dura is ready for parching. But before any grain is harvested a sort of first fruits' sacrifice is made, an old man and woman go to the various fields of the village and bring in some of the ripening ears of corn and heads of dura, and place them by the sacred house of the village. Some is later taken and ground and mixed with water and plastered on the side of the sacred tukl, the rest is taken by the people and some put on the door of their own houses, and some is carefully tied up within. When the dura is ready for harvesting, the heads are cut off short with a clam shell and heaped upon a rack made of poles resting upon forked posts about two feet above the ground. After drying a month it is flailed out with heavy clubs by the men and winnowed by the women and carried to the village, where it is stored in large barrel shaped bins made of coarse grass. The bottom of the large basket granary is oval, a grass band wrapped with rope is formed about the small base and resting in the forks of short stakes driven in the ground bears the weight of the filled basket and keeps it off the ground and free from ants.

There are very many varieties of dura. One man gave me the names of thirty-two varieties. It is probable however that the same variety has different names in different localities.

Dura is eaten in a variety of ways. The earliest heads are simply thrown on the fire and roasted. It is often merely boiled till softened and eaten so. A great deal is made into a mild beer and used as a regular food diet. The popular way of cooking it is to grind it into a fine meal and cook it into a mush and eat it with milk, or cook it up with meat. It is sometimes boiled with beans, and sesame is often eaten with it. A sort of dura bread is also made.

The Shulla retains all of his pastoral instincts and prizes his flocks and herds above all else. His sheep are very inferior in size and have no wool where wool ought to grow. His goats are small and few are good milk producers. His cows are also generally poor in milking qualities, but are fair in size and in beef conformation. They belong to the Indian breed of cattle, which have the hump on the wethers.

Tribal custom forbids the Shulla from riding upon a donkey, so he never possesses one. Cattle are never used for draught or carrying purposes, so he has no beasts of burden, and perhaps never will so long as women are plentiful.

The villages are full of hunting dogs. Unlike the Nuers and most of the Dinkas the Shulla raise chickens. They are a degenerate Mediterranean strain. Eggs are eaten only by women and children.

Animal life must be well guarded and carefully housed at night most of the year. If an animal loiters on the river bank it most likely becomes the food of a crocodile. If one strays off into the woods it probably becomes the prey of a hyena, leopard or lion. Myriads of flies and numerous varieties of ticks also prey upon the flocks and herds, tormenting them by night as well as by day, and transmit the germs of various diseases also. Texas or tick fever is nearly always present, and a trypanosome not so fatal as the one of dreaded tsetse fly is also prevalent. The plague is a frequent visitor too and the mouth and foot diseases often attack the cattle toward the close of the dry season. The annual loss from all these enemies of animal life is very heavy, but as no females, unless barren, are ever killed for food or sold, and grass is plentiful, on the whole there is an increase in the number of live stock raised.

As to the possibilities of agriculture in the Shulla land obstacles to be overcome have been mentioned. What the mission has done shows that many varieties of fruits and a considerable number of vegetables may be grown. Future generations may have lumber, if the right varieties of forest trees are planted. Cotton is not a sure rain crop, but with irrigation it has few enemies. Sugar-cane and rice can be grown in favorable places. The soil of this part of the Sudan is not generally deep, is deficient in nitrogen and very poor in humus. Nitrogen may be restored with legumes, but the humus problem is difficult, for the white ants devour very quickly all manure, mulch etc. spred upon the ground.

The Shulla in sticking to the one main crop of dura has after all adopted the grain which is naturally adapted to the soil and climate and yields best to his methods of farming.

5. Foods and food-stuffs.

kwę́n a kind of dura-bread or mush.
àkę́lọ́ a food of dura.
àpǫ́tọ́ a food of dura.
àréyọ́ a food of dura (prepared after Arab fashion).
àdǫ́lọ́ àdǫ́lọ́ a food of dura (prepared after Arab fashion).
mǫñandr a food of dura with fat, eaten without anything else.
a common dura-food.

Agriculture

	ótĕt	a food of dura, dainty.		ṭàbọ̀	dura, soaked, and then kept till it sprouts; for making beer.
	mọ́ké ṅàkị̀	a food of dura.			
	àṅọ̀ch	cooked dura.		àṭọ̀bóbò	beer before it is strained.
	àbẹ̀k	green roasted dura.		mọgọ	beer.
	òmọ̀t	dura roasted, then soaked and mashed.		mọ̀n àtẹ̀nọ̀	strained beer.
		dough.		ydwọ̀	a kind of beer.
	mọ̀ṅàbúr	a dura-food			

6. The seasons of the year.

	yéy jèrìá	about September, harvest of red dura.		ḷụ	hot season, January—February — no field-work
	ánwóch	about October; end of the harvest, people are waiting for the white dura to ripen.		dọ̀dìn	about March
				dókọ̀t	about April, "mouth of rain", beginning of the rains.
	ágwẹ̀rọ̀	about November—December; harvest of white dura begins.		shwèr	about May—July, time for planting red dura.
	wùdọ̀	December—January. Harvest of white dura continues.		adọ̀rìá	about July—September, beginning of harvest.

7. The months.

1. yér, ór (wor) — about September. 2. kọ̀n gàk 3. ṅyẹth 4. kól 5. akọch, akọn dụọn 6. akọn ṭẹn 7. áduọ̀n 8. àṭẹbór 9. àkọ́l dìt 10. bẹ́l dụọn 11. bẹ́l ṭẹn 12. lál.

8. The day-times.

	wọ́u è rùwọ̀	the first morning-twilight becomes visible.	chan a kẹ̀chì	the sun begins to sink, after noon.
	bạr	morning dawn	bọ̀rọ̀	afternoon;
	mwọ́l, mọ́l	morning;	feṅ fa b.	it is afternoon.
	feṅ fa mwọl	"the earth is morning"; it is morning.	a díkị wọ́u	the sun is setting.
			wan tyẹ́nọ̀	the sun has set.
	dè chàṅ	noon.	feṅ fa wọr	it is night;
	cháṅ yà màl	the sun is in the zenith.	kị wọr	at night, midnight.

9. Names of stars.

dwgi	moon	ákwòshèkàn	appears after the sun has set.
nèmân			
àdâk	three stars, the Uranus.	kyèlè jòp	a star ahead of the Venus.
nwòl			
dbáń	"4 northern stars".	kyèlè rùwòu	Venus.
shúrò		wèr	
tâfèrò		gyènò	"hen", Pleiades.
		àyép	comet.

10. Household-things.

tòdèt	a stick to fasten the door with.	kòdò	large basket for preserving dura.
tèt	the lower part of the door.	dònò	basket for dura etc.
tigo	door.	dwèch	a small kòdò.
tàk	hearth-stone, hearth.	adudo	a basket.
fèl	grinding-stone, whet-stone.	òtògò	pot for cooking food.
		fùk-fùkl	water-pot.
àdàu	small whet-stone.	dìdi	big pot for cooking large meals or beer.
tèni	neck-bench or support.		
pyèn	skin to sleep upon.	tàbò	dish.
pàu, pèn	hole for pounding dura.	fàrè	a mat for covering food in pots, dishes.
teanò	dura-stalk.		
dwayo	a frame on which spears are put, to protect them from the white ants.	lùi	a sieve for sifting dura.
		lèk	pestle for pounding dura.
		fèl	spoon.
dòlò	a grass ring on which the kòdò is placed.	fàlò	knife.
		gwèch	stick for stirring food.
lwol	calabash, gourd.	òbèrò	small pot for preserving beer.
àdàlò	gourd for churning milk.		
tègi	small calabashes for drinking water.	òkwànò	broom.
		tòl	rope.
dbèń	a spoon made out of a gourd, for taking the hot food out of the pot.	kàdì	a rope on which clothes, dancing-sticks, etc. are hung.
drèt	leaf of deleib or dom-palm, and basket made of it.	bwèt	mat of Arab making, to sleep on.
		òdòk	fence-mat.

	ókḗnȯ	a kind of mat made of ambach, as a seat for chiefs only.	wíjí grass for stopping up cracks in the wall, to keep out mosquitoes.
	dĩm	a sieve of cloth, for straining beer.	aṭiwi a pot.

11. Handicrafts.

bọ̄dọ means a skilful man, one who is particularly skilled in some work, and who, therefore, likes to do this work, and is asked by others to do it for them, so that this craft becomes "his work". Of course it is not his sole occupation, except perhaps in the case of the worker in metal. His is a trade held in high esteem, so that he has become the bọ̄dọ par excellence; if the natives simply speak of a bọ̄dọ, they mean the smith or metal-worker. He does not practice his craft in one place, but goes from village to village. The other craftsmen practice their craft only occasionally. But as a rule one man knows and practices only one of the arts enumerated below.

    bọ̀tẹ́ tọ́ń maker of spears; plural: bōtẹ́ tọń.
    bọ̀tẹ́ tyẹk kị́ tọń the man who files spears.
    bọ̀tẹ́ tẹẹ́ń kị́ bọ́l tọń the man who makes the spear-handles straight.
    bọ̀tẹ́ dạk tobacco-pipe maker.
    bọ̀tẹ́ yạ̣t kị bụ́l tọń the man who makes spear-handles.
    bọ̀tẹ́ twóóń kị́ púk potter, generally a woman.
    bọ̀tẹ́ gwẹ́tẹ jọ̀t who carves, makes figures on gourds.
    bọ̀tẹ́ yȯ̀r kị́ tyẹ̣l who makes the string on which the gourds are hung.
    bọ̀tẹ́ ẉich who makes the roof of huts.
    bọ̀tẹ́ kwȧdọ kiṛạ̣n who makes skin-clothes.
    bọ̀tẹ́ ógọ̀t who makes cotton clothes.
    bọ̀tẹ́ tẹẹń carpenter.
    bọ̀tẹ́ ṭái who tattooes.
    bọ̀tẹ́ tẹẹń kị loṭ who makes clubs.
    bọ̀tẹ́ chók kị kọ̀t shield-maker.
    bọ̀tẹ́ tẹẹń kị kwẹ̄r who makes shields to protect against clubs.
    bọ̀tẹ́ rọt kị lạ̣n tailor, sewer.
    bọ̀tẹ́ tẹẹń kị bụl drum-maker.
    bōtẹ kwọ́chȯ bụ̀l who covers the drum with a skin.
    bōtẹ fwótȯ bụ̀l who beats the drum.
    bōtẹ lẹu kị tḗgụ̀ who polishes beads.
    bōtẹ fích kị rẹk who makes ostrich shell beads.

bōte nálę́n who beats the small drum "nálę́n".
bōte gęt ki jè who knocks out the lower incisive teeth.
bōte twéch who cups.
bōte ndt ki waṭ who dresses the horn of cattle.
bōte róch who castrates bulls. [naments.
bōte nę́r who pierces the ears of cattle and men, to put in or-
bōte kwânǫ wúr the leader in singing.
bōte kúdǫ ki dán who makes the dancing-sticks.
bōte teęn kwǫm who makes chairs.
bōte ṭáni who makes the neck supports or rests.
bōte káké lwól who makes, carves calabashes, gourds.
bōte twoy kâl lùkǫ who makes giraffe-tail necklaces.
bōte teęn ki doke dǫt who makes mat-doors.
bōte shwǫy ki bǫ́yi net-maker.
bōte shwǫy ki ṭigǫ door-maker.
bōte shwǫn ki dyòm salt-maker.
bōte ṭǫ́kè ṭéàu maker of iron bracelets.
bōte fièdǫ lóṭ one who plaits stripes of skin at the end of the club-handle, to prevent the club from slipping from the hand.
bōte kyęre tyęle wǫt who makes the foundations of huts.
bōte wúnǫ diver.
bōte dǫ́k ki yei hair dresser who fashions the hair into small lumps.
bōte mēt hair dresser who makes the large artificial hair-dresses.
bōte nę́kè fàrǫ hippo-huntsman.
oyįnǫ crocodile hunter.

12. Tools of the bodo, or metal-worker.

ábán hammer.
kíkįt anvil.
tá yùjí file.
óbùk bellows.
chúr a cover for the pipe of the bellows, to prevent its growing hot.

dǫkúbí thongs.
tuón chisel.
tárę́k an instrument with which to pierce a hole into the spear-handle, to put the spear in.

13. Clothing and ornaments for the body.

láu skin-cloth, now also used for cotton-cloth.
óchyę̀nǫ loin-cloth for women.

obánǫ front-cloth for women.
dùt skin-cloth for dancing worn by both sexes

Clothing and Ornaments

	yör	skin cut into small stripes or fringes, worn round the waist.	bàkǫ́ a kind of beads.
			ddémǫ̀t a kind of beads.
			adék a kind of beads.
	áyǫ̀mǫ̀	ear-rings of tin.	áptù a kind of beads.
	gwęlǫ	metal ring worn on arm, wrist, feet.	óbǫ́ù white beads.
			tá̱tá̱ṅ black beads.
	gwęle yit	ear-ring.	kę̄n ówę̣dǫ̀ blue beads.
	yièl	bracelet for the wrist.	ɣèrǫ̀ red beads.
	gôk	knee-ring of skin.	ádwǫ̀gǫ̀ yellow beads.
	ógǫ̀nǫ̀	brown ambach-ring, worn on the upper arm.	wáṅ dgàk "crow's eye", a big bead.[1]
			gāgǫ cowry shell.
	gyęlǫ	ivory ring	tà̱myû̱gǫ̀ a string for tying together clothes. [the hair.
	achót	ivory ring.	
	węt	ivory ring carved in conical form.	gaṅ a kind of button worn in
			wěnǫ̀ brown giraffe-tail hairs.
	owę̣dǫ̀	ivory ring, a small strip.	óchı̀rǫ̀ white giraffe-tail hairs.
	órǫ̀mǫ̀	ivory ring, big.	achût tooth-brush.
	orǫ́k	knee-bells, used in dancing.	dwóp a head-dress.
	ótyaṅ	a small bell. [ing.	óchóch a head-dress.
	dtútúm	bell, similar to orǫk.	dę̀m a head-dress.
	òlôèlóé	dancing-bell	mèt a head-dress, "like a shield".
	òkǫ̀t	cow-bell, used in dancing.	
	agyęr	small cow-bell.	agêrǫ̀ a head-dress, "like a shield".
	tego, tęgǫ	a common name for beads.	
	amanjûr	blue beads, worn by women.	nwar bleached hair, long.
			dshíshwèl a chain, worn as ornament.
	rę̄k	ostrich shell beads.	gáṅkù rattle, made of leaves of the deleib, tied on leg or loin.
	gór	big beads, worn on the neck by men.	
	bǫl tęnǫ	a kind of beads.	ógǫ̀nǫ̀ } arm-ring of ambach.
	tę́dǫ̀	a kind of small beads.	adę́rǫ̀
	yèlǫ̀	green beads, round, small.	wál loin-ring.
	àbàtâ̱rǫ̀	a kind of beads.	shyl gwǫk "penis of dog" arm-bracelet of brass.
	óṅyę́ṅ	a kind of beads.	
	dèṅ	a kind of beads.	ṅwaṅ iron bracelet.

14. Names for cows.

dèàṅ	cow; common name. Plural: dǫk cattle.	wat bull.
		rōjǫ heifer.

[1] There are many more beads, each of which has its own name.

ńarōjọ	calf.	wû (waṭ) tyę́l rę̂k }	(ox) with white feet.
ólę̂k	grey-white spotted.		
ńeyọ̀m	head white, body black or yellowish.	dyòkàk	black with white tail.
		óchȏdọ̀	hornless cow.
ógǎk	belly and neck white, back and head black.	wárègọ̀t	an ox with one horn directed forward, the second backward.
ńdbę̂k	one leg white, the rest of the body yellowish.	óbyêch	a cow with ordinary, non-dressed horns.
tàkyèch	flanks white, the rest of the body black.	ọ́dệlọ̀	a cow with horns turned down.
ńdjàk	head yellowish, brown spots on the back, the rest white.	ógwę́l	an ox with horns turned towards the eyes.
ńdjók	head black, black spots on the back, the rest white.	ódų́lọ̀	a cow with horns pointing forward.
ńàkę̀r	flanks black, belly and back white.	ńát	a cow with horns cut off.
		àgwọ̀gnọ̀m	a cow with horns directed straight upwards, like a goat's.
ńádǎń	brown-black, small spots.		
ólât	brown-white, small spots.	bdń	a cow with one horn directed upward, the second downward.
ólę́ń	brown-white, large spots, females only.		
teduk	grey.	àbàch	a cow with horns directed straight sideways.
ńàkwâch	black-white.		
àjàlóń		wárnàmtài	an ox with horns directed straight backward.
tédígò	red-brown.		
tàbúr	ash-coloured.	ónệgò	a cow with horns directed straight backward.
tętań	black.		
ńdbǫ́ń	white.		
ńeńáń	striped white and red.		

II. SOCIAL INSTITUTIONS AND SCENES FROM DAILY LIFE.

15. Marriage.

Kwoౢpe ńwoౢm.

Ḍāṇ e wâjǫ̀ kị ńāne dāchǫ, ka kŏpì kịne: yá wḛ̆lì yi! Kịne: bḛ̆ ńǫ̀? Kịne: ya dwata kwǫf kị yin! Kịne: yi kǫ̀mǫ́ ńǫ̀? Kịne: ya dwata kwǫpe ńwǫm. Kịne: dé yì rè fa kḛ́tì fach yi tyḛń dǫ̀nǫ̀? Ka kḛta fach, ka tyḛń dǫ̀nǫ̀ kǫ̀pé. Ká gḛ̀ kò: wǫ́ bà kwǫ̀fé wǫ́n. Ká é dúǫ̀gǫ̀, ka e kạdǫ dyel mḛn kwǭbe ḍǫgḛ. Ka tyḛń dǫ̀nǫ ko: wá yèi kì kwǫ́pí, kḛ́t, kǫ̀l ḍǫ̀k. Ka ḍāṇǫ bḛ̀nǫ̀, ka ḍǫ (ḍǫk) kǫ̀l, ká é dúǫ̀gǫ̀; ka kǫ̀fì kịnè: kḛt, kǫ̀l dŭt! Ka dut kḛ̀l, dute tyḛń fà jwǫ̀k. Ka mǫgǫ tyḛń, ka tḛrǫ chwǫ́l. Ka wáḛ wòbò kǫ̀l yì tḛ̀rò bḛ̀nè, ka tḛrǫ kḛ́ḍǫ̀, ka waḛ dwai kị tón̂, mḛ́n kwàhì wúńǫ́, ká tḛ̀rò kḛ́tà fàch. Ká tḛ̀rò chǫ̀ńǫ̀. Ka ńálà ńwǫ́mí ka kịtǫ̀ wǫt kí jāl tón̂. Ńàn a dāchǫ yà gól gḛ́n kị ḍay tón̂. Ká tḛ̀rò chǫ̀ńǫ̀, ká nǎl a ńǫ̀mí ká kǫ̀l wǫ̀k yi wǫ̀té gḛ́n. Ka ńàn a dāchǫ kǫ̀l wǫ̀k yi wǫ̀té gḛ́n. Ká tḛ̀rò chǫ̀ńǫ̀ bḛ̀nè; ka ḍeań nḛk, mḛ́n châm yì tḛ̀rò; tḛ̀rò gĭr, kí mǫ̀gǫ̀ bḛ̀nè, kí kwḛ́n, ḛ́ gĭr, kwḛn ka chwǫ́pé kị mau (mǫu).

Ká tḛ̀rò ḍánǫ̀, tḛrǫ bia fach, ka jal ńwǫ̀m chyḛ̆k kífà ḍān. Ka kŏpì kịne: kạní jâm! Kạ̀l wèn, kí lāu, kị yiḛ̀l, gḛn a tǒjì! Ka mǫgǫ tḛ̀r, tḛr fa jàl, ka gḛ fḛka fǫ̀l bḛ hi bḛ̀nǫ̀ fàch. Ka gḛ dwai fǫ̀l kí dyèl, ká gḛ́ bḛ̀nǫ̀, ká gḛ báńà kḛ̀tǫ̀ kal. Ka kwḛ́ri kǫ̀l, ka lḛ́n fḛń; ka gḛ kḛta kal. Ká gḛ́ chúńǫ̀ màl, bàń yèchì fḛń. Ká kwḛ́r kǫ̀l, ka chɩ̀kè lḛń fḛń. Ká gḛ́ yechá fḛń. Ká nāne ńwǫm dǫ̀ńa dá kàl. Ka dyel fḛ̀ch, ka kḛta kal. Ka gḛ pḛ̀ká fḛń kí kàl. Ka yit dyèl nǫ́l, ká gḛ́ kḛ́tá wǫ̀t. Ka é bàńǫ̀ kị bùtǫ̀. Ka ńyḛ̀n kǫ̀l, mḛn bùtḛ, ká é bùtǫ̀. Ká dyèl kǫ̀l kị mwǫl, ká dyèl nḛk, ka wǫ́mán é gǫ̀pǫ̀ kúòjǫ̀. Ka kal mwǫ̀n, ká é rùmǫ kị mwǫ̀ńǫ̀, ka gḛ kǎ (kḛta) wǫ̀t bḛ́ chám. Ka ńàn ḛni é bàńǫ̀ kḛ̀tḛ. Ka ńyḛ́n kǫ̀l, ká é chámǫ̀. Ḍuki ká gḛ́ dwàtǫ̀ yŭk. Ká gḛ́ bḛ́n, ká gḛ́ tǫ̀nǫ̀, ka gḛ laȟa wûr gḛ́ tǎḍò. Ka gḛ rumǫ tàl, ká gḛ́ tḛ̀nǫ̀; ka kal mwǫ̀n kḛ́tḛ, gḛ kị wǫt. Ka ḍuki tḛrǫ bḛ̀nǫ̀ bḛ̀nè bḛ mát kí mǫ̀gǫ̀. Ká bŭl gǫ́ch, ká tḛ̀rò chǫ̀ńǫ̀.

Chǒtḛ́, ka óńwǫ̀k kǫ̀l, ka óńwǫ̀k nḛk, ká châm yì wǫ́mán. Ká gḛ́ dǫ̀gǫ̀, ka ńàn ḛni e dǫ̀ńǫ̀ kí wài gḛ́n. Ka wékè ńal ḛni, ká gḛ́ bḛ̀ḍǫ̀. Ka wài gḛ́n dǫ̀gǫ̀.

Ka yàjḛ́, ka kḛ̀l kí ḍeàń. Tyḛ́ń gḛ́n kŏfí kịne: ḍāṇ á rḛn, ka wiyḛ wḛ̆rò kị máyḛ̀. Ká ḍeàń kǫ̀l, kā chuńe gḛ́n mińǫ. Ka gḛ ko: dǫ̀kú kí ńà gól ún! Ka gḛ dúǫ̀gǫ̀. Ka rei gḛ́ witị fì. Sha mḛ̆kǫ kamd faḛ̀ fḛń wékè tyḛ́ń gḛ́n.

A man talks with a girl, and in the course of their conservation he says: "I have come to you." She asks: "What for?" He replies: "I want to talk with you." She asks: "What do you want?" He replies: "I want to marry you."

She says: "But why do you not go into the village, to the old people?" Then he goes into the village, and talks with the old people. They say: "We have nothing to say against it." Now he returns home, and brings a sheep, as a present for the old people. The old people say: "We accept your proposal, go, and bring the cattle!" The man goes, and procures the cattle, he returns with it to the old people, and they say: "Go, and bring the rest of the dowry!" And the rest of the dowry is brought, the part for the people in the village of God.[1] Now beer is strained, and the people are called. The ox of dowry is brought by all the people; the people go, and fetch the ox, and a spear, which is (a present) for the man who held fast the rope of the ox. The people go into the village. And the people dance. The bridegroom is put into a hut together with the arranger of the marriage; the bride stays with her family together with the woman-arranger of the marriage. While the people are still dancing, the bridegroom is led out by his friends, the bride also is brought out by her friends. All the people continue dancing, and a cow is killed, which is eaten by the people; and they drink plenty of beer; and they eat bread, bread which is mixed with butter. There are many people present.

At last the people scatter, and go home. The bridegroom is now instructed with regard to his wife (that is, he is told how much cattle etc. he has still to give). They say to him: "Bring goods, bring giraffe-tails, and skin-cloths, and bracelets for tying."

And (the next day) food (beer, and different foods prepared of dura) is brought; it is carried into the village of the bridegroom. The men who carry it, sit down outside in the bush before going into the village. The people of the bridegroom now bring a goat into the bush (to the carriers, as a present); after that the carriers come into the village, but they refuse to go into the yard of the bridegroom. Now hoes are brought forth, and are thrown on the ground (as a present for the carriers), and they go into the yard; they stand still in the yard with their food on their head, and again refuse to put their loads on the ground. So once more hoes are brought, and thrown down before them. Now they put their loads down.

The bride also, when she is brought by her friends into the home of the bridegroom, remains outside the yard. And a goat is led out (to those waiting outside), and then she enters the yard. They (she and her friends) sit down in the yard. The ear of the goat is cut off, and after that they enter the hut. — But the girl refuses to lie down; and metal ornaments are brought, which are to cause her to lie down, and then she lies down. The next morning a goat is brought, the goat is killed. The women dig for mud which is used in building; and the enclosure in besmeared with mud (is repaired). When they have

---

[1] for the deceased ancestors.

finished this, they go into the hut to eat. But the girl again refuses to eat. And metal ornaments are brought, and then she eats. The next day the women go out to bring fire-wood. When they come back, they put food on the fire, and spend the night in cooking. When they have finished cooking, they strain beer, and once more they besmear the enclosure with mud, and the hut also. The next day all the people come to drink beer. The drum is beaten, and the people dance.

That is all; and a ram is brought, the ram is killed and eaten by the women. Now they (the female relatives of the bride) go home, and the bride remains (in the house of her husband) together with her aunt. She is given to her husband, and they live together. The aunt too goes home.

When the wife is with child, a cow is sent to her relatives by the husband. Before this is done, her relatives (parents) say: "He (our son-in-law) is a bad man," and her father and mother are angry. But when the cow is brought, they are happy. And they say to the people who bring the cow: "Return to your family!" And they return. And they are sprinkled with water. And when the time comes that she is to be confined, she is brought to her family (to her parents; the child should be born in the home of the mother's parents).

16. Burial.

Ḏāṇ kęṅ a tówé, ka tēro dwai, ka gyēno kwaṅ, ka gǫ̇ch feṅ, ka gyēno t̯ǫ̇, ka lęṅ tátyęl, ka gyēno mēko mâk, ka gǫ̇ch feṅ, ká tặṇ wiy ḏāṇ; ka dyęl kậl, ka gǫchi[1] loṯ, ka wei budę ki kal. Ká wàṯ kậl, ka chwǫ̂p, ká jē chụ̀ kǫ̀, ka jam kwēr gwach. Ka dộrǫ́ kậl, ka tǫṅ kậl, ka kwęr kặl, ka atēgo kặl, ka lāu kặl; ka tyęṅ kędo bę ṇote kwoḍo, męn tât pęm; ka tēgo twoch tyęle gęṅ. Ká gę́ kę́ḍǫ̀, ka gę ṅùḍǫ̀ kwóḍǫ̀, ka kwoḍo kặl gę pach, ka wẹ̀kè tyęṅ kwoṅ, ka tyęṅ kwoṅ ko: kặl kǫ́ch! Ka kǫ̀ch kậl, ka gę ko: rǫmà ḏāṇ! Ka ręti kǫ́ṯ, ka ḏāṇ rǫ́m, ka ręṯe kặl, rǫm kę́y bùr ḏāṇ. Ka ḏāṇ e kwóṅ, ka jē mǭko ye kwoṇo ḏāṇ, ka jē mǭko yęchę́ ḍeàṅ. Ká pyęṅ kặl, ka rȇr (rêr), ká tất pęm, ká kiṯe feṅ (tabate). Ka ḏāṇ dwai kàl, ka chyęgę chwǫ́l, u miṯe tyęli ḏāṇ, ka ḏāṇ kiṯe wiy tabate. Ka nà gól gęṅ yęchę́ tyęli ḏāṇ, ka newęṅ chwǫ́l, u ḷṇé tŭk. Ká bùl kậl, ka dyęl kặl, ka dyęl gǫ̇che loṯ; ka bŭl gǫ̇ch. Ka jē ywǫṇǫ; a tini tēro fa ywoṅ, ka jē wùchǫ̀. Ka yài shăm, ka ḏāṇ é rùmǫ̀ kị́ kwöṅǫ̀. Ka bak e kóṯ, ka tēro lwǫké gaṯ, ka tēro duǫgo fach. Obwòyǫ̀ kặl kị́ gyęnǫ̀, ka jē fwót ki obwoyo. Ka jē kęṯi fach. Ka fặl rêp mach, ka kậl, ṅi gậsh bǭlé jē; jē e ṯậyǫ̀, ka jē rǖjo chdṅ gęṅ ánwęṅ. Ka mǫgo dwǫ́l, męn kiṯe kwǫm ḏāṇ ki kúbjǫ̀. Ká ḍèaṅ kậl, ká mǫ̀gǫ̀ tyęṅ, ka mǫgo kậl, kǫṅ kwǫm ḏāṇ. Ka kúbjǫ̀ dwai, ka kiṯe kwǫm ḏāṇ, ká mwoṅ ki fi, ka mǫgo chiki kặl, ka chiki kǫ̀ṅ, ka woṯ chwǫ̂p, ká bŭl fwót, ka tēro e wìchǫ̀, ká yài shăm, ka tēro tậyǫ̀. Ka dwan fâr, ka tēro kōbǫ ki

[1] gǫch yi loṯ.

kwo̱ fe̱ ywo̱k. Ka mo̱go̱ gwâch yi̱ t̯e̱ro̱ be̱n. Ka wôl, ká wá̱té ge̱n dwai. Ka mo̱go̱ tygn, ka būl gôch ki̱ bò̱̱rò̱. Ka wa̱ḭ chwóp, ká dye̱k ne̱k; ka jē ne̱nó̱. D̯uki̱ ka ywò̱̱ge̱ ywô̱̱k, ká d̯o̱k ánwe̱n ká né̱̱kè̱ kà̱l, ka d̯o̱k anwe̱n ne̱ke de (der) fach. Ka t̯e̱ro̱ bē̱̱no̱ bē̱n bē̱n bē̱n; Chôl gi̱r! Ka fen yi̱gó bò̱̱rò̱, t̯e̱ro̱ ywo̱n, ka d̯o̱k anwe̱n ne̱k ki̱ fa̱l yi̱ t̯e̱ro̱. Ka púki̱ yêch, ka bur ge̱n kwón ki̱ bátà wiy d̯a̱n. Ka atiwi dryà̱u ki̱ lwo̱l ki̱ obi̱rò̱ ki̱ fá̱rǫ́, ki̱ t̯a̱mi dryà̱u, ka ge̱ ne̱k ki̱ yey bur. Ka tune d̯o̱k ka ge̱ kâ̱l, kwoń fen, ge̱ lé̱té̱ yi̱ t̯e̱ro̱. Ka ywo̱ke e d̯â̱̱no̱. Ka kâ̱l ṯō̱̱ṯe yi̱ ré̱̱m, ka kâ̱l ṯō̱̱ṯe yi̱ bat, ka rino̱ pâ̱nè̱ bē̱ne. Tygn a kwoń d̯a̱n ke̱li chi̱n, ki̱ wich, ki̱ tyg̱l, ki̱ mútò̱.

When a man dies the people of the village are sent for; a fowl is taken and thrown on the ground, so that it dies; it is then thrown into the corner of the hut. Another fowl is seized and thrown on the ground, so that it dies; this one is put on the head of the dead man. A goat is brought, and beaten to death with a club, and then left in the yard. An ox is brought, and speared. And the people assemble, and the things necessary for burial are collected (from the people). An adze is brought, and a spear, and a hoe, and beads, and a skin-cloth. Then the people go to cut thorns with which to tie together boards (trees). And beads are tied round the feet of the men who do this work. They go and cut thorns, bring the thorns into the village, and give them to the grave-makers. The grave-makers say: "Bring an adze!" When the adze is brought, they say: "Measure the dead man!" And corn-stalks are tied together for a measure; now the man is measured; then they take the measure, and measure the place (size) of the grave.

The man is buried thus: Some men dig the hole, and some men skin the cow (which has been killed). And the hide is brought, and cut into stripes, and a bier is tied together with them, and the bier is put on the ground. The dead man is carried into the yard, his wife is called, she is to hold the feet of the dead man, and the man is laid on the bier. His wife (or: the women belonging to the family) sweeps the place where his feet lie; and a female relative of the dead man is called, she throws away the hearth-stones lying there. A drum is brought, a goat is brought, the goat is killed with a club; the drum is beaten, and the people begin to weep (mourn); as soon as the weeping stops, the people dance mourning-dances. Then the people assembled go around in a procession dancing. Now the burial of the man is finished.

A fence is made around the grave; the people wash themselves in the river, and then go back into the village. Oboyo̱ (a plant) is brought, and a fowl, the people are beaten (touched) with the oboyo̱. The people go back into the village. The eating-tools of the dead man are burnt, and the people rub the ashes on their forehead; the people now scatter and stay away four days. After that time beer is made, the beer for rubbing mud on the back of the dead

Burial. Inheritance

man.¹ An ox is brought, the beer is strained, the beer is brought, and poured on the back of the dead man (on his grave). Mud is carried, and put on the back of the dead man; the mud is prepared (made wet) with water. Again beer is brought, and again is poured on the grave. The ox is speared; the drum is beaten, the people take their arms and make war-plays, and go around in procession. When it is finished, the people scatter.

After one month has passed, the people talk about the mourning-festival. Dura for beer is collected from all the people, the dura is pounded, and the relatives are invited. The beer is strained, and in the afternoon the drum is beaten. An ox is speared, goats are killed. Then the people go to sleep. The next morning the mourning begins; four cows are killed in the yard, and four cows are killed in the middle of the village. Then all, all, all the people come, a great many of Shillūks. When it is afternoon, the people mourn, and four cows are killed by the people in the bush. Cooking-pots are carried out, and a hole is dug for them (and for the other household-things of the dead man) near the place where the head of the dead man lies. And two pots, and a gourd, and a small pot for beer, a mat for covering food, and two dishes, all these things are broken, and thrown into the hole. The horns of a cow are brought ("and the horns of cattle, and they are brought"), they are buried in the ground (on the grave), so that they may be seen by the people. Now the mourning-meeting disbands; one of the families receives a shoulder (of one of the butchered cattle), one receives a fore-leg, and all the other meat is also divided. The people who have dug the grave, receive the bowels, the head, and the feet, and the neck.²

17. Inheritance.

Ḍan ḳeń a ḳọ, wate nút, ka jámé kwań yi ńal duọń, ka ńal ṭēn wọté bẹ̌ḍọ. Ká ḍọk kwań yi ńal duọń bẹn, ka ńal duọń u yigé dọ̄ch, ká ḍọk fūnē én, u yige rach, ka ḍọk kwań yi ńal ṭēn. Ka ge ńāko, ka ḍọk kwań yi ńal ṭēn. Tēro bēno bēne bēne, ka kwọp kọ̄mi, ka ye kine: é, ere wuo, ena a tuóńi; yi chama ńo kẹ̌ti kí ḍọk? fūnē ḍọk! u bēno kwor, u chȯlè yi kẹ̌ti? Ka ḍọk fūnē tēro; ka ńal duọń wēkè mógé, ka ńal ṭēn wēke mógé. Ka kwọp kọ̄m chyḗ, ka ge ręp ki dkyèl, ka fi kọ̄ń feń, ka ge rępọ. Ńal duọń wēkè mánēńọ, kifa ená jáń kàl; ka mánọ̄k wēkè ńal ṭēn. Ka ńi bēn kwor gòńí, chȯlè, ka ńal ṭēn e bēdọ, fa chuḍọ. Ńal ṭēn ḍoge ńọmé ki ḍachọ. Chȯṭḭ, fēka feń.

Tyeń gole ka owiy jal eni e bēno, ka e kapọ ki akyęl, ka ómèn e kapọ ki akyęl; ńwọli gen fa mōk jal eni, wate jal eni, ḍān duọń; mayi gen e bēdọ ki jal duọń; kinau chèt.

When a man dies, and he has children, his property is taken by the eldest

---

¹ That is: for besmearing the grave with mud and smoothing the surface.
² Not everybody is buried so ceremoniously as this report tells, but only old, respected or rich people, chiefs of families or villages. — In almost every village one sees the horns of an ox buried projecting from the ground; this is the burial-place of such a man. *The Burial of a king vide page 128.*

son; the younger son (or sons) remains without anything. All the cattle too are taken by the eldest son; and if the eldest son is good, he divides the cattle between himself and his brothers, but if he is bad, he keeps all the cattle for himself. In this case hey fight, and the cattle is taken away (by force) by the younger brother (or brothers). But then all the people come, and they talk about the matter, and they say (to the younger brothers) thus: "Why, your elder brother, he refused to give you cattle, and now *you* want to keep it all? What for? If later on any debts (which your father may have contracted or which may fall on you) appear, you being his sole heir, will have to pay all; so the people divide the cattle; the elder brother gets his part, and the younger one gets his part. After that they again hold a big palaver, and they make friends; water is poured on the ground, and so they are reconciled. The eldest son gets many cows (or property), because he is the chief of the family, the younger one does not get so much. And if afterwards any debts are to be paid, the elder one will pay them, the younger remaining free. The younger brother marries a wife with his cattle; that is all, thus the matter is settled.

The wives of the dead man are treated (done with) thus: the elder brother of the dead man comes and takes one, and the younger brother also comes and takes one.[1] And if they beget children from these wives, they belong to the family of the dead man; they are (like) his (own) children (they live in the house of the eldest brother.) The eldest wife of the deceased, the mother of the children, remains with the eldest brother. — So is it exactly.

18. Murder.

Dạṅ lépè, ywódé, ẹ bíẹ wọ̀k, ka kệl, ka chíkì kèlọ̀, ka ṅan ẹni e rẹ́ṅọ̀, ka bíẹ bẹ kwóp: yá nẹka dạṅ a war! Ká bùl gộch, ka tẹ̄rọ bíẹ wọ̀k, ka tyẹṅ a mạn kẹṭe bẹ yẹ́ké jam, gẹ kân. Ka tyẹ̀kẹ̀ bẹ̄nọ, leṅ rị̈ṭ; ka fach yâk, gyẹn mâk, ka byẹl kệl. Ka tẹ̄rọ bẹ̄nọ, dọk a kệl fōṭe Jaṅ. Ka ṅị u dọk leṅe rị̈ṭ, ká dọk dùọk. Ka dọk aryau gộṅ yị jāgọ, ka mûje rị̈ṭ, ka rị̈ṭ e wèrọ̀, ká è kò: kẹ́ṭ, chól! Ka tẹ̄rọ chùdọ̀, ka mẹn e kāṅọ deaṅ, ka mẹn e kāṅọ deaṅ, ka dọk e tûmọ̀, ga pyārọ. Ka chwọk wúr, ka e bẹ̄nọ, ka bíẹ yị jāgọ, kịne: kwóp bẹ̀dà dì? Kịne: kwọf á ṭùm. Ka dọk kệl, ka gẹ ṭyêr, ka gẹ mûjọ kị dyẹk, mọk kwache tyẹṅ rị̈ṭ. Ka tyẹṅ rị̈ṭ yịẹ̀ṅọ̀, kịne: dạṅ rach! Ka nệkè kị deaṅ mẹ̄kọ, ka dọk kệl, ka tyẹṅ rị̈ṭ e bẹ̄nọ, kẹṭa Fashōdọ kị tyẹṅ dạṅ, tyẹṅ dạ̄ṅọ ṭōṭe dọk abich. Ka rị̈ṭ kạlọ dọk abich, waṭ akyẹl ywọk ṅál ẹṅí.

A man hides in an ambush; when he perceives his adversary, he comes out and stabs him, and he stabs him a second time. Then this man (the murderer) runs away home, and comes to tell the people of his village: "I have killed a man last night." Then the drum is beaten, the people come out from their houses, and

---

[1] The sons marry their father's wives, but not their own mother.

the women start to carry the valuable things away and hide them; the cattle are driven into the Dinka-country. Now a company of warriors come, the "army of the king"; they rob the village, all the fowls are seized, and the dura is carried away by them. When the "army of the king" turns back, they bring the cattle back from the Dinka-country. Two cows are loosened by the chief, and are given to the king. But the king is angry, he says: "Go, and pay (greater) amends!" Then the people pay; one gives a cow, and another one also gives a cow, till there are ten; then the cows are brought to one place. Now an ambassador from the king comes, he comes to the chief, and asks: "How is the matter?" The chief answers: "The matter is settled." The cows are brought and shown to the ambassador for examination. And besides they give some sheep to the ambassador and to the other people of the king (who have come with him), to please them. The people of the king take them, saying: "The matter of the man is bad! (that is: the gifts are not sufficient)". Now another cow is killed (and given to the ambassadors of the king). After that the cows (the ten cows mentioned above) are brought, and the people of the king go to Fashoda (with the cows), together with the family of the murdered one. The family of the man who has been murdered, receive five cows. The king gives them five cows and an ox, as a mourning (a mourning-fund) for their dead relative.

19. Blood Revenge.

Jal mękǫ, jal Mwǫmǫ, jal máddǫ̓ch, ka nękè yi rit Yǫ. Ka tyeṅ gęn é ywǫ̀ṅǫ̀. Ka jē ṅi lui yi fōte bwoṅ, ka gę ṅi makę, ka gę choṅ wǫt, ka jē e úgù pyar abi-kyęl, ka mụke tāṇ, ka gę dwǫl; ka gę rumǫ dwǫl, ka gę tyęṅ; ka gę rumo tyęṅ, ka būl kąl wǫk, ka ḍāṇ kąl, ka nęk, męn gǫy būl; ka būl tiṅ wǫt kị bar, ka būl tiṅ wǫt, ka ḍāṇǫ kąl, ka nęk; ka ywǫge ywǫk, ka pyar abi kyęl kąl wǫ̀k, ka gę nęk, (keṅ) ḍāṇ a nękè yi rit. Kā ęni anan, ka Chǫl e buǫgǫ bęne.

A certain man, a man of Mwǫmǫ, a very good man, was killed by king Yǫ. His relations mourned for him. — At that time people (Shilluks) used to run away from the country of the whites (i. e. Arabs), these were caught by the relations of the dead one, they were all put into a house, and when they numbered sixty, then beer was brewed, and it was mixed with flour; when they had finished mixing it, they sifted it; when they had finished sifting it, a drum was brought out, and one man was brought, and was killed; he was the one for beating the drum. Early next morning the drum was put into the house; when they had put the drum into the house, again a man was brought out and killed; and he was mourned. Thus all the sixty men were brought out and killed, in the place of the one man who had been killed by the king. That was the reason why the Shilluks were much afraid.

20. A Quarrel between Husband and Wife.

Jal mękǫ e ńwǫmǫ. Ka ńan a dachǫ bēnǫ, e kānǫ pî; ka jal ęni wěrǫ̀, kįne: à, ga pi nǫ̀? Ya by kęch. Ka ńan a dachǫ ka kwōna vǫk. Ka gę nęnǫ, ka gę tōrǫ yi kęch; chama ńi butǫ feń, ka ńińę báńá mèjò yi kęch.

Ka gę kędǫ bę̄ kwatǫ kį byęl, ka ńan a dachǫ lōńa wǫt (rǫt), e kānǫ gin cham. Ka gę bēnǫ, gę kātǫ byęl, ka gę pę̄ka péń; ńan a dachǫ kúchè gę́ń, ńan a dachǫ panǫ kį gǫre wǫt. Ká gę̀ ńàmǫ̀, ka ńi ko: á, ówá, chę (cha) duǫń a wan mēyi (mēi), ńwāl ę́ná! Ka gǫ ńwāle. Ka gę yűjǫ kį byęl. Ka ńan a dachǫ fęchǫ kįne: ńimta, a kįdi? a ya re wa reę? Jal e ko: ę̂ ńawǫ-tyau! gǫń dǫga! Kįne: kipańǫ? Kįne: chá re a wěke ya kęch? ko: ę̂, fa̧te yin a kōbį awa kįne: ga pi nǫ? Ka ńal ęni kę̧ta wǫk; ka węn chwǫ́l, ka e bēnǫ; e ko: á, pyeche ńa wun, wěke ya dǫga! kįne: kipańǫ? Kįne: ę̂, pyecho yau! A pyey ńan ęni, kįne: ńān! á kįdí? A kōp nate, cha wěkè yę dǫgę! Kįne: ę̂, kúchè ydń! Ńa tyau, tē kwóp! Ya ką̧la pi awa; a kōbį kįne: gęn a pi ń ǫ? Kęń ęni anan; ę́na (rę̧na) kędá. Kįne: nǫ̀! A tōre yi kęch, a kę̧ti gę bę̄ kwdle byę́l, a kį̧ta gin cham wǫt, gę tǫ̌k. Fa̧te kęń ęni anan? a bę̧ni, a kōbį kįne: ówá, cha duǫń a wan bygli! a ńām gę́ń, ę́ná kōbá, kįne: yá nę̀n! A kōbį: ńa tyau! gǫń dǫga! A kōba kįne: búh! na yín a kyęt dwá, kįne: ga pi nǫ̀? Fa̧te kęń ęni a bęn anan? A ką̧la gin cham; a yę́dé. A kōbe wiy ńǎn ę́ńi: yi kwata kapańǫ? Adi? chōl byę́lá a kwāl yi yin! A kōbe kįne: kipańǫ? Yā dę, a wěke ya kęch! Yi cha (yá) kűwa! dǫgi gōńa yin. A kędǫ, a kąle wa̧t, męn lǫ́gę́, a lǫ́gę́ lwǫge órè, a ̧tumi kwǫp.

A certain man had married a woman. One day his wife came and brought him water (to wash his hands, as is the custom before eating). But the man was angry, and so he said: "What is that water for? I am not hungry." Thereupon the woman went outside, she too was cross. When they went to sleep, they were troubled by hunger (both having eaten nothing). The man tried to lie down, but his eyes refused to close on account of hunger.

In order to get something to eat, the man with a friend (who lived in the same house) went to steal dura. But in the meantime the woman had prepared food and came into the house, after the men had gone. After some time they returned, bringing with them the stolen dura. They sat down in the house, but did not know that the woman too was there; she hid in a corner of the house. And the two men ate. They talked to each other: "Ah, brother, you have a thick ear of corn there, just let me touch it!" And he touched it. So they ate the corn from the ears. Suddenly the woman asked: "My brothers, how? Why do you bring such shame upon me (by stealing corn and not eating the food I have prepared)?" Then the man said: "You cursed woman, loosen my cattle."[1] She asked: "Why?" He said: "Why do you leave me hungry?" She

---

[1] This is the formula for: "I will be divorced from you." Loosen the cattle (give back the cattle) which I have paid your father for you.

replied: "Not so! did you not say yesterday: what is the water for?" The man went out, he called his wife's father. When the father came, he said to him: "Ask your daughter (what has happened), and then give me my cows." The father asked: "Why?" He said: "Just ask her!" He asked the girl, saying: "Girl, how is this? The man says he wants his cattle back!" She replied: "I don't know." The father said: "You cursed girl, tell me all about it!" So she told: "Yesterday I brought water, then he said: 'What is that water for?' That is the matter. Then I went out." The father said: "All right." The woman continued: "In the night he was troubled with hunger, therefore they went to steal corn; in the meantime I brought the food, and saw that they were gone. Is not that the matter? And then, when they were eating, one said to the other: "Brother, what a big corn-ear you have!" Then I said: 'Here am I!' And he said: 'You cursed woman, loosen my cattle!' And I replied: 'Dear me, was it not you who refused yesterday saying: what is the water for?' Is not that the whole matter? I brought food, and he cursed!" After that the father of the girl said to the husband of his daughter: "Why did you steal? How is that? Restore me my corn which you have stolen!"[1] The man said: "Why? why was I left hungry?" The father only replied: "You are a thief! I will give you back your cattle." — When the husband heard that, he brought an ox for reconciliation, with that he reconciled, he reconciled his father-in-law, and so the matter was settled.

21. The Husband who wanted to cook.

Jal mĕkọ ńi bẹ̆da gwạlọ; ka kōpa ḍane gólẹ̆ kịne: ẹ̆, ńān, ya lōńa ṭal![2] *Ka ńane ḍachọ ko: dọ̈ch! Ka e ko: bụ́h, ṭal dọ̈ch ẹ̆n! ḍāṇ yiga máchwē yị ṭàl. Ká è ṭāḍọ. Ka e keḍọ, ka kwẹn lẉẹ́, ka óbọ́i ṭwọra mal, ka gọ ńi yárẹ̆, ka gọ ńi kọńi pań. Ka kwẹne chẹ̄gọ, ka wiy pań rum yi pyẹn, ka kwẹn tọkẹ, ka lwọl duọń tōke ńa-gọl gẹn. Ka mẹn a gọ̄pe wótọ̀ṇò; ka e bẹ̆dọ gạn óbọ́i.*[3]

Ka gin cham e ṭum kị̆ chạ̀m, e bẹ̄di yau, ka ńan a ḍachọ kẹṭa wọk, ka pań ńwālẹ̆, ka gọ yóḍẹ̆ e tọ̄k, obọi ṭwọwọ. Kịne: bói, y ya tich adi? Ka ńi butọ péń, ka ńi dwọṭa mal, ka ńi gā yọ, kịne: bụ́h, hẹ̀! Kwọp a bań dwọ̄gò. Ka ńa gọl gẹn ko: á gìn ánọ̀? Kịne: ệ, faṭe gin ńi kwọp! mi ńa-ḍāṇ, chwọla: ńi chwē chwọla yi ńi chām óbọ́i, ka ṭāla gin cham a tin, a tọ̄ga obọi pań. Kẹn ẹni anan, dẹ chwọla yin chwé yi obọi. A kōbi ńan a ḍachọ kịne: wiy ńāra, yi neke mạre nọ chọ́ń? Ya fa dọ̄ge ṭal kẹ̆ṭe. Kẹn ẹni anan; a ḍwoṭi ńan a ḍachọ mal, a ṭāṇe gin cham, a chámị̆, ka chuńẹ̆ mịṇò.

A certain man was very thin, and he said to his wife: "I say, my wife, I will cook in place of you." The woman said: "All right!" He said (to himself): "Why, cooking is a good thing, a man grows fat from cooking." So he cooked.

---

[1] The man had — without knowing it — stolen the dura of his father-in-law.
[2] "I will come later", or: "do later, cooking": I will cook after, instead of you.
[3] He remained thinking of the foam.

He went and poured much water on the flour (to make bread), so that the foam floated on the surface. He skimmed the foam off and put it into the hole near the grinding-stone. When the bread was done, he covered the hole with a skin, and the bread he put into a large gourd for his wife, and what was left (in the pot), he scratched out for the children. (He did not take any food for himself, because) he was thinking of the foam. (He thought the foam was the best of the food, therefore he reserved it for himself).

When his people had finished eating, he sat quite still, waiting till his wife had gone out. Then he uncovered the hole and saw that the foam had gone, it had dried off! He said: "Dear me! what shall I do now?" He lay down, he got up again, he was quite perplexed. He could not say one word ("talk refused to return"). His wife asked: "What is the matter?" He answered: "Why, it is not a thing to be told; mother of my children, I thought because you are so fat, I thought it was because you used to eat foam, so I cooked the food today, and I put the foam into the hole. That is the matter. I thought you were so fat from eating foam. His wife said: "Father of my child, what greediness has been troubling you?" He replied: "I shall never cook again." That is it. The woman arose and cooked food, he ate, and was pleased.

III. SICKNESS.

22. Treatment of Sick People.

Ḍāṇ kɛ́ɑ mâgé yi jwọ̈k, ka jē dwai, ka jē kúfi̥ kine: ḍāṇ a lañi war ki jwọ̈k? Ká jè è kọ̈bọ̈: ḍāṇ e mâgè kidi yi jwọ̈k? Ká dyèl dwai, ka tɛ̄rọ lȧmò lȧma jwọ̈k, ka yi̥ dyèl ṅọ́l, ka pi weti̥ rɛ, ká dyèl e nɛ̀k, rɛmọ kɛḍọ feṅ, ka châm yì tɛ̀rò. Ka tɛ̄rọ tȧyò. Ka ḍuṅ u̥ bɛ̣t jwọ̈k è duọ́ṅ ki rɛ, ka ajwōgọ dwai. Ka ajwōgọ bɛ̄nọ, ka e kōbọ kine: kạni ki̥ kwɛ̀r, ka e ko: kạni ki̥ bɪ̣t, ka e ko: kạni ki̥ lāu, ka e ko: kạni ki̥ dyèl! Ká dyèl kū̥l, ka ḍāṇ e kite fɑ̣l, ká dyèl chibi wij ṭrò, ka dyɛl yeje kâk, ka yeje woúmà kàgò; ka ḍāṇ kita fach, ká jwọ̈k è wȧṅọ̀.

When a man is seized by sickness, people are called for, and the people ask: "Does he spend the whole night with sickness (is he troubled by night, so that he does not sleep)?" Again they ask: "How did the sickness come?" And a goat is brought, and the people pray, pray to God; then the ear of the goat is cut off; spittle is sprinkled on the body of the sick person; the goat is killed, its blood flows on the earth; the meat is eaten by the people. Now the people scatter (go home). If next day the sickness is still bad on him, a sorcerer is sent for. When the sorcerer comes, he says: "Bring a hoe!" and: "Bring a fish-spear!" and: "Bring a skin-cloth," and: "Bring a goat!"[1] When the goat is brought, the sick man is brought into the bush. The goat is put on the top of a white ant hill; its belly is cut open; when this is finished, the man is carried home, and the sickness disappears.

23. Another Report on Sickness.

Jwọ̈ṅ mēkọ ṅiṅ fà dwȧlọ̈. Ka ajwōgọ dwai, ka ajwōgọ bɛ̄nọ, ka e ko kine: kạni kwɛ̀r, mɛn kwoṅ yaṭ. Ka dyɛl kū̥l, ka lāu kū̥l, ka oṅwọk kū̥l, ká pàlò kū̥l, ka bɛ̣t kū̥l, ka yech kū̥l, ká lùi kū̥l, ká kɛ̀nò kū̥l, ka oṅwọk bô̥t feṅ ki̥ tàdò̥t, ka yeje tār mal. Ka ḍāṇọ kū̥l, ḍāṇ fɛka yeje, ka ṅa gô̥l gɛ́ṅ chi̥p ṅȧjɛ̀, ka ṅa wȧdɛ̀ chi̥p ṅime; ka oṅwọk mī̥tì̥, ka oṅwọk e tô̥. Ka gɛ ḍwò̥tȧ mâl, ká dyèl yéjɛ́ kâk, ka wȧi gâch réi gɛ́ṅ; ka mɛ̀nɛ̀ ṅọ́l, ka chíṅɛ́ ṅọ́l, ká dàtɛ̀ ṅọ́l, ka gɛ kwoṅ wiy tɛ̀t. Ka yaṭ tô̥k, ka ṅwò̥pɛ̀ pi̥, ka wɪ̣kò ṅȧṅ ɛ́ni, ká gò mȧtɛ̀ ɛ́n. Ka atɛ̀gò rôp, mȧkwȧrò, ṅiṅ ṭɛ̀rò, ka gɛ twôch ṅȧjɛ, ká lùi kâk, ká lúi̥l kâk, ka yech kwȧṅ, ka kite pȧl yi̥ yṳ̆, ka tɛ̀nò yì yṳ̆, ka pi kite yey lwọl, gɛ chḁ̂ò feṅ; ka bɛ̣t kwȧṅì̥ ɛ́n, ka kwɛ̀r kwȧṅi̥ ɛ́n, ka f āl̥ọ kwȧṅi̥ ɛ́n, ka riṅọ kwȧṅi̥ ɛ́n, ká dyèl kwȧṅi̥[2] *ɛ́n.*

Another sickness is called *dwȧlọ̈*. When this falls on a man, the sorcerer is sent for. When he comes, he says: "Bring a hoe to dig medicine with." Then

---

[1] These all are the fee of the witch-doctor.
[2] *kwȧṅ yì ɛ́n.*

a goat is brought, and a skin-cloth, and a ram, and a knife, and a round spear, and a certain (kind of) grass, and a fan, and a gourd. The ram is laid on the earth at the door of the hut, with its belly turned upwards. Then the sick man is brought, he sits down on the belly of the ram, his wife is placed behind him (on the ram), and his youngest son in front of him; thus they hold the ram fast, till it dies. Then they rise, the belly of the ram is cut open, the contents of the stomach are taken out and smeared on their bodies (of these three persons). The heart also is cut out, and the bowels. The hoof is cut off, and these things are buried at the door of the hut. Now the medicine is crushed, it is mixed with water, it is given to the sick man, and drunk by him. And they string beads, red ones, their name is rẹ̄rọ, they are tied about his back. The fan is cut in pieces, and the gourd too, and the grass is taken, and brought into the bush on the pathway, it is thrown on the pathway; water is poured into the gourd and thrown on the ground. The round spear is taken by the sorcerer, so are the hoe, the knife, the meat, and the ram.

24. Sicknesses.

dwālọ the abdomen is swollen, pains, diarrhoea.
tṹi heart-ache, pulmonary
áṅǫ̀nǫ̀ cold, catarrh. [disease.
dnẹ́kǫ̀ insanity, lunacy.
owin wich giddiness.
átọ̀gó teeth fall out, pains in the bones.
àlũt dropsy, hydropsy.
àdòn pains in the buttocks.
dkágó rheumatic pains, chiefly in the legs; feeling cold.
ṭẹ́ọu guinea worm, Ferendit of the Arabs; filaria medinensis.
àmwọ̀l swelling of knees and
lái leprosy [elbows.
nónò a disease of the head, the hair comes out in consequence of ulcerous inflammation.

ajañkobyet the skin peels off.
lẽr caries.
wàn a kind of light leprosy.
kwẹ̀m kwẹ̀m swelling of the shin-bone.
kamír salt-rheum, "lupus".
ajọ̀gọ̀ small-pox.
àbíp a sickness manifesting itself in strong fevers, generally mortal, chiefly children suffer from it.
gi bwọñọ "thing of the stranger", that is: of the Arab; siphylis.
kàjéjọ̀ inflammation of the finger-joints; parts of the finger rot off.
áñâch inflammation of the joints; of the toes.
ànṹn gonorrhoea.
bòr boils.

Names of Sicknesses

shǫ̀ltík the same as *àmwǫ̀l*, but it is curable, *amwǫl* is uncurable.

dwâdǫ̀ a kind of leprosy on the foot, takes a long time to heal.

miȩ̀m the skin becomes rough, squamous.

ṭàwó-shín diarrhoea.

ràm diarrhoea.

chǫ̀rǫ̀ blindness.

ṅi-ṅi̯n eyelashes get red, fall off.

ṅǫ̀lǫ lameness.

ákǫ̀n thigh-bone is affected, it is mortal.

duoṅ disease of the outer ear, chiefly of children.

gwǫ̀ṅǫ̀ itching.

àdwàṅ "a cripple who never walks".

àtàkǫ̀ hunch-backed.

byȩ́r a disease of cattle and men, pains in the back.

25. The Election of a King.

Ron rit.

Kẹn ron (ron) rit, ńi dwái kwáré dònò; ka wẹ́li ńa rit, ka gẹ mọ̀t, ka jē kẹdọ fōte dọnọ, ka lẹ̀lè kŭl, ka kite mach, ka búk. Ka wẹ̄ló lénò, lẹn yi mach, ka mach bẹdọ lŏch, fate rit; ka chiki mẹ̄kọ lẹ́nọ mach, ka e lyẹli nọk, fate rit, ka chiki lẹ́ño mach, ka e lyẹlọ duọ́n nọk, fate rit; ka mẹ̄kọ chiki lẹn mach, ka mach e ṣ̄ọ, fate rit; ka mẹ̄kọ lẹ́n mach, ka e lyẹl lyẹl duọ́n, ka pōtọ mal, ka tẹ̄rọ ńḕtò, rit anan! Ka tẹ̄rọ bẹ̄nò, ka nẹna pŭl. Duki ka jē bẹ̄nọ, ka jē wanọ pach; tyẹń lẹ̄l a bi, ka gẹ ńi tọńa pān, ka ńi gētí deań; ka gẹ bẹ̄nọ wani pan, ka gētí deań. Ka gẹ wita Báchôdò, ka jańe duọ́n e pẹ̀chò kine: amẹn a kwań yi lẹ̀lò ? kine: ńa rit ńate.

Chōti, ka jŭk dwái, ka gẹ dwai Mwọmó ki Tuńọ. Ka e bẹ̄nọ bẹne, ẹna jāge bẹne, ka kwó̂f kộm, ka tẹ̄rọ kẹ́dò, tẹ̄rọ keta fāre, ka pāre tyẹ̀k, tyẹk ákyẹ̀l. Ka jē nẹ́nò pŭl. Ka bar ẹni ka jē bẹ̄nọ, gẹ keta pach. Ka ton kwańi chińé, ka jē keta kal, ka tyẹńe man é ywọ́nò. Ni rŭn ẹni bẹdọ wọt; ka jake, kwā rit, a chwọ̄l, ka gẹ keta kal. Ka tedet ńǫ́lé ki ton; ka gẹ pota wọt, ka ńa rit kwáń gẹ wọk ki wọt. Ka e mujọ deań, ka deań nẹ́kè yi jŭk, ka gẹ chama deań. Ka kŭl ka tẹ̀rù ká Tàbàlò, ka jāgọ é kánò ki atút, ka atút chònè rit, ka kwọp kómé chẹ̀.

When a king is to be elected, they bring the descendants of the Nubians,[1] and the sticks of the princes are broken. And some people go to the Nubian country, and bring some flint stones; they are put into the fire; then the fire is blown up; and a stick (of the princes) is thrown into it, into the fire; if the fire remains black, then that one (the prince or pretendent who threw his stick in) is not the king. Another stick is thrown in (by another prince); if the fire burns (flames up) a little, then this one is not the king. Again another stick is thrown in; if the fire burns a little high, that one is not the king. Another stick is thrown in; if the fire dies, that is not the king. Another one is thrown in, and if the fire burns with a big flame, and blazes up, then the people laugh: "This is the king (the prince who threw in this stick, he is to be king)."

[Hofmeyer says concerning this: "According to an ancient use which existed before Nyikang's time, a number of little stones according to the number of princes which have been proposed for election are thrown into a fire. Each stone has its name; now the one whose stone remains in the fire without cracking becomes king. This test is repeated so long till only one single stone is left.]

After that the people come (from different villages); they sleep in the bush,

---

[1] The Shilluks say: "When Nyikang brought his people into the Shilluk-country, he brought some Nubians with him; these Nubians live in several villages among the Shilluks up to this day; they are known by the Shilluks, but in their outward appearance they do not differ from the Shilluks." According to the report given above they seem to play or to have played rather an important rôle in the constitution of the Shilluk dynasty. It appears that the Shilluks have been in some political connection with the Nubians.

the next morning they come near and enter the village. The people of the stones (those who brought the stones) come and turn to a certain village, and a cow is sacrificed; they go into the next village, and a cow is sacrificed (in each village which they pass, a cow is sacrificed). So they come to Fashoda. On arriving there, the great chief asks them: "Who has been elected by the flint stone?" They answer: "This or that prince" (calling the name of the elected one).

That is all, and then the chiefs are brought (are sent for); they all are brought, from Mwomo to Tungo (the chief from each district, from the extreme north [Mwomo] to the south end [Tungo] of the Shilluk country is sent for). And they all come, that is, all chiefs come, and they talk about the matter. Then the people go to the village (of the newly elected king), they surround his village all around; after that they pass the night in the bush. Early next morning they go into the village again. Their spears are taken from their hands. They go into the enclosure (where the new king lives). The women cry. The king remains in the hut. The chiefs, the descendants of the kings, are called, they too go into the enclosure. The door-stick (of the hut) is cut off with a spear. They rush into the hut, and take the prince (the new king) out. He gives them a cow, the cow is killed by the chiefs, and they eat the meat. Then they take the new king to Tabālo, and they adorn him with beads, with dancing beads of the king. And they hold a long palaver.

26. A second report on the Election of a King.

Jāk dwai; ka tero beno, ka ge chyko, ka kwop kómì. Ka rit mâk, dwai fări, ka kal fān duon, ka rón dok kal, ka kiti gol Ńikan, gol duon. Ka tero làmo, ka jwok lâm, ka Ńikan lâm; rit de mito. Ka rŭmi, ka pi lęn re yi tero bęn, ka kiti kal, ka lwok yi bāne rit. Ka e rŭm, ka re kiti lāu, lāne jāgo, ka tón jāgo ká wěki, ka keta mal yech atùtò-wish; keta mal, ka e rùo. Ru wou ter dwai, ka tyen Ńiekan ka ge dwai Akuruwar, fay Ńikan. Ka ge bęn, ge kala Ńikāno ki Dāk, é gwôgò ki okwon wudo ge gīr; ge twojo rye àbóbò, ge kal. Tero ko: Ńikan a bi. Ka dok kal, ka jal mēko yâp, ka kal, ka lāu lón wòk, ka twóch, ka chip fen ki yo. Ka tero beno bene bene, rit ya dlr, ka tero kelá kwom jal eni, é dè kùtò. Ka rŭmi, ka tyen Ńikan beno, ge kalo onwero, ka tero ren, rit e mito ki nan a dācho, ge rŭno kifa tyen Ńikan, kifa go u fwót yi tyen Ńikan, fwōti tero bęne; nān a góch, ká chip wāi, ka nāne ti góch ka chip wāi. Ka rit chyeti. Ka ge rena wot, ka dean kal, ka dean chwóp, ka rit kal wòk, ka tero e beno bene bene, jāgo bęne; ka chip dok gol duon, ka tero làm. Ka chyek: yi ku gók ki gí ràch! Yi kú nak ki jè! Ńach fen jāgo mat! Ka rit dwota mal, ka tero fęka fen, re bòde bęnè; de bān rit ya būtẹ. Ka e kōbọ kine: Shọ́lọ́, nẹ̀ni yán bẹne! fà fà wà kífà kwá! yú nẹni kị ria kị dọ̱ch. Ka ḍāṇ ye: wuò wuò wuò bẹ̄ne. Ka ḍean kạl, ka shwọp kifa kōbe riṭ. Ka ḍok kạl, wèkè tyẹn Ńikan. Ka jal ẹni gọ́n, ka e kẹḍọ. Ka ḍean shwọp, mẹ̀n tùmà kwọ́p. Ka riṭ e kiṭi kị lān mẹ̱kọ, lān duọn, lāne jāgọ. Ka tẹ̄rọ e kẹ̀tò, mẹn kẹḍọ fōṭe gẹn, mẹn kẹḍọ fōṭe gẹ́n

The chiefs are sent for; and the people (together with the chiefs) come, they assemble and talk about the matter. And the king is seized, and brought (back) into his own village. He is brought to a large place, and there he is (publicly) elected outside the courtyards. They assemble in the court of Nyikang, the large court; and the people pray, they pray to God, and they pray to Nyikang too; during this time the king is held fast. When this (praying) is finished, water is sprinkled on his body by all people; he is brought into a yard and is washed by the wives of the king. After that his body is covered with clothes, with royal clothes, and a royal spear is given to him; then he goes up to his royal hut, he goes up into it, and stays there one year.[1] When the year is passed, the people (the chiefs) gather, and the people of Nyikang are sent for. They are brought from Akuruwar, the village of Nyikang. They come and bring (the wooden statues of) Nyikang and (of) Dāk, they are beautifully adorned, many ostrich feathers are tied to them. When they are brought, the people cry: "Nyikang has come!" Now cattle is brought, and a man is sought, they bring him, strip his clothes off him, and bind him. He is laid on the ground in the midst of the road. And all, all the people come, the king in their midst, and the people pass over the back of this man, they step over him. When that is done, the people of Nyikang come, and bring a whip, and the people run away; — the king catches hold [2] of a girl — they run [3] away because of the

> [According to Hofmeyer (Anthropos V, page 333) this girl is always taken from the clan of the Kwa-okāl: "The Kwa-okāl come from the Bahr el Ghasal; their ancestor was a relative of Nyikang; but a crime committed by one among them against the house of Nyikang, reduced the clan. They were declassed to ordinary Shilluks, and as a punishment for their crime they were sentenced to pay a girl to the king. This contribution has to be delivered whenever a new king is elected, but in course of time it has become an honour and a profitable business ... This girl always stands at the king's side during the ceremonies of election. For this tribute the clan receives clothes, beads, bells, lances, and harpoons. A hole in the ground near Fashoda is filled with sheep; besides cows and oxen are driven into it, as many as may find place; these also belong to the relatives of the girl. This girl is now called nya kwer (i. e. child belonging to the authority. W.).

[1] or: "one day"?
[2] or: "is held fast by"?
[3] vide page 128, 2 a.

Election of King. Taxes 125

There are several other clans which have the privilege of performing certain ceremonies in connection with the election of a king. One has the duty of fanning the king with a feather of the king of birds, another has to secure the dura sticks with which the party of the king defeats the party of the enemies."]

people of Nyikang, lest they be beaten by the people of Nyikang; for they (the latter) beat all people, and every one who is beaten, is put into a separate place and has to pay a fine to the people of Nyikang. All the people try to run into a house.

Now a cow is brought, the cow is speared, and the king is brought out. All the people come, all the chiefs, and they place the king outside the door of the great court; the people pray. The king is given these commandments: "Do not do any wicked things! Do not kill people! Govern the country of the chiefs in peace!" And the king rises, and all the people go down, they kneel on the earth, but the wives of the king kneel beside him. And he says: "Ye Shilluk people all, look at me! This is the country of my father and my grandfathers; you will live a peaceful life through me!" And all the people say: "Our father, our father!" A cow is brought, and is speared on account of the prosperity (for the good speed) of the king. And cattle are brought, and given to the people of Nyikang. And the man (who was bound) is released, and goes home. Another cow is speared, which finishes the matter. And the king is covered with certain clothes, big clothes, royal clothes. Now the people scatter, each one goes to his own country.

27. How Clothes are secured for the Royal Court.

Ka tęrǫ kà bę̀ dwàr ki lai, lai kwer, gyęk. Ka tęrǫ e kędǫ bęn̥g, gę̇ gir, ka jāk e làmǫ̀: yina yik ḍàn, kwóbé péṅ ànàn, lai tyęk, lai kwer chę̄, u de tūṅ u twoye, u chudǫ chę̄. E lāmǫ: yina yik Ńikānǫ, kęṅ an páyà yî, wǫ ku țōțe kí kwǫ́p! E ko: ḕ, kwaye ḍàn, nak lai ki dǭch, u kur boṅ é gòn; nę̀kè dǭch, kàji-tę-bānǫ! Ka dyęl kậl, ka chwǫp, ka gyę̄nǫ kậl, ka ṅǫl, ka dwar e kędǫ, ka tūṅ dwar kęl, ka gyęk nęk gę gir, ka tęrǫ bę̄nǫ, ka jāk e chukǫ, ka lai tyęr, ka gę rūmǫ tyęrǫ, ka jāṅe duǫṅ, ka lai gǭché, ka e ko: jâgí, kęl mǫ̀k, ka e ko jāk ṅate: kęl mǫ̀k, ṅèṅ. Ka gę ṅèṅ. Ka gę rumǫ ṅèṅǫ, ka gę kęl, kițe bę tyęro; ka jāgǫ ko kịne: nǫ̀? E ko: ḕ dę wa bà kądǫ gén? Ka e kapǫ ḍeaṅ, ka ḍeaṅ kęl, ka jāk chóṅ, ka gę kędǫ ka Bachōdǫ. Ka rit ṅach, ka ko: jâk d bì. Kịne: wuo, wǫ bi! Wu kuli nǫ? Wǫ kuli jamé kwer. Kịne: gę̇ àdì? Kịne pyār abikyęl. E kǫ: dǭch! Ka rit e kanǫ waṅ (rwaṅ) duǫṅ, ka wę̀kè jāk, ka nęk. Ka jāk e ríjó, gę̇ chàmǫ̀ ki ḍeaṅ. Ka gę ṅèehǫ̀. Kịne: wuo, bà wịtǫ̀? Kịne: ḕ, mițú jwǫk! Ka jāk e bę̄dǫ, ka muki tyęṅ, ka gę ríjó, gę̂ màḍǫ.

Kine: à, dǭch, kęt, kąlú jwǫk! Ka gę bę̄nǫ. Ka gę wapę fō̤tę gęn, ka būl gǭch, ka tę̄rǫ chǭnǫ kí bùl. Ka gę lō̤gǫ: wuna yik tę̄rǫ, ê, wǫ́ dùȯ̤k, dę bę̤t peṅ mȯ̤t.

The people go hunting game, a game for the king, a gyek-antelope. And all the people go, they are many, and the chiefs address them: "O ye people, (hear) a commandment of the king, concerning the gyek-antelope, which belongs to the king: if any man let the game escape, he shall surely be fined!" Then they pray: "O Nyikang, this matter is under your auspices! Do not suffer us to have any mishap! You grandfather of man, kill the game well, so that we may incur no debts! May it be killed well, o Nyikang!" Then a goat is brought, it is speared; a fowl is brought and cut up. Now the hunting-party arises, each part (goes) in a different direction. And when many antelopes have been killed, the people come back, and the chiefs assemble, and the game is brought before them; when they have brought it all, the big (district-) chief divides the animals, and says: "This chief shall take this, and this one shall take that;" then he says: "Tan it!" And they tan it. When they have finished tanning, the skins are brought before the chief for examination. The chief (when he has examined them) says: "All right!" Again he says: "Shall we not bring them (to the king)?" He seizes a cow, which they take with them (to Fashoda); all the chiefs assemble, and go to Fashoda. When they arrive there, they ask for permission to enter (the royal court). It is said to the king: "The chiefs have come." They greet the king: "Our Lord, we have come." He asks: "What do you bring?" They answer: "Whe have brought royal goods." The king asks: "How many?" They reply: "Sixty." He answers: "Very well." Then the king brings a big steer, and gives it to the chiefs. The steer is killed, and the chiefs stay to eat it, together with a cow. Then they ask the king for permission to go: "Our lord, shall we not go now? (we will go now!)". The king answers: "Why, hold fast (to) God (that is: stay!)" So the chiefs remain; and beer is strained, and they stay to drink. Afterward the king says: "Well, all right, go now with God!"

When they come home and approach their villages, the drum is beaten, and the people dance to the drum; then they address the people; "O ye people, we have returned; may the country live in peace!" [1]

28. Making Boats for the King.

A kęt tę̄rǫ bę ṅwǫt ki yat, yętę kwėr, ka tę̄rǫ ṅùdǭ, ka yat kȧ̤l, ká tę̀rù bę̀nò, ka tę̄rǫ wapí fach. Ka jāgǫ chwǫ́l, ka yat tyęr ká è nę̄nǫ, ka e kapǫ mė̤, ka e ko: kwaṅ yęt ak! Ka kwȧṅ, ka e ko: mǫk an ba mǫk rí̤t, ka mǫk an tyęṅ, ka gę kwóch, ka gę bę̄nǫ gin keau Bachōdǫ.

[1] The dyęk-antelope belongs to the king, out of its hide clothes for the king's wives are made.

The people go to cut boats, boats for the king; and the people cut them, and bring the boats, all the people come (with the boats), and when they approach the village, the chief is called; the boats are put before him for examination. He looks at them, and seizes some, saying: "Take these boats!" They are taken, then he says: "These belong to the king"; they are hewn (carved), are sewn together, and after that they row them to Fashoda.

29. Provinces of the Shilluk country
beginning from south.

1. Tùṅọ̀	2. Ńejwàdọ̀	3. Dèṅọ̀
4. Dọr	5. Ńelòwák	6. Wóbò
7. Dyèl	8. Fèṅíkàṅ	9. Aryèkèr
10. Agunjwọ̀k	11. Ajọ̀gọ̀	12. Fákàṅ
13. Obàyàbwíjọ̀p	14. Obai-Dêgọ̀	15. Adịdeaṅ
16. Feṅidwái	17. Owọ́sht	18. Twọ̀ró
19. Awâu	20. Dur	21. Adọ̀dọ̀
22. Dọ̀t	23. Adọ́kọ́ṅ	24. Awáréjwọ̀k
25. Kwọ̀gọ̀	26. Obwâ	27. Málákâl
28. Famât	29. Ogọ̀t	30. Wâu
31. Fádèt	32. Fátâu	33. Bọ̀t
34. Ńéṅârọ̀	35. Bọ́l	36. Fábûr
37. Béó	38. Agọ̀dọ́	39. Yọ̀ṅ
40. Lụl	41. Kwọ̀m	42. Pàchôdọ̀
43. Agwọ̀rọ́	44. Ńegèr	45. Gòlbâṅọ̀
46. Fàdeaṅ	47. Lẹ̄mọ	48. Kódọ́k
49. Gọ̀lọ̀	50. Kwòchàṅ	51. Alẹl
52. Dètwọ̀k	53. Bùrbẹ̀k	54. Màl
55. Abyèṅài	56. Ogọ̀ṅ	57. Faṅíkàṅ-Otêgọ̀
58. Ńélyèch	59. Atwọ̀dwọ̀i	60. Tùrọ̀
61. Tọ̀mọ̀t	62. Akùruwâr	63. Abûr
64. Mâṅọ̀	65. Mwọ̀mọ́.	

The Clans or Divisions of the Shilluk People.

The Shilluks are divided into a number of clans or tribes, each of which is traced back to a common ancestor. In most cases this ancestor is a man, but some of the clans claim descendency from an animal.

The following names of the clans and all the remarks added have been procured by *Reverend D. Oyler, of Doleib Hill*, who collected them from an assembly of natives, and had them afterwards examined by some Shilluk men who are known for being well versed in the history and traditions of their people.

The names are given in the succession in which the natives enumerated them. If there are two different traditions of a clan, the second is introduced by: "Diff."

The word Kwa means "descendant."

[Hofmeyer in "Anthropos" enumerates 13 clans and gives some remarks on four of them.]

1. Kwa-Ajal, was founded by Jal, one of the men who came with Nyikang from his earlier home. They live at Nyelwak. They lay out the circle for building the house of Nyikang. — Diff.: the clan was founded by Milo, who named it after his son Jal. Milo waged war with the sun, and got a cow. When Nyikang saw it he was pleased and asked, where he got it. On learning it had been gained from the sun, he sent Milo back for more. The latter managed to steal several; but the sun became angry and burnt Milo and his people. Eventually a battle occurred, in which the sun succeeded in killing all the cattle except a pair of calves, which Milo saved by wrapping them in his cloth. He got them safely to earth.

2. Kwa Mal, was founded by a man and a woman who came down from above *(mal).* They left their children on earth and ascended again. — Diff.: they died on earth; their home is Malakal.

2 a. Kwa Lek, was founded by two celestial beings, a man and his wife. It gets its name from the large wooden pestle that the Shilluks use in crushing their dura. They quarrelled over a lek; the man wanted to use it to stir the cow dung, at the same time the woman said she needed it for crushing dura. Neither would yield to the other. Seizing the lek they fought over it. So violent was their quarrel that they fell to earth. Nyikang captured them and told them to settle at Malakal. The woman taught the people to make beer. Later they escaped and returned to the skies. At the crowning of the king their descendants strike the people with whips of sheep skin. The lek over which they quarrelled, is now at Malakal. — Diff.: they died at Malakal; and this is the same division as No 2, and should not be counted as a separate division. —

[This last remark is no doubt right, as both *2* and *2a* are of the same "celestial" origin; moreover Hofmeyer in "Anthropos" gives a description of the kwa Mal which is identical with that of our kwa Lek. W.]

3. Kwa Oman, was founded by a woman who was a wife of Nyikang. They do not appear to have a special function; live at Ogot. — Diff.: was founded by a man named Oman; they help to build the house of Nyikang. Oman was found by Nyikang in the Shilluk country.

4. Kwa Mon, was founded by Mon; Mon was found in the Shilluk country by Nyikang and became his servant. They help to build the house of Nyikang at Wau. They live at Ogot. — Identical with 3?

5. Kwa Ju, or *Kwa Jǫk,* was founded by Ju, a half-brother of Nyikang on his father's side. Ju built the house for Dak. The Kwa Ju build the three houses of Dak in Filo on the White Nile. When they have finished building the house, an ox is killed by a half-brother of the king.

They live at Mainam.

6. Kwa Nyadwai, was founded by Nyadwai, an ancient king of the Shilluks; he was the son of Tugo. They are found at Apio and Adit-deang. They help to build the house of the king. — The son of Nyadwai was a servant of Abudok.

7. Kwa Gwar, was founded by Gwar, a servant of king Dokot. They build the houses of Dokot in three villages. They give the skins of Mrs. Gray's waterbuck to the king. Their village is Chet-Gwok.

8. Kwa Nyikang, was founded by Nyikang, a servant of king Nyikang. They help to build the house of Nyikang. Their village is Fakang (the village of Kang). — Diff.: it was founded by Olam, a servant of Nyikang. Olam was captured by Nyikang in the river, and brought out. Nyikang settled him in the country. Olam is said to have been a man of tremendous appetite.

9. Ñwǫn, was founded by a hippo-hunter named *Ñwǫn.* He was found near Doleib Hill by king Abudok. The name *Ñwǫn* means to walk in a stealthy manner. They help to build the house of Abudok. Their village is Twara.

10. Kwa Reṭ (or *riṭ,* i. e. king), was founded by Nyikang. They all go to the crowning of a king. Their village is Filo.

11. Kwa Tŭki, was founded by a person that Nyikang discovered by the river. They taught the Shilluks to build the tuki (hearth-stones). It is made of three small pillars of mud built in a triangular shape. On the tuki the cooking vessel is placed. Before the Shilluks were taught to build the tuki, they used to dig a little hole in the ground for the fire. The Kwa Tuki help to care for the cattle of Nyikang. They live at Didigo.

12. Kwa Chwal, was founded by Chwal, who was found in the Shilluk country by Nyikang. They live in *Foṇe* Nyikang, and help to build the house of Nyikang. — Diff.: Chwal was found on his way here.

13. Kwa Jaṅ Nyikang; he had a Dinka wife, her people founded this division. They live at Ojodo, and help to build the house of Dak. — Diff.: it was founded by a Dinka, who was the son of Gok, and came of his own free will.

14. Kwa Tŭga, was founded by Tuga, a foreigner. They say he was an Arab. Nyikang married Tuga's sister, and her brother followed her.

15. Kwa Kęlǫ, was founded by *Okęlǫ,* a servant of Nyikang. He taught the

Shilluks how to prepare the mud for the tuki. They live at *Foṇe* Nyikang, and help to build the house of Nyikang at *Foṇe* Nyikang. — Diff.: Okelo was a Nuba, whose sister was married by Nyikang. Vide *11*.

16. Kwa Ogūti, was founded by *Gūti,* a servant of Nyikang. He came into this country. They live at Twara and tear down the old houses of Nyikang.

17. Kwa Dāk, was founded by Dak, a servant of Nyikang. They cut the first dura stalks for the house of Nyikang; they live at Owichi. — Diff.: Dak was the son of Nyikang; they build the house of Abudok.

18. Kwa Osḥọḷḷọ, was founded by Oshollo, a servant of Odak. They build the houses of Odak, and live at Malakal. — Diff.: Oshollo was the son of Dak; they build the house of Oshollo, and also the king's house.

19. Kwa Ñebọ̄dọ, was founded by Nyikang's blacksmith (*bọ̄dọ*). He furnishes the name for skilled workmen. They live at Nyelwak, and help to build the house of Nyikang at *Foṇe* Nyikang. Each year they give the king dried hippo meat.

20. Kwa Gūga, was founded by a man who once sat near Nyikang like a buzzard watching for meat. They live at Nyelwal and help to build the house of Nyikang.

21. Kwa Obọ̄gọ, was founded by Obogo, a servant of Nyikang that had come with him. When they arrived at the Nile, the current was blocked up with sudd, so that they could not find a crossing. Then Obogo told Nyikang to kill him. He was consequently thrust with a spear. When his blood touched the sudd, it parted, and a clear passage was furnished for Nyikang and his party. Obogo's self-sacrifice took place "at the end of the earth." They live in *Foṇe* Nyikang, and help to build the house of Nyikang. Vide *51*.

22. Kwa Ogẹkọ, was founded by Ogek, a servant of Nyikang. They get their name from the fact that they were the herders of the sacred cow that Nyikang got from the river. They are found at Wau.

23. Kwa Ñemwal ("the crawlers"), used to be a part of No. 10, but Nyikang became angry with them and said they could no longer belong to the Kwa Ret. They help to build the house of Nyikang and furnish hippo meat to the king. — Diff.: it was founded by Uwal, who was a member of No. 17. The division was effected peaceably, because the Kwa Dok had become too large for convenience. They help to build the house of Chal. Their residence is at Tonga.

24. Kwa Oḳạl, was founded by people that Nyikang found in the Shilluk country. They first dug in the ground. They help in building the house of Nyikang. When a king is crowned, the chief of this division gives one of his daughters to the king. — Remark. This division seems to be the same as Hofmeyer's

Kwa Okal, of whom he says, "They have come from the Bahr Ghasal; their ancestor was a relative of Nyikang. But a crime which they committed became the cause of their clan being decimated. They became common Shilluks, and as a punishment for their crime they had to pay a girl to the king. This tribute is repeated at each new election. The girl is called nya *Kwer*" (i. e. girl of the authorities, girl of taxes). Vide also *15*.

25. Kwa Lọbọ, or Oshū, was founded by Oshu, the son of Lobo, a servant of Abudok, who was found in the Shilluk country. They help to build the house of Abudok, their residence is in Owichi. — Diff. it was founded by Okola, the husband of Lobo; they were the parents of Oshu; servants of Nyikang.

26. Kwa Būṅa (Būṅọ?), was founded by foreigners who have come in. To become a member in good standing it was necessary for the member of each family to give a daughter to the king. The ancestors of the division were strangers who married Shilluk women and took up residence in the Shilluk country. They are found at Nyigir.

27. Kwa Orōrọ; are the same as 23 (?) Are found at Yonj.

28. Kwa Ḍokot, was founded by *Ḍokot,* a servant of Dak; they were found in the Sobat region by Nyikang. According to some they are the descendants of Dokot. They build the house of Dak. Their residence is at Gur.

29. Kwa Ńimọṅọ, was founded by *Ńimọṅọ,* who was found here by Nyikang, who married his daughter. They live in Gur.

30. Kwa Owẹn, was founded by a man who tried to deceive Nyikang. The name Owen means deceiver. They are servants of Nyikang, and help in building his house. Nyikang brought them from a distance; they live in *Fọṇe* Nyikang.

31. Kwa Orẹtọ, was founded by *Orẹtọ,* whom Nyikang found in the Shilluk country. They help to build the houses of Nyikang and Dak. Their residence is in Nigu and Wubo.

32. Kwa Wūṅ, was founded by a man who tried to hide all the fish of a certain kind *(eshura)* from Nyikang. When Nyikang asked for them, he said there were none; but his treachery was found out. If any of this division eat of this kind of fish, he will die. They are found at Tonga and furnish fish and other water animals to the king. They also help in building the house of Nyikang.

33. Kwa Ńishine, was founded by a man that Nyikang found near Tonga. They live at Tonga, and help to build the house of Nyikang.

34. Kwa Nai, was founded by Nai, a servant of Dak. They help to build the house of Dak that used to be on the mission ground at Doleib Hill. They are found at Obai and Abijop.

35. Kwa Dwai, was founded by Dwai, a servant of Dak. They help to build the house of Dak and are found at *Foṇe* Nyikang. — Diff.: Dwai was a servant of Nyikang. He was a Nuba, who came into the country and was taken by Nyikang.

[This last remark is probably right, as the Nubians are generally addressed: Nya Dwai.]

36. Kwa Agọ̄dọ, was founded by *Agọ̄dọ,* a servant of Nyikang. He was a foreigner that Nyikang found here. They live in Obuwa, and help to build the house of Nyikang. — Diff.: they build the house of Oshollo in Ditong.

37. Kwa Ńiḍeań, was founded by a Dinka who came into the Shilluk country. They live at Obai, and build the house of Dak.

38. Kwa Ńikọ̄gọ, was founded by *Ńikọ̄gọ,* a servant of Nyikang. Nyikang found him in this country. They build the house of Nyikang; their residence is at Didigo.

39. Kwa Duń, was founded by *Aduń,* a Dinka, who was a servant of Abudok. They are found at Owichi. — Diff.: he was a servant of Nyikang.

40. Kwa Okwai, was founded by Okwai, an ancient fisherman found in this country by Nyikang. They live at Adodo and build the house of Nyikang. — Diff.: he was a Dinka, and was found by Duwat.

41. Kwa Jalọ, was founded by Jalo, a servant of Odak. They live at Aditdeang, and build the house of Odak. — Diff.: he was a son of Duwat.

42. Kwa Ogwat, was founded by Ogwat, a servant of Odak. They build the house of Odak. Tonga is their home.

43. Kwa Omal, was founded by Omal, a servant of Odak. They build the house of Odak; their residence is at Malakal. — Diff.: They are the same as No. 2, and should not be counted as a separate division.[1]

44. Kwa Wań, was founded by *Wań,* who crowned Nyikang. Wang was found in the Shilluk country. They live at Okun and Dur; they have a part in the crowning of the king.

45. Kwa Okọ̄nọ was founded by *Okọ̄nọ,* a servant of Nyikang, who was found in the country by the latter. They live at Kakugo, and help to build the house of Nyikang. — Diff.: They build the house of Dak.

46. Kwa Duwạt, was founded by Duwat, a servant of Dak. They are the chief of the servants of Dak; they live at Filo.

47. Kwa Kū, was founded by Oku, a servant of Nyikang. Nyikang found him on the bank of the river in the Shilluk country. They build the house of Nyikang. Their home is Arumbwut.

48. Kwa Yọ̄dọ, was fonded by *Oyọ̄dọ,* a servant of Nyikang, found in the Shilluk country. They help to build the house of Nyikang. Their home is in

---

[1] They may, however, be a subdivision of 2, as Omal means "descendant of Mal."

Clans

Foṇe Nyikang. — Diff: Nyikang brought Oyodo from a distance.

49. Kwa Okọ̄gi, was founded by *Okọ̄gọ*, a servant of Nyikang. He was brought from the Nuba country. They help to build the house of Nyikang. Their residence is at Detwuk. — Diff.: he was found in the Shilluk country.

50. Kwa Mūi, was founded by *Omūi*, a Nuer servant of Nyikang. They live at Adit-deang.

51. Kwa Obǭn, was founded by *Obǭn*, a servant of Nyikang. He was found in the Shilluk country. He ate the meat cleaned off the skin of Nyikang's cattle. They live at Nyelwal. — Diff.: Obon was brought here by Nyikang.

52. Kwa Chwai ("soup"),[1] was founded by *Chwai*, a servant of Nyikang, who was found here. Their functions are the same as the preceding, except that when an ox of Nyikang is killed, they get the soup. They live at Nyelwal.

53. Kwa Riñọ, ("meat"), was founded by *Riño*, a servant of Nyikang, who was found in the Shilluk country. At the killing of an ox of Nyikang they get the meat.

54. Kwa Fyẹn ("skin"), was founded by *Ofyẹn*, a servant of Nyikang found in the Shilluk country. They get the skin of Nyikang's cattle. They live at Nyelwal.

55. Kwa Wich ("head"), was founded by *Owich*, a servant of Nyikang found in the Liri-country (Kordofan). They get the head of Nyikang's cattle. Their home is at Nyelwal. — Diff.: *Wich* was a Dinka.

56. Kwa Shịn, ("intestines"), was founded by *Shịn*, a servant of Nyikang. They get the intestines of Nyikang's cattle; live at Nyelwal.

57. Kwa Ńilẹnọ, was founded by *Olẹn*, a Nuer servant of Nyikang. They help to build the house of Nyikang. Their residence is Tonga.

58. Kwa Nyidọk, was founded by *Odọk*, a servant of Dak. They help in building the house of Nyikang. Their home is Dur and Obai.

59. Kwa Ayādọ, was founded by *Ayādọ*, a servant of Dak. They make a preparation of bean leaves and give it to the king, who puts it on his body. They are found at Dur. — Diff.: he was a servant of Nyikang, they help to build the house of Nyikang at Malakal.

60. Kwa Anūt, was founded by *Anūt*, a servant of Nyikang found in the Shilluk country. They taught the Shilluks to make fire by friction. At the crowning of the king they make fire. They are found at Fotou.

61. Kwa Nyerit̥, are descendants of Nyikang. They are the royal class. The king is chosen from among them. Their village is Yoyin. Vide *10*.

62. Kwa Ḍọn, was founded by *Odọn*, a Nuba, who came into the country. He was a servant of Nyikang. They help to build the house of Nyikang. Their village is near Tonga.

---

[1] These and some of the following as well as of the preceding names are apparently not really names of ancestors.

63. Kwa Odeno, was founded by *Odeni*, a servant of Abudok. They help to build the house of Abudok. Their village is Twara. He came into the country.

64. Kwa Wūbo, was founded by *Wūbo*, a servant of Nyikang. He was a brave man, who was never afraid. When the cows of Nyikang got into his dura, he watched them, and killed one cow. Nyikang told him that something bad would happen to him. As a result his village was attacked by the Nuers, and a large part of his descendants were killed; so it is a small division now. Wubo was very skilful in the use of weapons. — They do not rub ashes on their faces and bodies. They help to build the house of Nyikang. They live at Ajwogo.

65. Kwa Ńikāi, was founded by Kir, a servant of Nyikang. He was found at a distance. At the death of the king they beat the drum. They live in Gur. — Diff. he was found in the river by Nyikang.

66. Kwa Yǫ, was founded by *Yǫ*, a servant of Odak. They help to build the house of Odak. Their village is Obwo. — Diff.: he was a servant of Nyikang; they help to build the house of Oshollo.

67. Kwa Gau, was founded by *Ogau*, a servant of Odak. He was from the Anywak country. They help to build the house of Odak. Their residence is at Tonga.

68. Kwa Mwal, was founded by Mwal, a servant of Nyikang. He crawled away from battle. They do not eat of the flesh on the knee-joint. They help to build the house of Nyikang. Their home is at Ogot. Vide *23*.

69. Kwa Kam, was founded by Kam, a servant of Nyikang. He was a fish which Nyikang caught and changed into a man. They are found in *Fone* Dwai. — Diff.: he was brought in by Dak, and was his servant.

70. Kwa Okaṭi, was founded by *Okaṭi*, a son of Dokot. They help to build the house of Dak. Their home is at *Fone* Dwai. — Diff.: he was of Arabic descent. When a king is crowned, and the king starts to Tonga, they sweep the beginning of the road with a hen.

71. Kwa Bel, was founded by Bel, a servant of Nyikang. He was an Anywak. They are at Mainam. They help to build the house of Nyikang. — Bel once fought against Mui.

72. Kwa Ńiyǫk, was founded by *Oyǫk*, a servant of Nyikang. At the crowning they ring the bells.

73. Kwa Ńeyǫk, was founded by *Oyǫk*, a servant of Nyikang. At the crowning they ring the bells. They live at Fashoda.

74. Kwa Ńetyen, was founded by *Otyen*, a servant of Nyikang. He was sent on an errand by Nyikang and forgot; thus he got his name. They are found in *Fakań*; they help to build the house of Nyikang in *Fakań*.

Kings

30. The Shilluk kings.

1. Ńíkàṅọ̀ —	2. Dăk —	3. Shál —
4. Anọ̀nọ̀ —	5. Odăk —	6. Dywạt —
7. Bwọch ←	8. Dọ́kọ̀t	9. Abúdọk (queen)
10. Túgọ̀ ←	11. Okwọ̀n, Okōn	12. Ǹàdwài
13. Ǹạdọ̀kè	14. Kúdìt	15. Ǹàkwàchọ̀ ?o
16. Anèì?	17. Akwọ̀t	18. Awên
19. Akọ́ch o	20. Ǹẹ̀dók o	21. Kwaṭkẹr o
22. Ajañ	23. Kwòyìkwọ́n	24. Yọ̀r
25. Akọl	26. Kúr	27. Padyẹ̄t.

A. E. S. has the following list (according to Father Banholzer at Lul, and Dr. Giffen at Doleib Hill).

1. Nyakang	2. Dag	3. Odage
4. Kudit	5. Dokodo	6. Boj
7. Tugo	8. Nya Dwai	9. Nya Ababdo
10. Muko	11. Nya To	12. Nyakong
13. Okun	14. Nya Gwatse (Nkwaji)	15. Nyadok
16. Akwot	17. Ababdo A Kwot	18. Awin
19. Akoj	20. Nedok (Nyadok)	21. Kwad keir
22. Ajang	23. Gwin kun (Kwoe kon)	24. Yor Adodit
25. Akol	26. Kur Wad Nedok	27. Fadiet Wad kwad keir.

31. The Burial of a King.

Riṭ ka ńí wàńí, ńí kiṭe wọt. Ka ḍeaṅ chwọ́p, ka fyẹni yêch, ka rêr, ka wumi rēro, ka yẹn dwai, ka gẹ ṅọ̀t, gẹ́n á tàkúgì kạl, ka gẹ kwon feń. Ka dẹl ṇi ká gọ̀ tàdị̀ tǎt tabate. Ka gẹ rumọ ki tādọ, ka riṭ kạl; e kúchè tēro, ka kiṭe wọt, ka ruk ki lāno kwañ. Wọ̀mán aryau ka gẹ kạl, ka gẹ kiṭe wọt; ka mẹko miṭọ wijẹ, ka mẹko miṭọ tyelẹ; ka mẹn ṭọṭe ki atàbọ́ kí dăk, ka ńān ṭọṭe ki atābọ ki dāk. Ka wọt mūl, da bụ yọ mẹn yeje kạle yọ̀mọ̀. Ka gẹ bẹdọ wọt, maku dwat aryau. Ká gẹ ṭọ̀, ka kōnọ, ka rei gẹ yọ́kì tēnọ̀. Ka gẹ kẹ́là wiy wọt; riñ á ṭùm, ka gọ dọ̀ṇa chù. Ka jăk dwai bẹ̀ń wuṭe[1] Tūnọ, ka wuṭe[1] Mwọmọ, jāgi bẹ̀ń bẹ̀ń. Ka gẹ kẹdọ, mẹn e kàtọ́ ḍeàn; u wape gẹn, ka ḍok ẹni chọ́ń kách áky̱ẹl, ka gẹ chwọ̀p.[2] Ka gẹ kine: riṭ a wañ. Ka tēro ywọń, ka ḍeań mẹko yêch, ka fyẹn e ńêń, ẹn aṭẹp. Ka shū riṭ kitį yech aṭẹp, ka kóń feń; á kân, ka ywọk ywọk. Ka tēro bẹ̄nọ bẹ̄ne bẹ̄ne bẹ̄ne. Ka tọń shọ́ń gẹ gīr, ka gẹ twôch, ka gẹ kiṭe yi yẹi, ka okọt kiṭe yi yẹi gīr, ka tẹ̀k kiṭe yi yẹi gīr, ka puki kiṭe yi yẹi, ki tạ̀mì, ki lọ̀t. Ka jē kạl, gẹn aryau, mẹn aky̱ẹl ńāne dach, mẹn akyẹl ńāne jal, jē mọgẹ dọ́ch, ka gẹ kiṭe yi yẹi, gẹ túòjụ̀, chyẹń gẹn fá à tọ̄chọ́, ki tyẹli gẹ́n fá à tọ̄chọ́; mẹ̄ko ya ṭa yẹi, mẹ̄ko ya yẹt yẹi. Ka yẹi keau, ka

---

[1] *wiṭe*; reaching T., and reaching M., i. e. from T. unto M.   [2] generally: *chwọ̀p*.

wuṭi de nam, ka yɛi nɛ twóyɛ̀ y̨ fi kɛ̱ṯɛ gɛ yɛ̱jɛ̱. Ka yậ keau kɛ̱ṯɛ yi yɛi mḛkọ, ka yɛi a twoye, e mudọ kị jɛ̀ ki yejɛ̱, ki jam bḛn, ka gɛ ṯọwa nam.

When the king disappears (that is, dies),[1] his body is laid in a hut. A cow is speared, its skin removed, and cut into strips. When they have finished this, trees are brought, they are hewn with a certain ax, and then they are driven into the earth. With the strips (of skin) they unite these trees to a bier. When the bier is ready, they bring the body of the king — but without the people knowing it — lay it on the bier, and put it in the hut again. The body is adorned with a leopard-skin. Two girls are brought, and are put into the hut, where the body of the king is. One holds his head, and one holds his feet. Each of the girls is given tobacco and a pipe. Now the hut is walled (all openings are walled with mud), so that there is no way for the air to enter. They (the two girls) remain in the hut, and die there. The people wait two months; about this time the worms (who have eaten the flesh of the three bodies) have turned into bugs, and they come crawling out through the roof of the hut. Now (the people know that) the flesh (of the three corpses) is consumed and only the bones remain. Then all the chiefs of the Shilluk country are summoned, beginning from Tûngọ,[2] and reaching to Mwọmọ; all, all the chiefs. And they come, each one brings a cow; when they come near Fashoda, they gather these cows at one place; and the cows are speared. Now it is said publicly, "The king has disappeared." And the people weep. One of the cows is skinned, the skin is tanned and made into a bag. The bones of the king are put into this bag; and they are buried in a secret place. But still the mourning goes on, all, all, all the people mourn. And spears are gathered, a great many; they are tied together, and put into a boat; and cattle-bells are put into the boat, and beads, and pots, and dishes, and gourds. And two people are brought, a man and a woman, fine people, they are laid into the boat, they are bound, their hands and their feet are bound; one is laid in the back part, and one in the front part (of the boat). The boat is rowed into the middle of the river, there the boat is pierced, so that water enters into it. The men who row the boat, get into another boat, and the boat which they have pierced, sinks down with the people in it, and all the goods, together with the people, perish in the river.

32. The Man who took the Law into his own Hand.

Jal mḛkọ, ṅa riṭ, chwọla Buk Dē Jọk Buṅ Dāṅimọ, ka gɛ gōṅọ. Buk dọ̄ch; wạt bāṅɛ chwọla Okaṅọ. A gwọṅ ki Ayīk. Ka gɛ gōṅọ ki Bure Ṅakwachọ. Ka wạt bāṅɛ pạra bọ̄lɛ, ka kēl yi Ayīk ki tón, ká è ṭọ̄. Ka Agwōrọ chḛṯe yi riṭ, ka ṅwọle mâk, a kậl Ayīk Detạṅ.

---

[1] Of a king it is not said: "he dies", but "he disappears". — It is said: the king does not die of his own accord, but when he is very old, or sick, and the people think that his death is near at hand, his chief wife strangles him with a cloth.
[2] = Tonga.

A certain man, a prince, whose name was Buk Dē Jǫk Buin Dānyimǫ, carried on a law-suit. Buk was a good man; he had a slave, whose name was Oshangǫ. He carried on the law-suit with Ayık, in the court of king Nyakwachǫ. And his servant ran in front of him (or: came instead of him, viz. of his master), and was stabbed by Ayık with a spear, so that he died. (As a punishment for this misdeed) the village Ogwǫrǫ (which was the village of Ayık) was destroyed by the king; the children (of the village, or of Ayık) were caught, and Ayık was brought (banished) to Detang.

33. A killed Crocodile is the Property of the Magistrate.

Kęń mak nam, ka tęrǫ kędǫ[1], ka tęrǫ nini gat, ka bói mę̈n peń, ka rech e bęnǫ, ka boi ma̧go ki rech, ka jē t̬u̬dǫ, ka jē chāmǫ. Ka wǫu rū, ka maye bęnǫ, ka tęrǫ ma̧gǫ, ka ńan ka kęl, ka e makǫ ki ḍa̧n. Ka tęrǫ reńa wǫk, ka tygń tęk e dǫńǫ, ka ḍa̧n kul gę wǫk, ka ńan nęké. Ka tęrǫ ka̧ wǫk, ka jāke bęnǫ, ka gę pęchǫ: ńan a gwǫ̈k edi? Kine: e nęk! Kine: dę ę ya kęń? Kine: nut. Yech! Ka yech. Ka e ko: nólé, bā gik la̧gǫ. Ka kiṭe pach la̧gǫ, ka tęrǫ bęnǫ chę̈, ka ńan ṭal yi jāgǫ, ńańe la̧gǫ. Ka e chwǫtǫ jē, ka jāk dwai, ka e chām; tęrǫ ko: ō, ńan an dǫ̈ch. Ḍuki mękǫ ka ńań mękǫ kwáń, ka chām yi tęre yau.

Ka jāgǫ e chwǫ̈tǫ, ka tęrǫ bęnǫ, ka e pęchǫ kine: wuna yik jåk, ya peńa giche mękǫ, ęná kwāńu ki yey nam kå; kine: å gin áńǫ̀? Ya peńa kwǫ̈l. Kine: ę̂, kúchè wóń! Kine: ę̂, faṭe ńan a chām ki pay ńate? Kine: ę̂, e chāmǫ, twǫle ńań tǫnǫ. Kine: ę̂, chōlá! Ka e kyędǫ, kine: ya ba chudǫ. Kine: ę̂, wa kā Bachōdǫ. Kine: ę̂, wa kędǫ.

Ka gę kędǫ, ka gę wiṭa Bachōdǫ, ká gę̈ gòńǫ̀, kine: wuo (wuę), yá ḍálè yi kwóp kwǫfe ńate; kwǫ̈l a chámè ęn, kwǫl la̧gǫ. Kine: ę̂, yi chama ńǫ, ńate? Kine: wuo, kúchè yán. Riṭ e ko: ęrę (rédę), kęṭ chōl ki ḍǫk gá pyàrǫ, ki ḍa̧n! Ka e bęnǫ, ka e chudǫ ḍǫk gá pyàrǫ, ki ḍa̧n; ka gę kǫ̈l kōle riṭ, u tęre lińe[2], ka gę rūmǫ.

It was at the time when the river was barred (shut up for fishing), and the people slept on the river bank, and the net was sunk down on the bottom of the river, and the fish came, and the net caught fish, and the people cooked and ate them. And when it grew morning, the fishermen came, and the people went fishing again, then a crocodile was speared, and it seized a man; the people became afraid, and ran away, but those among them who were brave, remained; they brought the man who had been bitten by the crocodile out on the river bank. Then they killed the crocodile, and went out of the river (taking the crocodile with them). The chiefs came, and asked, "What about the crocodile?" They answered, "It is killed." They asked again, "But where is it?" Answer, "It is still here." The chiefs said, "Skin it!" And it was

---

[1] "When the river was caught, and the people went".
[2] that the people might hear.

skinned. The chiefs said, "Cut it up! It is the property of the magistrate." So the meat was put into the house of the magistrate. All the people came; the crocodile was cooked by he chief, the crocodile of the magistrate. He called all the people, and invited the neighbouring chiefs too; they ate the crocodile. The people said, "Ah, this crocodile is good!" Some days later they again caught a crocodile, and it was eaten by the people.

But the district chief had heard about the matter. He called all the chiefs of his district together; they came, and he began, "You chiefs, I want to ask you something, it is the thing which you got from the river there." They asked, "What do you mean?" He replied, "I am asking for some animal you killed." They said, "We do not know!" He asked, "Why, has not a crocodile been eaten here in somebody's village?" They answered, "Yes, that is true, it has been eaten by the little children." He said, "Make amends for it!" But they refused, saying, "We will not do that." Then he said, "Well, we will go to Fashoda (to bring the matter before the king)." They said, "All right, let us go!" So they went, and arrived at Fashoda. There they told their case, saying (the district-chief speaks first), "My lord, I am in difficulty about some matter, the matter of a certain man, he has eaten a killed animal, an animal belonging to the magistrate." The king asked the accused one, "Why did you eat it, man?" He answered, "My lord, I did not know." The king said, "Why! go, and make amends! You are to give ten cows and a man." The chief brought what was asked, into the enclosure of the king, so that all people heard it, and learned to be careful.[1]

34. How Fashoda became the Royal Residence.

Ka jāk riṯ Túgọ, jāk a pàrẹ, chwọla Ńewājọ. Ka waṯ ka gẹ ńí bẹ̄nọ, gẹ bēr[2] ga waṯe chôt, ka gẹ ńí gwọtọ wiy pach kị chāno. Ka riṯ e kōbọ kịne: bụ́h, gẹ rẹ ru waṯ, a rếi gèn gwōṯọ? Kịne: tyẹre pān ẹni. A gẹ̄r pān ẹni, a Pachōdọ; a dẹge Tugọ yẹjẹ, a kōbị Tugọ kịne: fān ẹni ụ chọ̄k á pà rọ̄ń! A bāne ńi rọ̄ń tẹ̀dọ yẹjẹ. A rǘm é jàgọ̀, a kōbị kịne: ka wạ̄da ụ rọ̄ń, a rọ́ńé.

King Tugo reigned, he reigned in his own village, which was called Nyewājọ. And there were oxen, they used to come (to some place), they were oxen without horns, called chod, they used to dig the ground of that place with their heads every day. When the king saw that, he said, "My! why are the oxen always digging the ground?" He said, "They like this place." So a village was built there, it was Pachōdọ. Tugọ moved from his place into this new village. He said, "This village shall always remain the village of election (the village of the king)." Since that time the people elect the king in it. When the

---

[1] Crocodiles belong to the king ("to the authority, magistrate,") nobody is allowed to eat them without permission of the king or the district chief. Here the chiefs of the villages try to usurp the privilege of the district chief.   [2] From *bẹ̄dọ* "to be".

king (Tugọ) had finished his reign, he said, "My son shall be elected!" And he was elected.

35. A Law-suit about Dowry.

Kẹṅ kẹt jē bẹ pidọ̀, ka jē kẹdọ, ka jē pẹka peṅ. Ka pān ẹni chọ́ṅ, ka ḍāṇ u̱¹ pẹ̱chọ̱, kine: ya̱ pidọ káché jâm! Kine: káchè jam kúchè yán!² Kine: yi nụti kọ̀pọ̱? Kine: yi mẹn an? Kine: yi wóu. Kẹye rọt kúchè yán! Kine: kipaṅọ kuche yin? Kine: jal tọṅ amẹn? Kine: jal tọṅ ṅate. Kine: kwáṅ jâm! Ka jame kwân. A, ṅate, yi re a pẹ̱m? ḍọk paṭe dyer? Ka jē kẹti bẹ gọ́ṅ. Ka jē kẹdọ, ka riṭ e yo̱t, ka gọ́ṅ gọ́ṅ kine: wuo, wọ chu̱ṭi ki̱ ṅál àn. Kine: wu kọma kwọf aṅọ? Wọ kọma kwọfe ḍọk. Atọ́, gōṅun! Kine: ȩ̂, wuo, wọ́ bì, cha wọ pyȩ̂jé ẹn ki kwọfe ḍọk, dẹ́ ȩ́ kyẹt, cha ḍọk kújẹ̱. A chọ́ṅà jẹ̱, a chọ́ṅ jẹ̱, a kọ́mà kwọ́p, a kwāṅ jam, ka ḍọk pẹ̱ka káché gẹ́ṅ. Ka jē yēyọ, jọ̀k ḍọ̀ṅ; dẹ chaka kẹr yau. Ȩ̀, arẹ lóṅé gọ́ṅ. Kine: wa tọu ya ṭẹ̱ṇ; dẹ ḍọk kache gẹ́ṅ kújà, dẹ nụti kỏ̀bȴ. Kẹ́ṅ ẹ́ni ànàn, a bāṅ kyẹ́dá. Ka riṭ e lọ̱kọ chyẹ̀, kine: rọ̱́, kinau, yi ba wéi jàl a kẹ̱r! yi re kẹ̱re ḍọk tẹ̱rọ? Kwọ́fi rach! kẹ̱t, chúdì ki̱ ḍāṇ! jal, ka yú³ múch ki̱ ḍọk abich. Ka e mūjọ ki̱ ḍāṇ, ka gọ ka̱lẹ́, ka tyẹṅ pān ẹni chọ́ṅ, kine: yá chúdì ki̱ ḍāṇ, kẹṅ ẹni anan. Dọ̀ch! A kẹ̱dẹ́, a tyẹṅi mọgọ, a chwọl tyẹṅ ẹni, a bẹ̱n, a tyẹ́re ḍāṇ tḥẹ̀ gẹ́ṅ. Ka gẹ yēi chyẹ̱, kine: dọ́ch, wá bà wàt. A kẹ̱t gẹ́ṅ, a kỏl ḍọk, ka ḍāṇ mẹ̱kè gẹ́ṅ.

At a certain time the people went to ask for indemnities, they went to the village (where the debtor lived), and sat down. The people of the village assembled. When the man began to ask, "I want indemnities for certain goods," the debtor replied, "I do not know anything about goods (which I owe you.)" The man asked, "Have you not been told?" He replied, "By whom?" The man said, "By your father." The debtor said again, "I do not know of anything concerning debts." The man said, "Why do you not know it?" Then it was asked, "Who is the judge?" The answer was, "That man is judge." He aid, "Count the goods (which you claim from this man)." All the goods were enumerated. The judge said tho the debtor, "Man, why do you deny? Is it not true what he said?" And the people went to bring the matter before the king. They found the king, and the matter was told. They said, "Our lord, we have come with this man." The king asked, "What a palaver do you have?" They answered, "We have a palaver about cattle." "Well," said the king, "tell me!" The accuser said, "Well, our lord, we came to ask him (the debtor) about the matter of the cattle; but he refused; he said, he did not know anything about cattle. So I assembled the people, and when the people were assembled, I talked to him, and enumerated the goods, and the cows (which I said he owed me) were found right; the people consented (to my statement), the old people. He refused again to acknowledge it." After

---

[1] *u̱* is here conditional: "when".
[2] "the place, i. e. the matter, of goods is not known by me".
[3] < *yí ú̱* "you will".

that the king said (turning to the accused one), "Well, now you also tell your talk!" He said, "My father died while I was a little child; but the cows, I do not know anything about them. I was not told; that is the reason, therefore I refused to give them." Then the king gave his judgment thus, "Well, so it is, you are a man who refused (to give what is due); why did you refuse to give the people their cows? Your matter is bad. Go, and pay a girl as amends, and you (turning to the accuser), man, give him five cows!" The debtor gave the girl, he brought her to the village (of the accuser). When the people of the village had assembled, he (the accuser) said, "I have been indemnified with a girl; thus is the matter now." The people say, "All right." Then he goes to strain beer; and he calls the people. They come; he presents the girl to the people to be examined (whether it is a sufficient pay). And they consent, saying, "Very well, we are friends now."

They go away, the cows are brought, and the girl is recognised by them. [A man has married somebody's daughter; after some time the girl, his wife, dies; now the father of the girl has to return part of the dowry which has been paid to him for his daughter. But in the meantime the father of the deceased wife has died too, and his eldest son has become his heir. The husband of the dead wife goes to this man, the brother of his dead wife, and wants his cattle back. But this man denies knowing anything about the matter, pretending his father did not tell him before his death. They therefore go before the king, who decides: the heir has to give his brother-in-law another girl instead of the deceased one; and in return the brother-in-law is to give the heir five five head of cattle, which is about half the usual price for a wife.]

V. HISTORICAL TRADITIONS.

36. Nyadwai.

Ńa riṯ mẹ̄kọ, chwọlá Ńadwai, ńi māyọ rech. Ka rech mẹ̄kọ dyẹ́rẹ̀ rẹ́ń, jal mẹ̄kọ ńiṅẹ ba Ogam. A kōbi Ogam kịne: kipańọ? Kịne: baṯẹ ńa riṯ? Kịne: ọ́¹ róń yí mẹn? Wijẹ duọń! Kịne: dọ̄ch yàu. A bẹ́dẹ́. A ḷarny
Ńadwai a róńe, Ogam ya Mạ̄ńọ. A úńí kịne: Ńadwai róńọ. A kōbi kịne: búh! Ko: a pẹ̄l Ogam! A kōbi Ńadwai kịne: dwai Ogam! A dwâi, a ṯóṯé ki dọk, a gẹ̄ri pārẹ, a ńọmi mạ́n, ka pārẹ dọ̄ńọ. Ka e ńwọli ńwọl mágîr. A chwọ̄lẹ́, a ńāgẹ́ ki ńwọle bẹ̀n yi Ńadwai, a paṯi pārẹ péń.

A certain prince called Nyadwai, was fishing. And he wanted a certain fish, the fish of Ogam (a fish which Ogam had caught). Ogam asked, "Why (should I give my fish to the prince)?" The people replied, "Is he not a prince?" Ogam said, "By whom will he ever be elected? He has such a big head!" The people replied, "Well, all right (do as you think best)." He refused.

But Nyadwai was elected king, while Ogam was at Manyọ. There he heard the talk, "Nyadwai has been elected." When he heard it, he said to himself, "Dear me!" (But Nyadwai) said (to himself), "This cursed Ogam!" Some time later Nyadwai sent word, "Bring Ogam!" Ogam was brought; the king gave him cattle, built him a village, he married a woman, and his village became large; he got many children. But one day he was called by Nyadwai, Nyadwai killed him and all his children, and he destroyed his village.

37. Golit.

Ńa riṯ Golit ka e bẹ̀ńọ, ka pẹ̄ka wiy Pîjọ, ko: ya dwata yey nam. Ka jańe lāgọ² e kyẹdọ kịne: nam yejẹ kọńọ ki yá! Kịne ya kyẹt. A múji dậṇ; a witi yaṯẹ pi, a kẹ́dẹ́, a pẹ̄ka yey nam bẹ̄ mạ́ńọ̀ ki dọk. A mạń wadẹ, a mâgé je bẹ̀n, a kẹ́dẹ́; a giti Lwańdẹ̄n, a mạgí gòn, a kōl dean pach bẹ̀nè, a kạli jań Ńōk a chibi gọ ka, a gẹ̄rẹ pārẹ Ńejōk, ńi kạbọ ki dọ ṯẹ̄rọ.

The prince Golit came, and settled at the mouth of the river Pîjọ; he said (to the chief there), "I want to settle (on the island) in the middle of the river." But the chief who ruled there refused, saying, "I myself like the island in the river, I refuse!" Then the prince gave him a man (slave), and on that the chief sprinkled the boats with water (that is, gave them permission to go on the island). The prince went on the island, and settled down there to steal cows. He sent his son to capture people (and their cattle), he captured all the people

---

[1] instead of the usual ụ́.
[2] "the chief of the magistrate", i. e. the ruling chief.

there, and after that went to Lwangdeng, and captured this village, he brought all the cows into his village. After that he brought Dinkas of Ngok,[1] and settled them in the place (of the village Lw.), he built them the village of Nyejōk; and those people too used to steal the cattle of the people.

38. Nyimo.

Ńa riṭ Ńimọ, gẹ ki ńa riṭ mẹkọ, ka gẹ ńí chwọl, ka gẹ ńi ryêch,[2] ka loḍe wêi gẹ́n, ka loḍe Ńimọ ńi kâp, kape yi ńa rāṇ ẹni. Ka Ńakwach e wêrọ̀, ka ńí dōgọ kẹ̄tẹ.

Ka pārẹ kyẹr, á tàdı̀r, Otudi, pa wụ̄t Ńakwachọ. Ka e jāgọ e dọ̣ch, ḍẹ ba war, ka ḍọgẹ ńi kâp yi ńiwẹn; a kōbi riṭ kı́ne: y tich adi? A ṭōṭẹ ki bān mánẹ̀nı̀ọ̀, mẹn gẹ̄ne rẹ, kifa ka bọ̣kẹ́; gọ[3] ńí kọn gọ̀[3] ẹn.

The prince Nyimọ was, together with another prince, invited to a meal. They had their clubs with them, and (in the course of the festival) the club of Nyimọ was taken away from him by force, it was taken away by that other prince. When his father, king Nyakwach (who was also present at the festival) saw that, he was very angry,[4] and he went home alone.

He built for his son a big village, Otudi, this was to be the village of the son of Nyakwach. And he (the son) reigned well, but he was a coward. His cattle used to be robbed by his brothers. The king said, "Ah, what is to be done?" He gave him a great number of slaves to protect him, on account of his fear. They were to help him.

39. Nyadoke.

A rōṅ Nàḍōké, a jāgẹ́, a kōbi kı̀ne: â, ya gēra fāra wọk! A gēre pār Pâbọ̀. Weya bẹ̀ḍà bute Ḍọṅ! A gēra pārẹ Ḍọṅ. A bẹ̄t gẹn ki Ḍọnọ, a jâgệ, a ńi nāgi lyẹch, a ńí chámà yi Ḍọnọ, a ńi kwáchẹ̀ yi Ḍọnọ. Ka Ḍọṅ ńi ṭōṭẹ lyẹch, a bẹ̄da rāṇ (rāṇ) Ḍọnọ. Ka ńi tōk kọṭ, ka Ḍọṅ ńi tōjọ ki jamẹ, chami kā wak, ka kọṭ ńi mọ̀kọ̀. A ńí koṅi bùr, mẹn chẹk lyẹch, ka lyeńe lúṭọ́ yẹ̀y bùr, ka Ḍọnọ ńi yàń, a chōga rāṇ dọch.

Nyadōke was elected. While he was reigning, one day he said, "Well, I will build my village in the bush!" He built the village of Pōbọ. Again he said, "Let me reside beside the Nubians!" He built a village in the Nubian country. He lived together with the Nubians, being their king. He used to kill elephants, the Nubians used to ask him for the elephants' meat, he gave it to them, and they ate it. So he was the king of the Nubians. — When the Nubians are without rain, they are accustomed to put on all their adornments, and go out into the

---

[1] *Ṅọk*, A Dinka-District south of the Sobat.
[2] "and they were called, and they were invited."
[3] *gọ* relates to the slaves, it has therefore the meaning of a plural.
[4] because his son allowed his club to be taken away from him.

bush; then it begins to rain. — Nyadōke used to dig holes for catching elephants, and the elephants tumbled into the holes. Thus the Nubians were satisfied, he continued to be a good king.

40. King Dokot.

Riṭ Dọ́kọ̈ṭ ká è mạ̈ṅọ̣, mạ̈ṅɔ fōṭẹ Dọṅ, ka ḍạ̈l yi Dọ̀ṅ, Dọṅ ṅi rẹ́ṅá mâl wiy kit. Ka e ko: búh, dẹ Dọṅ a ḍạ́lị́ yáṅ, ụ tích èdi̯? ě rei (γei) wá ṭach! Ka ṭay rêi, ka e ko: yey kit! Ka kit e yêch, ka dọgọ kọ́ṅé feṅ. A māgi Dọṅ, a kạ́lị́ gọ̀ṅ, a gẹ̈́rí gọ párẹ́, gọ lọgọ bạ̈ṅẹ́; a chạ̈gẹ́ ṅiṅe f ān ẹni gọ Adọkọṅ.

A kạ́lị́ mâr, a ṅwaṅ gọ bwóṅọ́, ka bwoṅọ mạ̈gẹ́, kạ́lị́ gọ̀ṅ, a lọgọ bạ̈ṅẹ́, a gẹ̈́rí pach, gọṅ Awarejwọk. Ka Chọ́lọ̣ kōbọ kịṅe: a rāṇe ṅọ, a rich mạ̈ṅ? A ko kịṅe: búh! Kịṅe: Chộl, bẹṅẹ́ kwọ́pí ànàṅ? A kwaṅ mâr, a lẹ̈ṅ gọ̀ nàm, ka Chọlọ e waṅ kị́ yù màr kị bōle párẹ́.

Pay mẹ̈kọ chwọlá Oṅg̈gọ̀, ka Chọl ṅi kẹ̈ṭò kị jụr, ka Chọle ṅi chyẹ̈́tị̈. Ka rāṇ e rōṅ, Chộl dẹ chyẹ̈̄ṭọ; a rọṅ Akwọṭ. Ka Akwọṭ e mạ̈ṇọ; ka lèṅ chyẹ̈̄ṭè, ka e bẹ̈ṅọ̀, ka e ko: búh, wá gg̈gọ̀ di? A bẹ̈ṅị́ bọl Oṅg̈gọ́, a chọ́ṅị́ bāṅe Dọ́kọ̈̇ṭ, a pyeje gin kịṅe: mạr e lẹ̈́ṅè kẹ́ṅ? A kōbi jal mẹ̈kọ kịṅe: ụ tích edi? Kịṅe: ụ dwái nâm! Kịṅe: búh, Akwọ́ṭ, dẹ̈ bá gèṅ? yi kụ waṅe kejẹ? A kōbi kịṅe: yá bà wáṅ! Kịṅe: ṅọ̣! A keau yụ̈ṭ, a keau gọṅ. A kạ̈l ḍọk, a mak ḍeaṅ Oṅg̈gọ, a kạ̈l ḍeaṅ mẹ̈kọ, a mạ̈gí Wajwọk, a kạ̈l ḍeaṅ mẹ̈kọ, a māge yi Aḍọkọṅ, a kạ̈l ḍeaṅ mẹ̈kọ, a kẹṭi tẹ̈rọ gọṭ, a lụ̈̄mị́, a chwộp ḍèaṅ. A kẹṭi Akwọṭ feṅ, a rọṅ ta pí, ká é chwọ̣̈ṅọ̀. Ka Chọlọ kōbọ kịṅe: riṭ tọ̣k, ba bi kẹ̈ṭẹ! Ka chaṅ wapọ mal, chaṅ e kẹ̈chọ̀, ka riṭ bẹ̈ṇọ, ka mạr kạ́lị́ kị ta pi. A kōbi kịṅe: tìṅ léṅ! A kẹṭ léṅ, a maṅ Diṅjọl, a ṅạ̈gẹ́, a maṅ ṅwọle, ka dọk e kōl kị mạ̈ṅé. A maṅa Agẹ̣̈r, a maṅi Chai, a māk peṅ bẹ̈ṅẹ̀, a kōbi Chọ́lọ̣ kịṅe: a rāṇe ṅọ, a chġgò kị́pà léṅ? A ko: búh, kwọ́pí, yina Chọ́lọ̣! A kwaṅ mâr, a lẹ̈ṅ gọ̀ nàm.

King Dokot went out to conquer, he went conquering into the Nubian country. But he failed to defeat the Nubians, because they used to escape upon their mountain. He said, "Why, the Nubians are too much for me! What shall I do? Well (he says to his people), make a pot ring!"[1] And a pot ring was made. Then he said, "Carry the mountain away!" So the mountain was carried away and put on the ground upside down. In this way he conquered the Nubians, he brought them (into the Shilluk country), he built them a village, and they became his subjects.[2] He called the name of this village Adọkọng.

He brought the silver pot[3] and swung it against (the army of) the strangers; thus he conquered the strangers, he brought them to his country, and they became his subjects; he built them a village, this is the village Awarejwọk.

But the Shilluks said, "What a king is this, that he is always conquering?"[4]

---

[1] a ring of grass, which is laid on the head for carrying water pots. The mountain was carried away like a water pot.

[2] This shows how Nubian colonies came into the Shilluk country.

[3] This pot is said to be an old heirloom. It was to be filled with "holy water" (*pi jwọk*), which was used for different religious rites. The possession of this pot was supposed to give fortune and victory.

[4] The Shilluks were tired of waging war, or they were jealous of the victories of the king

The king replied, "Why, ye Shilluks, is that your talk now?" He took the pot and thrust it (angrily) into the river. Thus the pot ("the way to the pot") was lost to the Shilluks in the front of the village of the king.

There was another village, called Ongogo; the Shilluks (of this village) fought with some foreign tribe, and were chased. Another king was elected, but again the Shilluks were chased. Then Akwot was elected, and Akwot went out to conquer (this tribe). But his army was defeated. When he came home, he exclaimed, "Why, what shall we do?" He came towards Ongogo, and the wives of Dokot, he asked them, „Where has the silver pot been thrown into the river?" Some man replied, "Why do you ask?" He said, "It is to be brought out from the river." The man exclaimed, "Oh dear, Akwot, is that true (is that what you are going to do)? Will you not miss the place where it lies?" The king said, "I shall not miss it." The man replied, "All right." They rowed boats, they rowed them towards the place where they were. Cows were brought, one cow was caught and given to the village of Ongogo, another cow was caught and given to Wajwok, another was given to Adokong.[1] Then another cow was brought, and the people went to the river, a prayer was spoken, the cow was speared (sacrificed), and Akwot went to the bottom of the river, he dived under the water; he stayed there a long time; the Shilluks said, "The king is away, he does not come back." The sun was rising, and when it began to sink, the king came from out of the water, he had brought the silver pot from the bottom of the river. He said, "Now raise an army!" The army was to defeat Dingjol (the Dinka country near Renk). They destroyed it, its children were captured, the cattle was taken away together with the women. He conquered Ager too, he conquered Chai (near Roseires), he defeated the whole country. When the Shilluks saw that, they said, "What king is that, that he is always continuing in warfare?" He replied, "Oh dear! is that now your talk, ye Shilluks?" He took the silver pot, and thrust it into the river.[2]

41. Nyakwach.

Riṭ Ńakwach ka e jękọ̀, ka wąte Ńadwai nágé kipa atèr; ka ńiwęn wąte mąne Ńadwai nágé; ka e chwọtọ kịne: wuna a yịk ńiwá, bi ṭẓrọ! Ka ṭẓrọ bẓnọ, ê katọ́ tọnẹ; ka e buọgọ, ka chọ̄ga kal. Ka e chwọtọ kịne: bi ṭẓrọ! Ka ṭẓrọ bia yịg. Ka e ko: yá (yāń) gọ́l, á kịdì? A chąṭu kịnau? Kịne: wọ wèrọ̀! yi nẹka nọ ki jē? Kịne: ẹrẹ (rędẹ) a ba nágé gẹ́n? Kịne: ba nẹka kị atèr; gọ̄le ka chyẹta wa, a bāńe nágá gẹ́n. Kịne: ḍúkị mẓkọ³ ú̧ lōńe gẹn kị́ jàgọ̀, wa, wa nẹ́kè nágọ̀! Paṭẹ ẹn, a bańe nágẹ gẹn? Kịne: ńọ̀, ê, dọch! Wiy gọl gẹn a faṭẹ feń. Kịne: Ńakwache, a bańi chọ́n kị́ jàgọ̀. Wọ ṭẓr an u chọ̄l yi mẹn? A dwọk ṭẓrọ.

---

[1] The cows were offered as sacrifices, one by the village Ongogo, and so on.
[2] From that time the silver pot is irreparably lost to the Shilluks.
[3] "some to-morrow", that is, in future time.

Nyakwach

A kōbi Ńakwach kine: gẹ́r féṅ kị̀ dọ̀ch. Ka ṅamạ̈ta, watẹ ṅiwá, chwọl ga ṅa riṭ. A chwọle gẹ (gi) Bachōdọ; a kẹṭ gẹn (gin), a yẹṅ kẹ́lé gin, a kwaṅe kwi gin, mọk jåk gẹ̀n ki Bachōdọ.

Ka jal mẹ̈kọ e kẹdọ kẹṭẹ, ka baṅe riṭ ṅí yạ̀jẹ̀, ka kur ṅi kụ̂lẹ́, ka ṅi chôl. Ka ṅi chịka kāṇọ, ka ṅi chôl. A bụ̈ṭ ko (kōr) ṅa riṭ, ka e ko: bụ́h! u tich adi? ẹ̀ dọ̄ch yau! A chika kāṅọ ki kur, a māk dọk yi riṭ, a kọl gẹ Bachōdọ, ka pach e dọ̄ṇọ é llù llù.

Ka wâdẹ ṅal duọṅ ka e kẹdọ, ka dọk yôdẹ́ yí tạ̀r, ka dọk kóje. Ka riṭ e fẹ̈chọ̀ kịne: dọk erẹ a kộl? yik Nakwach. Kịne: bụ́h, ụ ṅal a gwọk edi? ẹ̀, kwọfẹ rach. Dọ̄ch au, wei kẹdẹ gẹn.

A kẹ́lé gẹn, a pẹ̈chẹ wiyẹ kịne: dọk kộl gệ kẹ́ṅ? Kịne: kọ̄lá Bachōdọ. Kịne: ọ̀! a chọṇi wạ̈ṭẹ, a kōpi gin kịne: ṅaṅ ṅal ẹni! A kẹṭ jē, a chẹ̄ṭe, ka e rẹṇo, ka ṅan an ṅi wịṭẹ́ rẹ, go ṅí kẹ́lé kẹ̀lọ̀; ka ṅi pạ̈dọ, ka go ṅi kộpẹ́ kịne: ŕiṅ! A bẹn ṅal duọṅ, a kẹle gọn, a ṅạ̈gé gọ̀n. A bẹ̈na pach, a pyey gẹn kịne: yā (yāṅ) gọl, a kịdi? ṅamāyọ e tije wun edi? Kịne: ẹ nẹ̈k! Kịne: yi mén àn? Kịne: yi ṅal duọṅ. Kịne: bụ́h! wâdà a tộnùn? Ka e dụọdọ, ka kâ wọt, ka e rïjọ; e fa chāmọ kị gin cham, e ywọ̄ṇọ. A bẹ̈ni wọk, a chọṅ gin, a kōbi kịne: ṅal, baṅẹ yin a nẹk wạdà? Yi ụ chộk, góll ṅạ̈gi tóṅ! Chwọlá yín a rei ṅal ṅemāyọ́, dẹ ẹ tóṅ! Ko: ọ̀, chwọlá yin ṅal duọṅ, a yeji dide kwọp! ẹ̀, yi rach. A kẹṭi yi dọk, a ṅi kọchi gin, gin ṅi kọlọ pān akyẹlọ, a gin ṅi kāṇẹ.

When King Nyakwach reigned, he killed the children of (his brother) Nyadwai, because he feared their enmity; and his brothers who had been born by the women of Nyadwai's village, he also killed. Then he called out, "You, who are my real brothers, you people come!" The people came carrying their spears. When Nyakwach saw that, he was afraid and remained within his enclosure. Again he called out, "Come, you people!" And the people came to him. He asked them, "My children, how is it that you are walking thus (armed)?" They replied, "We are angry, why do you kill people?" He answered, "Why should I not kill them? I killed them because of their enmity, (and do you not remember that) their family chased us away? Therefore I have killed them. If at a future time they should have come to power, surely we should have been killed. Is it not for this reason that I killed them?" The people replied, "Well, eh, all right, their family has perished." Again they said, "Nyakwach, you formerly refused to be elected as king.[1] By whom should we have been avenged (if not by you)?"

The people returned home. Nyakwach said, "Restore the town well; and my nephews, the children of my brothers, shall be called 'children of the king'." He called them (his nephews) to Fashoda.[2] They went, and he picked some from among them, and the rest he took to be chiefs of Fashoda.

A certain man (one of these nephews of the king) went one day and slept with

---

[1] This seems to point to the preceding story.
[2] The chief town of the Shilluk country, and residence of the king.

the wives of the king. He paid the fine for adultery. But again he did an evil thing, and had to pay a fine. At last the king got tired of this, and he said, "Why, what is that? eh, never mind!" When this man once more did mischief, the king had all the cattle of that (man's) village seized and brought to Fashoda; so the village was left without a single cow.

The eldest son of this man (of the evildoer) went and found the cattle (of his father) in a pasture.[1] He separated those belonging to his father from the rest and drove them home. When the king heard that the cattle were away, he asked, "Why have the cattle been taken away?" So said Nyakwach. (When he heard that this same man's son had taken them) he exclaimed, "Why, what shall we do with this boy? eh, his affair is very bad! Well, never mind, let him go with them."

When the boy came home with his cattle, his father asked him, "From where has the cattle been brought?" He answered, "I have brought it from Fashoda." The father said, "All right." He assembled his sons and told them, "Kill this boy!" The people went away, they chased him, he ran away. And the pursuers came close to him, they were just near enough to stab him, then the boy (stumbled and) fell down. They told him, "Run!" (They did not want to kill him). But his eldest brother stabbed him, and killed him. When they came home, the father asked them, "Children, how is it? How did you deal with your brother?" They said, "He is killed!" The father asked, "By whom?" They answered, „By his eldest brother." The father exclaimed, "Why, my son has been killed by you?" He rose up, went into his hut, and remained there. He did not eat any food, he wept. And he came out again and assembled his sons, saying to the eldest, "My son, is it not you who killed my son? Your descendants shall always be killed by the spear! I thought you would protect your brother, and you have killed him!" Again he said, "Oh, I thought, you, the eldest one, had a heart which was wise! no, you are wicked."

Then he went to the cattle, he separated them: some he brought to another village, and some he hid.

42. The False Prophets.

Waṅ a bẹni rōr, ka gẹ chọṅ; rāṇ akyẹlọ chwọla Okwâ, rāṇ akyẹl chwọla Dâk, rāṇ akyẹl chwọla Ńikāṇọ. Ka gẹ bẹnọ, ka Chọli ńi kwòchò, chwọla riṯ; ki yi riṯ Ku. Ka tẹrọ chộṇọ, ka gẹ kẹdọ Bachōdọ, ka riṯ e ko: bụ́h! y rōr ṫich edi? Ka gẹ kẹdọ, ka bāńe riṯ kắpẹ́, ka riṯ wijẹ mūm, ka riṯ e ńāṇọ: ka dọk kắpẹ́, ka riṯ chuṅẹ rẹ̄ṇọ, ká è wệjẹ̀ ki mwọl, ka atẹgọ gǿdẹ́ yẹdẹ, ka gyẹ̄lọ bọḍi bādẹ, ka otyẹń kiṯẹ chiṅẹ, ka tọń kwāṅ, ka toch kwāṅ, ká é kẹ́dò, kẹti yi gin. Ka jal a Dāk gǿjẹ́ mach,

---
[1] where they had been brought by the king's people.

The False Prophets

ka paṭi peṅ, e ṭö; ka jal a Okwā ka kēl, ka e ṭǫ; ka jal a kōbi Ńikaṅo, ka e pạrǫ, é tǫ́ṅị yịnǫ; ká bûl gǫ́ch, ka tẹrǫ shǭnǫ.

Ka wudo chǫ́dǫ, ka byẹl e wāṅǫ, a mâk Chǫlǫ yi kẹch; a kẹṭi tẹri pōṭe Nuạr, a ńeau tẹrǫ byẹle Nuạr; ka Chǫlǫ ńi pǫ̀tǝ̀ yi Nuạr key kẹ́ch, ka Chǫlǫ ko: kwẹ ywach yi kẹch, ka mẹ̄kǫ ńārẹ ńị́ lwǭkị̀. A chyẹk byẹ́l, a bǫṭi tẹrǫ ṭjẹ̀.

At a certain time the "kings" came, they used to dance (the dances of Nyikang); one "king" called himself Okwā, one called himself Dāk, and the third called himself Nyikang. And they came (into the villages of the Shilluks); the Shilluks used to pray to them, calling them "king", — it was in the time of king Ku —, and the people danced.¹ They (the "kings") went to Fashoda. The king said, "Why, what is the matter with these kings?" And they (the would-be kings) went, and took the wives of the king by force. The king was much perplexed, he was in great confusion. They stole cattle too. Then the king became very angry, he sang a war-song early in the morning, he tied his bead-necklaces round his neck, put his arm-rings on his arm, fastened bells about his wrist, he took a spear, he took a gun, and he went, he went towards them. And the man who called himself Dāk he shot with the gun, he fell upon the ground and died. And the man "Okwā" was speared, and he died; the man who was called Nyikang fled, he turned towards the bush. Then the drum was beaten, and the people danced (for joy).

(About this time) a north wind blew, and the dura was burned, the Shilluks were seized with hunger. The people went to the Nuer country, to buy dura of the Nuers. And the Shilluks were beaten by the Nuers, in the time of this strong famine. The Shilluks say, ("In this time) some were starved, and some gave away their children for dura." — But when the next dura-harvest was brought, the people were relieved.

[In the first part of this story it is related, how some impostors pretend to be the ancient kings, who have come into this world again; the people believe in them and pray to them, and the "false prophets" take advantage of this to rob the people, till their procedings are brought to an end by the king.]

43. The Prince who refused to be King.

Ńa rān duǫṅ, chwǫla Alẹ́kè, ka dwai yi ụ rǫ́ṅ, ka e baṅ, ka tōtè, a kẹdẹ, a párẹ́ pōṭe Dǫṅ ki ńiwẹ́ṅ. Ka gẹ ńi rụ̀dǫ̀ (rǫdǫ) kị́ gìn chám; ńan ńal ṭẹṅ ńị́ kōpǝ̀ tḥmé pî. Ka ńa riṭ mẹ̄kǫ ńi kyẹdǫ kịne: wei bẹdẹ. Ka gẹ didǫ ki kwofe Dǫṅ; a bẹne pach, a gẹ́dẹ́ ki fārẹ, a chāgi fārẹ gǫn a Pwot. A pēka peṅ. A kōbị: ê, yá kyẹ̀t ki jāgǫ, ba dwata yáṅ. A rǫ́ṅ (rǫ́ṅ) wādé, a jāgǫ yáu. A ṭōmi lẹke lyech, a ṭōmi

---

¹ Thus worshipping them.

gyelǫ. Ka riṭ e wẽrǫ̀, ka nạ̀k kâ̧l gḗ gîr, ka ḍǫk chōl ga pyār aṅwen, ki̧ jḕ gá pyārǫ; riṭ kȩch; a dwǫk chwak, a chike chōl kḗ ḍǫk, ki̧ jḕ, a kōbi̧ riṭ ki̧ne: wei bḗdȩ̄̀, tū́ṅd yè kȩ́r.

The eldest son of a king whose name was Aleki, was brought to be elected king. But he refused, and when he was informed secretly that they were going to elect him by force, he went away and fled to the Nubian country, he with two of his brothers. And (during their flight, or in the Nubian country) they used to pound dura for food; the youngest of them was told (compelled) to bring water. (When they had gone) one prince (in the Shilluk country) said, "Let them stay there (in the Nubian country)." And they learned the Nubian language.

He came home again, and built himself a village, wich he called Pwot ("beaten"). He settled there, but he still continued saying, "No, I refuse to be chief; I don't want to." So his son was elected, and he reigned. He carved bracelets out of elephant-tusks.[1] When the king (at Fashoda) heard this, he became angry, and he sent an armed body to him, a great one. And he (the prince) had to make amends with fourteen cows and ten men; for the king was very much offended. Again an ambassador of the king was sent to the prince, asking for more cattle and men as compensation. Then the king said, "Now let him alone, the reason for his being so haughty as to cut ivory-bracelets was his wealth, and we have taken that from him."

44. The Cowardly King.

Jal mȩkǫ Akū́nǫ̀ Bàkù, ka e bḗnǫ, chama riṭ, e chyȩk, ka Chǫlǫ yēi, men an ka bȩda riṭ anan; wa yēi ki̧ en. Ka jal mȩkǫ kyedǫ: è, fa̧te riṭ! A rāṇ āṇǫ? A chyȩki nau, yạ̀ kyȩ̀t! Ka jal eni e bḗnǫ, ka pȩka tūṅ yǒ, bḗ lepe gǫ̀n. Ká gǫ̀ lḗpḗ, ka Akū́nǫ̀ Bàkǫ̀ bḗnǫ̀, ka e buǫgo, ka e reṅ. Ka jal eni ko: yi reṅa keṅ? Ma yi kōba yin, che yina riṭ? yi chyȩte nǫ kȩte? Ka tẓrǫ ko: à, wa chén ènà yi ḍāṇe nau? Ka Akū́nǫ̀-Bàkǫ̀ e bḗnǫ, ka tǭ̀ṅa fān, ka ye yi̧yí. Tẓrǫ kudi yau. Gǫy tǫ́m! Tẓrǫ kudi yau. Ka jāgǫ kōbǫ: gǭṅe wunǫ! Ka wunǫ gǭṅ yaṅ tǫnǫ. Ká é réṅǫ̀, ka Chǫlǫ nḗt̄ǫ: â, fa̧te riṭ! Ka Chǫlǫ ko: nȩk! Ka tǭ̀ṅa yinǫ, a par.

A man whose name was Akūnyo Bāko, came and wanted to become king. He was a short man. The Shilluks consented, "This man shall be king now, we are satisfied with him." But one man refused, saying, "No, he is not a king! What kind of king is he, this short man? I protest!" This man came and sat down on the side of a road, to lie in wait for the new king. While he was lying in wait for him, Akūnyo Bāko came. When he saw the man, he was afraid and ran away. The man asked, "Why do you run away? Was it not you who said,

---

[1] Formerly only the king was authorized to wear ivory bracelets.

he wanted to become king? What is chasing you?" When the people heard this, they said, "Ah, shall that man (this cowardly king) bring evil upon us?" And Akunyo Bako came, he turned towards the village, and he behaved like one possessed by a spirit.[1] But the people remaind silent. Then he said, "Beat the holy drum!" But the people remained silent. One of the chiefs said, "Loosen a rope!"[2] And a rope was loosened by a child. When he saw that, he ran away. And the Shilluks laughed, "Indeed, he is not a king!" The Shilluks said. "Kill him!" He ran towards the bush fleeing.

45. Queen Abudok.

Kẹn Dọ̀kọ̀t ka feṅ e bẹ̀dọ̀ e bu riṭ; ka Chọlọ wiẹ̀ṭ mùm; riṭ bogọn. Ka tẹro bẹno yi Abúḍọk, ka e ko: é wiṭe wọn a mum yi buṅe riṭ. A kōbi kine: kwáni riṭ! A kwáni, a ṛǝní. A kẹdọ, ẹn Abuḍọk, a dwai ṭẹnọ, a mȧjí, a wúdli, a pégi yẹṭe ṭȧp; ka a ṭẹme duọn, a pégi, ka aṭẹp e chù gò, e ba paṅ. A kal aṭem ṭẹn, a pégi, a páni; a kẹṭi Bachōdọ, a wei gọ feṅ. A kōbi kine: é, Chọlọ u núní yi kwa riṭ. A bāṅe ṅẹṅe kwa riṭ. A kōbi: é, kwa riṭ rẹ u lógó mùgò, ka ní gẹdi ki būte pári, fári ní doyi dòyó, ka e nuṅọ. U ṅẹṅ bat kẹnọ, u ṅẹṅ pal. A bāṅe nwọli a ṅẹni. — Kwọn Abúḍọk.

In the time of Dọkọt the country was without a king. And the Shilluks did not know what to do, because there was no king. And the people came to (queen) Abudok, saying, "Alas, we are in confusion from not having a king!" She said, "Take this one (pointing to one of her younger brothers) for a king!" So he was taken, he was elected. Abudok went away. She brought seeds of the water-lily, spread them out in the sun, and ground them. She put them into a bag, the bag was very big, so that, when she put the seeds in, the bag remained unfilled. Then she brought a small bag, poured the seeds in, and it was filled. Now she went to Fashoda with the bag, and put it down there. She said, "Ah, the Shilluks will be decreased by the descendants of the king. In future time the descendants of the king will become many. She said again, "Eh, the descendants of the king will be like a sickness (to the Shilluks), if they build their village beside your (the Shilluks') village, your village will become very small, it will decrease. But they (the royal family) will become many, just as the branches of the calabash plant become many in the bush." Therefore the descendants of the king have become so many. — This is the story of Abudok.

[*Explanation given by the man who told this story:* "Abudok was a bad queen, and the Shilluks did not like her; they wanted a king. So Abudok presented to them one of her two younger brothers, whom she raised (educated), saying, "Take this one for your king." Abudok went away

---
[1] When the new king is elected, the spirit of Nyikang takes possession of him; this is manifested by a shaking of the body, singing, etc.
[2] loosen a rope to thrash him!

angrily, she collected certain seeds, dried and pounded them, and brought them to Fashoda as a symbol, to show the Shilluks how they would be surpassed in number and in power by the descendants of the royal family." This story again shows that the royal family is not originally Shilluk, but of foreign origin. — But perhaps it was simply because she was a woman that the Shilluks did not want her to rule them. In the list of kings given by Banholzer Abudok is omitted.]

VI. WAR STORIES.
46. War.

Ka wọ wẹlọ, ka wọ nẹná ki yǔ, ka jē dwọgọ, ka wọ wanọ yǔ, ka wọ yȯtè jal mẹkọ, ga lyau, lyawe leṅ, ka e ko: wu kḁla kẹṅ? Wọ kḁla fōṭe bwoṅ. Kịne: wun a ya kẹṅ? Kịne: wa yȧ Penidwai. Kịne: fān ȧnọ̀? Wọ ya pache Chẹ́n. Kịne: yi Agōḍọ? Kịne: ȧwọ́! Kịne: dọ̄ch! A kḁl wọ́ṅ, a chip wọn pach mẹkọ, Duwȧt, a kḁl wọ́ṅ Agōḍọ, a yȯt jāgọ, a ṅute yi wọn kị́ dyẹ̀l, a lwȯk wọ́ṅ, a nẹ̇nȧ ki Bukyẹṅ, a bẹna dụki, ka wọ wanọ ki bȯ̀rȯ̀, a ṅute yȧ kị́ dyẹ̀l; a bẹ̇t tẹ̄di yau.

A kewu leṅ, a kẹ̇t tēṛọ, a kẹ̇te leṅ ki Aṭāṇọ, a nḁk Chọ́lọ̀ yi bwoṅ, a chyẹte tẹ̄ṛọ, a wiṭi bwoṅ Tūṅọ. Ka Gọkwach, jāgọ é yọ̇̀mọ̀. Ka chip feṅ yi bwoṅ, kịne: dọ́ch yȧu, wa fa wāt. A duọk bwoṅ, a tọ̄na ki bọ̄le Ṅelwāk, tọña muchọ̀, a buṭi ki muchọ̀, a nȧ́gé, ka chyẹt nam, ẹ gȋr.

A bẹ̇né, a pẹ̇́kị́ Óbȧṅ, a bẹ̇́di yau, ka nẹke dwat adẹk, a kẹ̇te, a lẹ́bé Tūṅọ, a nȧ́gé gọ̀n, a mȧ́gé gọ̀n, a dwọ́gé, a tōṅẹ Tāṛọ, a māgẹ Tāṛọ, a bẹ̇né, a tọ̄ṅ Kö-Bėlȗṭ, a mȧ́gé jē, a giṭi Wū, a māgi Wū, a giṭi Ṅọk, a mȧ́gị́ Ṅọk, a dwọgi Ṅọk, a pẹ̇ki Wiṅalwal.

A dọ̇́gọ́ fōṭe Joṅ, a jȧḍị́, a dwọ́gẹ́, a pẹ̇kḁ wiy Pich, a tọ̄́nẹ́ pach, a pẹ̄ka Tedigọ, a yọ̇́mẹ́ Ḍeṭim, a gwaịẹ ki ḍọk, kị́ jē. A kẹḍọ, a dụ̄gi Paḍean; a ṭȧ́bé Diṅjọl, ka Diṅjọl é yọ̇̀mọ̀. A nḁge gọn, a mȧ́ge ṅwọle gọn, a kẹ́ḍé. A māge Mwọmọ, a dọṅ pōṭe Chọl, é tịgụ̀ yi ràjọ̀ (rȧ̀jọ̀), dyel bogọn, ḍean bogọn, giẹ̄ne bogọn, byẹl bogin, pyẹn bogọn, kwot bogọn, wọt (ṛọt) bogọn, lwak bogọn; peṅ é dọ̇̀nọ̀, é ṅudọ̀̇ yi rājọ.

A rọṅ riṭ, riṭ Akọl, a kẹ̇te leṅ, leṅ Gẹr, ka Lwak chẹ̄te. A bẹṅ bwoṅọ, Alaṅṭaṛọ, a ṭȧbe riṭ, a mȧ́gé gọ̀n, a kite jē Bệl, a chȯge kún àn, a dọṅ riṭe Kū, é jȧ̀gọ̀, a bẹṅ Lir, ka gyẹ̄ne kụ́lẹ́, ka ḍean kụ́lẹ́, ka dyẹl kụ́lẹ́. A jāge riṭ Kū ki jaṅe dọ̇́ch; ka dọk ẹ ṅẹ̄nọ, ka gyẹno ṅẹ̄nọ, ka dyẹle ṅẹ̄nọ.

A liṅe kwọp yi bwoṅ mẹ̇kọ, a bẹ̇nọ, yiga bwoṅ mȧtẹ̇k, yé bẹ̇nọ, yé kẹ̇tọ̀ kị́ Alaṅṭar, ka Chọlọ ṅẹ̇ṭọ̀; kịne: ṅiṅe ȧnọ̀? yiga Túrùk, gẹ ki Nȋnẹ̇lẹ̇ṭ,[1] ye Alaṅṭaṛọ nẹ́kè nȧ̀gọ̀.

Yịk bwoṅ mẹ̇kọ kụ́lȧ́ wak, yiga Bȧkȧdi;[2] ka Bakadi bẹ̇nọ, ka tọ̄ña gat ki Ṭōbẹ̇t; a tōṅ gat, ka Chọl rẹṅa pach.

Ka tẹ̄ṛọ dwọgọ, ka kwọp lịṅ: Alaṅṭaṛọ nȧ̀gọ̀! Kȧ́ bùl gọ̇́ch, ka Chọlọ chọṅọ bûl; chuṅe miṇọ. A bẹṅ Turuk, a fẹ̇ka feṅ.

We were travelling, we slept on the road, and when the people (whom we had sent to look for the way) came back, we (found out that we) had lost our way. We found a man, a spy, a war-spy. He asked, "Where do you come from?" We answered, "We come from the country of the Shilluk people." He asked, "From which district (of the Shilluk-country) are you?" We replied, "From Penyidwai." He (asked), "From which village?" We (replied), "From

[1] that is, English.   [2] The Abyssinians.

the village Chen." He said, "Do you belong to Agǫdo? We replied, "Yes, we do." He said, "All right." He took us and brought us to some other village, Duwat, then he brought us to Agǫdo. He found out the chief, who (received us and) killed a goat for us, and then he accompanied us. We slept at Bukyeny. When the next day came, and it had become afternoon, he killed again a goat for me; the people (my companions and I) sat down.

A war signal was given. The people went, and there was a fight at Atāno, Shilluks were killed by the strangers, the Shilluks were chased throughout the country till the strangers came to Tonga. And the chief Gokwach surrendered; he was left alive by the strangers, they said, "All right, we are friends." The strangers turned back, and marched straight towards Nyelwāk. There they turned on an island (in the Nile), and while they were sleeping there, many of them were killed by the Shilluks, and many too were chased into the river, a great number.

After that they came and sat down at Obang; they remained quiet there for three months, then they went and attacked Tonga (again), some of the people they killed, and some they caught as slaves; they returned and marched towards Tāro; they captured Tāro and came marching towards Khor Filus, they caught people there; they came to Wū, they captured Wū, they arrived at Ngok and captured it; from Ngok they returned and sat down at Winyalwal.

They returned to the Dinka country, but there they had no success, and so went back, and sat down at the mouth of the river Pich. They turned to the next village, and then went (across the river) to Tedigo. The chief Detim surrendered, he paid tribute in cattle and men. From there the enemy turned back to Padeang. He cheated (the Dinka chief) Dingjol, and Dingjol surrendered. He was killed, together with his children. The enemies went away and captured Mwǫmǫ. While they remained in the Shilluk country, the country suffered very much, there were no goats left, no cattle, no fowls, no dura, no clothes, no shields, no drums, no houses, no cow houses; the land was ruined to exhaustion.

In that time a king was elected, king Akol, he fought a war, the war of Ger, and the people of Lwak (with their king Akol) were chased. Then came the strangers, the Ansars,[1] they outwitted the king and caught him. They arrived at Bel, and remained there. The (Shilluk-) king Kū[2] continued reigning during this time. And the Lir-people[3] came and brought fowls, and cattle, and goats. The king Kū[2] reigned well, so that the cows, and fowl, and goats became many.

About that time the fame of some other white people was heard of; they were coming, they were very strong white people, they came and fought the Ansars; when the Shilluks heard that, they laughed;[4] and it was asked, "What is their name?" And they turned out to be the Turks and the English. It was said, "The Ansars will surely be killed now."

---

[1] the people the Dervishes.
[2] = Kur.   [3] The Kordofan Nubas from Jebel Eliri.
[4] for joy.

And again there came white people, from the interior, they were Abyssinians. The Abyssinians came, and marched towards the river, the Sobat; the Shilluks ran away to their villages.

And the people returned to their villages, because there was a rumour, "The Ansars have been killed." Then the drum was beaten, the Shilluks danced to the drum, they rejoiced. The Turks came and remained in the country.

47. Tribal War.

Kal akyel e bẹno bia pạl, ka kal akyẹl e bẹnọ, ka leń kẹtọ̀. Ka ḍāṇ e kẹ̄l, ka ḍāṇ ńi fạ̣̀dọ̀, ka ḍāṇ mẹ̄kọ ńi chiki kẹ̀lọ̀, bẹr (bẹdọ) jē gẹ gīr, ka leń rẹṅọ, ka jē nẹk chyẹ, ḍāṇ chòp. Leń dèń, tyẹń a man bia bẹ ṭẹrọ ḍāṇ, ka gẹ ṭẹrọ pach. By ḍāṇ ma kẹtẹ ma ńi bẹ̄dọ wọk ki war. Jē ńi bia bẹ lìbọ̀ ki war. Jē ńi lācha wọt ki yey lwọl.

One family comes and goes out into the bush, and another family comes, and they begin fighting. And a man is speared, and falls down; again another man is speared, (so they go on till on both sides the dead are) many. At last one army runs away: many people are killed, they are speared. Now the warriors scatter. The women come to carry the dead home. No one is left out in the bush during night-time.

(After a war) the people come to lie in wait during the night.[1] — The people are accustomed to urinate in the house, in a gourd.[2]

48. The War of Nyeker.

Jal mẹ̄kọ chwọlá Ńekèr, wạde Dor, tẹ̀k, tẹ̀k, ka e kẹdọ, ka tọńa Tọṅọrọ bẹ manọ. Ka Tọṅọrọ nạ̣́gẹ́, ka gọ mạgẹ́. Ka ṅọye yi Yòdìt, ka e lōṅọ ki leń, ka mạńa Diṅjọl, ka leń chyẹt yi Diṅjọl; ka leń gọ̣́chẹ́ nam, ka leń nẹk; ka bia pach, ka e yẹwọ.

Some man whose name was Nyekēr, the son of Dor, was very, very brave. He went and turned towards Tongoro (in the Dinka country) to capture. He destroyed Tongoro and seized it (its people and cattle). And he was imitated by Yodit, he too raised an army and marched against Dingjol, but his army was chased by Dingjol, he drove the army into the river, so that they died. Yodit went home and repented what he had done.

49. The War of Deng.

Jal mẹ̄kọ chwọla Dẹń, ka fārẹ é kẹ̀tọ̀ ki Duwat; fa Ywéldìt. Ka léń tiń, tiń Yọń, ka leń e kẹ̀tọ, ka jē nẹk ga pyārọ. Ka Ojāṅọ dwai, ka e tẹ̀dọ̀, ka e ko: léń a ńi kẹta mwọl, ki mwọl chẹ̣t. Ka e mọ̄lọ, ka e butọ ki yọ̆, ka jē kā wọk, ka kọme

---

[1] This is blood revenge; if one tribe has more dead than the other, it tries to kill some people of the hostile village.
[2] for fear of being killed when going out.

gẹ́n pâr, ka gẹ nẹk, ka leṅ kẹ̣ta pach, ka e kẹ̣tọ, ka jē nẹk ga pyār aṅwẹn. Ka Dẹṅ kwachọ, kwachọ leṅ, ka tyẹk e bẹ̄nọ, ka lọgọ bâṅ gùn, ka fān ẹni e chyṅọ. Ka tyẹk chẹ̄tẹ, ka gọ nâ gẹ́; a kẹ́dẹ́, a tōṇa wọk, fōḷe riḷe Jaṅ.

There was a certain man with the name of Deng, his village fought with Duwat; the name of the village was Yweldit. The war began, it began at the village Yonj, the army fought, and ten men were killed. Then a Dinka man (a sorcerer) was brought, he made a charm, saying, "The war must be fought in the morning, early in the morning." So Deng arose early in the morning, and laid an ambush on the way; and when the people (the enemies) came out, he attacked them and killed (many of) them. The army of the enemy went back into the village, and when they came again, they killed fourteen men of Deng's. Then Deng begged, he begged for auxiliary troops; and an auxiliary army came. With them he went after the enemy, and the village (of Duwat) stopped fighting.

VII. TRADITIONS ON ŃIKĀŃO.

50. Nyikang's Parents.

Oshyāṅi ye Okwa, ye ṅǭma nam kį mayi Ńikaṅ, Ńakae, ṅa Ke. Ka jē ṅį kęta nam. Omya Ńakae fana ṅaṅ, będǫ kį ḍāṇ. Ka jē ṅį tugǫ kwǫmę, kįne: wáṅǫ́ yau! A kęt Dāk, a kwaṅ ṅa ṅaṅ, a nągé gǫ̀n, a búlį́, a yábį́, a kōbį Dāk kįne: á bùlà yàn! Kįne: è tích yí edi? Kįne: a chǎmá! Kįne: Ńakayǫ, kwárá a chám yi kwāri! Kįne: a chámè ręn? Kįne: yu kąla kęṅ? Kįne: ú ndmǫ̀! Kįne: ê! yí lǒṅi yi ręn kį́ chám̀ǫ̀, sha jē luǫ́ká nam. Ka ḍāṇ máké yì ṅàṅ. A kōbį ṅaṅ kįne: nam ba kélį yiṅ kę́tí! Dę̀ fa mąḍǫ fį! Kįne: dí dę́rę̀! ų ywódá yín, yí búdà wǫ̀k yí kę́lá kę̀lǫ̀. Yi fa ṅį nę̀nà wǫ̀k yi ṅį ṅwǫlu wǫ̀k. A tą̂t leṅǫ́, a ṅį bęn ṅaṅ wǫk, chę ḍǫke kwáṅǫ̀. Ka gę máké ṅàṅ. Ka chak mą̂nǫ̀ yi ḍą̂pǫ̀ kį́ ṅaṅ.

In ancient times Okwa (the father of Nyikang) married the (woman of the) river, the mother of Nyikang, Nyakae, the daughter of Ke. And the people used to go to the river. The brother of Nyakae was the crocodile, it lived with the men; and the people used to play on its back saying, "Our grandmother, eh!" One day Dak went, he took the children of the crocodile, he killed and roasted them. When the children were searched for, Dak said, "I have roasted them." Nyikayo (the brother of Nyakae) said, "How is that?" He replied, "I have eaten them." Then the mother of the crocodile said, "Nyakayo, my grandchildren have been eaten by your grandchildren." He replied, "Have they really been eaten by them?" He asked, "Where will you go now?" The woman replied, "I will remain in the river." Nyakayo said, "No, because you (and your children) will in your turn also be eaten by it (the crocodile), when the people (your children) come to wash." So the men now are caught by the crocodile. The crocodile said, "You (men) can never pass a river again, and you never will drink water from the river." Then Nyakayo (the man) said, "All right, if ever I find you (crocodile) lying outside the river, I shall surely stab you. You shall never sleep outside the river, you (shall only have sufficient time to) lay your eggs on the river bank." And a harpoon was made. During the time when the crocodile comes out of the river, the cows swim across the river; but (often) they are seized by the crocodile. This is the beginning of the enmity between man und the crocodile.

[Another Report on the Descent of Nyikang and on the origin of the Shilluk people, given in A. E. S. page 197:

In the beginning was Jo-uk (*jwǫk*), the Great Creator, and he created a great white cow, who came up out of the Nile and was called Deung Adok *(ḍeaṅ aduk)*. The white cow gave birth to a man-child whom she nursed and named Kola *(Kǫlǫ)*; Kola begat Umak Ra or Omaro *(Omarǫ)*, who begat Makwa or Wad Maul *(wat mǫ̱l)*, who begat Ukwa (Okwa). These people lived in a far-off country, nobody knows where.

Ukwa was one day sitting near the river when he saw two lovely maidens with long hair rise out of the river and play about in the shallows. He saw them many times after that, but they would have nothing to do with him and merely laughed at him. It should be mentioned that their lower extremities were like those of a crocodile.

One day Ukwa found them sitting on the banks, so he came up behind and seized them. Their screams brought their father, Ud Diljil, out of the river, to see what was the matter. Ud Diljil, whose right side was green in colour and in form like a crocodile, whilst his left side was that of a man, protested mildly, but allowed Ukwa to take away his daughters and wed them, merely giving vent to a series of incorrect prophecies regarding them.

Nik-Kieya *(Nyakae)*, the elder sister, gave birth to two sons and three daughters, and Ung-wad, the younger, to one son only, named Ju, or Bworo. The eldest son of Nik-Kieya, was called Nyakang (Nik-kang or Nyakam, = *Ńi̱kāṅ*) and inherited the pleasing crocodilian attributes of his mother and grandfather. Meanwhile Ukwa married a third wife, whose eldest child, a son, was named Duwat.

On Ukwa's death there was a furious quarrel between Nyakang and Duwat as to who should succeed Ukwa. It ended by Nyakang, with his sisters Ad Dui, Ari Umker, and Bun Yung, his brother Umoi and his half-brother Ju, acquiring wings and flying away to the south of the Sobat. Here they found the Shilluk country inhabited by wicked Arabs, so they drove them out and founded a most successful Kingdom. According to their genealogy this would have been about 1200 A. D., or later.

Nyakang had a creative power which he used greatly to the advantage of the Kingdom. In order to people the vast territory more quickly, he proceeded to create a people from the animal life he found in the forests and rivers. From crocodiles, hippopotami, and from wild beasts and cattle, he created men and women. When these had brought forth many children, the parent stock was removed by death, so that the children might not know of their origin.

The new creation and their offspring form the Shulla race or common people, in distinction from the direct descendants of Nyakang's family.

The latter continue to bear authority and fill the priestly function to this day. All outside the royal and priestly line are accounted Shullas.
Nik-Kieya still exists. She never died and never will. The western part of the Sobat and part of the White Nile is her favourite abode. She often appears, usually in the form of a crocodile, but at times in different forms and always in the river or on its banks. No sacrifices are ever offered to her: When she wishes, she takes what is required from among men and beasts; and when it is so, the people must not complain; indeed, it is an honour when Nik-Kieya is pleased to take her sacrifice of man or beast from a family.]

The Origin of the Shullas[1].
By Dr. T. Lambie, of Doleib Hill.

Nyikang, Duwad, Ju, Okil, Otin, and Moi were the sons of Okwa. Okwa was the son of Omara from heaven. Nyikang's mother was Nyikaya, Okwa's other wife was Ungwet. Nyikang and Duwad were twins, they lived far away to the south. Okwa was lost and his village was deserted, so the people asked, "Whom shall we elect king?" Part of the people said, "We will elect Nyikang," others said, "We will elect Duwad," so it came to pass there was war and the people were divided. Nyikang came and turned aside to the country of the Dim, and there he married the mother of Dak, and Dak was born. Dak was wicked and killed some people of the Dim, and the Dim said, "Booh! all the people are being killed!" So they agreed to kill him, saying, we will kill Dak." Another man, called Obogi, kept silence there at the council when they spoke, and when the people asked him, "Did you not understand our talk?" he said, "Ah!" like a deaf and dumb person. And they struck him and said, "This fellow dit not hear." Then Obogi went to Nyikang and told him about the plot. Nyikang replied, "Ah! very well, we shall see." So the father came and brought a wooden figure and put it up. And his son Dak played on the tom (stringed instrument), and when he had finished playing, he took off his bracelet and put it on the image in his house, and the Dim people came to his house and speared the figure. And when they thought they had finished killing it, they said, "He is dead, good!" They went away, and all the people came and began to lament saying, "Dak is dead." They killed a dog, and when they had finished, Dak came, while the people were dancing his funeral dance. Dak came in and saw them. And Nyikang said, "We will separate from you, we go to look for corn." So they came and stopped here in the home of the Shullas.

[1] i. e. Shilluks.

51. The Early Wanderings of Nyikang and his People. His Fight with the Sun.

Ka bẹ̀n jē kăké duọṅ, fōṇ ẹni ba Kẹ́rạu, fōṇ a bẹ̀ni Ńikåṅ; a dẹ̀ṅ gẹ̀n, gẹ ki Dụ̀wạt. A kōbi Dụwạt kịne: Ńikaṅ, yi kẹṭa kẹṅ? Kịne: ya kẹṭa kún ạ̀n. A kōbi: Ńikaṅ! Kịne: līḍe ṅåji. Ka Ńikaṅ e lịḍi ṅåjẹ́, ka dékúgi, ká gọ̀ lẹ̣́ṅẹ́ Ńikaṅ. Ka Ńikaṅ y bẹ̣no, a pyechị Ńikaṅ kịne: å gị ṅọ́? A kōbẹ́ kịne: kẹ́ṭ, ẹ́ ṅi kóṅ fằrï! A bẹ̣n Ńikaṅ, a pẹ̣ka fōṭe Ṭụ̀rọ̀, fōṭe nẹ̀yá Dāk.

Ka Dāk ṅi bẹ̣dọ wiy burọ, ḕ ṭōmọ ṭȍm. A kōbi nẹyí gẹ́n kịne: féṅ é tẹ̀rè yi Dāk. A kẹṭ nèyi gẹ́n, a tyẹ́kè tọ̀ṅ. A tōtè Dāk kịne: yi dwàtà nåḍgè yí neyọ. A kẹṭ Ńikaṅ, a dwai abọ̣̀bọ̀, a yiẹḍe bọ̣̀bọ̀, ka ṭōṭẹ́ chyẹne gọ̀n. A kẹṭ Dāk, a fẹ̣ki kẹṅ ẹni, a ṭǔmì ṭom. A bẹ̣n neyi gẹ́n, a kẹ̀li, ẹn abọ̣̀bọ̀. Dāk kẹṭa kal. A bẹ̣n Ńikaṅ, a kōbẹ́ kịne: nåră ẹ́ nåḍgọ̀ yí néyi gẹ́n. Ka neyi gẹn e buọgọ. A kōbi kịne: ẹ̀, riy ḍåṇ cháṅ åṅwẹ̀n! A rịji cháṅ åṅwẹ̀n, a ywóḍgi.

Ḍụki ká tẹḍọ̀ bẹ̣nọ̀ bẹ̣ne, gẹ́ gịr, ka Dāk blà wọk ki kàl. Ka kẹṭa yi mǔḍọ. Ka neyi gẹn e rẹ́ṅọ̀, ka ywọk ḕ rǔmọ̀.

Ka Ńikaṅ e ko: ya kẹḍọ! Ka e bẹnọ, ka kạla yi nam, nam mẹ̣kọ, chwọlà Faloko. A jē pẹ̣ka nam ẹni. Ká ḍeåṅ ē lòyọ̀, ḍe Ńikaṅ, kifa wáṭẹ́, wáṭẹ́ ṅi chåká chwọ̣̀bọ̀ yi Ńikaṅ; ká é kẹ́ḍọ̀, ka kẹṭi fōṭè chàṅ; ka ōjul ẹ́ kẹ́ḍọ̀, ka ḍeåṅ ywóḍẹ́, kẹ̀lẹ́ ḍọ (ḍọk) cháṅ. Ka e ko: yá yáfà ḍeåṅ. Ka Gårọ́, wạt chàṅ, ká ẹ́ kōbọ̀ kịne: jál, yi yàpà ṅọ̀? Kịne: yá yápà ḍeåṅ. Kịne: å ḍe mẹ̀n? Kịne: ḍe Ńikaṅ. Kịne: ḍe bẹ̣da kẹṅ? Kịne: kạlá fōṭe Ńikaṅ. Kịne: ẹ̀! paṭ! paṭe ḍe Ńikaṅ. A dúọgẹ́, ẹ̣n ōjul; a kōpẹ́ Ńikaṅ kịne: Ńikaṅ, ḍeåṅ a yōtè wọ́ṅ; ḍe ṅal mẹ̣kọ, bår (bǎr), pẹre Dāk, chyẹne då atẹ̣̀gọ̀. A kōbi Ńikaṅ kịne: tiṅ léṅ, a yōt ḍọk! A kẹ́ṭ Dāk, a måḡi Gårọ́, a tåyẹ́ gọ̀n fẹṅ; a ṅōḡle chyẹne gọ̀n, a kåp yịẹl wọk; a chyẹṭi léṅ. A bẹ̣n chaṅ, a chyẹṭe leṅ Ńikaṅ, a ṅåḡẹ́ gọ̀n; a bẹ̣n Ńikaṅ, a kwaṅ nẹ̀yọlọ̀, å ṅwåṅi chaṅ; ká chaṅ dọ̣̀gọ́ mål. A kẹṭ Ńikaṅ, a kwáṅẹ́ tẹ̀gọ̀, a pwōḍẹ́ jē, a påṛọ̀ jē mal.

A bẹ̣n tẹḍọ̀, a bẹ̣n wiy nam, ka jē dwoḍọ, ka gẹ bẹ̣nọ̀, ka gẹ wạnọ måné nåm. Ka nam yōt, å ṭik. A kōbi Ńikaṅ kịne: gọ kạla kẹṅ? A kōbi kịne: å kiḍì? A wåṅè yọ́. A påṛọ Obọ̣̀gọ̀ mål; a kōbi kịne: Ńikaṅ, yá wǔmì yi chám. Chwọ́bì yán ṭa tịk. A kōbi kịne: Ńikaṅ, y dẹ́ kûn, y kẹ́ṭi yi tịk, ka yi kạle båṅ tịk. A chwọ́bi ṭá tịk, a pyeṭe tịk, a bẹ̣nọ pách gẹ́ ki tịk.

A pẹ́kẹ́ Achyẹte-guok, a yōt fẹṅ, ẹ da bwō̄ṇọ, a dùọ̀k tẹḍọ̀ lọ̀ṅ, a pẹ́ki wiy Pìyọ, a pọṇi Dāk, a pọṇi wiy Pålọ. A kẹṭi leṅ pach. A chyẹṭe léṅ, a kẹṭ tẹ̣ḍọ̀.

A gẹ̀rẹ́ Ńelwal, a gẹ̀ri Pépwōjọ̀, a gẹ̀ri Adúẹ́lọ̀, a gẹ̀ri Tédigọ̀ Pālọ; a kẹṭ tẹḍọ, a gẹ̀ri Wau, Ochọ̣̄rọ, Peṅikaṅ Otēgọ, Akonwå, Mọ̀rọ̀, Óryàn; myere Ńikaṅ å ṭùm. A kẹḍọ, ena Ńikaṅ, a kōbi: ẹ́, Chọlọ dọ̣ṅọ.

A jágí Dāk, a kẹḍẹ, a jágí Ódāk, a kẹ́ḍẹ́, a låi yịnọ̀, a ṭòu. A mǔm tẹḍọ̀, kịne; e gwọk èdi? A duọk Ńikaṅ, a kōbi kịne: kụl ḍeåṅ, mẹn yik gí tabate. A wúmẹ́, a lŏni Duwat kí jàgò. A rúmí, a lóní Bwǫ́ch ki jàgò; a lŏní Dǫ́kǫ̈t ki jāgọ; a lŏní Tugọ ki jāgọ; a lŏní Okwọn ki jāgọ, a lŏní Kúdu kí jāgọ; a lŏní Ńakwachọ ki jāgọ.

In ancient times the people came to the country Kerau, this is the country into which Nyikang came. Here they separated, he and (his brother) Duwat. Duwat said, "Nyikang, where are you going?" He replied, "I am going to that place there." Again he said, "Nyikang, look behind!" And Nyikang turned round, and looked back, and he saw a stick for planting dura, which Duwat had thrown to him. When Nyikang came back to take it, he asked, "What is that?" Duwat replied, „Go, that is a thing with which to dig the ground of your village!" And Nyikang came, and sat down in the country of Turo. This is the country of his son Dak.

And Dak used to sit on the ashes of the village and to play the tom (a stringed instrument). But his uncles (the brothers of Nyikang) said, "The country is to be ruled by Dak alone? (being jealous of him). His uncles went to sharpen their spears. But it was told to Dak, "You are going to be killed by your uncles!" Then Nyikang went to fetch an ambach, he hewed it, and made for it hands (so that it looked like the statue of a man). Dak went and sat down in the same place again, and began playing his instrument. His uncles came and stabbed him — that is, the ambach statue; Dak went into his enclosure (unhurt). Nyikang came and said, "My son has been killed by his uncles." His uncles were afraid saying, "Let every man stay at home four days. When four days have passed, we may mourn him." The morning after four days were gone, all the people came (to mourn), there were a great many. Suddenly Dak came out from his enclosure and went to dance the mado dance. When his uncles saw this, they ran away, and the mourning was finished.

Nyikang said, "I will go!" And he came and went along a river, a certain river called Faloko. And the people settled on this river. Here the cow ran away, the cow of Nyikang, because of her calves, her calves used to be speared by Nyikang.[1] She went and came to the country of the sun. And Ojul ("the grey hawk") went to search for her; he found the cow among the cows of the sun. He said, "I am searching for a cow." Garo, the son of the sun, said, "Man, what do you search for?" He replied, "I search for a cow!" He asked, "What cow?" Ojul said, "The cow of Nyikang." Garo asked, "Where has it come from?" He answered, "From the country of Nyikang." Garo replied, "No, never! Here is no cow of Nyikang." He, Ojul, turned back and told Nyikang, "Nyikang, we have found the cow! among the cows of a certain man, he is awfully tall, just like Dak; on his hands he has silver bracelets." Nyikang said, "Raise an army, and find the cow!" Dak went and attacked Garo, he threw

---

[1] Whenever Nyikang came to a new place, he killed a calf.

him on the ground. He cut off his hands, pulled the bracelets off them, and chased the enemy's army; he came to the sun. But there the army of Nyikang was chased, and it was utterly destroyed. Then Nyikang himself came, he took an adze and aimed it towards the sun. He hit the sun, and it returned to the sky. Nyikang went and took the bracelet, with it he touched the dead of his army, and they returned to life.

The people came, they came to the head (source) of a river, there they arose and approached the junction of the river (in boats). They found the river full of sudd. Nyikang said, "Where does this come from? what shall we do?" Their way was barred. Then Obogo[1] arose saying, "Nyikang, I have finished eating. Spear me under the sudd!" He said again, "Nyikang, thus I shall part asunder the sudd, and if you come to any place where the sudd is, you just follow after it." So Obogo was stabbed under the sudd, and the sudd broke asunder, so they came to their place together with the sudd.

He settled (with his people) in Achyete-guok, but he found the country occupied by the white people, therefore the people returned to this side of the river. They settled at the head of the Pijo (i. e. *Sobat*), Dak passed on to Wij-Palo. The army went home (it scattered because the war was finished).

He, Nyikang, built the following villages: Nyelwal, Pepwojo, Adwelo, Tedigo, Palo. The people went on and built Wau, Oshoro, Penyikang Otego, Akuruwar, Moro, Oryang, these are the villages of Nyikang. Nyikang went saying, "Ah, there are still Shilluks left!"

Then Dak ruled, he went away;[2] (after him his son) Odak ruled, he went away[2] while hunting game. The people were perplexed, and they said, "What is that?" Nyikang returned saying, "Bring a cow, that we may make a bier." When that was finished, Duwat ruled after him; when he had finished, Bwoch ruled after him, after him Dokot ruled, then Tugo, then Okwon; then Kudit, then Nyakwacho. (For the complete list see page 135).

[A somewhat different report of this warfare is given by P. W. Hofmeyer in "Anthropos", 1910, V, page 332; it runs thus:

Nyikang heard of a country in which all ornaments and even the tools were made of silver. He made up his mind to go into this country with his sons and numerous armed people. The name of this country was wang garo i. e. the country where the sun sets and sleeps, and where the sun is so near that it may be seized with the fingers.

Nyikang arrived in the miraculous country; in truth, numerous cattle-herds were grazing here, and the young people were richly adorned with silver rings and silver sticks. Nyikang and Dag entered a hut, where a young woman was working. She was exceedingly beautiful; the Shilluk

---

[1] Obogo means "albino"; vide also page 157.
[2] i. e. he died.

heroes had never seen her equal. Dag asked the woman, whether she would like to marry him and go with him into his country. The woman was frightened, she sprang up, cursing the black fellows. But Dag replied, "Though we are black, and without silver ornaments, we shall show you that our arms are stronger than those of your men and that we may well venture to ask you for marriage." Thereupon the woman showed them the direction where her husband with his servants herded the cattle. Nyikang and Dag turned thither.

It was just growing dark and the herds were coming from the bush, the men with their costly silver ornaments following. Dag at once rose, went to meet them, and soon a great fighting was going on. The man who wore the heavy silver rings was defeated, and Dag stripped the ornaments off him.

In the heat of the fight and on account of the scorching sun all the Shilluks fell down. Nyikang ordered water to be brought, with which he sprinkled his fallen warriors, and they all came to life again. Even the sun he sprinkled that it might not burn so hot, and presently it ceased burning. Finally the Shilluks were victorious and drove away the cattle and men of the enemies. These people are the Quadshal (Kwa Jal).

When they had arrived in the Shilluk country, Dag once more proposed to the woman to marry her; but he was again rejected.

Nyikang offered the prisoners in his country cattle, but they declined. He offered them Shilluk women, but again they declined. So he gave them the privilege to seize and keep a number of Shilluk girls and to collect spears, sheep, and fat in the whole Shilluk country, as often as a new king would be elected. As this was a lasting privilege, they consented to accept it.]

52. Different Doings and Adventures of Nyikang.

Ńíkàṅo ńị́ ká (kẹdọ) tàn gat. Ka jē mōkọ ńi bẹnọ, gẹ̀ màyọ̀ ki yẹi. Ka yẹi ńí ɤóńa feń. Ka ńi lẹ̀di Nikań, ka Ńikań dẹ́li, ka e bẹnọ, ka e ko kịne: Dák, ya dẹ́li yị jē mōkọ. Ka Dák e kẹdọ̀, ka Dāk dẹ́lẹ́, ka Dāk e bẹnọ, ka e ko: yá dâl yí jọk ẹńí. Ka Ńikań ko: ẹ́, ǹàrà! gẹ di (ri) jē a ńí wèi gẹ́ń? Kịne: ẹ́, yẹi ńi wańa feń! A dẹ̀gí Dāk, a bẹn yị jọk ẹni, gẹ́ màyọ̀ ki yẹ̀. A lọk Dāk e ókộk, ka pẹka yey nam. Ka jọk ẹni e bẹnọ, ka gẹ kạla būte Dāk; ka gẹ mâk, ka gẹ kịtị fach.

Ka jọk ẹni e bẹdọ kị fach. Ká wọ̀t gêr yi Ńikań, ka gẹ kōbọ kịne: Ńikań, bẹnẹ́ wọti agak? Kịne: wọte wa fa ńi bẹdọ̀ nàu. A kōbi Ńikań kịne: ẹ́, de wọt ńi gêr edi? Kịne: wọte wa ńi gêr kị́ dạn! A kyẹdi Ńikań kịne: dạn bogọn. Kịne: ẹ́, dạn á gîr kị́ yí bẹ̀nè! A kōbi Ńikań kịne: ẹ́, bogọn. A kẹdẹ, chwọla Ólóâlọ. A kōbi kịne: kại dạn! Ka Ńikań é bàṅọ̀. A kẹt jal ẹni, a kạī ńārẹ, a chụ̀bí lạ̀bọ̀, a kyẹri

WESTERMANN, The Shilluk People. 11

wǫt, a chyɛk lɔ̰bǫ, ka tyɛle wǫt tɔ̰́gɛ́. A kōbǫ kịne: chuṅun! A māgi ṅārɛ, a gǫ̌chí gǫ̀n kḭ́ ɔ̀tɔ́ɔ̀, a ṯǫwɛ. A kōbi Ńikaṅ kịne: búh! Kịne: ɛ̰̀, Oloalǫ, kwǫfi rach! ɛrɛ ɖa̰ṉ a nɔ̌gí? Kịne: ɣédɛ̰? Kịne: ɛ̰̀, u̥ chǫ̂k ɔ́ gɪ̀ fɔ́ɔ́rɛ́ ɔ̀nɛ̰̀n: ka ṅi kyɛre wǫt Ńikaṅ, ɖa̰ṉ e ṅi ṯǫ̰ kifa Ólóɔ̂lǫ̰. A bɛṯ ṯɛrǫ, a kōbi Ńikaṅ kịne: ɛ̰́! Oloalǫ jēi u̥ chǫ̰̂gɛ́ ṯǫ̰ yi wǫn ɛni. Ka Oloalǫ kịne: dɛ̰̂dɛ̰̂ (dɛ̰ ɛrɛ), u̥ ṅyɛ̰̂n, ba ṯumi.

A wēkè jame kwɛ̰r yi Ńikaṅ, a ṅi kyɛre wǫt. Ka e ko kịne: wǫt ṅi kyɛl ki aɣṵ̄jǫ ṅita̰nǫ, ṅi châm a wâr, ṅi laṅa wǎr, ɛ̰̀ chɔ̰̀mǫ̰̀. Ka gōl akyɛ̰̀lǫ̰̀ gɛ kɛle bāṅe Ńikaṅ, ṅi chama chwai; ka gōl akyɛ̰lǫ chama riṅǫ, gōl akyɛl chama bāṅe. A rûmi, mǫ́k ɔ̀n a ṯum.

Ka Ńikaṅ ṅi ka wi kyɛr, ka jē mǫ̰kǫ ṅi yǒt gɛ tǔdǫ̰, jal ɛni ki ṅemɛn. Ka Ńikaṅ bɛṉǫ, ka gɛ ṅi rɛṅa nam. Ka Ńikaṅ ṅi ɖɔ́lɛ̰́, ka Dāk dwai, kɔ́ é bɔ̀ṅǫ̰̀; ka kwâch. Ka Ńikaṅ e kɛḏǫ, ka ṅārɛ wēki Dāk, chōl kɛy maye Dāk. A yei Dāk, a kɛḏǫ, ka jǫk ɛni yǒdɛ́. Ka gɛ rɛṅa nam, ka Dāk kɛla nam ki yɛi; ka gɛ gɛ̰̀ṅǫ̰̀ wǫk, ka gɛ riṅa nam, ka ṅān ɛni mǎgɛ́, ka gǫ kiṯi yi yɛi. Ka e bɛṉǫ, ka ómɛ̰n lúgɔ̄ bâṅɛ̂. Ka gɛ bɛ̰dǫ ki pach. E ṅwǫlɛ́ ki wǔdɛ̰. A kwali rēi gɛ́n, gɛ ki ṅɛmɛ̰n. A dǫn wǫḏɛ̰.

A kɛṯ ḏǫge nam. A kɛṯ Ńikaṉǫ bɛ chɛ́k, ka jal mɔ̰kǫ ṅi chōṯi ɣɛ̰n ki nam; ṅiṅɛ chwǫla ga Ochwâ. A kɛḏǫ, ɛna Ńikaṅ, a kónɛ̰́ jǫ́ch, jǫch Ochamdǫr, a yiɛri gǫn, a kiṯi Oḏǫp, a kiṯi mǫṅ ópún, kiṯi ḏǫk odǫp, a mɔ̂gɛ́, a bɛṉa wǫk, a ɖa̰ṉ. A bɛṉ ṅemɛn bāṅɛ. A bɛ̰da pach; a ṅi chāmǫ ṟǫ̂ch, ṟǫche Ńikaṅ, a ṅi châm mǫṅ adɔ̌ṯ. A wēri Ńikaṅ, a kōbi Ńikaṅ kịne: kyau kējǫ wiy Tor, jǫk kùn chámɛ́ kḭ́ jɔ̰́p. A ṅi chāmi jō̰p. A kɛṯ ṅɛmɛ̰n, a kōbi: ṯǫ̰ṯɛ yán ki riṅǫ! Ka e wēro̰ ki ṅɛmɛ̰n, a ṅākǫ. Ka gɛ ṅɛ̰lɛ̰́ nam, ka gɛ̰́lǫ̰̀, ka gǫ mǫ̰gɛ nam, ka gɛ kɛṯi nam.

Ka jǫk mǫ̰kǫ ṅi kɔ́ bɛ māi, gɛ bia ki Olam, ka Ńikaṅ ṅi ɖɔ́lɛ̰́, ka Dāk e kɛḏǫ. Ka gɛ rǫmǫ ki gin; ka gɛ mǎgɛ́. Ńikaṅ ko: wēki yan, ka Dāk é bɔ̀ṅǫ̰̀, kịne: bāṅd! Ka gɛ kɔ̰li Dāk, ka gɛ kɛṯa fach, ka gɛ wēki ḏǫ̀k ḏǫ̀nǫ̰̀; ka gɛ wēki tón alǫ̂dɛ́, gǫ ṅi gūtɛ dean. Kɔ̰l dean ki Bachōdǫ, gǫ ṅi lǫ́gǫ̀ mǫ̰́ gɛ́n.

Ka jǫk mǫ̰kǫ bɛ̰da, ga kwar bwoṅǫ, ka gɛ ṅi kɛḏǫ, ka ṅi ṅa baṅ; ka gɛ ṅi wēkḭ gyɛ̰nǫ, tyɛṅe a yǒt pɛ́n, ka ṅi kɔ̰l Ńikaṅ ki Akuruwar; gɛ ṅi maki gyɛ̰nǫ, gǫ ṅi gach ki fɛṅ kḭ́ yey ɖǫ́k. Chǫ̂ṯɛ́, mǫk ɛni ɔ́ ṯùm.

Jǫk mǫ̰kǫ ba yɪ̰t, gɛ ṅi kɛṯi gɛ yi nam, yi nam Abúḏǫk; gɛ ṅi chami ṅwǫle par. Nam ɛni chwǫlá Ńewɛk. Ka Abuḏǫk e bɛṉǫ, ka e pêchǫ̰ kịne: wúnɛ̰́ jǫ̰̀ kún? Kịne: wǫ́ bɔ́ yɪ̰t. Ka Abuḏǫk kuḏǫ. Ka gɛ chāmǫ kḭ riṅǫ; ka lwāṅǫ ṅi pɛka wiy riṅǫ, ka jǫk ɛni e baṅǫ; e ṅǫṅǫ. A kōbi Abúḏǫk kịne: wu rɛ a bāṅ woûn? Kịne: wǫ́ bǫ̰̀kǫ̰̀. Kịne: yi ṅǫ̰? Yi lwāṅǫ. Kịne: wí chákɔ́ ṅwǫ̀ṅǫ̰̀! Kịne: wǫ fa ṅi chɔ̰̀mǫ̰̀ gin kwǫmɛ da lwāṅǫ. A kiṯi gɛn pach yi Abuḏǫk. A kōbi Abuḏǫk kịne: wi chǫ̂k, wuna kwɔ̂re ṅwǫ̀ṅ! A bɛ̰dɛ́, ɛna bāṅ Abuḏǫk, a wēki kɔ̀l.

Nyikang used to go to the river-bank. And some people also used to come there, they were fishing in a boat, and suddenly the boat used to sink to the bottom. Nyikang saw it, but he did not know what to do (with these people), therefore he went home, and said (to his son), "Dak, there are certain people, I do not know what to do with them." Dak went, but he too could not manage them. So Dak came home saying, "I do not know what to do with these people." But Nyikang said, "My, why did you let the people go?" He answered, "Well, the boat went down to the bottom!" Dak returned and found the people again fishing in a boat. Dak turned himself into an egret and sat down in the middle of the river. The people came and were driven to the side of Dak; so he caught them and brought them into a (his) village (settled them).

These people now lived in a village. And Nyikang was building a house. They asked, "Nyikang, are these your houses? Our houses (the houses of our father) are not thus." Nyikang replied, "Eh, how then are (your) houses built?" They replied, "Our houses are built with human beings." But Nyikang protested, saying: "I have no human beings (for that purpose)!" They replied, "Why, you have a lot of people here with you everywhere!" But Nyikang said, "No, there are none!" The man (the chief of these water-people) went; — his name was Oloalo. — (But he came again) saying: "Bring a man!" But Nyikang refused. The man went and brought his own son; then he mixed mud, he marked the place where the house was to be built, he prepared the mud and dug out the foundations of the house. He said, "Bring mud!" And it was brought. He said, "Stop now!" He seized his son and struck him with a club, until he died. When Nyikang saw this, he said, "Ah, Oloalo, you are doing a wicked thing! how can you kill that man!?" Oloalo replied, "Why?" Nyikang said, "Well, it now will remain a custom of your village, always when a house of Nyikang will be built, a man will die because of Oloalo." The people remained there. Nyikang said, "Ah, Oloalo, your people will always die in building this house!" Oloalo replied, "Never mind, they are many, they will not be used up."

Nyikang gave him certain goods belonging to himself, with which to build the house (of Nyikang). And he said, "The house shall be built with a black heifer, which shall be eaten in the night; during the night it shall be eaten." One family — they are followers of Nyikang — eat the broth, and one family eat the meat, one family eat the meat on the skin. It is finished; this report is at an end.

Nyikang used to go to the river junction (of Sobat and White Nile), there he used to find some people who were cooking, a man with his sister. When Nyikang came near, they ran away into the river. Nyikang did not know what to do, and he called Dak. But Dak refused. He begged him. Then Nyikang went, and gave his daughter to Dak, as an indemnity for the mother of Dak. Now Dak consented, he went and found the people. They ran into the river, but Dak also drove a boat into the river and he drove them out onto the bank. They attempted to escape into the river again, but he seized the girl; he put her into his boat and came home. But her brother followed her, and they both remained in the village. (Dak married the girl), and she bore a son. After some time they stole away, the man and his sister. Her son was left in the village.

One day Nyikang went to fish with a hook. And a man (below the water) always used to break the fish-hook in the river, the name of this man was Oshwa. He, that is, Nyikang, now went to dig out the joch-plant, the joch of Ochamdor, he twisted it into a rope and tied the fish-hook to it, he fastened a piece of bread to the point of the hook, and so he caught the man in the river, he came out — it was a man! His sister came after him. They remained in the village, they used to eat calves, the calves of Nyikang, and they used to eat the corn which was cooked for making beer. At last Nyikang became angry, and said, "Row this man to the place of Witor, a place where he may eat buffaloes." (He was rowed thither, and) ate buffaloes. His sister also went there and she used to say, "Give me some meat!" He became angry with his sister, and they fought. And (while fighting) they rolled into the river, they tumbled down a steep slope, and so went into the river again.

Some people used to go fishing, to a place called Olam. Nyikang got into difficulties with them, and Dak went. He met them, and they were caught by him. Nyikang said, "Give them to me!" But Dak refused, saying, "They are my slaves." Dak took them along with him and brought them into his village. He gave them big cattle, and the spear Alodo with which to kill the cows. — When people bring cattle to Fashoda it is their (these people's) property.

There were some people, descendants of the white men; they became slaves. They used to give fowls. They were people found in the country before Nyikang was brought from Akuruwar. They used to catch hens, and to offer them to Nyikang as a tax, in the middle of Dok. — That is all, this report is finished.

Some people were fishermen, they used to go to the river, to the river of Abudok, they used to eat the calves of hippos. The name of this river was Nyewek. When Abudok came, he asked them, "From which place are you people?" They replied, "We are fishermen." Abudok was silent. And while they were eating meat, flies settled on the meat; but these people would not suffer it, they were proud. Abudok said, "Why do you refuse that meat?" They replied, "We are afraid." He asked, "Of what?" They answered, "Of the flies." He said, "You are proud, are you not?" They replied, "We do not eat anything on whose back there are flies." These people were taken home by Abudok. And Abudok said, "Ah, you will continue thus! You are the descendants of pride." They stayed there, they became adherents of Abudok, he gave them a setttlement.

53. The Man who sacrificed Himself.

Kẹṅ a bẹn Ńikāṅ, a kẹṯi Atulfi ki wạte bāṇẹ, a ywoda nam ẓ rígọ̀ yi tịk. Ka Ńikāṅ e jādọ yŏ. Ka jal ma óbọ̱gọ̀ e fẹchọ kịne: Ńikāṅ, yí rè chúṅ? Yi jati ki yŏ? Ye ko: àwọ́, yá játi̯ yọ. Ka e ko: kẹṅ ya rūmi̯ ki cham, yá ụ bí, ka ya chwọ̱p kị́ tọ́ṅ, ka rẹ̇má mọ̱lá nâm, tịk ụ chọ̱t. Ka Ńikaṅ chwọ̱bi̯ jal ẹni, ka rẹmẹ mọla nam, ka tịk e chọ̱dọ. Ka Ńikaṅ yịti ki yọ.[1]

When Nyikang came, he went to the Khor Atulfi with his followers; he found the river was shut up by the sudd, so that Nyikang did not find a passage. And a certain man who was an albino,[2] asked thus, "Nyikang, why do you stop? Is it because you do not find a passage?" He replied, "Yes, I do not see a way where to pass." The man said, "When I have finished eating, I shall come, I will be killed with a spear, my blood will flow into the river, and the sudd will break away." And Nyikang speared the man, his blood flowed into the river, and the sudd broke away. Thus Nyikang found a passage.

54. Nyikang and the River-people.

A kẹṯa Ńikaṅ wak, a máńi̯, a yōde yệ, riṅa wọk yi lyẹk, a kōbi̯ kịne: jọk, wei kátẹ́ (kẹ́ṯá) yi yẹi wun! jọk ẹni ko: kipaṇọ? Kịne yau. A kátẹ́, che yẹi ńi tọ̱ṅa peṅ, ka gọ ńi dẹ̱dí yi Ńikaṅ. A bẹn, a mágé gin, a kạle gẹ pach, a lâme gin, a lọgọ bāṇẹ, a wei gẹ tọṅ, gọ ńi lâm gẹn. A lọge tyẹṅ lām, a wei gẹ Ńibọ̱dọ; ka ńi bọ̱ti̯ Ńikaṅ. Chwọl gá kwar Waṅ, kwāre yẹi lyẹk.

Nyikang went into the bush capturing; he saw (at a distance on the river) a boat, he ran from the high grass to a place where the grass was burned, then he called, "People, let me get into your boat!" The people asked, "Why?" He replied, "Just let me go in." When he got into it, the boat went to the bottom (was about to sink, this being caused by the witchcraft of the people in the boat); but Nyikang pushed it up again; then he came and caught them. He brought them into a village; he taught them to pray; they became his slaves (his subjects); he gave them the spear and taught them to pray. So they became the people of prayer. He let them reside at Nyibodo; they keep the (religious) things belonging to Nyikang. They are called the descendants of Wang, the descendants of the boat of the grassless plain.

55. The Lost Cow.

Kwajụl e kwayi̯ dọk, dọk Ńikaṅ, ka dẹaṅ akyẹl e wáṅ, ka e kẹdọ kal dọ Dimọ. Ka e bẹṇọ: dẹaṅ agọn? Kịne: dẹaṅ tọ̱k! Ka Ńikaṅ wērọ, ka e ko: yap dẹaṅ! Ka

---

[1] Vide 51.

e kedǫ kun de chan̄, ka ye kedǫ, ka ye kedǫ, ka mákì wun; a kedǫ, a wiṭi fōṭe Dimǫ. Ka ḍean̄ ywodę ę wiṭi fach, ka fęki ṭd ryęk; a fyechę: yi kǫla kun â? Kǫle fōṭe Ńikan̄ bę yafe ḍean̄. Ka ḍuki mǫl a kęṭi kale ḍǫk, ka ḍe Ńikan̄, ka gǫ kǫ́lè ę́n. Ka e bę̄n, wanǫ fōṭe Chǫl. Ka ḍean̄ kǫ́lę́ kal ḍǫk. Ka fyęch Ńikan̄ kįne: ḍean̄ a kǫ́lè yin̂? Ka e ko: ḍean̄ d wani fach. Chwǫl ęna Kwajụl, bāne Ńikan̄.

Kwajul herded cattle, the cattle of Nyikang; and one cow disappeared, she went into the cattle-yard of Dimo. When Kwajul came home, Nyikang asked, "Where is the cow?" He replied, "The cow is away." Nyikang became angry, he said, "Search for the cow!" So he went westwards ("to the place of the sun"), he walked and walked, till he had been on his way a year; he arrived in the country of Dimo. There he found the cow, she had gone into the village, and was lying within the yard. They asked him, "Where do you come from?" He replied, "I come from the country of Nyikang, to search for a cow." The next morning he went into the cattle yard, and drove the cow of Nyikang away. And he came and approached the Shilluk country. He drove the cow into the cattle pen. Nyikang asked, "Have you brought the cow?" He replied, "The cow is here in the village." Therefore he was called Kwajul, the servant of Nyikang.[1]

56. The Liar.

Ojulǫ będa ga mąṭ, ka ńi węla kęń, ka ńi bę̄nǫ, ka ńi ṭǫdǫ; ka ńi węla fōne, ka ńi bę̄n, ka ńi tǫdǫ. A kōbi Ńikan̄, a fyechi kįne: Ojulǫ, yi re chǒk kifa tǫdǫ? Ko: â, mąṭ, tōdi ya! bęnę́ gin ńi yǫ́nį yá. Ka Ńikan̄ e ṅzṭǫ, e ko: jal, yi ų chǒk, yina twot. A chōgį anan, a tuòt, a n̄eau tōdǫ ki jach; a wǎki gǫ ę́n.

Ojulo was a friend (of Nyikang). When he went somewhere and came back, he used to tell all kinds of stories (lies) to Nyikang. Whenever he came to a country, he brought home a lot of stories. One day Nyikang asked, "Ojulo, why do you always lie so much?" Ojulo replied, "Ah, friend, let me lie! That is what makes me feel well." And Nyikang laughed, he said, "Man, you will always continue in this, you are a liar indeed!" And so he continued, he used to tell stories, he bought the story-telling with the shoulder of game, which he gave to Nyikang.[2]

57. Nyikang's Quarrel with Duwat.

Ńikàn̄ wèn Okwá, omęn Dụwąt, fōṭe Shǫ́lǫ fà Ṭùrǫ, yęna kách ákyę̄l. Kà Ńiekàn̄ e wę̀rǫ ki Dụwąt, Ńiekan̄ wądę Dāk, Dụwąt wądę Dìmǫ. Ka Dāk e n̄ākǫ ki Dimǫ ki bǎn rǫ̀ch Ńiekān̄, chama byęl, byęl Dụwąt; Dimǫ fwòt rǫ̀ch. Ńiekanǫ wę̀rǫ ki Dụwąt. — Ńiekan̄ e kedǫ, e ko: Dụwąt, dǫ̀ń! yá kędǫ̀! Ka Ńiekān̄ e kedǫ,

---

[1] Compare with this story No. 51.
[2] By giving the shoulder of the game he had killed, he "bought" from Nyikang the privilege to tell lies. (This is meant as a joke).

é chąṭǫ. Ka Dwwạt rena ban Ńiekan kine: Ńiekan, shụ̀ní! Ńiekań é ban. Kine: lịṭí! Ńiekano lịṭị. Ka tákǘgʰ lẹ́ní kine: Ńiekan, kwań tákǘgʰ bẹ kwon jẽi! Bẹn Ńiekan fōṭe Shǫ́lǫ̀, fa (fach) Ńiekan kị wǘdẹ Dāk kị Shal, wąṭe aryąu. — Wa (Wat) Ńiekan akyẹl ḷ yịgí nan nị māi kị́ rech.

Nyikang, his father is Okwa, and his brother is Duwat. The country of the Shilluks was (at that time) Turo; there they lived in one place. And Nyikang became angry with Duwat: Nyikang had a son whose name was Dāk, and the son of Duwat was Dimo. And Dak quarrelled with Dimo behind (or: on account of) the calves of Nyikang; they (the calves) ate the dura, the dura of Duwat, and Dimo beat the calves. Therefore Nyikang became angry with Duwat. Nyikang went away. He said, "Duwat, stay here! I go." And Nyikang went away walking. Duwat ran after Nyikang, saying: "Nyikang, stop!" But Nyikang refused. Again he called, "Look!" And Nyikang looked behind, and Duwat threw a digging stick towards him, saying: "Take this stick to bury your people with!"[1] Nyikang came into the Shilluk country, (and it became) the home of Nyikang and his son Dak and Shal; he had (these) two sons. — One son of Nyikang became a man who used to fish.

58. The Fish Ocholo.

Jal mẹkǫ niṇẹ chwǫla Ochǒlǫ, bẹda wat ban Ńikan. Kẹn lwǫke Ńikan nam, ka nị lǫ́gị́ rējǫ, ka nị dwaṇǫ kine: bųh! Ka Ńikan nị nàn, ka e bia pach, ka e ṭạḍǫ kị́ kǎk, ka wijẹ kịṭi kị apẹ̄r, ka kẹṭa nam; ka e dwaṇǫ, kine: bųh, ka nị kẹle Ńikan, ka rējǫ, ka gǫ nị bājẹ. Jal e bẹda jwǫk. Nị chịka dwaṇǫ, ka gǫ nị bājẹ. Ka Ńikan e pidǫ, ka bia pach, ka jal ẹni yōdi gǫ bẹn pach, dẹ twārǫ wéré ḍǫk.

Ḍụki ka Ńikan dǫgi gạt. Ka jal ẹni e lōgi kẹṭẹ, e chịka dwaṇǫ, kine: bųh! Ka nị kẹle yi Ńikan, ka bach, ka e gịtǫ bōrǫ, ka Ńikan bia pach. Ka Dǎk chwōlẹ, ka e ko: Dágí, na ḍạn, da rējǫ maduǫń kị́ yey nam kā; ya ḍàlị̀ ḍàlè, ka nị kẹ́lé ẹn, nị́ ḍàlǫ̀. Dǎk e ko: ẹ̀, a rech āṇǫ kị́ nam ṭẹn? Ko: è, u̯ lẹ́ṭe yin yau! Rējǫ ma chwake duǫń chārǫ; ka nị kēle ẹn, nị́ bạ̄jó bạ̄jó, dẹ ya ḍali ẹn, na ḍạn.

A kẹṭ Dǎk, ka gẹ ka (kẹṭ) nam; ka e dwan, kine: bųh! Ka e kẹ̣lị̀ ẹn, ka e bājǫ; ka e bia pach, ka e ko: ya ḍálị̀ ẹn! Ka Ńikan ko: ẹ́, dwẹn, yi nùtí ḍàlị̀ ẹn! Ka bọl kạ̊k ḍide, ka e kẹḍǫ, ka e dwan kine: bųh! Ka e kẹle (o kẹle) wịṭe pị gùn, ka kạ̊k paṭe rẹ. Ka jal ẹni dwǫta mal, ka e ko: hẹ̀, Dágí, kwofi rach, yi ba wen. Ka kẹṭa pache gǫn, e lǫgǫ ban, a gẹ̄re fārẹ, a chān niṇẹ Alẹ̄nǫ, a gẹ̄ra tǫk ḍǫk.

A certain man whose name was Ocholo (that is "Shilluk") was a slave of Nyikang. When one day he accompanied Nyikang to the river, he became a fish and he lifted his head above the water, saying, "buh!"[2] Nyikang did not know what to do; he went home, made a fish-spear (a harpoon), and tied a fish-line

---
[1] Vide page 159.
[2] a much used exclamation of surprise.

to its end. He went to the river again, the fish lifted his head above the water, saying, "buh!" Then Nyikang stabbed the fish, but he missed him; — this man was a jwok.[1] He once more lifted his head out, and Nyikang tried to stab him, but again missed him. At last Nyikang was tired, and he went home. When he came home, he found this same man gathering cow dung.

The next day Nyikang returned to the river bank; this man also returned; he lifted up his head out of the water, crying, "buh!" Nyikang stabbed him, but he missed him, so he went on till the afternoon, then Nyikang went home. He called Dak, saying, "Dak, son of man, there is a big fish in the river, I have failed to catch it, I tried to stab it, but I failed." Dak replied, "Well, what fish can there be in that small river?" Nyikang said, "Well, you just go and see it, it is a fish with a very strong voice. I stabbed it, but I always missed it. I do not know what to do with it, son of man."

Dak went, he went to the river. The fish lifted up its head, saying, "Buh!" He stabbed it, but missed it. He came home, saying, "I do not know how to stab it!" But Nyikang replied, "Oh, my cousin, you have not yet tried properly." Dak made his spear handle straight, and went again. The fish lifted up its head, saying, "Buh!" In this moment Dak threw the spear at the place where the splashing of the water was, and the spear fell on the fish (hit it). Then the man (the fish) arose, and said, "Ah, Dak, your talk is bad, you are a cunning one!" He (the fish-man) went home, he became a subject (of Nyikang), he (Nyikang) built him a village, and called its name Alengo, he built it beside the brook Dok.

59. Nyikang and the Sorcerers.

Ńikań ka e mąṅọ, ka e kẹdọ fōṭe mẹkọ, ka e ko: ẹ̀, wa kōbi ādi? Jē bẹdi gẹ ajwọk, ka Ńikań a dali, ka e ko: búh, u jē tich adi? Ko: ẹ̀! Ka e lọgọ yōmọ, ka Ńikań lọgọ òdinọ, ka peń nīmẹ, ka jē ẹni bẹ̄nọ, ka gẹ māgẹ́. Ka gẹ kąlẹ pach, ka gẹ gēṭẹ pā gin (gẹn).

Bẹr ga kwa wǒmán, gẹ̄r Twọlāń. Ka wěkí deań, dẹ nam, ogẹ́gọ̀.

When Nyikang was capturing (men), he went to a certain country, and he said, "Ah, what shall we say?" Because these people were witch-doctors, and Nyikang got into difficulties (trying to capture them). Again he said, "Why, what shall I do with these people? Ah, I have found out!" And he turned into a wind, and then he turned into a cloud-shadow, and covered the earth (so that it was dark and the wizards could not see anything); so he caught them. He brought them, and built them a village.

These are the descendants of the woman, they live at Twolang. Nyikang gave them a cow, a cow of the river, an ogego.

[1] jwọk = "God".

60. A War against Turtles.

Riṭ mẹkọ chwọlá Mói, omyẹn Ńikan̊. Ka e jẹ́kọ̀; ka kẹṭa bẹ manọ fōṭe jure mẹkọ, chwọla Bẹlọ. Ka gọ màn̊, ka gọ nágí.
Ka pōṭe mẹkọ chwọla Ótọ̀n, ka Otọn mǎn̊. Ka e lọgọ pùk. Ka fen̊e gọ̀lẹ́. Cha ḍānọ pẹ́ká pen̊, ko gọ n̊i kájı̣; ka len̊ nẹ̀kẻ pùk. A bẹnọ pach a dwai Dǎk; a kōbi Dǎk kine: a gin ánọ̀? Jal ẹni ko: len̊ mẹkọ, ya ḍálı̣ ẹ́n (rẹ́n), dẹ na n̊emēi ḍān̊, len̊ kẹ́ch, ḍān̊ n̊i kájé kájọ̀. Kẹ́ṭá gọ̀n, e ko: e bẹṭ ānọ? Kine: ẻ, kúchẻ yán. A ko Dāk kine: ẻ, faṭe gin lwẹn̊ au? E ko: nọt aṭẹ̀rı̣! A tyẹn̊ gẹ́n, a ṭaḍi bẹṭ, a tin̊ len̊. Ka Dāk e ko: wa kẹṭa mal! Ka kẹṭa mal, ka tẹrọ kōpe bẹne bẹne kine: kọ̀k pen̊! Ka tẹrọ chúṭọ kọka pen̊. Ka kwōkẻ Dǎk, ka gọ ɣalẻ wọk, ka len̊ é nẹk, duọ̀gọ pach.
Ka chika len̊ mẹkọ tin̊o, tin̊ fōṭe Bẹlọ, ka len̊ e kẹḍọ, ka len̊ kẹṭọ war ka o mı̀ḍọ̀ bẹne bẹne; pọn̊ ẹni e lọgọ mı̀ḍọ̀. Ka n̊i dẹme yi ḍān̊, ka ḍān̊ n̊i ṭọ̀. Ka Dāk chiki len̊ tin̊o kẹṭẹ, ka Dāk e kōbọ kine: kōde ɣẹḍọ̀! Ka ɣẹḍi kọ̀t, ka len̊ fẹka fen̊ ki bute fǎn ẹni, ka e lọgọ midọ kẹṭẹ, ka e bẹnọ, ka Dāk e ko: chwon̊ mach! Ka ɣẹḍe chwon̊ mach, ka omido bẹnọ, ka n̊i gọcha mach yi Dāk. Ka ɣáḍọ̀ midọ, ka len̊ nẹk yi Dāk, ka mak bẹne.
A bẹn̊ tẹrọ pach, a kōbi Moi, omya Ńikan̊, a kōbi kine: Dǎgí kwan̊ lǎu! A kwan̊ lǎu yi Dǎk. Yina rúmé n̊ẹ̀nọ̀; a n̊aji kwọp bẹn, a jẹ́kẹ́. A tin̊e len̊, a man̊i jur mẹkọ, a mǎgé gọ̀n, a lọgọ bǎn̊ẹ́.
A gẹra wọt ẹ tọ̀k, a kōbi Ńikan̊ kine: Dǎgí, wọt a gêr yi tọ̀k, dẹ yi jẹt kı̣́ kwàrọ̀. A kōbi kine: dẹḍẹ (dẹ ẹrẹ)? woda u gẹ̀rẻ yan yau ki lǎn̊ọ. A n̊i gẹ̀re kwāre lān̊ọ.

A certain king called Moi, a brother of Nyikang, ruled the Shilluk country. He went out to conquer some people called Belo (near Chai = Roseires). He conquered the tribe, and destroyed it.

Again there was another country, a country called Oton, he went to conquer this too. But the people of Oton turned into turtles, they buried themselves in the ground. And when the people of Moi sat down, they bit them; thus the turtles were victorious. Moi went home, and called for Dak. Dak asked, "What is the matter?" Moi said, "I have been defeated, I do not know what to do with them, you son of the sister of man! It was a very hard war indeed, my men were awfully bitten in the rear." He asked, "How so?" Moi answered, "Eh, I do not know." Dak replied, "Ah, is not that a simple matter?" He said "Cut sticks!" He sharpened the sticks, he made them like fish spears. Then he raised an army. Dak said, "Let me go ahead!" He went ahead, and he told all the people in the army, "Prick the ground!" So all the people, while they were walking, pricked the ground; thus Dak had the whole ground pricked, and the turtles came out, and the enemy was defeated, and they returned home.

Again he raised an army, he raised it against the country of Belo. The army went; it came to fighting during the night, the air was full of fireflies. It was the country of the fireflies. They fell upon the men, and the men died. When Dak fought against these people, he told his warriors, "Make grass torches!" They made grass torches; when the army came near the village and sat down there, the fireflies came; Dak said, "Light the torches!" They set fire to the torches, and when the fireflies came, Dak had the grass torches thrown at them; thus the enemy was destroyed by Dak, he caught them all.

When the people (the warriors) came home, Moi, the brother of Nyikang, said, "Dak, take the royal cloth (become our king)! You are a man of many thoughts, you know all matters!" Dak took the cloth, and he ruled.

He raised an army to wage war against a certain tribe, he destroyed them, and they became his slaves.

While Dak was absent, a house was built (by Nyikang and Moi); and when he returned, Nyikang told him, "Dak, we have been building a house (for you) during your absence, but there are not sufficient poles." Dak replied, "But what does that matter? I shall build my house with nabag poles." So it became a custom for the people to build with nabag poles.

61. Praising Nyikang.

Ka kwāyę ka e chwǫu, ka tūṅ leṅ tyęk, ka e kędǫ, ka e kętǫ. Ka leṅ nágę́. A bę̂n tęrǫ, a mạge dǫk, a kạl dǫk, a gę̄r peṅ. A wumę gę̄rǫ, a chip jɔ̊ kúrɔ̀, mǫk chip Mwǫmǫ, mǫk chip Tūṅ.

Our grandfather,[1] he roared, and he surrounded the enemies on all sides, and he went, and fought. He killed the enemies; then the (Shilluk) people came, they caught the cattle (of the enemy), they brought the cattle. They built houses in the country; when they had finished building, he appointed watchmen (men who had to watch the boundaries of the Shilluk country against their enemies), some on the northern boundary at Mwomo, and some on the southern boundary at Tonga.

---

[1] i. e. Nyikang.

VIII. PRAYERS AND RELIGIOUS CEREMONIES.

62. A Prayer to God.

Mālá yín, yina jwǫk, dę gǫ kwàchà yín ki̥ wǫr. A kòr jè ki̥dí chán bę̀n. Ka chä̱ṭi ki̥ kę́lé lûm, chä̱ṭá ré, a nèní ki̥ wǫt, nènd ré. Dę̱ gǫ̀ mǎlà yín ki̥ gin cham a ńi wèkè jē, ki̥ pik a ńi mä̱t, ki̥ wèl a kòrè yín. Bu̯ń an fó̱dę́ wi̥ji̥, yina jwǫk; yina lǫk kwa Ńikāṇǫ; fanę wún a chä̱ṭi ki̥ jwǫk; yina lǫk kwá, ki̥ ńāri Dâk. A yigę ryak, ryak fa mȗjé yin? Nami à chúńí ęná dèàń, fá ṯó̱, rę̱mę fa kę̱tę yi; yina jwǫk, dę gō̱ ńi̥ lǎmę̱ męn? fatę yin, yina jwǫk, ki̥ ęna yi̥k Ńikāń, ki̥ ńāri Dâk? Dę wèl fa mǫ́gí chę̀? Fanę yin u̱ tińi mâl.

Chō̱ṭi̥, ká dean chwǫ́p, ká wäl kwáń, ka lę̱ń re ńane a re da jwǫk, ki̥ pi̥ wętę rę̱. Ka yi̥ṭ dèáń ńó̱l, twoy tyę̱lǫ, ka bàt yáń ńó̱l, ka ṯál ànànànàn; fa bę̀l yi jè. Ká chwài mó̱ṯó̱ṇó̱, ka kǫń feń, mǫk jwǫk.

"I implore thee, thou God, I pray to thee during the night. How are all people kept by thee all days! And thou walkest in the midst of the (high) grass, I walk with thee; when I sleep in the house, I sleep with thee. To thee I pray for food, and thou givest it to the people; and water to drink; and the soul is kept (alive) by thee. There is no one above thee, thou God. Thou becamest the grandfather of Nyikango; it is thou (Nyikango) who walkest with God; thou becamest the grandfather (of man), and thy son Dak. If a famine comes, is it not given by thee? So as this cow stands here, is it not thus: if she dies, does her blood not go to thee? Thou God, to whom shall we pray, is it not to thee? Thou God, and thou who becamest Nyikango, and thy son Dak! But the soul (of man), is it not thine own? It is thou who liftest up (the sick)."

That is all; and the cow is speared; and the contents of her stomach are taken out, and are thrown on the body of the man who is sick ("is with God"); and water is poured on his body. And one ear of the cow is cut off, (it is cut into strips, these are tied together and the whole) is tied round the leg (of the sick one). And the right foreleg (of the cow) is cut off, and it is cooked at once; the people are not allowed to taste of it. They make a little broth out of it; that is poured on the ground: it is the thing (property) of God.[1]

63. A Prayer for Rain and the Ceremonies connected with it.

Tyęń a mán ńi̥ bę̱ṇǫ̀, ka gę bę̱n bę̱n bę̱n, kę̱ṭa bę̱ gúp ki̥ kúdjó, ka gę bę̱ṇǫ, ka ri̥ṭ e wâr, ka gę mwǫṇǫ, ka gę́ gwę̀dǫ̀ ki̥ bur kwārǫ, ki̥ bur lōjǫ, ki̥ bur tar, ki̥ chilǫ. Ka rûm gę gwę́t, ka gę chǫ̀ṇǫ̀, ka byęl e gút, ka dean kûl, ka dean chwǫ́p,

---

[1] This is said to be the only prayer to jwok. It is prayed on any occasion when a trial, as sickness, famine, war, falls on the people. The prayer is said by "old people", by the chief, or some other respected person of the village. The Shilluks were taught it by Nyikang.

ka ṭom kạ̈l wǫk, ka Chǫ́lǫ̈ (Chǫllǫ̈) bę̈nǫ bę̈ne bę̈ne, ká tȩ̈rǫ̀ chǫ̈nǫ̀, ka wēni ki wạr, ka tȩrǫ chǭnǫ, ka riṯ a kwach:

Ya kwache ki mátǫ́nô, má kạla ḍǫga. Peṅ e rȩ̈ṅ júr, Léṅ-dắrǫ́ chȩ dȩ wȩlǫ. Yá kȩ́tá yi máyȩ́ baṅda ṅa Ṅịdwai, Akolǫ, ṅaṅ Ṅikānǫ.

The women come, all of them go to scratch the ground for mud, then they come and besmear the temple of the "king", they prepare the mud, and make stripes on the temple with red ashes, and with black ashes, and with white ashes, and with soot. When they have finished this drawing, then they dance. After this dura is pounded, a cow is brought, the cow is speared; they bring out the little drum of Nyikango, and all the Shilluks come, and the people dance, and when the night comes, they continue dancing, and (while dancing) they pray to the "king":[1]

"I beg for some little things (food), to put into my mouth. The earth has been spoiled by the people; Lenydaro[2] is travelling (on the earth). I go to our grandfather, the chief of the daughter of Nyidwai, to Akolo, the children of Nyikango."

64. A Religious Ceremony.

The people went, the tom (the small drum belonging to Nyikang) was beaten, they danced to the tom; and the people were beaten by the king;[3] it was a very strong drum. When it was finished, the people put the drum on the ground; then they told stories about Nyikang. After that, the people went into the house of the women (or the slaves) (of the king). The spear of Nyikang was brought out, and the people bowed their heads. A sheep was brought, it was killed; the spear of Nyikang was washed with water; the people ran to the river bank. They beat the tom vigorously, then the people came back to dance. After that they scattered. The next day they beat the tom again, the people came again to dance, and after four days they dispersed.

65. How the Cattle is brought across the River.

When the chief of a village wants to talk about the cattle, he assembles the people, and addresses them, "Ye people, the grass is finished now, what shall we do concerning the cattle?" The people reply, "Ah, that is your business!" He says, "Well, bring the wizard!" The sorcerer comes, and a goat, a spear, and a hoe are given to him. And he says, "Milk the cows!" And the cows are milked, early in the morning. Then he says, "Loosen the cattle!" They take the ambach boats, and the cows come (are tied) behind the ambach boats. The sorcerer ties grass together, and he ties it a second time on the side of the river

---

[1] the "king" is Nyikang or any other ancient king, to whom the temple is dedicated.
[2] "the army of Daro", perhaps a mythical allusion.
[3] that is, they turned into a state of trance, being possessed by the spirit of the deceased king.

bank. Then the milk is poured into the river, and a club is stuck into the ground in the river. The sorcerer goes into the river, and says, "Bring the cattle!" Now the ambach boats are thrown into the river, and the sorcerer lies down in the middle of the river. The cattle swim (behind the boats). The sorcerer sings a song of the crocodile; the crocodiles belong to his family (to the family, the clan of the sorcerer).

When they have arrived on the other side, an enclosure is erected, and the cows are tied to their pegs. Then another sorcerer is called, and he performs his witchery on account of thieves (to keep off thieves). The cattle are seized, a cow-house is built, and that is all, the people settle in this place, a place with grass.

66. Preparation for War.

Leṅ keṅ é chágí, ajwo̱go̱ ńí de dwâi, ká do̱k go̱ṅ, ka e be̱no̱, ka dye̱k gwách, ka to̱ṅ gwách, ka yai be̱no̱, ká àke̱t ke̱t. Ka to̱ṅ me̱n péṅ, ka to̱ṅ akye̱l me̱n péṅ; ka ake̱t twôchè ré̱. Ka yai e be̱no̱, ka ke̱la t̯á àke̱t; ake̱te ya màl, e twojo̱ bwo̱l to̱ṅ. Nàno̱ mák yi ake̱t, ka ńi chi p wái, ka ńane a ńi mak ńi chi p wāi. Ka jē cha̱to̱ kí do̱ch. Ka tin, ka yai ko̱fí: fe̱ke féṅ. Ka oṅwo̱k kwáṅ, ka táye̱ féṅ, ka ye̱je̱ kák, ka wije̱ no̱l, ka wài ka̱l wo̱k, ka ńi léṅ ke̱le je̱. Ka wich aṅwo̱k ka kwáṅ yi ájwo̱gó, ka ńi léṅ fo̱ṅ eni ki ńim yāi. U¹ yik wiche oṅwo̱k u̱ ne̱no̱ kundo fo̱ṅ eni, ka yé ki̱ne: fo̱ṅ eni de chye̱to̱, kwo̱f ajwo̱go̱. U yik wiche oṅwo̱k u̱ ne̱nó kun adi léṅ, ye ki̱ne: leṅ rach! Ka ajwo̱go̱ e t̯e̱do̱ ke̱te̱, ka yech ka̱l, ka ko̱t, ka me̱ko̱ chiki ko̱to̱, ka ajwo̱go̱ ke̱do̱, ka oṅwo̱ṅ me̱ko̱ ka̱l, ka ne̱k, ka wije̱ chiki (che̱ki) we̱to̱, ká le̱t yi ajwo̱ṅ eni, ka e ko: do̱ch! Dwai te̱ro̱ be̱no̱! Ka te̱ro̱ be̱no̱. Ka wāi kwáṅé, ka go̱ lé̱ṅé ré te̱ro̱. Ka e ke̱do̱. Ka wich oṅywo̱k ka u̱ kwóṅí feṅ. Ka pi t̯a̱ṅ, ká go̱ lé̱ṅé re̱ te̱ro̱.

When a hostile army comes near, the sorcerer is sent for, and cows are loosened (are given to him), and when he comes, goats and spears are collected (and given him). Then the people come; a rope is made, and a spear is stuck into the ground; the rope is fastened to its top; now the people come, and pass below the rope. The rope is above, it is tied to the point of the spear. The man who is touched by the rope (in passing below it), is placed separately. (All these do not go into the war, because they would be killed). Thus the people walk (below the rope) a long time, till all have passed. Presently the sorcerer says to the people, "Sit down!" A he-goat is brought, and is thrown on the ground. It is cut up, and its head is cut off; the contents of its stomach are taken out, and are thrown among the people; the head of the he-goat is taken by the sorcerer, and thrown towards the hostile country, in the face of the assembled people. If the head of the he-goat points in the direction of the country of the

---
¹ if.

enemy, it is said: "The country (of the enemy) will be defeated;" that is the talk of the sorcerer. But if the head of the he-goat points towards their own army, they say, "It is a bad war!" In this case the sorcerer makes his witchery once more, grass is brought, and is tied on a rope, and after that it is tied again; then the sorcerer goes to bring another he-goat, it is killed, and its head is again thrown, and when the sorcerer sees (that it is in the right direction now), he says, "All right! Let all the people come!" The people come, the contents of the stomach are taken, and are thrown on the bodies of the people. Then the sorcerer goes. The head of the he-goat is buried in the ground; and water is put on the fire, and sprinkled on the people.

Now the army goes to fight. And people are killed, the army is defeated. The people come and bury their dead. Then they remain (in arms). Another sorcerer is sent for; cattle are given to him. And he works (his witchery), he is a most powerful sorcerer. When he has finished his doings, the army goes to fight again. Now they defeat the enemies and kill many people; after that they come and return home; they are satisfied. The people go to the king, a royal ambassador is called (and sent to the chief of the enemies), the people make amends for the men they have killed, they pay twenty cows; they go to loosen them, then they return home, and sit down.[1]

---

[1] After a war (among different Shilluk tribes) each army makes amends to the hostile tribe for the people that have been killed; these amends consist in a number of cattle.

IX. STORIES ABOUT SORCERERS.
67. The Cruel King.

Ka riṭ mẹkọ Ṅwọ-Bābọ, ka e jāgọ, kẹch, e nụgọ jē, ṅan a ḍachọ ká gọ̀ nụgẹ́. Ka e ko: gẹ̄r woṭ! Ka rọt (woṭ) gẹ̄r. Ka rọt ḍogẹ mū̀l, ka riṭ e kẹta woṭ ki ṅan a ḍachọ májùr. Ka rāṇ ẹni ko: tuk ḍọ woṭ! Ka Chọ́lọ̀ bàṅọ̀. Ka ṅi wurọ: Chọ́l a bàṅ! Ka e ṭọ.

Ka riṭ mẹkọ rọ́ṅ, chwọla Ṅaṭọ̄, kẹch. Ka jāk dwai; ka e fẹcho kịne: ẹrẹ (rẹ́dẹ̀) òwà á nụ̀gí? Jāgo ko: ḕ, kúchè wọ́ṅ! Ka jāk nụ̀gẹ́.

A certain king called Ngwo-Babo, reigned; he was very, very cruel; he killed people, even women he killed. One day he said, "Build a house!" And a house was built. When the door of the house was plastered (when it was finished), he went into it together with a young girl. (Then the door was walled up).[1] The king said, "Open the door!" But the Shilluks refused. The king began to sing, but the Shilluks refused; so he died.

And another king was elected, whose name was Nyato, he was very cruel. He caused all the chiefs to come, and asked them, "Why did you kill my cousin?" They replied, "Ah, we do not know." He killed all the chiefs.

68. King Nyadwai trying the Sorcerers.

Rọ́ṅ Ṅadwai, e jagi; a kwóni feṅ, a kiṭi yẹṇ feṅ, a kụli ṅọ̀r, a ṭạ́lị̀. A chóṅí djwọ̀k, ajwọgọ bẹ̄nọ, a pyechi gin, kịne: waṭe jāk, yá ḍálè yi gịnẹ wū (rū) féṅ. Ka ajwọgọ mẹkọ ṅi bẹ̄nọ, ka ṅi lịṅọ, ko:·gwátá pach. Ṅadwai ko: pẹ̀k pén! Ka mẹn ṅi bẹ̄nọ, ka ṅi lịṅọ, ka ṅi ko: gwátá pach. A bẹ̄n jal Ajwọgọ, a bẹ̄n jal Aḍọkọṅ, ka riṭ ko: à! A bẹ̄n jal Ṅỵ̀ṅdrọ̀, a kōbi kịne: ḕ, kụ̀l pi! Ka pi kụ̀l; ka e lọ̄gọ, lọ̄gi chịnẹ ki pi, ka byẹ̀l kwàṅé, ká è ṅàmọ̀. Ṅadwai ko: nụ̀gé djwọ̀k! Ka gẹ nẹk.

Then Nyadwai was elected, and he reigned. One day he had a hole dug into the ground, he ordered wood to be put into it, and to set it on fire (and to cover the whole with earth). Then he ordered beans to be brought and to be cooked. He assembled all the witch doctors, and asked them, "You children of chiefs, I do not know what this humming in the earth is!" (meaning the noise caused by the boiling of the beans). One of the witch doctors came, he listened and then said, "That is something bewitching (or cursing) the village." Nyadwai replied, "Sit down there!" Another came listening; he too said, "It is something bewitching the village." Then came the man (the doctor) of Ajwogo, after him

---

[1] In this way the Shilluk kings are buried. The king wanted to try his people, whether they were faithful to him.

the man of Adokong,[1] and the king said, "Ah!" Then came the man of Ningaro, he said: "Well, bring water!" And water was brought. He washed himself, he washed his hands (as a preparation for eating food); then he took the beans out and ate them. Nyadwai said, "Kill all the other witch-doctors!"[2] And they were killed.

In the time of the reigning of king Yo, some Dinka man whose name was Lengyang, came into the Shilluk country, and lived there. He was a sorcerer. Towards the end of his reigning Yo ordered the sorcerer to be brought, and he killed him (on account of his sorcery). On that a war arose with the Dinkas, and they fought at Tonga; Tonga was destroyed. Then the king said, "The whole army shall go!" And the Dinkas ran away.

69. The Vision of the Sorcerer.

There was a certain man whose name was Wet Kwa Oket, he was also called Agweratyep, a very strong man; he was a sorcerer. One day he had a vision, and he said," The white people come!" And the white people came, the country was destroyed by them. And he died, and was mourned; but before he died, he said, "Ah, the chieftainship shall be taken over by Ajalong after my death. But the man who kills me by his witchcraft, he too shall die after me." And he was mourned, and his steer fell under the dom palm.[3] And the man who had bewitched him, was struck by lightning, and died; for he had been cursed by the sorcerer. And all the people believed in him, saying. "Agweratyep is a strong man indeed!" The medicine men were afraid, and so the village lived in a peaceful condition.[2]

70. Agok.

Jwok chwola Agok, mạ̈ni ton jal yaṭ. Jal mẹko bẹda ajwogo, ka dean ywobẹ, ka deaṅ yẹ ta yi féṅ. Ka jē rẹna kal, ka jē ko: ê, Agŏk, deaṅ a tou. Kine: e nẹke yi nọ? Kine: kújả. Chọ̈n jẹ! Ka jē chọ̈n; ka e ko: ṅaté, faṭe yin a ywọp deaṅ? Kine: yan! Kine: kí paṅọ? Kine: yả pảṅi yín! Kine: hẹ̀, yi ba pyẹlọ, waṭ ṭyau, ṅiṅi lŏch! yi re chŏk yí yọ̀bọ̀ kí dọ̀ tẹrọ? Yả faṅe yiṅ àu, må kẹch. Kine, ê, de wâ ṭum! Kẹṭ, chŏl! A chŏlị́ ki dok ddẹk.

Ka jal ẹni e kẹdọ̀, ka bē gōte yi pwodọ. Ka jal ẹni tûk yi Agok, kine: ṅaté, kẹṭ jal yaṭ chíné! Ká è bẹdọ, chwola gọn a lị́k. Ka mwol ka e kẹdọ, ka gin ẹni ywode yi fwodọ. Gọ gŏl féṅ, ka bia pach. Ka e kōbọ kine: giche mẹkọ e gŏl yi fwodẹ yi jal yaṭ. E ko: dåpọ̀nọ̀ pyẹ́jí yán? Yi cha kŏpọ kŏpọ̀ kine: kẹṭ, jal yaṭ a yip pwodọ! Kine: kẹṭ! Kine: yi re bàn? Kine: chwọla ga lāke yau! Kine: ầ, chọ̈n tẹ̀rọ̀! A chọ̈n tẹ̀rọ̀, a pẹchẹ́ kine: jal yáṭ, yin nẹka ṅọ jē? A tyẹk

---

[1] They did not know the cause either, except the last, who found out the cause of the humming.
[2] The "medicine men" are the "bad sorcerers", who try to kill people by their witchery. They are called here "jọ yẹṛ" "men of medicine", as opposed to the ajwōgo, who is supposed to work for good.   [3] vide Introduction.

Agok

There was a jwok[1] who was called Agok; he was manifested by a certain wizard. A certain man was a wizard. He bewitched cows, so that the cows fell down. And the people ran to the house (of Agok) saying, "Ah, Agok, a cow has died." He asked, "By whom has it been killed?" The man said, "I do not know." Agok ordered, "Assemble the people." And the people assembled. Agok asked (the wizard), "Man, is it not you who bewitch the cattle?" The wizard answered, "Yes, it is I". Agok asked, "Why?" The wizard replied, "Because I want to try you (whether you are able to find out who did it)." Agok said, Ha, you are a cursed one! You cursed black-eyed one! Why are you always bewitching the cattle of the people?" He answered, "Only to try you whether you really are strong." Agok said, "Well, we have met. Now go and make amends!" He made amends with three cows.

Then the man went away and planted (a charm) in a field. The proprietor of the field was (while sleeping) wakened by Agok[2] with the words, "Man, go, there is a wizard in your field." But the man did not go, he thought he was dreaming. The next morning, when he went to the field, he found the charm which the wizard had put into the earth. He came home saying, "Something has been planted into my field by a wizard." Agok said to him, "Why do you ask me about this matter? I have told you already saying, 'Go, the wizard has planted a charm into your field. Therefore go!' Why did you refuse?" He replied, "I thought I was only dreaming." Agok gave order, "Assemble the people!" When all the people were assembled, Agok asked, "You wizard, why have you (tried to) kill people? you are going to kill the whole village" („you surround the village with killing"). He answered, "It is not I." But Agok replied, "You cursed one, I will surely kill you!" And he killed him. When the witch doctors saw that, they all repented, and they were much afraid. Then the people scattered.

And Agok was called king by the people. The people listened to his words (were obedient to him). They used to say, "If any man becomes sick, he goes to Agok, that he may be helped." He gives him (that is, the one who wants help gives to Agok) cattle, two cows, one cow is speared (sacrificed), and one he keeps alive, it becomes the cow of jwok.

---

[1] "god". [2] It is not meant that Agok went to wake him, but he wakened him in a vision.

X. CREATION.

71. The Creation of Men.

Dean fanɛ wáṅɛ,[1] *a ṅwọ́là kɛ̱nọ̀. Wiyɛ fanɛ jwọk. Wá ṅwọle jwọk gɛn áryáu, mɛ́n à lòjọ̀, mär yi máyɛ̱, mɛ́n à tàr, o chɛ́t. Kɛṅ bɛ̱n jwọk, e ṅōṭi mɛ́n à tàr, mɛ́n a lōjọ, ṅi kân. A kōbi jwọk kine: ɛ́rɛ̱ kâni? Kine: bógọ̀n!*[2] *A kōbi jwọk kine: ɛ́! wólé yin kû kâne yau! Yan márá mɛ́n à tàr, tyɛṅ à lòjọ̀, u̱ jâkè mɛ́n à tàr. A kậlị̱ wọk, ɛna mɛ́n à lòjọ̀. A kōbi jwọk: ɛ́rɛ̱ (rɛ́dɛ̱) kậlí? Kine: ɛ̂, cháká ká kậle yáu. A wékè wanɛ bwóṅọ́, a wékè twoch bwoṅọ, a wékè gōji, a wékè jam bɛ̱n, a márɛ́ yi jwọk. A jậk tyɛṅ a lōjọ yi obwoṅ anan.*

The cow is our grandmother, she bore a gourd. Our father is God. We were two of us born by God, (a black one and a white one). The black one was beloved by his mother; but the white [one was hated. When God came, she showed him the white one, but the black one she hid. God asked, "Why do you hide him?" She said, "For nothing." Then God said, "Well, do but hide him, I like the white one." The black people shall be ruled by the white people. On that she brought the black one out too. God asked, "Why do you bring him out?" She said: "Oh, I just brought him out (without any special reason)."

To the white one were given the book, and the gun, and the sword, and all kinds of goods, he is loved by God. So now the black people are governed by the white.[3]

71a. On Totemism.

Wudọ kị̱ àgàk kị Dɛ̱ṅ kâk kị yey kɛ̱nọ̀, gɛ́n a chwɛ̱k. Ka Dɛ̱ṅ bia pach, ka wudọ kɛ̱ta fậl, ka agak e fậrọ̀, ka a ṅwọ́lɛ̀ wóṅ yi Dɛ̱ṅ. A bɛ̱n Akwọɛ kị rei Duwọ̀t, a bɛ̱ne fōṭɛ Chọl, a yɛ̱ṅ jē riṭ. Ka ṅɛ̱ṅ wọn, ka mō̱kọ kɛṭi Feṅikaṅ Odurō̱jọ, a dḗṅà kị Feṅidwai, fanɛ dé̱ṅè wóṅ. Kwá fa Joṅaṅ, wọt Ńabíl, ka bɛ̱ne fōṭɛ Chọl, ena a ṅwọm Atọṅ, e ṅi riṭ, ɛna Adefậlọ anan.

Wudọ kị̱ àgàk wọt wọn, fa chậm yi wóṅ kifa dwậlọ.

The ostrich and the crow and *Dɛ̱ṅ*[4] were split[5] out of the gourd, all three are three-twin children. *Dɛ̱ṅ* went into a certain village, the ostrich went into the bush, and the crow flew up. We were born by *Dɛ̱ṅ*. *Akwọɛ* (the son of *Dɛ̱ṅ*) came in the time of *Duwọt* (a brother of *Ńikāṅọ*). he came into the Shilluk country to the people of the king (that is to Fashoda). And when we became many, some went to *Feṅikāṅ Odurō̱jọ*, but some remained at *Feṅidwai*.

Remarks see on page 179.

Totemism

Thus we separated from each other. Our grandfather was *Joṅaṅ*, a son of *Ṅabil*, he came into the Shilluk country; it is he who married *Atǫ̇ṅ*. He was king. That is the beginning of (the village of) *Adefālǫ*. — The ostrich and the crow are of our family. They are not eaten by us on account of the *dwālǫ*-sickness.

---

[1] *wǎṅę̆* "our grandmother". Here, as is sometimes the case, the pronoun of the third person sing. has the meaning of the first person pl.
[2] There is not, viz. a reason.
[3] With the exception of the first sentence this report is recent, because it relates to *white and black men*.
[4] These three are the "parents" not of the whole Shilluk people, but only of the tribe *Feṅikaṅ*, which lives at the mouth of the Sobat. Each tribe has its own "parents", which generally are animals.
[5] This means: the cow (see page 156) brought forth a gourd, the gourd split, and out of it went forth the ostrich, etc.

XI. ANIMAL STORIES.

72. Hare and Hyena.

Áfódjọ̀ é[1] *wẹ̀lọ̀ kí jwọ́k, è bẹ̀dọ̀ kí tá yât, jwọ́k é nẹ̀nọ̀, ká áfódjọ̀*
Hare he travels with *jwọk*,[1a] he stays in under tree, *jwọk* he sleeps, and hare
é bẹ̀dọ̀ mál. Ká jè bẹ̀nọ̀, gẹ́ gír; afoajọ ko: ḍwọ̀ṭí mál, lèn[2]
he stays upright. And people come, they many; hare says: rise up, war
á bì. Jwọ́k è kọ̀ kíné: bẹ̀dì yau. Ká lèn é bẹ̀nọ̀, kámá mak
has come. *Jwọk* he says thus: stay just. And war it comes, begins to seize
afoajọ ki jwọk. Jwọk è ko: afoajọ, mak tyálá,[3] *ká tyálẹ̀ mâk, ká*
hare and *jwọk*. *Jwọk* says: hare, seize feet my, and feet his seized, and
jwọk é wánọ̀. Ká lèn é kẹ́dọ̀, ká jwọ́k è ko: afoajọ, kẹ́ṭí! Ka afoajọ
jwọk he disappears. And war it goes, and *jwọk* says: hare, go! And hare
kẹ́dọ̀, afoajọ kẹ́ṭí[5] *yi óṭwóṇ, kō: óṭwóṇ! kine: ẹ̀? kine: wá fá wẹ̀lí?*[4]
goes, hare went to hyena, says: hyena! thus: eh? thus: we not shall travel?
é kọ̀: àwọ́! Ká gẹ́ kẹ́dọ̀. Ká gẹ́ kẹ́ṭí[5] *tá yât, ká lèn é bẹ̀nọ̀,*
he says: yes! And they go. And they went below tree, and war it comes,
afoajọ é nẹ̀nọ̀, óṭwóṇ bẹ̀dọ̀ mâl, óṭwóṇ e ko: afoajọ, lèn é bì! e ko:
hare he sleeps, hyena stays up, hyena he says: hare, war he came! he says:
bẹ̀dì yáù! Ká lèn é wáṇọ̀, afoajọ ko: mak tyálá! ka afoajọ
stay just! And war he approaches, hare says: seize my feet, and hare
ní gọ̀chá wijẹ féṅ; féṅ tẹ̀k, ka afoajọ rèṅ, ká
continually struck his head ground; ground was hard, and hare ran, and
óṭwóṇ mâk, ka oṭwọṇ pwót, ka pwót ki dọ̀ch. Ká
hyena was caught, and hyena was beaten, and was beaten thoroughly. And
wóñ, ka wèkè ḍeáṅ ki wát. Ka afoajọ bẹ̀nọ̀, kine:[6] *óṭwóṇ!*[7] *kine:*
got free, and was given cow and bull. And hare comes, thus: hare! thus:
ẹ̀? kine: jwọk é kọ̀ neya; kine ẹ̀? kine: wèkí yán wât. É kọ̀:
eh? thus: *jwọk* he says thus; thus: eh? thus: give me ox. He says:
kífọ̀nọ̀? kine: yá pwót tyàu. Ka waḍe wèki; ká gẹ́ kẹ̀dọ̀. Ká gẹ́
why? thus: I was beaten too. And ox gave; and they go. And they
kànọ́ lwọ̀l, mẹn ṅyẹ́t ḍeáṅ; ka afoajọ kụ̀lá lwọ̀lẹ̀, afoajọ e
bring calabashes, which milk cow; and hare brought cal. his, hare he
ko: yánà ṅyẹ̀dọ̀. Ka lwọ̀lẹ̀ kụ̀lẹ́, ká gọ̀ tòyẹ́, ka lwọle kụ̀lẹ́,
says: I it, milks. And cal. his brings he, and it pierces he, and cal. brings he,
ka lwọle oṭwọṇ chíp mál, ka lwọle afoajọ yẹna féṅ, ká ní
and cal. of hyena was put above, and cal. of hare was below, and continu-
ṅyẹ̀dọ̀, ká chàk ṭi kẹ́tá féṅ, yech lwọle afoajọ, ka lwọle oṭwọṇ
ally milked and milk cont. went below, middle of cal. of hare, cal. of hyena

Remarks referring to XI. vide on page 198.

ńí fàṅọ yì óbọ́i. Óbọ́i chàmị̂ yi oṭwọṇ, afoajọ ńí mụ̂ṭà chak. Afoajọ
filled with foam. Foam was eaten by hyena, hare drank milk. Hare

chwê.   Ka afoajọ e ko: nẹ̀k wà ṅarọ̄jọ! ka ṅarọ̄jọ   nẹ̀k,   ka oṭwọṇ
became fat. Hare he said: kill we calf,   calf was killed,   hyena

e ko: amẹn ụ ḍôṭ?
he said: who will milk?

Afoajọ e ko: yán! kịne: dọ̄ch! Afoajọ ko: ụ bẹ̀n óbọ́i, ka ḍeań
Hare he says: I! thus: allright! Hare says: if comes foam, then cow

a   ńẹ̀r;   óbọ́i bògọ̀n, ḍeań nụ̂tí; ka chak ńi ḍôṭ yi
has let down the milk; foam not, cow not yet; and milk was sucked by

afoajọ bẹ̀n, afoajọ chuṇg mẹ̀dọ̀. Chak bogọn, mẹn ńi mà̤ṭ yi oṭwọṇ,
hare all, hare his liver sweet. Milk not which was drunk by hyena,

oṭwọṇ gwāḷọ. Jwọk e bẹ̀nọ̀, kọ: yí rẹ̀ gwàl yìn? Oṭwọṇ ko:
hyena was thin. Jwok he comes, says: you why thin you? Hyena says:

chak ńi maṭe yi afoajọ bẹ̀n. Jwọk e ko: kwań wúṅọ́ àndn, mdk afoajọ!
milk is drunk by hyena all. Jwok says: take rope now, seize hare!

wuṇọ kậl kd màk afoajọ, afoajọ cha gọ̤́ńị, kd   gọ̀ń,
rope was brought and seized hare, hare wanted release, and was released,

ka oṭwọṇ e bẹ̀n, ka óbọ́i chàm é   waṅí, ka afoajọ ṭḁ̀l,
and hyena he came and foam wanted to disappear, and hare was tugged,

ka afoajọ é pạ̤̀ḍọ̀, kịne: búh! yà rẹ̀ nḁ́gé̤ yán kifa chak?
and hare   fell, thus: búh! I why kills he me because of milk?

oṭwọṇ ńí kudọ. Dụki ko: yá kd bẹ kwái. Kd e kẹ̣́dọ̀.
hyena was silent. To-morrow said: I go for herding. And he goes.

Ka tụ̀ńí ḍeań chwóchị̂   ẹ́n   ki lạ̀bọ̀. Ka é rìṇọ yiẹ,
Horns of cow is formed by him with mud. And he ran to him,

ko: oṭwọṇ! kịne: kạ̀l tàń àmàl, ḍeań a chán. Ka oṭwọṇ e
says: hyena! thus: spear waterbuck in front, cow is behind. And hyena he

bẹ̀n, ka ḍeań kạ̀l kd   é kò: búh! Yá kò: kạ̀l tàń
came, and cow speared, and (hare) says: búh! I said: spear waterbuck

a chán, wu chwak dṅọ ki ḍeań, a nḁ́gí, yu cham ọńọ? Ka ye ko:
behind, you do what with cow, killed you, you eat what? And he said:

kẹ̣ṭ dòté mách! Kịne: mach ágọ̀n? Kd è kò: a   chiṅệ. Ka oṭwọṇ e
go fetch fire! Thus: fire where? And he says: it is yonder. And hyena he

kẹ̣dọ, ka mach ywòdé̤ é bógọ̀n, ka e dúọ̀k, ka rìṇọ ywòdé̤ gọ
goes, and fire found he it was not, and he returned, and meat finds he it

kạ̀l yi afoajọ; ka afoajọ e ko: yí rẹ̀ dúọk? oṭwọṇ e ko:
was carried by hare; and hare he says: you why return? Hyena he says:

mach bógọ̀n; kịne: ḍeań d kạ̀l yi jwọk; ka wich kwóń féń; kd
fire is not; thus: cow was carried by jwok; and head was buried ground; and

è ko: kạ̀l mḁ́n mè̤ wọ́k! Afoajọ mẹ a kwoń yì ẹ́n, ka oṭwọṇ mẹ yik
he says: pull which his out! Hare his was dug by him, and hyena his was

maṯạk, ka afoajọ mẹ kạl wọk, ka otwọṇ mẹ d ḍàlị̀, ka otwọṇ kd̄ịd¹⁴
hard, and hare his pulled out, and hyena his was difficult, and hyena went
gólẹ̀, ka afoajọ kd̄ịd gólẹ̀, ka otwọṇ wora wū̃dẹ́, kịne: kẹ̯t, dwai
home his, hare went home his, hyena sent son his, thus: go, bring
mach gọl afoajọ. Ka ńa ńẹl ṯẹṇ e bẹ̃ṇọ, eko: yá kwàtjá maoh, ka afoajọ
fire home of hare. And the little child comes, says: I beg fire, hare
ko: bi dwani; ka afoajọ eko: yi kị́ ḷ̃ẹ màl, jiṯẹ̄ṯọ ụ̀ dẹ̀m
says: come, get; and hare says: you not look upward, pepper will fall
wańi, ka ńa ńẹl ṯẹṇ ḷ̃dá mal, ka kẹṯi yi wiyẹ̀; e ko:
your eye, and little child looked upwards, and went to his father; he says:
riṇọ gīr kị wọt afoajọ. Ka otwọṇ é kọ́pà loṯ ka wū̃dẹ e kọpa loṯ.
meat much in house of hare. And hyena he took club and his son took club.
Ka gẹ bẹ̃ṇọ, ka afoajọ kẹdọ ṯá pyẹ̀nụ̀, ka kọfa wū̃dẹ ko: pwótị
And they come, and hare goes under skin, and told his son, said: beat
ydn! Ka é ywọ̀ń, e ko: faṯ kị yan kẹ̄ṯá; wak otwọṇ. Ka otwọṇ é
me! And he cried, he said: not with me alone me; also hyena. And hyena he
rẹ̃ń, rẹ̃ńa pạl, ka otwọṇ ye bwọ̀gọ̀, afoajọ chuńẹ mẹ̀dọ̀.
ran, ran bush, and hyena he fears, hare his liver sweet.

The hare travelled with jwok. They rested under a tree; jwok was sleeping, and the hare remained awake. Then many people came and the hare said, "Arise! a war (an army) has come." "But", said jwok, "never mind." And the war came and was going to seize the hare and jwok. Then jwok said: "Hare, seize my feet!" He seized his feet, and suddenly jwok and the hare disappeared. The war passed by, and jwok said, "Hare, go!" The hare went; he went to a hyena and said to her, "Hyena!" "Eh!" said the hyena. "Shall we not travel together?" asked the hare. "Surely," replied the hyena. And they went. They went under a tree, and a war came; the hare was asleep, but the hyena was awake. "Hare", the hyena said, "war has come". "Never mind", replied the hare. When the war came, the hare said to the hyena, "Seize my feet!" The hare beat his head on the ground (wanting to disappear as jwok had done), but the ground was hard. The hare, seeing this, ran away, but the hyena was caught and was beaten pitifully. At last he got free; and they gave him a cow and a bull. Then the hare came, saying, "Hyena!" "Eh!" he replied. Said the hare, "Jwok has said thus"..... "Eh!" replied the hyena. The hare went on, "You must give me the bull." "Why?" said the hyena. "Because", replied the hare, "I also was beaten." He gave him the bull, and they went their way. Then they brought calabashes, such as are used for milking cows. The hare brought his calabash and said, "I will milk." And he brought another calabash (the hyena's), and pierced it, and he placed the hyena's calabash above, so that his own was below. When he milked, the milk ran down into his own calabash, and the calabash of the hyena became full of foam. The foam was eaten by the hyena, and the hare drank the milk. So the hare became fat. One day he said to the hyena, "Let us kill the calf!" And the calf was butchered. Then the hyena said, "Who shall suck now?" "I," answered the hare. "All right," said the hyena. "When the foam comes," replied the hare, "the cow has let down the milk; as long as there is no foam, it has not." (When the natives want to milk a cow, they let the calf suck the udder first, as without this the cow will not let down her milk. The hare wants to take the place of the calf, so that he may suck all the milk, leaving to the hyena only the small quantity of foam which comes out when the milk is finished.) So the hare sucked all the milk and was much pleased. But there was no milk left for the hyena, and he became thin. One day, jwok came and said, "Why are you so thin?" "The hare always drinks all the milk," said the hyena. Jwok said, "Take a rope and bind the hare." A rope was brought, and he bound the hare. The hare struggled to release himself, and he succeeded (but the loose rope was still round his neck. He ran to the cow and began sucking again). Then the hyena came, and when the foam was disappearing, he pulled the hare away by force, so that the hare fell on his back. "Oho," he said, "on account of a little milk he is going to kill me?" The hyena remained silent. The next morning, the hare said, "I am going to herd the cow." So he went. He formed cow-horns of mud (and placed them in the grass, so that they looked like the horns of a living cow). Then he ran to the hyena and said (pointing to the real cow), "Hyena, spear the waterbuck there in front! the cow is behind!" The hyena came and speared the cow; then said the hare, "Oho! (what have you done)! Did I not tell you to spear the waterbuck behind? What have you done with the cow? You have killed it! What will you eat now?" Then he said, "Go and fetch fire (that we may cook the meat)." "Where is fire?" asked the hyena. "Over there," answered the hare. The hyena went, but he saw there was no fire, so he returned. He saw that meanwhile all the meat had been carried away by the hare. "Why do you come back?" said the hare. "Because there is no fire," answered the hyena. Said the hare: "The meat has been carried away by jwok; but the head he has buried in the ground (as our portion)." And he said: "Let each pull out his part!" The hare pulled his part out, but the hyena's part was hard (would not come out). The hare got his part, but the hyena did not succeed in pulling his out. So he went home; the hare, too, went home. After some time, the hyena sent his son to the hare saying, "Go and bring fire from the home of the hare." The little child came and said, "Please give me fire!" The hare said, "Come and get it. But do not look up, lest pepper fall into your eye" (this was to prevent the child from seeing the meat of the cow which he had stolen and brought home). The child looked upward and saw the meat. Then he went home to his father and said, "There is plenty of meat in the house of the hare." When the hyena heard that, he took a club and said to his child, "Take also a club!" When they came, the hare went under his sleeping-skin and said to his son, "Beat me!" And he cried, "It was not I alone, the hyena too!"[15] When the hyena heard that, he ran away into the bush. The hyena was much afraid; the hare was very pleased.

73. The Monkey and the Lion.

Aywóm yà fạl; ká ǹù é bẹ̄nọ ki yiẹ bẹ̀ mā̰t ki pi, ka fạ̄dọ yey bur. Ka lại bẹ̄nọ bẹ̄ mā̰t ki pi; ká ǹù yôt ki pèǹ ki yéy bùr, ka lại ẹ́ rẹ̀ǹ. Ka aywom bẹ̄nọ, ká ǹù lṵ̀ẹ̀ ẹ́n, ka ẹ rẹ̀ǹ. Ka ǹu ko: kḁ̄léá wọ̀k! aywom ko: yí dúọ̀ǹ! e ko: ḛ̂, ya ṵ (yọ ṵ) kạl wọk i[16] yín. E ko: kạl yiẹ̀bi, ṵ[17] mákè yán tin, ká yí pạ̀r māl, ka ya pạ̄rọ māl báǹi, ká wá bi̍ḁ wọk. E kọ dó (dẹ̣ yi ṵ) chāmi yan! E ko: ḛ̂, yí fà chāmè yán, yín wotọ[18] di chọ̄n, yi fa chāmè yán. Ka aywom yiẹ̀bẹ kiẹ pèǹ, ká mák yí ǹù; ka aywom pạ̀ra māl, ka gẹ̣ bia wọk. Ká ǹù e ko: yá dâ kẹch. E ko: bútè[19] chaǹ ddẹ̀k, ya nḁ̄tí chām. E ko: yí kámá chāmi yán, gik aywom. E ko: nḛ̂; kine: wá kẹ́dọ̀ yi ógwọk, ogwọ̀k jāṇọ duọ̀ǹ. Ka aywom e ko: ógwộgí![20] Ye kudọ̄,[21] é chwọtọ: ógwộgí! Kine: ha! Kine: bi! Kine: à̰ǹọ̀? Kine: bi! wa da kwóp! Kine: ǎ gin à̰ǹọ̀? Aywom ko: ǹù kḁ̄lá wọk, ka a kḁ̀lé wọ̀k, dé chẹ (= chaka) chāmè yán, dẹ́ bẹ̀d ḁ̄dǜ àǹàn? Ogwọk e ko: ḛ̂, fà dúọ̀ǹ? Kwách wa jwọ̀k àǹàn í cham. Ka ogwọk chiǹẹ tiǹé māl, ki aywom ki ǹu, ká ogwọ̀k é lāmọ̀, kwaché jwọk, nḁ́ná māl. Ka ogwọ̀k e ko: yina jwọk, ḹní ki kwọ̄fá, fa yín a chwāch ǹù é duọ̀n kifa ṵ chām wọn? Ká ǹù chyẹn dkyèl tiṇa māl, chyẹn dkyèl mi̱t̰i aywom; ka ógwọ̀k è ko: faṭ ki kinau, kwọpa fa liṇ yi jwọk, tiṇ chini māl bẹ̀n, ká ǹù chiṇẹ tiṇe mal. Ka ǹeká bǖt aywom, ka ógwọ̀k e lāmọ̀, kine: Dẹ̀ fyech yín ye rẹ̀ǹ ki̱di̱; wá jȧṭ. Aywom kine: yán yá rẹ̀ǹ kine, ka rẹ̀ǹa māl wiy ya̰ṭ. Ógwọ̀k è kò: àwọ́, ki̱ǹâu. Ogwọk rẹ̀ṅa wọt. Ká ǹù è dō̰ṇọ kẹ̀ṭi̱. Ǹu ko: ka dẹ̣ ǹàjá nau! ogwọ̀k dẹ́ mákè yán kine. Ka aywom mákè yán kine; ka ogwọk chāmè yán ki̱ tyẹl amaḷọ, ka áywóm chāmè yán ki̱ chàn. — A tu̱mi̱.

The monkey was in the bush. And a lion came to him to drink water; and he fell into the well. Then some animal came to drink water; when it found the lion in the well, it ran away. The monkey came and saw the lion and ran away. The lion said, "Come to me." The monkey came, and the lion said to him, "Pull me out!" The monkey said, "You are heavy." He answered, "No, I want to be pulled out by you!" He said again, "Stretch down your tail, that I may seize it at once. Then you jump up, and I will jump after you; so we shall get out." The monkey said, "But then you will eat me!" He answered, "No, I will not eat you, you will live (stay) forever; you will not be eaten by me." So the monkey put his tail down, and it was seized by the lion. The monkey jumped up, and the lion too jumped up, and they got out. Now the lion said, "I am hungry; I remained three days without eating anything." The monkey replied, "You are going to eat me!" Talk of the monkey. The lion replied, "Yes". "Let us go to the fox, the fox is a great judge, replied the monkey." (They went, and when they had arrived) the monkey called, "Fox!" He was silent. He called again, "Fox!" He answered, "Ha?" He said, "Come!" The fox said, "What is the matter?" He answered, "We have something (to propound)." The fox asked, "What? The monkey answered, "This lion I pulled out, and when he was pulled out, he wanted to eat me; but how is that now?" The fox said, "Is he not great?"[22] (Then he said,) "Let us pray to God, (and after that) he may eat (you)." And the fox raised his hands up (praying). And the monkey and the lion and the fox, they all prayed; he (the fox) begged God, he looked upwards and said, "O God, hear my words! is it not thou who madest the lion to be big, that he might eat us?" And the lion lifted one paw up, and with one paw he seized the monkey."[23] Then the fox said, "Not so! or my prayer will not be heard by God; lift both your paws up!" The lion lifted both his paws up. And he moved towards the side of the lion. The fox prayed, saying, "We ask thee, how shall he run? (we pray thee, teach the monkey how to run) we do not know it." Then the monkey said, "As for me, I run thus." And he ran away along the top of a tree. The fox said, "Very well, just so!" and he ran home. So the lion as left alone. He said, "If I had but known about that, I would have caught the fox thus, and the monkey I would have caught thus, and the fox I would have eaten first, and after that I would have eaten the monkey." It is finished.

74. The Dog and the Fox.

The dog went into the bush; there he met the fox. And the dog said, "Friend, what are you doing in the bush? Go home (into the village)!" He said, "What shall we do in the village?" The dog said, "My master is accustomed to give one calf (whenever I come to him)." And he went with him. The dog went into the home, the fox remained outside the enclosure. The dog took some food, and he was beaten (by the people) with a club. He cried and ran into the bush. The fox asked him, "Why do you cry?" He answered, "O, I am (only) being educated (that's why I was beaten)." But the fox refused (to live with him), he ran away and ran into the bush, and he remained in the bush.

75. The Hare and the Hyena.

The hare went into the bush to make an ambach-boat, one for spearing fish. He sat down in it, pulled the fish out and roasted them. The hyena came and said, "To-day I have found you²⁴ ("you have been found by me")." The hare said, "Sit down, taste the food, my (elder) brother!" And he gave him fins of the fish. He asked him, "From where have you brought them?" The hare answered, "I have brought them from the river;" then he said to the hyena, "Put one of your members into this hole (then you will get fish)." The hyena went and put one of his members into the hole, and he was bitten, and he cried. He lay down (being sick from his wound). When he had recovered, he went into the bush and found the hare. He said to him, "I have found you (at last)!" The hare said, "Keep still, keep still!" He climbed a Nabag-tree, and threw Nabag-fruit down; the hyena remained under the Nabag-tree and ate the fruit; the hare went away and left the hyena eating.²⁵

76. The Lion and the Fox.

Ńù bệnọ̀, ye da ńyẹ́ń, biẹ yi bọ̀dọ̀, e ko: bọ̀dọ́, ṭaṭ tọ̀ńá agàk! ká ógwọ̄k é bệnọ̀, ye da ńyẹ́ń, biẹ yi bọ̀dọ̀, e ko: tọ̀ńá àgàk ṭaṭ gẹ́ń! Ká bọ̀dọ̀ kò: ńù tọ̀ńẹ̀ nútí yá,²⁶ ká ógwọ̄k è kò: ńù fàṭẹ̀²⁷ wát bâńá? Kịne: wat bâńí kịdì? E ko: kudi au, ụ bệń ńù ťiń kōpi kịne: ogwọ̄k è kò: yí fà wat bâńẹ̀? Ká ńù bệnọ̀, kịne: bọ̀dọ́!²⁸ Kịne: ẹrẹ tọ́ńa chọ̀ gị̀, fa ṭaṭè yíń?²⁹ Kịne: ógwọ̄k fan ẹn a kụl tọ̀nẹ̀, yi ṭaṭ mọ̀tí. Ya kịne: ńù kụ́ wêr? (ógwọ̄k) kịne: ê, fá wêr, fa wat bâńá? Ká ńù kò: mọ́k dọ̀ńi? Kịne: ńè. Ńù kò: yá dwai ẹ́n, ụ yik kwọfí (ẹ)ne fa fygṭ, yí chámè chámò̀,³⁰ kọ́fọ́ bọ̀dọ̀. Ká bọ̀dọ̀ kò kịne: dọ̀ch, kẹṭ dwai. Ka ńù kẹdọ̀, ka ogwōge yót, ê budọ̀ kí yụ́, e ko: chẹ (= chaka) da jwọk; dẹ̀ é chùdọ̀. Ká ńù ko: yí rè chúdí (chúrí)? nine dâ léń; yé kò: edi? E ko: áwẹ̀ń? Kịne: dwá; kịne ki mẹ̀ń? Kịne wú kú (= wú ki wú) bọ̀dọ̀. Kịne: dwọṭ! yú kwáńè yáń. Ká dwọṭá mâl, ká ńù kò: yẹ̀ṭí kwọ̀má. Ká è ko: pám má fáṭ,³¹ ẹ gwọ̄k è dì? Kịne: kiṭe kwọmá! Ká è kò: áchịchwệl má faṭ, é gwọ̄k ẹ̀dì? E ko: kiṭe dọ́gá! Ka e kiṭi dọ́gẹ̀, ká è ko: dẹ̀ dẹ̀l má fáṭ, é gwọ̄k ẹ̀dì? E ko: kwáń! Ka kwâń yi ogwọ̄k, ká yẹ́ṭá mâl, kwòm ńù. Ká gẹ́ bệnọ̀ kí ńù, ká gẹ́ kẹ́dọ̀; pach é cháńọ̀, ká ńù gọ́chẹ yi ógwọ̄k kí dẹ̀l, ká ńù é rẹ́ńọ̀, ka pwótè yi ógwọ̄k, ká gẹ rińọ̀, ríńọ yi bọ̀dọ̀, ká bọ̀dọ̀ dwọṭá mâl, ká ógwọ̄k è ko: bọ̀dọ̀,³² lẹ̀ṭẹ (lịṭi) yáń! fàṭè waṭ bâńá? bọ̀dọ̀ ko: àwó, waṭ bâńì! yi kama dìr. Ká gẹ́ kẹ́dọ̀, gẹ́ rińọ̀ kun a de wọṭ ógwọ̄k, ká woṭ ogwọ̄k é wáṇọ̀. Ka ogwọ̄k fáŕá féń, ka ŕéńá woṭ, ká máké³³ ńù ki yiẹbẹ̀, ka wiy yiẹbẹ́ é chọ̀dọ̀, ká ńù kò: kẹ́ṭ, yí rúm ki ṭọ̀ṭọ́ ki néjí. Ká é bọ̀dọ̀. Ká ńù kẹṭa fâŕẹ. Ká é kàńọ̀ ki lại, ká lại ṭâl, ká tẹ̀rọ̀ dwai é bệńẹ̀. Ká tẹ̀rọ̀ bệńọ̀ kí ogwọ̄k, ogwọ̄k gı̂r bệńọ ki ogwọ́ń ẹni, ẹn á pwóṭ ńu, nút ṭyáu. Ká gẹ́ kẹdọ̀ yi pwóḍọ́, ká óchó̧yọ̀ ywót é gı̂r, ka ógwọ̄k a fwóṭ ńù, e ko ne, tọ̀jọ̀ ki óchó̧yọ̀ ki yiẹpẹ́,³⁴ ka mẹ́ńọ̀ yiébẹ́ ńí twóch ke ri óchó̧yọ̀, ká ogwọ́ń ẹni, mẹ twóchè ẹ̀n ệ láńọ̀, ká e ko: rẹńe tẹ̀rọ̀ fá (= fach) ńù. Ká gẹ́ rẹ́ńọ̀, ka yiẹbẹ³⁵ bọ̀dọ̀, ká ógwọ̄kẹ mẹne yiẹbẹ́ ńí chọ̀dọ̀, ka yiẹpẹ́ gẹ́ń é ṭùmọ̀ kí chōṭọ. Ká gẹ́ wáṇọ̀, ká ńù ywót kí tẹ̀rọ̀ bệńè,

Lion and Fox

ká nù é pệchộ kịne: wú bì běnû? Kịne ê; ka ogwōk nájè ẹn, e ko: yí bì tyàu? E ko: ê. E ko: wá ụ yél wa mẹn? Ká é kò: yá chảm ddì? Kịne: faṭe yín a pwòtì yán? Kịne: ẹ! dwẹn? Kịne: ótyẹṇò; kịne: ẹ! yí chaka tổdộ! Nù kò: yiebi nụtı nộlè yan? Kịne: ágòn ẹn? Kịne: ánánộ! Kịne: dệ faṭe yan kẹta! Kịne: dá wú kí mẹn? Ogwōk e ko: faṭe wá běnâ? Kịne: àrá, bi lệṭ! Ka nu běnọ, ká gẹ lệṭ, mẹn yṭebệ chộdộ, ká mẹn yṭebệ chộdộ, ka gẹ běn yiepe gẹn chộdộ, ká nù wijẹ mum, ye ko: boṭu. Ká gẹ wéyẹ. Ká rìnộ wékè tệrộ, ká chảm yi tẹro. Chôṭi, ká tệrộ é dánộ, ká nù dộnọ ki fårẹ.

A lion came with some iron to the smith and said, "Smith, make me these spears!" The fox too came, bringing iron to the smith, and said to him, "These spears, make them." The smith said, "The spear of the lion is still with me (unfinished)." The fox said, "Is he not my slave?" He said, "How your slave?" He replied, "You just keep quiet; as soon as the lion comes, tell him, 'The fox has said, you are his slave'." And the lion came and said, "Smith, why have you not yet finished my spear?" He answered, "The fox brought his spear (and said), 'Make it (= mine) first'. I said: 'Will the lion not be angry?' He said: 'No, he will not be angry; for is he not my slave?'" The lion replied, "Is that true?" The smith (said), "Yes." The lion (replied), "I shall bring him, and if your talk turns out to be a lie, I shall surely eat you;" this he said to the smith, and the smith replied, "All right, go, and bring him." So the lion went; he found the fox lying on the road; he pretended to be sick, he groaned. The lion said, "Why are you thus groaning?" — He, the lion, became angry ("his eye had war"). — He said to the fox, "How did you speak (to the smith)?" The fox asked, "When?" He answered, "Yesterday." The fox asked, "To whom?" The lion said, "To the smith. Get up, we will go!" He said, "I am sick." The lion replied. "Get up! I will help you." So he rose, and the lion said, "Climb upon my back!" The fox said, "There is somebody's saddle (there is a saddle, I do not know to whom it belongs), what shall I do with it?" He answered, "Put it on my back!" Then the fox said, "Here is somebody's chain (bridle), what shall I do with it?" The lion said, "Put it into my mouth." Again the fox said, "Here is somebody's whip, what shall I do with it?" The lion answered, "Take it!" So the fox took it, and he climbed on the lion's back. He came with the lion; they went along. When they approached the village, the fox beat the lion with the whip, and the lion ran. Again he whipped the lion, and they ran gallopping to the house of the smith. The smith looked up ("arose"), and the fox cried, "Smith, is he not my slave?" The smith answered, "Surely, your slave is he, you have told the truth." They went on and ran to the place where the house of the fox was. When the house of the fox came near, he jumped down and ran into the house. But the lion caught him by his tail, and the end of the tail broke off. The lion said, "Go, I have given you a sufficient mark."³⁶ He, the fox, sat down.

The lion went into his village, he brought game and cooked the game, and he brought (invited) all the people (that is, the animals).³⁷ The people came, and the foxes, many foxes came, and the fox who had beaten the lion was also present. (On the way to the lion's village) they came into a field and found plenty of melons, and the fox who had beaten the lion, said (to his companions), they should tie melons to their tails. So each one tied melons to his tail. And this particular fox tied the melons very loosely to his tail. Then he said, "People, run to the village of the lion!" And they ran. (While thus running) the melon slipped off his tail, but the tails of the other's broke off, all of them. When they approached, they found all the people with the lion. The lion asked, "Have you all come?" They replied, "Yes." And the lion recognized the fox and asked him, "You too have come?" He replied, "Yes." The lion, "By whom shall we be reconciled (how can we, being enemies, eat at the same table)?" The fox asked, "What is the matter ("what have I become")?" The lion said, "Is it not you who beat me?" The fox said, "What? you do lie!" The lion said, "Did I not cut off your tail?" The fox replied, "Where is it?" The lion said, "Here it is" (showing the cut-off tail of the fox). The fox replied, "But that is not I alone (i. e. the case with me only). The lion, "Who beside you ("you and who")?" The fox, "Is it not all of us? why, come and look!" The lion came and looked at them, this one's tail was cut off, and that one's tail was cut off, all their tails were cut off. The lion did not know what to say ("his head was giddy"), and he said, "You have escaped!" He let them go, and the people were given meat, and the people ate. That is all. — The people scattered, and the lion was left in his village.

77. The Starling and the Centipede.

Ówầnọ bẹ̄dá (bẹ̄rá) riṭ; ye da ḍean, dẹ̄ ywộp. Ka winọ bẹ̄nọ bẹ̄ne bẹ̄ne, ka ówầnọ ko: yinẹ tẹ̄rọ, ḍea ywộ p, dẹ̄ kwộp nán á ywộbé! Ká tẹ̀rù mừmọ̀; é kọ: bựh! ẹrẹ (ẹdẹ) tẹ̄rọ á mừmị̂? Ka tẹ̄rọ ko: ywộp kúchị wộn. Ka ólyđù é kọ: yá-kị̂-yấn (yān?)-tẹ̣n nẻná³⁸ nút, ywọp de kwộp yị yán! Ka riṭ e ko: ṭọ́ṭu olyau kị́ nin; ká mện nị́ bànọ̀. Òtólè Kọ̀ṭ e ko: yi kwan nị́ná, ú gẹ́ lịḍọ́ ywộp, ú rúmé, ká gẹ́ wẹ̀ké yán. Ka olyau nị̀nẹ kwáné, ká lịḍọ́ kûn, ka chigị́ lịṭị́³⁹ kùn, ká lịḍọ́ mâl, ká lịḍọ́ yi tẹ̄rọ, ka lịḍọ́ yi túlọ̀, e ko: túlọ̀! Kịne: ẹ́? Kịne: ẹ́rẹ ḍe riṭ a ywộbí? E ko: dwẹ̀n? ya fa ywọp! Kịne yi re (ra) faṭ kị́ ywộp? Kịne: náyó kúchị yín? ẹ̀ná ywộp. Kịne: ná ámện? Kịne: náyó bẹ̄ṭ; ẹna nị́ nẹ́né rẹ̀jọ́. E ko: faṭẹ ẹn a chầlè yín? Chōṭị, ka tẹ̄rọ fầrd kwọ̀mẹ̀, ká pwót yị tẹ̄rù, ká é kẹṭị é rịnọ̀. Ka yoma wiy yaṭ. Á ńí chǫ́gí e búdǫ́ wiy yaṭ. Ká olyau é dùǫgò. Ká ótôl Kǫṭ e ko: wēki yan ńínd! E ko: ḙ, gḙ gwǫ̀gḙ́ nò̩? Ka owāno ko: wēki ńin olyau u go ńi tǫńé ywò̩p. Chǭṭṭ, ótôl Kǫṭ é kḙ́dò̩ ńin bógin. Ka riṭ e ko: yú (yi u) chàṭí kí dò̩ch; ḙ bógin u chàmḙ yin. Chǭṭi, a ńí ṭduwḙ́ e kḙ̄ṭḙ, e bogin chamḙ, a gyḙṭ yi riṭ.

The heron was king. He had a cow which was bewitched. And all the birds came, and the heron said to them, "Ye people, my cow is bewitched, tell me who has bewitched it." And the people were perplexed. He asked, "Dear me! why are the people so perplexed?" They said, "We do not know the wizard." Then the starling said, "O my goodness, if only I had my eyes, I would name the wizard." The king said, "Give the starling eyes!" But each one refused. At last the centipede *Kǫṭ* said, "Take my eyes, when the wizard has been found and the matter is finished, then give them back to me." The starling took the eyes, he looked in this direction and again looked in that direction; he looked upwards and looked at the people; and he looked at the owl saying, "Owl!" The owl replied, "Eh?" He said, "Why do you bewitch the cow of the king?" He said, "When? I am not a wizard." The starling replied, "Why should you not be a wizard? Do you not know your uncle? He is a wizard." The owl asked, "Who is my uncle?" He said, "The fish-spear is that uncle; it is he who sees the fish (in the water).¹⁰ Does he not resemble you?" — That is all, and all the people (= the birds) jumped on his (the owl's) back, and he was beaten by the people; and he went away running. He fled to a tree. There he is accustomed to stay, on the top of trees.

When the starling returned, centipede *Kǫṭ* said, "Give me my eyes!" But he said, "No, what for?" And the heron said, "Give (= leave) the eyes to the starling, that he may always make manifest the wizards." — That is all, centipede *Kǫṭ* went away without eyes. And the king said to him, "Walk in peace! There is nobody who will eat you." That is all; he (the centipede) is accustomed to die of himself (not killed by other people, or through violence); nobody eats him. He is blessed by the king.

78. The Hare and Tapero.

Afoajǫ a kḙṭa mal bē̩ ywótǫ́ búl; gò kí nąn Tāpḙ̄rò̩. Ka afoajǫ būl chǫ́n, ká būl chǫ́n ki mal. Ka Tāpḙ̄rǫ e dǫ̀nò̩ wò̩k, ḙ pá dwái yi nan a dāchǫ. Ka afoajǫ dwái yi nan a dāchǫ; ka gḙ chǭnó búl, ka Tāpḙ̄rǫ dǫ̀nǫ wǫk, ḙ́ fa dwái yi nan a dāchǫ; ka afoajǫ dwái ò̩ ḙ́n; ka būl dò̩n, ka afoajǫ é chwò̩tò̩ kine: nąn Tāpḙ̄rǫ, wa fa kḙṭ? Tāpḙ̄rò̩ ḙ kùdò̩, chuṇḙ rach kífa dwái afoajǫ. Ka Tāpḙ̄rǫ bia féń, afoajǫ á dò̩nò̩ màl. Ka afoajǫ ḙ́ lò̩nò̩ bḙ̄n, ka tyelḙ mak ki akḙ́ṭ, e ko: yá kḙ́ṭá féń, yá dò̩gú fò̩ṭḙ̀ wǫ́n. E ko: u yik yá ú wiṭḙ́ féń u jâk akḙ́ṭ, ya wiṭí fò̩ṭḙ̀ wǫ́n. Akḙt chò́ ńwò̩jó kí jàgù; ḙ́ nùṭí ki wiṭe féń, ka afoajǫ dḙ̄mò̩, ka e kḙ̄ṭò̩.

The hare went up (into the air) to find a drum; he and his uncle Tapero. And the hare danced to the drum, he danced up in the air. But Tapero remained outside (the ring of the dancers), he was not selected (for dancing) by a girl.[41] But the hare was selected by the girls, and he danced with them. Again Tapero remained outside, he was not selected by a girl, but the hare was again selected, and danced. At last the dancers scattered. Then the hare called, "Uncle Tapero, shall we not go?" Tapero remained silent, he was angry because the hare had been selected. Tapero went down, but the hare remained above. Some time after the hare also came; he fastened his foot with a rope, and said (to Tapero?), "I am going down, I will return to our country." Again he said, "As soon as I come down to the ground and (I) pull the rope, I shall arrive in my country (at once)." But he pulled the rope too early, before he had reached the ground. So the hare fell down and was dashed to pieces.[42]

79. Who is King?

Afoajǫ ṅǫmǫ dachǫ, gę kí ótwǫ́ṅ; dachǫ mārǫ ótwǫ́ṅ, dę afoajǫ chę́t yi dachǫ. Ká gę wę̀lọ̀, ka gę ko kine: nę́nì wǫt dyę̨k; ka gę nęnǫ, ka dyeṅ[43] nę̨k yi afoajǫ, ka ótwǫ́ṅ e nęnǫ, ká wài ka gę wóḍę́[44] ótwǫ́ṅ; ka wǫ́u è wuḍ, ka afoajǫ kęt, ka ótwǫ́ṅ dọ̀nọ̀, e nę́nọ̀. Ka ṅal tę̄ṅ bę̄nǫ, ka e ko: yá nę́ṅ! Ka ǫtwǫṅ ḍwǫta mal, ka līte rę, ka wài līte rę, ka e ko: afoajǫ á kǫ̆lę́ kę̣́ṅ? Ka ǫrę́ bę̄nǫ, ká è kò: dyęk á chám gę mę̨̀ṅ?[45] Kine: dyęk ba cham yi ǫtwǫṅ? Ka dę̀l è kǫ̆l, ka ǫtwǫṅ pwót, ká nǫmę̀ tàṅǫ̀.

Ka ǫtwǫṅ e kę́dọ̀, ka afoajǫ yótè yi ę́ṅ (rę́ṅ), é budę̀ rech, ka e ko: wíṅá teau,[46] yí yótè yáṅ! Ka e ko kine: ḍàṅ ṅí bę́lę́ gigę́ mǫ́tí, ka ókǫ̀k wēki ǫtwǫṅ, ka e ko: ówá, chà mę̀dò! Kine: gę mayi gę kidí? Kine: gę ṅi pǎdá (fāra) nam. Ka e ko: kęt pā (pár) nâm! Ka afoajǫ párá nam; ka ṅa pyęn deję wá ṅę̨̀tę̀. Ka ǫtwǫṅ e loṅǫ pāre nam, ka nę̨́kè ǫkǫk bę̄nę̨, ka e ywǫ̀nọ̀. Ka e kę́dǫ, ǫtwǫṅ, weyę gǫ ywǫ̀nọ̀.

Ka afoajǫ kędǫ é kę̀ję́,[47] ka ywoda lyęch, gǫ kudǫ kǫ̆dǫ̀ ki tyelę, ká è kò: ówá kǫlǫ kǫ̆dǫ̀. Ka tyęl lyęch ṅyę̀mę́ wǫ̂k, ka lyęch e kędǫ, ka è tǫ̀; ka afoajǫ kęta yey lyęch. Ka lyęch, afoajǫ meję yę́ję̀, ka èjàdǫ̀ kí kę̀n kǫ̆lę́,[48] ká è kò: yí rè ba kwǫ̣̂t? U ya kǫ̆lá baṅ kǫ̆tǫ́! Ka lyęch e kwǫ̀dǫ̀; ka bia wǫk.

Ka lyęch ya rit, ka ḍǫgę ṅí ṅǫṅę (ṅwaṅę) kwęt, ka dìet e ko: ęrę ḍǫ (ḍǫk) lyęch a ṅwaṅę kwęt ki chāṅǫ? Kine: paṭe ḍǫ rit? Ka atet e kę́dǫ, ká è tę̨̀nọ̀ kí àtę̀rǫu, ka kā (= kędǫ) chán; ka lyęch ká yìę, ka ụ kę̆lę́ kí ḍó gòṅ, ka lyęch pǎdǫ̀, ká kàl e kę̣̀tọ̀.

Ka ówǎnọ̀ ko: yá jękǫ̀, ya bàṅę rit! Ka rǫ́ṅ (rǫṅ), ka tę̀rọ̀ ṅí ká (= kęta) nâm bę̀ mài, ká lòt ṅí mena péṅ, ka nam ṅí bę̆dá târ, ka djē ṅí mǔl ki rech. Ka lǫt kwâl yi ògwàl, ka gǫṅ wékę́ kǫ́t; ka kę́lę yi kǫ̣t. Ka okwóm ka pyech[49] yi owāṅǫ, kine: lǫt e kwal yi mę̣ṅ? Kine: kúchì yán. Ka bǫ̣nọ̀ pyéch, kine: lǫt a kwâl yi

mɛn? Kine: loṭ a kwâl yi ògwàl. Ka okwóm pyech yi owāṅọ kine: dɛ kóbì ụ chame⁵⁰ kúchì yin? Cham⁵⁰ nùtí lîdɛ yin? Ka góch yi owāṅọ.
  Ka tan kōbọ ogwal: wá ràrọ! Ka tan ko: ogwàl, tyɛ́lí chɛ̀kọ̀, tyɛlá bàrọ̀. Ka ogwal e ko: wá ràrọ. Ka gɛ rɛ́ṅọ̀, mɛn ya kɛń, mɛn ya kɛń. Ogwal gîr ki yey pén bɛ̀nɛ̀, ka tan e ko: yọma ógwàl. Ká ògwàl è kò: yọmá tan. Ka tanọ pidọ, ka e pâḍọ̀, ka e ṭö̀ yi ṅwɛ̀ch.
  Ka ólɛ̀ṭ ka é jɛ́kọ̀ rọń (rọń) riṭ, ka rọ́ń, ka chip wij dbóbọ̀. Ka ḍeań nɛ̀k, ka olɛṭ e ko: buli riṅọ! Ka riṅọ bûl, ká è kò: kậl riṅọ! Ka riṅọ chwọ́ṅọ̀, ka chɛ́ká chwọ̀tọ̀; ka riṅọ e chwọ́ṅọ̀, ka pārá mâl, ka lāu lọń wij dbóbọ̀, ka riṅọ gwárɛ̀. A chógɛ́, a chɛ́kà gwar.
  A kwań lau yi atwâk. A rọ́ńé, a kúchî́ lāu yi jāgọ, à pâḍí. A kóp tɛ̀rọ̀ kine: wá rọ̀ṅè mɛ́nâ? Kine: rọ́ń ńdu! A lań ńau wộr ɛ́ ṅɛ̀ṭọ̀ ki fa kwọ́pé rọ̀ṅè. Ka dɛńɛ́ kwòdọ̀. Ka lɛ́ṭè mwọl, dɛń e kwódọ̀, ka tɛ̀rọ ko: buh! ɛ́dì ńdu? A bɛ̀ (= bɛ̄dọ) dɛńí ńdù? ńau ko kine: yá lànọ̀ wộr yá ṅɛ̀ṭọ̀, ká tɛ̀rọ̀ ko: buh! weì ki ụ rọ́ń!⁵¹ a wei, a kɛ́ṭ tɛ̀rọ̀.
  A yâp jāgọ, ka jāgọ ya mátộk. Ka tɛ̀rọ bɛ̄nọ, gɛ kōbọ kine: wá rọ̀ń mɛ́nâ? Rọ́ń dgàk!⁵² Ka agak rọ́ń, ka e jɛ̀kọ̀ kị jàṅè dọ́ch. Ṅị tọu lậì kị pal. Ka tɛ̀rọ ńi chukọ, kine: wá chwọl a mɛ́nâ? Kine: chwọl jâgọ! A chwọl jāgọ, a bɛ̀ṅe ɛ̀n agak, ka tɛ̀rọ kōbọ kine: jâgọ́, lại anaṅọ! Kwọṅ lậì! a kɛdọ bútè lậì, a kwań wdń gòn; ka e ḍùòḍọ̀, ka tɛ̀rọ chàm. A chốgi kí jàṅè dọ́ch; a kóp tɛ̀rọ̀ kine: dgàk ban ɛn jańe dọ́ch!
  A góy (= gọch) bûl, ká tɛ̀rọ̀ chǭ́ṅọ̀, ka bûl pwót; ka Ṭāpɛ̀rọ̀ ki túlọ̀ gɛ bɛ̄no, ka dwâi yi dāchọ.

The hare married a woman, he together with the hyena. The woman liked the hyena, but the hare was hated by her. And they travelled; and (the people to whom they came on their journey) said to them, "Sleep in the sheep house!"[53] So they slept, and sheep were killed by the hare, while the hyena slept, and he smeared the contents of the stomach on the hyena's mouth. When the day broke, the hare went away, he left the hyena sleeping. (In the morning) a boy came and asked, "May I come in?" Then the hyena arose, he looked at himself and saw the contents of the sheep's stomach on his body, he said, "Where is the hare?" The brother-in-law[54] came and asked the boy, "Who has eaten the sheep?" He answered, "Have the sheep not been eaten by the hyena?" Then a whip was brought, and the hyena was beaten, and his wife relinquished him (he was divorced from his wife).
  And the hyena went away. and he found the hare roasting fish; he said to him, "You cursed hare, I have found you!" The hare said, "Every one is accustomed to eat his food first (before doing anything else)."[55] He gave the hyena an okok (a certain fish with sharp pricks); the hyena said, "Father, it

seems to be good!" He asked again, "How do they catch it?" He answered, "They are accustomed to jump into the river (and thus catch it). The hyena said, "Go, jump into the river!" So the hare jumped into the river, but he bound a small skin around his waist (so that the thorns of the fish could not wound him). The hyena sprang after him into the river, but he was much bruised by the okok, and he screamed. And he (the hare) went away, he left the hyena screaming.

The hare went away to his place; he found an elephant who was taking a thorn out of his foot. The hare said, "My father is taking out a thorn." (He said to the elephant, "I will help you to take the thorn out", and) he cut the whole foot of the elephant off. Then the elephant went away almost dying from pain; the hare went into the belly of the elephant. The elephant shut the hare up in his belly, and he had difficulty in getting out. He said to the elephant, "Why do you not dung, that I may go out after your dunging?" The elephant dunged, and so the hare got out.

And the elephant was king. His cattle always scattered their dung on the road; and the ichneumon said, "Why do the cattle of the elephant always scatter their dung?" The people answered, "Are they not the cattle of the king?" And the ichneumon went and hewed a stick, and he went from behind to the elephant and stuck him in his trunk (stuck the stick into the trunk of the elephant); the elephant fell down (and died), and his house was destroyed.

Then the heron said, "I want to be king, I shall be king!" And he was elected, and the people went to the river to fish. They put a club into the river, which made the water clear, so the people used to catch fish. But the club was stolen by the frog; he gave it to the rain.[56] And the ibis was asked by the heron, "By whom has the club been stolen?" He said, "I do not know." Then the pelican was asked, "By whom has the club been stolen?" He answered, "The club has been stolen by the frog." Then the ibis was asked by the heron, "How could you say you did not know? Had you not seen it?" And he was beaten by the heron.

And to the waterbuck the frog said, "Let us run a race!" The waterbuck said, "Frog, your legs are short, but my legs are long." But the frog said, "(Never mind,) let us run!" And they ran. The one stood here, and the other stood there. But there were many frogs everywhere in the ground. And the waterbuck said, "I have beaten (surpassed) the frog!" But (always) a frog cried, "I have beaten the waterbuck." At last the waterbuck was tired, and he fell down and died on account of his running.

Then the hawk wanted to be king, and he was elected. He placed himself on an ambach-tree, and a cow was killed (on the occasion of the election of a new king), and the hawk said: "Roast meat!" And meat was roasted. Then he said: "Bring meat!" And the meat came not quickly; so he called again for meat, and yet it did not come. He flew up and left the (royal) clothes on the ambach, he snatched the meat; (from that time) he has always remained in the habit of snatching meat.

The royal clothes were taken by the atwak, but he did not know how to behave in royal clothes, therefore he was driven away. Then the people said, "Whom shall we elect?" It was said, "Let us elect the cat!" (When the cat heard that) she spent a whole night in laughing, because of the plan of electing her. And her jaws swelled from laughing. When the next morning the people saw that her jaw was swollen, they said, "Why! what is the matter with the cat? Why is your jaw thus?" She answered, "I spent a night in laughing." The people replied, "Leave her alone, she is not to be elected." The people went away.

They looked for a king; there was no one who might become king. So the people came saying, "Whom shall we elect? Let us elect the crow!" And the crow was elected. He reigned very well. The game died in the bush. And the people were at a loss, they said, "Whom shall we call?" It was said, "Call the king." The king was called; he came, he, the crow. And the people said, "King, here is a game, taste the game!" He went to the game and took (picked) its eye out. Then he arose, and the people ate. He continued to reign well. And the people said, "The crow, he is a good king."

A drum was beaten. The people danced. And the drum was beaten again, and Tapero and the owl came, and he was selected by a woman for dancing.[57]

80. The Hare.

Afoajǫ a wēli fōṭe riṭ, ka ywódá nǫ̈r; nǫr gir, ka fęka fen bę chám. Ká é rûm, ka gę chǫn kíní; ka aṭęp fan yi gęn. Ka amàlǫ dwâi, ka aṭęp kwan, ka gę chip wich amal, ká gò gǫ̈chí, kine: chǎṭí! Ka amalǫ (amǫlǫ) é bànǫ̀, ká gò chígí gǫ̈chò.

A kęṭí áfoàjǫ kęṭí, a dwâi kyèn, a yīj aṭęp, a kiṭí kwǫ̀m kyęn, à bán chǎṭǫ̀. A gǫ̈chí gòn; chámǫ́ kędę́ a chí gá fudǫ̀; a ko: bůh! Afoajǫ kine: bůh! aṭęp ú gwǫ́k ędì? A dęn ki kyèn, a kędǫ afoajǫ, a dwai dean, a yēj aṭęp wiję. A lęné aṭęp fen yi dean, a kōbǫ afoajǫ: yí rè lęni aṭęp fèn? Ko: yí rè nągí jè? yá będǫ̀! A kęṭi, a dęn afoajǫ, a nàn afoajǫ, aṭęp ú tich èdì? A chígí dǫ̀gò bę dwátǫ̀ nù; a ywódę́ ęn; a kǫ̀bí: yina nu! wá fà mąt? Kó û, yínè mǎdà! Afoajǫ kine: yá dál yi gìchò mękǫ̀. Ye ko: ú gìn ànǫ̀? Nǫr a yóte yán fōṭe riṭ, gę gír, a chǎmá, ká yá yànǫ̀, ká gę chína. A kǫ́p nu, yí chǎká tòtǫ̀, wálà a kwdlè yin? Kò: á kwdlè yán. Kō: yǎch! yá fà kęṭ! Kò: máṭ, bi kędǫ̀, kon yán! Kine: yá tęn, yí důǫn. A kęṭ nu, a yǒdí gìn ęní é pęk, a kyęde. A kędę afoajǫ tyau.

*A dwai ótwọ̀ṇ, ko: yin ótwọ̀ṇ, tẹ̀rọ̀ à dwâi yán bẹ̀nẹ̀, dẹ́ gẹ́ báṅ, dẹ bi, koṅ yan!
yu tọ̄tẹ kị́ nọ̀r, mọk ṳ́ chámè yín. A kẹti ótwọ̀ṇ, à yẹ̣ji kwọm ótwọ̀ṇ; a kạ́lẹ́ gẹ́n
pach, a wánọ̀ gọ́l gẹ́n, a lẹ̣̀ṅ gẹ̀ féṅ. Ká kwọ̀mé otwoṇ e fọ̀gọ̀. Ká afoajọ kọ̀mà
kịne: kwọm otwọṇ ṳ́ gwọ̀k ẹdí? Ka yịṭ yaṭ ká gẹ tọ́k yị̀ gẹ́n, a kịti kwọ̀m kẹṅ lẹṭ.
Ká ẹ́ tuyi yàṇ duọ́ṅ. Afoajọ lịṭà yáṭ, ẹ bạ̀r kị́ kwọ̀m ótwọ̀ṇ; a ṅwọ̄lị́; ka ṅwōlẹ
nị́ lịṭ afoajọ; e ko: búh! ụ bạ́lẹ kị́ àṅọ̀ (káṅọ̀)? A kwáṅị́ túk à bạ́lé gọṇ kị tuṅ
ẹni. Kẹṭ tuṅ ẹnā fáṭé dí nâm, a lọ́gị́ mùchọ̀.
Ye kẹdọ bẹ̣ fēṭ kị́ jâm, ká ṅwọ̣́lé ochọ̄ye ká gẹ́ fẹṭ. A bẹ̀nị́ òwêlè mẹ̣kọ, a kóbí
kịne: tọ̄ṭi yan kị́ gìn châm! A kyẹ́t afoajọ kịne: néwá, yà chẹ̀rá bẹ̀nọ̀ ànàn. Afoajọ
chàmá lēṭị nàjẹ̀. A ywòdé ochọ̄ye, é ṅẹ̣̀nọ̀, a dụoṭ afoajọ, ká fàlọ̀ kwàné, ụ kágọ́
gọ̀ṇ; ka fàl kẹdọ yéjé ochọ̄ye; ka afoajọ e ṅàṅọ̀: fàlọ̀ é kẹdọ kẹṅ āṇọ? Ka wijẹ
ṅọ̣̄li, kạ́ kẹdọ yéje ochọ̄ye, kạ́ ywode djè gẹ́ gịr, gẹ́ nẹ̀nọ̀. Ka é fẹdọ̀. A bẹ̀n wọk, a
ywóde wijẹ ẹ́ tyètọ̀ kị́ yúk, a chwọ̣́lí gọ̀ṇ, kịne: yine wich bí! Ka wich é bàṅ. A
chị́gị́ gọ̀ṇ chwọ̣́lé kị́ṭé, ká é bàṅ. Ká gụ̀ gọ̣́ché kị́ àtàl; a bẹ̀nẹ́ wich, a dọ́gé kẹ̀jẹ̀.*

    The hare travelled into the town of the king, and he found beans, plenty of beans. And he sat down to eat. When he had finished, he piled them (the rest) up in one place. He filled a bag with them. Then he brought a camel, took the bag and put it on the camel. He beat the camel saying, "Walk on!" But the camel refused. He beat it again saying, "Walk on!" The camel fell down and said, "The bag is too heavy." The camel went away.

    The hare too went away; he fetched a horse, lifted the bag and put it on the horse's back. The horse refused to walk; he (the hare) struck it, it tried to go, but it began to fall down saying, "Why!" The hare said, "Why! what shall I do with the bag?" He left the horse. The hare went and fetched a cow; he put the bag on it. But the bag was thrown down by the cow. The hare asked, "Why do you throw down the bag?" The cow replied, "Why do you kill people (by laying such a heavy load on them)? I refuse." He went away. The hare was left; he was perplexed, thinking, "What is to be done with the bag?" He once more turned back to fetch the lion. When he found him, he said to him, "You lion! Are we not friends?" He said, "Yes, you are my friend." Then the hare said, "I am in difficulty with a certain matter." The lion asked, "What is it?" He answered, "I found beans in the town of the king, plenty of beans. I ate some of them, and when I was full, I put the rest into a bag." The lion asked, "Were they given to you, or did you steal them?" He answered, "They were stolen by me." Then the lion said, "Never! I shall not go!" The hare said, "Friend, come, let us go that you may help me!" He said again, "I am small, you are big." So the lion went. He found the bag ("thing") very heavy; he refused and went away. The hare too went.

    He fetched a cock; he told him, "You cock! all (kinds of) people were

The Hare

fetched by me, but they have refused. But now come and help me, and I shall give you part of the beans to eat." The cock went, (the hare) put the bag on the cock, and it carried it home. When they came near the house, it threw it down. The cock's back was bruised (from carrying the bag). The hare said, "What is to be done with the back of the cock?" He crushed leaves of a tree and placed them on the sore place of the cock's back.

And there sprang up a large tree (on the sore place of the cock's back, some seeds having got into the wound by putting the leaves on it). The hare saw the tree was very high on the back of the cock. The tree bore fruit; when the fruit was seen by the hare, he said, "Dear me! by what (how) are they to be thrown down?" He took a stone and threw at them. The stone fell into the middle of a river and became an island.

The hare went to plant some vegetables (on the island), and he planted melon seeds. Then there came a traveller, he said, "Give me something to eat (the traveller saw the melons, which in the meantime had ripened)!" But the hare refused saying, "Cousin, I have come in this very moment (so I am not prepared to give you food)." The hare looked back; he saw there were many melons. The hare arose, he took a knife and split a melon. The knife went into the middle of the melon, the hare was perplexed, he said to himself, "Where has the knife gone?" Suddenly it (the knife) cut his (the hare's) head off. He (the hare) went into the melon and found there many people, who were alive. When he was tired, he came out; he found his head carrying firewood. He called it, "You head, come!" But the head refused. He called it again, but it refused. Then he struck it with the flat hand. The head came and returned to its place.[58]

[The Nubians have the same story; here, as in Shilluk, it forms part of a series of tales; only the part which coincides with the story in Skilluk is given here (translated from Leo Reinisch, Die Nuba-Sprache, Erster Teil, p. 232 ss). . . . The young man heaped up the eggs, squashed them, made a wind, and winnowed them, so that the wind blew away the egg-shells, and only the chickens were left. One of the chickens had a wound on its foot. They sent for the doctor, who said, "Take two ardeb of date-seeds, roast them and bind them on the wound, then it will heal. They did so. Now a date-tree grew out of the chicken's foot, it became large and bore fruit. When the fruit were ripe, a boy came and threw a stone at the tree; four fruit fell down. Thereupon the tree became angry, in its anger it fell down and formed an island. The owner of the island sowed sesamum on it; but afterwards he sowed melon-seeds. While they were still sowing, the melon-seds germinated and grew large. Then a

Turkish soldier came and asked the owner, "Give me one of the melons." The man replied, "They are not yet ripe." The soldier said, "If you don't give me one, I shall cut off your head." Then the man went, cut a melon and gave it to the soldier. This one took his knife and stabbed it into the melon; but the knife escaped into the belly of the melon. Then he drew his sword and stabbed into the melon, but the sword too escaped into the belly of the melon. The Turk became angry, pursued the owner of the melon, cut his head off and threw it away. The trunk of the man crept into the belly of the melon. But the head searched its trunk in vain. At last it went away into a barber's shop. Here he had his hair shaved. In the meantime the man (the trunk) crept out of the melon and went away. When he came to the barber's shop, he found his head, took it, placed it on his neck and went his way.]

81. The Camel and the Donkey.

Jal mẹkọ e ya da amalọ, gẹ kí adẹ̄rọ, gẹ ńi chọ̈k gẹ tyẹ̈tò̧ ki jam. De bogin ńi chámè gén, dẹ gẹ gwà̤lò̧ gwà̤lò̧. Ka amalọ ko: bụ́h! Kịne: adẹ̄rọ! Ka adẹ̄rọ yēi kịne: é! Kịne: wá chà ṭò̧! Kịne: àwọ́, wá chà ṭò̧. Amalọ ko: kẹń ụ fárị wá, yu (yịu) yēi! Ka adẹ̄rọ ko: àwọ́! yá yēi. Ka e ko: fār wọ!

Ka gẹ kẹdọ, gẹ chàṭò̧; ka gẹ wịṭa kẹch malạulạu; ká mùchò̧ lịṭé gén, ẹ yà di nam, di lũm gīr; ka gẹ ko: wa kẹ́dò̧ di? Ka adẹ̄rọ ko: kújà! Ka amalọ ko: wa ụ kwằńị! Ka adẹ̄rọ ko: wa kụ mát?³⁰ Kịne: ẹ́! Kịne: wa fa mut, gik amalọ. E ko: jwọk duọń! wa ụ wịṭi wọk. Ka gẹ kẹṭa nam, ka adẹ̄rọ kẹṭa bāńẹ, ka gẹ kwāńọ.

Ka gẹ wịṭi wọk, ka gẹ kẹṭa wọk; dẹ chuńe gén mẹdo; mucho bụ ḍàńẹ, ká gẹ chámò̧, ka gẹ ńi butọ. Ḍụki ka gẹ ńi chāmọ, ka ńi yụ̀dẹ̀ wóu, ka gẹ ńi bútò̧; kịnau chẹṭ ki chāńọ. Ka adẹ̄rọ chwēyọ, ka amalọ chwēyọ; dẹ ńzte gén fa tâdẹr; ka gẹ ńi māṭa gat ki pi; ka gẹ ńi bẹ̄ńọ.

Ka adẹ̄rọ kōbọ kịne: mát! Kịne: ẹ́! e ko: yi cha de gừgừ ki kẹch madọch; e ko: wija mûm; e ko: kẹń de búńị yịn, e ko: wá de ṭọ̀u, gik adẹ̄rọ. Amalọ ko: yi faṭe dẹ̈k? e ko: kwọp ńdjè yín? e ko: fa kúchì yin? gik amalọ. Ka gẹ bẹdọ chán àkyẹ̀lò̧; adẹ̄rọ ko: mátị! — kẹń chwọlé amalọ. Amalọ ko: ẹ̀! E ko: ya da ńwọl mótọṕọ́ ⁶⁰ ki wija, dẹ bẹṭ ẹdì? Amalọ ko: bụ́h! ńwọl motọnọ ⁶⁰ ga mọ̄ ńọ?⁶¹ Ká è kùdò̧. Ka gẹ ńeńọ, ká chịká kwóf kịne: mátị! Kịne: ẹ́! E ko: mọk ẹ́ni e ńwẹ̀ńọ́ ki wija. Kịne wịji chaka wịlọ! Kúchị yịn, kẹń mak wa, ka wá ńi pwôt kí lò̧ṭ? Dẹ yị chwẹ, dẹ da mó kọ́mí. Ka e ko: ará, yá kùt. Ka e kudọ. Ḍụki ka e ko: ya ḍálò̧ chám yi gik ẹ́ni, wịjâ ńwẹ̀ńò̧. Amalọ ko: bụ́h! Ko: yik chwaki ụ lịńè yàu yi tygń kg̣lé nam. E ko: á, wei ywọńa, gik adẹ̄rọ; ki ńwọl mótọṕọ́² yau! Ka amalọ ko: ẹ̀, ywọ́ńi! ya fẹt ki yí, ṭò̧ ụ bi kịfa wâ bẹ̄ńẹ, faṭe kịfa yá kẹ̈ṭà.

Camel and Donkey

Ka adẓrọ rẹ̄nọ, ká è kwoḍọ, ká é ywọ̀nọ̀ kí ywọk mágîr, ka ńi kwoḍọ; ká jè ma chậṭṭ ki yey yẹi, kine: adẓrọ ywọńẹ kẹ̇ti? Ka gẹ bia wọk, kine: muchọ yẹjẹ da jè.[62] *Ka gẹ yūbọ ki kẹle lūm, jē bogọn. Ka adẓrọ yôt, ka amalọ yôt, ka gẹ mak, ka ńi fwôṭt kí lòṭ, ka amalọ ko: yá ko kôp, yá ko: wa u yót; dẹ̀ ànànọ̀, yi kōbọ ádì? Adẓrọ kudọ. Ka gẹ kậl (kêl), ká gẹ́ máká kí wúnà yẹ̀i, yẹi fyéchà gẹ́n. Ka amalọ ka wune chôdậ, ka e rẹ̄nọ; ka tẓrọ rińọ bāńẹ, ka jē yọ̀mè ẹ́n. Ka adẓrọ dọ̄ńọ, gẹ ki bwoń, ka ńi gậchè lòṭ; yẹi fẓk, ka e tọ.*

Ḍyńi[62] *chinẽ ká àmàlọ̀ bia gạt bẹ mạṭ, ka adẓrọ yôdẹ, é tọ̀ ke yey pi; dẹ kúòdọ̀. Ka e ko: ḍwoṭi mâl! gik amalọ. Ko: ḍwoṭi, ywóni! Ọ́tyè̀nọ̀ yá kò: yi kú ywọ̀ni! yi kò: dā gin ńwẹ̀nọ̀ wiji; dẹ ḍwoṭ! Adẓrọ tọ̄. Ka amalọ kẹti bẹ̀ mạṭ ki pi, ka amalọ dọ̄ga kẹl ṭim.*

Somebody had a camel and also a donkey; they used to carry goods every day, but they got nothing to eat, so they were very thin. One day the camel said, "Dear me!" Again he said, "Donkey!" The donkey replied, "Eh?" The camel said, "We are going to die!" "So it is," replied the donkey, "we are going to die." The camel said, "Suppose we run away, would you consent?" The donkey replied, "Yes, I would consent." Then he said, "Let us flee!"

And they went travelling. They arrived in a very distant place; there they saw an island in the middle of a river. There was much grass. And they said, "How shall we get there?" The donkey confessed, "I do not know." But the camel said, "We will swim." The donkey asked, "Shall we not be drowned?" "No", said the camel, "we shall not be drowned;" talk of the camel.[64] He said again, "God is great! We shall arrive safely." They went into the river, the donkey went behind the camel. And they swam.

When they came to the bank, they got out of the water. They were very glad; there were no men on the island. They ate and then lay down; the next day they grazed again (the whole day), and when the night came, they lay down. Thus they did every day. The donkey and the camel became fat; their bellies became thick. They used to drink water in the river; and from there returned to grazing.

One day the donkey said to the camel, "Friend!" He replied, "Eh?" The donkey said, "You have indeed succeeded in bringing us into a good position; I am quite surprised; if it had not been for you, we should be dead now!" Such was the talk of the donkey. The camel replied, "Are you not a stupid fellow? Do you know anything? Are you not an ignorant one?" So said the camel. One day later the donkey continued, "Friend!" — So he used to call the camel. The camel replied, "Eh?" The donkey said, "I have some thoughts ("little seeds") in my head; how may it be with them?" "Dear me," replied, the camel, "what may be your thoughts!" Then the donkey was silent; and they went to sleep. But the next morning he began again, "Friend!" The camel said, "Eh?" The donkey said, "These things (thoughts) are still working in my head." "You begin to forget!" warned the camel; "do you not remember, when we were caught (every morning) and were always beaten with a club? But now you have become fat, you want to talk!" The donkey replied: "Well, I will be silent." And he remained silent. On the next morning he continued, "I cannot eat on account of this thing; my head is always wandering." The camel said, "Why, if you talk so loudly, the people who are travelling on the river will hear us." At last the donkey begged, "Let me bray just once; that is what is troubling me." Thus the talk of the donkey. The camel said, "Well, do bray! I am worn out by you. Death will come to all of us, not to me alone." And the donkey ran, snorting and braying exceedingly loud, and he snorted again. Some people who were travelling in a boat, heard him; they said, "Where does that donkey cry?" They went ashore saying, "There must be people on the island." They searched in the grass, but there were no people. At last they found the donkey and the camel. They seized them and beat them with clubs. The camel said, "Did I not tell you, saying: we shall be found? but now, what do you say?" The donkey was silent. They both were driven away and were bound with boat-ropes, in order to pull the boat. The rope of the camel broke, and he ran away. The people pursued him, but he outran them. So the donkey was left with the strangers. He was beaten with clubs; the boat was heavy, he died. Some days later the camel came to the river bank to drink; he found the donkey dead in the water; he was bloated. And he said, "Get up!" talk of the camel. He said again, "Get up and bray! formerly I told you, do not cry! But you said, something is ("working") in my head. Now get up!" But the donkey was dead. So the camel went to drink and then returned into the forest.[65]

---

[1] The animals, when acting like men, have in the English translations always been treated as persons.
[1a] In most of the texts the word "jwọk" is rendered by "God", where, however, it is used in rather a disrespectful sense, "jwọk" is kept in the translation.
[2] leṅ is "war", and "the army, host of war".
[3] tyal, more frequently tyẹl "foot".
[4] the future form of the verb, but without the future particle ʉ́.
[5] Very frequently the present tense is followed by the imperfect of the same verb, the first introducing the action rather as a state, the second showing the action as going on, as being in progress. "They go, when they were going below a tree. . .
[6] "he says" or "said" is: "e ko kıne"; but in fluent speech ko "to say" is often omitted and only "kıne" "thus" is said.
[7] vocative! see Grammar.
[8] chámı̣ was to be expected.

⁹ The "yin" lays stress on the subject: why are you so thin (while the hare is fat)?
¹⁰ *bŭh*, an expression used most frequently, cannot be well translated into English; it may mean any degree and shade of surprise, very often, as here, angry surprise.
¹¹ *Dụki* is not only "to-morrow", but simply "the next day".
¹² Instead of *"chwâch yị ến"*.
¹³ from *yi ụ*.
¹⁴ *kaţ*, more frequently *kęţ*, the stem for "go".
¹⁵ The hare wanted the hyena to believe that he, the hare, was being punished for his misdoings, and that the hyena, by coming near, might get a thrashing as well.
¹⁶ instead of *yi*.
¹⁷ in order that.
¹⁸ more frequently: *wiţọ* to arrive.
¹⁹ "beside" = since.
²⁰ vocative!
²¹ commonly: *kudọ*; here the *ọ* is long, as if to express the lengthened waiting for an answer — but all remained silent.
²² Is he, being great, not entitled to eat you?
²³ To prevent the monkey from secretly running away.
²⁴ Alluding to some old affair, for which he intended to take revenge now.
²⁵ Twice the hare escapes the threatened revenge of the hyena, and even injures him severely anew, taking advantage of the greadiness of the latter.
    The same story is told in Marno, Reisen im Gebiet des Blauen und Weißen Nil, under „Geschichten aus dem Sudan."
²⁶ the lion, his spear is still with me.
²⁷ *fa* and *faţ* are most frequently used in this way, to emphasize a sentence: is it not so? that is: it surely is so.
²⁸ vocative! the last vowel with high tone.
²⁹ "why remains my spear not cooked (forged) by you?"
³⁰ see Grammar.
³¹ "a saddle which is not": a saddle of somebody who is not present, somebody's saddle, I do not know whose.
³² vocative!
³³ instead of: *make yi ǹu*.
³⁴ one would expect: *yiepe wun*.
³⁵ one would expect: *yiepe gen*.
³⁶ "You are finished with your mark". "Whenever I meet you again, I shall recognize you and take revenge." This story of the lion and the fox is also told in Marno, l. c. The Hottentots have it likewise.
³⁷ He expected the fox to came too, and so to find an opportunity for finishing him.
³⁸ *yá-ki* . . . . an expression of assertion, the literal meaning is not clear; "I with my children?"
³⁹ from *lịdọ!*
⁴⁰ The fish-spear is a wizard, because "he sees the fish in the water"; he is thrown into the water at hap-hazard, and yet hits the fish.
⁴¹ In dancing the girl selects her companion, not the man.
⁴² The story seems to have some mythological relation.
⁴³ from *dyęk!*
⁴⁴ "and them (the contents) smeared he".
⁴⁵ goats are eaten they (by) whom?
⁴⁶ a curse; its literal meaning not clear.
⁴⁷ "the hare went, he (to) his place".
⁴⁸ "he was in difficulty with a place of his going out."
⁴⁹ and the ibis, and (he) was asked.
⁵⁰ In many cases like this the meaning of *cham* can hardly by rendered.
⁵¹ abstain from electing her! *ụ* is used here because the act of election lies in the future.
⁵² the people ask: "whom shall we elect?" (one among them exclaims), "elect the crow!"
⁵³ generally the *lwak*, the "cow house", is the place where strangers pass the night.

[54] Who that is, or why this designation is chosen, is not clear.
[55] "First let us eat, and then hold our palaver!"
[56] The frog is the friend of the rain.
[57] A number of stories are strung together under this head, most of them reflecting the political and dynastic life of the Shilluks with its intrigues and vicissitudes; some are told not without a certain grotesque humour.
[58] The mention of horse and camel in the beginning perhaps points to a foreign (Arab) origin of the story, or at least of the first part of it; though, of course, both horses and camels are not unknown to the Shilluks, as many of them have lived in contact with Arabs for a long time, in the north as well as in the west.
[59] The use of ky here is rather strange.
[60] more frequently: mat.
[61] $mok\ año$.
[62] "the island, its interior has people".
[63] from of $dyki$.
[64] This formula is often added after a verbal quotation.
[65] This story is evidently of Arabic origin.

XII. ADVENTURES BETWEEN MEN AND ANIMALS.

82. The Country of the Dogs.

Jě a kẹdọ bẹ dwar gá pyārọ, ka wiţa kùn à lḍu, ka dryàu é wáṅ. Ká gẹ́ máká chaṅ dryàu[1] wiţe gẹ́n á múm. Ká gẹ́ kẹti pach mẹko, ka gẹ ywoda mān kẹ́té gẹ́n.[2] Ka chwọu e bẹnọ pạl kị dọk, gẹ́nà gwôk, ka gẹ́ ṅi kẹti yẹţe kụ̄li, ka jal mẹkọ e pêchọ̀ kịne: chwọu ȧgọ̀ gẹn? Gẹ́ kudọ̀. Ka chịká fêchọ kịne: chwọu ȧgọ̀ gẹn? Ka gwok mẹkọ ka chuṅg é rẹ́ṅọ̀, ka pạ́rá kwọ̀mẹ. Ká gọ̀ ⁿȧ́gẹ́, ka ṅal ákyẹl e dọ̄ṅọ. Ká máká dwat (dwẹt) abich é bẹ̈dọ̀, a pyéch yi gwok: yi kụlá kûn? Ka e ko: yá kụlá fōţe Chọl; yá cháká wáṅọ̀. Ka wékè dọk gẹ́n ȧdẹ̣k, ka kẹl yi gwok kiţe kwọmẹ, ká gwòk é rẹ́ṅọ̀, ka wiţa bùtè fōţe Chọl, ka gwok e ko: fōţe Chọl á waṇ, à chínẹ̀; u[2] kẹdọ́ pach, ká yí wāch: yá yẹ́nà fōţe gwok, mān fá jẹ̀, chwọu fa gwôk; yí kị́ kùt, u kút, yi ţọ̄ (ţōu). Ka ṅȧl ẹ́ní è kudọ, ẹ fa kọ̄bọ; ká ẹ́ bọ̀kọ̀ kị wgr, ka ẹ́ lẹ̣kọ, gwok e bẹnọ, kịne: ṅal, yi re fa wāch? Kẹn ku wāch[4] ḍuki, yi ţọ̄! Ka ṅal duki mọl (mwọl) ka e wȧjọ̀, kịne: ka wáṅá ótyẹṇ, ya yẹ́nà fōţe gwòk kị́ mạ̣́dá bẹná, mān fa je, dẹ chwọu fa gwok, ka mạ̣́da nẹ́kì yi gwok, kefa jwanọ kị́ kwóp.

Some people went hunting; they were ten. And they arrived at a very distant place. Two of them lost their way, they walked for two days, then they became quite perplexed. They came to a certain village, where they found women only. After some time the men too came from the bush with the cattle, and they were dogs (the husbands of the women were dogs). They went into the enclosure (the homestead surrounded by an enclosure). And one of the men asked, "Where are the men (of your villages)?" They remained silent. He asked again, "Where are the men?" One of the dogs became angry[3] ("his heart turned bad"). He jumped on the back of the man and killed him. So only one man ("boy") was left. After five months ("he seized five months") he was asked by the dog, "Where did you come from?" He answered, "I came from the Shilluk country; I had lost my way." Then the dog gave him three cows, he was taken by the dog and put on his (the dog's) back, and the dog ran away with him. When they got near the Shilluk country, the dog said, "The Shilluk country is coming near; it is over there. Now when you reach home, tell (your people), 'I was in the country of the dogs, there the women are (real) people, but the men (males) are dogs.' Do not be silent! If you remain silent, you will die!" But the man ("boy") was silent, he did not tell (his story). And during the night he became afraid, he dreamed, the dog came and said, "Boy, why do you not

Remarks referring to XII. vide on page 222.

speak? If you do not speak to-morrow, you will die." And the next morning he spoke saying, "I was lost some time ago, and I lived with my friend in the country of the dogs; there the women are (real) people, but the men are dogs, and my friend was killed on account of his being hasty in speaking (on account of his indiscreet questioning, "Where are the men?" whereby he made the dog angry)."

83. Akwoch.

Jal mękǫ wątę fa abídęk. Ka ńal àkyęl dǭch. Ká fę̄rę̀ lɨ̀ńè yɨ̀ ńù, ká ńù màgǫ̀ kɨ́ bę́ŕ, ká ńù māgǫ kɨ́ lwaṅ, ká gę́ kìtę yéj ádàlǫ̀, ka bęi kitę yej ádàlǫ́. Ka e bęnǫ̀, ká é kò: yá ńèàwǫ̀! Kine: yí ńèàwǫ̀ ńǫ̀? Kine: ę́, ńɨ́ńę́ fà ńɨ́ kwôp. Ka ńɨ́ wēi kę̄dę́; ka bię yi jàl ę́ni, kine: yá ńèàwǫ̀! Kine: yí ńèàwǫ̀ ńǫ̀? Kine: ńɨ́ńę́ fà ńɨ́ kwôp. Ká è kò: lèdè ęn! Ka wēkę, ka dǫk ádàlǫ̀ yìębę́, ka bęi ríná wǭk, kine: wǭǒǒ; ka dǫk ádàl akyęlǫ, ká gǫ̀ yìębę́, ká lwáń ríná wǭk, kine: wǭǒǒ. Ká è kò: búh! bęr gá lwáṅ, gę́ kɨ́ bę́ŕ, e ko: yá fà kámá ńeau; — jal ęni fa rię —. Ká ńù kò: búh, fā dwǫk kęy gęn? Ka jal ęni ko: gę ywôdà gén kɨ́ kęń? Ká ńù kò: fa chǒl? E ko: chǒl kɨ̀ ón̂ǫ̀? Ńu ko: fa chǒl kɨ̀ dàn? Ka wąt bâṅ dwâi, ka chǒl, ka ńú[1] bàńǫ̀, ka ńa baṅ dwai, ka chǒl, ka ńù[2] bàńǫ̀. Ká jam bęn dwai, ká gę́ bàńǫ, ka wąt jal ęni chǒl, ká ńù bàńǫ. Ka rię e ko: yí dwátá ńǫ̀? ká è kò: yá dwátá Ákwǫ̀ch, — wąt jal ęni; ka jál ęni é ywǫńǫ̀. Ká ńù chuńę mędǫ kɨ́fà ńál ęní, ká gǫ̀ wēkɨ̀, ká gę́ kędǫ kɨ́ gòn. Ńu wądę bógòn, ka Akwǭch yigi wądę, ka ńu chuńę mędǫ.*

Ka ńu ńɨ́ kęta pąl, ka lại ńɨ́ mákè ęn, ka gę ńɨ́ kū̯lę́ pach. Ka mę̨ ńal ęní ka ńɨ́ tąl, ká gǫ̀ ńɨ́ wēkè, ka ńal ęni ńɨ́ chàm. Ka ńal ęni yiga machwê, ńu, chúńę̀ mędǫ. Ka gę ńɨ́ wę̄lò kɨ ńal ęni, ńɨ́ kędǫ fa (= pach) wątè ńu. Ká ńdjè yi ńù bęnę bęnę bęnę, dę chuńę gén mędǫ.

Ka chán àn chwǫlà dǭrǫ́; ye ko: màyó! Kine: é! Kine wēki yá dǭrǫ́! Kine: é gwōge ńǫ? Kine: u̯ nǫdà lōt̄. Ka wēkè, ka yat̲ maduǫń ńǫ̀tè ęn. Ka ńǫ̀tè ęn, ka e bęnǫ̀; ka dąn ęni ko: yi kęta kęń? Kine: ya kętę bę̨ ńǒt. Ńu ko: lǒtę́ rûm? Kine: nùtí. Ka duki è dǭgǫ̀ bę̨ ńǒt kɨ́ bùl. Ká gǫ̀ tyęń, ka e rûm, ká kū̯lę ęn, dę ńù chuńę mędǫ. Ká è ko: mâ, kòmí pyęń! Ka pyęn kū̯l, ká gǫ̀ kwō̄jɨ́ bùl, ka bùl é rûm, ka Akwǫch e kōbǫ kine: mâ! Kine: kęt chwǫl tyęń wún! Ńu kędǫ, ka kǫpę tyęń gęn, ka e ko: bùl a kwâch yi wądà, dę bi tęrǫ dukì! Ká è dǭgǫ̀, ka bùl kìtɨ yi chaṅ; bur máduǫń á kwǫń yi ńal ęni, ka yat̲ kìtɨ yéję́. Ka mach (may) kìtɨ yey yat̲, ka gǫ lę̄ńé yey bur, ka yęn é rụ̀pǫ̀ kɨ yey bur. Ká bùr rìk yi ńál ęní. Dę mach lyęlǫ kɨ pèń. Ká bùl gǒch, ká ńù e bęnǫ bęnę bęnę, ka ńɨ́ (yū̯) kine: ńǒl, yi fa dǫ̀ń? Kine: kɨ́fánǫ a dǭńá? yá fā ńǒl kɨ́ wáná. Kine: chwōr, yi fa dǫń? Kine: yá chwǫ̀rǫ̀ kɨ́ yìtâ? Kine: dę mìṅ, yi fa dǫń? à dé mę̀ṅ yàn, ya męn kɨ ńɨ́ńá? Tęrǫ bęnǫ bęnę, bu ńan a dǫ́ń kɨ pach.

Ka tęrǫ bię bę̨ bùl, ka ńal ęni yęta wiy yat̲, yat̲ máduǫń. Ka bùl fwôtè ęn, ká

tèrọ̀ biẹ bẹ chón, ka ṅu e chọ̄ṅọ. Ká ṅi dẹ̣má yèy bùr, ka gẹ ṭum ki faṭẹ yey bur.
Ka ḍạṇ ẹni dọ̄ṇọ. Ká kẹ́lè chán dẹ̣má yèy bùr. Ka ṇ̄ọt è dọ̄ṇọ̀. Ka ṅal ẹni bia wọk
ki wiy yaṭ, ka ṇ̄ọt ṇi ehọr yey bur. Ka ṅu ṭō bẹne. Ka e kẹḍọ, bāṅ nù mákè yi ṅal
ẹni ki ḍọ (ḍọk) ṅu; ká ḍẹ̣ṇ a bụ tūṅ ká ṅi nẹ̣k, ká ḍẹ̣ṇ a tuṅẹ nut, ṇi kẹ́lè ẹ́n. Ka
wạt baṅ mẹn a yiebẹ nut, ka ṅi nẹ́kè ẹ́n, ka wạt baṅ yiebẹ bogọn, ṅi wẹ̄l ẹ́n. Ká
gẹ́ ṭûm, ka gọ dọ̄ṅọ́ ṅù ákyẹ̀l. Ka e rẹṇọ, rẹ́ṇọ́ wák. Ka gẹ ᵏeḍọ ki jámẹ́ ke ḍọ.ṇẹ,
ka kẹṭi fōṭẹ gẹn, ká è gẹ̀rọ̀ kí fàrẹ̣ ki wāi.

Wẹn e ko: ẹ ú jàl kẹ́ṅ?° a ḍọkẹ gir kí bāṅi gir! Kuche wiyẹ, dẹ́ ẹ́n, wiyẹ ṅádjẹ.°
Ká gẹ́ bẹ̣ḍọ̀, ka peṅ ẹ yigi kẹch, ka wẹn byẹl bogọn ki yẹ, ka ṅal ẹni byẹl nūté yẹ,
ka némẹn ṅi bẹ̣n, ká è kò: ṇi ṭōṭẹ ow ak, ka gẹ ṅi ṭōṭẹ ki byẹl. Ka kẹṭẹ yi wẹn, e
ko: wụ́ ṭōṭẹ byẹ́l. Wẹn e ko: yi mẹn? Kịne: yi jal e kune chiṅé. Ka ḍykị wọné
kẹḍọ, kẹḍọ yi ṅal ẹni, ka gẹ ṭōṭẹ byẹ́l, ka ṅal ẹni ko: wiyẹ wúṅ nút? Kịne ệ nút;
kine ka kôf ùn kine: jal e wẹ̣̄lọ̀ yi chwọ̣lẹ́, ka wọne bẹ̣ṇọ, ka wiyẹ gẹn kôfẹ̀ gẹ́n, ka
wiyẹ gẹ́n ye bẹ̣ṇọ, ka bia yi wáṅẹ̣ chànọ̀. Ka ṅdl ẹni ko: yí rè bẹ̣ḍọ̀ wāṅi chāṅọ?
Kịne: wāṅa chán yika kạl wọ̀ḍà yị̀ ṅu. Kịne: de wạdi kẹṅ ywòdí, ú ṅájè yíṅ?
Kịne: nệ̂! Kịne: wạdi ṅiṅe mẹn? Ka jal ẹni ko: ṅiṅẹ Akwọch. Ká è ko: Akwọṅ
ṅdjè yiṅ? ṅal ẹni ko: faṭẹ yan Akwọch? Ka mákè yi wiyẹ, ka wiyẹ ywọṅọ, ká è
kạṅọ̀ kí ṅùwạ̣́t, ka wijẹ lyẹl, ka ṭōṭẹ ki lāṅọ kwach. Ka ṭōṭẹ ḍọ̀k, ka wiyẹ dọ̄ga
fārẹ. E ko: biẹ kẹḍẹ kach ákyẹ̀l. E ko: ệ, ya y bẹ̣ḍọ kẹn. Ká gẹ́ bẹ̣ḍọ̀, ṅal ẹni ya
fārẹ, ká gẹ́ ṅi wẹ̄lọ ki reyi gẹn.

A certain man had three sons. One child was pretty, and his fame reached
the lion. So the lion caught flies, and he caught mosquitoes too, he put them
into a gourd and came saying, "I am selling!" The people asked, "What
do you sell?" He answered, "Its name is not to be told." So they let him go.
He came to this man (the man the story treats of) and said, "I am selling." He
asked, "What do you sell?" The lion replied, "Its name is not to be told."
And he said, "Look at it!" He gave him the gourd, and he opened it; the
mosquitoes flew out with a loud buzzing; he opened the other gourd too, and
the flies flew out with a loud buzzing. The man said, "Why, they are but flies
and mosquitoes! I do not want to buy them." — This man was a king. The
lion said, "Why, will you not (put them back in) their place?" The man
replied, "Where should I find them?" The lion said, "Then will you not make
compensation?" The man asked, "What shall I give for compensation?" The
lion answered, "A man." So a slave was brought (and was offered) as compensation. But the lion refused him. Then a slave woman was brought and offered
as compensation, but the lion refused her too. He brought all his goods, but
they all were refused. (At last) a son of the man was brought, but the lion
refused him. The man said, "What then do you want?" He replied, "I want
Akwoch;" — he was the son of this man (Akwoch is the name of the pretty

boy whose fame had reached the lion). And this man wept. But the lion was glad because of this boy. He gave him the boy, and he went away with him. The lion had no child, and Akwoch became his child. The lion was very glad.

The lion used to go into the bush, to hunt game; and he used to bring it home. The portion of the boy he used to cook, and then give it to him. The boy used to eat it, and he became fat; the lion was much pleased. And they (the other people i. e. the other lions) used to walk with the boy and used to go into the village of the son of the lion (i. e. the village where the lion and his "son" lived). So all the lions knew him, and they all were much pleased.

One day the boy asked for an ax; he said, "Mother!"[10] She said, "Eh?" The boy said, "Give me an ax!" She asked, "What for?" He said, "I will cut a club." She gave it to him; and he cut a large tree. When he had cut it, he came. (The next day) this woman asked him, "Where are you going?" He replied, "I am going to cut." The lion asked, "Is the club finished?" He answered, "Not yet." The next day he went again to cut a drum. He carved it; and when it was finished, he brought it; but the lion was much pleased. And he (the boy) said, "Mother, bring me a skin (to fasten on the drum)." And a skin was brought, and he stretched it on the drum. When the drum was finished, he said, "Mother!" he said again: "Go and call your people" (i. e. the people of all the villages around, belonging to the lion's family). The lion went, and he told all his people, "A drum has been made by my son, now all people shall come to-morrow." Then he returned.

The drum was placed in the sun (to dry). Then a big hole was dug by the boy, and he put a tree into it; he put a fire into the (hollow) tree and threw the tree into the hole. The tree caught fire in the hole. The hole was covered by the boy, but the fire was burning in the ground. Then the drum was beaten, and all the lions came; and the people said, "Cripple, will you not stay at home?" The cripple replied, "Why should I stay at home? My eyes are not crippled!" Then they said to the blind one, "Will you not stay at home?" He replied, "Are my ears blind?" They asked the deaf one, "Will you not stay at home?" He replied, "Though I am deaf, My eyes are not deaf."[11] So all people came, there was no one left at home. The people came for the drum. Then this boy climbed upon a tree, a big tree, and he beat the drum. The people (= the lions) came to dance, and the lions danced. And (while dancing and not heeding the hole) they fell into the hole; they all fell into the hole. And this man (viz. the lion who was the boy's father, or his wife) was left; and he too was fetched and fell into the hole. Then the cripples[12] were left, and the boy came down from the tree and pushed them into the hole. So all the lions died (were burned in the hole).

Then the boy caught the slaves of the lion and his cattle. The cattle without horns he killed, and the cattle which had horns, he took with him. And the slaves which had tails, he killed, but the slaves, which had no tails, he let go.¹³ When he had finished them all, there was one lion left; that one ran into the bush. Then he went away with all his goods and his cattle, and he went into his native village, there he built his home in a place by itself.

The father (= his father, who at the same time is the father of the children whom he addresses) said, "To whom does this man belong? he has so many cattle, and so many slaves!" His father did not know him, but he (the stranger) knew his father. They remained some time, then it came to pass that a famine came, and the father had no more dura with him, but this boy (the stranger) still had dura. And his brothers (who did not know him) used to come to him, and he used to say (to his servants), "Give these boys dura." And dura was given to them. Then they returned to their father, saying, "We were given dura." He asked, "By whom?" They said, "By the man who is over there." On some other day these boys went again to this man, and they received dura. And the man asked, "Is your father still alive?" They said, "Yes, he is alive." Then he said, "Tell him, 'the stranger ("traveller") calls you'." The boys came. and told their father; and their father came, he came with a sorrowful face. The man (stranger) asked him, "Why is your face so sorrowful?" He said, "My eye is so sorrowful because my son has been carried away by a lion." The man replied, "If you met your son now, would you know him?" He said, "Yes." The man asked, "What is the name of your son?" He answered, "His name is Akwoch." Then he asked, "Would you know Akwoch now?" He said, "Yes, I would know him." The man replied, "No, you would not know him." Then he said again, "Am I not Akwoch?" And his father seized (embraced) him, and his father wept. And he brought a razor and shaved his head, and he gave him a leopard skin;¹⁴ and he gave him cows. Then his father returned to his village. And he said, "Come, let us go (= live) in one place." But he replied, "No, I will stay here. And they remained, the boy in his village, and the father in his village, and they used to visit each other.¹⁵

84. The Girl and the Dog.

Ñane ḍâchǫ fá bwǫch, ka kẹta fạl, e ywódá gwok; ká é kò kịne: yina jwǫk! e ko: ţōţi yán ke ñara! u nwǫmi gwok. Ka ţōţe ñarẹ yi jwǫk, ka ñarẹ é dḥnǫ̀. Ka ñârẹ kẹ́tá fạl, ka gwok ywodẹ́, gwok bẹ́dá ñabǫ́ñ. Ká gwók è ko: kẹ́ţi yi mảyí, gwok e ko, ye ḍâṇ u wẹ̀kẹ̀ yán ko-wẹ́ṇ? Ka ñan ṭẹṇ e bẹ̀ṇǫ̀, ko: māyǫ́! Ka mẹn yēyǫ. Ko: yá ywóta gwok fạl, dẹ gwók è ko ne: kẹ́ṭi māyi, kòpí kịne: gwok e ko:

dāṇ u wêkè yán ko-wẹ́n? Ká máyẹ́ ywọ̀n, ka kōpa wíyẹ̀; ka wiye e ko: kẹl muy (muj) gwok! Ka ńān ṭẹṇ kẹl muy gwok.

Ka gwok e yót, ẹ́ budọ̀. Ka ńān ṭẹṇ wêke. Ka gẹ ḍuodọ, ka gwok é kẹ̣dọ̀ ki ńāu ṭẹṇ, ka gẹ kẹḍọ ki gwok, ka gẹ kẹṭa féń; gwok bẹ̀dá jwọk, ka kẹṭa wọṭ gwok, yaṭ gīr bẹ̀nẹ̀, ka gwok e ko: ńí chám kí re yan, ka yi ńi kẹṭe gọl! Ka gọl ye ko: kẹṭi yejẹ! E ko: báń àgàk. Ka gwóń ẹní é kẹ̣ḍọ̀, ka ńān ẹni e ḍọ̄ṇọ. Ka ńān ẹni kẹṭa gọl gwok, gọl duọń, wọn ẹni wọṭ jwọk.

Ka ńān ẹni reña mal, ka e pạ̄rọ, ka peń e pyẹ̣dọ̀. Ka ńàn ẹní bia wọk, kẹṭi é rtńọ̀. Ka gwok e liṭọ, gwok e bẹ̣ṇọ é rtńọ̀; ńān ẹni reña wọṭ ki nam, wọṭ ma yeña nàm, wọṭ maduọń. Ka gwok e bẹṇọ, ka é bẹ̣̀dọ̀ ki tyẹle wọṭ. Ka tyẹń wọṇ ẹni gẹn abíryàu, ga yọgọ chwọgu, ḍācho bogọn ki kẹle gẹn. Gẹn ńi chama lại, ńi kẹṭi bẹ dwar.

Ḍān ẹni á fáńẹ́ wọṭ, ka jọk ẹni (ọni) e bẹṇọ, ká gẹ́ kọ̀: amẹn a ṭāl gin cham? Ka gẹ ńâńọ̀, ka gẹ kẹṭa bẹ yáf kị wọṭ, ka ńān ẹní ywót, chuńe gẹ́n mẹ̀dọ̀, e ko: yi yig namēi wọn. Ka gẹ bẹ̀dọ, ka ńān ẹni ko: yá chẹ̣́tè yi gwok. Ka gê kọ̀: ágọn ên? Kine: ya péń ṭa wọṭ, ka gẹ līṭá péń, ka gwok līṭẹ̀ gẹ́n, ka gwok gọ́ch ki toch. Ka gwok e ṭọu, ka wẹṭe fạ̄l.

Ka maka wun ga ábí ryàu, ka ńān ẹni ko: yá dwdtá kẹdọ bẹ lĩṭẹ chù gwok. Ḍań ẹni ko: bẹt, yi kú kẹṭ; ńan ẹni ko: yá kẹdọ! Ka gẹ kẹdọ, ka ńān ẹní é yạbọ, ká nẹ̀kè chọ̀gó ki tyẹle, ka ńān ẹni ṭọ̄. Ka ńań é ywọ̀ń, ka ńān ẹni kwáń yi gẹ́n kĩṭe nam; ńān ẹni kẹ́l yi nam. Ka wtṭé f òṭe gẹ́n, ka ywote jọ̄ (= jōg) chyẹk. Ka ńān ẹni kạl wọk, ka rĩṭ kópè, ka rĩṭ é kànọ̀ ḍáchọ̀ maduọń, ka ńān ẹni lwọk ki pi, ka chọ̄gọ yót yi ḍāṇ ẹní, ka kậl wọ̀k, ka ńān ẹni dwọṭa mal, é chàrọ̀; ka rĩṭ kópè: ḍāṇ a chêr! Ka rĩṭ e bẹṇọ, ka pyech yi rĩṭ, e ko: yi kậla kẹ́ń? Kine ya kạ̄la wọṭ ma yẹ́ńà nàm. Ka e ko: yi dwái yi ánọ̀? E ko: yá wékè gwọ̀k yi wiya, dẹ gwok é chńṭí yán, ya kẹ́ṭà wọṭ ki nam. Ka rāṇ ẹni ká é ywọ̀ń: ńàrẹ̀! Ka mẹn e bẹṇọ, ká é ywọ̀ń, ka ḍọk kại, ḍọk gẹ̀dè; ka kẹṭe wọṭ. Chōṭẹ, á ṭùm.

A woman was without child. She went into the bush and found a dog. She said, "O jwọk! give me a ("my") child! (If you give me one) it shall marry the dog." And a child was given to her by jwọk, and the her child grew up. And the child went into the bush; it found the dog; — this dog was a white one. The dog said, "Go to your mother and tell her, the dog says, 'When will the woman be given to me?'" The little girl came saying, "Mother!" The mother answered. The girl said, "I found the dog in the bush, and he said thus, 'Go to your mother and say to her thus, the dog says: when will the woman be given to me?'" Her mother wept; she told the (girl's) father; the father said, "Bring her to the dog." They found the dog lying. The girl was given to him.

And they (the dog and the girl) rose up, the dog went with the girl, they went into the ground; — the dog was jwǫk; they went into the house of the dog; there were many trees there everywhere. And the dog said, "You shall always eat with me; and you shall go into this enclosure." The people of the enclosure said to the girl, "Go to the center." The dog said to the girl, "These are slaves." Then the dog went away, the girl was left. So the girl had gone into the enclosure of the dog, a big enclosure; this house was the house of jwǫk.

One day the girl ran up, she jumped up, and the ground split. The girl came out; she went away running. The dog saw her, he came running; the girl ran into a house in the river, this house was (in?) the river; it was a big house. And the dog came; he remained at the foot of the house (below the threshold). The people of this house were seven; they were males, there was no woman among them. They lived on meat, they used to go hunting.

The girl hid herself in the house; and the people came (home and found their food cooked), they said, "Who has cooked the food?" They were astonished. They went searching the house; the girl was found, they were very glad. They said, "You have become our sister." So they remained. The girl told them, "I am chased by a dog." They said, "Where is he?" She said, "He is in the ground below the house." They looked into the ground and found the dog. They shot him with a gun. The dog died, and they threw him into the bush.

And seven years passed, then the girl said: "I want to go and see the bones of the dog." The boys (i. e. the men in whose house she lived) said, "Stay, do not go!" The girl said, "I will go!" And they (all) went; the girl searched, and she was hurt at her foot by a bone; the girl died. The boys wept. Then the girl was taken by them and put into the river; she was carried away by the river and came to her native country. There fishermen found her; they pulled her out of the water and told the king (what had happened). The king brought an old woman, she washed the girl with water; and the bone was found (in the body of the dead girl) by the woman. She pulled it (the bone) out, and then the girl rose up, she sneezed (became alive again). The king was told, "The girl has sneezed." The king came, he asked the girl, "Where do you come from?" The girl said, "I come from the house which is in the river." The king asked, "What brought you there?" She answered, "I was given away to a dog by my father; but the dog chased me, so I went into the house in the river." And the king wept, She was his daughter! Her mother too came, and she wept. Then cows were brought, they were sacrificed. They went home. — That is all, it is finished.

85. Anyimo and the Lion.

Ńan ńinę Ańimǫ e dǫ̂ch, kị ómęn Akwǫt, ki wiyę́; maye gęn bogǫn. Dǫ (dǫk) gę́n gir, dyęge gęn gir. Ká ńù e lińǫ, ká ńù e yigi d̨ān̨, ka ńu bę̄nǫ, ka bia yi ńal ęni, ka ryêch, ka kịți wǫt. Ka Ańimǫ kófí ómęn kịne: ţôţí ki ſik luōgǫ chińị́! Ka ńan ęni lịțe yi ńu, ká ńù chúńị mędǫ̀. Ka ńu ńachǫ kịne: yů kędǫ! Ka țôțè kị byę́l, ka ńal ęni ko: Ańimǫ, luǫk mâd̨â! Kịne: u wiți kā chińê, ka yi dúǫk! Ka gę kędǫ. Ka omia Ańimǫ e dǭnǫ bę̄ twar ki węr. Ka ńal ęni (ńu) kędǫ, gę chāți ki Ańimǫ. Ka ńal ęni ko: Ańimǫ, a kęń āńǫ ęn? Kịne: kęń ńi kwai ki rǭch. Ka gę kęți, gę chāțǫ. Ka țim maduǫń yót, ka ńu ko: a kęń āńǫ ęn? Kịne: kęń ńi kwai ki dǫk. Ka gę kędǫ gę chāțǫ, kędǫ kęń malaulau, kịne: a kęń āńǫ ęn? Ańimǫ ko: kęń ęni kúchè yán. Kịne: buh! ęna fańǫ a fyęń yan?

Ka gę wiți (woțí) būte tugǫ, tugǫ mâbâr; ka ńu ręńǫ, e ręńa kęle lûm, ka Ańimǫ ko ne: tuńǫ¹⁶ kwai d̨ān̨, bùtí ki féń, ya yęța wiji! Ka tugǫ bùtǫ̀, ka kęța wiy tugǫ. Ka e ko: tuń kwai d̨ān̨, kịne: d̨wóțí mál. Ka tugǫ d̨woța mal. Ka ńu bę̄nǫ, e rińǫ, ka Ańimǫ yôtè yi ęń, e tôk. Ka ńu ńùńǫ̀, ka e ko: Ańimǫ e kęța kęń? Ka yōmǫ ńwȯdchè ę́n; ka lịd̨â mál, ká gǫ̀ lịd̨ì mal; e ko: póe! yi fa țou tín? e ko: yi nùgà nùgǫ̀! ńan ęni ko: dę ęrę (dęrę)? Ká ńu gǫ̂dǫ̀ ki féń; ka tugǫ ka ńi bęńị́ a kama fûd̨ǫ̀. Ka Ańimǫ ko kịne: tuń kwai d̨ān̨, yí ku fât! Dǫk kęji! Ka tugǫ ńi dǫ̀gi kęję, ka ńu ńi gǫ̂dǫ̀ kęțę.

Ka dǫk lịțè yi ńan ęni, ka e ko: ńiwȯd kị ńimia, yana Ańimǫ, a chámì yi ńù ęn. Ka yań ęni é lịńǫ̀, a kęța pach. Ká gę́ kò: ńan mękǫ é chwǫ̀țǫ̀, kịne: yana chámì ńù ęn. Ka gę ko: ȧ, wú chágà tȯdǫ̀. Ka ńań dǭnǫ wûr, ka gę bę̄nǫ, gę kwai ki d̨ǫk, ka gę lēțę yi ńān ęni; kịne: ńewȯd kị́ ńimìâ, yana chám yi ńù ęn! Ka gę bia pach, ka Akwǫt kófe kịne: ńan mękǫ e kōbi kịne: yana Ańimǫ, â chám yi ńu ęn, dę pęr ki Ańimǫ. Ka leń tịń, ka tę̄rǫ bęnǫ. Ańimǫ kama ț̨ǫ̀ yi rȯd̨ǫ̀. Ka léń lịțè ęń, ká è ko: ńiwȯd kị ńimia, yana chám yi ńu ęn! Ka tę̄rǫ bęnǫ gę rińǫ̀; ka yót ńù ę́ yà féń, ę́ gǫ̂dǫ̀; leń fa nęnè ęń, ka kêl, ka ńu rińǫ wǫk; ka ńi kêl, ka ńu ęni fûd̨ǫ̀, ká è țǫ̀. Ka ńān ęni ko: tuń kwai d̨ān̨, buti, ya bia wǫk! Ka é bùtǫ̀, ka bia wǫk. Ka wiyę é kȧnǫ́ d̨ǫk, d̨ǫk dńwèn, mǫk chwǫ̂p kị ța tugǫ; ká chȧk kâl kị gin cham kị pi, ka d̨ǫk chwǫ̂p kị ța tugǫ. Ka Ańimǫ țôțę yi pi, ka e è mâd̨ǫ̀; ka țôțę yi mǫgǫ, ká è chȧmǫ. Węn chuńę mędǫ ki ómęn. Ka kâl pach; ka ńwǫm ka d̨ǫk kôl pyar-ȧnwèn, wiyę chuńę mędǫ.

There was a girl, her name was Ańimǫ; she was pretty; she lived with her brother Akwǫt, and her father; her mother was no longer alive. They had many cows and many sheep. The lion heard of her, and the lion turned himself into a man; he came to this boy (Akwǫt). He was received as their guest. When he came into the house, Ańimǫ was asked by her brother, "Give me water to wash his hands." So the lion saw the girl; she pleased him very much. After some time he took leave, saying, "I am going." They gave him dura, and the boy told his sister, "Accompany my friend a little way, when you have come to that place there, then return." So they went. The brother of Aṅimọ remained at home, he was sweeping the cow-dung. The boy (viz. the *lion*) went away with Aṅimọ. While they were walking, the lion asked, "Aṅimọ, what place is this?" She answered, "It is a place for herding the calves of the people of Akwọt." They went on and came into a great forest. Again the lion asked, "What place is this?" She answered, "A place for herding cattle." They went on walking and came to a very distant place. The lion asked, "What place is this?" She said, "I do not know this place; dear me, why are you always asking me?" They came to a deleib-palm, a very tall one. The lion ran away, he ran into the grass. Then Aṅimọ said, "Thou palm of the grandfather of men, lie down, that I may climb upon thu." The palm lay down, she climbed on it, and then said, "Palm of the grandfather of men, rise up!" The deleib-palm rose up. When the lion came running, he found that Aṅimọ was no more there. He was perplexed and said, "Were has Aṅimọ gone?" But her smell came into his nose, he looked up and saw her up in the tree. He said, "Póe! you will surely die in a moment!" Again he said, "I will kill you at once!" The girl asked, "Well, how?" The lion scratched the ground (round the deleib-palm), and the palm was beginning to fall down. Then the girl cried, "Palm of the grandfather of men, do not fall! return to thy place!" And the palm returned to its place. The lion began scratching again.

And the girl saw cows, and she cried, "My brother and my father, I am Aṅimọ, the lion is going to eat me!" The men heard it, they went home saying, "There is a girl crying, 'A lion is going to eat me.'" But the people said, "Nonsense, you are telling stories." Then the old men were sent for, they came herding their cattle (they drove their cattle near the place where the cry sounded); they were seen by the girl, and she cried again, "My father and my brother, I am going to be eaten by the lion!" They went home and told Akwọt, "There is a girl crying, 'I am Aṅimọ, the lion is going to eat me.' Her voice was like that of Aṅimọ." So an armed body was gathered, and they went. Aṅimọ was almost dying with thirst. When she saw the people, she cried, "My father and my brother, the lion is going to eat me!" The people came running; they found the lion scratching the ground; he did not see the people; he was stabbed; he ran away, but he was stabbed again, fell down and died. The girl said, "Palm of the grandfather of men, lie down, that I may get out." The tree lay down, and she came out. And her father brought four cows, they all were to be speared under the deleib-palm (as a sacrifice). And milk, food and water were brought, and the cows were speared under the deleib-palm. They gave *Aṅimọ* water to drink, they gave her milk too to drink; then they gave her food to eat. Her father and brother were very glad. She was brought home. She was married for forty cows,[17] so her father was much pleased.

86. An Adventure in the Forest.

E jal ęn ye kętį yey ṭim, bę̄ gwęn ki lâṅ, ka aṭẹp aryau ká gi pùṅè, ka lwọl ka gọ pùṅ. Ka lyẹch e bēnọ, ka ḍwoṭi yey ṭẹp, ká gù kọ̀ṅí chwāke, ka ḍwoṭi rię ṭẹm akyēlọ, ka gọ kọṅí chwāke; ka ṅwọle ṅiṅ aryau ka gẹ dōṅọ ki ṭa lwọl, ka lwọl dwọ gọ féṅ, ka ṅwọl ṅiṅ gni é ywòṅọ̀ ki yey lwọl, kine: kọ́r, kọ́r, kọ́r, kọ́r. Ka jal é líṭọ̀, ka lyẹch lēṭè ẹn, ka e búọ̀gọ̀, ka e rę̄nọ, ka ṅi pāra kwọm yaṭ, ka ṅi fyęt yi kwōṭ; kúchè ẹn, á bwọk ki mẹn duọṅ, ka ṅi kẹ́lè kẹle kwōṭ, ka lāṅg ṅí fyęt yi kwōṭ.

Ka wapa pach maduọṅ, ka ḍacho máduọṅ, máyù, ká gù yŏdẹ̋ (ywŏdẹ̋); ka e ko: wâṅộ, ṭōṭi ya fi! Kine: yi bia kęṅ? Kine: ḗ, yd kú fyẹch, ṭōṭi yan ki fi mọ̄té! Ka ṭōṭẹ fi mọ̄té. Ka ūḍí yi gwok, gwok māṅŏdẹ́; ka e ko: mā! Kine: wat bẹ̋n á ṅwọl? Ka gwok ūḍí yiẹ, ka gwok é ṅârọ̀; ka e ko: byh! Kine: fārá? Kine: ụ gọ̄ché ydṅ, yik yin fa káchè ydṅ! Ka ḍān duọṅ e ko: búh! wâdà, yi bia kęṅ? Kine: kút, mâ, yú chyęṭi[18] lyẹch, lyẹch maduọṅ; fúkẹ́ pẹr ki māné àgàk. Ka ḍachọ ko: bói! yi bia kęṅ a bẹ̄dí yi pẹr ki wuo! Ka e ko: wuọ ṅâjè ydṅ; faṭ ki gna, atēṅg da yẹṭ? Ka e ko: ḗ, kę́ṭ!

Ka e kę́ḍọ̀. Ka gẹ rúọmọ̀ pạr; ka par e rę́ṅọ̀, ka e rę́ṅọ̀, ka fẹṭi yi kuojọ, chwọle gn gna nam; ka é kwâṅọ̀ ki yey kúdjọ̀. Ka ṭēro bę̄nọ, ka māk; ka kậl pàch, ka fyẹwọ e fúḍọ̀ ki yey wârọ̀, ká è ṭō.

A certain man went into a forest to gather Nabag-fruits. He filled two bags and one gourd. (While he was gathering the fruit) an elephant came, he lifted up one bag and put it into his mouth, then he lifted up the other bag and put it also into his mouth; at last the contents of the gourd as well. But two seeds were left in the gourd; they kept rattling, *kọr kọr kọr kọr.* When the man heard this, he looked up and saw the elephant. He was frightened and ran away, he jumped upon a tree. The thorns of the tree pricked him, but he did not heed it on account of his great fear. He got right into the thorns, his cloth was torn by the thorns. Suddenly he came near a great house. There he met a big old woman; he addressed her, "My mother, give me water!" She asked, "Where do you come from?" He replied, "No, do not ask me, give me water first!" So she gave him water first. Then he was seen by a dog, a dog with young ones. (He saw the young dogs, but not the old one, the mother). He asked the woman, "Are they all your children?" Then he saw the old dog, he was growling. He exclaimed, "Oh dear! shall I run away?" The dog replied, "If you beat me, I shall bite you." After that the big woman asked, "Why, my son, where do you come from?" He answered, "Be silent, I am chased by an elephant, a big elephant. This pot is quite as large as his testicles."[19] The woman replied, "Well, you do come just from the same place where my father has come from." The man said, "I know your father; is he not the one who has a neck on his necklace?"[19] The woman said, "Now, go on!"

He went away and met with a hippopotamus. The hippo was running (towards him), so he too ran, he came to a place with white sand, thinking it was a river. He tried to swim in the sand. Then people came, they seized him and brought him home. But in the night his heart beat so violently (from excitement), that he died.

87. The Boy and the Hyena.

Ńal mḙkọ gḙ ki ówḙn gḙ wḙlọ̀; ka wọu é yúdọ̀. Ka ńál àkyḙlọ̀ e ko: bụh! e ko: mach ụ yŏtè kḙ́ṅ? Ka ówḙn e ko: kújà! Ka ńal ḙni ko: ya fa yḙ́fí (yáfí) mâch? Kine: ụ yâṅọ̀? gi [20] ńál àkyḙlọ̀. Kine: yi fa dọṅ ki būte jam? Kine: búh! ụ châmè yán yì ótwọ̄ṅ! Kine: ê, yi fa châm yi ótwọ̄ṅ. Kine: yá bḙ̀dọ̀. Ka ńal ḙni ko: dḙ yi re fa kḙ̣t bē yaf ki mach? Ká è kò: ụ châmè yán yi ótwọ̄ṅ. Ka kwọf ḙni wèi. Ka e ko: dḙ wâ bútḙ́! E ko: ê, ụ châmè yán yi ótwọ̄ṅ; ka ńal ḙni ko: ḙrḙ, buti ki fèṅ; ya buta ki kwọ̀mì. Ka e ko: dḙ ụ tằyí fèṅ yi ótwọ̄ṅ, ki ya châmè ḙ́ṅ! Ka e ko: ḙrḙ, bi, buti mál ki kwọmá, ụ kwáṅ yán yi ótwọ̄ṅ, ka yí wèi yì ḙ́ṅ. Ka ńal ḙni ko: á! yí gwǫ́k ḙdì? Yè kùdọ̀. Kine: dḙ yí fá kḙ́tḙ́ mâl? Kine: wiy yâṭ? Kine: àwǫ́. Ka yḙta mal. Ka ńal ḙni à tḙ̀k, ká èbúdǫ́ ki fèṅ.

Ka ótwọ̄ṅ e bēṅọ bḙ̄ṅe bḙ̄ne bḙ̄nè; ka otwoṅ e chàtọ̀ ki ṭa yaṭ. Ńál à tḙ̀k e nḙ̀nọ̀, ka ṅi ṅwàch yi otwoṅ, ḙ nḙ́nọ̀. Ńál à màl nḙ̀na fèṅ chḙ̀ṭ, dḙ bọ̄kọ bọ̄kọ; ká é dḙ̀mọ́ ṅàl yi wằrọ̀, dḙ̀mọ́ kwọm ótwọ̄ṅ, ka ótwọ̄ṅ mákè ḙ́ṅ ki yiṭḙ́, ká è kò: bói! yá kó kôp kine: yu (yiu) mákè yán! Ka ótwọ̄ṅ é ywòṅọ̀; ka otwoṅ ṅi kuodọ, ka ṅi dyabọ. Ka otwoṅ e rḙṅọ bḙ̀nè, ka kḙta kḙch malaulau, ka otwoṅ e tọ̄ ki yey wằrọ; ńal ḙni bḙ̄dō kí kwọ̀mè, ka ṅi ko: bói, yá kó kôp kine: yiu mákè yán! É kôbì kḙ̀tḙ́.

Dụki mwọl ka owen dwọta mal, ka lidá mâl, ńal ḙni tộk! Ka e ywọṅọ, kine: ówà châm yi otwoṅ! Ka e dúọdọ̀, ká é chàtọ̀ yej otwoṅ, otwoṅ chḙtḙ gìr, ka e kḙta kḙṅ malaulau, ka ńal ḙni yŏtḙ ḙ́ṅ, ḙ kôbì kḙ̀tḙ́. Dḙ bḙdọ kwọm otwoṅ, dḙ mḙ̣ti yiṭḙ otwoṅ, otwoṅ tọ̄ ki yey wằrọ̀. Ka ówḙn è kò kine: dwột! Kine: ê wèi yán! Yá ko kôp, ya ko: yi ụ mâgà! Kine: wu kôbì kí amḙ́ṅ? gik owen. Kwọp ówḙn fa líṅè ḙ́ṅ, ka mákè yi ówḙn ki chyènḙ̀; chyèṅḙ tḙ̀k ki rei yiṭ otwoṅ, ka yiṭè otwoṅ ṅôl ki yi ówḙn. Ka tíṅ mâl. Ka e duodọ, ka gḙ bḙ̄ṅọ ki owen, kine: ńal, wḙti yiṭ otwoṅ! Kwọf owen fa líṅè ḙ́ṅ; ka ṅi ko: bói, ya ko kōbḙ̀: yi ụ mâgà. Ka gḙ waṅa pach, ka tḙ̄rọ bḙ̄nḙ̀ bḙ̄nè, ka tḙ̄rọ ṅḙ̄ti bḙ̄nè, ka lwḙ́tḙ́ gǫ̀t ki rei yiṭ otwoṅ; ka yiṭ otwoṅ wḙ̀ṭì.

A boy went travelling with his uncle. When the sun went down, the one said, "Why, where shall we find fire (for the night)?" The nephew said, "I do not know." The first said, "Shall I not go to look for fire?" "What shall I do in the meantime?" was the reply of the other one. His uncle said, "You stay here with our goods." "No," said the nephew, "I would be eaten by the hyena." He replied, "No, you will not be eaten by the hyena." But he said, "I refuse to stay here." Then his uncle asked, "Why will *you* not go to fetch fire?" But he replied again, "No, I would be eaten by the hyena." So they left this matter. His uncle asked, "Shall we not lie down now?" He replied, "No, I would be eaten by the hyena." His uncle said, "Well, you lie down below, and I will lie upon you." He replied, "But suppose you are rolled down in the night from upon me by the hyena? Then I shall be eaten by her." His uncle said, "Well, then you lie upon me, so I shall be taken by the hyena, and you will be spared by her." The boy said, "Ah! what are you going to do?" Then he was silent. Again his uncle asked, "Will you not go up?" He said, "On a tree?" The uncle replied, "Yes, on a tree." So he climbed on a tree, and the brave boy (the uncle) lay down on the ground.

In the night came all the hyenas; they walked below that tree. The brave boy slept. A hyena came and sniffled at him, but he was asleep (and so she left him undisturbed). But the boy on the tree was awake, he was looking down staringly, he was awfully afraid, and at once he fell down, and fell on the back of the hyena. He caught the hyena by her ears and said, "Ha! did I not say I would catch you?" The hyena cried, and she dunged, she dunged very much. She ran away with the boy to a very distant place. There the hyena died during that night.[21] The boy was still on her back, and he still continued saying, "Did I not say I would catch you?" He said these words continually.

The next morning his uncle arose. He looked up, the boy was not there! He began to cry, saying, "My nephew has been eaten by the hyena." He arose and followed the way of the hyena. The dung of the hyena was on the whole way. He went to a very distant place. There he found the boy, he was still talking (the same words). He was still on the back of the hyena, holding fast her ears. But the hyena had died in the night. His uncle said, "Rise up!" But he said, "No, leave me alone! I did say, 'I would catch you (the hyena).'" He asked, "To whom did you say so?" He did not listen to the words of his uncle. Then his uncle caught his hands; the hands were tight around the ears of the hyena, so that the uncle had to cut off the ears of the hyena. Then he lifted him up, he arose, and they came. The uncle said, "Boy, throw away the ears of the hyena!" But he did not listen to his uncle's talk, he only kept repeating, "Well, I did say I would catch you." When they came near their home, all the people came; they all laughed. They loosened his fingers from about the ears of the hyena and threw the ears away.

88. Nyajak.

Ḍay[22] *mĕkọ yeję da ḍāṇ, ka e ṅwọlọ, ka būl gọ̈ch ki pach málọ̈wí, dẹ tẹ̄rọ ywotọ būl; fān ẹni fā fān ṅu. Ka ḍāṇ a chẹt ṅwọl; tẹ̄rọ ko: ẹ̇́, yi re kōbi? yi tẹṇ! E ko: ẹ̇́, ya kẹ́ḍọ̀. Ḍāṇ ẹni bẹ̄da jwọk. Ka e kẹḍọ ki tẹ̄rọ. Ka kọt é mọ̀kọ̀, ka gẹ nẹnọ gọ́l ṅù. Ṅu bẹ̄da ḍāṇ; ka ki wạr owọne é nẹ̀nọ̀, ḍāṇ a chẹt ṅwọl e nẹ̄nọ, ṅáje ẹ́n, ẹna ṅu. Ka ṅu chama yẹfa wọt, ka ṅan ẹni ko: yin amẹ́n â? Ka ṅu ko: Ṅàjàk! Ka ḍāṇ tẹṇ ko: ě! e ko: yi nụ̣ti nẹnọ? Kịne: ya nụ̣ti nẹnọ. Kịne: yi da kẹch? Kịne: awọ́! Kịne: yi fa nẹ́kè ki oṅwọk?*[23] *Kịne: awọ́! Ka oṅwọk nẹ́kè yi ṅu, ka tạ̈l yi ṅu, ka wēke Ṅajak, ka kwdṅì yi Ṅajak. Ka ṅu ko: Ṅàjàk! Kịne: ẹ́? Kịne: ka yi chám yau! Ka eko: awọ́! Ka yi nẹn yau! Kịne: awọ́! Ka ṅu kẹḍọ, ka kálá bẹ̀dọ̀, ka e duọgọ, chama yẹpa wọt. Ka Ṅajak ko: yín amẹ́n â? Ka e ko: Ṅàjàk, yí nụ̣ti nẹ̄no? Kịne: ṅẹ́! Kịne: yi da kẹch? Kịne: awọ́! Ka e ko: yi fa nẹke wạt? Ka e ko: awọ́. Ka wạt nệk, ka tạ̈le ẹ́n, ka wēki Ṅajak; ka ṅu ko: chám yà! Kịne: awọ́! Ka yi nẹni ya! Kịne: awọ́! Ka ṅu dọ̄gọ, ka e duọgọ, yẹfa wọt, ka Ṅajak ko: yin amẹ́n â? Kịne: Ṅajak, yi nụ̣ti nẹ̄no? Kịne: awọ́! E ko: yi dwata ṅọ? Rei da kẹch? Kịne: awọ́! Ṅu ko: nẹke yin ke dyẹl! Ṅajak ko: ẹ̇́, ya kụ nẹ́kè dyẹl; ya da rọ̄ḍọ. Kịne: dẹ kān ki ạ̀nọ̀? Kịne: ẹ̇́, kāni ki dọnọ. Ka rẹna gạt ki dọnọ, ka ṅi kẹpe ki pí, ka pi ṅi rāra pẹ́ṅ, ka chwê ṅi dọ̄na yeję, ki ṅwọl rech; ka gẹ ṅi mụti yi ṅu, ka ṅi chika tọ̄mọ, ka pi ṅi rāra peṅ. Ka ṅi fẹka feṅ bẹ̄ mụt ki chwê, ki ṅwọl rech.*

Ka Ṅajak wō gẹn túkè ẹ́n, ka gẹ ḏwọti mal, kịne: ạ̀nọ̀? Ṅajak ko: ṅu fa kama wá chàm? Ka e ko: chámun ki riṅọ anan! Ṅu ṅáje Ṅajak fa chẹt bẹ̄nọ. Ka wō gẹn kọ̈fè ẹ́n kịne: rẹ̇nun! Ka wọman e réṅọ̀, rẹna fọ̈tẹ gẹn. Ka Ṅajak e dọnọ. Ka ṅu kōrẹ e būḍọ,[24] *ka e bẹ̄nọ, ká é chwọ̀tọ̀ kịne: Ṅajak! E kudọ. Kịne: Ṅajak! e kudọ. Ka ṅu ko: adī? Ṅajak a nẹ̀ni. Ka bia wọt, ka e ko: Ṅajak! E kudọ. Ka mach kọ̈t, ka wọman yọte ẹ́n gẹ tọ̣̈k. E ko: búh! Ṅatyau Ṅajak! Wẹte gẹn a kọ̈lè ẹ́n! Ka Ṅajak ko: â, fạte yan ẹn? Ka fāṛọ kwọm Ṅajak, ka Ṅajak e wāṅọ. Kịne: ṅatyau Ṅajak, e kẹta kẹṅ? Ka Ṅajak ko: fạte yan ẹn? Ka ṅu ṅi fāra kwọmẹ, ka fa mákè ẹ́n, Ṅajak ṅi wāṅọ. Ka ṅu kōrẹ būḍọ. Ka Ṅajak e kẹḍọ, e kúchè yi ṅu.*

Ka wọne wịta pach, ka ṅu ẹni bẹ̄nọ, ka yigi yạt madọ̈ch, maduọṅ, ẹn olam: chuṅe gẹn mẹḍọ ki ẹn. Ka Ṅajak kọ: wu kụ ṅi kẹt ṭa yạt, yạṇ ẹni fa ṅu! Kịne: ẹ̇́, Ṅajak e chaka fyẹt. Ṅajak ko: ô, ya rum ki kwọp.[25] *Ka ṅwọle wọtạṇọ ṅi kẹta wiy yạt, ka ṅu e fārọ ki wọtạṇọ. Ṅajak ko: á, kwọfa a líṅè wún chị̂, ka jē wịte gẹ mûm, ka e kẹḍọ. Ṅajak kẹti yi ṅu, ka yige ḍāṇ maduọṅ yū yū yū. Dẹ e kwọmọ ki kẹ̄mọ; ka ṅu ko: ẹna ṅate ṅọ a yọ̄ ẹ́n? E ko: ṅan kwache fi! Ka tọ̈te ki fi; ka e*

mādọ, ka e dúọgụ̀, ká è dọ̀gụ̀, ka e lọgi yējọ. Ka ṅu kẹta gat bẹ̄ dwatọ (dwẹtọ) fi mẹn ṭāle ṅan ẹni. Ka kŏl yi Ńajak, ka gẹ rẹṅọ, ka gẹ waṇa fach.
  Ka ṅu bẹ̄nọ, ka·e ko: bụ́h! ṅaṅ ṭēṇ gẹ kẹta gẹ kẹṅ? Ko: faṭe ṅatyau Ńajak a kẹl gẹn? Ka e bẹ̄n ṅu bia pach Ńajak, ka e yigi ṅān madọ̄ch, bẹ̄ wājọ ki omia Ńajak. Ka ṅu ko: omia Ńajak dgọ̀n? Kine: ' chwộl! Ka omia Ńajak chwộl, ka gẹ wājọ. Ka Ńajak e bẹ̄nọ, e ko: bụ́h! e ko: omia, yi re rach kịnau? Kúchè yın ẹna ṅu? Ka ṅal ẹni ko: kẹ́ṭ, yi rach ki fyẹt. Ka Ńajak ko: mọgi, ya rum ke kwọf. Ka Ńajak e kudọ. Ka ṅal ẹni è nẹ̀nọ̀, ka waṅ gŏl yi ṅu.
  Chōṭi, ka ṅu kẹta fārẹ, ka dụki omẹn ywode ẹ́n, é ywọ̀nọ̀. Ńajak ko: yi re? Ko: waṅ a gŏl. Ka Ńajak ko: yá chá de kōbọ kine: mẹn ẹni (ani) fanẹ ṅu; dẹ anan yi kōbị adi? E kudọ. Ka Ńajak e kẹdọ, ka yigi ḍāṇ duọṅ, ka e bẹ̄n, é chàṭọ̀ kẹta fay ṅu; ka wiṭa (wuṭa) fach, ka e ko: wēl a ḍá kàl ẹ́n! Kine: kụ̀lí jwọk! Ka e bẹ̄nọ, ka e ko: bụ́h: oṅịmia, yi nụti bẹ̄dọ kẹṅ? Ka ṅu ko: yin amẹn? Ka e ko: ya faṭe ṅimiau, a kẹ́lè yọ̄mọ kāke duọṅ? Ka e ko: ọ̣, wija chaka wilọ, ka ṅu ywọṅọ, chuṅẹ mẹdọ. Ka gẹ wājọ, gẹ ki Ńajak; kúchè ṅu; e ko, chọgọ nẹ ṅịmẹn. Ka Ńajak lịda mal, ka waṅ omẹn lı̀ṭè ẹ́n ki mal, ka Ńajak e ko: ṅemia! Kine: é? Kine: āṅọ a yọm fẹ̄t ki wọṭ? Ńu ko kine: faṭe waṅ omia Ńajak? Ńajak e ko: á yŏtè ẹ yá kẹṅ? E ko: kụ dwai àn, ka ria yiga ṅan a ḍachọ. Ka ṅu ko: a gọ̄la wāṅẹ. Ńajak e ko: ẹna kụ̀l ẹ́n, ka.dẹ ẹrẹ a fu kiṭi wọk? Ka kiṭe wọk; ṅu ko: dẹ kụ gwârè agak? Kine: é, fa gwâr, ú kŏr yi wá. Ka Ńikaṅ e fẹ́chọ ko: dẹ kwọn ụ̄ ṭálè dgọ̀n? Ńu kine: a wŏl ẹ́n! Kine: á, dọ̄ch.
  Ka ṅu ko: ṅimia, ya kẹta gat bẹ̄ dwẹtọ pi. Ka Ńajak e ko: kẹ́ṭ! Ka ṅu e ko: kọ́ kŏṭ, kor waṅ omia Ńajak, kifa ọ̄ gwârè àgàk! wei ọ́ ṭàd wá ki gin cham. Ka Ńajak e dọ̄ṅọ kı́ ṭẹdọt, ka ṅu kẹta gat, ka Ńajak waṅ omẹn kwáṅè ẹ́n; ka rei gẹ agak, ka e fārọ, ka dọ̄gọ fōṭẹ gẹ́n. Ka omẹn yŏtè ẹ́n, ka waṅ omẹn kiṭe, ka omẹn e dọ̄ṅọ.
  Ka ṅu bẹ̄ni ki gat, ka waṅe yōde gọ tụ̄k, ka ḍāṇ ẹni yŏt ẹ tụ̄k. Ka ṅu ywọṅọ, kine: bụ́h! yeṅa ṅatyau Ńajak! E ko: Ńajak, kōra bụ́ṭ ki yẹ; ya fa dọ̄k kẹṭe! Chōṭi, ka Ńajak wei yi ṅu. Ka Ńajak e dọ̄ṅ gẹ ki ómẹn. Ńu e chōgọ, fa chiki dwọṅ.

A woman was with child, and she bore a child (which was named Nyajak). One day the drum was beaten in a village far away. The people went to dance to the drum, this village (where the drum was being beaten) was the village of a lion. And the child which had just been born (too wanted to go to dance). The people asked her (the child, a girl), "How, why are you saying, you also want to go? You are still so small!" She said, "Never mind, I will go." This child was a *jwọk*. It went with the people. When they arrived there, it began to rain, so they went into ("slept in") the house of the lion. This lion was a man.[26] During the night the other girls (who had come with Nyajak) slept, but the child which had just been born, was awake; she knew that the man was a lion. The lion wanted to open the hut (where the girls slept), but this child (Nyajak) asked (from within), "Who is there?" The lion replied, "Nyajak!" The child answered, "Eh?" The lion went on, "Are you still awake?" Nyajak said, "I am not yet asleep." The lion questioned, "Are you hungry?" "Yes, I am." The lion went on, "Would you not like to have a ram killed?" Nyajak answered, "Yes I would." So the lion killed a ram; he cooked it and gave it Nyajak; Nyajak took it. Then the lion said, "Nyajak!" She replied, "Eh?" "Do eat!" enjoined the lion. She answered, "All right!" The lion added, "And then sleep!" Nyajak replied, "All right!" The lion went away and waited some time. Then he returned, trying to open the house. But Nyajak again asked, "Who are you?" The lion replied, "Nyajak, are you still awake?" Nyajak said, "Yes, I am." The lion asked, "Are you hungry?" Nyajak replied, "Yes, I am." "Would you not like to have an ox killed?" asked the lion. Nyajak said, "Yes, I would." So an ox was killed and was cooked by him and given to Nyajak. The lion said, "Do but eat!" Nyajak replied, "All right!" The lion turned away. After some time he came back and tried to open the hut. Nyajak asked, "Who are you?" The lion said, "Nyajak, are you still awake?" Nyajak said, "Yes, I am." The lion inquired, "What do you want? Are you hungry?" Nyajak replied, "Yes, I am." The lion said, "Have a goat killed!" Nyajak replied, "No, I won't have a goat killed, I am thirsty." The lion asked, "In what shall I bring water?" Nyajak said, "Why, bring it in a basket!" The lion ran to the riverbank with a basket, he dipped it into the water, but the water streamed down on the ground, only leeches and small fish remained in the basket. He thrust them out and dipped the basket again, but the water flowed out on the ground, and the lion sat down a second time to pick out the leeches and the small fish.

In the meantime Nyajak awakened the other girls, and they arose asking, "What is the matter?" Nyajak said, "Is not the lion going to eat us?" Then she said to them, "Eat this meat (the sheep and ox which the lion had killed for Nyajak)!" Nyajak knew the lion would not come back quickly. When they had eaten, Nyajak said to the girls, "Run away!" They ran away home to their country. Nyajak alone remained. At last the lion was tired (of dipping water with a basket), and he came calling, "Nyajak, are you asleep?" He came into the hut saying, "Nyajak!" She remained silent. The lion lighted a fire, and he found that the girls had gone. He said, "This cursed Nyajak has led her comrades away." Nyajak replied, "Why, am I not here?" The lion sprang at Nyajak, but she disappeared. The lion cried, "This cursed Nyajak, where has she gone?" Nyajak replied, "Am I not here?" The lion sprang again at her, but did not catch her, Nyajak had disappeared. At last the lion was tired, and Nyajak went away; but the lion did not know it.

The girls arrived home. And the lion came to them; he had turned himself into a beautiful big tree, an olam (a sycomore fig); the girls liked him very much.[21] But Nyajak said, "Do not go under that tree! This tree is a lion!" They replied, "Why, Nyajak begins to lie!" Nyajak said, "All right, I shall say no more." The girls climbed on the tree; suddenly the lion seized them and fled away with them. Then Nyajak said, "Well, what did I say just now ("my talk has been heard by you exactly")?" The people were much perplexed; they went away. But Nyajak went to the lion, she turned into a very, very old man, she went limping on a crutch. When the lion saw her, he said, "What kind of man is this old person?" Nyajak replied, "A man begging for water." And he gave her water; then she went back. But presently she came back again, she had turned into a rat. The lion had just gone to the river-side to fetch water in order to cook the girls whom he had caught. Nyajak drove the children away and brought them home.

When the lion came back, he asked, "Why, where have the little children gone? Is it not this cursed Nyajak who has taken them away?" And the lion came into the village of Nyajak, he had turned into a very fine girl, he came to converse with the brother of Nyajak. The lion asked, "Where is the brother of Nyajak? Call him!" The brother of Nyajak was called, and they conversed together. But when Nyajak came, she exclaimed, "Oh dear, brother, how can you do such a wicked thing? Do you not know this is a lion?" The boy said, "Go away, you are a great liar ("you are bad with lying")." Nyajak replied, "It is your own affair, I shall say no more." And Nyajak remained silent. But while the boy slept, his eye was taken out by the lion.

That is all, and the lion went home to his village. But the next morning Nyajak found her brother weeping. She asked, "Why?" The boy answered, "My eye has been taken out!" Nyajak said, "Did I not tell you this man is a lion? what do you say now?" He was silent. Nyajak went away, she turned herself into an old woman, she went walking. When she arrived at the home of the lion, she cried, "Here is a traveller at the gate!" The lion replied. "Welcome!" She came in and exclaimed, "Oh, my brother, are you still here?" The lion replied, "Who are you?" Nyajak said, "Am I not your sister who had been carried away by the wind a long time ago?" The lion said, "Ah, my! I had almost forgotten!" The lion wept, he was very glad. And they talked together. The lion did not know that it was Nyajak, he believed her to be his sister. And Nyajak looked up and saw the eye of her brother. She said, "My brother!" The lion replied, "Eh?" She asked, "What is it makes such a bad smell in the house?" The lion answered, "It is the eye of the brother of Nyajak." Nyajak asked, "Where did you find that?" He answered, "I brought it, I had turned myself into a girl, and so I took out his eye." Nyajak said, "As you have brought it, will you not take it down (and show it to me)?" The lion took it down, saying "But mind, lest it be taken by the crow!" Nyajak said, "No, it will not be taken, we shall watch it." Then Nyajak asked, "But where is flour for cooking?" The lion answered, "It is just being pounded." Nyajak said, "Ah, that is good."

After some time the lion said, "Sister, I am going to the river-side to fetch water." Nyajak said, "Go!" The lion said, "Take heed, watch the eye of the brother of Nyajak, lest it be taken by the crow; we will cook it together with our meal." So Nyajak was left in the house, while the lion went to the river. But in the meantime Nyajak took the eye of her brother and then turned herself into a crow; she flew up and returned into her native country. She found her brother, put his eye into its place, and so her brother was cured.

When the lion came back from the river, he found that the eye had gone, and he saw that the woman was also gone. He began crying, "Alas, you cursed Nyajak!" Then he said, "My heart is tired with this Nyajak, I shall never return to her." That is all. And Nyajak was left alone by the lion, she lived with her brother. The lion remained in his place, he never returned anymore.

89. Ajang.

Dachọ mẹkọ wậdệ chwọ́lá Ajań. Rach ki órọ̀k, rọk gīr, dẹ tậrọ bẹ̀n chuńe gẹn rach ki ẹn; fa ńi furọ byẹl ńi chákd kwál. Māyẹ yejẹ fẹt, e ko: ńal ẹni gwọ́kẹ̀ ydn kidi? Ka e kẹdọ, é chậtọ̀ ki ńal ẹni, é kẹ́dọ̀ kị́ gọ̀n, kẹ́dọ̀ kúndó gạt. Kẹń ẹni láwà chàrọ̀ ki pach, ka gẹ bẹ̄dọ ki tậńe nàm. Ka máyẹ ywọ̀ńọ̀, e ko: bụ́h! Ya kōba kidi ki wậdà? A fụ̂dé yeja! ẹrẹ buńe ńań, mẹ̀n bì gọ wẹ̀kẹ̀ ẹ̀n!

Ka jal mẹkọ e bẹ̄nọ̀, ká ẻ kò: ḍận, yí rẻ ywọ̀ń? Kịne: yeja fẹt yi wậdà, wẹda ńi kwala jàmé tḥrọ̀; dẹ yan ya kẹ̣l ẹn, ụ dẻ ńań gọ wẹ̀kẹ̀ ẹ̀n. Ka jal ẹni ko: ụ wẹ̀ké yán, ụ fẹ̣tẹ̀ yán! Ka ḍáchọ̀ kùdọ̀. E ko: yí kụ̂ bọ̀kẹ̀, ụ fẹ̣tẹ̀ yán, ụ ńi tọ́tẹ́ ki jámẹ́, ụ fwóńe ydn kị́ gwọ̀k. E ko: kẹń fạr dwai, e ko: ńi bi, ka yi chwọti kịne: wiy nam! E ko: ya ụ bi wọ̀k. E ko: ụ jâm, jámé wậdi, gẹ ńi wẹ̀kà yín. Ka e ko: dọ̀ch yàu! Ka jal ẹni kẹ́ẹ̣́d nâm, gẹ́ lwọ̀tọ̀ ki ńa ńal ẹ́ni, ka kẹta nam. Ka gẹ rọ̀ńọ̀.

Chōti, ka ḍāṅ ẹni kẹta pach; ka ńa fạr dwai, ka ḍāṅ ẹni e bẹ̄no, ká é chwọ̀tọ̀: wiy nam! Ka jal ẹni yei, ka e bẹ̄no, gẹ ki ńa ńal tẹ̣n; ńál ẹ́ni chwé chàrọ̀; mayẹ chúńẹ̀ mẹ̀dọ̀. Ka gẹ maṭa ki mayẹ, ka mayẹ kẹta pach; ka jal ẹni dọ̀gá nàm.

Dẹ ḍāṅ a ḍachọ chuńẹ mẹdọ ki ńa ńal tẹ̣n. Ka ńal tẹ̣n é ḍọ̀ńọ̀, mayẹ ńi tọ́tẹ́ ki jâm kị́ chuń, ka ńal ẹni e didọ ki dọ̄ch ki gwọk jal ẹni; gwọk jal ẹni bẹ̀ńẹ a kwáńẹ̀ ńál ẹ́ni.

Ka ńal ɛni ṱậpè yi ńd gól jál ɛ́ní, u gɛ kɛ́pè gɛ́n. Ka gɛ kɛ́pò kí ńal ɛni. Ka ḍāṇ ɛni e ko: wá fa fȧ̂r? E ko: ê, wá fa fȧ̂r! Kine: dɛ anan, yi u (yu) gǫ̂k èdi? Kine: ɛ́, kúchè yán! Ka ńal ɛni wijɛ mûmò kí yi yǒ, mɛn kɛ́ṭí wǫ́k.

Jal ɛni kɛṭ bɛ̣ wɛ̣̀ld̥. Dɛ d̥ǫk gīr ki yɛ, wɑte bañ gīr ki yɛ, dyɛk gīr ki yɛ, jâm bɛ̣n ki yɛ. Ka e ko: dɛ ya kɛd̥a kid̥i? Ḍāṇ ɛni ko: kwań lōṭ jál ɛ́ní, ka yi kɛṭ, yi u yíte kí yǒ. E ko: u bɛ́nɛ́, yi ká nd̥k, u ṱówɛ́, ka yí bi wá bɛ̣̀d̥ò. Ka ńal ɛni e kɛd̥ǫ, ka mayɛ ywod̥ɛ, ka fyech yi mayɛ kine: yi re bɛ̣n? Kine: yá bi, chuńa rach ki jal ɛni yá rûm kí gwǫ̂k. Ká è gɛ̀d̥ò ki fậrɛ̣, ka tɛṛǫ ńi bia yɛ, ka tɛṛǫ bia (big) bɛ̣ ńeau ki fɪ ki yɛ, fígè à yìn yɛ̣, e mɛ̣d̥ò. Ka tɛṛǫ tòd̥ò kine Ajań ya fɑ̯l kun a chínɛ̂. Ka jal ɛni e bɛ̣no, ka e yǫgǫ obírò, ka e kíṭí fi, ka wếkè ńal ɛ́ní, e kuche yi ḍāṇ ɛni. Ka ńal ɛni e ko: máyó! Kine: ê! Kine: fùn àn ku kȧ̀l! Ka fuń ɛni wɛ́l ki yi mɛn. Ka ńal ɛni d̥wod̥ǫ chámá kɛṭa wok, ka reyi gɛ e yígó ḍāṇ, ka rḛ́ńd báń ńal ɛni. Ka ńal ɛni yigǫ chòr, ká è fậrò; ka jal ɛni e yigǫ chòr, ka fạ̄ra bāńɛ. Ka gɛ kɛd̥ǫ, gɛ́ rìńò. Ka reyi gɛn ńi mákɛ́, ka gɛ ńi fậd̥ǫ ki ńal ɛni. Ka ńal ɛni yík ágàk, ka jal ɛni yík ágàk, ka gɛ kɛd̥ǫ kí gùn, ka ńal ɛni dɛ̣md nam, ka ḍāṇ ɛni tǫńɛ a mēn féń yi ńa gól gɛn, ka jal ɛni dɛ̣md kwòm tɔ́ń; ka yɛjɛ tôyì yi tɔ́ń, ka jal ɛni ɛ́ tô, ka rɛp ki mach. Ka ńal ɛni kɛṭa bɛ̣ d̥wai mayɛ ki jámɛ́, ka ńa gǫl jal ɛni yigi chégɛ́, ka bāńɛ́ jal ɛni yigi mógɛ́ ki jam bɛ̣n.

A woman had a son whose name was Ajang; he was very wicked and did many evil things. All people were dissatisfied with him. Whenever they planted dura and it began to ripen, he used to steal it. His mother was tired with him, she said, "What shall I do with this boy?" She went away with her son and came with him to some river. The place was very far away from their home. They sat down on the river-bank, the mother began to cry, saying, "Alas, what shall I say concerning my boy? My heart is tired with him. Why, if only a crocodile would come, I would give him the boy!"

Then a man came, he asked, "Woman, why are you crying?" She answered, "My heart is weary with my son; he has a habit of stealing other peoples' property; so I have brought him here (thinking), perhaps there might be a crocodile to whom I could give my son." The man replied, "Give him to me, I will educate him." The woman remained silent. The man said, "Do not be afraid, he will be educated by me, I will give him goods, I shall teach him to work, and each month you may come to the river and call me, 'Father of the river!' Then I shall come out and give you the goods belonging to your son." The woman replied, "All right!" So the man went into the river with the boy. They waded into the water, went towards the middle, and dived there.

That is all, and the woman went home. When one month had passed, she came and called, "Father of the river!" The man at once replied to her call and he came out with the boy. The boy was very fat; so the mother was well pleased. They greeted the mother, and then she went home, and the man with the boy returned to the river.

The mother was very much pleased with her son; by and by he grew up, and each time (when she went to the river) the mother used to receive some goods; the boy was very diligent in learning the crafts of the man; he mastered all the crafts of the man.

But the wife of this man (of the father of the river) tried to persuade the boy to run away with her. She asked him, "Shall we not run away?" Again she asked, "What would you do here any longer?" The boy replied, "Why, I do not know." He was much perplexed, not knowing a way which might lead them out. — The man had gone on a journey. But he had plenty of cows, many goats, and all kinds of goods. — Now the boy asked, "But how shall I get out?" The woman replied, "Take the club of the man and go, and you will find the way. If he comes, kill him, so that he dies; then come back, and we will live together." The boy went; he found his mother and was asked by her, "Why do you come?" He answered, "I am very much dissatisfied with that man, I have stopped working with him."

The boy built a village, in which he lived; and the people used to come to him to buy water from him, because the water he had was sweet. But the people told the man (the father of the river), "Ajang is in the bush yonder." So the man came, he turned himself into a pot which he filled with water. The mother of Ajang gave him the pot, she did not know the pot was a man. But the boy warned his mother, "Mother!" She asked, "Eh?" He said, "Do not take this pot!" So every one left the pot alone. The boy arose to go out. Then the pot turned into a man and ran after the boy; the boy now turned into a vulture and flew away; the man also turned into a vulture and followed him flying. So they were flying in the air; the man seized the boy and fell on him. Then the boy turned into a crow, but the man also became a crow, always pursuing him; at last the boy fell into the river (in which the man's wife was still living, waiting for the return of the boy). The wife put her husband's spear into the ground, her husband fell on the spear, his belly was pierced by the spear so that he died; and he was put into the fire ("was seized by fire"). Then the boy went to bring some of the goods to his mother; and the wife of the man became his wife, the slaves and all the property of the man became his.

90. The Snake.

Ka jë mǫkǫ ḗ wḛlǫ, wḛlǫ Muŋǫ, ka gɛ kḛdǫ̣, ka gɛ witǫ, ka gɛ waṅǫ yǒ, ka gɛ tǭṅa yu ṅwel, ka gɛ fḛka feṅ, ka gɛ ko: bṳh! u peṅ tich edi? Ka ṭwǫl e bḛŋǫ. ṅwel, ka jal akyẹlo pạra mal, kịne: ṭwọl anan! Jal akyẹl ko: â, faṭe ṭwọl, bā riṭ! Kịne: faṭe ṭwọl duọṅ? Ka jal ẹni é rẹ́nọ́, ka pạna gọ̄di yaṭ; ka ṭwọl ẹ pẹ̄chụ̀, kịne: jal akyẹl a kẹṭa kẹṅ? Kịne: kúchọ̀ yán. Kịne: dẹ yí rè dọ́ṅ? Kịne: jal e cha e kōbọ kịne: yina ṭwọl, dẹ yâ kọ: dẹ yi ba riṭ, dẹ e ko: yi ba ṭwọl! Kịne: ē̩, ka gọ kậjẹ̣, ka e ṭọ̄. Ka ṭwọl e kẹdọ, ka jal e bẹ̄nọ e lépé lépụ̀, ka kẹjẹ kōṅẹ péṅ, ka nyẹña peṅ. Ka ṭwọl e bẹ̄nọ, ka e yūbọ, jal ẹni tọ̄k, ka ṭwọl e kẹdọ, ka ṭwọl kēlẹ tọ́ṅ. Ka ṭwọl pạra mal, ka jal ẹni rẹña peṅ, ka ṭwọl e yūbọ, yapa jal ẹni, ka e bẹ̄nọ, ka duọga péṅ; ka gūdẹ chọ̄te peṅ, ka e ṭọ̄.

Ka jal ẹni bia wọk, ka kẹṭa pach. Ka e ko: ṭwọl a nậgá. Jal acha a kậjẹ́! Ka jē ko: ẹ̣, ḍāṇ nẹ́kò yíṅ! Kịne: kụ kọ̀pè yà kōpọ, kịne: ṭwọl a bia cha, dẹ e rẹṅ wa. Ka e ko: che gọṇ a riṭ! Ka ya ko: ṭwọl duọṅ! A bẹ́né, a nậgé ḍāṇ, a kẹ́dá, a yōdá ḍāṇ d ṭọ̄. A kwóṅá kậjá, a bẹ̄ṅ ṭwọl, a kẹla ki tọṅ, a ṭóẉẹ́. A kōbi jē: kẹde lẹṭ wa. A kẹṭ jē, a yódẹ̣, é ṭọ̄. A kōbi jē kịne: ẹ̣, dọ̄ch, dwai waṭ! A kụl wạṭ, a límé, a chwǒp gẹ́ṇ, a gwẹ̄ṇ chúwé, a kụl ki pach. A ywọk ḍāṇ, a dwai chú ṅwẹ́l, a lọ́gé wál.

Some people travelled to Maṅọ. As they were walking and had reached a certain place, they lost their way. They turned aside at the trace of a snake. At last they sat down, saying, "Why, what shall we do in this country?" Then a snake came, a ṅwel; one of the men at once jumped up, crying, "There's a snake!" The other one said, "Oh no, it is not a snake, it is a king!" His friend said, "Is it not a big snake?" This man ran away, he hid himself behind a tree. The snake said to the one who remained, "Where has the other man gone?" He answered, "I do not know." Again she asked, "But why do you remain?" He answered, "That man said you were a snake, but I said you were a king; he said again you were a snake." The snake only replied, "Eh?" then she bit him, and he died.

When the snake had gone away, the other man came crawling cautiously; he had dug a hole at his place; he made it deep in the earth. The snake came and searched, but the man was not there. While she was going away, she was stabbed by the man; she jumped up, the man ran into his hole. The snake was searching, she searched for the man. At last she came down, in falling her belly was thrown violently on the earth, and she died!

Then the man came out and went home. He told the people, "I have killed a snake! The man who accompanied me, was bitten by her!" The people replied, "Ah, *you* have killed that man." He answered, "Did I not tell him, 'there is a snake coming, let us run!?' But he said, 'No, it is a king!' I said, 'No, it is a great snake!' The snake came, she killed the man, I ran away, and when I came back, I found the man dead. After that I dug a hole in the place where I was, and when the snake came, she was stabbed by me with the spear, and she died." The people said, "Let us go and see it!" The people went and found (him i. e. the man, or, the snake? probably the latter) dead. They said, "Why, all right, bring oxen!" And oxen were brought, they prayed, then the oxen were speared. They picked the bones of the man up, and brought them home. The women wept (mourned). They brought the bones of the snake too, they became a charm.

91. The Crocodile Hunter.

Ńań mẹkọ rach kí make jē; ka óyínọ dwai; ka oyinọ bẹ̃nọ, ka e kānọ gwok, ka gwok mȧk feń ki būte nam. Ka gwok e ywọ́nọ ywọ̃ń, ka ńań e linọ, ka e chīu, ka e bẹ̃n e rīnọ, cham é shāṅọ, ká è rọ̀nọ̀. Jal ẹni e budọ kị yey lūm, ka ńań pạra mal, ka kēl yi jal ẹni, ka ńań fạra nam. Ka jē bẹ̃n, ka mȧkè yi tẹrọ, ka tẹl yi tẹrọ, chama waṇe ḍa (dọ) wok. Ka chíkẹ̀ kẹ̀lọ̀, ka tọl shōte yi ńań, ka e kẹḍọ ńań.

Ka jal ẹni e dọ̀nọ̀, chuṇe rach. Ka ńań e kẹ́dọ̀, ka jal ẹni e kẹ́dọ̀, ẹ keau ki yẹi. Ka witạ pach mẹkọ, ka e ńeau ki gin cham, ka dọ̀gẹ́ yi yẹi, ká é châtọ̀, ka ńań yōt (yūt) e witi fōṭe gẹ́ń; ńań bẹda ḍāṇ. Ka jal bia wọ̀k, ka kẹṭa pach, ka kẹṭa gol ńań. Ka e bẹdọ ki ḍá kȧl, ká é chwọ̀tọ̀ kịne: wẹl a ḍá kȧl ẹń! Ka chwọl kịne: bi kal! Ka e bẹ̃nọ, ka fẹka feń, ka ṭōṭe kí gin cham, ká è châmọ̀, ka ṭōṭe ki mọgọ gȋr, ka e mụḍọ, ka e buṭọ. Ka lịḍa mal, ka leńọ lẹ̀tè ẹń ki mal; ka leń akyẹlọ lēṭe ẹń ki mal. Chōṭi, ka ńal ẹni e fẹ̣chọ kịne: ńan, ka e yēi. Kịne: jal gọl un e kẹṭe kẹń? Kịne a kẹṭ de pach! Kịne: chwọl! Ka e dwai. Kịne: ya chwọ́l yi mẹń? Kịne: yi chwọl yi wẹl! Ka e bẹ̃nọ, ka gẹ mȧtọ̀. Ka e ko: ómyȧ, yi bia kẹń? E ko: ya kẹla fōṭe mȧlḥulḥu; e ko: ya bi bẹ yafa leńọ. E ko: ya kẹla ńań, ńań marach ki cham ki jē; e ko: ya chaka yaf, kọ: fān ẹn a lēḍa leńọ ki mal, ki mẹn akyẹlọ. E ko: dẹ shwọla, ńań a tọ̄; dẹ yi kōbị adi? fa wẹ̀kì yan? Ka jal ẹni ko: ńań ẹni bẹdā ḍāṇ. E ko: faṭe yan ẹn, ẹna kẹle yin? E ko: tọn fa lēṭe yin ki wań būta? Kị men akyẹl a wań ywōṭḍ ẹń! Ka jal ẹni e buọgọ, e ḍali yi kwóp. E ko: yi u dọ̀k bẹ ṇeke ńań kẹti? E ko: ị, ya fa dọ̀k. Ka gẹ kwāńọ wọk, ka gẹ wẹki. E ko: ńa ńań mạṣẹṇ, e ko, kẹń u ńȧgí, e ko: gọli u tyẹ́kè yán. Ka jal ẹni ko: ị, ya fa dọ̀k ki ṇeke ńań. Ka ńań e ko: ara, kẹ́ị! Chōṭi, ka ńal e kẹ́dọ̀. Dẹ́ é bọ̀kọ̀, e chōgọ, fa chika ṇeke ńań.

A crocodile was very bad in catching people (caught very many people). And a crocodile hunter was sent for. The crocodile hunter came; he took a dog and tied it to the ground on the side of the river. The dog began howling at once; the crocodile heard it and came to the surface. It came running, and when it was near enough, it dived again. The hunter was lying amidst the grass. When the crocodile jumped up (to catch the dog), it was stabbed by the man; the crocodile jumped back into the river. But people came, and the crocodile was caught by them and pulled out. When they were near the river bank, they stabbed it a second time; but then the rope was broken by the crocodile, and it swam away.

The man was left on the river-bank; he was vexed. When the crocodile had gone away, the man also went; he rowed a boat and came to a village, and brought food, then he returned to his boat, and went on rowing. And he found out the crocodile had gone home to its own country. This crocodile was a man. And the man left his boat and went into a certain village. He went into the enclosure of the crocodile (but without knowing that it was the crocodile's). He remained outside the fence and called out, "A traveller is at the gate!" From inside some one called, "Come in!" He came and sat down. Food was given to him, and he ate, much beer was given to him, and he drank. Then he lay down. When he looked up, he saw a harpoon above (sticking in the roof of the hut); and he saw still another harpoon above. The man asked, "Girl!" She answered, and he went on, "Where has the man of your home gone?" (Only the girl was at home). She replied, "He has gone into the village." He said, "Call him." So she sent for him. The man asked, "By whom am I called?" He was answered, "By a traveller." He came, and they saluted each other. The man asked, "Brother, where do you come from?" The crocodile hunter answered, "I come from a very distant country, I have come to search a harpoon, I stabbed a crocodile, a crocodile which was famous for having eaten many people. When I was searching, I saw a harpoon in this place, above there; and I saw another one too. But I thought, the crocodile was dead (and now I find here my two harpoons with which I stabbed the crocodile)! What do you say of that? Will you not give them to me?" The man said, "This crocodile was a man! Is it not I who was stabbed by you? Do you not see the spear-wound in my side, and the other one in my arm-pit here?" When the man heard that, he was afraid; he did not know what to say. The other asked him, "Will you ever again go to hunt crocodiles?" He said, "No, I shall not do it again." Then the man took the harpoons down and gave them to him. But he said, "If you kill even a small crocodile child, I shall finish up your whole family!" But the crocodile hunter said, "No, I shall not kill crocodiles any more." Then the crocodile said, "Well, go!" That is all, the man went away. But he was afraid, he kept to his word, he never killed crocodiles again.

---

[1] "they seized two days": they passed two days, two days passed.
[2] "they found women only them": they found only women.
[3] if (you) go home.
[4] if you do not tell; in conditional negative sentences *ky* generally is used.
[5] Taking the stranger's question for an insult.
[6] "and the mouth of one calabash, and he opened it".

[7] *nù* has low tone; here a high tone is added to it representing the *é* "he", which is dropped, but its tone is preserved.
[8] "he is man where?" of which place is this man? *kęń* originally means place.
[9] "he was not known to his father, but he, his father was known to him."
[10] Probably the wife of the lion.
[11] This is to show that not a single person (lion), not even the cripples, the blind and the deaf, remained at home.
[12] They were left because they could not dance, and so did not fall into the pit.
[13] Who these slaves are, and why the cattle without horns were killed, is not clear.
[14] The leopard skin is the royal robe.
[15] This story vividly recalls that of Genesis chapter 37, and 42—46.
[16] from *tugǫ*.
[17] Such was the dowry in "the good old time."
[18] instead of *chygte yi*.
[19] of course he ought to have said, "his testicles are as big as this pot," and, "who has a necklace on his neck." Apparently from excitement and confusion the man misplaces his words.
[20] *gik*.
[21] From exhaustion.
[22] from *ḍachǫ*.
[23] will you not have killed a ram?
[24] and the lion, his breast was tired.
[25] I have finished with talking, that is: I shall say no more, (since you will not hear)!
[26] Was a man who was able to change himself into a lion, and into a tree; see below.
[27] The olam is a tree with a broad, beautiful shady crown.

XIII. ANECDOTES.

92. The Travellers.

Jǫk akyęlǫ é wḛlǫ, ka gę mákḕ yi kęch. Mǫgǫ nut ki yi gęn, męn ye da atęp, ḭ fȧṅ, ka jal akyęl chygṅg tḛ̄k, będa gŏró, jal akyęl ńi chȧm ki rei mǫkę. Ka gǫ ńi fyęjǫ kine: ŏwá, yi fa ṯōṯe ki rei mǫki? Kine: ȩ̂, ya kṳ ṯōṯę.[1] Ka jal ęni e kudǫ. Ka ńi wei będǫ ki kęch. Ka ńi chika fęchǫ ḍuki, kine: jal ŏwá, yi fa ṯōṯe? Ka e ko: Ki rei mǫka wala ki rei mǫki: Kine: ę̂, ke rei mǫki. Kine: ya kṳ ṯōṯę. Ka ńi chiki fyęchǫ kine: ŏwá, yi fa ṯōṯe? Kine: ki rei mǫka wala ki rei mǫki? Kine: ȩ̂, ki rei mǫka. Ko: ṯōṯe yan ki ńá-mátę̄ṅ,[2] ka ṯōṯe ki rei mǫkę. Kuche ęn, gǫn a mǫkę. E kǫmǫ ṯō̤; ká ȧ chȧmǫ̀, ka e yȧṅǫ, ka e ḍuodǫ̀, ka ńi wȧjǫ̀, ka chika fyęchǫ, kine: yi fa ṯōṯe yi mǫgǫ? Kine: rei mǫka wala rei mǫki? Kine rei mǫka. Ka ṯōṯe ki rȧi mǫkę, ka e chȧmǫ.

Ka ḍuki ko: wȧ kḛ́t! Kine: ȧwǫ́! Jal ęni ḭ́ chwḕ; chama ńwal ątḅę, ka ątḅę yōṯe én, mǫgę ḍoṅ e nǫk. Kine: ȩ̂, mǫk a cham yi męn? Ńal ęni ko: męn an ńi chȧmǫ̀ yin ki chȧṅi. Kine: ȩ̂, ęrę mǫka nūti wei yin? Kine: ḭ́, kęń de ḏōu ki yi kęch, mǫṅ ęni fa re ḍoṅ ki feń? yi re cham adi? Ká ȧ kùdǫ̀.

Chōṯi, ka kęti ṯōṯe gęn, ka wiṯa pach, ka tyęṅ gǫlę yŏtȧ ęn, e ńwǫl ki ńa-wǫḍe, ka ńal akyęl ńa-gǫl yŏtȧ gǫn ńwǫlǫ ki ńa-ńȧręg. Tyęṅ ęni chuńe gęn mędǫ, ki rei ę gęn yǫka (yǫga) mą̄ṭ, kine: ńa-wǫḍa ṭe ḍǭṅǫ cha męṅǫ, ki ńan ńȧri ke wei ńǫme rȧi gęn, kifa wa mą̄ṭ.

A ḍǭṅi ńal ṯēṅ, ka gę ńwǫm, ka gę bęḍǫ ki gól gęn, ka gǫl gęn ę yigi kyḛl. A chōk.

Two men were travelling together. On their way they became hungry, but they had food with them; each had a bag full of food. But one man was stingy, he was a niggard. But the other man used to eat of his food. And he asked his companion, saying, "Brother, shall I not give you of your food?" He replied, "No, don't give me!" His friend was silent; he left his friend hungering. But the next day he asked him again, "Man, brother, shall I not give you?" He replied, "Of my food or of yours?" The friend answered, "Why, of yours." He replied, "Don't give me!" Again he asked, "Shall I not give you?" He asked, "Of my own or of yours?" He answered, "Well, of mine." Then he said, "Give me a little!" And he gave him of his (of the stingy one's). But the stingy one did not know that it was of his own. He was almost dying of hunger, so he ate. When he had had enough, he rose and began to talk. The next day his friend asked him once more, "Shall I not give you some food?" He replied, "Of mine or of yours?" The friend said, "Of mine." But he again gave him of

---

[1] "I will not be given"; "may I not be given".
[2] "a small child", that is: a little bit.

his (the stingy one's), and he ate. The next morning he said, "Let us go!" His friend replied, "All right." He had recovered his strength; he wanted to feel his bag. When he found that there was but a little left in his bag, he asked, "Why, who has eaten my food?" His friend said, "You yourself have eaten of it every day." He replied, "How, did you not leave untouched my food?" The friend said, "If you had died of hunger, for what reason should that food have been left? what should you have done with it?" The man was silent.

That is all, and they went into their country. When they arrived in their village, they found that both their wives had born children, one a girl and one a boy. So they were both very glad, and they became friends. The stingy one said to his friend, "Friend, some day when my son has grown up, then let him marry your daughter, because we are friends."

The girl grew up, and they married, and they lived in both their homes (inhabited the homes of both their parents), and their homes became one. It is finished.

93. A Goat-story.

Dyẹl a kạ̈lọ̀ ki Tŭnọ̀ ki Achẹte-gwok, ka kita Akụ̈ru̇wâr, ka dyẹl é lŏyọ̀, ka ńi tọ́ńa fân, ka ńi nẹnọ̀, ka ńi ńwọ̈lọ̀. Ka d̶uki dyẹl ńi kẹd̶ẹ̀, ńi kẹd̶ọ fân, ka ńi ńwọ̄lọ, ka ńi d̶wod̶ọ, ka ńi kẹta fân, ka ńi ńwọ̄lọ. D̶uki ka ńi d̶wod̶ọ ki ńwọlẹ ki bāńẹ, ka ńi kẹta fân, ka ńi ńwọ̈lọ̀, ka ńi nẹnọ, ka ńi d̶wod̶ọ ki ńwọlẹ ke bāńẹ, ka gıtẹ́ Tŭnọ̀ Achẹte-gwok, ńwọlẹ gır.

A goat was brought from *Tuno Achete-gwok*, it was brought to *Akuruwar*; there the goat ran away and turned to a certain village, there it stayed (for some time) and brought forth young ones. The next day the goat went away, it went to another village and brought forth young ones again. After that it arose, went to some village and brought forth young ones. The next day it arose, with all its young ones behind it; it went to another village, there it brought forth young ones; it stayed there for some time and then arose with its young ones behind it. At last it arrived again at *Tuno Achete-gwok*, with plenty of young ones.

94. The Glutton.

Feṅ da kẹ́ch, kẹ́ch maduọṅ. Dẹ jal akyẹ̀lọ ye bụ byẹl, dẹ ńi chama bụp. Ka byẹl e d̶ọ̄nọ, ka byẹl e chạ̈gọ, ka dạke kẹch gen ki byẹl, ka ńi chām ki abwok, ki ṅọ̄r, ki ńim. Ka byẹl chạ̈gọ, ka ńa gọlẹ kŏfé kıne: t̶ạdi gin cham maduọṅ! Ka yi ṅọch ki byẹl, ka yi bạ̈k ki abwok, ka yi ṅọch ki ṅọ̄r, ka yi kyẹt ki omọ̄t, ka yi kyẹt ki ńim, ka yi t̶ẓ̈ṅ ki mańa mát̶ọ́! Ka gẹ t̶um, ka gik ẹni kạ̈l, ko: chip ńima kā! Ka fạ̀lọ̀ fạ̈ké ẹn, ka e chạ̈mọ̀; ka ńi chiki chạ̈mà kẹ̀ṅ, ka ńi chạ̈ká kẹṅ. Ká è yāṅọ, ka e ko:

chaṁ! e kōbḙ kḙtḙ. Yejḙ báṅ châm, ko: yi tọ̄ tiṅ! Yejḙ baṅ. Ka fālọ kwáṅè ḙn, e ko: ótyèṇ yi ṅi chama bup, dḙ kōra būt ki yí, ê, chăm! Yejḙ baṅe cham; ka yejḙ chwọ́pè ḙn, ka e tọ̄.

There was a famine, a great famine. One man had no more dura, he used to eat mud. When the (new) dura had grown up and it ripened, and the time had come for the people to rub dura-ears in their hands, and they ate the new dura, and maize, and beans, and sesame, and the dura was quite ripe, then this man said to his wife, "Prepare a great meal, boil dura, and cook maize, and boil beans, and roast green dura, and roast sesame, and prepare vegetables too." When all these things were ready, the woman brought them. He said to her, "Put them before me!" Then he sharpened his knife and began to eat. He ate, now from this, now from some other dish. When he was filled, he said, "Eat!" — He said this to himself. — But his belly refused to eat any more, it said, "You will die at once!" His belly refused. Then he took the knife and said, "Formerly you (belly) used to eat mud, and I was tired with you, why, eat!" But his belly refused to eat. He took his knife and stabbed his belly, and he died.

95. Bachet.

Ye¹ jal mâ rit, ye da wat bâṅḙ, ṅíṅḙ Bachet; wḙn chuṅḙ mḙdọ. Ka Bachet gḙ̀tè ki fārḙ, ká è bḙ̀dọ̀ wâi, ḙn a jâgọ̀. Ká tḙ̀rọ chùṅọ̀ gḙ́n yígí márâch ki Bachet; ka gḙ ṅi biḙ bḙ̀ góṅ. Ka Bachet ṅí chwộl, ka e bḙ̄nọ, é tyḙ̀tọ̀ kí kôt. Ka ṅi fyḙ́t chè yi rit kine: áṅọ̀ a tyétí? Kine: wuo! Kine: ya biḙ bḙ̄ gyḙ́r kí kàl. Ká rit è kò: wat bâṅd, wiji nḁ́ti wilọ̀ ki gyḙr ki gòlà? Ka rit chuṅḙ yiga márâch kí tḙ̀rọ̀, kine: wu chaga fyḙt. Ka ṅal ḙni wêt dọ̀gḙ́ fârḙ, ka kḙta fârḙ.

Ká tḙ̀rọ̀ ṅi fôtè ḙn, ká jámè tḙ̀rọ̀ ṅi kápè ḙn. Ka tḙ̄rọ ṅi biḙ bḙ̄ góṅ. Ka ṅi chwộl, kine: kôfı Bachet, kú bì ḙ́ yà wiy kyḙ́ṅ, ka kú bì è chàtà tyḙ́lḙ́. Ka Bachet bḙ̀n, e chàtọ ki wiy kyḙṅ, chà fàch è chãṅọ̀, ká yípá wộk kí wíy kyèṅ, ka tyḙ̀l àkyḙ̀lọ̀ weyḙ wiy kyḙṅ, ká tyḙ̀l àkyḙ̀lọ̀ yḙṅa féṅ, ka e bḙ̄n é chàtọ̀. Ka rit e ko: á gìn áṅọ̀ à gwọ́k ki yín kḙ̀nàu? Ká è kò: fatḙ yin a kōp kine: yá kú chàtı ki wiy kyḙṅ, kine: yá kú chàtı ki féṅ? A wéyá tyḙlá àkyḙl kí wíy kyḙ̀ṅ, a weya tyḙla akyḙl ki feṅ. Ka rit é ṅḙ̀tọ̀, ká è kò: yí bột, yí fa ṅḙ́kè yán; kḙt dọ̀k fāri!

Ka Bachet dọ̄gọ. Ka dọ̄gọ́ yi kwọ́pḙ́, ka tyḙ́ṅ ḙni biḙ bḙ̄ góṅ yi rit. Ka rit e ko: Bachet y ṅḙ́kè yán de chaṅ tiṅ! Kine kḙdun! Ká gḙ kḙ́dọ̀. Kine: kànè mḙṇọ ki tọṇ gyḙ̄ṇọ! wu bḙ̀ṇọ̀! Ka mḙn ṅí kàṇọ̀ (kàṇọ̀). Ka Bachet dwâi, Bachet fa kòpè yi rit. Ká è bḙ̄ṇọ, e bu tọṅ gyḙ̄ṇọ, má kḁlè ḙn. Ka rit è kò: ṅān ku ṅwọl ki tọṅ gyḙ̄ṇọ, nḙ̀gà nḁ̀gò! Dwoṭi mal! Ka d̨āṇ ṅí d̨wọtá mâl, ka tọṅ gyḙ̄ṇọ ṅi wêi féṅ. Tḙ̀rọ bḙ̀ṇè á d̨wotı mal, ka Bachet è d̨ḁṅọ̀. Ka rit e ko: Bachet, yi re fa d̨wọt? E kudọ. Kine: Bachet, yi re fa d̨wọ́t? Ka Bachet d̨woṭa mal, ka tọṅ gyḙ̄ṇọ bògọ̀n, mḙn dọ́ṅ

---

¹ *Ye* "he" has here rather the sense of "there was".

kị féṅ. Ka Bachet chyẹ́nẹ́ ḍẹ̀nẹ̀, ká é ywòṅ, kịne : ó, ó, ộ! Ka rịṭ e fẻcho kịne! dṅọ̀, Bachet, ẹn a gwọ́kò yí kịnàu? Bachet kịne: gyẹn ńị ńwọ̀ḍlọ̀ gẹ́ kẹ́tè gẹ́n, gẹ bụ́ṅ ọ́ṭwọ̀ṇ? fa ńị ńwộl! Ká è kò: ará (ẹrẹ́), yá fá ọ́ṭwọ̀ṇ? Ka rịṭ e ḳọ̄ yi ṅyẹ́rù̀, e ko: yi bộṭ, kẹṭ, ḍọ̀k fārı́!

There was a man, a king, he had a slave whose name was Bachet. He liked him much. He built a village for Bachet at a separate place, where Bachet became chief. But the people of the village were dissatisfied with Bachet, and they came to the king to complain. Bachet was called by the king, and he came carrying thorns (such as are used in house-building). The king asked him, "What are you carrying there?" He answered, "My lord, I come to make a fence (for you)." The king replied, "Ah, my slave, you still think of building me a fence?" And the king became angry with the people and said, "You lie!" He let Bachet return, and he went to his village.

And (again) the people were beaten by their chief Bachet, and their property was taken by him. So they went again to complain of him. The king gave order to call him, saying, "Tell Bachet, he must not come on horseback, and he must not come on foot either." And Bachet came riding on horseback, but when he approached the village, he alighted from the horse; he left one foot on the horse, and one foot was on the earth. So he approached walking. The king asked, "What is that? why are you doing thus?" He answered, "Did not you give order, I must not come on horseback, nor on foot either? Therefore I left one foot on the horse, and am walking with the other." The king laughed saying, "You are a clever one! you shall not be killed, go, return to your village."

Bachet returned, but he went on in the same manner (troubling his people). The people came again complaining to the king. The king replied, "Bachet shall be killed this very day!" Then he said, "Go! every one of you bring a hen-egg, and then come back." So every one brought an egg. But this order of the king had not been told Bachet, and so he came without an egg. When they were all assembled, the king said, "Every one who does not lay an egg, shall surely die! Rise up!" So every one rose up, leaving his egg on the ground. All the people rose up, only Bachet remained seated. The king asked, "Bachet, why do you not rise up?" He was silent. Again he asked, "Bachet, why do you not rise?" Then Bachet arose, but there was no egg under him. Bachet stretched out his hands crying, "O o oh!" The king asked, "What is it, Bachet, that you are doing thus?" Bachet replied, "Do you think all these could have laid an egg by themselves, if there had not been a cock? Well, I am the cock!" The king almost died with laughing; he said, "You are a clever one, go, return to your village!"[1]

---

[1] As the name of the hero shows, this story is of Arabic origin.

96. The Country Where Death is Not.

Jal mękǫ mayę nut. Dę mayę ko, chamę bǭkǫ tǭ, chama dwata fwōṇe bu tǭ. Wadę ko: fwōṇe buṅ tǭ e yeṅ kun? Kịne: ê, kụl yan, nut! Dāṇ ęni ba yū.
 Ka gę kędǫ̀, fōṇ ęni lạulạulạu, fwōṇe yey bu tǭ. Ka ńí tōńa pach mękǫ, ka ńi kwachǫ pi, ka gę ńi tǭtę, ka ńal ęni pęchò kịne: tǭ nut ki fōṇ? Kịne: ê, yi kụla kęṅ, ęna fygrię tǭ? Ka e ko: maya bǭkǫ tǭ; maya dwata fōṇe bu tǭ. Kịne: ê, kędun! Ka gę ńi kędǫ, ka gę ńi tǭńd fān kętę, ka gę́ ńi fę́chǫ̀. Kịne: ê, yina ńate nǫ̀, ęna fyeń tǭ? ê, kędun; tǭ nut. Ka kętạ fǫ́dò máláuldu, ka e fęchǫ kịne: fǫ́tę wun bęt adi? yeję da tǭ? Kịne: ê, jē fá ńi tǫ̇u. Ka mayę chuṅę minǫ, e ko: dǫ̀ch, wụ̂dà, yá kụl yi yíṇ fōṇe fa ńi tǫu yeję.
 Wạdę mękǫ mụ̀dę̀, ka mayę kịtị gǫl ęni. Ka e ko: máyá ànàn, wei bę̀dę ki yiṅ; yá kęti fōtę wóṇ, ya u makị run gę ádę̀k, fanę kę́ṅ u bę̄nd bę lę̀tę̀ wun ki maya. Muyę chuṅę medǫ.
 Ka ńal ęni e dụ̂gụ̀, dụ̀gụ̀ fǫtę gę́ṅ. Ka e bę̀dǫ fōtę gę́ṅ.
 Ka ḍāṇ ęni wiję kāgǫ; ká è kòbò: müṭ wụ̂dà, wijá kāgǫ. Ka ńal ęni dwodǫ, ka e dwatǫ jē. Ka jē bę̄nǫ, ka jē pęka péṅ, ka ńal ęni ko: wú chwǫ́lé yáṅ kifa mayę mụ̇da anaṅ. Wu gwachǫ ki ńyęṅ, mǫk u yǫ̀de wụ̂dę, dę ko: wiję kāgǫ, dę riṅǫ u ręṅ; dę fana fa kịne: u ńal. Ka ḍāṇ ęni ywǫ̀ṅ, kịne: ê, jwǫk bógǫ̀ṅ, wija fa kāgǫ! Tęrǫ ko: ê, mâk, reję riṅǫ! Ka mâk, ka kụ̂l, ka táyi féṅ, ka ńâl, ka riṅo pụ̂ńị. Ka tęrǫ chāmǫ ki riṅǫ. Dụki ka ńyęṅ gwâch, ka ńyęṅ kâṅ yi maḍę wụ̂dę.
 Ka wụ̀dę bę̄nǫ, ka fęka feṅ, ka tǫ́tę gịn cham, ká è chàmǫ̀. Ka e pęchǫ kịne: maya agǫṅ ęṅ? Ka mụ̀dę ko: mụ̂dá, mayę mákè yi jwǫk, wú gwǫ̀djǫ̀ ńyęṅ, dę ńyęṅ ak; dę ńâl kifa riṅǫ u ręṅ; dę wǫṇ, tǭ bogǫṅ ki fōtę wóṇ, ḍāṇ kęṅ a mâk yi jwǫk ńi chaka ńālǫ. Ńal ęni ko kịne: buh! ya ńeau māya!? eko: yá bę̀dǫ̀; ko: ya u kęt yàu! Ńal ęni ko: yi gǫ̂tù. Ńal ęni ko: ê, ya fa gǫ̂tù. Ka tęrǫ bę̄nǫ, kama cham ki ńal ęni; ka lwǫ̂k ki yi muḍę. Ka gę kętạ kun malạulạu, kifa u (tǫ̀) chàm. Ka tęrǫ wịtę́ mùm,[1] kịne: ę kęti kęṅ? Ka mụ̀dę edụǫgǫ; ka e ko: kęt, yi u cham tyau nami mayi. Ka ńal ęni bia fōtę gę́ṅ, ka e kōbi ki pach kịne: máyá a châm yì ńù.
 Chōtị, ká tę̀rò e ko: mayi fa ńa-ḍái òrǫ̀k. Tǭ fa nut ki yey féṅ bę̀ne? dá kun tǫ̀k yi tǭ?

There was a man with his mother. The mother was much afraid of dying, therefore she wished to go into a country where there is no death. The son said, "Where is a country without death?" She answered, "Well, there is such a country, bring me there!" The woman was very old.
 So they travelled into a very, very distant country, to (reach) the country where there is no death. They turned into a village and asked for water. When it was given them, the son asked, "Is there death in this country?" The people answered, "Dear me, where do you come from that you ask such a

[1] the people, (their) heads were perplexed.

question concerning death?" He answered, "My mother is afraid of dying, so she wants a country where death is not." The people said, "Why, go away!" They went and turned to another village. There they asked again and received the answer, "Why, what kind of man are you that you ask about dying? Go away! There is death here." Then they went to a very distant country and asked, "How is your country, is there death in it?" The answer was, "No, people do not die here." The mother was very glad, she said, "Well done, my son, you have brought me to a country where there is no death."

Her son had a friend in that town, and to his home he brought his mother. He said, "Here is my mother, let her live with you. I shall go to our country, and after three years I shall return to see you and my mother." His mother was satisfied.

So the boy returned to his native country and stayed there for some time.

But his mother became sick; she got a head-ache; she said, "Friend of my son, I have a headache." On that the boy arose and called the people together. The people came and sat down. The boy said, "I have called you because of the mother of my friend, who is here. Now collect money, that we may give it to her son (when he returns). For she says her head is aching; and because of that (because of her sickness) her meat (flesh) will spoil. For that reason," he said, "she must be killed (at once)." When the woman heard this, she began crying, "I am not sick! I have no head-ache!" But the people said, "Never mind, seize her, or her flesh will be spoiled." So she was caught, brought, thrown on the ground and killed; her flesh was divided among the people, and they ate it. The next day they collected money and brought it to the friend of her son.

And her son came back. He sat down, they gave him food, and he ate. He asked, "Where is my mother?" His friend answered, "My friend, our (your) mother was seized with sickness, so we collected money, — here is the money! — and killed her, lest her meat should be spoiled. For as for us, we do not die in our country, if a man is seized with sickness, we kill him." The boy replied, "Why, should I sell my mother? Never!" Then he said, "I will but go." His friend said, "You are angry?" He replied, "No, I am not angry." In the meantime the people came and wanted to eat the boy too. His friend therefore went to him saying, "Go, or you also will be eaten like your mother." He accompanied him into a distant country. When the boy came home, he said to his people, "My mother has been eaten by a lion."

That is all; and the people said, "Your mother was a sinful woman. Is not death in all the world, and should there be a place where there is no death?"

97. The King and the People.

Jal mɛkọ bà riṭ; kôp tɛ̀rọ̀: gɛ̀r wọ̀t! Ká wọ̀t ŧí gɛ̀r, ká yè ko: gɛ̀r kàl! Ká yè ko: fŭr fwódọ́! Ká fwódọ́ ŧí fŭr, ká byɛ́l ŧí chɛ̀gọ̀. Ká gɛ́ ŧí kâch. Ká ê kò kine: kíṭí wí pàm (pɛ̀m)! Ká ŧí kò: mwọn rɛ̀rọ̀! Ka ye kō ne: fwọ̀t byɛ́l! Ká yè kò: chwách òkọ̀dọ̀! Ka dwai ŋ̂ột. Ká yè kò: chwách ṭagọ̀! Ká ké chān kíndù. Ká wàṅ àkyɛ̀lọ̀ chàmá dwāta fwọdọ kí mâl. Ká tɛ̀rọ̀ é kɛ́dọ̀ bɛ̀ yáf kí yọ̀, mɛ́n kɛ̣ṭe mâl. Ká tɛ̀rọ̀ kámá dúọ̀k pach: yọ́ bógọ̀n. Ká dān mâyú yót, ka dān ɛni é fɛ́chọ̀: wú kɛdu kun? Gɛ̀ kò: fáṭé riṭ yè kō, chàmá dwátá fwọ́dọ́ kí mâl? Dɛ́ yọ̌ bógọ̀n. Ká dān duọ́n è kò: wá! wú fà dɛ̀k! yọ̌ nút ki màl mo-chāne. Tínú ṭàkâgı mâl, ka kōṭ l̥ɲù mâl bānɛ̣! O ṭúmé gɛ̂n, ká gɛ́ kɛ̣ṭ gèn fàch. Ká gɛ́ pyɛ́ch yi riṭ kine: fwọ̀dɛ́ á yót? Ǹɛ̀, á yót. Dɛ̀ a kɛ̣k? Kine: nɛ̀, a kɛ̣k. Dụki ka tɛ̣rọ kɛ́dọ̀ bɛ̣ fŭr. Ka dān duọ́n kà yót, kà fyɛ́ch: wọ́ fúr wọ̀n kidí? Furu mâl yàu! Ka tɛ̀rọ̀ ŧí furọ̀ mâl yau. A duọ̀k gɛ̣n, a fɛ́chí riṭ, è kò: á rŭm kí furọ̀? Kine: àwọ́! Kɛ̣de kàchú byɛ́l! Ká námí dùwà. Ka riṭ ye ko: duki ya ká (= kɛdọ) bɛ̄ kɛ̀mọ́ kí fwọ́dọ́. Ká tɛ̀rọ̀ é bọ̀kọ̀. Kine: fwọ̀dọ́ àgọ̀n ɛn? Wá jàt kí yọ̌ mɛ̀n kɛ̣ṭ wọ̀n mâl. Wú chàkà fyɛ̣̂t. Wú rè fà kōbùn: fwọ̀dọ́ bógọ̀n?

A man was king; he said to his people, "Build a house!" And a house was built. And he said, "Make a fence!" Then he said, "Hoe a field!" A field was hoed, (dura was sown and) the dura ripened. They harvested the dura. Then he said, "Lay it on the drying-ground!" He said again, "Make a threshing-place!" After that, "Thresh the dura!" He ordered, "Make a corn-basket!" So pegs were cut for fastening the corn-basket. He said, "Make a cover (for the basket)!" And so (he troubled his people) every day.

One year he wanted to make a field up in the air. And the people went to look for a way which led up into the air. At last they turned back, there was no way. Then there was an old woman, she asked them, "Where are you going?" They answered, "Did not the king say he wanted a field up in the air? But there is no way!" The old woman said, "Dear me! how stupid you are! There has been since early days a way up into the air. Lift up your dura-stick, and throw up seeds after it!" (They did so). When they had done so, they went home. And they were asked by the king, "Have you found a field?" They answered, "Yes, it has been found." He asked. "Is it planted?" They said, "Yes, it is planted." The next day they went to hoe. They found the old woman and asked her, "How shall we hoe the field?" She answered, "You just hoe up into the air!" So the people just hoed up into the air. When they returned, the king asked them, "Have you finished with hoeing?" They answered, "Yes." Then he said, "Go and harvest the dura." And so on as on former days (so he always found some new idea how to trouble the people).

And the king said, "To-morrow I shall go to look at the field." The people were afraid. He asked, "Where is the field?" They answered, "We could not find the way which leads up into the air." The king said, "You have been telling lies! Why did you not say, 'there is no way?'"

98. Wealth cannot be imitated.

Wi jăn mẹko chwọlá Ayọ̆mọ, bẹda jal kẹr, wûdẹ́ chwọlá Awan; mắrẹ ẹ́n; ka waṭe pyau kị ḍọ̀rè pyar abíkyẹ̀l; kat waṭ mọ̄kọ ka pyar ắnwẹ̀n; ka gẹ kậl, ka wạde ńọ̀k ka gẹ kậl; ka waṭ pyau, ka waṇ akyẹl chwọp, chịkị chwọpọ, ka gẹ chộp bẹ̆n, ká gẹ́ rûmọ, ka ḍọk gọ́ń, mọk kọ́l bẹ ńwọm, ka pyar abídẹ̀k. Ka jal de ńarẹ é chwọ̀ù; kịne: búh, ga ḍọ̄ ńọ, a kōle ydu gẹ gír ńau? O lọk ńara ụ tọ́wọ̀, ụ líne ńara kị́ kún, ka ye kịne: kịpańo a ńwọmị kị dọk gír? Ko: ḕ, ya bẹ̆dọ̀. dwọ̄gun ḍọ̀ [1] *wún!*

Ka ńal ẹni kyẹdọ, kịne: ḍọk ba dwọk! Ka jal ẹni e yeyọ, ka kẹtị kẹ́lé ḍọ̀k, ka kwańa pyar ắnwẹ̀n, ka ḍọk bẹ̆n dwọk. Ka waṭ nẹ̆k, ga pyar ádẹ̀k, mọk cham yị tẓrọ. Ka ńān ẹni ká wêkè, ka gẹ bẹ̆n kị́ gùn. Jal ẹni ko: ńắrà bá dọ́ń; ka ńwọm e ṭumọ, a bẹ̆ne pòṭẹ gẹ́n.

A ńọ́yí yi jāne mẹ̆kọ, chamẹ́ lūńọ, chamẹ́ pyauwe, chamọ ńọye waṭ Ayọ̄mọ. Ká èjàdọ̀ kị waṭ mọń nẹ̆k, ka wiṭe múm yi nọke ḍọk. Ka wāńe yi dyẹk. Ka Ayọ̄mọ nẹ̆to, kịne: họ họ, chama nōyọ wada chọn! ya ba dùọn! ya fạṭe jal kẹr? Dẹ a ńan pẹr wiṭe wọn? Ya ba gịta kun, ko kọ́mà ńińá, bāda ba bạr! dẹ yi re jắt anan? Kẹr ńị ńọyẹ róù; kāka ba duọn. Fạṭe ḍọk ochāni?

There was a rich Dinka-man whose name was *Ayọmọ*; his son's name was Awan. He loved his son and pierced the horns of sixteen of his cows and stuck tail-hairs into the holes.[2] Again he brought fourteen more oxen, and rams he brought, and he put hairs through the horns of these oxen too. One ox he speared, again he speared another one, and when he had finished spearing them all (those which he had set apart for being speared), he loosened the cattle which were to be given as dowry; they were eighteen. When the man for whose daughter these cows were to be given, heard the cows mowing, he exclaimed, "Oh dear, what do all these cattle mean which are being driven to me? Why are they so many? If my daughter (should marry the son of this man, and after that she) should die, the name of my daughter would be heard all over the country,[3] and the people will say, 'why was she married for so many cattle?' No, I don't consent; go home with your cattle!" But the boy (Awan, who wanted to marry the girl) said, "No, the cattle will not be returned." So at last the man consented. He went among the cattle and selected fourteen; the rest were sent

Remarks see on page 233.

back. Then the thirteen oxen were killed as a feast for the people. And the girl was given to him, they came with her, her father said, "My daughter shall not stay with me any longer (because the dowry has been paid)." When the marriage-festival was finished, they returned to their country.

Now this man was imitated by a certain chief, who wanted to do the same thing; he too wanted to pierce the horns of his cattle, and wanted to imitate the son of *Ayọmọ*. But he lacked sufficient cows to kill, and he got into straits, because his cows were so few. He took goats instead of the cows, and when *Ayọmọ* saw that, he laughed, "Họ họ, he really wanted to imitate my son! I am great! Am I not a rich man? Is there any one so rich as to attain to us? My fame has spread everywhere, all people know my name; my arm is long! Why do you try such a thing, being short of cattle? Wealth can never be imitated; it is not a thing of one day. I have been raising my cattle since a long time ago."

99. Increase of Cattle.

Jal mẹkọ bẹda jal kẹr, bẹda kway Jọ́nọ̀, wạtẹ gîr, kākẹ ba chắkí, ńi chaka tiń mal, ka e yọ̄, ka e rūmọ jāgọ, ka wạtẹ chwọlẹ, ka e ko: u tọ́wá, ya kú kọ́ńè pach. Tẹ́rẹ́ yán, tẹre ya kâl dọk, ka ya kwōńe yejẹ, u dọk ńi ńwọlẹ.

A tọwẹ, a tẹ́ri kal dọk, a kwōńe yejẹ, ka dọk ńí ńwọ̄lọ, a chôk pān ẹni, a pa kẹr, Odwojọ.

A certain man was very rich, he was a descendant of the Dinkas; he had many sons. His time was not near (that is, he was very old); he was so old, that he was carried (he could not walk any longer). Because he was so old, he gave up his chieftainship, he called his sons and told them, "If I die, do not bury me in the village; carry me, carry me to the cattle place and bury me in the midst of it, so the cow will bring forth many calves."

When he had died, he was carried to the cattle fence and was buried in the midst of it, and the cattle brought forth many calves. This village always remained a rich village, it is *Odwojọ*.

100. The Haughty Prince.

Kwakadwai bẹda jal kẹr, ka e kẹdọ, ka e ńọmọ, e ńọmọ ńań rịṯ. Ka dọk kộl, ga pyār abíkyèl. Ka chịki ńọmọ kị pyār abíkyèl.

Ka ńị kọ̄tọ Tộr, ka lūm ńị tùmọ̀, ka kọ̄tọ Dộr. Ká dộk è yàńọ̀. Ka ńa rịṯ e wẹlọ, wẹla yiẹ, ka gẹ ryẹjẹ, ka alẹtọ bện, kị́ chāk, ki kwẹn mau, kị rīńọ. Ka ńa rịṯ mẹkọ kyẹdọ: ya ba dwata gik ak! Kifańọ? A bẹ̄t Ochôlộ, kẹ́rẹ gîr, ka e kwọnọ.

Kɛn mōla kal mǫl, ka ńarōjǫ ńi nɛ̽k, gǫ ńi chăm. Ka e ko: wate ḍān, nɛku ḍān, ki ria u chŏla! Ka wǫde é nɛ̽kỵ, ka gǫ chōlɛ.

Kwakadwai was a rich man. He started to marry, and he married the daughther of a king. He brought sixty cows as a dowry. He married a second wife for sixty cows.

He used to drive his cattle to *Tǭr* (a place of pasture), and when the grass was finished there, he drove them to *Dǫr* (another pasture).

One day some princes were travelling, and they came to him. He entertained them as his guests; dura and dried meat were brought, and milk, and bread baked in butter, and meat. But one of the princes refused, "I don't want these things!" "Why not?" (asked the people). "Because he is a (mere) Shilluk (not one belonging to the royal family), and yet he is so rich!" He did not touch the food.

This (rich) man, when he went to his cattle place early (every) morning, he used to kill a calf and to eat it. And he said to his people, "Sons of men, kill a man! I myself will make amends for him!"[4] And they killed a man, and he made amends.

101. The Hyena with the Bell.

Ka jal mɛ̽kǫ ńa rit, chwǫla Lwal Pōlkóe, ka dyɛkɛ chăm yi ótwŏn. Ka burǫ kwŏńɛ, ka ǫtwǫn mâk yey bur. Ka Lwal bɛnǫ, ka ǫtwǫn kyɛdǫ, ko: wei, kụ nɛ̽k. Ka wei, ka yɛdɛ gǫn kiti mālo, ka ǫtwǫn e kɛdǫ ki mālǫ yɛdɛ. Chami ńi maka lai, ka lai ńi rɛńǫ, ka kōrɛ būdǫ yi kɛch, ka e tǭ.

There was a certain man, a prince, whose name was *Lwal Pōlkoe*; his goats were being eaten by the hyena. Therefore he dug a hole and caught the hyena in the hole. When Lwal came, the hyena begged him, "Leave me, do not kill me!" So he let her go, but he tied a bell to her neck, and the hyena went away with the bell about her neck. But now whenever she wanted to catch game, the game (heard the bell ringing, and) ran away. At last the hyena became tired with hunger and died.

---

[1] *dǫk.*
[2] A sign that these cows were to be reserved as dowry for buying his son a wife.
[3] If the wife dies, the dowry paid for her has to be returned by her family; in this particular case it would be difficult for the father of the girl to give back so many cows, as some would die or perish in some other way in the meantime, and so the affair would turn out a shame to the father and the girl.
[4] to show his immense wealth; it was a bagatelle for him to pay a slave.

XIV. REPORT ON A HUNTING MATCH, AND A JOURNEY.

102. Elephant Hunting.

Wá kệt kí àkīm ki wate chŏl gén àbi-dèk, wate bwon gén àryàu ki Abat kí obwoṅ yẹi, ká wá kệtá pōtẹ Nuạr, lŭm gīr, ka wa kệtá wọk, Abat ye dọṅọ nam ki obwoṅ yẹi; ká lyech ywótì wón, gén àdẹ̀k; ka wọ pẹka péṅ, ka yā tōtẹ ki toch, ka Akwọkwan tōtẹ yi toch, ka Ṅaṅ tōtẹ toch, ka toch (twoch) akīm màkè lŭm, ka toch mwōjọ; ká lyech é rẹ́nọ̀, ká wọ́ dùọgọ̀, lyey bógòn. Dụki ka wọ dọ̄gọ; ka lyech ywótè wón; ka wọ́ riṅọ, lyech fídè wón; ka yòtè wón, é mạdọ̀ pi mẹn an lŭm bogọn. Ká wá kẹta yi lyech, wate bwoń àdẹ̀k, wóṅẹ̀[1] chǒl wón àdẹ̀k, ká wọ́ kẹdọ̀, ka Akwọ̄kwán é pàṅọ̀, ka Aryaṅ ká é paṅọ, wọ́ dọ̀ṅọ̀ wón dǹwọ̀n; yán ki akīm ki wate bwoń ryẹt, ká wọ́ kẹti yí lyech e shǎkí shǎkí, ka akim e kò: wá gọ̀chà lyech àkyẹ̀l, ka wọ gọ̀chọ̀, ka lyech é rẹ́nọ̀, ka yán rẹna bằṅẹ̀, lyech wón kámá tọ̄, ka yá kẹdọ, ya riṅọ, ka gọ̀chè yán tyẹl àdẹ̀k,[2] wọ́ kẹdọ kẹ́ṅ, wọ́ kẹta kẹlẹ tim, ka lyech e chǔṅọ̀, yá bi, yá nẹn, yá nẹn, yẹn gîr, ka lệtẹ yán, ká yá lệtẹ ẹ́n, ká gùjá ki mach. Lyech é ywọ̀n, ka lyech e bẹ̀n, é riṅọ, ka ya chyẹ̀tẹ ẹ́n, ka tyẹlá nẹ́kè ydṭ, é kúché yán, fa rụ̀mọ̀. Ka lyech é chǔnọ̀, cha (= chama) yá gọ̀chè ẹ́n, ka é rẹṅọ, ká wọ́ kẹtí kí ẹ́n, ka yá mák yi rọ́dọ̀, ká yá duọgọ, lyech á kệt, ya duọgọ, ya châtọ; rẹmọ gîr, dẹ yụ́ kúchè yán, ká yá kǎlá yi yu lyech, yá waṅ kí gén, ldù bógòn kí dọga, pi bogọn, ka ya pẹka ta yaṭ, lŭm gîr; ka yá bwọ́gọ́, ka yá dwodọ, ka toch gọ̀ch yi akim, ka toch lṭnè yán ldu ldu ldu, yá kẹdọ, ya riṅọ, ka toch ní gọ̀ch gẹ́ gîr. Ka ya bẹ̀nọ̀, ka toch gọ̀chè yán, ká toch líṅ yì gén. Chuṅẹ gẹ́ mẹ̄dọ, chuṅa ṭyau mẹ̄dọ; ká yâ bẹ̀n, ká gẹ́ yọtè yán, gẹ́ gọ̀ch aṅwak, ká yà tōtẹ yi pî; rọ̀dọ̀ baṅi tụm, ka ya tọtẹ yi mọgọ (gin cham), ká chwàká é bánọ̀; ka yá kẹta nam, ka ya budọ ki yẹjẹ. Ká yá màkè yi kọjọ̀, yá bẹ̀t ki dọ̀ch ki nam; ka ya ṅi mụdọ ki pî; ka yá bìá wọk, ká wọ́ bẹ̀n wọ́ bìá gat. Ka wọ́ bē̤dọ dụki, ka wọ bẹ̀n wọ́ bỉẹ̀ tōtẹ chǒl, wọ́ màk jẹm àryàu, wọ bẹ̀nọ̀, gin cham bogọn, wọ́ ṅi chámá rìṅọ ẹ kẹ́tẹ̀, ka wọ bia Atằrọ̀, ká tàṅ yòtẹ̀ wón gẹ́ gîr. Ká wọ́ kẹtá wọk, ká tàṅ pwót, àbí-dẹ̀k, mẹ̀k a gọ̀chè yi akim, gọ̀tjè wiy tụṅẹ, ká è tọ̄. Ka yẹì é pàṅọ̀ yi riṅọ, ka wọ bẹ̀n.

We went (by boat), the doctor, eight Shilluks, two white men, Abbas, and the white men of the steamer. We went into the Nuer country, there was much grass along the river. When we left the boat, Abbas remained near the river with the white men of the steamer. We found three elephants, when we saw them, we sat down on the ground, they gave me a gun, *Akwokwan* and *Nyaṅ* too received a gun. The gun of the doctor was entangled in the grass, and

---
[1] more frequently *wọna*, see Grammar.   [2] "three feet", that is: three times.

it suddenly exploded. When the elephant heard it, it ran away; we returned because the elephant was no more (i. e. the elephants disappeared). The next morning we went again and found again an elephant. We ran pursuing the elephant. We found it drinking water in a place where there was no grass. We went towards the elephant. We were three white men and three Shilluks. While we were going, *Akwọkwan* and *Anyan* stooped down (i. e. hid, being afraid); so we four were left, I, the doctor, and the other two white men. We went to the elephant and approached it closely, then the doctor said, "We have got one elephant!" We shot, the elephant ran away, and I followed it; our elephant had received a mortal wound. I followed it running and shot it three times. We ran into a place where there was a forest; there the elephant stopped, I came and looked and looked, there were dense trees; at last I saw it, and it saw me, and I shot it with the gun. The elephant cried, it came running, and I was chased by it, I knocked my foot against a tree, but I did not heed it, it did not make a wound. The elephant stopped and I intended to shoot it. It ran again, I ran with it; and I was seized with thirst; I turned back, the elephant ran away, I turned back and went; there was much blood. But I did not know the way. I went along the elephant's path, I was quite lost to my companions; there was no more spittle in my mouth (from thirst), I had no water. I sat down under a tree in the midst of much grass. I became afraid and arose. Then there was a gun fired by the doctor, I heard it very, very far off. I went running and heard them fire many guns. At last I too fired a gun, it was heard by them. Then they rejoiced, and I too rejoiced, and I came and found them, they had shot an anwak; they gave me water. My thirst would not cease, and they gave me food, but my throat refused to take it. I went into the river and lay down in the water. So I became cool, I lay in the water a long time. Then I drank water. At last I came out. And we came to the river-side. We stayed there till the next day, then we came back into the Shilluk country. We had been away two weeks. During our return we found no food, so we ate nothing but meat. We came to the river Ataro, there we found many waterbucks. We went out of the boat and shot eight waterbucks. One was shot by the doctor between its horns, and it died. The boat was quite full of meat; so we came home.

103. A Journey.

Ka wọ́ wẹ̀lọ̀, wẹ̀lọ Tūnọ, ka wọ ka pōṭe Nuạr, ka wọ kẹ́lẹ̀ yi nam mẹ̄kọ, chwọla Ńẹyẹrọ, ka wọ ka Teryau, ka wọ tọ̄ńa wok, ka wọ budọ rech, ka wọ kẹdọ, ka wọ tọ̄ńa kal riṭ, chwọla Pẹ̀dỏ, ka wọ tọ̄ńa lwāgẹ, ka ẹ pẹ̀chọ̀ kịne: wạte Chọ́lọ̀, wu kạl wu kɛṅ? wǫ kò: wa kḁla fōt̪e Chóly! Kịne: wich apǫṅǫ? Kịne: wa chaka ṅeau wǫ byɛ̣l. Kịne: búh, a t̪ō wun yị kɛ̱ch? E ko: kɛ̱tu lwak! Ka wǫ kɛ̱ta lwak, ka oṅwǫk kạ̈l, ka nɛ̱k, ká châm yị wón; ka chak kạ̈l, ka wǫ châmǫ̀, ka ṅyɛṅ a kạ̈le wǫn, ṅeau ki byɛ̣l. Ka wǫ bɛ̄nǫ, ka kɛ̱ti yị yạ̈t̪, ka wǫ bɛ̄nǫ, ka yɛi mákò yị pàr, ka yɛi mudǫ, ka wǫ kwāṅǫ wǫk; a bɛ̱ná, a t̪ǭṅa Ńebǭdǫ̀, a bɛ̱na pach, a bɛ̱na Peṅidwai; kɛ̱ch kɛ̱ch!

We travelled to *Tonga* and from there came into the Nuer-country; we were travelling on some river, whose name is *Ńeyɛrǫ*. We came to Teryau, there we landed; we roasted fish. We went and turned to the home of the king, whose name was *Pɛ̣dō*. We turned towards the cow-house. He asked us, "You Shilluk children, where do you come from?" We answered, "We come from the Shilluk-country." He asked, "What for?" We replied, "We want to buy dura." He said, "Why, are you suffering ("dying") from hunger?" Then he said, "Go into the cow-house!"[1] So we went into the cow-house. A ram was brought and killed, and was eaten by us; and milk was brought, and we ate. Then we brought forth money to buy dura. (After we had bought it and brought it into our boats) we went into the boats and returned home. But one boat was seized by a hippo, it sank, and we swam to the bank. So I came home turning towards *Ńebǭdǫ*, I came home to *Peṅidwai*; the famine was very great.

---

[1] the cow house serves as a residence for guests.

XV. SONGS.
104. War songs.

A chip tuṅ lḗṅ, leṅ a chip shin Aṅǭnǫ; Bal kḙchǫ! Yana bāṅ Ńikaṅ; chḙ ya dǫ́ṅ á bḙ̄r; kōfá yín ki mǫk jwǫk; riḙ e kḁl jwǫk. Wora ḍwǫ̀ṇ kwom lḗṅ! Yana bāṅ Ńikaṅ! Leṅ a chip shine kwḁyḙ́, ki Otḙgǫ tuṅ leṅ Ńàbǭdǫ̀. Ńikaṅ a yḁ̂ti̥, kuro gḙ̄k Jaṅ.

The wings of the army are drawn up; the army is placed in the hands of *Aṅǭnǫ*. Bal is strong. I am a servant of *Ńikaṅ*, I was nearly left desolate. I tell you the tidings of God; the king comes with God. The kings arose against the enemy's army. I am a servant of *Ńikaṅ*. The army is placed in the hands of our grandfather, in *Otḙgǫ*, as far as *Ńabǭdǫ* war is raging.

Fāri y̧ laki mḙn, ṅa Ńikaṅ? fāri y̧ gḙ̂r ki tǫ́ṅ!

Who shall inherit your village, you son of *Ńikaṅ?* Your village will be built by spears!

Wei yiḙgḙ yūḙgò! Fa Ńikaṅ fa ṅi țùmí, lwḁgá á kyḙ̀t, ki Wy̧rokwar á kyḙ̌t; lwḁgá fa tūgǫ! akyḙl a dǫ̀nǫ̀, ka lǭkǫ bāṅ gḙ́n, Areoṅiḍi̥ṅ, fa wḁ̂tḙ́ Gḙ̄ṅjwǫ̀k, fa wḁ̂tḙ́ Abōl! wei yiḙgḙ yūḙgǫ, fa Ńikaṅ fa ṅi țùmí.

Let them carry (people) away! The house of *Ńikaṅ* will never be finished, my people refuse (to surrender), *Wy̧rokwar* refuses; my people are not to be played with! One will always be left; and he will follow them (the enemies), *Areoṅiḍi̥ṅ*, from the village of the children of *Gḙ̄ṅjwǫk*, the village of the children of *Abōl.* Let them carry away, the house of *Ńikaṅ* will never be finished.

Agǭgjdṅ Aṅǫ̂ṅ-wán, wa teau dḙ́rūk. A waṇi, a waṇi yǫ, dḙ kḁ̄lá F'tjǫ̀. Máchḙ́ rḙ́ fa dǭgé rḙ̣́, mache rḙ fa dǭgé rḙ. Akōlḙ́-Ńákwḙ́, a kḁl jwǫ̀k. Mache yǫ fa dǭge rḙ.

Agogjang Anongwan is cursing the Turks, they are coming near, they are approaching on the way, they come up the mouth of the Sobat. But the fire of their guns will return on themselves, their fire will return on themselves; Akole Nyakwe he comes (against them) with God. Their fire will return on themselves.

Yá fìt lyà fǫ̀, ya fìt lya féd, Ńikaṅ, ya fìt lya fǫ, ya fìt lya fǫ, jal duǫṅ, ya fìt lya fǫ.

I am tired of being waylaid, I am tired of being watched upon, *Ńikaṅ*, I am tired of being waylaid, my master, I am tired of being waylaid.

Ká dé bṳ́n Ágwęt, wat Jǭk, ya re (de) ḷǫ́nị yinǫ, yá yiḝlḕ Kḛ̀ch Alál, yá yiḝlḕ yị kwāyǫ, kech Alal, wúrú Wạt.

But for *Agwęt*, the son of *Jǭk*, I should have left my country, and gone far away; I have been saved by the strength of Alal, I have been saved by our grandfather, the powerful Alal, the son of *Wạt*.

Ńá Dāk, yi kwacha ṅǫ? Ya kwacha ńḕdǫ̀! Chḛ ya kḛṭị kun, fura yán. Ya yiḝlḕ yi kwá Ayádǫ̀. Wanǭ Ńa Dāk gḕrǫ pach kị́ tŭk, ówâu fa lén mḛkǫ.

You son of *Dāk*, what do you ask for? I ask for a hoe, for wherever I go I hoe the ground. I have been preserved by our grandfather *Ayādǫ*. The mother of the son of *Dāk* has built us a house under the deleb palms; the branches of the deleb are like an army.[1]

Mǫ́ké byḛl Ńakāyǫ, ya chạ̀ṭị, ya yànǫ̀, mǫke byḛl Abuk, man Dḛn, ya chạ̀ṭị yá yànǫ̀.

By the dura-beer of *Ńakāyǫ* I walk, I am filled with it, by the beer of Abuk, the mother of *Dḛn*, I am walking, I am filled with it.

Akōl a duǫ̀k mal; yá nḛna rḛ̀. Ki nḛni gwach, rūme yḛjà ńḛ̀nǫ̀. Dāk a shwǫu, shwǫu obwoṅ Dǭrǫ̀.

Akōl has returned. I live through him free from oppressors. The anxieties of my heart were many. But *Dāk* roared, he roared the white people away to *Dǭrǫ*.

Mḛnǫ ki gyḕnḛ̀, mḛnǫ kị́ gyḕnḛ̀, gyḕne Dāk yǫ̀, mḛnǫ kị gyḕnḛ ....

Each one has his own fowl, each one has his own fowl, but all fowl belong to *Dāk*.

Ya rǫyi rǫi! ęnḛ gin ānǫ? bwonǫ! Tḕrǫ ywǫgǫ mal. byel a kḛl yi obwoṅ. Kwaye fa tǫ̀k, ńa Dāk a kạ̀l jwǫk. Ńá gól kwańé kót ún, wa kela wiy tuṅ! Obwoṅ chama yákà yán. Tḕrǫ bḛ̀n nụtí yạ̀k ḕn. Ńan a tón yán? Yan a rạ̄t lābǫ. Shàgê, dǫk lwāgi, yi ṳ ńàké ki ńan mḛkǫ̀.

I am fleeing away, shouting loud! What is the matter? "The white people!" the people are shouting loud. "The dura is being carried away by the white people!" — But our grandfather is not absent. The son of *Dāk* is coming with God. Ye people, take your shields! We will go this way! The white people want to take away all our property. Other people have not been robbed by them! Who ever dared to take away my goods? I, the king of the people! Ye Arabs, turn back your hosts, fight another tribe!

---

[1] The rustling of the leaves of the deleib palm is like the rustling of an army; so that when the enemy approaches the village, they imagine they hear an army, and flee.

105. Mourning songs, and others.

Abâ na Ńikań, Amyęle wa tǫ́k. Fà nęná ya dǫ̀nǫ̀ twàlǫ̀. Lwǫn fan ǫ́tû, fà jań wǫ́n. Amyęle lwǫń, wạt Kwâjèriù, dę kâl, dǫn é twàlǫ̀, fay dǫn é twàlǫ̀, fay dǫn e yȧ̀rǫ̀. Agûmwél fanę jȧ̂gǫ.

Aba, the son of Ńikań, my father Amyęle, is no more. Look at me, I am left poor. Lwǫń is away, he, our chief, Amyęl Lwǫń, the son of Kwajeriu. Our family is left destitute, our village is left destitute, our home is left reproached. Agumwēl, he was a great chief.

Afyęk wat Deń, liawǫ́ tǫ̀r. Aryal-bęk gǫń dean, u kwaya Ajwǫt-ńimin.

Afyek, the son of Deń, is waylaying in the grassy place. Aryalbek loosens a cow and gives it to Ajwǫt-ńimiń, to herd (= to possess) it.[1]

Ayidǭke, wạt Ryal-dwęt Wun-diȧ̀rò, Ayikǫ́, Wúnė-gêń-bęl, ya wań ki yŭ kun a kạl ęn.

Ryalawet Wundiāro, Ayiko, Wunegenbel Ayidoke, I lost the way in which he went.

Akwǫ̀néyǫ̆r, yina mâń júr, de ya dǭn bęr! Jińbęk, Akwǫneyǫr, kwārę fa tǫwa pal. Gę ki rache weya dǫń á bęr. Akwǫt a lęnǫ fạl; ya yafa jāgǫ Duńkǫk, ya yafa Okwoni, Ajāl-ńabań gwań, Ńámâilȧi.

Akwoneyor, you captured people, but I was left poor! Jingbek, Akwoneyor, their grandchildren are dying in the wilderness. They live in misery, are left destitute. Akwǫt threw me out into the bush. I am searching for chief Dunkok, I am searching for Okwoni, Ajalnyaban-gwań, Nyamailai.

Akwǫneyǫr, yi kiţa kęń ki lwāgi? Akwǭtǫ nụtí jȧlǫ. Olām-bęń a gęl chōr. Olam na Ńikań, Dulại wạt Kēr, Kwālại a gęl chōr. Na Ńikań ki mayi Bęk.

Akwoneyor, where have you brought people? Akwǭtǫ has never been cursed by his subjects,[2] Olām-bęń is a preserver of men in the famine. Olam, son of Nyikang, Dulai, son of Ker is a preserver of people in hunger, a son of Ńikań and of his mother Bęk.

Agwęt-ńanedǫń, feń a fȧ̂ţ chyę̄, lwak a reń, Agwęt ńa Ńikań! Dę ywǫgǫ mal labǫ tánę́ chíńę́.

Agwetnyanedong, the country is starved, the people are dying. Agwet, son of Nyikang, they are mourning, stretching up their hands.

---

[1] A song of cattle stealing.   [2] has always been loved.

Adǫl-tuṅ, yi kǝ̱ta kęṅ? Nuǝr a waṇi, ya kǝ̱ta fáné láṅà jwǫk, Awen, ṅa Yǫr.
"Adoltung, where are you going?" "The Nuers are approaching, I am going to the town of God, oh Awen, son of Yor."

Akol Dāk ṅa Ńikaṅ, Kaye-Dūrǫ, Akolų́ku, Akol-Kwālai, ṅa Ogāk Fǭlǫ, kwai ḍāṇ, ya yięlé yín, a yięda yin shǫ̱n ki dyę̇rí, ya yięlé. Yákǫ̱l, maye Dàké, Amǫl ṅa Ogāk (= Shal), lwagi ṅi̱ fyę̀n ṅi̱ fyèṅǫ̀: Shal kǝ̱ta? Kęṅ ma wāṇǫ; ṅan ṅi̱ gōṇi̱ kǫ̱t? naṅe chi̱ṇǫ ywóda̋ ki̱ Dèṅǫ̀, watė́ shwai ywoda, lwāk Amǫ̋l, ṅa Ńikaṅ.

Akol, Dak, son of Nyikang, Kaye Duro, Akoluku, Akol Kwalai, son of Ogak Folo, you grandfather of men, I am preserved by you, I have been saved by you in ancient times, I have been preserved. Yakol, you father of *Dāk*, Amol, your people are continually asking me, "has Shal gone?" Hunger is approaching; where has he gone, he who preserves the descendants? Licking of hands[1] I found at *Deṅǫ*, eating of soup found I, you people of *Amǫl*, the son of *Ńikaṅ*.

Ajàk-bàṅ-wèl-jǫk, kwacha kwārǝ, kwacha tygṅ fa jwǫk, ri̱t e duǫk mal. Kwacha kwayǝ yau. Tǫ̀m è gǫ̀jǫ̀; yan da Ńikaṅ, ri̱t e duǫk mal; tǫ̱ná fa yǝṅa shi̱ṇá? Yan da Ńikaṅ; feṅ a yięl, a yięl é rę̀ṅ; ya fura byęl, ya fàkǫ̀, ya tǝ́ṅa shi̱ṇa, Wuro-kwá, kǫṅ bà̋dá̋!

Ajak-banweljok, I am praying to our grandfather, I am praying to the people of the place of God, the king[2] has returned. I am praying to our grandfather. The holy drum is being beaten, I am with *Ńikaṅ*, the king[1] has returned to us. Is not my spear in my hand? I am with *Ńikaṅ*. The country is saved, it is saved, though it was desolate. I am planting my dura; I thank (my ancestors), I lift up my hands, Wuro-Kwa, strengthen my arms!

---

[1] "licking of hands" is an expression for plenty of good food. [2] *Ńikaṅ*.

XVI. RIDDLES.

106. Riddles.

Adùk gọ́nọ́ lùyì : mọ̀n ófŭn.	The gray one is going under a pond: Loaf of bread, which is put into the fireplace.
ńịṅ gúwd nẹ́né lọ̣kọ̀ : táté kâl.	my necklace is seen beyond the river: The unbarked, white fence sticks.
ńēmẹ̣i kị́ rei gẹn fa gúl̀ẹ̀: tụ́né ḍeaṅ.	Brothers who never hurt each other: The two horns of a cow.
Ajwọ̄gọ laṅ war, ị́ yāwọ: yiep ḍeaṅ.	which sorcerer spends the whole night in swinging?: The tail of the cow.
Anor-nor kēmọ wẹn Fashōdọ: dlệ̄yọ̀.	Anor-nor visits his father (the king) at Fashoda: The grass called alẹyọ, which is used in making ropes. When taxes, cows etc., are brought to the king at F., the rope with which the things are bound, gets to F.
Fwôt, fa fyêl : bùl.	It is beaten, yet is does not ease: The drum.
A rik a rik, fẹra manị : tẹdét.	(Dinka-language, except the last word.)
Akur jọ́n dẹṅ : chọ̄gọ.	white pigeons: Bleached bones.
A pō ṭok ṅa tyẹk okọ̄dọ: Ṭọ ḍāṇ.	
Adùk obọ̣̄gò kwóté nẹ́gẹ́ : gyẹ̄no.	The gray one who is spotted is driving her little ones: The hen.
Aduk chọ̣̄r yi f^woḍọ̣̀o: ótọ̆k.	The gray one is running towards the fields: The mist.
Ṅejók gwotị feṅ: dwẹi.	The black-white cow is making white the earth: The moon.
Ṅwọli yaṅ tẹnọ chọ̣̄gò toke bur: yịt̪.	Little children stand continually at the side of the heaps of ashes: The ears of man.
ńemẹi ḍọgẹ lùṅ féṅ : Órọ̀m.	Two brothers, their mouth is turned down: The nose.
Adāle jwọk yigẹ lùṅ féṅ : t̪au.	The calabash of God which is turned downward: The fruit of the heglig-tree.
Agar agar, yat̪ wiṅ: lẹ̣k.	A long row of trees full of white birds: The teeth. Along the rivers one sees frequently trees which are literally covered with snow-white birds.
Wệt̪ feṅ, kōrọ fa tōr: aṅọ̄nọ.	Thrown on the ground, yet not broken: Mucus from the nose.

Tetel pōte rate: chūl ḍāṇ.	
Yēn lọ̈n kị yēn lọ̈n: wan ḍāṇ.	It is on this side and on the other side: The eye of man.
Ya wẹ̄li yi kẹti kẹn? ṭẹpọ́ ḍāṇ.	I am travelling, where are *you* going?: The shadow of man.
Wâ dàgù, ẹ́ bà kẹ́ṭ: bùr.	We remove, he does not go: The ashes. If people leave a home-stead, the ashes remain behind.
A rigi rik pẹre maṇi: Tedẹt.[1]	

---

[1] Some of the riddles have not been translated, their meaning being obscene, some have for this reason been omitted altogether.

THIRD PART
DICTIONARY

SHILLUK ENGLISH.

Remark. Different dialectical forms of a word are not given here. If corresponding forms of a word in other languages than Shilluk are noted in the Comparative List in Part I, they are not repeated here.

A.

a my; see Grammar.
á denotes the past tense.
ā it is; ā gin ānǫ̀ which thing (what) is it?
ā which? á jàl ā which man is it?
ā́ yes
àbàch a cow with horns directed straight sidewards
ábǎmách a bird, living on fish
àbán-àbán hammer
àbār a kind of reed. a. á yá nàm the a. is on the river
abaratāṛǫ̀ a big worm, living on the heglig tree
àbát (ar.) fishhook
àbàtūrǫ̀-àbàtūrí the iguana-lizard
ábíck five
ábídèk eight
ábíkyèl six
àbìn a gourd out of which spoons are made
ábínwèn nine

ábíp small-pox
ábíryàu seven
àbǫ́bǫ̀, also àbwóbǫ̀ ambach, Herminiera elaphroxylon; the plant as well as things made of it, as arm-rings, boats, statues
àbǫ́kǫ̀-àbǫ́kí a very poisonous snake
àbú poor; yá fà àbú I am poor. see bú, búnǫ̀
àbúrǫ̀-àbùr the bushbuck (Ba. aburi)
àbwòk maize, corn; gệ fûr a. kí fwòdǫ́ they planted corn in the field
àbwǫ́nè toch the butt of the gun
àchà that there, those there
achak-achák poet
àchán behind, back; see chán.
àchán-àchàn a fish
àchệm straight
áchíchwêl (ar.) chain

àchǫ̀yǫ̀ melon
áchùnǫ̀-áchúní the small black house-ant
àchút-àchút arm-ring of ambach; syn. ogệnǫ
àchwàtǫ̀-àchwàtí loincloth for women
àchwát-àchwát guineafowl
áchwík a bird
áchwík-áchwèk anus; syn. opap
àchyệnǫ̀-àchyện black winged ant, lives in houses, its bit is painful
ádàlǫ̀-ádǎlí gourd, calabash
ádèk three
àdệrǫ̀-àdệr an arm-ring of ambach; syn. ogệnǫ
àdệrǫ̀-àdệr donkey; a chạti wich adệrǫ he rode on a donkey
adệrǫ serf
ádí, ádì, also ệdì how, how much? chàn ádí

how many days? (Di. di)
àdımọ̀-àdımı̀ beak
ádínò-àdìn an electric fish
ádọ̀lọ̀-àdọ́l a fish
àdúdọ́-àdút a basket
áduk grey
àdúkê a kind of red dura
àdùọ̀n, also àdúọ̀n a month, about March
ádwọ̀rọ̀-ádwarı̀ a fish
àdwât chicken-pocks
àdı̣́t-adat (ar.?) bottle
ádı̣́ù pistol
ádẹ̀dẹ̀k armour, armament
àdùrọ̀k a kind of white dura [son
àdwẹ̀n an honourable per-
afa in order that
áfẹ̀dọ̀-áfẹ̀t stink-cat, skunk
áfệ, also áfı hail, hail-
stone; a. dyèmò it is hailing
áfòàjọ̀-áfọ̀àchı̣̀ hare, rabbit
àfọ̀kệ husk, as of cotton
áfùdọ̀-áfútı̀ a fish, with
big belly, four large upper and lower front teeth
àgàk these, those (Di. kak)
ágàk-àgẹ̀kı̀ crow; àgànè chwâi a little black crow (Bo. gaki)
àgẹ̀k uncultivated land
ageṅ lyech a herb with a blue blossom
àgẹ̀rọ̀-àgẹ̀r a hair-dress of the men

àgẹ̀tọ́ blessed; see gẹ̄tọ
àgòn, gòn where? àgòn ẹ̀n where is he? àgò gẹ̀n where are they?
àgọ̄nọ̀ general name for white dura
àgọ̀rọ̀-àgọ̀r neck-bone, cervical vertebra
àgwẹ̀n-àgwẹ̀n bastard child
àgwẹ̀rọ̀ a season, about November-December, harvest of white dura
àgwọ́lọ̀-àgwọ́lı̀ a fish
àgyẹ̀n ṅwọ̀n nàm a small bird with a white bill
ayọ̄jọ heifer; see ṅayọ̄jọ
àjàlọ́ṅ proper name for men (also name for a cow?)
àjúl grey hawk
àjwọ̀gọ́-àjwọ̀k medicine-man, witch-doctor, sorcerer
àk these
àkâch a kind of white dura
akộl-àkọ̀lı̀ bird-trap
akánọ̀ verandah, shed
àkâr-àkâr a bird, eating dura
àkâre yàt branch of a tree
àkẹ́yò-nékèı the child of my sister; niece, nephew
àkẹ̀ch the dura-bird
akẹchmwọl morning-dawn
àkẹ̀n tyẹ̀lò calf of the leg
àkọ́ch a month; àkọ́n duọn

about January, àkọ́n ẹ̀n about February
àkộkọ̀ a basket
àkộl-àkộlı̀ drum-stick
àkọ́ldìt (Dinka?) a month, about May
àkọ̀ṅ-àkọ́nı̀ gazella rubi-frons
àkúr (àkúrọ́)-àkúrı̀ wild pigeon; àkúr-jwàt a small bush-pigeon (Turkana akuri)
àkwâirọ́ch a bird ("it herds the heifer")
àkwân-àkwân ear-lap
àkwọ́l a kind of red dura
àkwộr husk
àkyẹ̀l one; alone, single
àkyẹ̀n-àkyẹ̀n cock or spanner of a gun
alâbọ rice
àlâl a kind of white dura
àlẹ̀bọ́-àlı̣́pı̀ a bird
àlẹ̀bôr a month, about April
àlẹ̀nọ̀-àlẹ̀nı̀ a fish
alẹ̀tọ a food: dura with dried meat
àlẹ̀yọ̀ a grass, used in making ropes
àlílı̣̀t bat
àlọ́dọ́ the (holy) spear of Ńikaṅ, which he brought into the Shilluk country, is said to be kept at Feṅikaṅ
àlùṅ-àlùṅ somersault
àlútọ̀-àlútı̀ fist; buffeting
àlwẹ̀dọ̀ a kind of white

dura, it has four ears, like four "fingers"; its stalk is chewed like sugar cane; see *lwēdǫ*
ama because
ámágák a dance, accompanied by singing and clapping of hands, but without drum.
amal in front of; see *mal*
àmálǫ first; *tyèl a.* at first, the first time; see *mal*
àmálǫ (ar.) - *àmáli* camel
àmàrǫ fárǫ́ rhicinus
ámáṭ-ámáṭi a stork, black with white breast, nests on trees
àmę́n, (also *àmę́n*) - *àmǫ́k* who?
ámwól-ámwóli a large black fish
ànàn, *ànàn-ànàn*, here, now, just now, presently, at once
ànànǫ, *ànànǫ̂* = *ànàn*; also : here it is
ánę́kǫ́ spirit of a deceased person; *wiję da a.* he is possessed by a spirit, he is senseless, mad; see *nūgǫ*
ànǫ́n quarrel
anor-nor a certain grass, used in making ropes
ánáni brown earth
ánwóch a season, about October, end of the red dura harvest
ànàdǫ-ánàni breast-bone

ánękǫ́ red sand
ánę́nǫ-ánę́ni a small red ant, feeds on carrion
ánǫ̀-ǫ̀nǫ̀ what, which? (Teso *ńo*, Nr. *ńy* what, Ba. *ńa* who)
anǫl a mocker
ánǫ́n-ánǫ́ni a knife for cutting grass
ánǫ́nǫ́ snot, mucus
ánwák-ánwáki water-buck
ánwǫn four (Nr. *ńwān*, Masai *uńwan*, Teso *woŃono*, Ba. *uńwan*)
àpę́r fish-line
àrá well! why! by God! see *re*
àròch-àròch a shell
arū an exclamation
àryàu two (Madi *erí*, Abokaya *iri*, Teso *arai*, Masai *āre*
àtábǫ́ - átǫ̀m (a foreign word) tobacco
àtál a slab
átái-átái a large pot
àtę̀gò, also *àtéègǫ - àtę̀k* (finger-)ring of metal;
àtę̀nè duǫn big ring (Nr. *tę̀k*)
àtę́n-àtàn hat
ater enmity
àtèt, also *átèt-àtę̀t* mangouste, ichneumon
àtíni just now, to-day;
àtǫ́ well!   [see *tin*
àtùdǫ-àtùti a wild goose (Di. *twot*, *atwol*, Nr. *twǫr*)

Atúlfi the Sobat
àtúnǫ́ wind, gale, blast
àtúń-ákyèl("one-horned") rhinoceros
àtút a bead, worn by the king
àtwák-àtwàk a bird
àṭábǫ́ a kind of red dura
aṭach ḍǫn a very tough grass
àṭędǫ́ (foreign word?) bamia
àṭéi ḍān the buttocks
àṭęp-àṭęp, also *àṭęp* bag, sack (Di. *atep*)
àṭę́r forever, for a long time
àṭę́rǫ́-àṭę́ri, also *àṭę́r* a small stick or spear of wood, such as were in use formerly; used in digging eatable roots etc.
àṭíwí-àṭíu a small waterpot, in shape of a cooler
àṭùṭèwìch a small hut for the new elected king(?)
àwà, *àùwà* yesterday
áuwàr-áuwà the day before yesterday
àwdi a kind of red dura
àwák-àwák a bird
àwáńít a bird
àwǫn when?
àwęt a kind of white dura
àwǫ́ yes
àwǫ́ch-àwòch a large, cylindrical shell

àwǫk nǫ̀m a cow with horns directed straight upwards, like a goat's
àwúṇǫ̀ marrow, as of bones
áyâch bǫ̀r a bird
àyéch sand, dust [ridge
àyi̯ęr-àyi̯ęrì quail, part-
àyǫ̀lkàk a cow, black with white tail
áyǫ̀mǫ̀ - áyǫ̀m tin, ornaments of tin
àywák-àywák tuft, crest of birds
áywóm-áywòmì monkey

B.

bá, bà 1. to be; 2. not. syn. fà
Báchódǫ̀, Páchódǫ̀ Fashoda
bāgǫ to make a fence; pt. á baka bak he made a fence, pe. bák, n. bàk
bāgǫ to boil (eggs, corn), to stew (meat); a baka nwǫl gyęnǫ he boiled eggs; pe. a bęk
bai buttermilk
bājǫ to tie together; pt. á bęchà lāu, pe. á bęch, bęch, n. bęch
bājǫ to miss; yá báchà lai I missed the game
bák-bâk fence, palisade
bálǫ̀ to throw; a bala gwok he threw at the dog; see batǫ
bànę́ syn. bęnę́n
bānǫ to make a mistake, to be confused, vexed; to scold; to dispute
bànǫ̀-bàni the meat on the skin of killed animals
bānǫ to roll up (?)

bàń a cow with one horn directed downward, the other upward
bànǫ̀ to refuse, to prohibit; pt. á bànà gwǫk he refused to work
bànǫ̀-bàń locust
bàń 1. behind, after, back, 2. slave, servant, person belonging to one; more frequently: wǫt bāń (Nu. abāk hind part)
bāpǫ to ask for a thing, to beg; pt. a bapi gin cham he asked for food; pe. a bâp
bàr, also bǫ̀r long, far
bǫr early in morning, morning-dawn
bǫrǫ to be long, far
bàt-bât arm, fore-leg, trunk of the elephant
batǫ to throw; pt. a bala kit he threw a stone, pe. kit a bâl the stone was thrown
báyǫ̀ mosquito see bęyǫ
bę̀ for, in order to; from
bia to come

bęch, also bach bundle
będǫ to remain, stay, be; to refuse; pt. a będa wǫt he stayed in the house
bę̂ mosquito; see bęyǫ
bęjǫ̀ to wring out; lāu da pi, bęch! the cloth is wet, wring it out
bę̀l a month, bę̀l tę̀n July, bę̀l dúǫ́ń June
bęlǫ to taste; pt. a bę́là gin cham; pe. a bę̂l; n. bę̀l (Nr. bęl)
bę̀n, also bę̀nè all, quite (Di. eben)
bę̀nę́n that is, he is, that is why, from bà "to be", and ę̀n "he, it"
bę̀nǫ̀ to come; á bę̀n jal a man came (Nr. bęn)
bę̀r (ar.) flag, banner
bę̀r poor, destitute, wasted; from bę̀dǫ̀?
bę̂ 1. round spear, fishspear. 2. (sharp?)
bęyǫ-bę̂ mosquito
bì, bìà to come

bĭ white ant
bĭá, bĭę to come (Teso bia to come)
bigin = bogǫn
bǫch barren; see bwǫch
bōdǫ to cast iron, to work in iron; to be clever, to escape a danger; pt., pe. a bǫ́t; n. bǫ̀dǫ̀
bǫ̀dǫ̀-bǫ̀tĭ blacksmith, craftsman
bógǫn (from bú and gǫn) there is not
bǫ́i-bǫ̀i net; bǫ́i óráf cobweb (Bo. boi)
bōkǫ to fear, to be afraid; pt. a bǫ̀kĭ (Kuamba bokǫ)
bǫl a mat for closing a door; used by chiefs
bǫ̀lǫ̀-bǫ̀l face, front, frontside, in front of; bǫ̀l tǫ́n the shaft of the spear
bǫ̀lǫ̀ to have misfortune, disaster, to be bereaved
bǫl ḡenǫ neck-ring of pearls
bōmǫ to be bent, crooked; yat á bǫ̀m the tree is crooked
bǫ̀nǫ̀ to laugh; pt. a bǫ́n; see nǣtǫ
bǫ̀nǫ́-bǫ̀nĭ pelican
bǫ̀nǫ̀-bǫ̀nĭ a small lizard
bŏr-bǫ̀r boil
bǫ̀rǫ̀, also bǫ̀r afternoon; tín kĭ bǫ̀r this afternoon

bǫ̀t-bǫ̀tĭ bachelor
bú to have not, to lack
Buda-Chǫl native name for Taufikia; also Bura-Chǫl; Bura is the same as burǫ "open place"; the meaning of the name is: "the open place of the Shilluks", Tauf. being situated in a free place, not covered with grass or bush
búdǫ̀-bút a shell
búdǫ̀ part, half
búdǫ̀, also búdǫ̀ to lie, to lie down, to be sick; pt. á bútǫ̀; n. bútǫ̀
budǫ to roast, to bake; pt. a but he roasted; also a bul; a budĭ rêch he roasted fish; pe. rech a búl (Nr. bulǫ)
búdǫ̀-bútĭ a small melon, sweet, eatable
būdǫ to be tired, troubled, vexed; to tire; kǫ̀rá búdǎ "my breast", that is "I, am tired"
búgĭn there is not; wó gǫ̂k yętĭ chàn ádęk, búgĭn a wékĭ wǫn we worked three days there was not a thing he gave us: he gave us nothing
bugǫ to press the bellows; pt. á bùk kĭ óbùk; pe. á búk

búh exclamation of surprise
būl-būlĭ drum (Karamojo bur)
bun part
búnǫ̀ to have not, to lack
búp mud, Somal bōr hole
búr-búr cave, well
búr abwok the blossom of the corn
búr ashes
bùrǫ̀ = búr ashes; also: free, open place in the village, covered with ashes (Di. bur, Nu. but)
būte side, beside; from budǫ to lie?
bwǫ̀bǫ̀ uncooked butter
bwǫch sterile; syn. bǫch
bwǫ̀dǫ̀ = bōdǫ to be clever, pt. a bǫ́t
bwǫ̂gǫ̀ to frighten; pt. á bwǫk; n. bwǫ̂gǫ̀, see bōkǫ
bwǫ̀nǫ̀-bwǫn white man, European, Arab; bwǫn jwǫk missionary (Nr. bwoń)
bwǫ̀nǫ̀ a kind of red dura
bwǫ̀nǫ̀-bwǫ̀nĭ a fish
bwǭp-bwǭp the lower part of the belly
bwǭrǫ to make a mistake, to err; lębę é bwǭrǫ he makes a mistake in talking; ká yígí yá bwǫ̀rǫ̀, nĭ kòfí yán if I make a mistake, tell me! pt. bwǭri

byę́dò to follow; pt. *a byęta ḍaṇ*; pe. *a byę̌t*; n. *byędò*

byęl dura; pl. of *byę̀ló byę̀ló*, also *byę̀lò-byę̀l* dura

byę̀rò-byę́r belly, womb
byę̀rò-byę̀r root

Ch.

chà, probably short for *chan* "day"; sometimes used for "when", and in the composition "*sha męko*" some time, at some future time, in future

chà short for *chāgo, chaka* to begin, intend

chabo to mix, knead, tread; pt. *a chàpà (chàpà) labo* he mixed mud; pe. *a chập, chấp*; n. *chập*, or *chấp*

chabo to kick; pt. *á chàpì gwok* he kicked the dog; pe. *a chập*; n. *chậpò*

chāgo wor to compose a song, n. *chấk*

chāgo to approach, come near; to be near; *a chấkí* he approached; *a ch. keń mēko* he changed his place, residence

chāgo to begin, pt. *a chaki* (or *á chaka*) *gwok* he began to work, pe. *a chấk*

chāk milk; *ch. ṇoyo* cheese

chấkí near; see *chāno* and *chāgo*

chấl wax

chālo to be similar, like; to resemble; pt. *á chấlì yín* he is like you

chấlò a kind of white dura

chậm left, left handed (Di. *chām*, Nr. *chậm*)

chấmì-chấmì (chậmì) bait; see *chāmo* to eat; *ya kita ch. ḍok abat* I put a bait on the hook

chāmo to eat; to outwit, cheat, deceive; pt. *á chàmà byę́l* he ate dura; pe. *á chấm*; n. *chấm*

chamo to be going to, to wish, intend, want; often shortened into *chà* or *chè*

chấn behind, *ya kędo chấn* I am going behind

chấn (chấnò)-chấnì sun, day, time; *ki chấn* every day, daily; *de chấn tịn* to-day (Nr. *chan*)

chāno, also *chấnó* to approach, to come or be near, pt. *a chấnì*,

or *chấnì*; n. *chấnò*, and *chấkò*

chấnó shallow place

chấnó - chấnì the upper part of the inner thigh

chāo pi ki feń to pour water on the ground

chấp a rat

chấrè, or *chấrò* very, in a high degree

chấrè mach light of fire, beam

chāto (chấto) to move in a direction; to walk, go; to ride, drive; pt. *a chāti nau* he went naked (Di. *kat, chǫt*)

chayo to blame, abuse, insult

chę short for *chamo* to be going to, and for *chāgo* to begin

chę just, now

chędo (chyędo) to hate, pt. *a chętí ḍacho* he hated the woman, pe. *chę̂t*, n. *chę̀t*

chęgo (chyęgo) to command, pt. *a chękà ḍaṇ*, pe. *a chę̂k*, n. *chę̀k (chę̂k)*

chęgo to catch (fish with

a trap or hook), pt. á chẹ̀kà rech, pe. a chệk, n. chẹ̀k; see chigọ
chẹgọ to be ripe, see chyẹgọ
chẹgọ, chyẹgọ to be short
chẹgọ to repeat, see chigọ
chẹk, chyẹk (to be) short
chẹm straight
chẹmọ toch to aim a gun
chẹ́né wọt dripping-eaves
chẹ̄nọ to curse, to kill by witchcraft
chẹ̀rọ to do or be done at once, just now, just before; e chẹ̀rọ bẹ̀nọ̀ he comes at once; a chẹt ńwọ́l he had been born just before
chẹ̀t straightway, just, exactly; see chẹ̀rọ
chẹt, chyẹt excrements of man or animals; chẹ̀tẹ́ gyẹ̄nọ dung of fowls (Nr. chyẹt); see chiḍọ
chẹ̀tánà a kind of white dura
chẹ́tẹ̀ tyẹ̀lọ̀ foot-sole (?)
chì-màn wife
chiḅọ to put, place; pt. a chip fūk feń he put the pot on the ground, ya chípà aṭẹp chyẹnẹ I put the bag into his hands
chiḍọ̀ to suffer from diarrhoe, pt. a chiṭ, n. chét
chigọ to lay a trap, to catch fish in a trap or crawl, pt. a chika rech, pe. a chyệk, n. chyẹk
chigọ to repeat, continue, a chika gwọk he repeated, continued his work
chigọ, chyẹgọ to command
chílọ dirt, soot (Bo. shi)
chínẽ over there, yonder
chịnọ̀, also chịnọ̀-chịn intestines, bowels (Nr. chin)
chin obāṅọ "hands" i. e. string, of apron
chiu to come to the surface
chōdọ, chōdọ to break off, to rend, pt. a chōta ṭọl he broke the rope; pe. a chót; n. chót
chōdọ to blow (of wind)
chọdọ to put (into), to push
chōgọ, chōgọ to remain, continue, go on; a chôk, a chōga (chōka) gwọk n. chôgọ̀; see chigọ
chōgọ to abstain from; to stop, finish
chôgọ̀-chôk a fish, ńí chảm yi jẹ́ it is eaten by people
chôgó-chú bone (Nr. choākh)
chōjọ to beat, wound with a sword; a chōch jal ẹni he wounded this man, pt. a chọ́ch
chōk it is finished

Chôl, Chôl Shilluk; see Ochōlọ
chōl dirty (Ju. chol black, Nr. chōl black)
chōlọ to avenge, to give compensation, to pay a fine; n. chôlọ̀
chọn, chọn formerly, sometimes
chọ̀nọ̀ dé kwòm the backbone; see chọ̄gọ
chọ̄nọ to dance; gẹ chọ̄nọ būl they are dancing to the drum
chọ̄nọ to assemble; to gather, pile up, store up; jal duọn a chọ̄na jẹ̄ ki búrọ̀ the chief assembled the people in the open place (Nr. chwọk); see chukọ
chọr blind; see chwọr
chọ̀r-chọ̀r vulture
chọrọ to move towards, to go into; e chọrọ dẹ fach he goes into the village; pt. á chọ̀r, n. chọ̀r
chót a steer without horns
chôtị that is all! past tense of a verb whose present is not used
chudọ to groan, moan
chudọ = chōlọ to make amendments; pt. a chút, a chôl, n. chòl
chūdọ to clean, polish; chūdọ lẹk to brush, clean the teeth; see chùt

chùgọ̀-chúk charcoal
chukọ to assemble
chúl-chúl penis (Olukonyo eisulu, Nu. sorot); ch. gwok copper-bracelet; ch. ótwǫ́n a certain plant
chuṅọ liver, chúṅá mẹ̀dọ̀ "my liver is sweet": I am satisfied, happy; chuṅa rach I am vexed, unhappy
chúṅ pl. chǫ́ṅ s. knee (Ba. kọnọ, Karamojo akuṅ, Teso akungi)
chuṅọ to stand, stop, wait, be quiet, be silent; pt. a chúṅí; chúṅí, chúṅí! be quiet! (Nr. chuṅ); compare chōgọ
chuṅọ to assemble; see chukọ and chōṅọ
churọ to be bald; wija chùr my head is bald
chúrọ̀-chùr a fish
chute gin cham (?) to ask for food; from chwọtọ
chùt-chút tooth-brush
chwāgọ to absolve, justify, pt. jāgọ a chwàkà ṅán àn the judge absolved this man, pe. á chwákè yí jāgọ
chwài-chwàyì soup, broth (Di. chwai); vide chwê
chwājọ to form, create, make, build; pt. a chwáchà tạbọ she made a pot; pe. a chwách, n.

chwách (Di. chwech, chak)
chwàk-chwàk ambassador of the king
chwāk throat, voice, self
chwàrọ̀-chwàr bug
chwayọ to pierce, perforate; pt. á chwài yạt, pe. á chwâi
chwê leeches
chwê (to be) fat (Di. chwai, Nr. chwaṭ)
chwējọ to suck out (a wound), to bleed a man; to absorb, suck up; pi a chwêch yi péṅ the water was sucked up by the earth
chwęk, chwọk ambassador of the king; see chwạk
chwẹ̄k twins
chwẹlọ to circumcise; pt. a chwẹ̄la ḍāṅ, pe. a chwẹ̄l, n. chwẹ̄l
chwèr a season, about May-July; the dura is being planted
chwēyọ to become fat
chwiṅọ to begin to rot, decompose; pt. riṅo á chwìṅì
chwiṅọ liver; see chuṅọ
chwọ̄bọ to be visible, clear, distinct, kwọfẹ chwộp his speech is clear
chwọbọ to mix, a chwọpa kwęn kí mau he mixed the bread with fat, n. chwộp

chwǭbọ to spear, to pierce violently; pt. gẹ chwọpa ḍeaṅ they speared a cow; pe. a chwộp
chwọ̀gọ̀-chú bone
chwǭgọ to stay, = chōgọ
chwọlọ to call; see chwọtọ
chwoṅọ mach to light a fire
chwọ́ṅ chaff
chwọṅọ to be late, to stay behind, yí rè chúọ̀ṅ why are you late? n. chwǫ́ṅọ̀
chwọr vulture
chwọr blind (Nr. chọr)
chwọrọ to be blind
chwọtọ to call; to ask for; to mean; pt. a chwọta jal, or a chwọla jal, pe. jal a chwộl (Nr. chwọl, Di. chọl)
chwọu male, man (Nr. chau)
chwọwọ to roar; pt. a chwǫ́wì, n. chwǫ́wọ̀
chyẹdọ-chyẹt excrement, dung; see chẹt
chyẹdọ to hate; see chẹ̄dọ
chyẹ̄gọ 1. to ripen, to be well cooked, be done; 2. to be short; pt. á chyẹk
chyẹ̄gọ to shut, close
chyęgọ lạbọ to knead mud for building
chyęgọ to command (Di. chyek)
chyẹk short (Di. chyek)

chyẹk-mȧn wife, chyẹgẹ́ chwọ́l his wife was called, see chi wife (Nr. chyek)

chyẹnǫ-chyẹ́n, chín hand, forearm (Di. chyẹn, Turkana ekaṅ)
chyẹ̄rǫ to sneeze; chyẹ̄rǫ

yȧt to take snuff
chyẹtǫ to chase
chyóu-chyowí porcupine

D.

dȧ to have, yá dâ ḍèàṅ I have a cow
dafōl rat
dāgǫ to move into an another place, to emigrate; pt. á dȧ̀k; n. dȧ̀k; see denǫ
dȧk-dȧ̀k tobacco-pipe, small pot
dȧ̀kȧ́gì-dȧ̀kȧ́kí a stick for digging the ground or planting dura
dāmǫ tọ́ṅ (Di.) to avoid a spear
dȧṅ the gums (Somal dāṅ)
dānǫ see denǫ
dȧ́rù to be overtired, to break down, to be afflicted with, pt. a dȧ́rì yi jwǫk
dȧtǫ̀-dȧt hoof
dẻ forms the perfect tense
dẻ short for dyẹ́r middle, in, into
dẹ̀ but
dẻ chȧ́ṅ noon
dẻ chȧ́ṅ tíṅ to-day
dè chȯ̀ṅ forever
dẹ̄dǫ to lift up, as a boat from the ground

dėdǫ̇t door
deduk grey; see aduk
dẹ̄gǫ to move into, e dẹ̄gǫ . yey wǫt he moves into the house; see dāgǫ
ḍẹk stupid; see ḍẹgǫ
dėkúgì = dȧ̀kȧ́gì, stick for digging the ground
dẹl-dẹ̌l skin, hide, whip, dẹl ḍọ́k lip, d. ṅiṅ eyelid; dẹla bẹn a fẹt "my whole skin is tired": I feel very tired (Ga. odwel, Di. del)
dẹ̌mǫ̀ to fall down, pt. a dệm, n. dẹ̌mǫ̀; see dyẹmǫ; perhaps dẹ̌mǫ̀ is not properly a verb of its own, but the infinitive of dyẹmǫ (Nr. dẹ̄mǫ to rain) [bone
dėṅ-dėṅì the lower jaw-
dėṅǫ̀, also denǫ to scatter, to part, to separate, pt. dẹ̄ṅ, dẹ̄ṅ
dẹ̄rè why, when? (from de erẹ "but why")
dėtȧ̀ṅ-dėtȧ́ṅ the spitting snake
didǫ to learn, to be ack-

nowledged with, to know; pt. a dít ki dǫ Chọl he learned the Shilluk language, n. dídǫ̀
diko: a díkí wọ́u the sun is setting, darkening
dimǫ to dry, to wipe; á dim chyẹṅ he wiped his hands
dip-díbí a fish
dir middle, truth, true, upright; see dyẹ́r
dīt (Dinka) large, big
dọ̈ch (to be) good, nice, agreeable, right; yá bẹt kí dọ̈ch I remained a good (a long) time
dọ̈chǫ to twist, to wring
dọ̄dǫ mǫgǫ to brew beer, pt. a dwǫla m.; pe. mǫgǫ a dwǫ́l; n. dwǫ́l
dọ̈dǫ̀ black earth; ṅyeṅ a dọ̄dǫ iron
dōgǫ to go back, to turn back; pt. a dọ̄k, n. dọ̈gǫ̀, see duǫgǫ
dǫ́gǫ́lpǫ́ù chameleon
dōjǫ to be good, to become good; n. dọ̈jǫ̀

dǫk gum-sap, caoutchouc
dŏl circle
dōlǫ to make round, a circle; n. dŏl.
dǭlǫ mǫgǫ to make beer, pe. a dwǫ́l; see dǭdǫ
dǭṅǫ to be or become good, well; see dōjǫ
dǭṅǫ to remain, be left; pt. a dǭṅ (Di. dǫṅ)
dǭṅǫ to grow up, become large; to be large, big, great (Nr. dǫṅ)
dǭrǫ-dǫ̀r wall
dǭrú, dǭrɔ̀-dǭrì ax, adze
dɔ́yɔ̀ to decrease, be decreased, pt. a dǒɩ
dúànɔ̀ to evaporate, to steam away, to dry up; — to rise above the water; pt. a dùàn; n. dúònɔ̀; see dwǫnǫ
dúnɔ̀ to smoulder, mach e dunǫ, ja lyel, the fire is smouldering, it does not burn
dúɔ̀gɔ̀ to come back, to return back, to repeat, continue, to accept, duǫgǫ wǫk to miscarry; pt. a dúɔ̀k, n. dúɔ̀gɔ̀; ú dúɔ́k kɩ̀ ŏwén when will he return? (Di. dwǫk, Nr. jok)
dúɔ̀kɔ̀, dúɔ̀gɔ̀ to ruminate; pt. ḍeaṅ a duǭkɩ lūm
dúǫ́ṅ big, great, large, old, respected, jal duǫṅ honourable address to a respected person
dúp-dûp a mouse
dút-dút loin-cloth of skin for men, worn in dancing
dút a present to the relatives of the bride; same as dút loin-cloth?
dútɛ̀nè a skin-cloth; see dút
dùwàt a herb, used as medecine against dwālǫ
Dùwàt name of a brother of Ńikaṅ [month
dwài (dúài)-dwàt moon, Dwai Nubian; used in addressing
dwai to bring, see dwāyǫ
dwăr hunting
dwārǫ to hunt
dwātǫ to wish, to want; to call, pt. dwátá
dwāyǫ to bring, to carry; to send for, to let come, pt. gɛ dwáyá, or gɛ dwái, pe. a dwái
dwęi moon; see dwai
dwęnǫ, or duanǫ to be shallow, to evaporate
dwǫchǫ to wring (a cloth); pt. a dwǫcha lāu; pe. lāu a dwǫ́ch; see dǭchǫ
dwōdǫ chyęn to cross the arms; pt. a dwótá ch., pe. ch. a dúòt, chyęnǫ a dúòt ɛ̀n his arms are crossed
dwǫlǫ to mix beer with flour, see dǭdǫ
dwotǫ to seek, to want; pt. a dwotɩ yûk he searched firewood, pe. yùk à dwái, n. dwɛ̀tɔ̀; see dwātǫ
dwynǫ to dry out, to evaporate; see duanǫ, dwęnǫ
dyɛbǫ to suffer from diarrhoe; pt. a dyɛ̀p; pe. a dyɛ̂p; n. dyɛ́bɔ̀; ḍǫgɛ dyɛ̀bɔ̀ he talks too much, is talkative
dyɛ̄gǫ to rain a little: kǫt e d. it is raining a little, drizzling, syn. ṅwęyǫ
dyɛ́l-dyɛk goat; e kwayǫ kɩ́ d. he herds goats (Nr. àḍɛ̀l)
dyɛl jwǫ̀k "God's goat", butterfly
dyɛ́l wɔ́tè bɔ̀ṅ a bird
dyɛmǫ to fall; pt. a dyɛm; kǫt é d. it rains in large single drops, afei e d. its hails; see dɛ̀mɔ̀
dyɛṅ a grass, used in tying the house-poles
dyɛ́r middle, truth, true, certain; often shortened into dè with the meaning of "in, into", (Nr. dar, Ba. diri)
dyɛrǫ to desire; see dwātǫ
ḍǎchɔ̀-mǎṅ woman
ḍăkàù-mǎṅ woman
ḍálɔ̀ to fail, to be in difficulties, at a loss (Ba. dāra, Somali dāl)

dăṇ, also dăṇ man, person, human being, mankind; woman, mother, dāṇ ṭeṇ baby
dāṇ nwọ̆m bride
dăṅ-dăṅì dancing-stick
dèdṅ, sometimes shortened to dè-dọ̀k cow, cattle
dẹgọ to be stiff, paralyzed, lweta a dẹ̆k my fingers are paralyzed
dẹgọ to be slow in talking or thinking, to be stupid, ignorant; pt. a dẹ̆k, n. dẹ̀gò; see the preceding word
dẹ̄nọ to vex one, pt. a dẹ̀nì ẹ́n he vexed him; pe. yâ dẹ̀nì ẹ́n I was vexed by him, n. dẹ̀nò
dẹ̆k, dēk stupid
dẹ-twọ̀rọ́ a dry place
didọ to make straight

dọ̄dìn the hot season, about March
dọ̀dọ̀ to suck (milk); pt. a dọ̀t; a dọta chak; pe. a dọ̀t
dọ̀k-dọ̀k mouth, bill; border, edge, language; dọ̀ Chọl the Shilluk-language; dọ̀ kal outside the yard, before the yard; dọk dkyẹl one mouth-ful; with one mouth, at once, unanimous; (Nr. tok, Masai gu-tuk, Teso akay-toko)
dọ̀k reply to a call
dọ̀-kọ̀t "mouth of rain", the beginning of the rainy season, April, May
dọ̀l a kind of white dura
dọlọ to swing n.; pt. a dọ̀l, n. òdọ̀lọ

dọ̀nò-dọ̀nì a big basket
Dọ̀nò (from Dongola) Nubia, Nubian
dọ̄rìd a season, July-September, the beginning of the red dura-harvest
dúkì to-morrow; dùnè chínê the day after tomorow
dúòdọ̀ to rise, to get up; pt. a dwòṭì mal, or: a dwòṭá mal; n. dúòdọ̀
dụ̀rụ̀ fẹ́ṅ to destroy, pt. a dụra feṅ, n. dụ̀rụ̀
dwayọ-dwái pegs, driven into the ground round the big dura-basket
dwẹṅ sorrow
dwọ̀dọ̀ to suckle a child; pt. a dwọt ńal ṭeṇ, pe. a dụ́òt
dwọ̀r buffalo's hair hung on the horn of a cow

E.

ę his
ệ he, she, it
ê no
èdì, ẹ́dì how?

ẹ́lẹ́ì a grass out of which ropes are made
ẹ́n he, him, she, her, it, that one

ẹ́nd = ẹ́n
ẹ́nì this, that, these, those
ẹ́rẹ̀ why?

F.

fà 1. to be, 2. not
fàch-myẹ́r home, village,

settlement
fạdọ to be tired, to be

loath of; p. fạt, more frequently fẹt, sometimes *fit, yeja fęt yi gwęt* my heart is (that is: I am) tired with writing, n. *fądǫ*

fądǫ to fall, fall down; to die (said of a chief); pt. *a fất, a fęti; wiję fất* his face fell = he was disappointed, *a fąti feṅ* she bore a child; n. *fądǫ̀*

fągǫ̀ to be sharp, to sharpen; pt. *a fąk* he sharpened, *a fąká fal* he sh. the knife, pe. *fal a fąk*

fąk sharp

fąl bush, desert, uninhabited and uncultivated land

fąl-fęt spoon (Bo. *fala, pali*)

fąlǫ̀, also *fąlǫ̀-fąl, fąl* knife

fąm-fąmi 1. board, table; 2. saddle

fąṅę it is he, that is it

fąṅǫ̀ to stoop down, to hide; pt. *a fąni, a fęni,* n. *fąn*

fāṅǫ to try, test, examine, pt. *a fąṅi*

faṅ, faṅ full

fąṅǫ̀ to be full, to become full; to fill, pt. *a fąṅ ki pi*

fāṅǫ to divide, to distribute

fąr-fęri hippo

fāṛǫ to fly, to jump, to run away, to pass by, to flee; pt. *á fāra*, or *a fāṛ kwǫmę* he jumped on his back (Di. *par*, Nr. *bar*)

fāṛǫ to remember; pt. *a fąrá kwǫp*, pe. *a fąr*

fąrǫ́-fąri a small mat for covering plates or dishes

fąt skin, peels of fruit; *fąte ṅwǫle yąt*

fąt it is not, not present, not here; no; *fąté ęn* not he

fāyǫ 1. to fear; 2. to make fear; pt. *ya fāya jal ęni* I frightened the man

fęchǫ to ask; pt. *a fęchi ęn*; pe. *a fyęch*

fędǫ to lie, tell lies; pt. *a fęt*, or *a fyęt*, n. *fędǫ̀*

fędǫ̀ to plant, raise, grow; educate; pt. *a fętá byęl*, pe. *a fęt*; n. *fędǫ̀*; see *fidǫ*

fęjǫ̀-fech peg, nail of wood

fęjǫ to lead (as a sheep); pt. *a fęcha dyęl*, pe. *a fęch*, n. *fęch*

fęk (to be) heavy (comp. *fękǫ*)

fękǫ to sit, sit down, pt. *a fęká feṅ* he sat down, *a fęki; a fęka witi chǫṅ* he sat down on his knees

fęmǫ to gainsay, denie; pt. *a fęm*, n. *fyęm*

feṅ earth, ground; down, below, *feṅ e rú* one year passed

feṅ gąi the first twilight (probably from *feṅ*)

fęr equal, alike, identical, *fęr bęn* it is (they are) all alike; *fęr ki męn* the same as that one

fęrǫ to catch, take hold of; pt. *a fęri ęn*, pe. *a fęr*, n. *fęrǫ̀*

fęrǫ̀ to sweat, perspire; pt. *a fęr*

fi-fik water (Somali *biyo*)

fidǫ to be tired; pt. *a fit; yá fiti yin* I am tired with you, see *fądǫ*

fidǫ to follow, persecute, pe. *fit*, n. *fidǫ̀*

fidǫ̀ to raise, educate; pt. *a fętá ḍąṅ* he raised a man, pe. *a fęt*, n. *fidǫ̀*

fięmǫ̀ to denie, to gainsay, n. *fyęm*; see *fęmǫ*

fięrǫ̀ to be close together, to stand in a line

Fijǫ̀ the mouth of the Sobat-river

fijǫ mach to rub fire, pt. *a fichá m.*, pe. *a fich*, n. *fich*

finǫ̀ to be pretty, beautiful, pt. *a fin*

finǫ̀ (finǫ̀)-fini cheek

fit (to be) tired, see *fidǫ*

fǫdǫ̀ to surpass, to be

more than, pt. *a fŏṭi; a fōṭi jal* he surpassed the man; *mach fōṭi mal* the fire rose up (Ba. *put*)

fŏdọ̀-fŏṭ country, *fōṭe wọn* our country, *fōṭe chọl* the Shilluk country; see also *fwōdọ*

fọ̄gọ to be bruised, pe. *a fŏk*, n. *fọ̀gọ̀*

fōjọ to brush, rub, clean, pt. *a fóchà lāne jal duọń*, pe. *a fwóch; fōjọ chak* to make butter

fọ̄lọ̀-fọ̄l cloud

fọnọ lŭm to weed grass, to pull out ill-weeds; pt. *a fọna l.*, pe. *a fọ́n*, n. *fọ̀n*

fōṭe country, native country, home; this form used only when a genetive follows: *fōṭe wọ́n* our (my) country; see *fŏdọ̀*

fuḍọ to pull out, as a pole; pt. *a fuṭi yaṭ*, pe. *a fúṭ*, n. *fúṭ*; see *fọnọ*

fuḍọ̀-fúṭ a lame person

fuḍọ to be lame, to become lame; to palpitate violently, to be seized with apoplexy, *fygwọ e fuḍọ* his heart beat violently

fujọ yēi to comb, dress the hair; pt. *a fucha yēi*, pe. *a fúch*

fŭk-fŭgi (*fuki?*) tortoise

fŭk-fŭki pot; *fuke fi* water-pot

funọ same as *fọnọ*

furọ to till the ground, to plant, pt. *a furi feń*; (Somal *abūr* farming)

fwŏdọ̀ to beat; pt. *a fwota éń*, pe. *a fwŏt* (Di. *pwot*, Ba. *but*)

fwŏdọ́-fwŏt place where the ground is tilled, field, farm

fwọjọ, fŭdjọ̀ to praise, to thank; pt. *a fwōcha ẹ́n, a fwōchi ẹ́n*, pe. *a fwọ́ch*, n. *fwọ́ch*

fwōjọ chak to butter; pt. *a fwocha chāk*; see *fōjọ*

fwōnọ to teach

fyàrọ̀ ten

fyẹchọ to ask; see *fẹ̄chọ* (Ba. *pija*)

fyẹdọ to lie, to tell lies, n. *fyẹ́t*

fyẹ̄dọ to split, rend, break; to sting, hurt, prick, pt. *a fyẹta tịk* he broke the sudd, pe. *a fyẹ̄t; féń á fyẹ̄t* "the ground was split": the day broke, n. *fyẹ́t*

fyẹjọ yẹi to pull a boat; to lead; see *fẹ̄jọ*

fyẹ̀lọ̀ cacare, *a fyẹ̀lị̀*, *a fyẹ̀l*, n. *fyệlọ̀* (Nandi, Kamasia, Ndorobo *piek* excrement)

fyẹnọ̀, fyẹ̀n-fẹ̀ni skin, for clothing, sleeping on

fyẹ́r-fẹ́ri or *fẹ́r* backbone, *fyẹ̀rá á tót* my b. is stiff, aches

fyẹ́t a lie

fyẹ́t (to be) torn

fyóu-fyẹ̀ṭ heart; *fyowa dwata kẹḍọ fōṭe Chọl* my heart wants to go to the Shilluk country (Di. *pwou*)

G.

gà piece, copy, number; it, they; *ga adi* how many (pieces, copies)? *jē ga adẹk* "men they three" = three men (Nu. *gar*)

gàgọ̀ to belch; pt. *a gâk* *gàgọ̀ — gâk* cowrie-shell

gài an exclamation of surprise; see *gāyọ*

gājọ 1. to touch; *g. féń* to "touch the ground"

gāmǫ—giwí

with a sacrifice, to lay a sacrifice on the ground, to sacrifice; to leave a sacrifice on the ground; 2. to smear; chiefly in a religious sense, to smear mud on a building dedicated to Ńikaṅ; pt. *a gącha ląbǫ yi wǫt*, pe. *a gắch*, n. *gắch*

gāmǫ to hand, reach; *gami yán gín àn* hand me that thing!

gāmǫ wórǫ́ to accompany a song; pt. *gę́ gâm*; see preceding [*gầm*

gầmǫ̀ to capsize; pt. *á*

gānǫ to think, to think of; to trust; to respect, honour; pt. *a gąna jal ɛ̨ni*; n. *gầnǫ̀*

gầnǫ̀-gàṅ, also *gàṅį* metal-button, worn as adornment in a string on the brow etc.

gàt (*gàt*)-*gắt* river, riverside, river-bank (Somali *gar*)

gāyǫ to be amazed, perplexed, astonished, to utter an exclamation of amazement; pt. *a gá̀i*; n. *gầyò*

gę́ they, them

gēdǫ to build; see *gēro*

gedǫ to tickle; pt. *a gęt*

gēdǫ to chirp, twitter, warble, sing (of birds)

gę̄lǫ̀ chòr to sustain people (in times of need); pt. *a gę̂l*; n. *gęl*

gę̨́lǫ̀-gę́lį̀, or *gę́lį* a steep slope or river-bank; *gę̄l nam* steep river-bank; *gę̄l* (or *gę̄lǫ*) *waṅ* eye-brow

gę́n they, them (Nr. *kę́n*)

gēnǫ to drive, drift, float; *a gę̀ṅ*

gēnǫ to besiege; pt. *a gẹ̄na pach*; pe. *a gę́ṅ*

gēro to build, to erect a building, to found a settlement; pt. *a gę̀rá wǫt*; pe. *wǫt a gę̂r*

gę̀t red-brown stuff with which the face is smeared

gētǫ, gītǫ to besmear (the face); see preceding

gẹ̄tǫ to kill, sacrifice; to treat a guest

gi, short for *gin* thing, only in compositions

gi bwǫ́ṅ "thing of the strangers": siphilis

gìchǫ̀ something (from *gin, gi* thing); *g. mę̨̀kǫ̀* something else, something

gi chwak ornaments of the neck

gi chyę̨́n misfortune, mishap; see *chygnǫ*

gidǫ to be wanting (of teeth); pt. *a gidí lęk* he has no (or few) teeth; *a gęta lęk* he pulled out teeth, pe. *lęk a gę̂t* the teeth were pulled out (?)

gįę̨́dǫ̀ to sacrifice (as a cow); to bless; to treat a guest; pt. *a gįęta* (*gyęta*) *dęaṅ*; pe. *a gį̨ę̂t*; see *gę̄tǫ*

gi fę́n "thing of the earth": something

gi gwę̨́t writing material, pen, pencil

gi gwǒn bribery

gin-gik thing

gin sometimes instead of *gę́n*, and *gòn*

gin châm food

gin dúǫ́n womb

gin lâk inheritance

gin mą̂t beverage

gin mûch alms

gin myshą̨́nį old, antique, ancient things

gin ṅâk arms

gin tûk toy, plaything

gin ɛ̨ę̨p little thing, baby

gìnį̀ǫ̀ to rub; pt. *a gínị̀ ɛn ki mau* he rubbed him with oil; *á gìn* he rubbed; pe. *á gìn*

gír much, many, plenty of

gi rǫ́m measure, ruler

gitǫ to reach, arrive, to last till; *gitǫ dųki* till to-morrow; *e gitǫ bę̄rǫ* it lasted till afternoon

giwí stone

gỉ wich head-ornament,
gẹ̀ he, it, him [hat
gōbọ kwojọ to scratch mud together (for building etc.); pt. a gẹ̀pà or gẹ̀pỉ k.; pe. a gọ́p; n. gọ́p
gōdọ fẹ́n to scratch the ground, to dig; pt. a gẹ̀là fẹ́n; pe. a gọ́l; n. gọ́l
gēdọ to loosen (?); pe. lwetẹ gẹ̀t his fingers were loosened
gāgọ to work, to do, make, practise; pt. a gẹ̀kà wọt; pe. a gwẹ̀k
gōjỉ-gòchỉ sword; from gōjọ (Nr. gōjọ̀)
gōjọ to strike, beat; to fire a gun, to hit; pt. a gọ̀chà nal; pe. nal a gọ́ch
gọ̀k-gọ̀k a ring of skin, worn round the leg below the knee
gọ̀l enclosure, home, homestead; family; tyẹn gọla the people of my family, belonging to me; espec.: "my wife"; tyẹn gọ̀l gẹ̀n his, or their wife (Di. gọl, Nr. gọl, Somali gola)
gọ̀l: kẹ̀n gọ̀l boil, abscess
gọ̀lọ̀-gọ̀l side-arm of a river, bay, bight
gọ̀n where? a kẹt yi gọn where did he go?

gọ̀n he, him, it
gōnọ to keep, preserve; pt. a gōna jam he kept the goods; pe. a gọ̀n; n. gọ̀n
gōnọ to loosen; much used in the sense of loosening a cow, that is giving it away; pt. a gọ̀nà lāu he loosened the cloth; pe. dọk a gọ́n the cattle was l.
gōnọ to complain of, to accuse, to carry on a law-suit against one; pt. a gọ̀nỉ; n. gọ̀n
gōnọ to scratch; pt. a gwọ́nà dẹlẹ he scratched his skin; n. gwọ́nọ̀; see gwọ́nọ̀
gọn a dry place (?)
gōnọ to stoop down, to dive; pt. a gọ̀n he stooped down; a gọ̀nỉ ta pyẹn he hid himself under the skin; n. gọ̀nọ̀
gọ̀pọ see gōbọ
gọr corner
gúr-gọ̀r, or gọ̀rỉ a kind of big white beads worn as necklace
gōró niggard
gōrọ to tattoo, to make incisions; pt. a gōra jal
gọ̀t corner, hiding place; behind; syn. gọr; a fanỉ gọ̀t wọ́t he hid in the corner of the house

gōtọ to dig, see gōdọ and gwotọ
gōtọ̀ to be vexed, angry, to sit down vexed, not saying a word; pt. a gōtỉ
gú-gú a big fish
gudọ (gụdọ) to knock, to hammer, to pound; to hurt, to kill; pt. á gụtà byẹ́l he pounded dura, pe. byẹ́l á gút or: a gúr, n. gụt
gúk (to be) blunt
gúl, gụ́là wọt the corner between roof and wall of the house, see gọ̀t
gúlọ̀-gụ̀l (ar.) cannon
gụnọ to bribe; pe. a gụ́n he has been bribed
gúr-gúr, also gúr a very large fish, weighing up to 2—300 lbs.
gúr, kẹ́y gúr tattoo, brand; scar of tattooing; see gārọ
gārọ to tattoo, see gōrọ
gút-gụt navel, umbellicum
gụt-gụt a wooden hammer
gwàch taxes
gwāi rough; yat magwāi a rough tree
gwājọ to collect or to pay taxes; pt. a gwàchà nyẹn; pe. a gwàch; n. gwàch
gwālọ to be thin; pt. á gwàl

gwănọ to scratch, see gwọnọ

gwānọ to err, to make a mistake, to do something by chance, unintentionally; e gwānọ tŏdọ he told a false report, a lie; kit chaka gwānọ ẹn a stone hit him by chance; pt. and pe. gwẹ́n

gwārọ to snatch, snatch away; pt. a gwāra rĭnọ he snatched the meat; pe. a gwâr; n. gwárọ, or gwérọ

gwatọ to bewitch, curse

gwāyọ to bark, bay; pt. a gwāi

gwāyọ to be coarse, rough; kwọmẹ gwāyọ his back is rough

gwẹdọ to carve, to write; pt. yá gwẹt I wrote; a gwẹta, or gwẹti wańọ; pe. a gwệt; n. gwẹ́t

gwẹjo to kick; pt. a gwẹcha ḍāṇ; pe. a gwẹ́ch; n. gwẹ́ch

gwẹlọ to wink (with hands); é gwẹlọ kí chyẹnọ; pt. a gwẹ́l

gwẹ́lọ́-gwẹ́l ring

gwēnọ to pick up, to gather, to collect; a lŏ́tẹ́ yán e gwēnọ yák I saw him collecting firewood; pt. a gwẹ́nà yuk, pe. a gwện

gwērọ to peel off, as skin; dẹlẹ gwērọ his skin peels off; pe. a gwêr

gwẹt carvings

gwidọ lẹp to give a sign with the tongue, to "wink" with the tongue; pt. á gwit; see gwẹ́lọ

gwòk-gúòk dog (Karamajo eńok, Elgumi ekińok, Teso akińoko)

gwọk work; ẹ́ gwọ́k èdì what kind of work is that? what is here to be done? what shall we do? see gōgọ

gwọńọ to scratch; pt. yá gwọńa rea I scratched myself

gwotọ to dig up the ground; see gōdọ

gyèk-gyòk Mrs. Gray's waterbuck

gyẹ́lọ́-gyẹ́l ring of ivory; see gwẹ́lọ

gyẹ̀nọ̀-gyẹ́ń hen, fowl (Mundu ńgo)

gyērọ to build; see gẹ̄dọ

Γ.

rúdọ king; comp. rit, rōr

rālọ wọk to bring out

rám-rḿn thigh (Nr. ram)

rārọ thrashing-place; gẹ pwótà byẹl ki wiy rārọ

rédò-redi grass-torch

rējò fish; comp. rēju

rér, wór September

rèrò-rèri a red bead

rèrọ to cut into strips; pt. a rêr pyẹnọ he cut the skin into strips

ret spirit = rit king

rọ́ well! all right!

rōdọ to pound; cf. widọ

rōjọ to bask, to sun oneself; pt. a rōch

rọ̄nọ to elect; see rọ̄nọ

rọ̄nọ fen to sink, to dive; pt. a rọ̄n fen; n. rọ̄nò

rúrò-rúr relations by marriage, see órò; rúrí his brother-, sister-, father-in-law

rùt house; see wọt

H.

há exclamation of fright

J.

jàch-jǎch shoulder-blade
jādǫ to be in or to get into difficulties, to be at a loss, to be short of, to fail; pt. *a jati̧ ṅygṅ* he is short of money, also *a jęt*; n. *jàdǫ̀*
jāgǫ kęt to pull a rope
jāgǫ to rule, to govern, to be chief; *é jāgǫ féṅ* he rules the country; pt. *a jākà f.*, pe. *a ják jǎgǫ-jǎk* chief; *jāṅ duǫṅ* big chief, district-chief
jal-jǫk man; see *jālǫ*
jal fyęt a liar; *jal f. fęr ki̧ kū* a liar is like a thief
jàl gǫ̀l husband; *jàl gǫ̀lá* my husband
jal gwǫ̀k workman, labourer
jàl léṅ warrior, soldier
jale lwǫ̀k washerman
jàl mǫt robber, waylayer
jal ṅwǫ́mi̧ bridegroom
jal ṅal butcher
jal ṅgau trader, merchant
jàlǫ̀, also *jàl-jǫk* man (vir); for the plural *tygṅ* is also used; in compositions the sing. is always *jal*, the plural, if the following word begins with a consonant: *jǫ*
jalǫ itching
jālǫ to curse
jal tŏdǫ̀-jǫ t., or *tygṅ t.* liar
jalyat̜ medecine-man; the "bad" wizard
jàṁ, jáṁ goods, property, valuable things; *wú dà jam gi̧r* you have plenty of goods
jame gwǫ̀k tool
jame kwęr things belonging to the community, to the king, or which are reserved for religious purposes
jam léṅ 1. arms, armour for war; 2. booty, spoil
jǎṅǫ̀ to lean against; *e. j. wǫt*
japǫ (jabǫ?) mǫgǫ to stir the beer
jĕ people; *jĕ fōṇ* the people of this country
jękǫ to reign, rule, govern; pt. *a jéki̧*; n. *jékǫ̀*, or *jàgǫ̀*; see *jāgǫ*
jęm (ar.) week
jęriá a season: about September, the time of harvesting the red dura, *yey j.* in the *j.*
jęt to be short of; see *jādǫ*
jí̧mǫ̀ to have colic; *yēja j.*
jóch, jòch-jǫ̀ch a plant, its root is used in making ropes and fish-lines
jōgǫ to turn something back, to prevent, to chase or drive away; *jógì ḍǫk* drive the cattle away, pt. *a joka léṅ* he turned the war back, prevented war
jǫ̀k pl. of *jal*, men, people
jǫ̆ ṅǎk warriors
jǒp, jòup-jǒpi̧ buffalo
jōr-jǫr a small fly or gnat; a bug
jûdǫ̀ to be over-tired, perplexed

jŭr, jŭr people, tribe (Ba. jur country)
jŭṭ: woou á jŭṭ, chan a kęṭ the sun has set, the day is gone
jwāno to hasten, hurry; to be hasty, rash, é jwàno kwóp he is hasty, without deliberation, in his talking
jwǫk-jwok God; sickness; ę̀ dà jwǫk he is sick

K.

kà 1. place; 2. there, here; chíp kà put it there; 3. and, and then; chan aryau ka yi bi in two days, then come again; kà connects only sentences, kí single words; 4. kà, kà logo if, when kà = kędò to go; yá kà bę̀ gwǫk I go to work
kābo to take by force, to rob; pt. á kàpà deań; pe. deań a kâp; n. kępò (Somali qab).
kàch = kà, kęch place; in the place of, instead of
kādǫ salt (Masai makat)
kādo, or kądǫ to bring; see kāno, pt. á kù̀t, a kùdi gin cham, pe. a kę̀l; (Somali qād to take)
kądǫ to twist, plait, braid; pt. a kù̀t; á kù̀dì lum he twisted grass; also: a kętà yei he plaited the hair; pe. yei á kę̀t, n. kęt
kādǫ to go, to step on; syn. kędǫ

kāgo to cut open, to split; to rend; pt. a kàkà deań he cut open a cow; a kaka yaṭ he split the tree; a kak, pe. a kâk, n. kâk
kāgo to plant; pt. ya kaka yaṭ; pe. a kâk
kāgo dǫk to gainsay, debate, dispute; pt. ya kàkà dǫk; the same as kāgo to cut open?
kâgò bush-cat
kâgo sand-bank, chiefly a small stretch of sand uniting two islands
kągǫ, sometimes kāgo to ache, to pain violently. wija kągo my head aches; pt. á kùk, n. kę̀k
kājo to pluck, to pick, to gather, to strip off (as dura-corns from the ear); pt. gę kàchà byęl they harvested dura; pe. a kâch; see kājo to bite
kājo to bite, to sting; to pain, ache; pt. ṭwǫl á kàchà dāṅ the snake bit the man; pe. dāṅ a kâch; chīna á kàch my bowels ache; n. kàch (Di. kach, Nr. kach)
kù̀k a fish-spear; see bęṭ
kàké time, chiefly the ancient time, k. fà chàkí a time not near: a long time ago; k. féń (long) time; k. dúǵn the ancient time, the time of old, a long time ago, formerly
kàl-kù̀lí fence, enclosure, court, court-yard (Di. kal; Somali qalo castle)
kąlo to carry, bring; to be carried, brought; to ride, drive; to come from; ę kąlǫ gin cham woṭ he carries the food into the house; ya kąlǫ wich adᶚro I am riding on a donkey; kąl ya wǫk carry, pull me out! pt. a kąl gin cham he carried the food; yi kąla kęń where do you come from? a kęla gin cham he carried the

food; pe. *a kḗl* it was carried

kṵlọ bḙdọ to wait

kámá (pt.) to be going to, to wish, to begin; *yá k. gwḙt*

kân while; see *ká* place

kānọ dom-palm (Nr. *kân*)

kānọ, kạnọ to bring (Somali *kēn* bringing, Nr. *kẹn* to take)

kanọ to hide; pt. *a kana nygá*; pe. *n̄. a kân*; n. *kân*

kân-kânḭ trumpet (Nr. *kân*)

kân = kâká time; for inst., *kān a tịnḭ* some time

kārọ to have branches, to branch off; *dọ Chọl a kâr* the Shilluk language has many branches, i. e. is rich in structure

kạtọ to bring, pe. *a kâ̰l*; see *kādọ*

kātọ to step over, see *kādọ*

kàwó-kàwḭ beam for building a house

kāyọ address for a descendant of a king

kàyò-kâi elder brother; see preceding

kāyọ appetite, desire for meat

kẹch hunger; *yá dà k.* I am hungry

kẹch strength, power; strong, powerful, severe; bitter, sour (Nu. *kagal* sharp, Nr. *kẹch'*)

kẹchọ: *chan̄ a kẹchḭ* the sun is turning downwards, it is afternoon

kḙdọ-kḙt a fish

kẹdọ to twist a rope

kḙḍọ to go; pt. *a kḙ́t*; *a kḙ́t wọt* "she went into the house": she is going to bear a child

kẹgọ to plant, see *kāgọ*

kḙl, kḙlé middle, midst, in the midst of, amidst, between, among; *kḙl tḙ̄rò* among the people, *wàt bògòn ki kḙlé gɛ̄n* there is no child among them; *kḙlé bât* the place between the shoulders

kēlọ, kạlọ to throw a spear, to spear, to stab, pt. *a kēla ḍā̰n̄*, pe. *a kêl*, n. *kḙ́tò*

kẹmọ crutch

kḙmọ to visit; pt. *a kḙma ḍā̰n̄*; pe. *a kḙm*; n. *kḙmò*

kẹnọ to stroke, caress, fondle

kḙnò-kḙnḭ gourd, calabash

kẹn̄ (from *kẹch*) place; time; reason; here, where, when, if; Nr. *kan*

kẹn̄ bòl itch, place where a gnat has stung, blister

kẹn̄ gwọn̄ itching

kẹn̄ kwọn̄ burial-place

kẹn̄-kwọte path of the cattle

kẹn̄ lḙ́t "hot place", wound, boil

kenọ yaṯ to shake a tree

kḙnọ to be strong; pt. *a kḙnṵ̄*; n. *kḙnò*; see *kẹch*

kẹn̄ rin̄ — *kache rôr* "place of the king", a small hut where a deceased king is adored

kḙnọ = kẹn̄ rin̄

kḙò-kḙó boundary, border

kḙpọ to take a thing out of a larger quantity, to choose, pick out; to take away, to steal; to whore, to prostitute oneself; *kḙpi* choose! pt. *a kẹpi*; n. *kâp*; see *kạbọ*

kẹr rich; *ya fa jal kẹr* I am a rich man; *ya faṯ ki jal kẹr* I am not a rich man

kḙrọ to dig out; pe. *tyẹle wọt a kyêr* the foundation of the house is dug out

kḙ́t alone, self; again; *yá kḙ́tá* I myself, I alone

kḙ́t rope, plait of hair

kḙ̄tọ to throw a spear, to spear, stab; to thrust; to fight; pt. *á kḙ̄là ḍā̰n̄* he stabbed a man; *á kḙ̄tḭ ton̄* he threw a

kḕṭọ—kú 263

spear; pe. tón á kḙl; n. kḙṭọ̀; see kḙlọ
kḙṭọ to dash, to shatter, to split; pt. a kḙṭi̥, n. kḙṭọ̀
kḙti-kǒṭ breast
kewọ leṅ to give a war-signal
kḙwòu edge, boundary
kḙy bḕdọ a place for sitting down (from kḙṅ)
kḙy kwai pasture
kḙy nen sleeping place
ki fish-eagle
kí with, and; connecting words
kich bee
kídi, kídi how? (Nu. kir manner)
kidọ colour; kite lōjọ black colour
kífá in order that, on account of, because of
kífáṅọ̀, kífọ̀nọ̀ why?
kḙ̀mọ̀ to lean the head, to be thoughtful, to ponder, meditate; pt. á kḙ̀m; see kḙmọ
kíndù thus, like that, just so
kíné thus; often introducing the direct speech
kinkín a fish
kirọ to tremble, shiver, dẹla kir my skin shivered (Nu. kerkere)
kit-kiti̥ stone, rock, hill, mountain (Nu. kit)
kite colour; see kidọ

kiṭọ to put, to place, a kiṭi jam woṭ he put the things into the hut
kǒ, kọ̀ short for kọ̄bọ to speak
kọ̄bọ to take
kọ̄bọ to say, to speak; pt. a kọ̀p; a kọma kwọp he said a word; pe. a kwọ̀p
kǒch-kùchi a small ax
kǒdọ̀ to fasten, tie; to wrap, as a wire round the spear-handle; k. bak to make a fence, n. kûdọ̀.
kōdọ to blow, as an instrument; k. mach to blow the fire; pt. a kōdi mach; a kōti kāṅ he blew the trumpet
kōdọ-kǒṭ, kọ̀ṭ seed
Kódọ̀k the town of Kodok, near Fashoda
kāgọ to rent, hire (Nr. kokh to trade)
kāgọ to blossom
kọ̀i breast of woman (a word used only in the royal court)
kǒjọ̀ cold (Nr. kọch')
kọjọ to separate [man
kó kàl-kōṭḙ kàl̥ unmarried
kọ̄kọ (kọ̄gọ?) feṅ to stick into the ground; pe. a kwǒk
kọ́ kǒṭ be quiet! take care!
kól a month, about December

kọlọ to pull out, extract; pt. a kọla yaṭ; pe. a kôl; n. kọ̀l
kōlọ to drive, as cattle
kọmọ to be going to; syn. kama
kǒn-gàk a month, about October
kọnọ to stimulate, affect, to excite desire; to be excited; e kọnọ fyowa it stimulates my heart, I want it; yèjḙ kọnọ he is excited; pt. a kyni̥, n. ọ̀kọ̀n
kōnọ worm
kọ̀ni̥-kọ̀ni̥ a niggard
kọ̄nọ to help; kọ̀ṅ áṅ help me! pt. á kọ̀ni̥ éṅ he helped him
kōnọ, kọ̄nọ to pour out; pt. a kōni̥ fi he poured the water on the ground
konọ to dig; see kwọṅọ (Nr. kwọṅ)
kọ̄nọ to blow; syn. kōdọ
kōrọ to keep, preserve, to care for, to watch; pt. a kórà gi féṅ he kept the thing; pe. a kór; n. kor
kọ̀rọ̀ cotton, see kwōrọ
kọ̄tọ to drive, see kwọ̄tọ
kọ̀ṭ rain; k. e mọkọ it is raining (Madi ikodí)
kōṭ trumpet; see kōdọ
kù-kùwi̥ thief
kú not, prohibitive (Bako)

kúchɛ̀ not to know, to ignore; past form of *kujǫ*; generally this form is used, and almost always in passive; *kúchɛ̀ yán* I do not know

kudǫ kōdǫ to pull out a thorn, pt. *a kǫla k.*, pe. *a kǫ́l*, n. *kǫ́l* — see *kǫlǫ*

kudǫ to be quiet, silent; pt. *a kùt; kudi* be quiet! *yí kú kùt* do not be silent! (Nu. *kite, huse*)

kujǫ not to know, to ignore, *kújà* I do not know (Nr. *kuy'*)

kŭlǫ to bow; *e kŭlǫ wijɛ pen* he bows his head, pt. *a kula w.*

kūmǫ to cover; pt. *a kuma dak ki ṭāgǫ* he covered the pot with a cover

kùn place; there, where; *yi kŭli* (or *kǫla*) *kun* where did you come from? (Nu. *kul*)

kun de chan west

kun do direction

kun dwōgǫ wań Ńikan east ("the place from where returns the eye of *Ń.*", i. e. is the sun)

kun dwōgǫ wań wude north

kun dwōgǫ wań lwal south

kun dwōgǫ wań odǫn west

kŭnɛ̀-dǫ̀nɛ̀ pig (*dǫnǫ* = Nubia)

kúnǫ̀ - kúní a younger child, younger brother

kŭṇǫ mach to blow up the fire; see *kōdǫ*

kúòdǫ̀ - kúòt tick; *k. ya yiṭɛ gwok* there are t. in the ear of the dog

kúòdǫ̀ to be swollen, bloated, as a dead body; pt. *a kùòt*; n. *kúòdǫ̀*

kúòjǫ̀-kúòch a place with white sand in or near a river; mud for house-building

kúǫ́nǫ̀ to taste, to take first of the food; pt. *a kwǫna gin cham*, pe. *á kwǫ́n*, n. *kwǫ̀nǫ̀*

kyr a fine (imposed by the king or magistrate)

kūrǫ to watch, see *kōrǫ*

kūwājǫ address for a foreigner [descendant

kwá grandfather, ancestor;

kwach fins of the fish, see *kwáṅǫ̀*

kwachǫ to beg, ask, pray, request; pt. *a kwacha ḍāṇ*, pe. *a kwách* (Ba. *kwat, kwache*)

kwàch-kwáṅí leopard

kwāgǫ to embrace, to carry in the arms; pt. *a kwaka ḍāṇ*; pe. *á kwák*; n. *kwák* (Di. *kwak*)

kwāgǫ to decompose, putrefy; pe. *rīṅǫ a kwák*

kwǫl killed, butchered animal

kwālǫ to remain, n. *kwál*

kwālǫ to steal, pt. *a kwāla gin an*; pe. *a kwál* (Ndorobo *achǫr* thief)

kwàṅɛ̀ chàṅ watch, clock; from *kwāṅ* "to count", and *chan* "sun, time"

kwáṅí a stick for scratching the head (probably a plural form)

kwáṅǫ̀-kwáṅí solo-singer

kwāṅǫ to count, enumerate; read; pt. *á kwàn*

kwáṅǫ̀-kwach the fin of fish

kwāṅǫ to take (Di. *kwań*, Nr. *kan*)

kwáńḍɛń a bird, eats fish

kwaṅǫ to be the first in doing something; *e kwaṅǫ bɛ̄nǫ* he comes first

kwáṅǫ̀ a very large red ant

kwāṅǫ to swim, pt. *á kwàń*

kwa riṭ descendant of a king; from *kwārǫ* grandchild

kwárǫ̀ - kwɛ́rí poles for making the house-roof

kwárǫ̀ red

kwārǫ-kwàr 1. grandfather, ancestor; 2. grandchild, descendant (Nr. *kwar* chief)

kwātǫ to steal; see kwālǫ
kwāyǫ 1. to herd cattle; pt. á kwài; a kwaya d̥ǫk; 2. to be well, to have slept well
kwāyǫ-kwài grandfather, ancestor; see kwá
kwe some (Nr. kwei)
kwę̂kò (kwę́ę̂kò) to open the eyes; pt. a kwę̂kò wane he opened his eyes; pe. wana kwę̂k
kwę̄le riṭ the hair (of a king)
kwęn a kind of bread or pudding (Nr. kwǫn)
kwǫnǫ fingernail
kwę̄r: jam kwę̄r things belonging to the community or the magistrate, or the king, or which are reserved for religious purposes; also part of the dowry
kwęr poles for the thatch
kwę̄rǫ-kwę̂rì hoe
kwętǫ to steal; pt. a kwętì he stole, a kwętà (or kwęti) d̥ean he stole a cow; see kwālǫ
kwę́t-kwę̂t dung-hill; cow-dung piled up
kwęyó wound
kwi some; see kwę
kwodǫ to drive, to herd
kwod̥ò-kôṭ thorns, sticks, poles for house-building
kwod̥ǫ mach to make a fire; see kōd̥ǫ and kwǭd̥ǫ
kwǭd̥ǫ to fart, to ease oneself; pt. a kwǫ́ṭ; yí rè kwǫ́ṭ? n. kwǫ́ṭ (Nr. kwǫt, kōṭ)
kwogǫ to sweat
kwōgǫ to take; pt. a kwoka yaṭ, pe. a kwók, n. kǫ̀nò
kwǫjǫ to sew together, to tie by sewing or binding; to stretch a skin on a drum; pt. a kwòchà làu, pe. a kwóch, n.
kwok sweat [kúòjò
kwòm-kòm back; on, upon
kwòm-kúǫmì board, chair, table
kwǫmǫ to carry on the hip; p. a kwǫma nal ṭēn
kwǭmǫ to limp, lame, hobble; pt. a kwǫ̀mì; n. kwǫ̀mò
kwǫn flour
kwonǫ to be sulky, capricious, moody, to refuse eating
kwònè yíṭ the place behind the ear
kwǫnǫ to bury, pt. a kwǫna d̥āṇ; pe. a kwǫ́n (Nr. kwon)
kwōnǫ to help (Di. kon)
kwǫ́n-kwòn history, report
kwǫnǫ lwę̄dǫ fingernail
kwǭnǫ to begin, pt. a kwǭnì
kwǫp talking, talk, speech, word; matter, affair
kwor debts, fine; see kur
kwǭrǫ-kôr cotton, thread (Masai karash cotton cloth)
kwǭrǫ: mach kw. lamp, torch; see kwǭrǫ cotton
kwǫrǫ to winnow, to clean the corn by winnowing, pt. a kwǫra byę́l, pe. a kwǫ̂r, n. kúòd̥ò
kwòt-kôt shield
kwǫtǫ to drive, lead; pt. a kwǫtì d̥ǫk, or: a kwǫla d̥ǫk he drove the cattle, pe. d̥ǫk a kǫ́l, n. kǫ́l
kwǫtǫ to blow (wind), pt. yǭmǫ a kwǫ́ṭ, or: a kwǫti the wind blew; pe. a kǫ́l yi yǭmǫ he was driven by the wind; see kwǫrǫ to winnow, and kwǫtǫ to drive
kwǭṭó-kwǫ́ṭ farting
kyàu border, as between fields, see kę̀wù
kyawǫ to row a boat; pt. a kyau; n. kèò
kyèch right hand, on the right hand
kyędǫ byę́l to roast dura
kyędǫ to refuse; pt. á kyę̀ṭ he refused, a kyędi kęd̥ǫ he refused to go, n. kìòd̥ò, kyę̀r; a refuse is often expressed by clicking of the tongue (Ga. kwero)
kyę̄gǫ to cackle (fowls), pt. a kyę̂k

kyél together; gé kedọ kyél they are going together; from akyel
kyélọ-kyél fence (?)
kyélọ-kyél star
kyēnọ to squat, cower (lifting one knee higher than the other)
kygnọ yit to listen, pay attention; pt. a kygna y.

kyéń-kyéńí, or kyéń horse (Madi kainō donkey, Abokaya kańer donkey)
kyer the water of two uniting rivers
kyerọ to leak, trickle, drizzle, bleed; remọ k. the blood is trickling; rea kyerọ I am bleeding; pt. a kyér

kyerọ wọt to mark out the (circular) fundamental lines of a house; a kyérà, or: kyérí kal he marked the circle of a fence; pe. a kyér, n. kyérò
kyét-kyét 1. a fish, 2. the space between the cut-out teeth

L.

làbọ̀ mud, clay; l. ya yŏ there is mud on the road
làbọ̀ people
lách urine (Turkana alot, Masai galak)
lach broad, wide
lachọ to be broad, wide
lagọ to inherit; pt. a làkà jam; pe. a làk; n. làk (Nr. lakh)
lagọ to dream; n. làkọ̀ (Nr. lakh)
lagọ magistrate, authority, community
láí-láí game
lāi yino to be lost, to die (said of men only)
lājọ to piss
làkọ̀-làk dream
lál a month, about August
lāmọ to pray to God, to worship; pt. á làm; á làmà jwọk; pe. á làm

lańọ́-lańí, lańí the nabag-tree
lańọ war to spend the night waking; a lańa war; n. lańe war
lāńọ to be loose, to be not strong, durable, to rend easily
láú-láńí skin, cloth; láńé dān cloth of man (Bo. lao, Ba. labo, Turkana elau, Karamojo elou)
láú spittle
láú far away
láwè-láwí oar of boats
láwọ́-láń, also láńí skin, cloth, syn. láú
láwọ́ to be far away; pt. a láwí
láyò: wijẹ l. he is ashamed; pt. w. á láí; n. láí wich
lèbọ̀ to lie in wait for; pt. á lepà dāń, pe. á lep,

n. lébọ̀
lędọ to shave; e l. tiga he shaves my beard; see lyel
lēdọ, also lìdọ to see, pt. a léta dāń, or: a léta d., pe. a lét
léjò-lék tooth; lek lyech ivory (Nr. lech, Nandi kelek, Ndorobi kelek, Masai ala, Somali ilik)
lék déń a kind of white dura [see lagọ
lękọ to dream, pt. á lék;
lèlò-lél flint-stone (Di. alel, Ba. lele)
lèlọ̀ to be smooth, even, pretty, nice, good, pt. a lèl, n. lèlọ̀
léń war, army, danger; leń a tíń an army was raised, a war arose; nińẹ da l. "his eye has war": he is angry

lęnọ to become or feel hot; see lęt

lęnọ to throw; pt. *a lęna tuk*, or: *a lęni tuk* he threw a stone; pe. *tuk á lęn*

lęp-lęp tongue (Di. *lyęp*)

lępọ 1. the junction between wall and roof, 2. = *labọ* mud

lępọ ręk to crawl, creep, go stealthily

lęt, also lęt (to be) hot, sore, *ńina l.* my eye is sore; *fen lęt* it is hot: *rea lęt* I feel tired, unwell, feverish, am lazy (Nr. *lęt*)

lęu the hot season, January-February

lęu-lęwi (sing. also *lęu*) a small lizard (Di. *aleu*)

lęwọ wiy wọt to make the upper edge of the roof even, smooth

libọ to be cool, cold; pt. *a limi*; n. *libọ* (Ba. *libi* wet)

libọ to steal upon, to come stealthily upon; pt. *a lępa ńu*, pe. *a lęp*, n. *libọ*; see *lępọ*

lidọ to see; see *ledọ*

linọ to hear; pt. *yá lin* I heard; *a lina kwọp*, or *lini kwọp*; pe. *á lin* (Nr. *lin*)

liu liu (to be) destitute, bereft, without cattle (Nr. *liu* to die)

lọch-lōjọ black; *tyęń lōjọ* black people; *bwọn l.* black Arabs

lōdọ to wade in water; pt. *a lwọ́t*; pe. *pi a lwọ́t*

lọgọ to become, pt. *a lọka ḍạn* it became a man

lọgọ (lọ̄kọ) to follow; *e l. bán gọn* he follows after him; pt. *a lók b. g.*, n. *lọgọ̀*

lọgọ (lọ̄kọ) to answer, to interpret; pt. *a lọ́ki kwọ́p*, *a lọ́kà kwọ́p*; pe. *kwọ́p á lọ̄k*; n. *lọgọ̀*

lọgọ to reconcile, compensate

lọgọ to wash, pt. *a lọgi lau*, *a lwọ̄ka lau*, pt. *a lwọ̄k* [ing dura

lọ̀i-lọ̀i a fan used for sift-

lōjọ to be black

lọ́kọ̀ this side (Di. *lon*)

lól deep

lọn sticks

lōnọ (lūnọ) to do a thing later, after somebody else, to follow one in doing something, pt. *a lōna bęn* he came later, after him; n. *lọnọ̀*

lọnọ to pull out, pluck, as feathers, hair; to loosen; to get off (clothes); pt. *a lọ́ná gyę̄no*, pe. *a lọ́n* (Nr. *lon*)

lọ́n àn this side, *lọ̄ne chinê* that side; see *lọ́kọ̀*

lọ́t-lọ́t club

lōyọ to run away, flee; pt. *a lōyi*, n. *lōyọ̀*

lugọ to come after somebody, to follow; *e lugọ bán gọn* he follows him; pt. *a luk bán gọn, a luka ḍạn*; pe. *á lúk*; n. *lugọ̀*; see *lōnọ*

lûgọ̀ to turn, to be turned towards; *a lógi lọ̀gi* he turned (himself), he turned round; *ńaję ę́ lọgę* he turned his back; n. *lọ́k*; see *lōgọ*

lûmọ̀-lûm grass

lūnọ to turn (down), to be turned (down), *alilit e lūnọ fen* the bat hangs upside down, pt. *á lún*; n. *lúnọ̀*, see *lûgọ̀*

lúọ̀bọ̀ to be in company, to converse with a person, to have intercourse with, to deal with; pt. *gę luọ̄pa rei gęn* they conversed with each other; *a luọbi* he c.; *a luọ́p*

luọn gwók the blossom of the dura

luṭọ to fall into (?)

lûyi-lûyi pond, small lake

lwọ́k-lwọ́k cow-house (Di. *lwak*, Nr. *lwak*)

lwak people

lwàlį̀ the general name for red dura (probably a plural form)
lwānǫ to be or have become poor, destitute, bereft
lwàṅǫ̀-lwàṅ fly (Di. lwaṅ, Nr. lwaṅ, Ba. alouṅo)
lwędǫ̀-lwęt finger; l. tyęlǫ toe; lwęn duǫṅ thumb, lwęn ţęṅ little finger
lwęṅ worthless, insipid, cheap, simple; see lwāṅǫ and lwęṅǫ
lwęṅǫ to be insipid, tasteless, worthless, cheap, simple, senseless
lwęṅǫ to be soft
lwijo (lwîjǫ́) to whistle

lwōgǫ to exchange
lwǫgǫ to accompany; espec. to acc. a guest a short way; a lwǫka ęṅ; see lǭgǫ
lwōgǫ to wash (oneself or something); a lwǫki rę he washed himself; a lwǫka ḑāṅ he washed a man; pe. a lwǫ́k, n. lúǫ̀gò; see lǭgǫ (Teso ake-loṅgo)
lwôl-lǫ̂t a gourd, pumpkin, calabash
lwǫṇǫ scrotocele
lwoṅ gwok "molar tooth of the dog": the blossom (or the sprout?) of the dura

lwóp-lwòbį́ company; see lúǫ̀bò̧
lwǫtǫ to wade in water; pt. a lwǫ̀tį̀, n. lwǫ̀tǫ̀; see lǭdǫ
lyawǫ to spy, to lie in wait for
lyęch-lięch elephant
lyęfǫ to want something but being ashamed of asking for it
lyęk a place where the grass is burned
lyęlǫ to burn, to flame; pt. a lyęl, n. lyęl
lyęlǫ to shave; pe. a lyęl; see lędǫ and preceding
lyęṅò cooked butter

M.

má because, for; whether
má which, who, rel. (Nu. ma, man)
má-męk aunt, sister of the mother
mach fire (Nandi māt, Kamāsia māt, Ndorobo māt, Suk mā')
madírǫ́ (ar.) Mudir, Governor
mądǫ̀ a certain dance; first part of a dance
mądǫ to drink; pt. a mą̂t, a mą̂tà pi, pe. pi a mą̂t (Teso akai-mata)

māgǫ to catch, to get hold of, to seize, to hold fast; pt. a maka ḑāṅ; a maki ḑāṅ; pe. a mâk
mąjǫ to spread out in the sunshine; pt. a mą̂chà lāu, a mą̀chà lāu, pe. a mą̂ch
mál, or mâl, often short mál heaven, the upper region, surface; above, on, onward, forward, at the head
mālǫ to adore, to pray, to offer thanks (to God); pt. a māla jwǫk, pe. jwǫk a mâl
málǫ̀-mę́l, mál bell
malǫ to roast, broil; pt. a mą̂là riṅǫ, pe. a mą̂l
mán, wǫ̀mán women
mànǫ̀-mán testicles; máné ḑāṅ
máné nam junction of two rivers
mąnǫ to hate, detest, to be inimicous, to wage war against; to forbid, prohibit; pt. a mąni, n. mą̂nò̧

ma̱no̱ to capture, to besiege; pt. a ma̱na pach; pe. a ma̱n; n. ma̱no̱

máò fat, oil, see mau

mar green; ńińi mar kifa ńyeń your eye is green on account of money: you are greedy after money

már, also má because, because of, on account of

ma̱r a silver pot which plays a rôle in the history of the Shilluks; it does not exist now

ma̱ro̱ to love; pt. a mári jal gni; pe. a már; n. ma̱do̱

ma̱ro̱ to thunder; pt. mal a mari the heaven thundered, it th.; n. ma̱ro̱

ma̱t slow, slowly; also a form for excusing oneself or of asking attention or precaution: take care! excuse me!

mát-ma̱ti female

ma̱t-ma̱t friend; ma̱da̱ my fr. (Di. mat, Nr. ma̱t)

ma̱to̱ to greet, salute; pt. a ma̱ti en, a ma̱ta en he saluted him; n. ma̱to̱, or má̱t (Di. mat, Teso akai-mala, Somali mōd)

má̱tó̱nó̱ small, little, a little

màu fat, oil, m. deań butter, m. kich honey, m. cho̱gó marrow

may-kwor candle (from kwōro̱ cotton)

mayo̱-mài the mother's sister, aunt

māyo̱ to fish, to catch fish

māyo̱ mother?

me property; forms possessive pronouns; mé tero common property of the people

me̱do̱ to increase, augment, add; met ńyeń give more money

me̱do̱, also me̱do̱ to be sweet, flavorous, savoury; agreeable, joyful (Nr. me̱th to taste)

mejo̱, me̱jo̱ to shut up, shut in, to hide, to close; pt. a mecha ńiń he shut the eye; pe. a méch; n. méch

mējo̱ to make straight, even, to pull, drag, tear; to adjust by pulling, tearing; pt. a me̱chà yat, a me̱ch; pe. a me̱ch; n. me̱ch

me̱ko̱-me̱ko̱ some, some other, someone, somebody else, jal m. some man, another man

mén his mother (from mi en)

me̱n, mén which, the one who, whose

mēno̱ to put into, to stick into, to press into; pt. a ménà yat feń he stuck the tree into the ground; pe. a mén

me̱no̱ to twist; pt. a mye̱n; a mye̱na weno̱ he twisted his beard; pe. a mye̱n

me̱no̱ the one who, syn mén

me̱no̱-me̱ni heart

me̱no̱ hind part of the head

me̱ńo̱ to be pretty, beautiful; bo̱l è m. the face is pretty

me̱no̱ to be deaf; pt. a me̱ń (Nr. mēń)

me̱r a kind of white dura

méri charcoal

me̱ro̱ to be reconciled, to reconcile; pt. ge me̱r; n. me̱ro̱

met sweet

me̱t-me̱t big hair-dress of the men

me̱t ótwo̱n crest of the cock

mi mother; miá my mother

mino̱ to be pleased; chuńg m. he is pleased, satisfied; n. mino̱

míno̱ (minno̱?): mal a míni, kot é míno̱ a heavy rain-shower is coming, it is going to rain heavily, it is getting dark; n. mino̱

mịṅ deaf, deafness; see
meṅọ (Nr. měṅ)
mịọ̀ mother, see mī
mịṭọ to hold fast, to keep,
chyęṅg tẹ̈k kị mịṭe ṅyęn
his hands are tight in
holding fast money: he
is close
mọdọ to cohabit; pt. á
mọ̀t; á mọta ḍāchọ; pe.
a mọ̀t, n. mọ̀t
mōdọ to break (?), pe. mọ̀t
mōdọ dark; feri fù m. it
is dark; see mūdọ
mọ̀gọ̀ any food prepared
of dura, dura-beer; m.
mátẹ́ beer, m. bùr flour,
m. gin cham bread,
pudding, mọn a wach
dough (Di. mọu)
mō̱gọ to crumble off, as
the bank of a river;
to glide into; pt. a mọ́k,
n. mọ̀gọ̀
mōjọ to boast of, to be
proud of
mōjọ to give; see mūjọ
mọ́k these, these ones, see
mēkọ (Nr. mọk) [fish
mọk-mwōk the dog-head
mọ́k dọ̱n truth, true, verily,
mọ́k = pl. of mēkọ, dọ̱n
pl. of duọn
mōkọ pl. of mẹkọ

mọkọ (sometimes mọkọ)
to rain, to drizzle, drop;
kọ̀t é mọ̀kọ̀ it is raining,
kọ̀t á mọ̀kị̈ it rained
mọ́l, mwọ́l morning
mọlọ to flow
mọlọ to come early; pt.
a mọ́l bę̄nọ he came
early, n. mọ̄lọ
mōṇọ to swallow; pt. a
mōṇa gin cham; pe. a
mọ́ṇ
mọrọ red ant (Nr. mwọr
mwọr)
mọ̀t adultery, see mọdọ
mọ̈tẹ́ to pick out, to gather,
to pluck; pt. ḍāchọ mọ̈ta
abwok, pe. a mọ̈t
mọ̈té, mọ̈tẹ́ first, at first
mọ̈tọ̀ sterility (of the soil)
mọ́tálọ̀ (foreign word?)
onion
mōtọ to hold fast; pt. a
mọ̈ti̧, pe. a mō̱ta yat,
n. mịtọ̀
mùchọ̀ island
mudọ to drown, to be
drowned
mūdọ darkness; m. e. bę̄nọ
d. is coming; feri bá
m. it is dark, feri fáṭẹ́
m. it is not dark (Bo.
mul) [witchery
mùgọ̀ disease caused by

mūjọ to give, a mūcha
ṅyęn (Nr. moch')
myke beer, see mọgọ
mūlọ to creep, crawl (Di.
mol, Nr. mwāl)
mūlọ to plaster with mud,
to wall, to wall up
mūlọ̀ to tame, to be tame,
a múl kị fach it was
used to the house, it
was tame
mūmo to be perplexed,
confused; pt. wija mùm
I am perplexed (Nu.
mumur deaf)
mùtọ̀ neck; mune ḍān
neck of man
mwōjọ to be stingy (?)
mwōjọ to explode; pt. a
mwóch, n. mwōjọ̀,
mwōche toch the ex-
plosion of the gun
mwọ́l, mọ́l morning, feri
fù m. it is morning
mwọṇọ to plaster with
mud, to wall; a mwọna
rārọ (Nr. mun mud)
mwọ́ṇi scutiform cartilage
mwọ́ṇọ̀ to whisper
myer pl. of pach village
myęrọ to be worth, to
deserve, to be becom-
ing; pt. a myęr, n.
myę́rọ̀

N.

No word begins with ṇ

N.

nả (also nà) as, like, nà én like him

nägǫ to kill, to hurt, to put out, extinguish; to break; e nägǫ tǫbǫ feṅ he throws the dish on the ground; pt. a nęka ḍāṅ, pe. a nęk, n. nảgǫ̀; yi nägǫ wun adi how many years have you killed: how old are you? (Nr. nakh)

nảm-námí river

námí as, like, just as

nāṅǫ to lick; pt. a náṅ, n. nảṅ

nau thus, without anything, without clothes, naked; e chāṯǫ nau he walks naked (Nr. nô)

nāyǫ, nēyǫ uncle, nēyả my uncle

né thus, as, just as, like né jal gni as this man (Nr. éné thus)

nębǫ to be wet; pt. a nę́p, n. nè̱bǫ̀

nēnǫ to look; a nęnà mal he looked up; pe. a nę̣n, n. nę̣n, n. yǫ to see a way, to hope

nēnǫ to wait

nęnǫ to live, a nę̣n

nęṅǫ to sleep, é nę̣nǫ̀ he is asleep; pt. á nę̣n; yi nę̣n did you sleep (well)?

nèyà thus

ndí right! all-right! very will!

nimo to cover, to shade

ninǫ to sleep; p. a nę̣n, n. nę̣n; see nęnǫ

niṅǫ to move, to shake, be moved by the wind

nòk, nǫ́k (to be) little; a little

nǫkǫ to recover, to heal; pt. á nǫ̀kị, n. nǫ̀kǫ̀

nōnǫ to be or become little, to diminish; pt. á nòṅ, n. nự̣ńǫ̀; see nǫk

nūmǫ to lick, to kiss; n. nûmǫ̀ [exists

nút, nụ̂t there is, there

nự̂tí not yet, not

nwajǫ mǫl to breakfast; pt. a nwach kị mǫl

nwāṅǫ to aim at

Nwảr The Nuer-country or people

Ń.

ńả-ńwọ́lị̂ child, young one, seed, egg; ńa is also used in expressing a deminutive form; in these cases it is frequently pronounced ńę or even ńe

ńả báṅ slave, servant, person belonging to somebody; also "wife"

ńả bóṅ a white cow

ńa chóḷǫ́ a kind of red dura

ńa diṅ a cow with small brown and black spots

ńa ḍai chwǫu a whore

ńảḍáṯ bottle (ar?); see aḍaṯ

ńaḍęi feńidwai a kind of red dura

ńả-fégyę̣nǫ̀ a kind of red dura

ńa féluộṯ a kind of red dura

ńả giṅ ḍę̣ṅ baby

ńa gól-tyę̣ń gól 1. wife, people belonging to the family; 2. used in addressing a higher person, as a chief

ńá (ńe-) ṛóḷǫ̀ an axe

ńà-jăgò child of a chief
ńá ják a cow with a fallow head, small brown spots on the back, the rest being white
ńa jók a cow: head black, small black spots on the back, the rest white — same as ńa ják?
ńakḍi-ńíkḍi niece, nephew
ńa kęr a cow: sides black, belly and back white
ńa kįnǫ a kind of red dura
ńākǫ to struggle, wrestle, fight; pt. á ńàk, n. ńàkò
ńà-kòrò cotton-seed
ńà kwách a cow, speckled black white
ńá kwâń rìį loose woman
ńal, also ńęl-ńań boy
ńal dúǫ́ń-ńań dǭnǫ young man, youth
ńa lẹ́ń-ńwǫl líń a small drum
ńa lęį a brown or grey cow
ńąli-ńąlį python
ńamāyǫ brother
ńamio-ńemęk sister
ńāmǫ to chew (Bo. ńa)
ńa múdwęlò a bird; syn. okǭge nam
ńàn, also ńàn-ńwǫl girl, daughter (Di. ńan)
ńan ęn small girl
ńan ńwǫ́m bride
ńan kǎyò elder sister
ńane dǎchǫ, sometimes ńan a dǎchǫ girl

ńa ńań young crocodile
ńàn-ńąńį crocodile (Karamojo agi-ńań croc., Elgumi ati-ńań croc., Masai ki-ńań croc., Lendu ńa hippo
ńa ómà tír a large duck
ńa pygn-ńwǫl pyḡni a small hide or skin
ńarįį child of a king, prince
ńārǫ lŭm to cut, mow grass
ńàrò gums
ńàrǭjò-rǭch calf
ńáu hair on the genitals
ńáu-ńáwį cat (Di. ańao, Nr. ńau, ńau, Masai ńau cat, Lendu ńau hyena)
ńa wąį young bullock
ńa wúmètír a bird
ńayąį a small tree, shrub, bush
ńá yǫm àbwòk a kind of red dura
ńè = ńà child, young, little
ńek posterity, pl. of preceding
ńèkǎyó elder brother
ńemei sister
ńemęk a kind of white dura
ńemia-ńemęk brother
ńemiáu sister
ńemię tygn gǫl sister-in law [striped
ńe ńań a cow, white-red

ńéń, ńiń eyes; see wań
ńgnǫ pèń to make a deep hole into the ground
ńe tǫnǫ black cow
ńewá female cousin
ńè yǫ́m a cow: head white, body black or bay
ńí to use to; expresses the habitual form of the verb
ńièdò to milk; pt. a ńiẹį
ńigį a month, about November
Ńį́kànò the ancestor of the Shilluk nation
ńim genitals of woman
ńim face, in front of, facing (Nr. ɲyam)
ńimò-ńìm sesamum (Di. ńum, Teso ika-ńumu)
ńiń, also ńiń name, ńińí ámęn which is your name?
ńiń eyes; see wań.
ńiń small part, atom; ń. yąį a fǎįį wańa a chip of wood fell into my
ńińe chú joint [eye
ńòdò to bear young ones; pt. á ńòt, n. ńwòdò; see ńwǭlǫ
ńódò to show, see ńudǫ
ńǭdǫ to be soft; syn. lwǭnǫ
ńǫ́rǫ́lǫ̀-ńẽwúlį an axe; see ńarǫlǫ
ńǭjǫ byél to cook dura
ńǭmǫ to marry; pt. a ńǭmi dǎchǫ; a ńǭma dǎchǫ; pe. a ńwǫ́m

ṅō̱nọ to pound, crush; e
ṅō̱nọ lạbọ he pounds,
kneads the mud; pt.
a ṅō̱ni̱ l., pe. a ṅó̱n, n.
ṅó̱n
ṅō̱nọ to scatter, to tread
on; pt. a ṅō̱na kwọt;
pe. a ṅó̱n; n. ṅó̱n;
same as the preceding
ṅó̱ṅ see ṅụṅọ
ṅóty̱ẹ̱nọ̱ some time, some
days ago, the other
day
ṅụḍọ to show; pt. ạ ṅót̠ạ́
wọt he showed the
house; pe. a ṅót̠; n.
ṅóḍọ̱
ṅụṅọ to rub (as a wall,
to make it smooth);
pt. a ṅụ́ṅi̱ wọt; pe. wọt
a ṅó̱ṅ
ṅúọ̱gụ̱, ṅwọ̱gụ̱-ṅúọk louse
ṅwāgọ to take part (in a meal), to agree, consent, to be of one opinion; pt. á ṅwákạ́ gin
cham; n. ṅwák, wá
ṅwaka kwọp we were
of one opinion
ṅwālọ to touch; pt. a
ṅwáḷá kwọ̱mẹ̱; a ṅwati̱
kwọmẹ̱, n. ṅwạtọ; see
ṅwạtọ
ṅwaṅ-ṅwaṅi̱ bracelet of
metal, iron
ṅwaṅọ to be able, clever,
to be able to work
with both hands, the
left and the right, alike
ṅwạtọ to touch; pt. a
ṅwáti̱ gin an, a ṅwál
gin an, n. ṅwạtọ; see
ṅwālọ
ṅwayọ to doze
ṅwẹ̱lọ̱-ṅwéḷi̱ earth-worm
ṅwē̱nọ to walk around
ṅweyọ to rain a little, to
drizzle; kọt e ṅweyọ
ṅwọbọ to knead, as mud,
dough, to mix with
water; pt. a ṅwọpa
lạbọ̱; pe. a ṅwọ́p; n.
ṅúọ̱bọ̱
ṅwọḍọ to be weak; pt. a
ṅwọ́n
ṅwọ́li̱ young ones, children, seed, ṅwọle jwọk
twin-children
ṅwō̱lọ to bear young or
fruit; pt. á ṅwọ̱́l
ṅwō̱mọ to marry; pt. a
ṅwō̱ma gn; pe. a ṅwọ́m;
n. ṅwọ́m; see ṅō̱mọ
(Bo. ṅo)
ṅwọṅọ to crouch, squat,
cower; pt. a ṅwọ́ṅ
ṅwọt weak; see ṅwọḍọ
ṅwọtọ to show; see ṅụḍọ

Ṅ.

ṅach back, behind, backward; ya cháṭa ṅájá I
went backward
ṅạchọ to take leave, to
ask for permission to
go; pt. a ṅacha ḍā̱n;
pe. á ṅách; n. ṅách
(ṅách)
ṅādọ to cut, to butcher;
a ṅát (ṅát); pe. á ṅát,
or: á ṅál; see ṅālọ
ṅāḍọ to rely on, to trust;
pt. a ṅát̠i gn
ṅājọ to know; almost exclusively used in passive: a ṅáchè yán; also:
a ṅáchè yán I know
him; n. ṅájọ̀
ṅālọ to butcher; pt. a
ṅálá ḍeaṅ, pe. a ṅál,
n. ṅál; see ṅāḍọ
ṅāmọ to yawn; pt. á ṅám;
n. ṅámọ̀ (Nr. ṅām)
ṅan, ṅane, from nate "man,
person" often occurs
in compositions, in
plural generally tyṅ
"people" is used
ṅane chwọr blind person
ṅane ḍachọ̱, also ṅan a
ḍachọ̱ woman
ṅan dwār hunter
ṅan kọk a hired person

ṅan kŏr guardian
ṅan kwȯdi shepherd
ṅan kwal thief
ṅan lę̆dǫ̇ barber
ṅan lōjǫ black man
ṅan lōk kwǫ́p interpreter
ṅan máṅę̇ ṅǫ̇lǫ̇ eunuch
ṅan mâr beloved one, friend
ṅan márâch a bad person
ṅan męn enemy; from mąnǫ
ṅan mŭl apprentice
ṅan ṅwǫm bridegroom
ṅan ṅâr boaster
ṅānǫ to be perplexed, astonished; pt. a ṅáṅ
ṅārǫ (also ṅarǫ) to gnarl, growl; to bluster, boast, brag; a ṅâr, or: a ṅǫ̇rì; n. ṅárǫ̇
ṅát a cow with horns cut off
ṅátȯ-tyę́ṅ man, person (Nr. ṅāk, Ba. ṅǫtǫ)
ṅate bȧpȯ beggar
ṅate budę a lying, a sick person
ṅate fach inhabitant, citizen
ṅate fwȯṅ teacher
ṅate gwǫ̇k workman
ṅate jwāṅǫ kwǫ́f one who is hasty, rash in his words, an arrogant person
ṅate jwǫ̇k 1. a "man of God"; 2. a sick person
ṅate kę́r rich person

ṅate kú thief
ṅate kwáchǫ́ beggar
ṅate kwāyǫ́ herdsman
ṅate lę̇ṅ one who beats the small drum
ṅate mǫt a lewd person
ṅate nęk murderer
ṅate ṅál butcher
ṅate ṅę̆nǫ̇ an unconscious, a swooning person
ṅate rępe kwǫp mediator, conciliator
ṅate ṭǫ́l cook
ṅátȯ węlǫ̇ traveller, stranger
ṅátȯ yáf kí mȧn one who seeks intercourse with women, lewd person
ṅate yát an abuser
ṅate yięȯdǫ helper
ṅȧyǫ́ a kind of red dura
ṅę́ yes
ṅęawǫ to trade, to buy, sell; pt. a ṅęau, a ṅęawi byę́l
ṅędǫ-ṅę̆t, ṅę̆t rib; see the following
ṅędǫ̇-ṅę̆t a hoe, made out of bones, now seldom
ṅęgǫ to bleed a person
ṅę̇jȯ a mark
ṅejǫ to recognise, see ṅājǫ
ṅę̆lǫ to roll; pt. gę́ ṅę̆lá nam they rolled into the river; n. ṅę̆lǫ̇
ṅęmǫ to cut off, take off; pt. a ṅę̆ma yił; pe. a ṅę̆m; n. ṅę̆m
ṅēnǫ to be unconscious,

to swoon; pt. á ṅę̆n n. ṅę̆nǫ̇
ṅę̆nǫ to tan, to prepare a skin by tanning
ṅę̄nǫ (to be) much, many (Nr. ṅwan)
ṅę́r-ṅę́r the white-ear cob
ṅę̆rǫ to let the milk down (said of a cow); pt. á ṅę́r; see ṅyę̇dǫ
ṅę́t brain
ṅę̆tǫ to laugh; pt. á ṅę̆tì; pe. á ṅę̆tì; n. ṅyę́rǫ̇
ṅę́ allright! well!
ṅǫbǫ to hang up
ṅǭdǫ to cut; pt. á ṅȯl, á ṅȯt, á ṅǫla (ṅǫta) yat; pe. á ṅǫ̇t, or: a ṅǫ́l (Nr. ṅǫt)
ṅǭgǫ to vomit, pt. yá ṅǫ̇k (Nr. ṅǫk)
ṅǫ́l a lame person, a cripple; from ṅǭdǫ
ṅǫ́l-ṅǫ̇lą̇ a large watersnake
ṅǫlǫ to cut; see ṅǭdǫ
ṅǫlǫ to avoid; the same as ṅǫlǫ, ṅǭdǫ to cut?
ṅǫ̇ṅ the rectum; ṅǫ̇ṅí pyę̄lǫ an invective, injurious word
ṅǫ̇rȯ-ṅǫ̇r, also ṅǫ̇r bean (Nr. ṅǫr)
ṅǫ̆t cripple; from ṅǭdǫ, see ṅǫ́l
ṅotǫ to spit; pt. a ṅota, or: a ṅola láù; pe. a ṅól; see ṅwotǫ
ṅō̄yǫ to curdle, coagulate

ṅọ̄yọ to imitate
ṅù-nùwí lion
ṅụdọ to cut, to kill; see ṅọ̄dọ
ṅudọ to surpass in something, to be too much: *e ṅudọ yi rājọ* he is very bad
ṅùwât razor
ṅwājọ to smell v. n., yọ̄mọ d ṅwdchi̥ ẹn the wind smelled towards him: he smelled the wind; n. ṅwâjọ̀ (Nr. ṅwẹch')

ṅwāṅọ to aim at; pt. *a ṅwâni̥ lai*; pe. *a ṅwân*; n. ṅwânọ̀
ṅwẹch-ṅwẹch a large lizard, lives in the water and on land
ṅwẹch, also ṅwẹ́ch running
ṅwẹ́ch a kind of red dura
ṅwel a snake
ṅwọ̄jọ to hasten, make haste, to be the first in doing something; pt. *a ṅwọ́ch*; n. ṅwọ̄jọ̀

ṅwọnọ to be prudish, coy, simpering, conceited, presumptuous, proud; pt. *d ṅwọn, a ṅwọni*, n. ṅwọ́n, or: ṅọ̣nọ̀
ṅwotọ lâù to spit; pt. *d ṅwòti̥ L*, pe. *a ṅól*
ṅyẹ̀dọ to milk; pt. *a ṅyẹ́t, a ṅyẹ́ti̥ ḍeaṅ*, or: *a ṅyẹ́ti̥ ḍ.*; pe. *a ṅyẹ́t*; n. ṅẹ̀dọ̀
ṅyẹmọ wọk to cut off
ṅyẹ́ni metal, money (Bo. gaṅa)

O.

óbânọ̀ front-apron of women
òbạu-òbâu̥i the lungs
òbẹch-òbẹ́ch reed
òbẹr-òbẹri feather, wing
obẹt womb
òbírọ̀-òbi̥r a small pot for beer
óbọ̣gọ̀-óbọ̣k spotted, speckled; an albino
óbọi foam, froth
òbọu lungs, see obạu
óbu̥k bellows
óbwọniọ̀-bwọn stranger, foreigner; chiefly the white man, Arab, Turk, European; obw. wok, obw. lōjọ "white man of the bush", "black white man": Sudanese

Arab, black Arab
óbwọ́rù grass for thatching
óbwóyọ̀-óbwòu̥i a shrub with thick, fleshy leaves, very frequent in the bush
óbyẹ́ch a cow with ordinary, non-dressed horns
óchôdọ̀ a hornless cow, a cow with short horns
óchôlọ̀-watẹ chôl or chọl Shillukman
óchọ̣yọ̀-óchọ̣yi melon
óchùn liver; see chuṅọ
óchyẹṅọ̀-óchyẹn a loincloth, "back-apron", for women
ódàn chyẹṅọ the palm of the hand

ódẹk-ûdíki̥ a large-mat (Nr. ódẹk)
ódẹ̣lọ̀-ódẹ̣l 1. a cow with horns turned down; 2. anchor; see ódú̥lọ̀
ódẹ̣rọ̀-òdẹ̣r kiddle, garth, crawl
ódibọ̀-ódip, ódip blanket
odiṅọ cloud-shadow
ódọ̣n west-wind
ódú̥lọ a cow with horns pointing forward
ódọ̣n a kind of red dura
òfàdọ̀ a tree, its fruit is eaten by goats
ofạdọ wọl mask
ófwọn-ófùn loaf of bread
ofyẹt lyẹch a kind of white dura
ógâk a cow: back and

head black, belly and neck white
ógâl-ógàl (ar.) mule
ógál̥-ógál̥, or: ógàl mule; see ogal
ògḷ̇dgḷ̇ a bird
ògl̥gò a cow; see ógâk
ógĭk-ógìk buffalo
ógn̥l̥̀-ógn̥l̥̀ bracelet of ambach
ógót a cotton-cloth
ógwàl-ógwḷ́l̥̇ frog
ogwal calf of the leg; o. bat "calf of the arm": the fleshy part of the upper arm
ógwé-ógwé̂ bow (for shooting)
ógwḷ́l on ox with horns turned towards the eyes; female: agwḷ́lò
ógwòk-ógòkl̥ jackal, "fox"
ógwól-ògwòl a black bird
ògwòrò-ògwòrt, also ógwê-rl̥ the blue (grey?) heron
ójàn̥ò-wate jàn Dinka-man, barbar
ókòdò-òkòtl̥ a big basket
ókòdò-òkúṭl̥ hedgehog
ókòk-ókòk, also ókògì a fish with three thorns
òkòk (also ókòk) — òkòk egret, also name of the little white heron
òkòk-òkòk flower, blossom (Di. gak)
ókót-òkòt bell; o. e ṭò̄no the bell rings

òkút papyrus
Ókwá Nyikang's father
òkwàn̥ò-òkwán̥l̥ broom
òkwêk, also òkwòk-òkwôk a kind of goose
ókwèn fì a kind of red dura
ókwól-òkwòl̥̇ an eatable gourd, is cultivated
òkwóm-òkúóm the sacred ibis
ókwòn-ókòn long feathers, such as are used as ornaments in the hair
ókwûr-ókòrì the spotted serval, and its skin, worn as dancing-cloth
ókyl̥l-ókyèl̥ black, grass-eating ant, they live in armies, build large hills
olách mâch a kind of white dura
ólák-òlékl̥ a fish [fig
òlám-òlémì the sycomore-
óléáu the starling
ólḹk a cow, grey and white spotted
òlḹl̥ò-òlḹl̥̇ a club ending in a ball, knob-kerry
ólḷn (ólḷn ?) a cow with large brown and white speckles; see ólḹk
óll̥, òll̥-ólétì brown hawk
òléé-òlòé, also òlélòé duck (Di. olului, Nr. lwélwè, Ba. wilili)
ólút a cow with small brown and white dots

ólwĕ a kind of white dura
ólwè-ólwè marabou-stork
ómâ cousin
ómàdò-némàdò the child of my brother, niece, nephew, ómàdá my n.
ómâyò-ómái the child of my mother's sister, cousin, see ómâ
òmèdò-òmèt fire-fly
ómḷlò (ar.) salt
ómèn his brother
ómèrù a kind of red dura
ómi-némi brother
ómòdò a cow (or other animal) black and white spotted [lope
ómòrò-ómòr roan ante-
omòt green dura
ònáu-ònáu a snake, not poisonous, eats frogs
ónàyò-ónái the child of my mother's brother, cousin
ónògò a cow with horns directed straight back-ward, like those of the young buffalo
ònwáṇi̥ large black ant, eats termites, bites painfully
óṅèló red earth on river banks, used for making pots
onemia my brother
ṓṇò to dive; see ṛōṇò
óṅwí drizzling rain
óṅwòk-óṅwòk male goat or sheep

òṅwẹrọ̀ a whip
óṅyẹṅ - óṅyẹṅì a green snake, not poisonous, catches chickens
ópáp-ópáp the hip-bone
òpárọ̀ a gourd
ópŭn-ópùn loaf; see ófwọ̀n
óráp - óráp spider (Nu. korābe)
órạ̀t-órạ̀t a snake, not poisonous, eats chickens
óràt-óràt calico-cloth
órọ̀-òr white ant-hill
órọ̀ (òrọ̀)-ọ̀r relatives by marriage
ōrọ to send; see wōrọ
óróch-óròch ram
órụ̀gó hollow
òrọ̀k-òrọ̀k craft, astuteness, wrong, sin
órọ̀k - órọ̀k, órụ̀gì small bells worn round the knee in dancing
órụ̀mọ̀ male sheep or goat, see rụ̀mọ̀ (Masai oro he-goat)
órwọ́mọ̀-rwōm male sheep or goat, see órụ̀mọ̀
ótạ̀t-ótịtì a pot for water or beer
ótịnọ̀ - ótìnì, ótịn stones heaped up, a dam, embankment, bridge
ótọ́k mist, fog; feṅ da o. it is misty
òtọ̀lọ̀ centipede
òtọ̀lọ̀ a kind of white dura
ótwọ̀l-ótwẹ́l̄ a river-fish, resembling a snake
òtyệm-ótyẹ̀m dragon-fly
ótyẹ̀nọ̀-ótyẹ̀n a fish
otyẹn bells
óṭạ̀gọ̀-óṭạ̀nì 1. a flat fish; 2. a gourd used as a dipper
óṭọ̀i a kind of red dura
óṭọ̀r-óṭọ̀r a ford
óṭọrò a kind of red dura
óṭụ́ a humble, poor person
òṭwól blue
óṭwọ́ṅ-óṭwọ̀ṅi hyena
óṭwọ̀ṇ-óṭọ̀ṅ 1. cock; 2. male animal (Di. wton)
óṭyẹ̀n old time, ancient time, a long t. ago
òwá - ńéwá the child of my father's brother, cousin
òwảjọ̀-ńéwảjọ̀ the child of my father's sister, cousin
òwáṅọ̀-òwáṅì a heron
òwáù-òwáu 1. the black ibis; 2. branch of deleibpalm
òwẹ̀dọ̀-òwẹ̀t a fish
òwẹk a toothless person
òwẹ́t-òwẹ̀t some kind of mat
óyíṇọ̀ crocodile-hunter
oywái-oywáì worm, caterpillar
óywák-óywákì, also óywẹ́-kì the golden-crested crane

P.

pàch-myẹ̀r village, home (Di. pan)
pāgọ to sharpen
pākọ to thank
pām-pắmì board, table, saddle (Bo. pam millstone); see pẹ̀m
páṅọ̀ to hide
paṅ the hole below the mill-stone
pāṅọ to trie a person
paṅ full
pāṅọ to divide; pe. pák
pàṅọ̀ ear-wax
pàr-párì, pẹ́rì hippo
payọ to depend on, to be under somebody's auspices or responsibility
pẹgọ to fill, to fill into; pt. a pẹka byẹ́l yech aṭẹp he filled dura into the bag; pe. a pẹ̀k; n. fẹ̀k; see fāṅọ
pẹ̀k (to be) heavy
pèl-pèl grinding-stone
pẹlọ to drizzle; kọt e p.

pȩm drying-place for dura, in the fields; thrashing-floor
pȩmo to denie
per like, alike, similar
pėr news
pėt bad smell
pi, pí-pik water (Nandi pek, Somali piyi, Turkana aki-pi, Karamojo agipi, Teso aki-pi)
pido̧ to persecute, follow, to demand debts; n. pidȩ
pido̧ to get tired
pik water; see pi
po̧no̧ to pull out
po̧no̧ to pass somebody; pt. a po̧n, a pōna ėn; n. fȯn; see fōdo̧
puk turtle
pwȯdȯ-pwȯt a place prepared for a field, farm, field
pwono̧ - pwȯch tendon Achilles
pyȧr-ȧryȧu twenty
pyȧrȯ ten
pyēlo̧ to cack

R.

rȧch-recho̧ bad, r. kí rań dúȯń "bad with great badness": very bad; rach may also mean: very much, in a high degree (Di. rach)
rājo̧ to become or to be bad; n. rȧjȯ
rȧm-rȧm thigh; also rȧm (Nr. ȷȧm)
ra̧m diarrhoe
ra̧mo̧ to pain, ache; pt. a ra̧m; n. ra̧m (Di. rem)
rȧnì-rėnì looking-glass
rāno̧ to see by witchcraft
rȧrȯ a thrashing-place
rāro̧ to run, to stream; to run a race; pt. a rȧri; n. rȧrȯ
rȧrȯ-rȧr sinew, nerve, vein
ra̧t la̧bo̧ king of the people; see rit
ra̧u hippopotamus (Di. ro̧u, Nr. ro̧u, Madi robi, Abokaya arua hippo; Lendu ra croc.)
rȧwȯ duchn
ra̧wo̧ to blacken poles in order to make them hard; n. ra̧u
re-rek body, rȩ lėt his body, that is: he, is hot, feels unwell, is lazy (Nr. ro̧, Madi rū, Abokaya amarū)
rė why? yí rè kėt why did you go? (Nu. rė interrogative particle)
rė expresses casus irrealis
rȩbo̧ to bring together, mix, unite, associate, reconcile; pt. á rė́pà jė he reconciled the people; pe. jė á rėp, also a rêp; a rêp yi mach it was caught by fire
rȩbo̧ to be thin, not strong, not durable
rėf, rėp thin, not durable, see rȩbo̧
rejo̧ to be bad, to spoil; see rach
rējo̧ to receive a guest, to be hospitable; pt. a recha dȧn; pe. a ryêch
rėjo̧-rech fish (Teso agaria)
rėm thigh; see ra̧m
rėmȯ blood (Madi ari, Abokaya ari)
rȩno̧ to become or be bad, to spoil; pt. ȧ rė́ni, also ȧ rė́ni; n. rė́ni; chunȩ r., yejȩ r. he is angry; see rȧch
rēro̧ to cut into strips
rėtȯ-rėt corn-stalks
reyo̧ tach to make a potring
rīgo̧ to be shut up, barred,

as the river by sudd;
to fill up (as a hole),
to bury; pt. *a rika ḍāṅ*
rĭjǫ to stay, remain; pt.
á rĭch; n. *rĭjǫ̀*
riṅǫ to run; pt. *á rḗṅ*
(Di. *riṅ*, *ryaṅ*, Nr. *riṅ*)
riṅǫ́ meat (Masai *aki-riṅ*,
Teso *aki-riṅ*)
riṯ (also *raṯ*)-*rōr* king
(Ju. *rwot*, Nu. *arti* god,
Somali *ga-rat* chief)
robǫ to string (beads);
pt. *a ropa tḗgǫ*; pe. *a
rŏ́p*; n. *rŏ́p*
rǫ́bǫ̀ (ar.) one shilling, ¹/₄
Riāl
rŏ́ḍǫ́, rŏ́ḍǫ́ thirst; *yḍ̀ dâ
r., ya máke̥ yè̥ r.* I am
thirsty (Teso *ako-rai*,
Nr. *rḗṯ*).
rōgǫ to hollow, to scoop
out; pt. *a rǫ̀kà yaṯ*;
pe. *a rŏ́k*
rōjǫ-rōch heifer, see *ṅa-
rōjǫ*
rōjǫ to castrate
rŏk-rŏk a small gourd
rǫmǫ pi to fetch, to dip
water; pt. *á rwǫ́mà pi*;
pe. *á rwǫ́m*; n. *rwǫ́m*
rǫmǫ to meet; to measure,
to weigh; to be suffi-
cient; to think, under-
stand; to overleap; pt.
a rǫma kwǫ́p he ponder-
ed on the word; n. *rǫ̀m*
rǫ́mǫ̀ female sheep
rōṅǫ to sink, to dive (Di.

rwaṅ)
rō̱ṅǫ to elect (a chief,
king); pt. *gɛ rō̱ṅa riṯ*;
pe. *a rŏ́ṅ*; see *yō̱ṅǫ*
rǫ̀ṅǫ̀-rǫ̀ṅǫ̀ a large, poisonous snake, eats rats
rǫ̀ṅǫ̀ rain-bow; see preceding
rōṅǫ to be or do wrong,
to be astute, to sin; pt.
a rŏ́ṅ, n. *ŏ̀rŏ̀k* (Ba. *lo-
rok*, *lo-ron*, Teso *irono*)
rǫṅǫ-rǫnii kidneys
rorǫ to be sterile (of animals)
rǫtǫ (rǫdǫ) to sew; pt. *a
rǫta láu*
rǫyǫ to spill; *a rǫya pi*
he spilled water; pe.
pi d rŏ́i, n. *rŏ́i*
rǫyǫ to cry (in running)
away), n. *rŏ́i*
rûdǫ̀ north-wind, the time
while it is blowing;
winter
rûgǫ to put on clothes or
ornaments, to adorn;
pt. *a rùkà lāu*; pe. *a
rúk*
rúm-ŏ̀rǫ̀m, wǫm noose
rumǫ to turn (up); pt. *á
rùm dǫ̀ṅǫ feṅ* he turned
the basket (on the
ground) upside down
rūmǫ to finish, be finished;
pt. *á rûm* it is finished
rūmo to measure, to think,
to be thoughtful, anxi-
ous; pt. *d rûm*; n. *rûmǫ̀-

rûmḭ*; see *rǫmǫ*
rūmǫ yaṯ to tread over
a tree; to overleap a
tree; pe. *yaṯ d rǫ́m*
rūn year (Di. *rwon*, Nr.
rūn)
rūrǫ to hum; *lwaṅ e r.*
ruwǫ to pass away; *run
ákyḛl d rû* one year
has passed away, n.
ruwǫ
ruyǫ: *a rúyi̥ wǫ́u* he went
after sunrise (?); see
ruwǫ
rwǫmǫ to catch with both
hands; see *wǫmǫ*; same
as *rwǫmǫ* to meet?
rwǫmǫ to meet, measure;
see *rǫmǫ*
rwǫ̀t house; syn. *wǫt*
ryak (Dinka) famine
ryēbǫ to hire or rent for
money, to bribe; pt. *a
ryɛpa jâgǫ̀* he hired
(bribed) the judge; *a
ryɛpa ḍāṅ* he hired a
man for work; pe. *wǫt,
yɛi a ryɛ́f* the house,
the boat was hired, rent
ryejǫ to invite, to receive
as guest, to entertain,
treat; pt. *a ryecha ḍāṅ*,
pe. *a ryèch*, n. *ryèch*;
see *rējǫ*
ryek a mat, fence of mats
ryḗmǫ to drive or to chase
away, to banish; pt. *d
ryɛ́mà ḍeaṅ*, pe. *d ryḗm*
ryɛrǫ to hang up, to

suspend, to be hanging, suspended; *riṅ r. mal* the meat is hanging above; pt. *a ryɛra riṅo mal* he suspended the meat

ryɛrǫ to come forth, to rise; *chán a ryɛ̂r* the sun has risen; see the preceding

ryɛt both; see *áryàu* (Di. rēk, Ba. *mu-reke*)

T.

tábátè bier; *gɛ kíṭi ḑā̄n wíḷe t.* they put the man upon the bier

tɑdǫ to tie boards or laths together; *gɛ tátà wǫt*; n. *tàdǫ̀*

tādǫ-tátí sticks, laths for building a house; *tátɛ́ wǫt*; *t. kal* fence-sticks

tádǫ̀t door

tagjte chain; *á tùòchì ḷn kí t.* he was bound with a chain

tagǫ to dig the foundations of a house

tàkḯgì planting-stick see *dàkḯgì*

tàkyèch a cow with white flanks, the rest being black

tálál-tàlál brass, anything made of brass

tàlál-tàlál a reddish, poisonous snake; vide preceding

tánǫ̀ roof

taṗǫ to put on fire

taṅ along, *ɛ kɛḑǫ t. nam* he goes along the river

tán hartebeest

taṅɛ nam river-side

tāṅǫ to stretch out (the hand)

tɑṅǫ to be divorced, to divorce, *a tɑ̄ṅa ḑâchǫ* he was divorced from the woman, n. *tán*; see preceding

tár, târ white

tár pasture-place

tārǫ to turn (a thing); pt. *ya tāra mal* I turned upside; n. *târǫ̀*

tátɛ́ kál fence-sticks

tátyɛ́l the corner of the wall opposed to the door

tátwól a cow of bay colour

tɑyǫ to throw, to scatter, v. a. and n., n. *tâyǫ*

tɛ̣bámì (also *tɛb.*)-*tɛ̣bámì* girdle, belt

techǫ to be wet

tɛ̣dɛ̣t-tɛ̀dɛ̣t door-stick; see *tàdǫ̀t*, an *dédǫ̀t*

tédígò a red-brown (bay) cow

teduk a gray cow

tɛgǫ to be or become hard, strong; n. *tɑgǫ*; see *tɛ̣k*

tɛ̣gǫ̀-tɛ̀k chain, string of beads, ring

tégúdì-tégúṭì poles or sticks, about 2½ foot long, serving as supporters for the house-poles

tɛ̣k to be hard, strong, brave, tenacious, perseverant, cruel

tɛ̣k the cavity below the scutiform cartilage

tɛ̣kǫ wǫt to dig out the foundation of the house, *a tɛ̣k*, n. *tɛ̣ke wǫt*; see *tɑgǫ*

tɛ̣kǫ to smack with the tongue; *a tɛ̣k dyɛ̣l* he called the goats by smacking

tɛ̣lǫ to pull, to pull out; pe. *lum á tɛ̣l* the grass was pulled out

tɛ̣mǫ to take without asking; n. *tɛ̣mǫ̀*

tɛ̣nǫ̀ bug

tɛ̣nǫ to pour out drop by drop; *a tɛ̀nì pi* he poured out the water

tệnọ-tện oribi-gazelle
tệnọ mọgọ to strain beer; pt. á tyệná mọgọ, pe. mọgọ á tyện; n. tyện
tện̥ọ to be hard, strong; a tện̥ì, n. tệgọ
tện̥ọ to stamp (with the foot), to shake, to clap (hands), to hew, carve; pt. á tệná lau he shook the cloth; a tện̥i chygn he clapped the hands; pe. a tện̥, a tyện; n. tện̥; see tyệnọ
tệr straight, yaṭ máṭệr a straight tree
tệrọ̀, tệdọ̀ people (Ba. tir people, Nu. ter they)
tẹrọ to carry; see tyẹṭọ
tệṭ door; see tệdệt
tệtán a black cow
tệwídi-tệwìtì fish-hook
tẹwọ to wag; pt. á tệù, n. òtệu
tídọ (gin cham) to covet after (food); n. tídọ̀
tigọ: ẹ tigọ yi rājọ he is very bad, spoiled; yọ̄mọ tigọ the wind, air smells bad
tijọ to do; pt. a tich, n. tich
tịk-tịk 1. sudd; 2. chin
til (to be) clear; pik til the water is clear
timọ ḍạṇ seton, fontanel
tín at once, soon, presently, just now
tín̥ọ to lift up, to raise;
pt. a tện yaṭ; pe. á tện;
n. tện (Nr. tun)
tipọ̀ 1. shadow of man; 2. an apparition in a dream, a spectre (Nr. tif, Massai o–ip)
tọbọ to be soft
toch-tòdách gun
toch narrow
tōdọ to tell stories, to tell lies; pt. a twótá kwọ́f, pe. kwọ́f á twót, n. tòdọ̀, or twot (Di. twot)
tọgọ to castrate (as a goat)
tọ̀gọ̀ a grass growing in the river; papyrus ?
tọgọ to hatch; gyẹnọ é tọ̀gọ̀ ñwọ́ḷí the hen hatches eggs
tọ̀gọ̀ the occipital bone
tọ́gọ̀ to wound (?)
tọ̀gọ to put into
tọ̀jọ mau to rub with oil or fat
tōjọ, tọ̀jọ to tie; pt. a tōchi lūm, pe. á twóch
tọk to be absent, to be wanting (Di. wtok)
tọk-tọki side, part, middle; tọk nam, tọké nam side of the river
tọkọ to crush, to beat soft, to knead
tōmọ lẹke lyẹch to carve ivory
tọ̀mọ pi to fetch, dip water; see rọ̄mọ
tọ̄nọ to rob, pillage; pt. a tọ́ná pach; pe. a tọ́n;
n. tọ̀nọ̀
tọ́n-tọ̀n, also tọ́n spear; jal-tọ́n (day tọ́n), the man (woman) who performs the wedding-customs for the bridegroom (and bride) (Di. tọn)
tọ̀nọ̀-tện̥, also tọ́n egg (Di. twọn, Nr. twọ̀n)
tọ̄nọ to turn (towards, aside); a tọ̄ni fạl he turned into the bush; tọ̄nọ chán to go to ease oneself
tọ̄nọ to pick; witọ t. fẹn kí adịmọ̀ the bird picks the ground with its bill (same as tọ̄nọ to turn?)
tọ̄nọ kwọf to tell the truth (same as tọ̄nọ to turn?)
tọr, also tôr-tòrì waterpool, grassy place
tọr dust
tōrọ to trouble, to be troubled
tōrọ to break; pt. a tōra yaṭ; pe. a tôr; n. tôr
toyọ to pierce, perforate, to sprout, germinate
tuígọ̀ - tùk deleib - palm (Orunyoro, Oruhima, Luganda, Lunyara: akatugu; Lusese katugọ, Madi itu)
tugọ witọ̀ to scare up birds; pt. á tùká w.
tugọ lûm to crush grass;

pt. á tùk, pe. lūm á tǫ̂k, n. tǫ̂k; see tǫkǫ
tugǫ to open; see tukǫ
túgò to play; pt. a tuk tûk-tûkị̂ stone, cooking-stone, hearth; gệ ṭàḍò gin cham wiy t.
tukǫ dédǫ̀t to open the door
tukǫ to awaken, to be awake
túlò owl
tūlǫ to rise (sun); n. túlò (Ba. tule)
tūmǫ to gather, assemble, v. n. and a.; jē a tūm the people assembled
tûṅ, also twuṅ horn (Nr. tuṅ)
tûṅ side, end
túòjò to bind, tie; to dress (a wound); pt. a túòchà kęṅ lęt he dressed the wound; pe. a twôch
túọ̀ṅò to withhold, detain from; to get nothing; pt. á túọ̀n gin cham he did not get any food
tùóṅ-tùọ̀nị̣ chisel
tùọ̀nị̀-túọ̀ṅ worm
tugǫṅǫ a small red insect; see preceding
tùt matter, pus

twāgǫ wiy wǫt to beat the roof of the house even; n. twâgò
twālǫ to be poor, helpless; pt. á twàl, n. twàlò
twǎrò to snore, snort; pt. á twǎr
twarǫ to float on the water, as foam
twārǫ to gather, pick up; to clean, to sweep; pt. a twara wẹl he picked up, cleared away the grass, n. twǎr
twējǫ to be bald; wijẹ twẹjò
twẹl fore-arm, lower fore-leg
twēlǫ to remain small, not to grow well
twǭṅ ankle
twǫlǫ to bubble (as water)
twot false report; n. of tōdǫ
tyaṅ corn-stalk
tyau: wi na tyau! also: na tyau! a curse
tyęgǫ to surround; pt. gę tyęka lǫi they surround-ed the game; pe. á tyę̆k; n. tyę̆gò
tyęgǫ to file, polish (the spear); pt. a tyęka tǫ̀ṅ;

pt. a tyę̆k; n. tyę̆k
tyęgǫ to finish; pt. a tyęki gin cham; n. tyę̆gò
tyęk company of warriors; army
tyę̆k-wedding ceremony
tyękǫ to continue in; de chán àn bę̄ne a tyę̆kè yán yá chāṭǫ, dè ànàn yá nṳ̀tí fęḍǫ this whole day I have continued walking, but I am not yet tired
tyęlò-tyęl foot, foundation, basis, root; times, meaning; tyęl ádęk three times; tyęl amalǫ the first time; tyęle wǫt the foundation of a house (Ga. tyeno, Suk kel)
tyęṅ people, persons
tyęṅ leṅ warriors
tyęṅ a màn women
tyęṅǫ to strain; s. tę̄ṅǫ
tyęṅǫ ygi to hew, carve a canoe; see tę̄ṅǫ
tyęrǫ to show, to present for examination, to ex-hibit; see tyęrǫ
tyętǫ to carry; pt. a tyęti yat, a tę̄ro yat he car-ried a tree; pe. a tę̆r; — see tę̄rǫ

Ṭ.

ṭá the lower part, the hind-part; below, under, behind, beneath (Nr. ṭar)

ṭá (ṭáù) the heglig-tree and its fruit (Nr. ṭǫu)

ṭabọ—ṭyɛrọ 283

ṭabọ to cheat, outwit; pt. a ṭapa ḍāṇ; pe. a ṭáp; n. ṭabọ̀
ṭách a wreath or ring made of a cloth or of grass, laid on the head for carrying loads; also laid on the ground to put the pot upon
ṭāḍọ to cook; to smelt metal, to forge; pt. a ṭāla gin cham she cooked food, pe. a ṭál (Di. wtal, Nr. ṭal)
ṭāgọ̀-ṭáni̇̀ a cover (mat) for the big dura-basket
ṭai wich the tattooing of the fore-head
ṭâk-ṭákì, also ṭákì (ar.) cap, hat
ṭákúgì a little ax
ṭāṇọ chyɛn to stretch up the hands; pt. a ṭańa ch., n. ṭāṇọ̀
ṭāṇọ̀-ṭáni̇̀ the temples
ṭāṇọ to put (under or on); pt. a ṭāṇi yaṭ wiy ḍāṇ he put a tree on his head; pe. a ṭāp; n. ṭāṇọ̀
ṭar the buttocks
ṭátyɛ̀lọ̀ heel
ṭaṭéḍì a pole for pulling boats (rowing)
ṭáu-ṭâṭ the buttocks; see ṭar
ṭau to die; see ṭọu
ṭàyèdè gàk, also ṭàyèt gàk a cow, black with white throat
ṭɛḍọ to make a bad, hurtful charm; pt. a ṭyɛ́ṭ; n. ṭyɛ́ṭ
ṭɛ̀ṇọ̀-ṭɛ̀ṇ a water-lily, its seeds are eaten
ṭɛ̀ṇọ̀-ṭìṇ the meat on the breast (of animals)
ṭɛ̀ṇ-ṭɛṇọ small, little; a little, few
ṭɛṭel dura-stick
ṭɛ́wọ̀ the current
ṭìḍọ to drizzle, to rain a little; kọṭ e ṭ.
ṭìgọ̀-ṭìk a mat for closing the door-hole, a door
ṭìm trees, forest (Di. tim, Masai en dim, Nandi timdo)
ṭìṇọ̀-ṭìṇ woman's breast
ṭọ́ buttocks; see ṭau
ṭọ̀ch dew; ṭ. wiy lūm dew is on the grass
ṭọ̀l-ṭọ̀l, also ṭọ̀l rope
ṭọ̀m-ṭọ̀m 1. a musical instrument, guitar; 2. a small drum, dedicated to Nyikang (Di. tom, Nr. ṭom)
ṭōmọ ṭom to play the guitar
ṭomọ to cut off, cut open
ṭoṇọ to put on fire for cooking or boiling
ṭōrọ to make even, smooth, by filling up with sand; to make a road, a ford; gɛ ṭōra nam the made a ford across the river
ṭōṭọ to give
ṭọwọ to die; pt. á ṭọ̀u, also á ṭọ̀ he died (Teso twan-ary, Ba. twan)
ṭùmọ̀ to be finished; pt. á ṭùm, á ṭùmi̇̀
ṭùrọ̀-ṭùr mahogany-tree
ṭwôl-ṭólì snake, serpent; ṭ. a kachì ḍāṇ the s. bit the man (Nr. ṭọ̀l)
ṭwomọ: ṭyɛlɛ ṭùòm ɛ́n, he sits on the ground with the knees drawn high
ṭwońo to blow one's nose; pt. a ṭwôń; n. ṭwôńọ̀
ṭwọwọ to dry, be dry; pt. lúm á ṭwọ́ú the grass is dry; see ṭọwọ
ṭyàu also, likewise, too
ṭyàu-ṭyàu guinea-worm
ṭyɛḍọ to bewitch
ṭyɛṇọ: wań ṭ. the sun has set
ṭyɛrọ to show, exhibit for examination; pe a ṭyêr, n. ṭyêr

U.

ú sign of future and of conditional

ýnù-ýńwǐ a rat

ùwệlè traveller, stranger

W.

wá we, us

wāi aunt; syn. wājǫ

wầl separate, by itself

wḋi, also wḋi the contents of the stomach

wájàl fá dímǫ̀ a kind of red dura

wájàl-ńéńảrǫ̀ a kind of red dura

wâjǫ̀ to talk, converse, to tell stories; pt. á wàch: a way kwóp, pe. á wâch; n. wách

wâjǫ̀-wắch father's sister, aunt (Nr. wach)

wak outside, the bush, uninhabited country; bwoṅǫ wak Europeans or Arabs living far away in the interior

wàlà or

walǫ to grind

wālǫ to boil (of water), v. a. and n.

wḋlǫ̀-wàl loin - ring, of ostrich egg shells etc.

wàṅ-ḙn: ḙ w. to squat

waṅǫ-wach paper, letter, book, mohammedan amulet

waṅǫ to be lost, to disappear; to die (said of a king only); to lose; pt. jwǫ̀k á wàṅ the sickness disappeared

wapǫ to approach, come near; pt. á wàp, á wàpḭ pach

wáṅ-rūn year, time; wáṅ mēkǫ some (future) time

wáṅ-ńḭṅḭ eye; direction; grain (Nr. waṅ, Turkana ekǫṅ, Suk kǫṅ, Elgumi akǫṅ, Teso akoṅo)

waṅgu-ṅiṅgu a big-sized white bead

wáṅ ágàk "crow's eye", a kind of red dura

wáṅ àwảch pl. àwảchḭ window

wáṅ kājǫ point of the roof

waṅ-Nikaṅ "eye of Nikaṅ", east

wáṅ ṅḙ̀dǫ̀ side of the human body

wáṅ ṅù "lion's eye" a kind of red dura

wáṅǫ̀-wáṅ grandmother; wāṅg our grandmother

wāṅǫ to smoke (tobacco); pt. á wàṅ kḭ́ ảảk he smoked a pipe

wāṅǫ to burn, be burned (Nr. wāṅ)

wáṅǫ̀ = wak bush

wáṅ ódǫ̀ṅ west

waṅ wǫt window

waṅ wurǫ lwal south

wáṅ ywódǫ̀ arm-pit

war-wárḭ night; feṅ fa wár it is night, kḭ́ wár at night (Suk ǫruǫ, Karamojo akoar, Teso kwari, Massai kawarie)

wár nàmtài an ox with horns directed straight backward, like a buffalo's

wắrè gǫ̀t an ox, with one horn directed forward, the other backward

wārǫ to smear (with mud); pt. *a wara kęnǫ*
wārǫ-war shoe
wǫsh talk, s. *wạjǫ*
wǫt-wati, or wǫt son, one belonging to our family, wati wǫn those belonging to the family, the relatives
wǫt bạn pl. wǫté bạn servant, slave
watǫ to depart, start, set out; pt. *á wǫtì*; n. *wǫtò*
wû tyǫl ryęk a cow with white feet
wǫt-wǫt steer, bull
watǫ chwai to eat soup
wau time (?)
wędǫ chwai to eat soup; pt. *a węta chwai*; pe. *a węt*; n. *węt*; see watǫ
węi-węyi soul (Di. *wei*, Nr. *yei*)
wējǫ to sing a war-song
wękǫ to give away
węl piece, copy, number
welǫ to change; pt. *a węlà jam, a wętà jam*
wẹlǫ a stick (of the royal princes), which is used in electing a new king
welǫ to travel, to journey; *a węli* he travelled
węlò-węl traveller
wǫn his father
wǫn, kó wǫn (ki ówǫn) when? *yi kęti fōte chǫl kó wǫn?* when shall you go into the Shilluk country?
wǫn dbwók the hairs of the maize-ear
wǫn dǫk bristles about the mouth
węni ki wǫr the night has come
wẹnǫ-wẹn hair, bristle, wire; hair of the giraffe-tail
wẹnǫ to live in a foreign country, among a foreign tribe
wenǫ to be cunning
wẹr-wǫr giraffe
wérǫ-wér dung of cows and goats; *were dǫk*
węrǫ to be angry; pt. *á węr; ku wǫr* do not be angry (Ba. *woran*)
wętǫ (wętǫ?), also wętǫ to throw, throw away, fling; pt. *á węti; á wętì gin féń, á wętà gin féń* he threw the thing on the ground; pe. *á węt*, or *a węti*, n. *wętò*, or *witǫ*
węt-witi, or węt arrow
weyǫ to leave, to let, let alone, let free, let go; *á wẹl ẹn*
wî, wú father
wich-wǫt, wį head, top, surface; *wija yót ki kwǫf ęnì* "my head has found this matter": I understand this matter; *a kęti wija* "it went into my head": I understand it; *wija tęk ki kwǫfe chǫl* "my head is hard in learning the Sh. language": I have difficulties in ...; *wija wil* I have forgotten; *wija dà mǫgò* "his head has beer": he is drunken (Nr. *wich*, Somali *wej* face)
wichǫ to take weapons (?)
wįdǫ to exchange, borrow; pt. *a wẹlà tǫn* he exchanged the spear, pe. *a wẹl*, n. *wil*; see *wẹlǫ*
wijǫ to make the roof of a house; n. *wich*
wil exchange, trade
wilǫ: *wija wil* I have forgotten
winǫ to be giddy, dizzy; *wija winǫ* my head is giddy
wi ńa tyau a curse
winǫ-wiń bird
wītǫ fi to sprinkle with water; pt. *a wīti fi*; pe. *fi a węt*; n. *wītǫ*; see *wętǫ*
witǫ, sometimes watǫ to arrive (Nr. *ręt*)
wiy tǫk-wįté tǫk shoulder
wiy kyęń "horse's head" riddle
wiy ńu "lion's head" story, tale
wiy wǫt roof
wǫ́, wǫ́ we, us

wọ̀bọ̀ youth?
wōcho (wūchọ) to dance; pt. á wóch; n. wójọ̀; see chǭṅọ
wōdọ byél to pound dura; pt. a wólà byél; pe. a wól; n. wól
wódọ̀-wóṭị buttocks
wōdọ to pull out; pt. a woṭa gin an wọk
wodọ to plaster, smear, besmear; pt. a woṭi woṭ; pe. a wóṭ; n. wódọ
wójùl-wójùl a fish
wọ́k, wọ̀k outside, out
wól-wọl channel
wọlọ to cough; pt. á wọ̀l; n. wólọ̀
wōlọ̀ to lean
wōlọ to pound (dura); pt. á wólà byél; pe. a wól; n. wól; see wōdọ
wọ́mǎn woman
wọmọ, rọmọ to carry water
wọmọ, also rwọmọ to catch with both hands
wọ́n we, us
wọ́ṅ sly, cunning
wọṅọ to be sly, cunning; to outwit, cheat; pt. á woṅa én, pe. yá wọ́ṅ

wòṅọ̀-wòṅị the swallow
wor kings; see rị́ị̀
wọr-rọ̀rì, ṭrì a pole in the midst of the village, on which the drum is fastened
wòrdu a kind of red dura
worọ to send; n. wór
wōrọ to sing (Teso ayori)
wòrọ̀-wōr termite-hill
worọ wọk to pull out, as a pole; to take away; n. wór, ór
woṭ-woṭi house (Di. roṭ, Nandi kōṭ)
woṭ dyẹk goat-house
woṭé wọ̀m the nostrils
woṭ fwoṅo-woṭé fw. school
woṭ kich bee-hive
wōtọ to hollow; yaṭ a wót the tree is hollow
wótól, or útól a kind of reed
wōṭèṇ-wōṭọ̀nọ̀ child
woṭọ to arrive; see wiṭọ
wọ́u the daylight; w. a yúṭ it is getting dark; w. e rùwọ̀ it is dawning (in the morning); w. a. wá (or rú) it is light
wọwọ to be noisy, make

a noise, to talk much and noisily
wú, wuy father
wú 2. p. pl. you; wú nín did you sleep (well)? = good morning!
wúch = wich head
wúdọ̀ I. north-wind; w. e chǭdọ the n. is blowing; 2. a season during which this wind blows, following agwērọ; harvest of the white dura
wúdọ̀-wút ostrich (Di. ut)
wué yes
wüjọ to make a mock-fight; n. wúch
wúm nose (Madi om-va, Abokaya omvọ, Bari kume, Masai en gume, Teso ekumi)
wúmì, also rúmì a cover
wümo = rūmọ to finish
wún 2. p. pl. you
wun-run year
wúṅọ̀-wúṅ rope (for tying cows)
wúọ̀rọ̀, also wọ̀rọ to sing; pt. á wúọ̀r, n. wúr
wúr song

Y.

yà to be somewhere or somehow; seldom: to be something; jwọk ya

mal God is above
yá I
yạbọ to open; pt. a yạbi

woṭ; pe. a yáp (same as yạbọ search?)
yạbọ to search for; pt. á

yap; á yabi dọk he searched cattle; pe. a yáp (Di. yap)

yách-yách a person of equal age, contemporary, companion, friend; yáche wón my ("our") friend

yado to curse, insult; pt. á yeti

yāgo to take away; to rob, pillage

yai a company of people, espec. of warriors; vide yach

yājo to be pregnant, be with child; pt. á yách; n. yech

yalo to curse; see yado

yán I, me

yańo to boil v. n.; pt. pi á yàn

yaña = yęña to be

yāno, yánò to be full, filled; to be satisfied with food; pt. a yán; n. yáno

yár-yári a ring or wreath of (cow-, antelope-) hairs, worn in dancing

yāro to skim off

yaro to reproach, insult; pt. á yár, n. yárò; see yado

yato to be merciful, gracious; jwok á yati

yat-yęn 1. tree; 2. medecine; yan ęni this tree (Nr. yat, jat, Any. jat, Teso aki-ya medecine, Massai jata tree)

yau, also yau just, nothing particular, quietly, bedi yau "you just remain quiet"; bogon yau there's nothing particular

yawo to swing, wag; pt. á yau; n. yáwò

ye he, it

ye, yey = yech middle, in yeach oh no! never!

yebo to open; pt. a yepa wot; pe. a yap; see yabo

yech-yet the interior of the body, the belly; interior, inside, middle; in, amidst, among (Di. yich, Nr. jach').

yech-yech a grass used as medecine

yedo to climb; aywom yeta wiy yat the monkey climbed upon the tree (Di. yit)

yego adalo to clatter with a rattle; see yęgo

yęgo to carry many (little) things, to be laden with many things; á yeka yen he carried sticks; pe. á yek

yei-yat boat, ship; yei mách steam-boat; y.wok railway; y. nam riverboat

yei hair; y. dan hair of man; y. tik beard; y. wan eye-brow, eyelashes

yejo to skin, to peel off; pt. á yechá deàn he skinned the cow; pe. deàn á yech, n. yech

yējo, also yęjo to sweep; pt á yechá wot; pe. á yech, n. yech

yejo-yech rat

yējo to help one in lifting a load on the head; also: to carry a load; pt. a yecha dan he helped the man; yá yech áap I carried a bag on my head

yęno (yino) to dismount; a yena wok ki wiy kygi he dismounted from the horse

yęno to pick up, pick out, choose; pt. á yęná gi fen; pt. á yęn, n. yen

yęña, yena to be; syn. ya (Ba. yen)

yęto to abuse, insult; pt. a yáni (yęni) ęn, a yánà ęn he abused him, n. yęn; see yado

yęt-yit a well

yęt-yięt neck (Di. yet)

yęt-yit scorpion; á kách yi yęt he was bitten by a scorpion (Nr. jit)

yęto to climb; see yędo

yęwo to repent

yey often before a consonant instead of yech: in, inmidst of, among

yey yęriá a season, about October — December tệrọ nị́ kàjọ̀ byẹ́l y. y. the people use to harvest in the autumn

yẹ́yọ̀ to assent, believe, trust; pt. yá yẹ́i (Ba. yeye)

yʰyò-yẹ̀i hair

yɛ̱yọ, yēyọ, to be able, to can; yá ú yēi kị́ gwɛ̱dọ̀ I am able to write

yì by, through, with; towards (Bo. hì)

yí you, sing.

yiɛbọ to open; pt. á yíɛpà wọt he opened the house; pe. a yiɛ̱p; n. yiɛ̱p

yiɛ̱dọ̀, also yíɛ̱lọ̀ to arbitrate, make peace, stop a quarrel; to save, deliver, liberate; pe. á yiɛ́l

yiɛdọ to cut, chip, carve; to point, sharpen; pt. a yiɛ̱tị yɛi, á yiɛ́rà yɛi he carved the boat; pe. á yiɛ̱t, á yiɛ̱r; n. yɛ̱t

yiɛgọ to help one in lifting up a load; to carry; pt. a yiɛgi labọ, á yiɛ́ka labọ; pe. a yiɛ̱k, n. yɛ̱k; see yɛgọ

yiɛ́gọ̀ to breathe aloud, to moan, groan; pt. á yiɛ̱k

yiɛ̱l-yiɛ̱lị jackal

yiɛ̱l-yiɛ̱l (also yɛ̱l-yìl) bracelet, anklet; y.tyɛ̱lọ anklet

yiɛ̱lọ̀, yɛ̱lọ̀ = yiɛ̱dọ̀

yiɛ̱nọ to pick up; see yɛ̱nọ

yiep, tail y. rọ̱mọ̀ "sheeptail" a red dura, y. wan the angle of the eye; y. kyện "horsetail": a red dura

yiɛrọ to twist; pt. á yiɛ́rà tọ̣l he twisted a rope; pe. á yiɛ̱r; n. yiɛ̱r

yigọ to rattle with the rattle; pt. a yɛka kị́ ddàlọ̀, pe. a yɛ̱k; see yɛgọ

yiɛ́gọ́ to become; pt. á yíká dāṅ

yín you, sing.

yíná, also yíná, you, it is you

yinò-yɛ̱t fisherman

yinọ far away, in the bush, outside

yìrò smoke; y. kẹ́tá mál the smoke rose up

yitọ to find, pt. a yitị gi feṅ he found something; see yōdọ

yíṭ(yíṭ)-yɛ̱t ear, leaf; yiṭé yat leaves of the tree (Mundu je ear, Suk yit ear, Di. yet, yid, Nr. yiṭ)

yiyí to be possessed by a spirit, to be in ecstacy

yō̱ old

yŏ-yɛ̱t road

yōbọ to bewitch; pt. a ywọba jal mɛ̱kọ; pe. a ywọ́p

yōdọ to find; pt. a yōta ɛ́n; pe. a yót

yógọ́ to become; pt. a yókd dāṅ; see yigọ

yō̱lọ to mix (?)

yō̱mọ to surpass, beat one, to overcome, to be victorious; pt. a yọ́m; n. yọ̱m

yọ̱mọ̀ air, wind, weather, y. é kwọ̀tọ̀ the wind is blowing (Di. yō̱m, Suk yomat, Turkana ekurwam, Karamojo eguwam, Kamasia yō̱me, Teso ekwamu

yú, yùòṭ-yùóṭị person of old age; see yō̱

yú = wú you

yūdọ to pass away (sun, time) to get dark; yūdị wọ́u the day has gone

yú fyɛ̱l tín an insult, an injurious (obscene) word; see fyɛ̱lọ, pyɛ̱lọ

yūjọ to pluck off the grains from the ear with the teeth

yúk firewood; ɛ́ kẹ́dọ̀ bɛ̱ gwɛ̱ni yúk she goes to gather f.

ywachọ to pull, drag, tear

ywachọ to be starved

ywɛnọ to step on, walk on; see ywoṅọ

ywǫbǫ to bewitch, curse;
see *yǭbǫ*
ywōdǫ to find, see *yōdǫ*
ywō̄gǫ to comfort, console (?); *yă yǫ́kĭ ɛ́n* I comforted him
ywǫ̂k, ywǫ̂k a cry, crying
ywoṅǫ to tread under foot, to step upon; pt. *á ywóṅà ḍā̱ṇ; á yúȯṅ;* pe.
á ywóṅ; n. *ywóṅ.*
ywō̄ṅǫ to utter a loud sound, to cry, weep; to rattle; pt. *á ywǫ̀ṅ*
ywǫ̀p-ywǫ̀pĭ bewitcher

ENGLISH SHILLUK.

A.

abhor v. *mạnọ*
able, to be ~ *yēyọ*
above adv. *mal*
absent a. *tǫ̈k*
absolve v. *chwāgọ*
absorb v. *chwējọ*
abuse v. *ygtọ, chayọ*
accompany v. *lọgọ, luọgọ*
accuse v. *gọ̈nọ*
accuser n. *ṅate gọṅ*
ache v. *kạgọ, kājọ, rạmọ*
add v. *mẹdọ*
adore v. *malọ*
adorn v. *rūgọ*
adze see ax
affair n. *kwóp*
afraid, to be ~ *bọkọ*
after prep. *bán*
afternoon n. *bǫ̈r*
again adv. *kẹte*
agree v. *ṅwāgọ*
agreeable a. *dǫ̈ch*
aim v. *ṅwāṅọ, chẹmọ (toch)*
air n. *yọmọ̀*
albino n. *óbọ̣gọ̀-óbọ̀k*
alike a. *fẹr*
all a. *bẹ̈n, bẹ̈nè*
alms n. *gin mūch*
alone *ákyèl, kẹte*
along, prep. *tan̄*

also adv. *ṭyàu*
amazed, to be ~ *gäyọ*
ambach n. *ảbọ̣bọ́, abwọ̣̈bọ*
ambassador n. *chwǫ̀k-chwǫ̀k*
amidst prep. *kẹ́l, yech*
among prep. *kẹ́l, yech*
ancestor n. *kwá*
ancient time n. *ótyè̩n*
and conj. *ká, kí*
angry a. *wę̣rọ̀*
anklet n. *yìẹ́l-yìẹ̀l*
another *mẹ̈kọ*
answer v. *lọgọ, luọgọ (kwóp)*
ant n., black house — *áchùnọ̀ - áchúnị̀*; red *mọrọ*; black winged *achyè̩nọ̀-áchyè̩n*; white *bí*
ant-hill n. *òrọ̀-òr*
anus n. *áchwịk-áchwǫ̈k*
apparition n. *tipọ*
apprentice n. *ṅan mũl*
approach v. *wanọ, chāgọ, chānọ*
apron n. *óbánọ̀*
arise see rise
arm n. *bàt-bǫ̈t*
armour n. *ádẹdẹ̈k*

arm-pit n. *wán ywódọ̀*
arm-ring of ambach n. *áchùt̄ - áchúṭ, ogọ̈nọ, ádẹ̣̈rọ̀*
arms n. *gin ṅāk*
army n. *lán, tyę̣k*
arrive v. *witọ, watọ, gitọ*
arrow n. *wę̂t-witi*
artist n. *bọ̀dọ̀-bọ̣̈tị̣̀*
as adv. *ná, námí* [*láyọ̀*
ashamed, he is ~ *wijè*
ashes n. *búr*
ask v. *fẹ̣cho; ~ for kwachọ, bạpọ*
ass n. see donkey
assemble v. *chukọ, chọ̈ṅọ, tūmọ*
assent v. *yẹ̈yọ*
associate v. *rę̣bọ*
astonished, to be ~ *gäyọ, ṅāṅọ, mūmọ*
astuteness n. *òrọ̀k-òrọ̀k*
at once adv. *tị́n, ànàn*
augment v. *mẹ̈dọ*
aunt n. *wàjọ̀-wǎch; mâyọ̀-māi; mǎ-mę̈k*
avenge v. *chōlọ, chudọ*
avoid v. *ṅọlọ*
awaken v. *tukọ*
ax n. *dẹ̣̈rú-dẹ̣̈rì*

B.

baby n. *gin ṭēṇ; ña gin ṭēṇ*
bachelor n. *bòṭ-bòṭì*
back n. and adv. *kwòm-kòm; bǎṅ; ṅǎch*
backbone n. *fyęr-fęri*
backward adv. *ṅǎch*
bad a. *rach;* to be ~ *ręṅǫ*
bag n. *ǎṭęp-ǎṭęp, ǎṭęp*
bait n. *chǎmì-chǎmì*
bake v. *budǫ*
bald a. *twęch;* to be ~ *churǫ*
bamia n. *ǎṭędǫ́*
banish v. *ryęmǫ*
banner n. *bęr*
bar v. *rīgǫ*
barbarian n. = Dinka
barber n. *ñan lędǫ*
bark v. *gwāyǫ*
barren a. *buǫch*
basis n. *tyęlǫ̀-tyęl*
bask v. *rǭjǫ*
basket n. *ǎdúdǫ́ - ǎdút; dǫ̀nǫ̀-dǫ̀nì; ǎkǫ́kǫ̀*
bastard n. *ǎgwęn-ǎgwęn*
bat n. *ǎlìlìṭ*
bay n. see bight
bay v. *gwāyǫ*
be *ya, yęña, bà, będǫ*
bead n. *tęgǫ-tęk*
beak n. *ǎdìmǫ̀-ǎdìmì*
beam (wood) n. *kāwǫ-kāwì*
bean n. *ñǫ̀rǫ̀-ñǫ̀r*

bear (young gones) v. *ñǒdǫ̀, ñwǫlǫ*
beat v. *fōdo, fwodǫ; gǭjǫ*
because conj. *mǎ, mǎr, ama*
because of *kḷfà*
become v. *lǫgǫ, yigǫ, yǫgǫ*
bee n. *kìch*
bee-hive n. *wǫt kich*
beer n. *mǫ̀gǫ̀*
beg v. *kwachǫ*
beggar n. *ñate bǎpǫ̀, ñate kwachǫ*
begin v. *chāgǫ, kǎmǎ, kwǭñǫ*
behind adv., prep. *ṅǎch, bǎṅ, chǎn*
belch v. *gǎgǫ*
believe v. *yęyǫ*
bell n. *ǒkǫ́ṭ-òkǫ̀ṭ; mǎlǫ̀*
bellows n. *òbu̧k* [*męl*]
belly n. *yech-yęṭ*
below prep. *ṭà;* adv. *fǒṅ*
belt n. see girdle
beneath prep. *ṭà*
bent, to be ~ *bǒmǫ*
beside prep. *bùte*
besiege v. *mąṅǫ, gęṅǫ*
besmear v. *wǫdǫ, wārǫ, gēṭǫ, gǎjǫ*
between prep. *kęl*
beverage n. *gin mǎṭ*
bewitch v. *yǒbǫ, gwaṭǫ, chęṅǫ, tędǫ, ṭyędǫ*

bier n. *tǎbǎtǎ*
big a. *dúǫñ, dǫ̀ṅǫ̀*
bight n. *gǔlǫ̀-gǔl*
bill n. *dǫ́k-dǫ̀k*
bird n. *wiṅǫ́-wìṅ*
bird-trap n. *akǎl-ǎkǎlì*
bite v. *kājǫ*
bitter a. *kęch*
black a. *lǒch-lōjǫ*
black man n. *ñan lōjǫ*
blacken v. *rąwǫ*
blacksmith n. *bǒdǫ́-bǒṭì*
blanket n. *ǒdǐbǫ́-ǒdǐp*
blast n. *ǎtǔṅǫ̀*
bleed v. n. *kyęrǫ;* v. a. *ṅęgǫ*
blind a. *chǫ́r, chwǫr*
blind person n. *ñan e chwǫr*
blister n. *kęñ bǫ̀l*
bloat v. *kúǒdǫ̀*
blood n. *ręmǫ̀*
blossom n. see flower
blossom v. *kǒ̄gǫ*
blow v. *kǒ̄dǫ;* of wind: *chǒ̄dǫ;* to ~ the nose *ṭwoṅǫ*
blue a. *ǒṭwōl*
blunt a. *gǔk*
bluster v. *ñąrǫ*
board n. *kwòm-kùòmì; pǎm-pǎmì*
boast v. *mǒ̄jǫ*
boat n. *yèl-yǎṭ*
body n. *re*

boil v. *wālọ, yańọ*; eggs, corn: *bụgọ*
boil n. *kẹń lẹ́t, kẹń gòl*
bone n. *chọ̈gọ̀-chú*
book n. *wańọ-wạch*
booty n. *jam lén*
border n. *dọ̈k-dọ̈k*; see also boundary
borrow v. *wiḍọ*
both *rygt*
bottle n. *àḍát-aḍát*
boundary n. *kẹ́ò-kẹ́ó*
bow v. *kũlọ*
bow n. *ógwé-ógwé*
boy n. *ńal-ńań*
bracelet n. *ńwań-ńwańị; yiẹ́l-yiẹ̀l*
brag v. *ńārọ*
braid v. *kạḍọ*
brain n. *nẹ́t*
branch off v. *kārọ*
branch of tree n. *akáre yaṭ*
brass n. *tálâl*
brave a. *tẹ̣k*
bread n. *kwẹ́n*
break v. *tōrọ, chōḍọ, fyẹ̄ḍọ*

breakfast v. *ńwajọ mọl*
breast n. *kẹ́ú-kọ̀ṭ* (woman's) n. *ṭịńọ̀-ṭịń*
breast-bone n. *àńḍò-àńáńị*
brew v. *dọ̄ḍọ, dwọ̄lọ*
bribe v. *gụńọ, ryẹ́bọ*
bribery n. *gi gwón*
bride n. *dạ̄ń ńwọm, ńan ńwọm*
bridegroom n. *jal ńwómí, ńan ńwọm*
bring v. *kạḍọ, kạlọ, kāńọ, dwayọ, dwai*
bristles n. *wẹ́ń*
broad a. *lach*
broil v. *mạlọ*
broom n. *ókwāńị-ókwāńị*
broth n. *chwái*
brother n. *ńamāyọ; ńẹmiańemẹ̄k; ómí-ńémi*; elder ~ *kạ́yọ̀-kạ́i*
bruise v. *fụ̄gọ*
brush v. *fōjọ*
bubble v. *twọlọ*
buffalo n. *jòp-jòpị; ógik-*

ógik
bug n. *chwàrò-chwàr; tẹ̀ńò*
build v. *gẹ̄ḍọ, gẹ̄rọ*
bull n. *waṭ-wāṭ*
bundle n. *bẹch, bach*
burial-place n. *kẹń kwọńi*
burn v. *lyẹ̄lọ, wāńọ*
bury v. *kwọńọ, rīgọ*
bush n. *fạ̈l; wak, wọk*
bushbuck n. *àbúrò-àbùr*
bush-cat n. *kạ̄gò*
but conj. *dẹ̈*
butcher n. *jal ńal, ńate ńal*
butcher v. *ńāḍọ, ńālọ*
butt of the gun n. *ábwóńẹ̀ toch*
butter v. *fwojọ chāk*
butter n. *mau chāk*; cooked ~ *lyẹ̄ńọ*
butterfly n. *dyẹl jwọk*
buttermilk n. *bai*
buttocks n. *wòḍò-wóṭị; ṭar; áṭéi dạ̄ń*
buy v. *ńẹawọ*
by prep. *yị*

C.

cack v. see ease
cackle v. *kyẹ̄gọ*
calf n. *ńárọ̈jù-rọ̄ch*
calf of the leg n. *dkẹ́ń tyẹ́lò, ogwal*
calico-cloth n. *òrát-òrát*
call v. *chwọ̄lọ, chwọṭọ*
camel n. *àmàlò-àmàlị*

can v. *yāyọ*
cannon n. *gúlò-gùl*
caoutchouc n. *dọk*
capricious, to be ~ *kwońọ*
capsize v. *gāmọ*
capture v. *mạńọ*
care for v. *kōrọ*
caress v. *kẹńọ*

carry v. *kạlọ, tyẹtọ, tẹ̄rọ*; ~ on the hip ~ *kwọmọ*
carve v. *gwòdọ, tẹ̄ńọ, yiẹḍọ*
carvings n. *gwẹ́t*
cast iron n. *bọ̄dọ*
castrate v. *rọ̄jọ, tọgọ*
cat n. *ńdu-ńdwị*
catch v. *māgọ*

caterpillar n. *oywái-oywái*
cattle n. *dǫk*
cave n. *búr-búr*
centipede n. *ótǫ́lǫ́*
chaff n. *chwǫ́n*
chain n. *áchíchwêl, tagīte*
chair n. *kwǫ̀m-kúǫ̀mì*
chameleon n. *dǫ́gólpóù*
change v. *wídǫ, wēlǫ*
channel n. *wǫ́l-wòl*
charcoal n. *chùgǫ̀-chúk, mêrì*
chase v. *chyętǫ, ryēmǫ*
cheap a. *lwēń*
cheat v. *tābǫ, woñǫ*
cheek n. *fìnǫ̀-fìnì*
chew v. *ñāmǫ*
chicken-pocks n. *ádwât*
chief n. *jâgǫ̀-jâk*
child n. *ñà-ñwǫ́lí*
chip v. *yięḍǫ*
chirp v. *gēdǫ*
chisel n. *tùǫ́n-tùǫ̀nì*
choose v. *yēnǫ*
circle n. *dôl*
circumcise v. *chwęlǫ*
clap v. *tęńǫ*
clatter v. *yęgǫ*
clay n. *làbò*
clean v. *fōjǫ, chúdǫ, twārǫ*
clear a. *tíl,* to be ~ *chwōbǫ*
clever, to be ~ *bǭdǫ*
climb v. *yędǫ*
clock n. see watch
close v. *chyęgǫ, męjǫ*
cloth n. *láu-lánì; fyęn-fęnì*
cloud n. *fǭlǫ̀-fǭl*
cloud-shadow n. *odíńǫ*

club v. *lòt-lòt; òlęlǫ̀-òlęlí*
coagulate v. *ńǭyǫ*
coarse a. *gwāyǫ*
cob n. *ńęr-ńêr*
cobweb n. *bǫ́i-bǫ̀i*
cock n. *ótwǫ̀n-ótǫ̀n*
cock of the gun *àkyęn-àkyęn*
cohabit v. *mǫdǫ*
cold a. *kōjǫ, líbǫ*
colic, to have ~ *jīmǫ*
collect v. *gwēnǫ*
collect taxes *gwājǫ*
colour n. *kídǫ*
come v. *bęnǫ, bi, bia*
come back v. *dúǫ̀gò*
come early v. *mǫlǫ*
come near v. *waṅǫ*
command v. *chęgǫ*
company n. *lwòp-lwòbí*
compensate v. *lōgǫ, chōlǫ*
complain v. *gǭńǫ*
compose a song *chāgǫ*
conceited a. *ńwǫṅǫ*
conciliator n. *ñate repe kwǫp*
confused a., see perplexed
consent v. *ñwāgǫ, yēyǫ*
contemporary n. *yàch-yàch*
continue v. *chōgǫ, chígǫ*
converse with v. *lúǫ̀bò, wājǫ*
cook v. *tádǫ, tālǫ*
cook n. *ñate tál*
cool a. *líbǫ*
copy n. *gà, wél*
corn n. *àbwòk*

corner n. *gǫr, gǫl, tátyęl*
corn-stalks n. *rętǫ̀-ręt; tyań*
cotton n. *kǫ̀rǫ̀, kwǭrǫ*
cotton-cloth n. *ógǫ́t*
cough v. *wǫlǫ*
count v. *kwāṅǫ*
country n. *fódǫ̀-fǒt*
court n. *kàl-kǎlí*
cousin n. *ǒwâjǫ̀-ńéwâjǫ̀; ǒwá; òñâyǫ̀; òmâyǫ̀, òmâ*
cover n. *wúmì, rúmì*
cover v. *kūmǫ, nìmǫ*
covet v. *tǐdǫ*
cow n. *dèàn-dǫ̀k*
cow-dung n. *wérǫ̀-wér*
cower v. *kyēnǫ, ńwǫṅǫ*
cow-house n. *lwôk-lwâk*
cowrie-shell n. *gâgǫ̀-gâk*
coy a. *ńwǫṅǫ*
crane n. *óywâk-óywákì*
crawl v. *lępǫ ręk, mulǫ*
crawl n. see kiddle
create v. *chwājǫ*
creep v. *lępǫ ręk, mulǫ*
crest of birds n. *áywâk-áywâk;* of the cock *mēt*
cripple n. *ńǫ́l*
crocodile n. *ńân-ńánì*
crocodile-hunter n. *óyíṅǫ̀*
crooked, to be *bǭmǫ*
crouch v. *ńwǫṅǫ*
crow n. *ágàk-ágękì*
cruel a. *tęk*
crumble off v. *mōgǫ*
crush v. *ńǭṅǫ, tǫkǫ, tugǫ*
crutch n. *kęmǫ*
cry v. *ywǭṅǫ, rǫgǫ*

cry n. *yuɔ̧k*
cunning a. *weṅo̧, woṅo̧*
curdle v. *ṅo̧yo̧*
current n. *țɛ̧wɔ̀*

curse v. *jālo̧, chɛ̧no̧, gwato̧, yādo̧, yālo̧*
cut v. *ṅo̧lo̧, ṅudo̧, ṅālo̧, ṅādo̧*

cut grass v. *ṅāro̧ lūm*
cut off v. *ṅẓmo̧*
cut open v. *kāgo̧*
cut into strips v. *rēro̧*

D.

dam n. *ótịṅo̧-ótịṅ*
dance v. *chɛ̧no̧, wōcho̧*
dancing-stick n. *ḍàṅ-ḍāṅì*
danger n. *lɛ́ṅ*
dark a. *mōḍo̧, mūḍo̧*
dash v. *kɛ̧țo̧*
day n. *chǎṅ-chǎṅí*
daylight n. *wo̧u*
deaf a. *mẓṅ, miṅ*
deal with *lúɔ̀bo̧*
debate v. *kāgo̧*
debts n. *kwor, kur*
deceive v. *chǎmo̧*
decompose v. *kwāgo̧, chwịṅo̧*
decrease v. *dóyo̧*
deep a. *lól*
deleib-palm n. *túgò-tùk*
demand debts *pído̧*
denie v. *fɛ̧mo̧*
depart v. *wạ̄țo̧*
descendant n. *kwāro̧-kwǎr*
desert n. *fạ̈l*
deserve v. *myɛro̧*
destroy v. *ḍuro̧ feṅ*
detain from v. *tùọṅò*
detest v. *mạ̈no̧*
dew n. *țòch*
diarrhoe n. *rạ̈m*; to suffer

from ~ *chịḍò, dyɛbo̧*
die v. *țowo̧, țou*
difficulty, to be in ~ *ḍalo̧*
dig v. *koṅo̧, kwoṅo̧, gōdo̧*
diminish v. *nōṅo̧*
Dinka-man n. *ójǎṅo̧-wạte jǎṅ*
dip water v. *ro̧mo̧, țōmo̧ pi*
dirt n. *chīlo̧*
disappear v. *wāṅo̧*
dismount v. *yɛ̧no̧*
dispute v. *kāgo̧ ḍo̧k*
distant a. *lạ́ú*
distribute v. *fạ̈no̧*
dive v. *rōṅo̧ gɛ̄ṅo̧*
divide v. *pạ̈no̧*
divorce v. *țạ̈no̧*
dizzy a. *wịṅo̧*
do v. *gōgo̧, tịjo̧*
doctor n. *jal yaț*
dog n. *gwòk-gùok*
dog-head fish n. *mòk-mwòk*
dom-palm n. *kāno̧*
donkey n. *àḍɛ̧rò-àdɛ̄r*
door n. *tádò̧t, țạ̈t*
door-mat n. *țịgò-țịk*
dough n. *mo̧ṅ a wach*

down adv. *féṅ*
doze v. *ńwayo̧*
drag v. *ywacho̧*
dragon-fly n. *òtyɛm-ōtyɛ̧m*
dream v. *lạ̈go̧, lɛko̧*
dream n. *lɔ̀ko̧-lǎk*
dress v. *rūgo̧*; ~ hair *fujo̧ yēi*
drift v. *gēṅo̧*
drink v. *mạ̈ḍo̧*
drive v. *kạ̈lo̧, kōlo̧, chạ̈țo̧*
drizzle v. *kyɛro̧, ńweyo̧, țēdo̧*
drown v. n. *muḍo̧*
drum n. *būl-būlì*
drum-stick n. *ákòl-ákóli*
dry v. *dimo̧, țwo̧wo̧*
drying-place n. *pɛ̧m*
duchn n. *rà̧wò*
duck n. *òlóé-òlò̧é*
dung n. *chɛ̧t*
dung-hill n. *kwéț*
dura n. *byél*
dura-bird n. *ákɛ̧ch*
dura-food n. *mo̧go̧*
dura-stick n. *ḍạ̈kǎ̧gì - ḍạ̈kǎ̧kì*; *takǎ̧gì*
dust n. *tò̧r, àyéch*

E.

ear n. *yíṭ-yìṭ*
ear-lap n. *ákwán-ákwàn*
earth n. *féń*
earth-worm n. *ńwọ̀lọ̀-ńwọ́ḷḷ*
ear-wax n. *pànọ̀*
ease one's self v. *fyẹ̀lọ*
east n. *kun dwọ̄gọ waṅ Ńikaṅ*
eat v. *chāmọ*
eat soup v. *waṭọ chwai*
ecstasy n., to be in ~ *yiyi*
edge n. *ḍộk-ḍộk*
egg n. *tộnọ̀-tộṅ; ńwọle gyẹ̄nọ*
egret n. *òkộk-òkộk*

eight *ábídẹ̀k*
elder brother n. *ṅèkūyọ̀*
elder sister n. *ṅan kūyọ̀*
elect v. *rọ̄nọ, rọ̄nọ*
elephant n. *lyẹ̀ch-lìḍch*
embrace v. *kwāgọ*
emigrate v. *ḍāgọ*
enclosure n. *kàl-kūlì, gọ̀l*
enemy n. *ṅan mẹn* ←
enmity n. *aṭẹr*
enumerate v. *kwānọ*
equal a. *fẹr, pẹr*
err v. *gwāṅọ, bwọ̄rọ*
escape v. *bộdọ*
eternal a. adv. *àṭẹ́r*

eunuch n. *ṅan mánẹ̀ ṅọ̀lọ̀*
European n. see white man
evaporate v. *dwẹnọ*
exactly adv. *chyẹ̀t*
examine v. *fāṅọ*
exchange v. *lwọ̄gọ, wīḍọ*
excrements n. *chẹ̄t*
exhibit v. *tyẹrọ (tyẹrọ?)*
exist v. *nūt*
explode v. *mwōjọ*
extinguish v. *nẹ̄gọ*
extract v. *kọlọ*
eye n. *wáṅ-ṅiṅ*

F.

face n. *ṅim; bọ̀lọ̀-bộl*
fail v. *ḍalọ*
fall v. *dẹ̄mọ, dyẹ̄mọ*
family n. *gọ̀l*
far away *lḗú*
farm n. *fwộdọ́-fwộṭ*
fart v. *kwọ̄dọ*
Fashoda n. *Báchộdọ̀*
fasten v. *kōdọ*
fat n. *mảu*
fat a. *chwé*
father n. *wí, wú, wúó*
father-in-law n. see" relatives by marriage"
fear v. *bộkọ*

feather n. *òbẹ̀r-òbẹ̀rí*
female n. *mât-màṭi*; see also woman
fence n. *bák-bậk; kàl-kūlì*
fence in v. *bāgọ*
fence-sticks n. *tátè kāl*
fetch water v. *rọmọ pi*
field n. see farm
fight v. *ṅākọ*; n. *léṅ*
fig-tree n. *olām-ọ́lẹ́mì*
file v. *tyẹgọ*
fill v. *fāṅọ, yāṅọ*; ~ up *rīgọ*
fin n. *kwáṅọ̀-kwach*
find v. *yitọ, yōdọ*

fine n. *kur*
finger n. *lwẹ̀dọ̀-lwẹ̀t*
fingernail n. *kwọṅọ lwẹ̀dọ*
finish v. *tyẹgọ, rūmọ, ṭumọ*
finished, it is ~ *chộṭí*
fire n. *māch*
fire a gun v. *gẹ̄jọ toch*
fire-fly n. *òmẻdọ̀-òmèt*
firewood n. *yák*
first n. *amalọ*; adv. *mọ̣ṭé*; to be the ~ *kwaṅọ*
fish n. *rējọ*
fish v. *māyọ*
fish-eagle n. *kí*
fisherman n. *yíṅọ̀-yíṭ*

fish-hook n. *tȩwídɨ-tȩwítɨ̀;*
  ɨ̀bɨ́ɨ̀
fish-line n. *ɨ̀pḝr*
fish-spear n. *bêɨ̀*
fist n. *ɨ̀lútɨ̀-ɨ̀lútɨ̀*
five *dbich*
flag n. *bȩ̀r*
flame v. *lyḝlọ*
flee v. *fɨ̄rọ, lōyọ*
fling v. *wȩtọ*
flint-stone n. *lȩ́lɨ̀-lȩ̀l*
float v. *gȩ̄no, twarọ*
flour n. *kwọn*
flow v. *mọlọ*
flower n. *òkọ̀k-òkọ̀k*
fly v. *fɨ̄rọ*

fly n. *lwɨ̀nọ̀-lwɨ̀n*
foam n. *óbọ́i*
fog n. *ótọ̀k*
follow v. *lọgọ, lugọ, pídọ,*
  byḝdọ̀
fondle v. *kȩnọ*
fontanel n. *tɨmọ dɨ̄n*
food n. *gin cham*
foot n. *tyȩ̀lɨ̀-tyȩ́l*
foot-ankle n. *twȩ̄ñ*
for conj. *mɨ́, mɨ̀r*
forbid v. *mɨ̀nọ*
ford n. *ótọ̀r-ótọ̀r*
fore-arm n. *twèl*
foreigner n. *óbwọ̀nọ̀-bwọñ*
fore-leg n. *bɨ̀t-bɨ̀t*

forest n. *ɨ̀im*
forever adv. *ɨ̀ɨ̀r, dè chọ̀n*
forget v. *wich wil*
form v. *chwɨ̄jọ*
formerly adv. *chọ̀n*
forward adv. *mal*
foundation n. *tyȩ̀lɨ̀-tyȩ́l*
four *ɨ̀ñwȩ̀n*
fowl n. *gyȩ̀nọ̀-gyȩn*
friend n. *mɨ̀ɨ̀-mɨ̀ɨ̀*
frighten v. *bwọ̀gò*
frog n. *ógwɨ̀l-ógwȩ́lɨ̀*
front n. *bọ̀lɨ̀-bọ̀l*; *ñim*; in
  ~ of *amal, ñim*
froth n. *óbọ́i*
full a. *fañ, yañ*

G.

gainsay v. *kāgọ dọk, fȩ̄mọ*
gale n. *ɨ̀tûnọ́*
game n. *lɨ́ì-lɨ́í*
garth n. see kiddle
gather v. *twɨ̄rọ, tûmọ,*
  gwȩ̄nọ, chọ̄nọ, mōtọ
gazella rubifrons n. *ɨ̀kọ̀n-*
  ɨ̀kọ́nɨ̀
genitals of woman *ñim*
germinate *toyọ*
get up v. *dúòdọ*
giddy a. *winọ*
giraffe n. *wȩ̀r-wȩr*
girdle n. *tȩ̀bɨ̀mɨ̀-tȩ́bɨ́mɨ̀*
girl n. *ñɨ̀n-ñwọ̀l*; *ñane*
  dɨ̄chọ [*fọtọ*
give v. *wēkọ, mōjọ, mūjọ,*
glide into v. *mō̄gọ*
gnarl v. *ñārọ*

gnat n. *jōr-jọr*
go v. *kȩdọ, kɨ̄dọ, chūtọ*
go back v. *dọ̄gọ*
goat n. *dyȩ́l-dyȩk*; male ~
  óñwòk-óñwọ̀k
God n. *jwọk-jwòk*
good a. *dọ́ch*
goods n. *jɨ̀m*
goose n. *òkwọ̀k-òkwɨ̀k*;
  ɨ̀tùdọ̀-ɨ̀tùtɨ̀
gourd n. *ɨ̀dɨ̀lọ̀-ɨ̀dɨ̀lɨ̀,*
  kȩ̀nọ̀-kȩ̀nɨ̀; òpɨ̀rọ̀; ɨ̀blɨ̀;
  lwọ́l
govern v. *jāgọ*
grandchild n. *kwārọ-kwɨ̀r*
grandfather n. *kwɨ́, kwɨ̄yọ-*
  kwɨ̀i
grandmother n. *wɨ̄ñ*
grass n. *lùmọ̀-lùm*

great a. *dúọ̀ñ, dọ̀nọ̀*
greedy a. *ñiñe mɨ̀r*
green a. *mɨ̀r*
greet v. *mɨ̄tọ*
grey a. *ɨ̀dùk*
grind v. *wɨ̀lọ*
grinding-stone n. *pȩl-pȩ̀l*
groan v. *yiȩ̀ọ, chudọ*
ground n. *fȩ́ñ*
grow v. a. *fȩ̄dọ, v. n. dọ̄ñọ*
growl v. *ñārọ*
guardian n. *ñan kȩ̀r*
guinea-fowl n. *ɨ̀chwɨ̀ɨ̀-*
  ɨ̀chwɨ̀ɨ̀
guinea-worm n. *ɨ̀yɨ̀u-ɨ̀yɨ̀u*
guitar n. *ɨ̀òm-ɨ̀òm*
gum n. *dọ̀k*
gums n. *ñɨ̀rọ̀, dɨ̀n*
gun n. *toch-tòdch*

H.

hailstone n. *áfét*
hair n. *wěnǫ-wén; yéyǫ-yèi*
hammer v. *gudǫ*
hammer n. *ábáń-ábáń; gút-gūti*
hand v. *gāmǫ*
hand n. *chyenǫ-chyén, chíń*
hang up v. *ryerǫ, nǫbǫ*
happy, to feel ~ *chuńǫ medǫ*
hard a. *tęk*
hare n. *áfóájǫ-áfóáchí*
hartebeest n. *tán*
harvest v. *kājǫ*
hasten v. *jwānǫ, nwōjǫ*
hat n. *átęń-átáń; ták-táki*
hatch v. *tǫgǫ*
hate v. *mąnǫ, chędǫ*
have v. a. *da*
hawk n. *ólét-ólétí; grey ~ djál*
he *é, yé, én*
head n. *wích-waṭ*
heal v. n. *nǫkǫ*
hear v. *lińǫ*
heart n. *mènǫ-mèní; fyóu-fyét*

hearth n. *túk-túkí*
heaven n. *mal*
heavy a. *fęk, pęk*
hedgehog n. *òkǫdǫ-òkúti*
heel n. *tátyèlǫ*
heglig-tree n. *tá*
heifer n. *rǫjǫ-rǫch*
help v. *kǫ́ńǫ, kwǫ́ńǫ*
helpless a. *twālǫ*
hen n. *gyènǫ-gyen*
herd v. *kwāyǫ*
herdsman n. *ńate kwāyǫ́*
here adv. *kęń; kú; ánán*
heron n. *ògwǫ́rǫ̀-ògwǫ́rí; òwáńǫ̀-òwáńí*
hew v. *tęnǫ*
hide v. *fanǫ, mejǫ, kanǫ*
hide n. *dęl-dę́l*
hill n. *kít-kíti*
him *é, én, gǫn*
hind-part n. *tá*
hip-bone n. *òpáp-òpáp*
hippo n. *fár-fęrí*
hire v. *ryębǫ, kǭgǫ*
history n. *kwǫ́ń-kwǫ́ń*
hit v. *gū̃jǫ*
hobble v. *kwǭmǫ*
hoe v. *furǫ*

hoe n. *kwę̄rǫ-kwę̄rí*
hold fast v. *mīṭǫ, mōṭǫ, māgǫ*
hole n. *búr-bűr*
hollow v. *rǭgǫ, wōtǫ*
hollow a. *órǭgó*
home n. *pàch-myęr; gǫ̀l*
homestead n. *gǫ̀l*
honour v. *gąnǫ*
hoof n. *dátǫ-dát*
horn n. *tuń*
horse n. *kyę́ń-kyę́ń*
hospitable, to be ~ *rējǫ*
hot a. *lęt*
hot season n. *lęu*
house n. *wǫt-wǫti*
how, how much *ádì, kịdi*
hum v. *rūrǫ*
hunger n. *kęch*
hungry a. *da kę̀ch*
hunt v. *dwārǫ*
hunter n. *ńan dwār*
hurry v. *jwānǫ*
hurt v. *nągǫ*
husband n. *jal gǫl*
husk n. *áfǫ̀ké, àkwǫ́r*
hyena n. *ótwǫ́ń-ótwǫ́ńí*

I.

I *yá, yán*
ibis n. *òkwóm-òkúóm,* black ~ *òwáù-òwáu*
identical a. *fęr*
if conj. *kęń*
ignore v. *kujǫ*

iguana n. *àbàṭūrò-àbàtūrį*
imitate v. *ṅọyọ*
in prep. *yech*
in order that *kįfà*
in order to *bį̇*
increase v. *mẹdọ*
inherit v. *lạgọ*
inheritance n. *gìn lâk*

inside n. *yech-yẹį*
insipid a. *lwẹ̇n*
insult v. *yẹṭọ, chayọ*
intend v. *chamọ*
interior n. *yech-yẹį*
interpret v. *lọ̇gọ*
interpreter n. *ṅan lọ̱k kwọ́p*

intestines n. *chịnọ̇*
invite v. *rējọ, ryejọ*
iron n. *ṅyẹ̈n*
island n. *mùchọ̇*
it *d. yẹ́, ẹ́n*
itch n. *kẹ̇n bọ̇l*
ivory n. *lẹke-lyẹch*

J.

jackal n. *ógwọ̈k - ógọ̈kį; yįẹ̇l-yįẹ̇lį*
journey v. *wẹlọ*

jump v. *fạrọ* [*nàm*
junction of rivers n. *mâné*
just *chẹ̣t*

just now *ànàn*
just so adv. *kịnau*
justify v. *chwāgọ*

K.

keep v. *kōrọ, gōnọ, miṭọ*
kick v. *chạbọ, gwẹ̇jọ*
kiddle n. *ódẹ̈rò-ódẹ̈r*
kidneys n. *rọṇọ-rọṇi*
kill v. *nạgọ*

king n. *rį̇į-rôr*
kiss v. *nụmọ*
knead v. *ṅwọbọ, ṭọkọ, chạbọ*
knee n. *chúṅ-chọ́ṅ*

knife n. *fàlọ̇-fàl*
knob-kerry n. *òlẹ̈lọ̇-òlẹ̈lį*
knock v. *gudọ*
know v. *ṅājọ*

L.

lack v. *bụ̇ṅọ*
lake n. see pond
lame v. *kwọ̈mọ*
lame person *ṅọl, fuḍọ̇-fúṭ*
lamp n. *kwọ̈rọ*
language n. *ḍọ́k-ḍọ̇k*
large a. *dúọ́ṅ, dọ̈ṇọ*
late, to be ~ *lōṅọ, chwọṇọ*

laugh v. *ṅẹ̈ṭọ, bọ̈ṅọ̇*
leaf n. *yíṭ-yiṭ*
leak v. *kyẹrọ*
lean v. *wōlọ, jạṇọ;* ~ the head *kimọ*
learn v. *didọ*
leeches n. *chwé*
left hand *châm*

leopard n. *kwàch-kwàrį*
let alone v. *weyọ*
let go v. *weyọ*
let the milk down *ṅẹ̈rọ*
letter n. *waṅọ-wạch*
liar n. *jal fyẹ̇į, jal tôdọ̇*
lick v. *nāṅọ, nūmọ* [*tôdọ*
lie n. *twot, fyẹ̇į;* tell lies

lie — my

lie down v. búdọ̀; lie in wait for lēbọ.
lift up v. tiṅọ
light a fire chwoṅọ mach
like adv. nà, námí
likewise adv. tyàu
limp v. kwọ̄mọ
lion n. ṅù-ṅùwí
lip n. dẹ̀l dọ́k
listen v. kyẹnọ yiṯ
little a. ṯẹ̀n-ṯọnọ; nọ̀k
live v. nẹnọ

liver n. óchǔṅ, chuṅọ
lizard n. lẹ̀u-lẹ̀wì; large ~ ṅwẹ̀ch-ṅwèch
load-ring n. ṯâch
locust n. bǎṅọ̀-bǎṅ
loin-cloth n. óchyẹ̀nọ̀-óchyẹ̀n
loin-cloth for women n. àchwàtọ-àchwàtì
loin-ring n. wọ́lọ̀-wọ̀l
long a. bạr
look v. nẹ̄nọ

looking-glass n. râṅì-rẹ́nì
loose, to be ~ lāṅọ
loosen v. lọnọ, gọ̄ṅọ
lose v. wāṅọ
loss n., to be at a ~ ḍalọ
lost, to be ~ wāṅọ
louse n. ṅúọ̀gọ̀-ṅúòk
love v. măṛọ́
lower part ṯà
lungs n. òbọ̀u

M.

magistrate n. lạ̄gọ
mahogany-tree n. ṯùrọ̀-ṯùr
maise n. àbwòk
make v. gọ̄gọ, chwājọ
make straight mẹ̄jọ
maker n. ṅan a gọ̄gọ
male n. chwọu
male animal óṯwọṇ-óṯậṇ
man n. ṅàtè-tyẹ́ṅ; jal-jọk; ḍâṇ
mangouste n. dtèt-àtẹ̀t
mankind n. ḍậṇ
marabou n. ólwě-ólwè
marrow n. àwúṇọ̀
marry v. ṅọ̄mọ
mask n. oṯậḍọ lwọl
mat n. ódẹ̀k-ǔdíkì
mats for fence ryek
matter n. kwọ́p
me a, yán
mean v. chwọ̄lọ

meaning n. tyẹ̀lọ̀-tyẹ́l
measure v. rọmọ
measure n. gì rọ́m
meat n. riṅọ́
mediator n. ṅate rɛpe kwọṛp
meditate v. kǐmọ̀
meet v. rọmọ
melon n. òchọ̀yọ̀-òchọ̀yì
merciful a. to be ~ yậtọ
metal n. ṅyẹ́ṅ [yech
middle n. kẹ́l, kẹ́lé, dǐr, midst n. kẹ́l
milk n. chàk
milk v. ṅyẹḍọ
miscarry v. dúọ̀gọ̀
misfortune n. gi chyɛn
mishap n. gi chyɛn
miss v. bájọ
mist n. ótọ̀k
mistake, to make a ~ bwọ̄rọ, bậṇọ, gwāṅọ

mix v. chwọbọ, chậbọ, rɛbọ
moan v. chudọ
money n. ṅyẹ́ṅ [mì
monkey n. àywóm-àywò-
month n. dwọ̀ḍì-dwọ̀ṯ
moon n. dwọ̀ḍì-dwọ̀ṯ
morning n. mọ́l, mwọ́l
morning-dawn n. akɛch mwọl
mosquito n. bɛyọ-bɛ́ḷ
mother n. mì, miọ
mountain n. kìt-kǐtí
mouth n. ḍọ́k-ḍọ̀k
move v. n. niṅọ
move into v. dậgọ
mow grass ṅārọ lūm
much a. gǐr, nɛ̀nọ̀
mud n. lậbọ̀
mule n. ógâl-ógàl
murderer n. ṅate nɛk
my a

N.

nabag-tree n. *lăńǫ́-lăńį*
nail n. *fèjǫ-fech*
naked a. *nau*
name n. *ńiń*
narrow a. *toch*
navel n. *gût-gût*
near a. *chăkí*
neck n. *yèṭ-yieṭ*; *mútǫ̀*
neck-bone n. *ágǫ̀rǫ̀-ágǫ̀r*
neck-ring n. *bǫl ṭẽnǫ*
nephew n. *ómậdǫ̀-ńémậdǫ̀*;
ńàkái-ńíkái
nerve n. *rầrǫ̀-rầr*
net n. *bǫ́i-bǫ̀i*
nice a. *dǫ́ch*
niece n. *ómậdǫ̀-ńémậdǫ̀*;
ńàkái-ńíkái
niggard n. *kǫ̀nǫ̀-kǫni*; *gǫ̀rǫ̀*
night n. *war-wàrį*
nine *ábínwèn*
no! *fà̇ṭ!*
noisy a. *wǫwǫ*
noon n. *dè chán*
north n. *kun dwǣgǫ wań wude*
north-wind n. *rǎdǫ̀*
nose n. *wúm*; *rúm-órǫ̀m*
nostrils n. *wǫ̀té wǫ̀m*
not *fà*; prohib. *kí*
not yet *ńǫtí*
now adv. *tín, ànàn*
number n. *gà*

O.

oar n. *ṭáṭéḍi*; *lăwè-lăwį*
offer thanks *mālǫ*
oil n. *màu*
old a. *yǭ*
on prep. *kwòm*
on adv. *mal*
one *ákyèl*
onion n. *móṭdlǫ̀*
onward adv. *mal*
open v. *yębǫ, yąbǫ*
open eyes v. *kwękǫ*
or conj. *wàlà*
oribi-gazelle n. *tę̀nǫ̀-tę̀n*
ostrich n. *wúdǫ̀-wùt*
outside adv. *wak, wǫk*
outwit v. *chä̃mǫ, ṭąbǫ, wōńǫ*
overcome v. *yǭmǫ*
overleap v. *rǎmǫ*
overwhelm v. *ńuḍǫ*
owl n. *túlǫ̀*

P.

pain v. *kājǫ, kągǫ, rąmǫ*
palm of the hand n. *ódàń*
paper n. *wańǫ-wąch*
papyrus n. *òkút*
paralyzed, to be ~ *ḍągǫ*
part v. *dęnǫ*
part n. *tǫ̀k-tǫ̀ki*
pass away v. *yūḍǫ, ruwǫ*
pass by v. *fąrǫ*
pasture n. *kęy kwai, tą̀r*
pay taxes *gwājǫ*
peel off v. *gwęrǫ, yępǫ*
peg n. *ḍwayǫ-ḍwai*; *fèjò-fech*
pelican n. *bǫ̀ńǫ́-bǫ̀ńį*
pen n. *gì gwèṭ*
penis n. *chùl-chúl*
people n. *tąrǫ, jè, lębǫ, lwak, jùr*
perforate v. *chwayǫ, toyǫ*
perplexed, to be ~ *wich*

e mümǫ, ńānǫ
persecute v. pīdǫ
perseverant a. tẹ̈k
person n. ńàtò-tyẹ́n; dạ̈n
perspire v. kwǫgǫ, fẹ̈rǫ
pick v. kājǫ
pick out v. mōtǫ, yẹ̈nǫ
pick up v. gwẹ̈nǫ, twārǫ
piece n. gà, wẹ̈l
pierce v. toyǫ, chwō̱bǫ, chwayǫ
pile up v. chō̱nǫ
pillage v. tǫ̈nǫ, yāgǫ
pig n. kùnè dọ̀nọ̀
pigeon n. àkúr-àkúrí
piss v. lājǫ
pistol n. àḍàù
place v. kiṭǫ, chịbǫ
place n. kả, kẹi, kun
plait v. kụdǫ
plait of hair kẹ́t
plant v. kāgǫ, fẹ̈dǫ
plaster v. mūlǫ, mwǫnǫ, woḍǫ
play v. túgǫ̀

play guitar ṭōmǫ ṭom
plenty gír, ńẹ̀nù
pluck v. kājǫ, mō̱tǫ
poet n. achak-achāk
pole n. kwòḍò-kò̱ṭ; kwàrò-kwẹ́rí
polish v. tyẹgǫ
pond n. lùyì-lùyì
ponder v. kìmǫ
pool n. tò̱r-tò̱rì
poor a. twālǫ, àbù́
porcupine n. chyou-chyowi
posterity n. ńek
pot n. fŭk-fŭkị́; dàk-dạ̈k; ótẹ̀t-ótẹ̀tì; óbírò-òbẹ̀r; àtài
pound v. wōḍǫ; ńō̱nǫ; gudǫ; wōlǫ
pour out v. kō̱nǫ
power n. kẹch
powerful a. kẹ́ch
practice v. gō̱gǫ
praise v. fwō̱jǫ
pray v. lāmǫ, kwachǫ, mālǫ

pregnant a. yach
presently adv. tín, ànàn
preserve v. gōnǫ, kōrǫ
press into v. mēnǫ
pretty a., to be ~ mẹ̈nǫ, lẹ̈lǫ
prick v. fyẹdǫ
prince n. ńariṭ
prohibit v. banǫ, mạnǫ
property n. jàm
proud a. ńwǫnǫ, mō̱jǫ
prudish a. ńwǫnǫ
pudding n. kwẹ́n
pull v. ywachǫ
pull a boat fyẹjǫ yei
pull out v. wō̱dǫ, kǫlǫ, tẹ̈lǫ
pumpkin n. lwòl-lọ̀t
pus n. tùt
put v. chibǫ, kịṭǫ
put into v. mēnǫ
put on (clothes) v. rūgǫ
put on fire ṭǫ̈pǫ
putrefy v. kwāgǫ
python n. ńạ̀lí-ńạ̀lì

Q.

quail n. áyiẹ̀r-áyiẹ̀rì | quiet, to be ~ chuńǫ, kudǫ | quite bẹ̈n, bẹ̈nè

R.

rabbit n. see hare
rain v. kò̱t é mò̱kò̱
rain n. kò̱t

rain-bow n. rò̱ńò̱
raise v. tivịǫ; ~ cattle etc. fẹ̈dǫ

ram n. órǫch-órǫch
rat n. yèjò-yèch; chāp; dafōl

razor n. *ṅùwậį*
reach v. *gāmọ, gitọ*
read v. *kwānọ*
reason n. *kẹń*
reconcile v. *rẹbọ, lọgọ, mērọ*
recover v. *nọkọ*
rectum n. *ṅộń*
red a. *kwàrộ*
reed n. *òbẹ̀ch-óbîêch; àbâr*
refuse v. *bańọ, kyẹdọ*
reign v. *jāgọ, jẹkọ*
relation n. *wạt-wạti*
relatives by marriage *órộ-ộr*
rely on v. *ńâdọ*
remain v. *dộńọ, bẹdọ, rijọ, chōgọ*
remember v. *fārọ*
rend v. *kāgọ, fyẽdọ, chôdọ*
rent v. *kōgọ, ryēbọ*
repeat v. *chigọ, dúộgộ*
repent v. *yẹwọ*

report n. *kwộń-kwộń*
request v. *kwachọ*
resemble v. *chālọ*
respect v. *gāńọ*
rhinoceros n. *átúń ákyẹ̀l*
rib n. *ṅẹdọ-ṅẹ̀t*
rice n. *alābọ*
rich a. *kẹr*
ride v. *chātọ, kạlọ*
riddle n. *wíy kyẹ̀ń*
right a. *dộch*
right hand *kyộch*
ring n. *átẹ̀gộ-átẹ̀k; gwẹ̀lộ-gwẹ̄l*
ripen v. *chẹgọ*
rise v. *dúộdộ*
river n. *nàm-nàmị*
river-bank n. *gát-gât*
road n. *yǒ-yẹ̀t*
roan antelope n. *ómộrộ-ómộr*
roar v. *chwọwọ*
roast v. *mạlọ*

roast dura *kyẹdọ byẹl*
roast fish v. *budọ*
rob v. *yāgọ, kābọ, tộńọ*
robber n. *jàl-một*
rock n. *kìt-kìtị*
roll v. *ṅẹlọ*
roof n. *wiy wọt, tàńộ*
root n. *byẹ̀rộ-byẹ̀r*
rope n. *tộl-tộl; kẹ́t; wúńộ-wáń*
rot v. *chwiṅọ*
rough a. *gwāi*
round a. *dộl*
row v. *kyawọ*
rub v. *ńyńọ, giṅọ, fōjọ*
rub fire *fíjọ mach*
rub with fat *tộjọ*
rule v. *jāgọ*
ruminate v. *duộgọ*
run v. *rīńọ*
run away v. *fārọ, lōyọ*
run (a race) v. *rārọ*

S.

sacrifice v. *gẹ̄tọ*
saddle n. *pậm*
salt n. *kādọ, òmẹ́lộ*
salute v. *mạ̄tọ*
sand n. *àyéch*
sand-bank n. *kậgộ*
satisfied a. *yáń*
save v. *yiẹdộ, yộlộ*
say v. *kộbọ*
scare up v. *tugọ*
scatter v. *tậyọ, dẹńọ*

school n. *wọt fwońọ*
scoop out v. *rōgọ*
scorpion n. *yẹ̀t-yịt*
scratch v. *gwāńọ*
scratch mud *gōbọ kwojọ*
scrotocele n. *lwọńọ*
search for v. *yậbọ*
season, hot ~ *dộdìn*
see v. *lẹdọ, lìdọ, nẹ̄nọ*
seed n. *ṅà-ṅwộlị; kōdọ-kột*

seize v. *māgọ*
self *kẹ̀te, re*
sell v. *ṅẹawọ*
send v. *worọ*
send for *dwāyọ*
senseless a. *lwộń*
separate a. *wâì*
serval (spotted) n. *ókwộr-ókộrì*
servant n. *wạ́t bâń, ńà bâń*
sesamum n. *ńìmộ-ńìm*

settlement n. *făch-myęr*
seven *dbíryḍu*
severe a. *kḁ́ch*
sew v. *rǫtǫ, kwǫjǫ*
shade v. *nīmǫ*
shadow n. *tipǫ*
shake v. *tḛ́nǫ, ninǫ*
shake a tree *kenǫ yaṭ*
shallow a. *dwęnǫ*
sharp a. *fak*; to be ~ *făgǫ*
sharpen v. *păgǫ*
shatter v. *kḛ́tǫ*
shave v. *lyḛ́lǫ, lḛ́dǫ*
she *ḭ, yḭ, ęn*
sheep (male) n. *ónwǫ́k-ónwǫ̀k*
sheep n. female ~ *rǫ́mǫ̀*
shell n. *àrŏch-àrŏch*
shepherd n. *ńan kwai*
shield n. *kwŏt-kŏt*
Shilluk-country n. *fōŕę chǫ́l*; ~ language *dǫ chǫ́l*; ~ man *óchǒlǫ̀-waṭe chǒl*
ship n., see boat
shiver v. *kirǫ*
shoe n. *wāṛǫ-war*
short a. *chęk, chęgǫ*
shoulder n. *wiy tǫ́k-wiṭe tǫ́k*
shoulder-blade n. *jàch-jǎch*
show v. *ńudǫ, ńwoṭǫ, tyęrǫ*
shrub n. *ńayaṭ*
shut v. *mejǫ*; ~ up *rigǫ*
sick a. *da jwǫk*
sick, to be ~ *búdǫ̀*
sick person *ńaṭe jwǫk, ńaṭe budǫ*

sickness n. *jwǫ̀k*
side n. *būte, tún*; *tǫ̀k, tǭki*
silent, to be ~ *kudǫ, chuńǫ*
simple a. *lwęń*
sin n. *òrǫ̀k-òrǫ̀k*
sin v. *rōnǫ*
sinew n. *rǎrǫ̀-rǎr*
sing v. *wúǫ̀rǫ̀*
single *ákyę̀l*
sink v. *rōnǫ, rōnǫ*
siphilis n. *gi bwǫń*
sister n. *ńamio-ńemęk*
sit down v. *fęka ṕeń*
six *dbíkyęl*
skim off v. *yārǫ*
skin v. *yḛ́jǫ*
skin n. *dęl-dḁ́l, fyęn-fḁ́ńi*; *lău-lḁ́ńi*
skunk n. see stink-cat
slave n. *ńa bǎn, waṭ bǎn*
sleep v. *nęnǫ*
slow a. *mǎṭ*
sly a. *wǫ̀ń*
smack v. *tękǫ*
small a. *tęń-tǫńǫ*
small-pox *dbíp*
smear v. *wǫdǫ*
smell v. n. *ńwājǫ*
smell n. bad ~ *pęt*
smoke v. a. *wānǫ*
smoke n. *yìrǫ̀*
smooth a. *lḁ̈́lǫ̀*
smoothe v. *nyńǫ*
smoulder v. *dunǫ*
snake n. *ṭwól-ṭól̃*
snatch v. *gwārǫ*
sneeze v. *chyḛ́rǫ*
snore v. *twārǫ*
snort v. *twārǫ*

snot n. *ánǫ̀nǫ̀*
Sobat n. *Átúlfi*
soft a. *nōdǫ, tǫbǫ, lwḛ́nǫ*
soldier n. *jal lḛ́ń*
some *mękǫ́-mǫ̀kǫ̀*
somebody *ńàtè*
someone see some
something *gichǫ mękǫ*
somersault n. *dlúń-dlùń*
son n. *waṭ-waṭi*
song n. *wúr*
soon adv. *tíń*
sorcerer see witch-doctor
sore a. *lęt̃*
soul n. *wei-wéyi*
soup n. *chwài*
sour a. *kḁ́ch*
south n. *kun dwǭgǫ waň lwal; wań wurę lwal*
speak v. *kōbǫ*
spear v. *kēlǫ, chwǭbǫ*
spear n. *tǫ́ń-tǫ̀ń*
speckled a. see spotted
spectre n. *tipǫ*
speech n. *kwóp*
spider n. *óràp-óràp*
spill v. *rǫyǫ*
spirit (of deceased) n. *ánę́kǫ̀, ręt*
spit v. *ńotǫ*
spittle n. *lău*
split v. *kāgǫ, kḛ́tǫ, fyḛ́dǫ*
spoil n. *jam lḛ́ń*
spoon n. *fǎl-fḛ́t*
spotted a. *óbǭgǫ̀-óbǫ̀k*
sprinkle v. *witǫ*
sprout v. *toyǫ*
spy v. *lyawǫ*

squat v. *ńwọ́nọ, kyɛ̀nọ*
stab v. *chwọ̄bọ, kēlọ*
stamp v. *tɛ́nọ*
star n. *kyɛ́lɔ̀-kyɛ̀l*
starling n. *ólêâu*
start v. *wāt̪ọ*
stay v. *bɛ̄dọ, rījọ*
stay behind *chwọńọ*
steal v. *kwālo, kwāt̪ọ*
step on v. *ywɛńọ*
sterile (of animals) a. *rorọ*
sterility (of the soil) n. *mɔ̀t̪ɔ̀*
stick v. *kɔ̄kọ*
stick into v. *mēnọ*
stick n. *kwôdɔ̀-kôt̪*
stiff, to be ~ *d̪ɛ̄gọ*
stimulate v. *kọnọ*
sting v. *kāj̪ọ, fyɛ̄dọ*
stink-cat n. *áfídɔ̀-áfɛ̀t*
stone n. *kít-kítí; tűk*

stoop down v. *gōnọ, fańọ*
stork n. *ámát̪-ámát̪*
story n. *wíy ǹù*
straight *àchɛ́m, t̪ɛ̂r*
straightway *chɛ̀t*
strain v. *t̪ɛ́nọ*
stranger n. *obwọ́ńọ̀-bwọ́ń; ńate wɛ̀l̪ɔ̀*
stream v. *rārọ*
strength n. *k̪ɛ́ch*
stretch out v. *tānọ*
stretch up (hands) *t̪ańọ*
strike v. *gɔ̄jọ*
string beads v. *robọ*
strip off v. *kājọ*
stroke v. *kɛńọ*
strong a. *t̪ɛ̂k, k̪ɛ́oh*
struggle v. *ńākọ*
stupid a. *d̪ɛ̂k*
suck v. *d̪ọ̄dọ* [*chwêjọ*
suck out (a wound) v.

suckle v. *d̪wọ̄d̪ɔ̀*
sudd n. *tɪ̂k-tɪ̀k*
suffice v. *rọmọ*
sulky, to be ~ *kwonọ*
sun v. *mɛ̄jọ*
sun n. *chán*
surface n. *wich-wat̪; mal*
surpass v. *fōdọ, ńud̪ọ*
surround v. *tyɛgọ*
suspend v. *ryɛrọ*
swallow v. *mɔ̄nọ*
swallow n. *wǒńɔ̀-wòńí*
sweat v. *kwọɛgọ, fɛ̄rọ*
sweat n. *kwok*
sweep v. *yɛ̄jọ*
sweet a. *mɛt*
swell v. *kùòd̪ɔ̀*
swim v. *kwāńọ*
swing v. *d̪ɔ̂lọ, yāwọ*
swoon v. *ńēnọ*
sword n. *gôjɪ̀-gòchɪ̀*

T.

table n. *kwǫ̀m-kúǫ̀mì pὰm-pάmí*
tail n. *yiep*
take v. *kwańọ*
take by force *kābọ*
take leave *ńgchọ*
talk v. *wājọ, kɔ̄bọ*
talk n. *kwóp*
tale n. *wíy ǹù*
tame v. *mûlɔ̀*
tan v. *ńeño*
taste v. *bɛ̄lọ kúǫ̀ńọ̀*
tattoo v. *gɔ̄rọ*

Taufikia *Bura Chọl*
taxes n. *gwàch*
teach v. *fwōńọ*
teacher n. *ńate fwoń*
tear v. *ywachọ*
tell v. *kɔ̄bọ*
tell lies *fɛ̄dọ*
tell stories *tōdọ*
temples n. *t̪áńɔ̀-t̪áńí*
ten *pyārọ*
tenacious a. *t̪ɛ̂k*
tendon Achilles n. *pwońọ-pwòch*

termite n. *bǐ*
termite-hill n. *wôrɔ̀-wōr*
test v. *fāńọ*
testicles n. *máńɔ̀-máń*
thank v. *pākọ, fwōjọ*
that pr. *àchà, ɛ́ní*; conj.
them *gɛ́, gɛ́n* [*kifa*
then *kú*
there adv. *kùn*
these *àgàk, àk, ɛ́ní, mọ́k*
they *gɛ́, gɛ́n*
thief n. *kú-kúnoi; ńàtè kú; ńan kwal*

thigh n. *γάm (rám)-γáṁ*
thin a. *rêf, rêp, gwâl*
thing n. *gin*
think v. *rǫmǫ, gānǫ*
thirst n. *rŏḍó*
thirsty a. *mak yi rŏḍó*
this *ẹ́ní*
thorn n. *kwŏḍǫ̀-kŏṭ*
those *àchà, àgàk*
thrasing-place n. *rȧ̀rǫ́*
thread n. *kwǭrǫ*
three *áḍẹ̀k*
throat n. *chwāk*
through prep. *yì*
throw v. *bạlǫ, bạtǫ, wẹtǫ, tạyǫ, lẹ̄nǫ*
thunder v. *mạ̄rǫ*
thus adv. *neya, kị́ndù*
tick n. *kùóḍǫ̀-kúót*
tickle v. *gẹḍǫ* [*bājǫ*
tie v. *kōdǫ, tōjǫ, twōjǫ,*
tie together v. *tạdǫ*
till v. *furǫ*

time n. *chȧ́ṅ, wȧ̀ṅ, kẹṅ*
tin n. *dyǫ̀mǫ̀*
tired, to be ~ *būḍǫ, fạdǫ, fẹt*
tobacco n. *àtābǫ́-àtǡm*
tobacco-pipe n. *dàk-dạ̀k*
to-day *dė chȧ́ṅ tị́ṅ*
toe n. *lwẹdǫ tyẹ̄lǫ*
to-morrow *ḍùkì*
tongue n. *lẹ̀p-lẹ̀p*
too adv. *tyàu*
tool n. *jame gwǫk*
tooth n. *lẹ́jǫ̀-lẹ́k*
tooth-brush *chùṭ-chùṭ*
toothless person *ówẹ̀k*
top n. *wìch-wạṭ*
tortoise n. *fùk-fùgì*
touch v. *ṅwālǫ, gạjǫ*
towards prep. *yì*
toy n. *gin tūk*
trade v. *ṅgawǫ*
trader n. *jal ṅgau*
travel v. *wẹ̄lǫ*

traveller n. *ṅate wẹ̄lǫ̀*
tread on v. *ṅǭnǫ, chạbǫ*
treat a guest *gẹ̄tǫ*
tree n. *yȧ̀ṭ-yẹ́ṭ*
tremble v. *kirǫ*
tribe n. *jùr*
trickle v. *kyẹrǫ*
trouble v. *tōrǫ*
troubled, to be ~ *būḍǫ*
true a. *mǫ́k dị̄ṅ*
trumpet n. *kȧ̀ṅ-kȧ́ṅì*
trunk of elephant *bàt-bạ̀t*
trust v. *yēyǫ, ṅāḍǫ, gạnǫ*
truth n. *mǫ́k dị̄ṅ ; dỉr*
try v. *fāṅǫ*
tuft of birds *áywàk-áywàk*
turn v. *lūgǫ, luṅǫ, tǭṅǫ*
turn back *dǭgǫ*
twenty *pyār dryàu*
twins n. *chwẹ̄k*
twist v. *kạdǫ, kẹdǫ, mẹ̄nǫ*
twitter v. *gẹḍǫ*
two *dryàu*

U.

uncle n. *nāyǫ, nēyǫ*
under prep. *ṭà*
unite v. *rẹbǫ*

upon prep. *kwǫm, wiy*
urine n. *lách*

us *wá, wàn, wǫ́n*
use to v. *ṅí*

V.

vein n. *rȧ̂rǫ̀-rȧ́r*
verandah n. *akȧ́nǫ̀*

very *chȧ̀rẹ̀*
vex v. *ḍēnǫ*

vexed, to be ~ *būḍǫ, gōtǫ, chuṅǫ rach*

victorious a., to be ~ *yọ̄mọ*
village n. *pàch-myɛ̀r*

visit v. *kɛ̣mọ*
voice n. *chwāk*

vomit v. *ñọ̄ụọ*
vulture n. *chòr-chọ̀r*

W.

wade v. *lọ̄dọ, lwọtọ*
wag v. *tɛwọ, yạwọ*
wage war v. *mạnọ*
wait v. *kạla bɛ̣dọ, chuṅọ, nēnọ*
walk v. *chātọ*
walk around v. *ṅwēnọ*
walk on v. *ywɛnọ*
wall v. *mūlọ*
wall n. *dọ̄rọ-dọ̀r*
want v. *dwātọ*
war n. *léṅ*
warble v. *gēdọ*
warrior n. *jal léṅ*
wash v. *lwọ̄gọ, lọ̄gọ*
washerman n. *jal lwọk*
watch v. *kōrọ*
watch n. *kwàné chàṅ*
water n. *pi, fi-fik*
waterbuck n. *áṅwâk-áṅwáki; gyèk-gyèk*
water-lily n. *tɛ̣nọ̀-tɛ̣n*
water-snake n. *ṅọ́l-ṅọ̀lị̄*
way n. *yọ́-yɛ̣̀t*
waylayer n. *jàl mọ́t*
wax n. *chál*
we *wá, wán, wọ́n*
weak, to be ~ *ṅwọdọ*
weather n. *yọ̀mọ́*
weed v. *fọnọ*
week n. *jɛm*
weep v. *ywọ̄ṅọ*

weigh v. *rọmọ*
well a. *dọ̣ch*
well! *àrá*
well n. *yɛ̀ṭ-yḷt*
west n. *(kun dwō̱gọ) waṅ odọṅ; kun de chaṅ*
west-wind n. *ódọ̀ṅ*
wet, to be ~ *nɛbọ, techọ*
what *áṅọ̀*
when conj. *kɛṅ*
when adv. *wọ̀ɛn, ówɛṅ*
where adv. *ágọ̀n, gọ̀n, kɛṅ, kun*
whether conj. *má, már*
which interr. *áṅọ̀, mɛ̂n, ậ*; rel. *má*
while conj. *kān*
whip n. *dɛ̣l-dɛ̣l*
whisper v. *mwọṅọ*
whistle v. *lwijọ*
white a. *tàr*
white man n. *óbwọ̀ṅọ̀-bwọṅ*
who interr. *ámɛ̣n*; rel. *má, mɛṅ*
whore n. *ṅa ḍai chwọu*
why *rè, ɛ̣̀rè, kífáṅọ̀*
wide a. *lach*
wife n. *ṅà gọ́l-tyɛ̣̀ṅ gọ́l; chì-màn*
wind n. *yọ̀mọ́*
window n. *waṅ wọt*
wink v. *gwɛ̣lọ*

winnow v. *kwọrọ*
winter n. *rùdọ̀*
wipe v. *dimọ*
wire n. *wɛ̣nọ̀-wɛ̣n*
wish v. *dwātọ*
witch-doctor n. *àjwọ̀gọ́-djwọ̀k*
with conj. *kḷ*
withhold v. *tùọ̀nọ̀*
within prep. *yech*
wizard n. *jal yaṭ*, see also witch-doctor
woman n. *dâchọ̀ - màn; dàkàu*
womb n. *byɛ̀rọ̀ - byɛ́r; obɛt; gin duọṅ*
work v. *tijọ, gō̱gọ*; n. *gwọk*
workman n. *jal gwọk, ṅate gwọk*
worm n. *tùọ̀nọ̀-tùọ̀ṅ, kōnọ, oywái*
worship v. *lāmọ*
worth, to be ~ *myɛrọ*
worthless a. *lwɛṅ*
wound n. *kɛn lɛ̣́t, kwɛ̣yó*
wrap v. *kōdọ*
wrestle v. *ṅākọ*
wring v. *dwọchọ*
wring out v. *bɛ̣jọ̀*
write v. *gwɛ̣dọ*
wrong n. *òrọ̀k-òrọ̀k*

Y.

yard n. *kàl-kḁlḭ*
yawn v. *ṅāmǫ*
year n. *wun-rūn; waṅ-rūn*
yes *awǫ́*
yesterday *áwà*
yonder *chinȇ*
you pl. *wú, wún*
you sing. *yí, yín*

REGISTER.

Aba (a man) 239
Aba Island XX
Abaka 34
Abijop 131
Abo-Kaya 34
Abouré 43
Abudok 129, 131, 149, 164
Abu Shoka LVIII
Abwong (village) 30
Abyssinia 30, 35
Abyssinians XXVII, 153
Achetegwok 160, 225
Acholi L, LI, 30, 31, 34
Ad Dui XL, 156
Adefalǫ 179
Adlan LVII
Adǫkǫn (village) 143, 144, 176
Aduṅ 132
Adwelo 160
Afyek 239
Agǭdǫ 132, 152
Agok 177
Agweratyep 176
Agwet 238 f.
Ajang 218, 219
Ajwogo (village) 134, 175
Akobo (river) 30
Akol (king) 152, 240

Akole Nyakwe 237
Akolo 172
Akūnyo Bāko (a man) 148
Akuruwar XXII, XLII, 124, 160, 164, 225
Akwai Chakab LV
Akwǫe 178
Akwoneyor 239
Akwot (king) 144, 239
Akwoto 239
Alaguiang 43
Alęki (a man) 148
Alenǫ (a village) 168
Aloa (Alwa) LV
Aluǫ 32
Alur, Aluru L, 31, 32
American Mission LX
Amol 240
Ansar LXII, 152
Anūt 133
Anyimo 209
Anywak XL, 10, 11, 13, 14, 16, 30, 32, 33, 34, 37 ff., 44, 46, 134
Anǭnǫ 237
Arabs XXVII, XXVIII, XLVIII, 115, 129, 156

Ari Umker XL
Atāno 152
Atara XLIX
Atbara LXI
Atong 179
Avikam 43
Awan (a Dinka) 231
Awarejwǫk 143
Awǫn 240
Ayā̇dǫ 133, 238
Ayǫmǫ (a Dinka) 231, 232
Baadi LV
Bachet 226, 227
Baggara Selim LVIII
Bagirmi 36
Bahr el Asraf = Sobat XX
Bahr el Jebel L
Bahr Ghazal 34, 131
Bahr Zeraf XX, 45
Bakedi 31
Baker S. LVIII
Bal 237
Bálăk = Anywak 44
Banholzer 135, 150
Bạr 32, 44
Bari L, 10, 11, 12, 13, 17, 29, 35, 36, 38 ff., 56, 57
Baro (river) 30

Baumann, O. 32
Beir L, 31
Bęk 239
Bel (a man) 134
Belanda LI, 31, 32, 44
Belo (a people) 169
Ber *(Bę̄r)* LI, 31, 32, 44
Beri *(Bę̄ri)* L, 31, 32
Bertat LVII
Black water fever XXI
Blue Nile 35
Bongo LI, 10, 17, 31, 32, 36, 38, 44, 45
Bǫr LI, 32, 34, 45
Bruce, J. LIII
Bukedi 31
Bukyęn (village) 152
Bunyoro 31
Bunyung XL
Burkeneji 35
Bwoch 160
Bwǫrǫ XL
Cailliaud LV
Cameroons 35
Carson, R. LXIII
Chai LVI, 144, 169
Chęn (a village) 152
Chopi 31, 32
Church Missionary

Chwol—Jur 309

Society LXf.
Chwol (a man) 129
Cows of Nyikang XLIV
Crowther 60
Dāk XVII, XLIII, 124, 129, 130, 131, 132, 133, 147, 155, 157, 159, 163, 164, 167, 168, 170, 238, 240
Dar Fung LIII
Darfur LVI
Dembo LI, 31, 32
Deng (a man) 154, 178, 238, 239
Dervishes XXVII, LIX
Detim (chief) 152
Detwuk (a village) 133
Dĭdĭgǫ (a village) XLII, 129
Dim 157
Dimǫ XLI, LI, 166f.
Dingjol 144, 152, 153
Dinka XXVIII, XXIX, XXXIX, XLIX, 10, 11, 12, 13, 14, 17, 30, 35, 36, 37, 45, 46, 48, 60, 115, 129, 132, 133, 142
Dokot 129, 131, 134, 142f, 144, 149, 160

Doleib Hill LXI, 131
Dongola 45
Dǭr = Bongo 31
Dor (a man) 153
Dǭrǫ 238
Dunkok 239
Dur (village) 132f.
Duwat XLI, 132, 152, 154, 156, 157, 167, 178
Dwai (a man) 132
Dwai 134
Eafeng 43
Efik 43
El Dueim XXf.
Elgumi 35
Eliri LVII, 152
Emin Pasha 32
Ewe 43, 44, 49, 60
Fabuchak L
Fadiang XLIX, 152
Fadibek LI
Fadyet XLVI, LX
Fadjulli LI
Fagak L
Faggeir LI
Faina XLIX
Fakang 129, 134
Faki Mohammed Kher LVIII
Faloko (river) 159
Famir L
Fandikir LI
Fanyikuara LI
Fashien LI
Fashoda 124, 126 et passim
Fatil L

Fawer L
Fayak L
Fayot L
Fazogli LIV
Fenyidwai 151, 178, 236
Fenyikang XLII, 160, 178
Filo 132
Fort Sobat LIX
Fotou (village) 133
Fulfulde 73, 88
Funj LII et passim
Gā 43, 44
Gaadi Abu Shilluk LV
Gǎnǎg = Nuer 44
Gang (language) L, 11, 12, 13, 17, 27, 30, 31f, 37ff, 60
Garo 159, 160
Gaya L, 31
Ger 152
Gessi LIX
Gezira LIII, LIV, 35 [XX
Gezira Wad Beiker
Giffen,Dr.XXXIIX, XLVII, LXI f, 135
Giffen Mrs. XXV
Gok (a man) 129
Gokwach (a man) 152
Golīt 141
Golo 45
Gordon, Ch., LVIII f.

Gur (village) 134
Guthrie, C. B.
Gūti 130
Gwar 129
Hameg LVII
Hamitic (influence, languages) 33, 48, 49, 56f, 88
Hartmann, R. LIII
Haussa 88
Hebrew XX, 72, 73
Herbagi LV
Hofmeyer 122, 124, 130, 160
Hollis 48, 75
Hottentot 73
Ibo 43
Ismail Pasha LVIII
Isoama 43
Jafalu L, 31
Jal (a man) 128
Jalo 132
Ja-Luǫ L, 31f, 37ff
Jambo = Anywak 30, 44
Jebel Gule LVI
Jebel Dyre = Eliri LIV
Jebel Tegla = Tagale LIV, LV
Johnston, Sir H. 31, 32, 37
Jǭk 238
Jonyang 179
Ju XLf, 129, 157
Jur (language) LI, 10, 11, 17, 30, 31, 32, 37 ff, 44

Kaka XX ff	Kwakadwai 233	Mek = king XLVI	XLIV, LIV, 10,
Kakugo 132	Kwa Lek 128	*Mékyibǫ* 43	17, 25, 29, 36,
Kam 134	*Kwa Obǭgǫ* XLIV	Merowe LXI	38 ff, 45 f, 130,
Kamasia 35	*Kwa-okāl* 124	Milo (a man) 128	133, 142 f, 148,
Kang (a man) 129	Kwat Ker XLVI	Mitterrutzner 37,	195
Kāṅǫ XLI	Lado 31	48	Nuer 10, 11, 13, 14,
Karamojo 35	Lake Albert 31	Mittu 34	16, 17, 26, 29,
Kavirondo 31	Lake Kioga 31	Mohammed Ahmed	30 ff, 44 f, 60, 236
Kawa XX, L f	Lake No XX, XXI,	LIX	Nun XXII
Ke 155	XXII	Mohammedanism	Nupe 43
Kelge XL	Lake Victoria 31	XLV	Nyabil 179
Kenana Arabs	Lambie Dr. 157	Moi (king) 157,	*Nyadōke* (king) 142,
XLIX	Lango L, 31 f., 37 ff.	169 f	143
Ker 239	Latuka L	Mon (a man) 128	Nyadwai 129, 141,
Kēr = Bahr Jebel	Lendu 34	Mongalla 31	145, 175 f
45	*Leṅdarǫ* 172	Moro 160	Nyagir XLIX
Kerau 159	Lori 152	Moru 34	Nyagwado XXII
Khalifa XLIX	Luba 34	Mui (a man) 134	Nyajak 214, 215
Khalifa Abdallah	*Luǫ* LI, 31 f, 44	Mwal 134	Nyakae 155, 156
LIX	Lur L	Mwomo XX, 115,	Nyakayo XL f, 238
Khartum LVIII ff.	Lwak 152	123, 136, 176	Nyakwach 142, 144,
Khor Atar XX	*Lwal Pōlkoe* 233	Nagdyeb XX	145, 160
Khor Atulfi 165	*Lwǫṅ* 239	Nai (a man) 171	Nyato (a king) 175
Khor Filus 45, 152	Madi 34	Nama 73	*Ńedǫk* XLVI
Kich L	Madi-Kaya 34	Nandi 35, 37	*Ńekēr* (a man) 153
Kir (a man) 134	Mahdi LIX	Nasser LVII, 34	Nyelwak (village)
Kitchener LX	Mainam 134	*Nāt* = Nuer 44	128, 152
Kitching 31 f, 48	Makwa 156	Ndorobo 33, 35	Nyelwal XLII,
Kodok LVIII, LX	Malakal 128, 132	Ngishu 35	XLIII, 133, 160
Kǫlǫ XL, 156	Malaria XXI	Nielwag XXII	*Ńewājǫ* (village)
Kordofan XXVII,	Malek LXI	Nigu (village) 131	138
LIV ff.	*Mǡṅǫ* 141, 220	Niloto-Sudanic	Nyewek (river) 164
Kū (King) 147, 152	Marchand LIX	group 33, 34, 35,	*Ńeyērǫ* 236
Kudit 160	Masai 30, 33, 35,	36	*Ńibǭdǫ* XLII, 165,
Kunama 43, 46	37, 56 f, 75	Niloto - Hamitic	236 f
Kur Wat Ńedǫk LX	Masran Island XX	group 33, 35, 36	Nyidwai 172
Kwa Ajal 128	McCreery LXIII	*Nimǫṅǫ* 131	Nyifwa L, 31
Kwajeriu 239	McLaughlin LXII	*Niñarǫ* 176	Nyikayo 155
Kwajul (161), 166	Meinhof, C., 33, 48	Nuba, Nubian	Nyimo 142

Ṅǫk 30, 142, 152
Ṅwǫ-Bābǫ (a king) 175
Ṅwǫṅ (a man) 129
Obai 131, 133
Obang (village) 152
Obogi = Obogo 157
Obogo (a man) 130, 160
Obǫ̈n (a man) 133
Obwo (village) 134
Ochamdor 164
Ocholo 167
Odak 132. 134, 160
Odęṅ 134
Odimo 44
Odok 133
Odwojǫ (a village) 232
Ogam (a man) 141
Ogan (a man) 134
Ogek 130
Ogot 134
Ogwet (a man) 132
Ojul 159, vide Ojulo
Ojulo 166
okāṅǫ XX, XLIXff
Okati 134
Okę̈lǫ 126
Okil 157
Okōgǫ 133
Oku (a man) 132
Okun (village) 132
Okwa XLf, 147, 156f, 167
Okwai 132 [239
Olam (a man) 129,

Olam (a place) 164
Olęṅ 133
Oloalo (a man) 163
Omal (a man) 132
Omarǫ XL, 156
Omdurman LXff
Omǫi XLf
Omǫrǫ 157
Omūi (a man) 133
Ongwat XL
Oṅōgǫ (village) 144
Orę̈tǫ (a man) 131
Oryang 160
Oshārǫ XLII
Oshollo 130, 134
Oshoro 160
Oshu (a man) 131
Oshwa (a man) 164
Otęgǫ 237
Otigǫ XLII
Otin 157
Oton 169
Otǫṅǫ XLII
Otudi (village) 142
Otyęn (a man) 134
Owichi (village) 131
Oyler, Rev. D. XLII, 127
Oyǫ̈dǫ (a man) 132
Oyǫ̈k 134
Pálǎk = Anywak 44
Palo 160
Pedo (a Nuer King) 236
Pepwojo 160
Petherick 32
Pijo 152, 160
Plaoui 44

Pōbǫ (village) 142
Port Sudan LXI
Prophets XLIII
Ptoemphanae LIII
Red Sea 35
Reinisch 195
Renk 144
Rǫ̈l (Rohl) L, 34
Roseires LVI, 144, 169
Schweinfurth 31 f, 34, 45
Selim Baggara XLIX
Semitic languages 72
Senegambia 35
Sennar LIII et passim
Shakwa el Shilkawi XX
Shal (Chal), 130, 167, 240
Shilkawi = Shilluk XX
Shuli L, 31 f
Sobat XX et passim
Songhai 56, 57
Struck, B., LI, 31ff
Suakin LXI
Sudan languages 24, 26, 33, 35, 46, 48, 56
Sudd XXI
Suē (river) 31, 34
Sūk 35
Sun-service XLV
Tabālǫ (village) 123
Tabi LVII

Tapero 190
Tāro 152
Tatoga 35, 37
Tedigo 152, 160
Téoui 44
Teso 35
Tęt = Shilluk 44
Tidrick, R. W., 97, 99
Tonga XX et passim
Tǫṅǫrǫ 153
Totemism 178
Tuga (a man) 129
Tugo 138, 160
Turkana 35
Turks XXVII, XXVIII, LVIII, 45, 152, 195f, 237
Turo 159, 167
Twara 129, 134
Twi L
Twi 43, 44, 60
Twolang 168
Ud Diljil 156
Umak Ra 156
Um Dubreka LIX
Umiru 31
Umoi 156
Unyoro 32
Ungwad 156
Vai 43
Wad Dakona Island XX
Wadi Halfa LXI
Wad Medani LX
Wat Mǫ̈l (Maul) XL, 156

Wajwǫk (village) 144	Wet Kwa Oket 176	Wira 34	115, 134
Wang 132, 165	Wed Agub LIII	Witor 164	Yodit 153
Watson, Rev. A., XLXI	White Nile XLI, 30 34 f,	Wū (village) 152	Yonj 131
Wau XLII ff, 130, 160	Wij-Palo 160	Wubo village 131	Yǫr 240
	Winyalwal (village) (152)	Wūbǫ (a man) 134	Yoruba 43, 44, 60
		Wuro Kwa 240	Yoyin 133
		Yǭ (King) XLVI,	Yweldit 154